# The Restatement and Beyond

# The Restatement and Beyond

## The Past, Present, and Future of U.S. Foreign Relations Law

*Edited by*

PAUL B. STEPHAN

AND

SARAH H. CLEVELAND

OXFORD

UNIVERSITY PRESS

# OXFORD
## UNIVERSITY PRESS

Oxford University Press is a department of the University of Oxford. It furthers the
University's objective of excellence in research, scholarship, and education by publishing worldwide.
Oxford is a registered trademark of Oxford University Press in the UK and certain other countries.

Published in the United States of America by Oxford University Press
198 Madison Avenue, New York, NY 10016, United States of America.

Library of Congress Cataloging-in-Publication Data
Names: Stephan, Paul B., editor. | Cleveland, Sarah H., 1965– editor.
Title: The restatement and beyond : the past, present, and future of U.S. foreign relations law /
Paul B. Stephan, Sarah H. Cleveland.
Description: New York : Oxford University Press, 2020. | Includes bibliographical references
and index.
Identifiers: LCCN 2020008365 (print) | LCCN 2020008366 (ebook) | ISBN 9780197533154 (hardback) |
ISBN 9780197533987 (updf) | ISBN 9780197533994 (epub) | ISBN 9780197534007 (online)
Subjects: LCSH: Restatement of the law, the foreign relations law of the United States. | United States—
Foreign relations—Law and legislation.
Classification: LCC KF4651 .R463 2020 (print) | LCC KF4651 (ebook) | DDC 342.73/0412—dc23
LC record available at https://lccn.loc.gov/2020008365
LC ebook record available at https://lccn.loc.gov/2020008366

1 3 5 7 9 8 6 4 2
Printed by Integrated Books International, United States of America

**Note to Readers**
This publication is designed to provide accurate and authoritative information in regard to the subject
matter covered. It is based upon sources believed to be accurate and reliable and is intended to be
current as of the time it was written. It is sold with the understanding that the publisher is not engaged
in rendering legal, accounting, or other professional services. If legal advice or other expert assistance is
required, the services of a competent professional person should be sought. Also, to confirm that the
information has not been affected or changed by recent developments, traditional legal research
techniques should be used, including checking primary sources where appropriate.

*(Based on the Declaration of Principles jointly adopted by a Committee of the
American Bar Association and a Committee of Publishers and Associations.)*

You may order this or any other Oxford University Press publication
by visiting the Oxford University Press website at www.oup.com.

# Contents

## IV. THE RESTATEMENT AND INTERNATIONAL LAW'S LIMITS ON DOMESTIC JURISDICTION

## V. THE RESTATEMENT AND IMMUNITY

*Note on references*: Throughout this book, references in footnotes to the THIRD RESTATEMENT and the FOURTH RESTATEMENT, respectively, should be understood as referring to THE RESTATEMENT (THIRD) OF THE FOREIGN RELATIONS LAW OF THE UNITED STATES (Am. Law Inst., 1987) and THE RESTATEMENT (FOURTH) OF THE FOREIGN RELATIONS LAW OF THE UNITED STATES (Am. Law Inst., 2018). Following the convention used in the Fourth Restatement, all uses of the word "State" to refer to one or all of the entities that the United States comprises are capitalized, while references to sovereign states under international law are not.

# Contributors

**Anthony J. Bellia Jr.** is the O'Toole Professor of Constitutional Law and Concurrent Professor of Political Science, University of Notre Dame. He participated in the Members Consultative Group for the Fourth Restatement.

**John B. Bellinger III** is a partner in the Washington, D.C., Office of Arnold & Porter. He was Legal Adviser, U.S. Department of State (2005–2009), and Legal Adviser, National Security Council (2001–2005). He served as a Counselor to the Fourth Restatement and is a member of the ALI Council.

**Pamela K. Bookman** is Associate Professor of Law, Fordham University School of Law.

**Gary Born** is the author of *International Commercial Arbitration* (3d ed. 2020), *International Civil Litigation in United States Courts* (6th ed. 2018), and other works on international law. He is a partner in the London Office of Wilmer Cutler Pickering Hale and Dorr LLP. He was an Adviser to the Fourth Restatement.

**Curtis A. Bradley** is the William Van Alstyne Professor, Duke University School of Law, and co-Editor in Chief of the American Journal of International Law, and was Counselor on International Law to the Legal Adviser, U.S. Department of State (2004). He was a Reporter for the Fourth Restatement.

**Hannah L. Buxbaum** is Vice President for International Affairs, Indiana University, Professor and John E. Schiller Chair in Legal Ethics, Maurer School of Law, Indiana University Bloomington, and Member of Curatorium, Hague Academy of International Law. She was an Adviser to the Fourth Restatement.

**Donald Earl Childress III** is Professor, Pepperdine School of Law, and currently serves as Counselor on International Law to the Legal Adviser, U.S. Department of State.

**Bradford R. Clark** is the William Cranch Research Professor of Law, George Washington University Law School. He was an Adviser to the Fourth Restatement.

**Sarah H. Cleveland** is the Louis Henkin Professor of Human and Constitutional Rights and Faculty Co-director of the Human Rights Institute, Columbia Law School. She served as Member of the European Commission for Democracy Through Law (Venice Commission) (2010–2019), Vice Chair and Member of the U.N. Human Rights Committee (2015–2018), and Counselor on International Law to the Legal Adviser, U.S. Department of State (2009–2011). She was a Coordinating Reporter for the Fourth Restatement and a Reporter for the Treaties part.

**Kristina Daugirdas** is Professor of Law, University of Michigan Law School, and served in various capacities of the Office of the Legal Adviser, U.S. Department of State (2006–2009).

**Ashley Deeks** is Professor, E. James Kelly Jr.—Class of 1965 Research Professor, Senior Fellow, Miller Center, University of Virginia, and a member of the Board of Editors for the American Journal of International Law. She served in various capacities of the Office of the Legal Adviser, U.S. Department of State (1999–2010).

**William S. Dodge** is Martin Luther King Jr. Professor and John D. Ayer Chair in Business Law, University of California Davis School of Law, and was Counselor on International Law to the Legal Adviser, U.S. Department of State (2011–2012). He was a Reporter for the Fourth Restatement.

**Samuel Estreicher** is Dwight D. Opperman Professor of Law, Director of the Center for Labor and Employment Law, and Co-director, Institute of Judicial Administration, New York University School of Law. He participated in the Members Consultative Group for the Fourth Restatement and was the Chief Reporter for the American Law Institute's Restatement of Employment Law (2015).

**Jean Galbraith** is Professor, University of Pennsylvania Carey Law School and a member of the Board of Editors for the American Journal of International Law.

**John C. Harrison** is the James Madison Distinguished Professor, University of Virginia School of Law. He was Counselor on International Law to the Legal Adviser, U.S. Department of State (2008), and Deputy Assistant Attorney General, Office of Legal Counsel, and other positions, U.S. Department of Justice (1983–1993).

**Chimène I. Keitner** is the Alfred and Hanna Fromm Professor of International Law, University of California Hastings College of the Law. She was Counselor on International Law to the Legal Adviser, U.S. Department of State (2016–2017). She was an Adviser to the Fourth Restatement.

**Harold Hongju Koh** is Sterling Professor of International Law, Yale Law School. He was Legal Adviser to the U.S. Department of State (2009–2013), and Assistant Secretary of State for Democracy, Human Rights and Labor (1998–2001). He served as a Counselor to the Fourth Restatement and is a member of the ALI Council.

**Thomas H. Lee** is Leitner Family Professor of International Law at Fordham University School of Law and currently serves as Special Counsel to the General Counsel, U.S. Department of Defense. He participated in the Members Consultative Group for the Fourth Restatement.

**Ralf Michaels** is a Director of the Max Planck Institute for Comparative and International Private Law, Hamburg, Chair in Global Law at Queen Mary University, London, and a Professor at Hamburg University. He was formerly Arthur Larson Professor, Duke University School of Law. He was an Adviser to the Fourth Restatement.

**Jide Nzelibe** is Professor of Law, Northwestern University Pritzker School of Law.

**Austen Parrish** is Dean and James H. Rudy Professor of Law, Maurer School of Law, Indiana University Bloomington.

**George Rutherglen** is the John Barbee Minor Distinguished Professor, University of Virginia School of Law.

**Paul B. Stephan** is the John C. Jeffries Jr. Distinguished Professor, University of Virginia School of Law, and was Counselor on International Law to the Legal Adviser, U.S. Department of State (2006–2007). He will become Special Counsel to the General Counsel, U.S. Department of Defense, in August 2020. He was a Coordinating Reporter for the Fourth Restatement and a Reporter for the Jurisdiction part.

**Beth Stephens** is Distinguished Professor, Rutgers Law School. She was an Adviser to the Fourth Restatement.

**David P. Stewart** is Professor from Practice, Georgetown University Law Center. He is currently Chair of Board of Directors and formerly President, American Branch of the International Law Association (2014–2018), and served in various capacities of the Office of the Legal Adviser, U.S. Department of State (1976–2008). He was a Reporter for the Fourth Restatement.

**Edward T. Swaine** is the Charles Kennedy Poe Research Professor, George Washington University Law School, and was Counselor on International Law to the Legal Adviser, U.S. Department of State (2005–2006). He was a Reporter for the Fourth Restatement.

**Bakhtiyar Tuzmukhamedov** is Vice President of the Russian Association of International Law, a member of the Committee Against Torture, and served as a judge on the U.N. Criminal International Tribunals for Rwanda and the Former Yugoslavia (2009–2015). He was a member of the International Advisory Panel for the Fourth Restatement.

**G. Edward White** is the David and Mary Harrison Distinguished Professor, University of Virginia School of Law. His works in legal history have been awarded the Silver Gavel Award from the American Bar Association, the James Willard Hurst Prize from the Law & Society Association, the Littleton-Griswold Prize from the American Historical Association, the Scribes Award, and the Association of American Law Schools' Triennial Coif Award.

**Stephen K. Wirth** is a senior associate in the Washington Office of Arnold & Porter.

**Ingrid Wuerth** is Helen Strong Curry Chair in International Law, and Director, Cecil D. Branstetter Litigation & Dispute Resolution Program, Vanderbilt Law School. She was a Reporter for the Fourth Restatement.

# Introduction

## The Roles of the Restatements in U.S. Foreign Relations Law

*Sarah H. Cleveland & Paul B. Stephan*

That foreign relations law exists as a field owes a great deal to the American Law Institute's Restatements. This may seem strange to someone not immersed in U.S. legal culture. The Institute is a private organization that does not purport to speak with official authority, however august its members may be. Nor is it, strictly speaking, an academic enterprise, at least by U.S. standards. Its Restatements are not meant to be speculative or groundbreaking, but rather distillations of the best of contemporary legal practice in a particular area. Yet Restatements have enormous impact on the development of the law in the United States, nowhere more so than with respect to foreign relations.

Foreign relations law is no little thing. One can provisionally define the field as the legal institutions, rules, and norms that govern a state's engagement with foreign persons, transactions, and activity, counting the international legal system as "foreign." In Curtis Bradley's succinct formulation, "the term is used to encompass the domestic law of each nation that governs how that nation interacts with the rest of the world."[1] For the United States, constitutional transformation in the mid-twentieth century, based on changes in both the Supreme Court's doctrine and the practice of the executive and Congress, drew widespread attention to the role of law in managing these interactions.[2] The half-century since the end of the Warren Court has, if anything, seen an even more profound development of the law, accompanied by greater interest among lawmakers, public actors, civil society, and the legal academy.[3]

---

[1] Curtis A. Bradley, *What Is Foreign Relations Law?*, in THE OXFORD HANDBOOK OF COMPARATIVE FOREIGN RELATIONS LAW 3 (Curtis A. Bradley ed., 2019).

[2] See G. Edward White, *From the Third to the Fourth Restatement of Foreign Relations: The Rise and Potential Fall of Foreign Affairs Exceptionalism*, in this volume.

[3] The literature is vast. For an overview, see Sarah H. Cleveland, *The Plenary Powers Background of Curtis-Wright*, 70 COLO. L. REV. 1127 (1999). For more recent work, some but not all triggered by the U.S. response to the 9/11 attacks, see BRUCE A. ACKERMAN, BEFORE THE NEXT ATTACK: PRESERVING CIVIL LIBERTIES IN AN AGE OF TERRORISM (2006); ANTHONY J. BELLIA JR. & BRADFORD R. CLARK, THE LAW OF NATIONS AND THE UNITED STATES CONSTITUTION (2017); CURTIS A. BRADLEY,

Sarah H. Cleveland & Paul B. Stephan, *Introduction* In: *The Restatement and Beyond*. Edited by: Paul B. Stephan and Sarah H. Cleveland, Oxford University Press (2020). © Oxford University Press.
DOI: 10.1093/oso/9780197533154.003.0001

The issues are myriad. In a global economy, states impose conflicting regulatory demands, often motivated by opposing economic and political interests. The executive and Congress tussle over the authority to regulate, whether in trade (such as recent U.S. import barriers on steel and aluminum), the environment (such as the Paris Agreement, which the Obama administration signed and from which the Trump administration intends to withdraw), national security (such as the Joint Comprehensive Plan of Action with Iran, which the Obama administration crafted and the Trump administration has cast aside),[4] or the use of force (such as debates surrounding the 2001 Authorization of the Use of Military Force, which still serves today as the basis for U.S. military actions around the world).[5] The federal government and the States claim inconsistent prerogatives, for instance over the treatment of undocumented aliens and the right to sanction foreign regimes for human rights abuses. The power of the judiciary to resolve these disputes, especially but not only with respect to the elaboration and enforcement of the rights of persons against foreign and domestic state power, is contested and evolving. Foreign relations law comprises all this and more. The Restatements have done much to shape it.

The first (confusingly called Second) Restatement of the Foreign Relations Law of the United States brought widespread attention to the term "foreign relations law."[6] It appeared at a time when the Warren Court was opening up new vistas for judge-made public law. It staunchly defended the proposition that

---

INTERNATIONAL LAW IN THE U.S. LEGAL SYSTEM (2013); JACK L. GOLDSMITH, THE TERROR PRESIDENCY—LAW AND JUDGMENT INSIDE THE BUSH ADMINISTRATION (2007); ERIC A. POSNER & ADRIAN VERMEULE, TERROR IN THE BALANCE: SECURITY, LIBERTY, AND THE COURTS (2007); SAIKRISHNA PRAKASH, IMPERIAL FROM THE BEGINNING: THE CONSTITUTION OF THE ORIGINAL EXECUTIVE (2015); MICHAEL D. RAMSEY, THE CONSTITUTION'S TEXT IN FOREIGN AFFAIRS (2007); THE CONSTITUTION IN WARTIME: BEYOND ALARMISM AND COMPLACENCY (Mark Tushnet ed., 2005); Richard H. Pildes, *Conflicts Between American and European Views of Law: The Dark Side of Legalism*, 44 VA. J. INT'L L. 145 (2003); Jed Rubenfeld, *Unilateralism and Constitutionalism*, 79 N.Y.U. L. REV. 1971 (2004). For a contemporary historical perspective, see G. EDWARD WHITE, LAW IN AMERICAN HISTORY—VOLUME III: 1930–2000, at 444–509 (2019); G. Edward White, *The Transformation of the Constitutional Regime of Foreign Relations*, 85 VA. L. REV. 1 (1999); G. Edward White, *Observations on the Turning of Foreign Affairs Jurisprudence*, 70 Colo. L. Rev. 1109 (1999).

⁴ On the Paris Agreement and Joint Comprehensive Plan of Action, see Harold Hongju Koh, *Could the President Unilaterally Terminate All International Agreements? Questioning Section 313*, in this volume.

⁵ On the possibility of a future project addressing the international law of armed conflict or the separation of powers with respect to the use of force outside the country, see Bakhtiyar Tuzmukhamedov, *Constitutional Authority for the Transboundary Deployment of Armed Force*, in this volume; Ashley Deeks, *Sleeping Dogs: The Fourth Restatement and International Humanitarian Law*, in this volume.

⁶ RESTATEMENT (SECOND) OF THE FOREIGN RELATIONS LAW OF THE UNITED STATES (Am. Law Inst. 1965). The project got under way in 1955, and its preliminary draft received Institute approval in 1962. The naming convention then used by the Institute numbered the Restatements in relation to each other, conceiving of them as forming generations. Because it already had begun a Second Restatement in another field (torts, on which work commenced in 1952), the Institute titled this

foreign relations, no matter how imbued with discretion and prerogative, still must rest on law. Louis Henkin's great treatise, which appeared seven years later, confirmed that the legal regime that governs foreign relations is fundamentally constitutional law over which the Supreme Court holds sway.[7] Not long after, Henkin took over the drafting of what became the Third Restatement.[8] Prepared during a period of what to many seemed constitutional retrenchment and a loosening of judicial supervision over public life, it offered a robust defense of the proposition that, "In conducting the foreign relations of the United States, Presidents, members of Congress, and public officials are not at large in a political process; they are under law."[9] Moreover, it made clear that the judiciary, as much as the executive and Congress, creates and enforces this law.[10]

The Third Restatement became, by many measures, the most influential of all the Institute's projects. More than a thousand federal and State judicial decisions have cited it, the Supreme Court twenty-nine times, four times in the 2017, 2018, and 2019 terms alone. Practitioners rely on it constantly, and scholars have used it as the launch pad for intense controversies.[11] For foreigners, it is the principal source for understanding how law and foreign relations mix in the United States. And for those committed to judicial protection of individuals, especially the marginalized and downtrodden, in the modern world, it confirms and bolsters the duty of the courts to proclaim law in the service of justice.[12]

The Institute launched a partial revision in 2012. Not everyone agreed with this decision. Some feared that revisiting the Third Restatement would lead to a retreat from its core commitments to judicial development of the rule of

volume Restatement (Second), even though it had no predecessor. On the history of the term "foreign relations" before the Second Restatement, see Bradley, *supra* note 1, at 8–13.

[7] LOUIS HENKIN, FOREIGN AFFAIRS AND THE CONSTITUTION (1972).

[8] The project was initially titled The Restatement of the Foreign Relations Law of the United States (Revised) and was led by Professor Richard R. Baxter of Harvard Law School. Henkin replaced Baxter in 1979 upon the latter's election to the International Court of Justice. It was given its final title as Restatement (Third) in recognition of its place in a new generation of Restatements. In that form, the Institute approved it in 1986.

[9] THIRD RESTATEMENT intro. at 5.

[10] See Paul B. Stephan, *Courts, the Constitution, and Customary International Law—The Intellectual Origins of the Restatement (Third) of the Foreign Relations Law of the United States*, 44 VA. J. INT'L L. 33 (2003).

[11] Compare, e.g., Curtis A. Bradley & Jack L. Goldsmith, *Customary International Law as Federal Common Law: A Critique of the Modern Position*, 110 HARV. L. REV. 815 (1997), with Harold Hongju Koh, *Is International Law Really State Law?*, 111 HARV. L. REV. 1824 (1998); Gerald L. Neuman, *Sense and Nonsense About Customary International Law: A Response to Professors Bradley and Goldsmith*, 66 FORDHAM L. REV. 371 (1997). The debate has crept back into the courts, which have cited the provoking article seventeen times (including two Supreme Court opinions), the Koh response eleven times, and the Neuman response once.

[12] THIRD RESTATEMENT intro. at 4:

In recent years, principally as a result of reinterpretations by the Supreme Court and adjustments by Congress, there has been some redistribution of power among the three

law in foreign relations and protection of individuals from state power. Others argued that the field was in flux and that any effort to codify it would frustrate its progressive evolution.[13] Proponents of the project contended that the transformation of the international environment and the U.S. role in it since the Third Restatement compelled the Institute to do something. Globalization had become a thing, the Cold War had ended (only to be succeeded by a multifaceted struggle against nonstate armed attacks), and the Supreme Court had rethought many of the suppositions underlying the jurisprudence of the Burger, as well as the Warren, Court. The Court in particular had revisited questions of structural constitutionalism that go to the heart of foreign relations law, namely, the constitutional separation of powers within the national (federal) government and the boundaries between federal and State authority.[14] The Third Restatement, the proponents argued, no longer fully reflected the present state of the law, whatever its heroic interventions had achieved.

The Institute responded by authorizing three significant, but limited, projects. The reporters addressed the U.S. approach to treaties, but not other forms of international agreements; U.S. views on jurisdiction, but not generally on separation of powers or federalism; and jurisdictional immunity of states, but not other immunities required or regulated by international law. These three drafts received final Institute approval in 2017 and, after integration into a single text, were published in 2018.[15] Even before publication of the final product, the drafts had an impact, eliciting U.S. twelve judicial citations, including two by the Supreme Court, and dozens of references in legal periodicals.[16]

---

branches of government, and some increased protection for the rights of the individual, in matters relating to foreign relations as well as in other matters.
See Sarah H. Cleveland, *Our International Constitution*, 31 YALE J. INT'L L. 1 (2006).

[13] For ongoing concerns along these lines, see Jide Nzelibe, *Can the Fourth Restatement of Foreign Relations Law Foster Legal Stability?*, in this volume.

[14] Representative cases from the period before the start of the project include Medellín v. Texas, 552 U.S. 491 (2008) (separation of powers); Rasul v. Bush, 542 U.S. 466 (2004) (judicial review in national security cases); American Insurance Ass'n v. Garamendi, 539 U.S. 396 (2003) (federal preemption of State law); Crosby v. Nat'l Foreign Trade Council, 530 U.S. 363 (2000) (preemption).

[15] Because of the initial division of the projects into three parts, there were a total of eleven preliminary drafts, eight Council drafts, and eight tentative drafts. The membership approved the tentative drafts at the May 2017 annual meeting, and the reporters then combined them into an integrated text.

[16] For all citations to the Fourth Restatement, including drafts as well as the final product, see Gamble v. United States, 139 S. Ct. 1960, 1975 n. 12 (2019); Upper Skagit Indian Tribe v. Lundgren, 138 S. Ct. 1649, 1659 (2018) (Thomas, J., dissenting); Bolivarian Republic of Venezuela v. Helmerich & Payne Intern. Drilling Co., 137 S. Ct. 1312, 1321 (2017); United States v. Garcia Sota, 948 F.3d 356, 362 (D.C. Cir. 2020); In re del Valle Ruiz, 939 F.3d 520, 532 (2d Cir. 2019); United States v. Park, 938 F.3d 354, 366 (D.C. Cir. 2019); Mountain Crest SRL, LLC v. Anheuser-Busch InBev SA/NV, 937 F.3d 1067, 1080 nn. 63 & 64 (7th Cir. 2019); United States v. Dávila-Reyes, 937 F.3d 57, 66–67, 70 (1st Cir. 2019) (Lipez, J., concurring); In re Sealed Case, 932 F.3d 915, 940 (D.C. Cir. 2019); United States v. Prado, 933 F.3d 121, 133 n. 6, 136 n. 7, 137 n.8 (2d Cir. 2019); Philipp v. Federal Republic of Germany, 894 F.3d 406, 416 (D.C. Cir. 2018); Doe v. Mattis, 889 F.3d 745, 755–57 (D.C. Cir. 2018),

Meanwhile the leadership of the Institute has indicated an intention to extend the project.[17] If this happens, the reporters most likely will consider some of the issues addressed by the Third Restatement but left out from the published Fourth Restatement, but certainly not all. We thus have arrived at a moment of both reflection and anticipation. There is a completed project that requires assessment, but also the prospect of future action that wants direction. And revision of the new Restatement aside, one cannot expect that foreign relations law will reach a stable equilibrium going forward, any more than it remained unchanged during the remarkable transformation of international relations over the last quarter-century. The field is dynamic, and we must try to anticipate the directions in which it might evolve.

## I. The Fourth Restatement's Past

The American Law Institute's Restatements do not emerge *ex nihilo*. They reflect the times in which they are produced, at best crystallizing the essence of legal doctrine that reflects the beliefs and aspirations of a significant portion of the American legal community. By significant we do not necessarily mean representative: The American Law Institute comprises the U.S. legal élite and expresses the views of leading members of the profession, which need not be the same as those of the rank and file. The Restatements also become a platform for shaping

---

reissued, 928 F.3d 1, 11–13, 21, 23 (D.C. Cir. 2019); *id.* at 35 (Henderson, J., dissenting); Leidos, Inc. v. Hellenic Republic, 881 F.3d 213, 220 (D.C. Cir. 2018); Republic of Marshall Islands v. United States, 865 F.3d 1187, 1193 (9th Cir. 2017); De Csepel v. Republic of Hungary, 859 F.3d 1094, 1112 (D.C. Cir. 2017); Jerez v. Republic of Cuba, 775 F.3d 419, 423 (D.C. Cir. 2014); Simon v. Republic of Hungary, 2020 WL 1170485, at * 4 n. 3 (D.D.C. 2020); Fulmen Company v. Office of Foreign Assets Control, 2020 WL 1536341, at * 9 (D.D.C. 2020); Mulugeta v. Ademachew, 407 F. Supp. 3d 569, 583 (E.D. Va. 2019); Continental Transfert Technique, Limited v. Federal Government of Nigeria, 2019 WL 3562069, at * 14 (D.D.C. 2019); In re Grand Jury Investigation of Possible Violations of 18 U.S.C. § 1956 and 50 U.S.C. § 1705, 381 F. Supp. 3d 37, 66 n. 15 (D.D.C. 2019); KT Corporation v. ABS Holdings, Ltd., 2018 WL 3435405, at * 5 (S.D.N.Y. 2018); Simon v. Republic of Hungary, 277 F. Supp. 3d 42, 50 n. 4 (D.D.C. 2017); Jiménez v. Palacios, 2019 WL 3526479, at * 13 n. 85 (Del. Ch. 2019); AlbaniaBEG Ambient Sh.p.k. v. Enel S.p.A., 160 A.D.3d 93, 104 n. 12, 73 N.Y.S.3d 1 3306 (App. Div. 2018); JPMorgan Chase Bank, N.A. v. Herman, 168 A.3d 514, 518 n. 5 (Conn. 2017). The British judiciary also noted its awareness of the project and called on lawyers to cite to it in the future. R on application of the Freedom and Justice Party v. Sec'y of State for Foreign and Commonwealth Affairs, [2018] EWCA Civ. 1719 ¶ 97:

> For completeness, the ALI is currently working in this field and the Restatement of the Law Fourth, Foreign Relations Law of the United States, approved by the ALI in 2017 awaits publication. It is not a point of criticism of the parties that we were not shown the published drafts of this Restatement but a signal to future readers of this judgment that there may be more up to date and valuable material from the ALI in future.

[17] In his introduction to the Fourth Restatement, ALI Director Richard Revesz says, "My hope is that, in the not-too-distant future, we will undertake a new project designed to complete the Restatement Fourth." FOURTH RESTATEMENT intro. at xvii.

developments in the law going forward as well serving as a foil for critics pushing for change.

Certainly the Restatements of the Foreign Relations Law of the United States have done this. The Second and Third Restatements provided invaluable technical knowledge to a general audience, but they also embraced and to some extent amplified the general approach of what G. Edward White calls "foreign affairs exceptionalism."[18] White traces the origins of this approach to a wish on the part of leading figures in the legal establishment to reconcile resistance to the growth of the federal government with legal support for the assumption by the United States of a leading role among the nations of the world. Then, in the years after World War II, the legal establishment wanted to provide the nation with a structure for the exercise of U.S. power and influence within the West as well as an unencumbered hand in dealing with its Cold War adversaries. White regards the Third Restatement as the apogee of that conception of foreign relations as a field governed by distinct constitutional rules.

White also traces the retreat away from exceptionalism as technological, economic, and political changes combined to blur the line between domestic matters and foreign affairs. The Third Restatement, grounded as it was on a conviction about the distinctiveness of the two domains, invited a reaction and revisionism. What had been taken for granted by most scholars became contested territory. Meanwhile, an emerging majority on the Supreme Court began to pull away from some of the arguments and holdings that the Third Restatement had embraced and in some cases sought to extend.

White sees the influence of this history in the Fourth Restatement. He depicts it as straddling a possible turn in the broad cultural understanding of the law of foreign relations. In his view, it neither leads a revisionist charge nor fights an irredentist struggle against any surrender in the commitment to exceptionalism, but it does expose a shifting of the foundations of the field. As he puts it,

> the Fourth Restatement can clearly be understood as signaling that although foreign affairs exceptionalism has not disappeared from cases and commentary, the broad support for it reflected in the Third Restatement can no longer be said to exist, and in some of its pivotal areas it might be said to be in jeopardy.[19]

White provides a historical context for the Fourth Restatement. He explains the presence of both continuity and the change in the Fourth Restatement, and indicates how it carries its particular historical burden. This anchors the remaining chapters in the volume, which engage directly particular claims made by the Fourth Restatement as well as considering more broadly the possible

[18] White, *supra* note 2.
[19] *Id.* at 58.

futures of the issues it addresses and those that the American Law Institute might confront going forward.

## II. The Fourth Restatement's Present

The business of restating law invites controversy, both as to what gets in and what is left out. The Fourth Restatement is no exception. The contributors to this volume frame the ongoing debates that surround the project. Some of the controversies focus on claims made in the Restatement, while others stake out positions in matters yet to be addressed. We have organized their interventions thematically, largely following the project's organization. Thus we look first at treaties, the subject of the Restatement's Part III.[20] We then consider the allocation of federal and State authority in foreign relations law, an issue that runs through Part IV, Chapters 1–3, but receives only interstitial treatment there. We next explore the role of international law in limiting a state's exercise of jurisdiction. The last set of contemporary debates involves the construction of the kinds of immunity from jurisdiction that a foreign actor might receive in the United States. The Restatement's Part IV, Chapter 5, addresses the immunity of states from adjudicative and enforcement jurisdiction, but not that of international organizations and foreign officials, including diplomats.

With treaties, a fundamental issue is the manner and extent that a court may derive from a treaty in force a rule of decision to apply in a case before it. By most measures, the United States has entered in treaties (defined as international agreements to which the Senate consents to ratification) at a lesser rate recently.[21] The Obama administration saw relatively few Senate consents to ratification, and the Trump administration gives little indication that it wants new international legal commitments in that form.[22] Yet a large inventory of treaties remains in

---

[20] The reporters of the Fourth Restatement decided to follow as best as they could the numerical structure of the Third. A collateral benefit of this approach is to leave room for future additions, if the American Law Institute decides to extend the project. As a result, it begins with Part III, leaving future reporters to develop parts that (more or less) track what the Third Restatement covered in its first two parts.

[21] Oona A. Hathaway, *Treaties' End: The Past, Present, and Future of International Lawmaking in the United States*, 117 YALE L.J. 1236 (2008).

[22] From 1981 through 2008 the Senate gave consent to ratification to an average of 16.36 treaties a year. It gave consent to 9 total in President Obama's first term, and 11 in his second, for an average of 2.5 over his time in office. Since President Trump's inauguration, the Senate has consented to the ratification of seven treaties, all submitted by the Obama administration. One, an amendment to the NATO Treaty to allow the accession of Montenegro, has come under a shadow due to remarks by President Trump raising the possibility of U.S. withdrawal from that organization. See Koh, *supra* note 4. The current administration has withdrawn from two Article II treaties, the Treaty of Amity, Economic Relations, Consular Relations with Iran and the multilateral Optional Protocol to the Vienna Convention on Diplomatic Relations. In both cases the consent to jurisdiction of the International Court of Justice was unacceptable to the United States in light of recent cases filed

force, presenting ongoing questions of interpretation and implementation. How should courts, as well as government officials and legislators, glean meaning from these agreements and participate in their enforcement?

For a semi-monist country like the United States, treaty interpretation and application present problems. On the one hand, uniformity across treaty parties seems a worthwhile goal. It would be odd if the same text created different legal obligations for some of the parties. On the other hand, because at least some treaties have direct effect in the U.S. domestic legal system, and others exercise a kind of gravitation pull on domestic law due to canons of construction informed by policy, one might expect rules for interpreting domestic law also to be relevant. But what happens when these interpretive principles push in opposite directions?

The response of the Fourth Restatement to this problem leans on the side of international uniformity. Its section on treaty interpretation emphasizes the principles articulated in the Vienna Convention on the Law of Treaties, an instrument to which the United States is not a party but which, in the view of the United States, captures the basic elements of the customary international law of treaty interpretation.[23] The Restatement acknowledges the competing concern of respecting domestic lawmaking, but seems to endorse the criticism that excessive reliance on statements generated in the course of the advise-and-consent process would put the United States out of step with international practice.[24] At the same time, it supports the U.S. practice of expressing exceptional treaty interpretations through the adoption of conditions in the course of ratification.[25] This endorsement necessarily is limited to domestic law, as U.S. treaty makers lack the authority to impose an interpretation on other parties.[26]

The Restatement also endorses the principle that the United States may enter into treaties that prescribe rules that Congress, in the absence of a treaty, could not adopt.[27] At the same time, it is carefully noncommittal as to the proposition that the structural constitutional limitations of federalism play no role in the making or application of treaties.[28] It similarly elides the controversy

---

under those treaties. The administration most recently terminated the Intermediate-Range Nuclear Forces Treaty with Russia.

[23] FOURTH RESTATEMENT § 306 & cmt. *a*, reporters' note 1. For a prior article advocating this approach, see Jean Galbraith, *What Should the Restatement (Fourth) Say About Treaty Interpretation?*, 2015 B.Y.U. L. REV. 1499.

[24] FOURTH RESTATEMENT § 306 reporters' note 11.

[25] *Id.* § 305. See Edward T. Swaine, *Reserving*, 31 YALE J. INT'L L. 307 (2006).

[26] FOURTH RESTATEMENT § 305 cmt. *e*. A reservation may alter the international obligations of the United States, but international law governs both the effectiveness and consequences of reservations.

[27] *Id.* § 312.

[28] *Id.* §§ 307 (discussing individual-rights constitutional constraints); 305 cmt. *b* (separation-of-powers limitations); 312 cmts. *b* & *c* (federal authority to prescribe through treaties exceeds that of Congress). For the debate on federalism constitutional limitations, compare Curtis A. Bradley, *The*

over another structural constitutional limitation, namely, whether the treaty provisions of Article II provide an exclusive means of concluding at least some international agreements.[29] This leaves open an extensive discussion over what one might call treaty exceptionalism, namely, the different status of treaty-making as a positive power of lawmaking under the Constitution. Whether this is an important conversation, or instead merely interesting, turns on whether the recent decline in treaty adoptions by the United States is transitory or structural.

The essays in this volume concentrate on the separation-of-power issues that international agreements pose. Article II treaties, the focus of the Fourth Restatement's Part III, dispense with the House of Representatives but depend on a supermajority of the Senate to provide consent as a condition to the president's subsequent ratification. Since the founding of the nation, however, presidents have also entered into international agreements either on their own constitutional authority or on the basis of legislation adopted by Congress. The coexistence of these mechanisms, one expressly provided by Article II of the Constitution and the other implied from the competences pricked out by Articles I and II, leads to many problems. Are the two mechanisms in any sense exclusive, in the sense that certain kinds of international agreements by the nature can be joined by the United States only by employing one, but not the other?[30] What kinds of powers do executed international agreements give the executive, and what kinds of controls may Congress retain over the executive authority established by an agreement? What role do the courts have in holding the executive to limits imposed by Congress in the course of implementing an agreement.

Harold Hongju Koh considers the question of exit from international agreements. The Trump administration came into office vowing to transform U.S. relations with the rest of the world, in particular by challenging the many commitments crafted by earlier presidents both during and after the Cold War. It has withdrawn from several treaties (of both the Article II kind and the others) and has threatened to pull out of still more. Koh proposes to revise how presidents can exit international agreements by construing Articles I and II as to require, roughly speaking, the same degree of congressional involvement in the

---

*Treaty Power and American Federalism*, 97 MICH. L. REV. 390 (1998), and Curtis A. Bradley, *The Treaty Power and American Federalism, Part II*, 99 MICH. L. REV. 98 (2000), with David M. Golove, *Treaty-Making and the Nation: The Historical Foundations of the Nationalist Conception of the Treaty Power*, 98 MICH. L. REV. 1075 (2000).

[29] FOURTH RESTATEMENT § 310 cmt. *f* & reporters' note 11 (discussing constitutional requirement of legislation, but not addressing constitutional requirement of a treaty). The lack of a mandate to discuss nontreaty international agreements explains this gap. For the debate, compare Bruce Ackerman & David Golove, *Is NAFTA Constitutional?* 108 HARV. L. REV. 799 (1995), with Laurence R. Tribe, *Taking Text and Structure Seriously: Reflections on Free-Form Method in Constitutional Interpretation*, 108 HARV. L. REV. 1221 (1995).

[30] See Curtis A. Bradley, *Article II Treaties and Signaling Theory*, in this volume.

exit process as was required to authorize U.S entry.[31] As to Article II treaties, this entails a criticism of the Fourth Restatement, which, he argues, too readily embraces the conventional wisdom of the last forty years about the president's authority unilaterally to terminate a treaty in the absence of any legislatively imposed limits. As to treaties derived from legislatively adopted authority, he proposes adoption of an interpretive template that would read into legislation bestowing competences a requirement that the undoing of any resulting international commitments requires symmetrical legislative participation.

Samuel Estreicher argues that Congress already has substantial control over executive authority under international agreements.[32] He sees a trend toward domestic implementation of treaties through legislation, rather than by regarding treaties as adopting rules that apply directly in the domestic legal system. He argues that all three branches need to do a better job of crafting, adopting, and applying treaty-implementing statutes. He looks at cases where, in his view, Congress and the courts missed an opportunity to clarify the domestic significance of particular treaties, as well as one instance, the Refugee Act of 1980, where Congress built upon and extended the rights proclaimed in the international instrument.

Koh's second claim and Estreicher's argument open up issues that an extended Fourth Restatement is likely to address, namely, the relationship between international agreements of all sorts and domestic legislation. Jean Galbraith argues that the Restatement's focus on Article II treaties is unexceptionally conventional but misses the most important problem, namely, the role of international law as both a foundation of and a constraint on the modern administrative state.[33] She suggests that, rather than seeing international agreements as presenting exceptional separation-of-powers issues, we should use the lens of contemporary administrative law as a means of sorting out matters of executive prerogative, legislative control, and judicial oversight. In this sense, her chapter underscores White's speculation about a waning of foreign affairs exceptionalism.

Curtis A. Bradley steps back to consider a structural question, namely, what impact does the choice between Senate consent based on a supermajority vote and authorization grounded on a legislative act have on presidential interests and authority?[34] He assumes that we still observe constitutional limits on the choice, in the sense that, by well-established convention if not by a judicially enforceable rule, the executive must submit at least some kinds of treaties to the Senate for a supermajority vote of consent. He questions, however, what this choice means

[31] Koh, *supra* note 4.
[32] Samuel Estreicher, *Taking Treaty-Implementing Statutes Seriously*, in this volume.
[33] Jean Galbraith, *The Fourth Restatement's Treatment of International Law and Administrative Law*, in this volume.
[34] Bradley, *supra* note 30.

to the United States' international partners. He effectively disposes of one popular argument, that a treaty signals an administration's stronger commitment to
an international project, by demonstrating all the ways that treaties can be un-
done. Like the other chapters on international agreements, Bradley documents
the ways in which the law of U.S. international agreements rest on general bodies
of domestic law, rather than distinctive international norms.

As White notes, the Third Restatement made ambitious and ultimately controversial claims about the status of international law as the domestic federal law
of the United States. The Fourth Restatement did not confront those claims directly, as they fell outside the reporters' remit. This did not preclude them from
addressing particular applications of those claims, to some extent opening space
between its position and that of the Third Restatement.

Several chapters in this book address the status of international law in U.S. law
head on. Given the enduring debate that the Third Restatement touched off, one
should not be surprised that they do not agree. Gary Born delivers perhaps the
most comprehensive defense of the position that the U.S. legal system should
open itself up to the domestication of international law, pushing back against
several decades of recent Supreme Court jurisprudence.[35] He would go further
than even the Third Restatement in assimilating all private international law—
conflicts of law, the law governing the choice of forum, the rules for recognition and enforcement of foreign judgments, the *forum non conveniens* doctrine,
and the like—to federal common law. One of the authors of this introduction
pushes in the opposite direction, defending and seeking to extend the judgments
memorialized in the Fourth Restatement about the limited scope of federal
common law.[36]

This debate turns on perceptions of the history of these doctrines and disagreement about the context that the history imposed, as well as functional
arguments about the role of judicial discretion and concerns about various kinds
of legal risk. One might see State legislatures and courts alternatively as incom-
petent when not predatory, or as subject to bracing market discipline of a sort
from which the federal courts are largely free. One might draw either sweeping
conclusions or make carefully limited interventions in the law.

In the latter category is the chapter authored by Anthony J. Bellia Jr. and
Bradford R. Clark.[37] They provide a critique of one particular conclusion
of the Third Restatement, namely, that the long-standing presumption that
Congress does not intend to put the United States in violation of its international

---

[35] Gary Born, *International Law in American Courts*, in this volume. For a fuller exposition of his
views, see GARY BORN, INTERNATIONAL LAW IN AMERICAN COURTS (2020).

[36] Paul B. Stephan, *The Waning of the Federal Common Law of Foreign Relations*, in this volume.

[37] Anthony J. Bellia Jr. & Bradford R. Clark, *Restating* The Charming Betsy *as a Canon of Avoidance*,
in this volume.

obligations extends to all duties imposed by international law, not just those to which the United States owes other states.[38] They argue that the doctrine, as developed by the Marshall Court and applied since by the Supreme Court, is one of constitutional avoidance, not of international law protection. As a result, it applies only to statutes that might lead the judiciary to intrude into the management of relations with other states, what they call the law of state-to-state relations. They do not deny the power of Congress to mandate such intrusions, but interpret the doctrine as seeking to raise the barrier to such acts. They express the hope that further work on the Fourth Restatement will clarify that point.

Chimène I. Keitner touches on an issue that did not have a substantial practical manifestation until after the Fourth Restatement went to press.[39] Congress, in the course of expanding the power of victims of terrorist acts to seek recourse in U.S. courts, has significantly revised the rules for *in personam* jurisdiction with respect to certain foreign states and foreign officials. These moves have made concrete a question that previously had lurked around the edges of certain litigation, namely, whether the Constitution limits in any way the power of Congress to invite suits against foreign states and their representatives in a manner that, if applied to other potential defendants, would raise significant questions of constitutional due process. Keitner sketches the case for imposing constitutional limits, in part to bolster international legal constraints on the assertion of judicial jurisdiction over foreign states.

Thomas H. Lee also considers the ongoing role of customary international law as a source of rules of decision that U.S. courts might apply.[40] He criticizes the Third Restatement for what he regards as an excessive and unfounded embrace of this body of law as federal common law, but argues that the Fourth Restatement goes too far in the other direction. He contends that federal courts can resort to customary international law in some contexts in a way that does not exceed the constitutional and jurisprudential limits on federal judicial power or otherwise upset the constitutional separation of powers.

John C. Harrison approaches the same problem from the perspective of constitutional theory. He observes that the best historical evidence indicates that the references to "the Laws of the United States" in the portions of the Constitution dealing with judicial power did not include judge-made law. He recognizes that the modern Supreme Court in a handful of cases has reached the contrary conclusion, but seeks to chart a course correction. In particular, he seeks to counter what he regards as excessive inferences drawn from the famous decision of *Erie*

---

[38] THIRD RESTATEMENT § 114.

[39] Chimène I. Keitner, *Personal Jurisdiction and Fifth Amendment Due Process Revisited*, in this volume.

[40] Thomas H. Lee, *Customary International Law and U.S. Judicial Power: From the Third to the Fourth Restatements*, in this volume.

*Railroad v. Tompkins.*[41] He particular regards as unfounded the Supreme Court's mandate that a federal court always must apply the conflicts-of-law rules of the State in which it sits with respect to all nonfederal rules of decision.[42] He argues that development of conflicts rules by federal courts in their role of expounding general law can achieve many of the desirable outcomes of managing international litigation without the constitutional infirmity of federal common law.

On matters of jurisdiction, the Third Restatement famously made ambitious claims not only about the status of international law in U.S. courts but also about the existence of bodies of customary international law regulating transnational legal conflicts. Two in particular provoked pushback from both the U.S. government and foreign commentators—the claims that customary international law regulates assertions of national prescriptive jurisdiction through a "rule of reason" that relies on multifactored balancing applied on a case-by-case basis, and that customary international law regulates assertions of adjudicative jurisdiction even in instances where neither jurisdiction to prescribe nor jurisdiction to enforce is implicated. The Fourth Restatement, by contrast, avoids using claims about international law as a vehicle for reforming U.S. law. To a greater degree than the Third Restatement, it distinguishes the question of best practice from that of what international law requires. For example, it recognizes that in an interconnected world, with fundamental features such as the World Wide Web that were unimaginable to the framers of the Third Restatement, regulatory and policy conflicts based on overlapping assertions of prescriptive jurisdiction are prevalent and significant. It shifts the means for judicial mediation of these overlaps from the development of customary international law to the implementation of strategies of statutory interpretation.[43]

One might think that these techniques, customary international law creation and interpretation of domestic law, collapse into the same thing. Both give courts a role in avoiding conflicts between competing national regulatory regimes by raising the cost to lawmakers of enacting such conflicts. Focusing on interpretation of domestic law, rather than on pronouncing rules that presumably bind all states, has its advantages. It allows national courts to address their own sovereigns, rather than imputing to other states a legal standard that governs the world. This shift in focus makes the dispute-avoidance strategy less threatening to other states and may do a better job of inducing their restraint and cooperation. The cost, some argue, is to remove U.S. judges from international conversations that privileges judges of all nations over other lawmakers.

---

[41] 304 U.S. 64 (1938).
[42] Klaxon Co. v. Stentor Elec. Mfg. Co., 313 U.S. 487 (1941).
[43] Compare FOURTH RESTATEMENT § 405 (ascribing reasonableness in exercise of prescriptive jurisdiction to international comity), with THIRD RESTATEMENT § 403 (ascribing reasonableness in exercise of prescriptive jurisdiction to customary international law).

Consider the controversial practice of "tag" jurisdiction. The Third Restatement indicated that assertion of judicial power over a person based on fleeting presence within the jurisdiction transgressed an emerging norm of customary international law.[44] Embarrassingly, the Supreme Court in 1990 held that service on a natural person temporarily present in a forum satisfies the standards of constitutional due process.[45] Rather than finding U.S. doctrine in conflict with international law, the Fourth Restatement accounts for current domestic doctrine and does not indicate whether international law requires anything else.[46] Instead it indicates that the law of foreign judgment recognition and enforcement, concededly not based on international legal obligation but nonetheless highly salient, provides a satisfactory response to excessive assertions of adjudicative jurisdiction.[47]

This shift in emphasis raises a broader question, on which views can differ. One can assume the desirability of the progressive development of rules of prescriptive jurisdiction to manage conflicts caused by competing demands by different sovereigns. Is the adoption of international rules necessarily the optimal response? If all sovereigns recognize and apply the same rules identically, then the answer surely is yes.

In a world where sovereigns advance competing claims about the content and limitations of international law, however, this conclusion may not follow. Given the opportunity to make a rule that purports to bind many or most other states, each state may assert claims that reflect its particular interests and culture.[48] Assigning a role to international law in managing prescriptive conflicts then might, perversely, increase international friction, as competing claims about the content of what is supposed to be a universally binding rule pile up. The alternative approach, of each state seeking within its domestic legal system to increase international harmony without insisting on exact equivalence or reciprocity from other states, might achieve greater progress.[49] One might respond, however, that softening the obligation to cooperate more likely will produce confusion and recriminations, not harmony.

Two of the chapters here champion the Third Restatement's approach to these issues. Hannah Buxbaum and Ralf Michaels argue that a general embrace of the

---

[44] THIRD RESTATEMENT § 421(2)(a) & cmt. *e* ("not generally acceptable under international law").

[45] Burnham v. Superior Court, 495 U.S. 604 (1990). Four Justices held that presence alone was sufficient; the concurring opinion of Justice Brennan, who supplied the fifth vote for the decision, focused on voluntariness and sought to leave the door open for exceptions.

[46] FOURTH RESTATEMENT § 422 cmt. *c* & reporters' notes 5, 7.

[47] *Id.* § 484(f), cmt. *h* & reporters' note 7.

[48] ANTHEA ROBERTS, IS INTERNATIONAL LAW INTERNATIONAL? (2017); COMPARATIVE INTERNATIONAL LAW (Anthea Roberts, Paul B. Stephan, Pierre-Hugues Verdier, & Mila Versteeg eds., 2018).

[49] William S. Dodge, *International Comity in American Law*, 115 COLUM. L. REV. 2071 (2015) (international comity as an alternative to binding international legal obligation).

"rule of reason" in the academic community and repeated references to the Third Restatement by the courts show that, however innovative the doctrine might have been in 1987, it has evolved into a rule of law.[50] Austen Parrish follows on with a similar defense of the Third Restatement's conclusion that customary international law limits the power of national courts to assert jurisdiction over persons, even when the courts do not purport to prescribe rules of decision for such disputes or impose material sanctions on the persons brought within their jurisdiction.[51]

William S. Dodge argues that the Third Restatement, as well as its contemporary defenders, failed to appreciate the useful distinction between an international legal obligation and a norm of international behavior that signals a cooperative, rather than law-abiding, disposition.[52] The concept of international comity, he argues, provides all of the needed rules of the road for international transactions and litigation without putting the Restatement's reporters in the role of imposing legal rules that many if not most states regard as desirable but not mandatory.

Pamela K. Bookman offers a forwarding-looking perspective on the problem of adjudicative jurisdiction. She explores the springing up of specialized courts for international litigation around the world, largely detached from traditional state judiciaries although rooted in the authority of particular states. These bodies inevitably will challenge traditional conceptions of prescriptive and adjudicative jurisdiction, requiring the international regime. She is agnostic as to the choice between customary international law and international comity, instead expressing confidence that the need for a new round of restating the law will be manifest sooner rather than later.

Donald Earl Childress III draws a comparison not between the Third and Fourth Restatements, but rather between the Fourth Restatement and the much earlier Second Restatement of the Conflict of Laws.[53] Both address the doctrine of *forum non conveniens*, a mechanism that allows a domestic court with jurisdiction over a civil suit to dismiss a case in favor of a foreign venue. Childress notes the growing significance of the doctrine in allocating jurisdiction among states, the failure of the Conflict Restatement to provide any useful guidance on the matter, and what he considers the limited success of the Fourth Restatement to channel what otherwise might be unconstrained judicial discretion. He looks

[50] Hannah Buxbaum & Ralf Michaels, *Reasonableness as a Limitation on the Extraterritorial Application of U.S. Law: From 403 to 405 (via 404)*, in this volume.
[51] Austen Parrish, *Adjudicatory Jurisdiction and Public International Law: The Fourth Restatement's New Approach*, in this volume.
[52] William S. Dodge, *International Comity in the Fourth Restatement*, in this volume.
[53] Donald Earl Childress III, Forum Non Conveniens *in the Fourth Restatement*, in this volume.

to the American Law Institute's ongoing Third Restatement of the Conflict of Laws as a possible source of further legal development.

Finally, George Rutherglen considers the ongoing problem of territoriality as a concept on which to ground various forms of state jurisdiction.[54] On the one hand, growing international connectivity and the dematerialization of interactions in a cyber world confound the practical consequences of the territorial concept. On the other hand, no other concept comes readily to hand to allocate assertions of state legal authority, whether prescriptive, adjudicative, or enforcement. Rutherglen leaves us with a sense of grudging respect for territoriality as a limiting principle, however out of date it might seem.

One area of international jurisdiction where Congress has taken an active role in defining U.S. obligations under international law is state immunity. That states enjoy some kind of immunity from the adjudicative jurisdiction of other states is a fundamental feature of contemporary international law. It rests on the core principle of sovereign equality, expressed in the maxim that no state's courts have the right to stand in judgment of another state's actions. This basic proposition leaves open a host of questions, however. How complete is this principle? May a state make an irrevocable waiver of its rights and thus submit to another state's courts? What about state acts that do not rest on a state's character as a sovereign to have legal effect, that is private acts that happen to be undertaken by a state? What about actions that are attributable to a state under general international legal principles of state responsibility, but which are antithetical to the international legal order (such as torture, genocide, or acts of aggression)? When an otherwise lawful civil judgment is entered against a state, how can that judgment be enforced?

Until adoption of the Foreign Sovereign Immunities Act in 1976, the executive branch had the leading, and perhaps exclusive, role within the U.S. constitutional system for answering these questions. With this legislation, Congress took over the subject, with the inevitable statutory ambiguity leaving a substantial role for the judiciary. The executive went from the center of power to an occasional amicus curiae with only limited success in bringing the courts around to its understanding of what the statute, as well as international law, requires.

How this system would evolve, and in what directions the courts would take the statute, were largely unclear at the time of the Third Restatement. The Fourth Restatement's reporters, by contrast, confronted a welter of decisions, many by the Supreme Court.[55] Much of their work consisted of making sense out of the

---

[54]  George Rutherglen, *Territoriality and Its Troubles*, in this volume.

[55]  The Court has delivered twenty opinions in cases involving the interpretation of the Foreign Sovereign Immunities Act since adoption of the Third Restatement, eight of those since the Fourth Restatement got under way. There were only two for the reporters of the Third Restatement to consider.

highly technical, sometimes confused decisions, rather than filling in gaps and trying to push the law in directions not clearly indicated by the statute.

The Fourth Restatement generally maps the approach of the U.S. courts, the Supreme Court in particular. As the Court has repeatedly emphasized, the Foreign Sovereign Immunities Act occupies the field of state immunity, leaving no room for implied exceptions or extensions.[56] Within that field, it sets a default of immunity and puts a plaintiff to the task of finding an exception within the four corners of the statute. It has done this not only with respect to adjudicative jurisdiction but also as to the enforcement of judgments against a foreign sovereign's assets.[57] The Court accordingly has paid less attention to the issue of whether customary international law demands immunity in particular cases and has not considered whether customary international law might forbid immunity in some instances. The Restatement consistently compares and contrasts the requirements of international law with those of the Foreign Sovereign Immunities Act, but does not indicate that a court should follow the former where it departs from the latter.[58]

One chapter in this book criticizes the Fourth Restatement for its failure to confront the inconsistency between contemporary international law and one significant aspect of the contemporary statutory structure, the so-called terrorism exception to state immunity. Various amendments to the Foreign Sovereign Immunities Act over the last quarter-century have removed immunity for states that, in the view of the U.S. executive, are sponsors of terrorism. Beth Stephens observes that this criterion is essentially orthogonal to any plausible argument for recognizing an exception's to international law's default rule of state immunity.[59] Foreign policy considerations dominate, so that the transgressions of friendly states are overlooked, while those of adversaries are magnified. She would welcome recognition of exceptions to state immunity that bolster human rights enforcement, but maintains that U.S. practice with respect to terrorism conflicts with established international law and brings with it no moral weight that might justify efforts to forge a new norm.[60]

---

[56] Argentine Republic v. Amerada Hess Shipping Corp., 488 U.S. 428 (1989) (no exceptions to immunity from adjudicative jurisdiction outside statute); Republic of Argentina v. NML Capital, Ltd., 134 S. Ct. 2250 (2014) (no immunity from discovery provided by statute for cases within exception to immunity from adjudicative jurisdiction); FOURTH RESTATEMENT ch. 5, intro. note, at 323.

[57] Ministry of Defense and Support for Armed Forces of Islamic Republic of Iran v. Elahi, 546 U.S. 450 (2006); Rubin v. Islamic Republic of Iran, 138 S. Ct. 816 (2018); FOURTH RESTATEMENT § 464 reporters' note 10.

[58] FOURTH RESTATEMENT § 451 cmt. a (adjudicative jurisdiction); id. § 464 reporters' note 16 (enforcement jurisdiction).

[59] Beth Stephens, The Fourth Restatement, International Law, and the "Terrorism" Exception to the Foreign Sovereign Immunities Act, in this volume.

[60] Kristina Daugirdas, in the course of her more general critique of the Fourth Restatement's approach to international law, makes similar arguments about the U.S. terrorism exception to state immunity. Kristina Daugirdas, The Restatements and the Rule of Law, in this volume.

Two other chapters explore topics in the international law of immunity that an extension of the Fourth Restatement might address. David P. Stewart and Ingrid Wuerth look at the immunity of international organizations and their officials.[61] In the United States, a statute addresses the question, but its fails to provide clear answers to the most important questions about the scope of those immunities. The Supreme Court recently stepped into the gap, but its interpretation of the statute leaves open as many questions as it answers. Stewart and Wuerth seek to clean this mess, and in the course of doing so guide future reporters of an extended Restatement.

Finally, John B. Bellinger III and Stephen K. Wirth address a significant problem that the American Law Institute thought too undeveloped to be incorporated into the first version of the Fourth Restatement, namely, the immunity of foreign officials from judicial jurisdiction.[62] In the United States, these cases almost always involve suits seeking compensation for alleged violations of international human rights law. As Bellinger and Wirth show, ongoing issues highlight the role of the executive in determining the scope of common law immunity and the inferences to be drawn from legislation, in particular the Torture Victim Protection Act, that establishes a federal cause of action for such violations. As they note, these questions may soon command the attention of the Supreme Court, although there is no reason to expect that the Court will put everything important to rest.

The significance of the debate is enormous. If immunity exists whenever a foreign state refuses to disavow the acts of its officials, civil litigation as a means of condemning and seeking reparations for grave human rights abuses would mostly disappear. But allowing suits to go forward whenever plaintiffs can obtain jurisdiction over foreign officials creates a hole in the principle of immunity, which is supposed to provide states, and arguably those through whom states act, freedom from litigation, not just from liability.

## III. The Fourth Restatement's Future

However one assesses the accomplishments of the Fourth Restatement, what remains to be done? The Third Restatement had two volumes, the first comprising a kind of general part of foreign relations law, the second a series of special parts covering topics such as the law of the sea, international environmental law,

---

[61] David P. Stewart & Ingrid Wuerth, *The Jurisdictional Immunities of International Organizations: Recent Developments and the Challenges of the Future*, in this volume.

[62] John B. Bellinger III & Stephen K. Wirth, *Foreign-Official Immunity under the Common Law*, in this volume.

human rights, international economic law, and remedies under international law. Should the Institute take on all or any of these subjects? What about international humanitarian law, the relevance of which to the United States has grown enormously since 9/11? Something that the reporters of the Third Restatement could not have imagined is the rise of cyber conflicts, both militarized and politicized. Do we need a Restatement of the law of cyber relations, whether governing state-backed attacks, nonstate vandals, political interference, espionage, economic injuries (including theft of intellectual property), or censorship? Have particular areas of economic law, such as international trade, international financial regulation, or anticorruption, developed to the point where they demand separate treatment as elements of foreign relations law?

There are at least two schools of thought about the desirability of extending the Fourth Restatement to specific bodies of foreign relations law. On the one hand, these subjects give content to the concept of foreign relations law. They demonstrate concretely how the general framework laid out in the general part affects critical choices in areas of law that have evolved from esoteric to mainstream over the last thirty years.

The opposing view concedes the great significance of these areas of law and argues that for this reason they deserve separate restatements by specialized experts.[63] During the 1980s it might have been possible for four scholars, admittedly giants of the field, to stand astride such diverse topics as the law of the sea and human rights. But as these fields have deepened, the need for a firm command of their specifics has grown. As so often occurs, this argument goes, the emergence of a field makes it harder for generalists to remain relevant.

Two chapters flesh out the opposite positions on this question as to one especially salient topic, international humanitarian law. Bakhtiyar Tuzmukhamedov provides a survey of comparative international practice regarding authorization to deploy force outside a state's boundaries.[64] He indicates that patterns exist and the need for stronger legal foundations is clear. Ashley Deeks, however, looks at the fundamental instability of this body of law in the face of new technologies for conducting armed conflict and the profound divisions among states about the

---

[63] Current Institute projects that cover topics addressed in the Third Restatement include The U.S. Law of International Commercial and Investor-State Arbitration (Proposed Final Draft, Apr. 24, 2019), the Restatement of the Law Third Conflict of Laws (Preliminary Draft No. 5, Oct. 23, 2019), and Principles for a Data Economy (Tent. Draft No. 1, May 22, 2020; joint project with European Law Institute). Completed projects include PRINCIPLES OF THE LAW, INTELLECTUAL PROPERTY: PRINCIPLES GOVERNING JURISDICTION, CHOICE OF LAW, AND JUDGMENTS IN TRANSNATIONAL DISPUTES (Am. Law Inst. 2008); PRINCIPLES OF THE LAW, TRANSNATIONAL CIVIL PROCEDURE (Am. Law Inst. 2004); PRINCIPLES OF THE LAW, TRANSNATIONAL INSOLVENCY (Am. Law Inst. 2012); RECOGNITION AND ENFORCEMENT OF FOREIGN JUDGMENTS: ANALYSIS AND PROPOSED FEDERAL STATUTE (Am. Law Inst. 2006); LEGAL AND ECONOMIC PRINCIPLES OF WORLD TRADE LAW (Am. Law Inst. 2012).

[64] Tuzmukhamedov, *supra* note 5.

feasibility of legal regulation, much less the content of such law.[65] She suggests that abstention would keep the reporters of a future Restatement out of trouble, and that plunging into the fray is not likely to lead to a positive outcome.

Edward T. Swaine reviews basic questions of methodology and ambition implicated in restating the law of foreign relations.[66] When considering state practice, for example, what weight should be given to the views of the government? It enjoys authority and experience, but also is disinclined to take a critical perspective or to own up to its own transgressions. Kristina Daugirdas also takes up this point.[67] She argues that reporters should assume, if not an adversarial stance, at least greater skepticism and detachment when faced with official accounts of encounters between domestic and international law. She envisions a Restatement as functioning somewhat like a judicial tribunal, disinterested, skeptical, and fair.

Jide Nzelibe ends the book with a set of more existential questions.[68] Does it make sense to restate a body of law that both shapes and reflects many dynamic processes, both international and domestic? Is there any reason to expect that forces that transformed the world between the adoption of the Third Restatement and the launching of the Fourth to slow down in the near future? It seems not only unrealistic but undesirable to freeze a body of law that must adapt broadly and quickly to a fluid environment. But if it is not to freeze the law, what else can a Restatement do?

* * *

It is our hope that the Fourth Restatement, of which we take personal responsibility as well as professional pride, can serve as a focus for the progressive development of the law and a means to illuminate some of the difficult issues that the law confronts, even if it cannot aspire to definitive resolution of anything. The essays in this book challenge that hope. It brings us great personal satisfaction that such a distinguished body of scholars agreed that the topic deserves their attention. Our fascination with and enthusiasm for the law of the foreign relations of the United States remains undiminished.

---

[65] Deeks, *supra* note 5.

[66] Edward T. Swaine, *Consider the Source: Evidence and Authority in the Fourth Restatement*, in this volume.

[67] Daugirdas, *supra* note 60.

[68] Nzelibe, *supra* note 13.

# PART I
# THE FOURTH RESTATEMENT AND THE PAST

# 1

# From the Third to the Fourth Restatement of Foreign Relations

## The Rise and Potential Fall of Foreign Affairs Exceptionalism

### G. Edward White

The Restatements of legal subjects promulgated by the American Law Institute are issued in successive editions for a reason. The primary purpose of a Restatement of a legal field is assumed to be that of providing an authoritative overview of its controlling doctrines. Ever since the ALI decided that its first editions of Restatements, promulgated in the 1930s, needed revision, successive editions of Restatements have emphasized unsettled and evolving doctrinal issues in addition to presumptively settled "black-letter" doctrinal propositions. Yet it seems fair to say that mere uncertainty about the application of core doctrinal propositions to future controversies has not been enough to generate a decision to issue a new Restatement. What seems needed is a sense that court decisions and commentary issued after the publication of a Restatement do not seem to be reinforcing its core doctrines, and may well be undermining them.

That sense appears to have brought about the ALI's decision to commission a Fourth Restatement of the Foreign Relations Law of the United States.[1] The last published edition of the Third Restatement of Foreign Relations appeared in 1987.[2] By 2011 the ALI had agreed to commission a Fourth Restatement, selecting Sarah H. Cleveland and Paul B. Stephan as Coordinating Reporters a year later. Between 2014 and 2017 eight Tentative Drafts of the Fourth Restatement were produced, and in 2018 the Fourth Restatement, after approval by the ALI membership a year earlier, was published. Although twenty-five years between the publication of a Restatement and the decision to commission to a successor is not unprecedented in the ALI's history,[3] we will see that in the case of

---

[1] FOURTH RESTATEMENT.

[2] THIRD RESTATEMENT.

[3] The "Second" Restatement of Foreign Relations Law (so-called because the ALI then numbered restatements in relation to each other and a Second Restatement of Torts was already under way) was published in 1965. By 1980 Louis Henkin's revisionist treatise of the constitutional dimensions of foreign relations law, FOREIGN AFFAIRS AND THE CONSTITUTION (1972) had appeared, the ALI

G. Edward White, *From the Third to the Fourth Restatement of Foreign Relations* In: *The Restatement and Beyond*. Edited by: Paul B. Stephan and Sarah H. Cleveland, Oxford University Press (2020). © Oxford University Press.
DOI: 10.1093/oso/9780197533154.003.0002

the Third Restatement it represented the startling collapse of a long-established orthodoxy about foreign relations jurisprudence.

This chapter traces and analyzes the course from the Third to the Fourth Restatement of Foreign Relations Law. It is primarily about why the Third Restatement, arguably the most authoritative embodiment of a particular approach to the law of foreign relations in America to appear in the twentieth century, should have had that authority suddenly, and decisively, questioned at that century's end, and subsequently repudiated, at least in part, by judicial decisions and commentary in the first two decades of the twenty-first century. It is about what I am calling the twentieth-century rise, and the twenty-first-century potential fall, of foreign relations exceptionalism.

## I. The Hegemony of Foreign Affairs Exceptionalism

### A. Origins

In 1910 George Sutherland, then a senator from Utah, published in the *North American Review* an essay entitled "The Internal and External Powers of the National Government."[4] In it Sutherland argued that there was a critical distinction between "the Federal powers of the general government, which are exerted in its dealings with the several states and their people, and the national powers which are exerted in its dealings with the outside world."[5] Over the next nine years Sutherland would continue to emphasize that distinction, suggesting that there was an important difference between the federal government's role as an actor within the American constitutional system and its role as a sovereign in the international order.[6] In that latter capacity, he argued, many powers of the federal government were not derived from the Constitution, but from "extra-constitutional"[7] sources, such as the acknowledged capacity of sovereign nations

---

had commissioned a Third Restatement of Foreign Relations Law, with Henkin taking over from Richard Baxter as Chief Reporter following the latter's appointment to the International Court of Justice, and the First Tentative Draft of that Restatement had been issued, with six more Tentative Drafts appearing through 1986.

[4] George Sutherland, *The Internal and External Powers of the National Government*, 191 NORTH AM. REV. 373 (1910). Sutherland had introduced this as a Senate Document a year earlier. Sen. Doc. 417, 61st Cong., 2d Sess. (1909).

[5] *Id.* at 374.

[6] In 1919 Sutherland published lectures he had delivered at Columbia University as CONSTITUTIONAL POWER AND WORLD AFFAIRS (1919). The lectures repeated and expanded upon the "internal"/"external" division of powers he had first fashioned in 1909.

[7] Sutherland, *supra* note 4, at 384.

to advance their interests and defend their sovereignty in relations with foreign powers.

Why would Sutherland, who remained an advocate of constitutional limits on the power of the federal government to encroach on the prerogatives of the States throughout that time interval, have wanted to fashion his "internal"/"external" powers distinction? Two reasons, both connected to developments in early twentieth-century American jurisprudence, suggest themselves. First, beginning in the late nineteenth century, Congress began experimenting with delegating power to the president to enter into executive agreements with foreign nations that did not take the form of treaties. In the orthodox nineteenth-century regime of foreign relations jurisprudence formal relations between the United States and foreign powers was typically conducted in the form of treaties, negotiated by the executive branch and approved by the Senate. Confining foreign relations policymaking to the treaty form presumed that the States, being represented in the Senate, would retain some influence on foreign policy. More significantly for present purposes, it also presumed that all exercises of foreign relations would be undertaken within a constitutional framework.

The late nineteenth-century delegations to the executive to enter into agreements with foreign powers that did not take the form of treaties largely involved economic matters, such as reciprocal agreements involving tariffs under which the president could adjust the customs duties imposed on import of products from foreign nations in response to those nations' treatments of U.S. imports.[8] The constitutionality of one such congressional delegation on tariffs, ratification of which did not require Senate approval, was challenged before the Supreme Court in *Field v. Clark*, an 1892 case.[9] A 7–2 majority sustained it, even though by the standards of orthodox foreign relations jurisprudence the legislation granted the president power he did not have under the Constitution, that of entering into agreements with foreign powers that were not treaties and did not require Senate consent.

Executive agreements then proliferated in the years between 1892 and World War I.[10] Under orthodox conceptions of late nineteenth- and early twentieth-century constitutional jurisprudence, the discretionary authority granted the

---

[8] For more detail on the emergence of executive agreements in the late nineteenth century, see G. Edward White, *The Transformation of the Constitutional Regime of Foreign Relations: The Old Regime Under Stress*, in HISTORY AND THE CONSTITUTION: COLLECTED ESSAYS 217–19 (2007).

[9] 143 U.S. 649 (1892). The challenged legislation, the McKinley Tariff Act, 26 Stat. 367 (1890), authorized the president to implement a series of reciprocal commercial agreements between the United States and foreign producers of sugar, tea, coffee, molasses, and hides. The agreements anticipated those producers not establishing duties on U.S. imports in exchange for the United States allowing free trade in the designated products, and allowing the president to suspend the free trade treatment if foreign nations began imposing duties on American products imported into their countries.

[10] John Bassett Moore, *Treaties and Executive Agreements*, 20 POL. SCI. Q. 385, 417 (1905).

executive to enter into a series of agreements with foreign powers that were not treaties was in sharp contrast to the perceived constitutional constraints on the federal government's exercise of its powers in the domestic arena. Although the president had enumerated constitutional authority to make treaties with foreign nations, and Congress had a like authority to regulate foreign commerce, no provision of the Constitution gave the executive authority to enter into agreements with foreign powers that were other than treaties, and no provision gave Congress authority to delegate to the president power it did not possess in the foreign relations areas, such as authorizing him to enter into protocols with foreign nations. In the period when executive agreements in foreign relations were becoming the norm, the prevailing model of constitutional interpretation in the domestic realm remained one in which federal regulatory power was treated as limited to the exercise of enumerated powers, with States being perceived as retaining a residuum of power to regulate the affairs of their citizens unless being expressly forbidden by the Constitution.

But executive agreements in the area of foreign relations were convenient and congenial with the growing international economic and political presence of the United States in the late nineteenth and early twentieth centuries. After the conclusion of the Spanish-American war the United States acquired major overseas "colonies," Puerto Rico, Guam, and the Philippines, for the first time in its history. The advent of steamship travel made the passage of people and goods between America and overseas nations far more efficient and profitable, inducing the United States to make a considerable investment in international trade and commerce. Executive agreements meant that commercial relationships with foreign nations could be more responsive to rapid changes in commercial markets and need not be affected by senatorial oversight or perceived demands of domestic American politics. They also meant that if the United States encountered political or even military opposition from foreign powers because of its international contacts and policies, such conflicts might be negotiated informally rather than being addressed by the cumbersome process of treaty formulation and ratification.

Thus there were practical reasons why Sutherland might have been attracted to a view of foreign policymaking that emphasized executive discretion and avoided constitutional complications. But a theoretical hurdle remained for him. Throughout the first two decades of the twentieth century, while he was fashioning what he would call a "radically more liberal"[11] rule of constitutional construction for the federal government's exercise of its foreign relations powers, he retained the orthodox view that in the domestic arena the federal government's

---

[11] SUTHERLAND, *supra* note 6, at 47.

activity was reserved for areas where it had been granted enumerated powers, the States retaining residual authority over all other areas. In order to justify a much greater exercise of federal power, including constitutionally unconstrained executive discretion, in foreign relations, Sutherland needed to posit a bright line between what he called the "internal" and "external powers" of the federal government.

Sutherland would derive the existence of such a line from two sources. First, he had been taught that it was necessary to allocate all of the powers of sovereign entities identified in the Constitutions throughout the entire corpus of the document.[12] This meant that in domestic affairs, only enumerated powers in the federal government could be exercised by that government, resulting in a potentially large number of governmental powers being retained by the States. In foreign affairs, where the States were specifically prohibited by the Constitution from conducting foreign relations, those powers provided by the Constitution were granted to the federal government.

This principle, however, did not aid Sutherland in justifying the exercise of federal foreign relations powers that did not seem specifically authorized by the Constitution. Executive agreements seemed an illustration. So he resorted to another basis for the exercise of these powers. He turned to what had come to be called "plenary power" theory, the idea that certain powers exercised by the U.S. government did not rest on an authorization by the Constitution, but on what Sutherland called an "extraconstitutional but not unconstitutional" basis. Plenary power theory, as it emerged in the late nineteenth and early twentieth centuries, posited that the United States occupied a dual role, as a nation whose conduct was guided by a Constitution and as a sovereign power in the international arena. In the latter capacity it had "plenary powers" that followed from its sovereignty, which included the power to protect its interests when engaging with foreign sovereigns. Such powers did not arise from constitutional grants, but from the inherent responsibilities attendant on surviving and thriving in a world of international conflict. They were derived from the necessity of sovereign nations preserving their own existence.[13]

Plenary power theory had emerged in three other areas of late nineteenth- and early twentieth-century American jurisprudence before Sutherland adopted it as a way of reinforcing his distinction between the "internal" and "external" powers of the federal government. The three areas were relations between the federal government and aboriginal American tribes, immigration, and the relationship

---

[12] FRANCIS PASCHAL, MR. JUSTICE SUTHERLAND 15–20 (1951).

[13] For more detail on the emergence of plenary power theory in the late nineteenth century, see G. EDWARD WHITE, LAW IN AMERICAN HISTORY, VOLUME 2: FROM RECONSTRUCTION THROUGH THE 1920s 71, 77–86, 103–11, 157 (2016).

of the United States to its overseas territories. In all of those areas, in a series of cases decided between 1886 and 1905,[14] the Court recognized the power of the federal government to make laws affecting tribes that were not treaties, and to which tribes had not consented; its power to exclude aliens from the nation, even in contradiction to treaties with foreign governments that had accorded protected status to citizens of those governments; and its power to incorporate acquired territories into the Union without ensuring that residents of those territories would be accorded the same constitutional protections as American citizens. These authorities rested, as one decision put it, on the "inherent and inalienable right of every sovereign and independent nation, essential to its safety, its independence, and its welfare."[15] Sutherland would later describe this "inherent" sovereign power as "very delicate, plenary, and exclusive" in "the field of international relations."[16]

## B.  The Eradication of Reserved State Powers in Foreign Affairs

The orthodox nineteenth-century regime of constitutional foreign relations jurisprudence had treated decisions made by the federal government in the foreign affairs arena as constrained by what might be called a "reserved power consciousness." That consciousness, which emphasized the limited enumerated constitutional powers of the federal government and the presence of an accompanying residuum of State powers alongside them, was reflected in the assumption that virtually all federal exercises of foreign policy would take the form of treaties which required the Senate's consent to ratification as a representative of the States. But the emergence of federal foreign affairs policymaking in the form of executive agreements that did not require senatorial approval and the emergence of "extraconstitutional" plenary powers in the federal government to make decisions affecting immigration or overseas territories suggested that the reserved powers of the States were occupying a diminished role in foreign relations. One commentator suggested in 1922 that if the reserved powers of the

---

[14]  United States v. Kagama, 118 U.S. 375 (1886) (tribal affairs); Chae Chan Ping v. United States, 130 U.S. 581 (1889), and Fong Tue Ying v. United States, 149 U.S. 698 (1893) (immigration); and eleven "Insular Cases" decided between 1901 and 1905: DeLima v. Bidwell, 182 U.S. 1 (1901); Goetze v. United States, 182 U.S. 221 (1901); Dooley v. United States, 182 U.S. 222 (1901); Armstrong v. United States, 182 U.S. 243 (1901); Downes v. Bidwell, 182 U.S. 244 (1901); Dooley v. United States, 183 U.S. 151 (1901); Fourteen Diamond Rings v. United States, 183 U.S. 176 (1901); Hawaii v. Mankichi, 190 U.S. 197 (1903); Kepner v. United States, 195 U.S. 100 (1904); Dorr v. United States, 195 U.S. 138 (1904); and Rasmussen v. United States, 197 U.S. 516 (1905) (territorial relations).

[15]  Fong Tue Ying, 149 U.S. at 711.

[16]  United States v. Curtiss-Wright Export Corp., 299 U.S. 304, 320 (1936).

States "restrict the exercise of national [foreign relations] powers at all, they do so simply by virtue of constitutional understandings."[17]

Between 1920 and 1942 a series of Supreme Court decisions appeared to make the eradication of State interests from foreign policymaking explicit. The first of those decisions was *Missouri v. Holland*,[18] where the Court considered whether a treaty between the United States and Canada for the protection of migratory birds[19] could serve to regulate a subject matter—hunting such birds—that had clearly been understood to be within the province of the States. Congress had passed legislation regulating the killing of migratory birds in 1913, prompting an immediate challenge on the ground that it exceeded the federal government's commerce powers, migratory birds not being regarded as articles in interstate commerce. In that litigation counsel for the United States had conceded that the legislation could not be supported on Commerce Clause grounds.[20] In debates on the 1913 legislation, Senator Elihu Root suggested that negotiation of a treaty protecting birds might give "the Government of the United States . . . constitutional authority to deal with this subject,"[21] and that same year a resolution recommending such a treaty passed the Senate. By 1916 the treaty with Canada had been negotiated and ratified.

Congress then passed enabling legislation to enforce the treaty.[22] The State of Missouri challenged its enforcement. A trial judge dismissed the suit on the ground that the 1918 legislation was constitutional because it had made pursuant to a treaty, even though legislation without a treaty would have violated the Constitution. Missouri appealed to the Supreme Court, which in a 7–2 opinion, written by Justice Oliver Wendell Holmes, sustained the legislation.

The way in which Holmes framed the constitutional issue in *Missouri v. Holland* would not have been comforting for those who believed that foreign relations should be conducted within a reserved powers framework. He suggested that limitations on the treaty-making power of the United States needed "to be ascertained in a different way."[23] This meant that neither the enumerated/reserved powers framework nor the framers' understanding of which subjects were properly "matters requiring national action" would be controlling. The only test for whether a treaty was constitutionally legitimate was whether

---

[17] QUINCY WRIGHT, THE CONTROL OF AMERICAN FOREIGN RELATIONS 86 (1922).

[18] 252 U.S. 416 (1920).

[19] Convention with Great Britain for the Protection of Migratory Birds, 39 Stat.1702 (1916)

[20] United States v. Shauver, 214 F. 154, 160 (E. D. Ark. 1914).

[21] Quoted in 51 Cong. Rec. 8349 (May 9, 1914). Root's comment, made in January 1913, was omitted from the published record of Senate proceedings that year. See CHARLES A. LOFGREN, GOVERNMENT FROM REFLECTION AND CHOICE: CONSTITUTIONAL ESSAYS ON WAR, FOREIGN RELATIONS, AND FEDERALISM 121 (1986).

[22] 40 Stat. 755 (July 3, 1918).

[23] 252 U.S. at 434.

it governed a "matter requiring national action." He then maintained that even though the framers had not said that the protection of migratory birds was such a matter, the "whole experience" of the United States since the founding of the Constitution apparently demonstrated that there was a national interest in the protection of migratory birds.[24] Although Holmes had signaled that he was interested in ascertaining "qualifications to the treaty power,"[25] his treatment of migratory birds, whose regulation had hitherto been thought of as centered in the States, did nothing to suggest that any existed.

Eventually Holmes mentioned some constitutional limitations on the treaty power—treaties that were inconsistent with "prohibitory words to be found in the Constitution" preventing the federal government from exercising specific powers, or "some invisible radiation from the general terms of the Tenth Amendment."[26] There were few illustrations of direct prohibitions on the conduct of the federal government in the constitutional text, and Holmes's characterization of the Tenth Amendment's restraining federal power as operating only through some "invisible radiation" seemed to reverse the presumption in orthodox constitutional jurisprudence that power was retained in the States or the people unless it had been specifically conferred on the national government. Indeed Holmes hinted in *Missouri v. Holland* that the treaty-making power of the federal government might rest in part on inherent sovereign powers, making it not subject to constitutional limitations at all.

At least one commentator noted that the question of whether a "national interest of considerable magnitude" was implicated in a treaty was typically treated as a "political" one in which courts would accept the judgment of Congress or the executive. Quincy Wright's conclusion that after *Missouri v. Holland* "[t]he 'reserved powers' of the states . . . do not limit the treaty-making power"[27] might have seemed like a recognition of the displacement of the States from foreign relations policymaking. But Wright, in the course of his discussion of *Missouri v. Holland*, emphasized that, so long as foreign policy continued to be conducted by the federal government mainly in the form of treaties requiring Senate consent to ratification, "[t]he practice of the Senate, the opinions of statesmen and dicta in the courts indicate that . . . the treaty power ought to exercise its powers in such a way as not to interfere with the States in the control of their own land, natural resources, and public services and not to interfere unnecessarily with the enforcement by the State of its own policy with reference to the protection of public safety, health, morals and economic welfare."[28] Those comments

---

[24] *Id.*
[25] *Id.*
[26] *Id.*
[27] WRIGHT, *supra* note 17, at 87–89.
[28] *Id.* at 93.

suggested that Wright did not see *Missouri v. Holland* as quite as revolutionary as his initial comment suggested. Perhaps it was just a case finding a "national interest" in the protection of migratory birds.

The difficulty with this interpretation of *Missouri v. Holland* was that foreign policy did not continue to be conducted primarily in the form of treaties after 1920. A vivid illustration was the United States' 1933 agreement with the Soviet Union to grant that nation diplomatic recognition in exchange for a partial settlement of claims the Soviet Union, as a successor to previous Russian governments, had made against American nationals. The Litvinov Agreement, named for Soviet Commissar of Foreign Affairs Maxim Litvinov, assigned the amounts of those claims to the U.S. government. In addition, the Soviets agreed not to make any claims against the United States for damage from American troops supporting the White Armies in their efforts to prevent the Bolsheviks from coming to power after the Russian Revolution in 1918.[29]

In the nomenclature of early twentieth-century foreign relations law, the Litvinov Agreement was a protocol, not requiring significant congressional oversight or Senate approval. It arguably raised three potentially momentous issues for the twentieth-century constitutional jurisprudence of foreign relations. One was whether it enjoyed the same constitutional status as a treaty despite the lack of legislative branch participation in its formation. Another was whether, if it did, it had the same potential to displace competing State law should any of its provisions conflict with State policies as to the disposition of assets assigned by the Russian government to the United States. A third was the effect of the agreement on State common law cases in which international subjects were parties.

Prior to the agreement State courts, most prominently those of New York, had treated such cases as "domestic," meaning that they were governed by State common law rules. Because New York City was the center of economic transactions involving Russian banks, American banks, the Soviet Union, and American and Russian citizens in the years between the Bolshevik Revolution and the Litvinov Agreement, New York courts entertained a number of legal disputes involving assets, allegedly owned by banks, corporations, or individuals, that were affected by the Soviet government's treatment of Russian corporations and property in Russia during those years. In that period the United States consistently declined to recognize the Soviet government, maintaining instead that the "Russian government" consisted of refugee representatives of the czarist or provisional regimes that had been displaced by the Bolsheviks.

---

[29] For more detail on the Litvinov Agreement, see White, The Triumph of Executive Discretion in the Constitutional Regime of Foreign Relations, in HISTORY AND THE CONSTITUTION, *supra* note 8, at 253–54.

In a series of "Russian recognition" cases decided between 1924 and 1933, the New York Court of Appeals treated the nonrecognition of the Soviet government by the United States as leaving New York courts free to decide for themselves how the "private rights and obligations" of citizens affected by dealings with the Soviet government would be disposed of in that State. Questions raised in cases affecting those rights and obligations, the Court of Appeals concluded, were neither questions of "foreign relations," requiring deference to the policies of the federal government, nor "international political questions" that should be withdrawn from the courts. They were simply domestic State common law cases. In deciding them, the New York courts could make independent determinations about the status of the "Russian government" and about whether decrees by that government confiscating the property of American or Russian citizens were consistent with State policies regarding the disposition of that property. In short, New York judges could treat the "official" attitude of the United States toward the Soviet government between 1918 and 1933 as having no legal effect on cases involving the actions of that government which affected the assets of persons within the State.[30]

*Missouri v. Holland* had held that enabling legislation implementing a treaty which had been approved by the Senate could displace competing State law grounded on the exercise of State police powers even though that legislation, absent the treaty, would have been an unconstitutional invasion of State prerogatives. *Field v. Clark* had held that executive agreements in the area of foreign policy could be constitutionally valid without Senate consent to ratification. An unanswered question raised by the interaction of those two decisions was whether an executive agreement not taking the form of a treaty could prevail over competing State law in the fashion of *Missouri v. Holland*. That question first came before the Supreme Court in 1937.

But before resolving that issue, the Court decided another constitutional foreign relations case that squarely injected into twentieth-century American foreign relations jurisprudence Sutherland's distinction between the "internal" and "external" powers of the federal government. The effect of the case, *United States v. Curtiss-Wright Export Corp.*,[31] was to suggest that the power of the executive to enter into agreements with foreign nations was in part grounded on the "inherent" powers of sovereignty, and thus "extraconstitutional." It was also "not unconstitutional" because the president's authority to conduct foreign affairs was to

---

[30] The cases were Sokoloff v. National City Bank of New York, 239 N.Y. 158 (1924); Fred S. James & Co. v. Second Russian Insurance Co., 239 N.Y. 248 (1925); Russian Reinsurance Co. v. Stoddard, 240 N.Y. 149 (1925); First Russian Insurance Co. v. Beha, 240 N.Y. 601 (1925); Petrogradsky Mejdunarodny Kommerchesky Bank v. National City Bank of New York, 253 N.Y. 23 (1930); and Salminoff & Co. v. Standard Oil Co., 262 N.Y. 220 (1933).

[31] 299 U.S. 304 (1936).

an important extent not just "plenary" but "exclusive": Its exercise did not raise constitutional separation of powers concerns.

*Curtiss-Wright* challenged a 1934 joint resolution, introduced by Franklin D. Roosevelt and approved by Congress, that gave the president power to suspend American arms sales to the Paraguayan and Bolivian governments, which had been at war with one another since 1932.[32] It authorized the president to impose an embargo on the shipment of arms from American manufacturers to either Paraguay or Bolivia if he found that the embargo might "contribute to the establishment of peace between those countries."[33] It also provided that violators of the embargo could be subject to fines and imprisonment.

In January 1936, four corporate officers of the Curtiss-Wright Export Corporation, the corporation itself, and two affiliated companies were indicted for conspiring to sell aircraft machine guns to Bolivia in violation of the joint resolution. Among the grounds under which the defendants contested their indictment was that the joint resolution amounted to an unconstitutional delegation of power from Congress to the executive branch. Such arguments had emerged in constitutional cases since the mid-1930s, when the Roosevelt administration attempted to create a number of administrative agencies to manage sectors of the economy, and used delegations of power from Congress to those agencies to do so. The District Court agreed that the joint resolution effected an unconstitutional delegation of power to the executive, and the government appealed directly to the Supreme Court.

Sutherland opened the principal portions of his opinion for the Court in *Curtiss-Wright* as follows: "Whether, if the Joint Resolution had related solely to internal affairs it would be open to the challenge that it constituted an unlawful delegation of legislative power to the executive, we find unnecessary to determine."[34] This was because, in Sutherland's view, the case involved an exercise of the "external" powers of the federal government, and those powers were conceptually distinct from its "internal" powers. The external powers of the federal government were derived partially from the Constitution and partially from its "inherent," plenary, sovereign powers. The latter powers were "extraconstitutional," stemming from the identity of a nation as a sovereign power among other international sovereigns, and as such were apparently not subject to constitutional constraints at all. Sutherland stopped short of saying that the exercise of executive power in foreign relations was wholly unconstrained: He conceded that, "like every other governmental power," it need to be "exercised in subordination to the applicable provisions of the Constitution."[35]

---

[32]  48 Stat. 811 (1934).
[33]  *Id.* at 1744.
[34]  299 U.S. at 315.
[35]  *Id.* at 320.

But Sutherland's opinion in *Curtiss-Wright* did not provide any *constitutional* grounding for the executive's exercise of plenary and exclusive power in foreign affairs. He advanced three reasons for the proposition that the executive was the primary repository of foreign relations policymaking. One was to rehearse the "inherent power" basis for the president's authority, functioning as commander-in-chief of the nation or the head of an international sovereign. Another was practical considerations of international policymaking, such as the fact that the president alone negotiated treaties with foreign powers, that he was in a better position than representatives of other branches to gain "confidential sources of information" affecting foreign affairs, and that oversight from other branches might impair the secrecy and confidentiality necessary for delicate diplomatic bargaining. The third was what Sutherland called the "unbroken legislative practice" of deferring to executive discretion in foreign affairs. In support of this last claim he cited numerous joint resolutions of Congress authorizing the president to take action on various foreign relations matters.[36] In short, Sutherland's justifications for unfettered executive discretion in the realm of foreign affairs were each extraconstitutional in their nature.

But *Curtiss-Wright* produced only one dissent, a two-sentence opinion from Justice James McReynolds stating that he "did not agree" with the majority, and was "of opinion that the court below," which had dismissed the indictment, ostensibly on delegation grounds, "reached the right conclusion."[37] Neither did it elicit much critical commentary.[38] The decision may have initially appeared as of less significance than it came to be regarded because the Chaco war between Paraguay and Bolivia ended in 1936 and Roosevelt's proclamation, issued in connection with the joint resolution, had been withdrawn in November 1935. *Curtiss-Wright*, however, would emerge as the first linchpin in a chain of decisions that would have the dual effect of elevating executive agreements to the constitutional status of treaties and virtually displacing States from the arena of foreign relations policymaking.

The latter effect of *Curtiss-Wright* began to take shape in *United States v. Belmont*,[39] a case decided by the Court a year after *Curtiss-Wright* was handed down. In *Belmont*, assets of the Petrograd Metal Works, a Russian corporation, had been deposited in the New York banking house August Belmont & Co. before the outbreak of the Bolshevik revolution. When the Soviet government

---

[36] As to this last point, Chief Justice Hughes had pointed out in one of the Court's early domestic delegation cases that all those examples were only indications that Congress had wanted the president to implement particular policies it supported, as opposed to fashioning them on his own. Panama Refining Co. v. Ryan, 293 U.S. 388, 422 (1935).

[37] 299 U.S. at 333.

[38] For a summary of reaction to *Curtiss-Wright*, see White, *supra* note 8, at 264.

[39] 301 U.S. 324 (1937).

came to power in 1918, it began appropriating the assets of private companies, including the Petrograd Metal Works' account in New York. The Litvinov Agreement treated all assets of American nationals appropriated by the Soviets as "amounts due the Soviet government" for the purposes of their assignment to the United States. Relying on the agreement, the United States made a demand on Belmont's executors for the assets.

The executors refused. When the United States sued in federal district court, the executors sought to dismiss the suit. They argued that the account of the Petrograd Metal Works was located in New York, and, not being property located within Soviet territory, was not subject to any nationalization decree. They also argued that the public policy of New York State was not to give effect to extraterritorial claims on property owned by American citizens within its jurisdiction. Finally, they argued that to enforce the Soviet nationalization decree was to take property without just compensation. The district judge granted their motion, and the U.S. Court of Appeals for the Second Circuit affirmed. The Supreme Court granted a writ of certiorari and reversed. Sutherland wrote for five other justices, with Stone, joined by Brandeis and Cardozo, concurring separately.

Sutherland began his opinion in *Belmont* by stating that "[w]e do not pause to inquire whether in fact there was any policy of the State of New York to be infringed, since we are of opinion that no state policy can prevail against the international compact here involved."[40] That sentence was startling, because the Constitution had granted the States power to "enter into . . . Agreement[s] or Compact[s] with . . . a foreign Power," albeit with the consent of Congress,[41] and because reserved-powers constitutional jurisprudence treated the States as having very strong interests in the disposition of property within their borders, especially property held by American citizens. Sutherland treated those considerations as irrelevant to the disposition of the assets in *Belmont*.

They were irrelevant, Sutherland concluded, for two reasons. First, "international compacts and agreements" made by the federal government had the same constitutional status as treaties, and were thus supreme over competing State laws.[42] Second, "complete power over international affairs is in the national government and is not and cannot be subject to any curtailment or interference on the part of the several states." For the latter proposition he cited *Curtiss-Wright*, but that case had only been about the former proposition. Nonetheless, Sutherland maintained that "[i]n respect of all international negotiations and compacts, and in respect of our foreign relations generally, state lines disappear."[43] By Sutherland's account, the States had ceased to become actors in the

[40] *Id.* at 327.
[41] U.S. CONST., art I, § 10, cl. 3.
[42] 301 U.S. at 330–31.
[43] *Id.* at 331–32.

realm of constitutional foreign affairs jurisprudence, and the federal execu-tive had virtual carte blanche to establish plenary control of foreign relations. As for the Just Compensation Clause argument, Sutherland claimed that the Constitution had no extraterritorial effect except with respect to American citi-zens, and the assets under dispute in *Belmont* were owned by a Russian corpora-tion, the executors being mere custodians of them.[44]

Despite Sutherland's broad language in *Belmont*, the case only decided that the United States had a cause in action against the August Belmont bank. It thus did not reach the question of whether, if New York public policy about the dis-tribution of Russian assets within the State conflicted with any distribution con-templated by the Litvinov Agreement, the former had to give way. That question was raised in *Moscow Fire Insurance Co. v. Bank of New York & Trust Co.*,[45] a case brought before the New York Court of Appeals in 1939 and entertained by the Supreme Court that same year. But only six Justices heard it, and they were evenly divided.[46] Thus it fell to *United States v. Pink*,[47] heard by the Court only a few days after the Japanese attack on Pearl Harbor and the United States' declara-tion of war against the Axis powers, to decide whether an international executive agreement purporting to dispose of assets within the United States could be en-forced in the face of a conflicting State policy.

The *Pink* case arose out of the same set of transactions implicated in *Belmont* and *Moscow Fire*. It involved the assets of the First Russian Insurance Company, which had been established in New York in 1907 and ceased to do business in the State in 1925. When the company's New York business ended, the New York Superintendent of Insurance, Louis Pink, took possession of its assets, paid off the claims of its domestic creditors, and retained about a million dollars. Various foreign creditors then filed claims. In a 1931 decision, the New York Court of Appeals determined that those claims should be paid and any surplus distributed to a quorum of directors of the company.[48]

---

[44] *Id.* at 332.

[45] 280 N.Y. 286, 20 N.E.2d 758 (1939).

[46] United States v. Moscow Fire Ins. Co., 309 U.S. 624 (1940). Justices Stone, Reed, and Murphy did not participate. The Court's order affirming the New York Court of Appeals' decision only stated that it was affirmed by an equally divided Court, not identifying the votes of the Justices who partic-ipated. At that point in the Court's history the participating Justices would have been Chief Justice Hughes and Associate Justices McReynolds, Roberts, Black, Douglas, and Frankfurter. Hughes and Roberts had joined Sutherland's opinion in *Curtiss-Wright*, and Hughes, Roberts, and Black had joined Sutherland's *Belmont* opinion. So if one were to extrapolate from those decisions, Hughes, Roberts, and Black might seem candidates to support reversing the New York Court of Appeals in *Moscow Fire*, and McReynolds a candidate for affirming it. But that extrapolation fails to account for Douglas's subsequent very strong statement of plenary federal power in foreign affairs in *United States v. Pink*, 315 U.S. 203 (1942), a case discussed later.

[47] 315 U.S. 203 (1942).

[48] Matter of People (First Russian Insurance Co.), 255 N.Y. 415 (1931).

When the Litvinov Agreement was executed in 1934, most of the million dollars remained in Louis Pink's possession. Pursuant to the agreement, the United States claimed a right to all of those assets on the ground that they had been confiscated by the Soviet government in one of its nationalization decrees and been assigned to the United States. After an unsuccessful resort to the federal courts,[49] the United States brought suit in a New York State court, naming Pink and the foreign creditors of the company who had presented claims in the earlier New York liquidation proceeding as defendants. The Court of Appeals dismissed the case based on the authority of *Moscow Fire*.[50] Undaunted, the United States filed a petition for certiorari with the Supreme Court, which was granted: The Justices evidently wanted an opportunity to resolve the issue of whether the Litvinov Agreement trumped competing State policies.

The posture of *Pink* required the Court, before it could resolve the choice-of-law issue, to find that the Litvinov Agreement actually "competed" with New York policies with respect to the distribution of the assets of Russian companies located in the State. That would be the case only if Soviet nationalization decrees extended to property of Russian corporations located outside the Soviet Union. In 1918 the Soviet government had issued a nationalization decree as to insurance companies, and the United States in the *Moscow Fire* argument had produced an after-the-fact declaration by the People's Commissariat for Justice in the Soviet Union that it applied extraterritorially. But the decree itself had no language suggesting that it was intended to have this effect, and it offered no ostensible reason why the Soviets would have been interested in confiscating the property of a Russian insurance companies they could not reach because of its location. Moreover, international law, American common law, and the U.S. Constitution all supported the principle that American courts would not enforce the confiscatory decrees of other nations when those decrees affected property located within the borders of the United States.[51]

Nonetheless Douglas, writing for an attenuated Court,[52] summarily concluded that the 1918 Soviet nationalization decree was intended to have extraterritorial effect, resulting in the property of Russian insurance companies outside the United States being among the assets the Soviets assigned to the United States

---

[49] United States v. Bank of New York & Trust Co., 296 U.S. 436, 479–80 (1936).

[50] United States v. Pink, 284 N.Y. 555, 32 N.E.2d 552 (Ct. App. 1940).

[51] For support for that conclusion, see, on international law, Edwin Borchard, *Confiscations, Extraterritorial and Domestic*, 31 AM. J. INT'L L. 675 (1937); on common law, a line of cases collected in United States v. Director of Manhattan Co., 276 N.Y. 396, 403 (1938); and on the Constitution, WILLARD B. COWLES, TREATIES AND CONSTITUTIONAL LAW 75–88 (1941).

[52] Justices Jackson and Reed did not participate, and Frankfurter wrote separate "observations," the equivalent of a concurrence in the judgment. Justices Stone and Roberts dissented. Although Douglas's opinion was the "opinion of the Court" inasmuch as it represented the views of the majority of Justices participating, only Black, Byrnes, and Murphy joined him.

in the Litvinov Agreement. That conclusion prepared the way for the Court to consider the issue it had avoided in *Belmont* and failed to resolve in *Moscow Fire*: Whether an international executive agreement purportedly affecting property held within a State could override that State's common law rules about the disposition of that property.

Douglas quickly concluded that it could, and did. His reasoning was summary. First, he noted that "the contest" in *Pink* was between "the United States and creditors of the Russian corporation who, we assume, are not citizens of this country and whose claims did not arise out of transactions with the New York branch."[53] That statement may have been accurate, but the New York courts had already determined that foreign creditors who could establish claims against the First Russian Insurance Company after it ceased doing business had priority in the disposition of the company's assets. Because it was clear that *Pink* had been brought to the Court to determine whether a federal executive agreement prevailed against State policies when it conflicted with them, Douglas cited *Curtiss-Wright* and *Belmont* for the propositions that executive agreements had the same constitutional status as treaties.[54] His description of the "contest" only served as a reminder that Americans would win and foreigners lose if the Litvinov Agreement prevailed.

Turning to that issue, Douglas next cited *Curtiss-Wright* and *Belmont* for the proposition that the president was the "sole organ of the federal government in international relations."[55] He then turned to the "reserved powers" issue in *Pink*. "We repeat," he announced, referring to *Belmont*,

> that there are limitations on the sovereignty of the states. No state can rewrite our foreign policy to confirm to its own domestic policies. Power over external affairs is not shared by the States; it is vested in the national government exclusively . . . And the policies of the States become wholly irrelevant to judicial inquiry, when the United States, acting within its constitutional sphere, seeks enforcement of its foreign policy in the courts. For such reasons, Mr. Justice Sutherland stated in [*Belmont*], "In respect of all international negotiations and compacts, and in respect of our foreign relations generally, state lines disappear. As to such purposes the state of New York does not exist."[56]

The only remaining issue in *Pink* was whether, by enforcing an assignment of property from the Soviet Union of assets of Russian nationals located in

---

[53]  315 U.S. at 227.
[54]  *Id.* at 229–30.
[55]  *Id.*
[56]  *Id.* at 233–34.

New York, the United States had violated the Fifth Amendment's just compensation clause, which applied to aliens as well as citizens. Douglas argued that so long as an international executive agreement embodied a federal policy of giving the United States and American nationals "priority against . . . creditors who are nationals of foreign countries and whose claims arise abroad," there was "'no Constitutional reason" why the federal government "need act as the collection agent for nationals of other countries when it takes steps to protect itself or own assets." This apparently meant that the federal government could decide for itself what was "just compensation" for resident aliens of a particular country by using an international agreement with that country to "regroup . . . assets."[57]

All told, *Pink* seemed to signal the end of reserved power participation by the States in foreign affairs. From Wright's supposition that after *Missouri v. Holland* "[t]he 'reserved powers' of the states . . . do not limit the treaty-making power," American constitutional foreign relations jurisprudence had moved to the point where apparently any exercise of foreign policy by any branch of the federal government could displace State policies on the subject of that exercise. It was not merely that the reserved powers of the States did not limit the conduct of foreign affairs by the federal government; they were not even relevant to foreign policy-making. In respects to "foreign relations generally," Douglas and Sutherland had announced in *Belmont* and *Pink*, the States did not exist.

## C. The Emergence of the Federal Courts in the Realm of Foreign Affairs

In the period of its origins, from the early years of the twentieth century through the 1940s, American constitutional jurisprudence seemed to treat the conduct of foreign affairs as "exceptional" in three interconnected respects. First, the conduct of foreign relations was no longer a joint venture of the executive and legislative branches, illustrated by the previous emphasis on treaties, negotiated by the executive and approved by the Senate, as the predominant mode under which foreign policy was conducted. By the time *Pink* was decided, not only did executive agreements that did not involve Senate oversight, or even congressional oversight, enjoy the same constitutional status as treaties, they had become more common than treaties. Foreign policymaking had become largely the province of the executive.

Second, the concepts of separation-of-powers limitations and "reserved power" federalism limitations on the federal government did not appear to exist to any significant degree in the realm of foreign affairs. The negotiations and

---

[57] *Id.* at 228.

exchange of letters between the United States and the Soviet Union which produced the Litvinov Agreement illustrates both propositions. The Constitution gave the president power to negotiate treaties, specifying at the same time that such treaties were to be made with the advice and consent of two-thirds of the Senate. It did not give the president any power to enter into executive agreements with foreign nations. Both the principle of separation of powers and the theory that the Constitution only granted enumerated powers to the federal government, with a residuum of power remaining in the States or in the people, suggested that the executive had no power to enter into agreements with foreign powers on its own. But when Congress authorized the president to suspend American arm sales to Paraguay or Bolivia if he thought such an embargo might contribute to peace between those warring nations, the Supreme Court summarily dismissed the argument that such an arrangement, because it lacked any constraints on the president's discretion, was an unconstitutional delegation of power to the executive branch, even though a Court with identical personnel had found delegations without clear standards in the domestic realm unconstitutional.

Moreover, once an executive agreement with a foreign power was in place—even one, such as the Litvinov Agreement, in which Congress had not participated at all—any policies embodied in that agreement trumped competing State policies, even when the policies in question affected matters, such as the disposition of property within a State, that had traditionally been regarded as within the province of States. Moreover, we have seen that the sorts of federalism-based constitutional objections to executive policymaking that were routinely taken seriously by courts in the domestic realm, such as executive takings of property without compensation, were finessed by the Court in *Pink*.

Third, Sutherland's distinction between the "internal" and "external" powers of the federal government had become a leading principle of constitutional foreign relations jurisprudence, buttressed by the proposition that foreign relations policymaking did not involve just the exercise of constitutionally enumerated powers but also of "extraconstitutional," "inherent" powers, ones that flowed from the role of the United States as an international sovereign dedicated to its preservation and advancement in the world community. The power of the federal government to conduct foreign affairs was to an important extent "plenary," that is founded on sovereignty rather than constitutional grants, and was to an important extent "exclusive," not only because the States had been forbidden by the Constitution from conducting many foreign policy measures but because States had no "plenary" power to advance or defend the sovereignty of the United States. When those propositions are combined, the idea that the conduct of foreign policy by the federal government, especially its executive branch, was "exceptional" in being far less subject to constitutional constraints than federal policymaking in the domestic realm, seemed entrenched by the 1940s.

Nothing in the international relations of the United States seemed to call for a reconsideration of foreign affairs exceptionalism from the 1930s through the 1960s. If anything, the continuing involvement of America in the international disputes of other nations before World War II; in the diplomatic and military forays which immediately preceded that war; in the war itself, first as an ally of nations resisting the aggression of the Axis powers and then as a full-scale belligerent; and, after the surrender of Italy, Germany, and Japan, in "Cold War" hostilities with the Soviet Union, its satellite nations, and Communist China, seemed to suggest that the realm of American foreign affairs was constantly changing, volatile, dangerous, and increasingly affected by considerations of confidentiality, secrecy, and the use of executive agencies specializing in intelligence and counterintelligence. The federal government appeared to be, in many respects, particularly well suited for the exercise of plenary discretionary power by the president and executive officials, in keeping with the president's role as commander-in-chief of U.S. military forces and as the head of an international sovereign.

When the Warren Court came into being in the mid-1950s, the thrust of what I am calling foreign affairs exceptionalism had largely been in two directions, moving away from traditional separation-of-powers and federalism constraints on executive branch exercises of foreign policy and buttressing the view that the discretionary character of those exercises was justifiable because they were often "extraconstitutional," grounded on plenary powers stemming from sovereignty. Those moves, although instituted by the Supreme Court, were seemingly not designed to carve out an enhanced role for the federal *courts* in the realm of foreign affairs. To the contrary, they appeared to constrict the role of the courts, either as constitutional overseers of the executive branch in cases such as *Curtiss-Wright* or as the sources of independent common law doctrines that could limit the hegemony of the executive in foreign affairs in cases such as *Belmont* and *Pink*.

To be sure, Warren Court majorities had, by the early 1960s, demonstrated their willingness to scrutinize the actions of other branches for possible constitutional violations and something of a fondness for the role of federal courts as sources of creative and modernizing legal doctrines. But the Warren Court's constitutional and statutory activism had been almost exclusively in the domestic arena until 1964. An article that year by Louis Henkin, who would serve as the Chief Reporter for the Third Restatement of Foreign Affairs, noted that "the foreign relations of the United States do not cry for the courts to fill an obvious lack of law left for them by the Constitution or by necessary implication from the works or the silences of the political branches."[58] Henkin went on to add that

---

[58] Louis Henkin, *The Foreign Affairs Power of the Federal Courts: Sabbatino*, 64 COLUM. L. REV. 805, 824 (1964).

"the courts are not equipped or competent to make foreign policy, or to judge the impact of their rulings in occasional cases on the vital concerns of the nation."[59]

But between 1962 and 1968 the Warren Court decided two cases, and entertained a third, in which federal courts were asked to consider whether State policies that had the effect of discriminating against foreign nations or their residents amounted to efforts by the States to engage in foreign policymaking. The first of those cases was *Ioannou v. New York*.[60] A New York surrogate court denied the power of Victoria Miculka, a resident of Czechoslovakia who was the beneficiary of a New York estate, to assign her interest to her niece, a resident of London. The court applied a New York statute that prevented payments by or to persons "residing behind the iron curtain." This decision was ultimately appealed to the Supreme Court of the United States, where a majority dismissed the case for want of a substantial federal question.

Douglas, dissenting in *Ioannou*, argued that although States had traditionally regulated the disposition of estates within their boundaries, "[t]he practice of state courts in withholding remittances to legatees residing in Communist countries, or in preventing them from assigning them, had become notorious," and "the issue is of importance to our foreign relations." He thought that if the purpose of prohibiting assignments of funds made in "unfriendly foreign governments" was to preclude those governments from "obtaining funds that will assist their efforts hostile to this Nation's interests," it might "have some basis in reason," but then it would be "an attempt to regulate foreign affairs."[61]

Six years later, in *Zschernig v. Miller*,[62] a majority of the Court endorsed Douglas's view. An Oregon statute provided that when alien heirs claimed inheritance rights to real and personal property in the State, they needed to establish, as a condition to inherit, proof that they "may receive the benefit, use, or control of money or property from estates of persons dying in this state without confiscation, in whole or in part, by the governments of such foreign countries."[63] When a resident of Oregon died intestate in 1962, her heirs, residents of East Germany, claimed real and personal property located in the State. The Oregon State Land Board petitioned a probate court for an escheat of the property under the Oregon statute. That court held that, although the East German residents were entitled to the real property under a 1923 Friendship Treaty between the government of the United States and the then government of Germany, they could not claim the

---

[59]  *Id.* at 832.
[60]  371 U.S. 30 (1962).
[61]  *Id.* at 31–32.
[62]  389 U.S. 429 (1968).
[63]  *Id.* at 432.

personal property because the treaty covered only realty and they could not offer proof against confiscation.

When *Zschernig* reached the Supreme Court, the East Germans argued that the Oregon statute was unconstitutional because in practice it interfered with the foreign relations powers of the federal government. The U.S. government had not expressed any position on the eligibility of East German residents to inherit personal property in the United States. In effect the argument presumed that there was a "dormant" foreign relations power in the federal government that prevented the States from taking any actions affecting the inheritance status of nonresident aliens.

The Court in *Zschernig* had three options. It could conclude, overruling an earlier case, that the States had no power to affect the inheritance rights of nonresident aliens because to do so was to exercise power in the area of foreign relations.[64] It could conclude that because the practice of the United States in entering into treaties with foreign nations giving reciprocal rights to the citizens of both was to include the inheritance of both real and personal property, the 1923 Friendship Treaty should be understood as doing that, removing any potential constitutional issue from the case. Or it could distinguish the earlier case by concluding that here the Oregon statute's impact on foreign relations was more than "incidental" and "indirect."

The Court chose the last option, with Douglas writing the majority opinion, Harlan concurring separately, White dissenting, and Marshall not participating.[65] Douglas's opinion stressed the "minute" judicial inquiries into the practices of foreign banks and the composition of the government of foreign nations apparently triggered by the Oregon statute. He alluded, as he had in *Ioannou*, to the tendency of State courts to prevent residents of Communist countries from receiving or assigning assets. Because the U.S. government had fashioned no policy about the inheritance rights of nonresidents aliens, *Zschernig* could have been read as a strong statement of foreign affairs exceptionalism. But it could also have been read as a "Cold War" case, precipitated by concerns about fears that Communist governments would inevitably confiscate the assets of their residents who inherited personal property in Western nations.[66]

---

[64] See Clark v. Allen, 331 U.S. 503, 516–17 (1947).

[65] Stewart and Brennan joined Douglas's opinion, but in a concurring opinion expressed the view that the case for foreign-relations field preemption was even stronger than the majority opinion argued. 389 U.S. at 441–42.

[66] The doctrine of dormant foreign relations powers, when applied to routine exercises of State functions such as the probating of wills disposing of property in the State, seemed to make a great many such exercises constitutionally vulnerable whenever they affected foreign nations or individuals. The Court was to reconsider those implications of *Zschernig* in *Crosby v. National Trade Council*, 530 U.S. 363 (2000).

The third 1960s case prompting the federal courts to involve themselves in foreign policy decisions was in one respect the opposite of *Ioannou* and *Zschernig*. Instead of nonresident aliens being discriminated against by a policy of an American State, American citizens were discriminated against by an act of a foreign government. *Banco Nacional de Cuba v. Sabbatino*[67] involved the seizure of a shipment of sugar lying off Havana, Cuba, by the Cuban government in retaliation for a reduction of Cuba's sugar quota by the United States in July 1960, approximately six months after the Castro government had displaced the Batista regime in Cuba. When the sugar was seized from a carrier, it belonged to C.A.V., a Cuban corporation principally owned by Americans. C.A.V. had entered into contracts with Farr, Whitlock & Co., an American commodity broker, to purchase Cuban sugar. The contracts provided that Farr, Whitlock would pay C.A.V. for the sugar upon presentation of the bills of lading in New York.

Once the Cuban government seized the sugar shipment, Farr, Whitlock entered into contracts, identical to those it had made with C.A.V., with a representative of the Cuban government, which then assigned the bills of lading for the sugar shipment to Banco Nacional de Cuba, another representative. The Cuban government then instructed its agent in New York, Societe Generale, to deliver the bills of lading to New York and to seek payment from Farr, Whitlock. On learning from C.A.V. that it claimed to be the rightful owner of the sugar and thus entitled to payment under the purchase contract, Farr, Whitlock declined to pay Banco Nacional.

At this point the New York Supreme Court ordered Farr, Whitlock to transfer the funds due under the purchase contract to Sabbatino, whom it had appointed temporary receiver of C.A.V.'s assets in New York. Banco Nacional filed suit in federal district court in New York, claiming that Farr, Whitlock had converted its bill of lading and that it was entitled to the proceeds from its purchase contract. The district court found, among other things, that C.A.V. had a property interest in the sugar subject to the Cuban government's claim of title, and that under customary international law Cuba's seizure of the sugar was invalid. It granted Sabbatino summary judgment against Banco Nacional, meaning that he retained the funds on C.A.V.'s behalf. The U.S. Court of Appeals for the Second Circuit upheld the district court on the customary international law issue. The Supreme Court granted certiorari "because the issues involved bear importantly on the conduct of the country's foreign relations and, more particularly, on the proper role of the judiciary in this sensitive area."[68]

A Court majority, in an opinion written by Harlan and joined by all the other justices save White, then reversed. It held that the "act of state" doctrine, which

---

[67]  376 U.S. 398 (1964).
[68]  *Id.* at 407.

holds that a court in one nation will not sit in judgment on the acts of another done within its territory, meant that the Cuban expropriation decree confiscating C.A.V.'s sugar had to be upheld, with any redress of grievances resulting from such acts to be obtained through diplomatic means. The act of state doctrine, the Court declared, was part of the corpus of federal common law, and thus binding on States, so that the views of New York courts on the lawfulness of Cuba's seizure of the sugar were irrelevant. Further, even if the doctrine was taken not to apply to acts of state that violated customary international law, it was not clear that Cuba's actions did; application of the doctrine did not require specific endorsement by the executive; and there was no reason to think that a foreign plaintiff could not invoke the doctrine in American courts. As Harlan put it, "the judicial branch will not examine the taking of property within its own territory by a foreign sovereign government . . . in the absence of a treaty or otherwise unambiguous agreement regarding controlling legal principles, even if the complaint alleges that the taking violates customary international law."[69] He argued that a judicial finding that an expropriation was valid, when the executive branch had asserted that it was not, would result in conflict between the branches, while a judicial finding that an expropriation was unlawful might trigger resentment on the part of a foreign government, interfering with diplomatic efforts to compensate Americans whose property had been appropriated. Thus the act of state doctrine kept American courts from injecting themselves into the "very delicate" arena of diplomatic foreign relations.

Although it was clear from *Sabbatino* that foreign affairs exceptionalism was to receive support from the courts, it was not immediately apparent what that meant. Louis Henkin's initial reaction to *Sabbatino* was that "[e]ven accepting Justice Harlan's assertion of an independent common law power in the [federal] courts, surely that power is subordinate to legislators. And the foreign policy of the United States is 'legislated' mainly by the President."[70] But it was clear, after *Sabbatino*, that, at least with respect to the "act of state" doctrine, which was entirely a judicial creation, federal courts could establish common law principles in foreign relations cases that overrode any conflicting State common law decisions. By 1972 Henkin had concluded that "*Sabbatino* establishes foreign affairs as a domain in which federal courts can make law with supremacy." He added that whether the courts could "make law without the invitation of the political branches in foreign affairs" was a question "only the courts can tell us."[71] Henkin felt that although customary international law had long been seen as

---

[69] *Id.* at 428.
[70] Henkin, *supra* note 58, at 823.
[71] HENKIN, *supra* note 3, at 220.

part of the common law of States, the "implications" of Sabbatino seemed to have changed that.

## D. The Apogee of Foreign Relations Exceptionalism: The Third Restatement

In the 1970s the American Law Institute began considering whether to begin a Third Restatement of foreign relations law, and eventually resolved to do so, even though the Second Restatement had not been approved until 1965.[72] Between 1980 and 1986 seven Tentative Drafts of the Third Restatement appeared, and it was eventually adopted by the Institute in 1987. Of all the indices of foreign relations exceptionalism since its early twentieth-century origins, the Third Restatement was the most marked. It codified all the elements of exceptionalism that had emerged since the first decades of the twentieth century—Sutherland's bright-line distinction between the "internal" and "external" powers of the federal government, Curtiss-Wright's equating of the constitutional status of treaties and executive agreements without congressional oversight, Belmont's and Pink's eradication of any role for the States in the exercise of foreign policy, and Sabbatino's and Zschernig's conclusion that the federal courts should displace State common law rules whenever "foreign policy interests" were present in a case, however domestic its setting—and added two elements of its own.

One of the elements involved the status of customary international law in the federal courts. We have noted that Louis Henkin's understanding of Sabbatino evolved from 1964, where he thought that any role played by the federal courts in fashioning principles of customary international law would be a modest one, to 1972, where he anticipated the possibility of larger federal court participation in "foreign affairs" generally. In 1980 the First Tentative Draft of the Third Restatement appeared. In it, not only had the anticipated role for the federal courts in declaring and applying principles of customary international law expanded, the status of customary international law rules in American foreign relations law had grown as well. One needs to bear in mind that Sabbatino's conclusion that the "act of state" doctrine was binding on American State courts involved a doctrine that had long been formulated by U.S. federal courts, not one derived from customary international law. It was thus arguable that Sabbatino had little effect beyond the "act of state" context, and Henkin's initial reaction to the decision seemed to take that argument for granted.

---

[72] The ALI's decision to commission a Third Restatement in the 1970s was itself unusual: Typically the intervals between successive Restatements had been much longer.

But when the First Tentative Draft, with Henkin as its Chief Reporter, appeared in 1980,[73] a much more expansive version of customary international law's effect on U.S. courts, and of the relationship of customary international law to international agreements made by the United States, was proposed. The First Tentative Draft stated that "[i]nternational law in the United States has come to be regarded as federal common law, and no less than treaties and other international agreements, therefore, it is afforded supremacy over state law by Article VI of the Constitution." It added that "determinations of international law by the Supreme Court of the United States" were "binding on the states" in the same manner as treaties or executive international agreements, and that cases "arising under" customary international law were "laws of the United States" and hence within the Article III jurisdiction of the federal courts.[74] Although the 1980 Tentative Draft stopped short of suggesting that *all* principles of customary international law needed to be applied in U.S. courts and were binding on U.S. officials,[75] what it proposed was still a quite broad conception, especially as it did not rest on any case law save *Sabbatino*.

In addition, the 1980 Tentative Draft treated the status of customary international law doctrines as identical to that of treaties or executive agreements when U.S. courts recognized them. This meant that just as a treaty or an Act of Congress or an executive agreement, enacted subsequent to the recognition of a customary international law doctrine, displaced that doctrine if inconsistent with it, a later-enacted rule of customary international law trumped existing provisions of other foreign affairs enactments if it was inconsistent with them. Although conceding that the latter situation had "never been authoritatively determined," the Tentative Draft proposed that "[a] rule of international law or a provision of an agreement that becomes effective as law in the United States supersedes . . . .any inconsistent preexisting provision in the law of the United States."[76] That proposition invited the federal courts to invalidate statutes that they believed inconsistent with their understandings of customary international law doctrines.

The other major element of foreign relations exceptionalism added by the Third Restatement came in constitutional law, specifically in the apparent conclusions by the 1982 Third Tentative Draft that the protection of the U.S. Constitution could apply to foreign nationals who claimed that actions by

---

[73] Foreign Relations Law of the United States (Revised) (Tent. Draft No. 1, 1980). I identify subsequent references to the First and Third Tentative Drafts of the Third Restatement (the Third appeared in 1982) by the year of their appearance.

[74] Third Restatement, 1980 Draft, ch. 2, intro. note at 41.

[75] The 1980 Tentative Draft stated that not all customary international law addressed "activities, relations, and interests of the United States." Section 131 cmt. *c*.

[76] *Id.* § 135 (1).

U.S. officials abroad which affected them had violated constitutional standards. As in the First Tentative Draft's invocation of *Sabbatino* for propositions about customary international law as federal common law which went well beyond that decision, the Third Tentative Draft based its conclusion about the Constitution on an extrapolation of language in the plurality opinion in the 1957 Supreme Court case of *Reid v. Covert*.[77] Henkin's 1972 treatise had taken that case to state that "wherever it acts the United States 'can only act in accordance with all the limitations imposed by the Constitution,'"[78] and had used it to claim that an older view that the Constitution imposed no limits on the United States when it acted outside its territory was "dead."[79] But Henkin's treatise stopped well short of suggesting that inhabitants of foreign nations could invoke the Constitution anytime they were disadvantaged by U.S. policy, or even that U.S. officials were bound by constitutional safeguards when they acted abroad.

But by 1982 the Third Tentative Draft was prepared to claim that "the Constitution probably governs . . . at least some exercises of authority in respect to some aliens abroad," although acknowledging that "the matter has not been definitely adjudicated."[80] A reporter's note added that "[j]udicial statements declaring that any exercise of authority by the United States is subject to constitutional limitations" would "seem to apply . . . to acts in respect of any alien anywhere."[81] To illustrate, the draft stated that if the apprehension of subjects abroad, either by U.S. or foreign officials, involved conduct that "shocked the conscience," or if evidence allegedly pertinent to apprehensions had been obtained in violation of Fourth Amendment standards, accused subjects would be immune from prosecution in U.S. courts or the evidence obtained would be inadmissible in U.S. criminal trials.[82] Those conclusions had potentially broad implications, for they assumed that constitutional protections could extend to foreign nationals as well as American citizens and apply to the extraterritorial activities of U.S. officials, and that the U.S. Constitution could not simply be made a basis for preventing action by the U.S. government that violated its provisions, but also for authorizing individual suits arising out of that action.

In summarizing the state of foreign affairs exceptionalism at its high-water mark, the Third Restatement anticipated that the federal courts would play a significant role in establishing its propositions. This was a marked change from foreign affairs exceptionalism at its origins, whose thrust had been to confine most of foreign relations lawmaking to the federal government, displacing the

---

[77] 354 U.S. 1 (1957).

[78] *Id.* at 6.

[79] HENKIN, *supra* note 3, at 266.

[80] Foreign Relations Law of the United States (Revised) § 721 cmt. *b* (Tent. Draft No. 3, 1982).

[81] *Id.* § 722 reporters' note 16.

[82] *Id.* § 433 (3), (4) & cmts. *c, d.*

States, and to the executive branch of that government, minimizing the role of the Senate or of Congress. By the early 1980s, with the Third Restatement's readings of *Sabbatino* as a general charter for the federal courts to apply rules of customary international law to displace competing State rules in cases with international dimensions, and with *Reid* as a comparable charter for those courts to discern and to apply the exterritorial reach of provisions of the U.S. Constitution, the federal courts had been installed as the leading architects of an exceptionalist program. Other-branch checks on the role of the federal courts in that capacity were minimal. If Congress or the executive disapproved of a rule of customary international law being applied in those courts, they could hypothetically displace it with some statutory enactment, but that required securing the joint assent of both branches. And even that check was contingent on the enactment's not raising any constitutional objections, a matter to be determined by the courts. Meanwhile the courts, according to the Third Restatement, had considerable flexibility to allow citizens or aliens affected by unconstitutional extraterritorial conduct to pursue civil remedies.

It has been suggested that the Third Restatement was the product of dual developments, in the decades of the 1960s and 1970s, that combined to create a distinctively optimistic orientation toward the capacity of the federal courts to establish themselves as lawmakers in the arena of foreign affairs.[83] One development, under way since the years after World War II, was the emergence of what might be called "Cold War cosmopolitanism" in foreign affairs: an attitude that combined a rejection of the isolationist tradition of American foreign policy for a more expansive role of the United States in foreign affairs, as was befitting the global "leader of the free world," with a marked determination to treat the Soviet Union, and its purported ally Communist China, as antidemocratic adversaries comparable to those of the Axis powers in World War II. By identifying principles of customary international law that reflected the democratic aspirations of members in the global community, and helping integrate those principles in domestic American law, the courts could confirm the United States' role as a leader of enlightened international opinion. And by signaling that the U.S. Constitution had a global reach and could be invoked by American courts to protect the rights not only of American citizens abroad but of foreign nationals as well, the courts were underscoring that the Constitution could be seen as a bulwark against official misconduct everywhere.

The other development was the rise in the 1970s of skepticism about the capacity of the American political branches to function effectively in the

---

[83] Paul B. Stephan, *Courts, the Constitution, and Customary International Law: The Intellectual Origins of the Restatement (Third) of the Foreign Relations Law of the United States*, 44 VA. J. INT'L L. 33, 57–58 (2003).

international arena, combined with a legacy of confidence about the capacity of "activist" American courts to infuse the legal order with principles of fairness, justice, and equality. By the end of Earl Warren's tenure as Chief Justice in 1969, the Supreme Court had become recognized as the most prominent, and arguably most successful, reformist institution of the American political and legal order, far outdistancing, in areas such as race relations, criminal justice, and legislative reapportionment, the other branches. And in the next decade, after arguably having demonstrated their ineffectuality in the domestic arena in the 1950s and 1960s, the political branches appeared to demonstrate it as well in foreign affairs, allegedly blundering in Vietnam, Latin America, Africa, Iran, and Afghanistan, to the benefit of the Soviet Union and its allies and to the unsettling of prospects for global peace and the democratization of the international order.[84]

Those developments combined to suggest that a systematic effort by the federal courts to inject Cold War cosmopolitanism into American foreign relations jurisprudence might result in a reorientation of that jurisprudence analogous to that which the Warren Court had produced in domestic constitutional law. But that reorientation failed to materialize, and when the Third Restatement of Foreign Relations Law was officially endorsed and published by the ALI in 1987, the long hegemony of foreign affairs exceptionalism had begun to exhaust itself.

## II.  Cracks in the Exceptionalist Paradigm

### A.  Critical Commentary

Even before the Third Restatement was officially approved, some criticism of its aggressive treatment of customary international law had appeared. Additional critiques of its treatment of customary international law and its general approach to separation of powers issues would surface in the 1980s.[85] But on the whole the Third Restatement's readings of *Sabbatino* and *Reid*, and all of the defining elements of foreign affairs exceptionalism, were treated as mainstream features of what came to be called the "modern position" on foreign affairs jurisprudence, "modern" not only for its twentieth-century arrival in the history of that jurisprudence but because it supposedly harmonized with the stance of Cold War

---

[84]  For more detail, see *id.* at 53–54.

[85]  Philip R. Trimble, *A Revisionist View of Customary International Law*, 33 U.C.L.A. L. REV. 665 (1986); Arthur M. Weisburd, *The Executive Branch and International Law*, 41 VAND. L. REV. 1288 (1988); Stewart Jay, *The Status of the Law of Nations in Early American Law*, 42 VAND. L. REV. 819 (1989).

cosmopolitanism thought best suited for the United States' place in "modern" international relations.[86]

But then, suddenly, came a barrage of critical commentary, initiated by Curtis Bradley and Jack Goldsmith's 1997 *Customary International Law as Federal Common Law: A Critique of the Modern Position*.[87] Bradley and Goldsmith subsequently produced a series of additional articles expanding their critique.[88] Defenders of the mainstream position responded,[89] setting off a debate that has continued up to the present.[90]

The critique of Third Restatement–style foreign affairs exceptionalism advanced five arguments. First, it maintained that the history of American foreign affairs jurisprudence prior to *Sabbatino* and *Zschernig* was neither consistent with customary international law being regarded as a form of federal common law trumping the decisions of State courts when inconsistent with them, nor with the view that dormant foreign affairs preemption had been established in the same manner as dormant preemptions in the domestic arena, such as in Commerce Clause cases. In short, there was no "originalist" case for *Sabbatino* or *Zschernig*; those decisions were jurisprudential novelties.

Second, the critique maintained that although one might seek to justify *Sabbatino* or *Zschernig* functionally, on the ground that the involvement of

---

[86] Louis B. Sohn, *The New International Law: Protection of the Rights of Individuals Rather Than States*, 32 Am. U. L. Rev. 1 (1982); Louis Henkin, *International Law as Law in the United States*, 82 Mich. L. Rev. 1555 (1984); Richard B. Bilder, *The Role of States and Cities in Foreign Relations*, 83 Am. J. Int'l L. 821 (1989); Larry Kramer, *The Lawmaking Power of the Federal Courts*, 12 Pace L. Rev. 263, 288 n.84 (1992); Howard N. Fenton, III, *The Fallacy of Federalism in Foreign Affairs*, 13 Nw. J. Int'l L. & Bus. 563 (1993); Lea Brilmayer, *Federalism, State Authority, and the Preemptive Power of International Law*, 1994 Sup. Ct. Rev. 295; Bradford R. Clark, *Federal Common Law: A Structural Reinterpretation*, 144 U. Pa. L. Rev. 1245, 1292 (1996); Andreas Lowenfeld, *Nationalizing International Law*, 36 Colum. J. Transnat'l L. 121 (1997). In the second edition of his treatise, which appeared in 1996, as in his first, Henkin declared that "[a]t the end of the twentieth century as at the end of the eighteenth, as regards foreign relations, 'the states do not exist.'" Henkin, *supra* note 3, at 227; Louis Henkin, Foreign Affairs and the United States Constitution 149–50 (2d ed. 1996).

[87] Curtis A. Bradley & Jack L. Goldsmith, *Customary International Law as Federal Common Law: A Critique of the Modern Position*, 110 Harv. L. Rev. 815 (1997).

[88] See, e.g., Jack L. Goldsmith, *Federal Courts, Foreign Affairs, and Federalism*, 87 Va. L. Rev. 1617 (1997); Curtis A. Bradley, *The Treaty Power and American Federalism*, 99 Mich. L. Rev. 98 (2000); Curtis A. Bradley & Jack L. Goldsmith, *Treaties, Human Rights, and Conditional Consent*, 149 U. Pa. L. Rev. 399 (2000); Jack L. Goldsmith, *Should International Human Rights Law Trump U.S. Domestic Law?*, 1 Chi. J. Int'l L. 327 (2001).

[89] Most prominently, Harold H. Koh, *Is International Law Really State Law?*, 111 Harv. L. Rev. 1824 (1998).

[90] For recent contributions supporting the Third Restatement's view, see Donald E. Childress, *When* Erie *Goes International*, 105 Nw. U. L. Rev. 1531 (2011); Michael Glennon & Robert D. Sloane, Foreign Affairs Federalism 247–75 (2016); William S. Dodge, *Customary International Law, Change, and the Constitution*, 106 Geo. L.J. 1559 (2018). Recent literature supporting the critique includes Paul B. Stephan, *Inferences of Judicial Lawmaking Power and the Law of Nations*, *id.* at 793; John Harrison, *The Constitution and the Law of Nations, id.* at 1659; and Ingrid Wuerth, *The Future of the Federal Common Law of Foreign Relations, id.* at 1825.

American citizens and the U.S. government with international affairs has been far more extensive in the twentieth century than previously, and that there are therefore more opportunities for States to undermine a comprehensive national foreign policy, or interfere with the relationships between American citizens and foreign governments, *Sabbatino* and *Zschernig* invited the federal *courts* to police State interference with foreign affairs, a task that courts were arguably far less well suited than the political branches to perform.

Third, the increasing participation of American individuals and corporations in foreign affairs, taken alongside the increasing number of international organizations that were not sovereign nations but whose policies potentially affected those individuals and corporations, meant that the bright lines Sutherland and other early advocates of foreign affairs exceptionalism drew between the "internal" and "external" affairs of the United States had become blurred, and consequently more "domestic" issues, traditionally the province of the States, were surfacing in international relations. Thus one of the working assumptions of foreign affairs exceptionalism—that the States "disappear" in the arena of foreign relations—was no longer empirically sound.

Fourth, carving out a potentially large space for the federal courts to fashion customary international law rules binding the States, or to subject Americans and foreign officials acting abroad to constitutional constraints on their conduct, rested on two assumptions that were wrongheaded. One was that the political branches needed help from the federal courts in monitoring the activities of States that might interfere with their opportunities to effectuate foreign policy because they were incapable of such monitoring themselves. Another was that the costs of political branch silence in responding to State intrusions were greater than the costs of federal judicial lawmaking. The first assumption was arguably misplaced because State intrusions on national policy making in foreign relations tended to have a broader impact, and consequently be more discernible, than intrusions affecting domestic commerce. Moreover, in addition to Congress as a potential monitor, the executive branch had significant powers that it could enforce in the form of executive agreements or orders designed to override State actions that it perceived as undesirable. And the second assumption was also arguably misplaced because there was no reason to think that if federal courts were given widespread power to determine when customary international law rules trumped arguably competing State rules, they would do a better job of determining when a "federal interest" worthy of displacing State law was implicated in a particular customary international law doctrine and when it was not. The comparatively recent existence of *Sabbatino* and *Zschernig*, and the limited number of opportunities federal courts had had to decide when customary international law applied, suggested that judicial "errors" might result. In any event it was hard to understand why, if the federal government found itself vexed by a particular

State intrusion into its foreign policymaking prerogatives, it would not be able to respond through the political branches.

Fifth, Supreme Court decisions after *Sabbatino* and *Zschernig* suggested that far from embracing the foreign affairs exceptionalism of those decisions, the Court was moving in the direction of reducing their impact. In *Barclays Bank PLC v. Franchise Tax Board of California*,[91] the Court considered the validity of a California method for taxing multinational corporations. A number of foreign corporations objected to the method, and its opponents spent several decades urging Congress to preempt it, but without success. Consequently, Barclays Bank and other foreign corporations challenged the taxing method in court, citing *Zschernig* and asserting that "federal uniformity was essential" in the area of multinational taxation. They noted the large number of diplomatic communications sent to the United States protesting against California's tax scheme and received the support of several amicus briefs from foreign nations.

The Court rejected those arguments. It ruled that, when determining whether a State law was implicitly preempted by federal policy, courts had no authority, where the national government had not enacted any such policy, to balance "effects" of a State law on foreign relations against competing interests of States. It also concluded that some communications by officials of the federal government about the undesirability of the California method of taxation could not, in the face of congressional or executive inactivity, be given weight simply because of the purported value of the federal government's speaking with "one voice" in the area of foreign policy. Finally, it held that congressional inaction in the face of ostensibly adverse State activity regarding a matter touching foreign affairs should be taken as creating a presumption that Congress was prepared to tolerate the activity. *Barclays Bank* seemed to check significantly the expansionist potential of *Zschernig*.

A second case involved another dimension of the Third Restatement version of foreign affairs exceptionalism, the extraterritorial effect of American laws, whether constitutional or statutory. In *EEOC v. Arabian American Oil Co.*,[92] a naturalized U.S. citizen, working in Saudi Arabia, challenged his discharge by his employer on the ground that he had been discriminated against because of his race, religion, or national origin in violation of Title VII of the Civil Rights Act of 1964. A federal district court dismissed the suit on the ground that Title VII's protections did not extend to U.S. citizens employed abroad by American companies. The Fifth Circuit affirmed, as did the Supreme Court.

The Court applied a presumption against the extraterritorial effect of U.S. laws absent a clear statement by Congress of that effect. It maintained that the

---

[91]  512 U.S. 298 (1994).
[92]  499 U.S. 244 (1991).

presumption served to "protect against unintended clashes between our laws and those of other nations which could result in international discord."[93] It added that Congress, rather than the courts, was the appropriate body to "calibrate" the provisions of its statutes.[94] A third case involved the act of state doctrine emphasized in *Sabbatino*. That case had invited courts to make assessments of the "foreign relations implications" of acts of a foreign nation, and lower courts had applied its reach in an inconsistent fashion. In *W.S. Kirkpatrick v. Environmental Tectonics Corp.*,[95] an unsuccessful bidder on a construction contract in Nigeria sued in district court for damages on the ground that the contract had been obtained through bribes, in violation of Nigerian and U.S. law. The district court held that the act of state doctrine barred the suit because application of the statute on behalf of the unsuccessful bidder would require imputing improper motives to foreign officials and thus might embarrass the executive in its conduct of foreign relations. The Third Circuit reversed, concluding that the case did not require U.S. courts to determine the *validity* of a foreign statute, only its application, and any finding that Nigerian officials had participated in bribery in the awarding of construction contracts was insufficient to embarrass the executive in its conduct of foreign policy. The Supreme Court affirmed the Third Circuit, concluding that the act of state doctrine was applicable only where U.S. courts needed to determine the validity of a foreign law, and that such an inquiry was not necessary to decide the unsuccessful bidder's claim. The decision thus not only narrowed the meaning of the act of state doctrine, it served to eliminate a number of potential instances in which courts, in the absence of guidance from the political branches, might be asked to speculate about the implications of applying laws of other nations for the conduct of U.S. foreign policy.

Finally, in *United States v. Verdugo-Urquidez*,[96] the Court rejected the Third Restatement's contention that the Constitution applied to the extraterritorial acts of U.S. officials against foreign persons. The case involved Rene Martin Verdugo-Urquidez, a Mexican citizen, believed to be a leader of an organization smuggling narcotics into the United States, who, pursuant to an arrest warrant issued in the United States, was apprehended by Mexican officials in Mexico and brought to the United States, where he was arrested. Following his arrest, U.S. Drug Enforcement Administration (DEA) agents, along with Mexican officials, searched his residence in Mexico and seized certain documents, including a tally sheet allegedly reflecting the quantities of marijuana he had smuggled into the United States. In a trial before a federal district court in California,

---

93   *Id.* at 248.
94   *Id.* at 259.
95   493 U.S. 400 (1990).
96   494 U.S. 259 (1990).

Verdugo-Urquidez moved that evidence of the documents be suppressed under the Fourth Amendment, citing *Reid v. Covert*. The district court agreed, and a divided panel of the Ninth Circuit affirmed, stating that "the Constitution imposes substantive constraints on the federal government, even when it operates abroad," and that the DEA agents had failed to obtain a search warrant before seizing the documents.[97]

A five-Justice majority of the Court, with Stevens concurring separately, reversed, concluding that at least with respect to the Fourth Amendment, *Reid* did not govern because the defendant was not only a foreign national but one whose presence in the United States was not voluntary.[98] It also held that were the Fourth Amendment to apply to all actions of U.S. officials abroad,

> aliens with no attachment to this country might bring actions for damages to remedy claimed violations of the Fourth Amendment in foreign countries or international waters, and Members of the Executive and Legislative Branches would be plunged into a sea of uncertainty as to what might be reasonable in the way of searches and seizures conducted abroad.[99]

The Court maintained that "[a]ny restrictions on searches and seizures incident to American action abroad must be maintained by the political branches through diplomatic understanding, treaty, or legislation."[100]

The critiques of the "modern position" on customary international law as federal common law, on dormant federal preemption in foreign affairs, on the extraterritorial effect of American laws, and on the act of state doctrine had the cumulative effect of providing reasons why foreign affairs exceptionalism might be inapposite in those areas, and in suggesting that the Supreme Court had been inclined to narrow, rather than to broaden, the scope of *Sabbatino*, *Zschernig*, and *Reid*. The critiques served as a brake on the momentum of foreign affairs exceptionalism that had been building since the 1960s.

## B. Historicization of Exceptionalist Jurisprudence

Bradley's and Goldsmith's *Customary International Law as Federal Common Law*, and some of their subsequent work around the turn of the twentieth century, contained sections in which they engaged in historical analysis in order to

[97] *Id.* at 263.
[98] *Id.* at 270.
[99] *Id.* at 274.
[100] *Id.* at 275.

show that the purportedly established status of the federal government as the sole architect of foreign policy had not in fact been in place until the twentieth century and had not been grounded on accurate historical research. They used history as a technique for subverting "mainstream" contemporary jurisprudential propositions by demonstrating that their mainstream status was more contingent, and time-bound, than might first appear.

On the heels of those historical inquiries came another line of scholarship that sought to use history in another fashion, not so much as a basis for undermining the pedigree of doctrines associated with foreign affairs exceptionalism but as a way of emphasizing that foreign affairs exceptionalism was a distinctive, time-bound jurisprudential development. That scholarship proceeded from two vantage points. One, anticipated by Bradley's and Goldsmith's work, was to consider exceptionalism against the backdrop of American foreign relations jurisprudence since the founding era. When the coverage of foreign relations decisions and commentary was expanded in that fashion, it turned out that few of the propositions asserted about foreign affairs jurisprudence by exceptionalists were of long-standing duration.

For example, there was no established tradition of federal exclusivity in foreign relations before the twentieth century. Foreign relations was almost exclusively conducted in the form of treaties, which needed to be approved by the Senate, until the last years of the nineteenth century. Before *Missouri v. Holland*, commentators assumed that the "reserved powers" of the States limited the treaty power, so that the federal government could not enter into treaties with foreign nations on subjects that were beyond its domestic reach. And States had involved themselves throughout the nineteenth century in areas such as quarantine restrictions and "head" taxes on ships carrying passengers that embarked in U.S. ports, which affected foreign commerce.[101]

Further, there was also no established tradition of federal plenary power, following from the inherent powers of sovereign nations in the international community, to conduct foreign affairs. Plenary power theory had first made its appearance in what might be called "domestic" contexts involving the exercise of some "foreign relations" powers by the federal government, such as treaties with Indian tribes, decisions to exclude entrant or deport resident aliens, and the projected reach of constitutional protections to residents of overseas U.S. territories.[102] Although Sutherland asserted, in both *Curtiss-Wright* and scholarship preceding that decision, that the inherent powers of the United States as a sovereign nation had been recognized since the Articles of Confederation, historical

[101]  For more detail, see White, *supra* note 8; WHITE, *supra* note 13, at 124–30.
[102]  For more detail, see Sarah H. Cleveland, *The Plenary Power Background of* Curtiss-Wright, 70 U. COLO. L. REV. 1127 (1999).

support for that assertion was dubious.[103] The effect of those historical inquiries was to suggest that *Curtiss-Wright, Belmont,* and *Pink* were products of the discrete historical circumstances that were affecting the conduct of foreign policy by the United States as World War II was foreshadowed and then unfolded.

## C. Additional Court Decisions

One of the unanticipated consequences of the 2001 attack on the World Trade Center and the subsequent initiation of a global "war on terror" was the Supreme Court's consistent refusal to embrace exceptionalist arguments in situations where the power of the political branches to conduct foreign policy seemed entrenched. When persons accused of terrorist activities after 2001 challenged their detentions, the U.S. government consistently advanced exceptionalist arguments in support of its actions.[104] Some commentators initially predicted that the courts would be highly deferential to the political branches after 9/11.[105]

But the Court, in a series of decisions between 2004 and 2008,[106] consistently sided with detainees who sought judicial review of their status, rejecting arguments by the government that detention of aliens in U.S. facilities had been committed to the political branches and that the government's conclusion that a detainee was an "enemy combatant," eligible for indefinite detention without trial while hostilities continued, was conclusive. In the second of those decisions the government argued that "military necessity" justified the indefinite detention of enemy combatants." Justice Thomas accepted that argument, but as the sole dissenter.[107] In the third decision the Court found a military commission established by the president to try detainees unconstitutional, rejecting government arguments that the case raised "political questions" and was hence not justiciable, that the commission had been authorized by a congressional statute, and that it was not governed by the Geneva Conventions.[108] In the last of the cases, the Court held that detainees in a U.S. base in Guantanamo Bay, Cuba, were entitled to petition for habeas corpus relief under the U.S. Constitution, and that a 2005

[103] For a near-contemporary critique of Sutherland's historical analysis of the "inherent powers" of the Articles of Confederation, see David M. Levitan, *The Foreign Relations Power: An Analysis of Mr. Justice Sutherland's Theory,* 55 Yale L.J. 467 (1946).

[104] For a summary of those arguments, see Robert M. Chesney, *National Security Fact Deference,* 95 Va. L. Rev. 1361, 1366–77 (2009).

[105] See, e.g., Owen Gross, *Chaos and Rules: Should Responses to Violent Crises Always Be Constitutional?,* 112 Yale L.J. 1011 (2003).

[106] Rasul v. Bush, 542 U.S. 466 (2004); Hamdi v. Rumsfeld, 542 U.S. 507 (2004); Hamdan v. Rumsfeld, 548 U.S. 557 (2006); Boumediene v. Bush, 553 U.S. 723 (2008).

[107] Hamdi v. Rumsfeld, 542 U.S. at 509. See *id.* at 579 for Thomas's invocation of exceptionalist arguments in his dissent.

[108] Hamdan v. Rumsfeld, 548 U.S. at 558–64.

congressional statute outlining their treatment was not an adequate substitute for habeas.[109]

There have been some additional decisions, in the areas of justiciability, federalism, and executive dominance, that might be seen as retreating from an exceptionalist posture. One article has offered those decisions, as well as the detainee cases, as support for an argument that "normalization" has largely replaced exceptionalism in contemporary foreign relations jurisprudence.[110] That argument has been criticized,[111] and seems overstated: There is also evidence that lower courts have continued to treat foreign affairs as a sphere distinct from domestic affairs and to demonstrate a receptiveness to exceptionalism in foreign relations cases.[112]

So it seems too early to say that foreign affairs exceptionalism has passed out of existence, or even that it now has a marginal status in foreign affairs jurisprudence. But it seems plain that the aspirations for an exceptionalist-dominated regime of foreign relations reflected in the Third Restatement have not been realized, and that the commissioning of a Fourth Restatement of Foreign Affairs partially reflects that fact. The last section of this chapter takes up the Fourth Restatement's prospective treatment of foreign affairs exceptionalism.

## III.  Toward the Fourth Restatement

Restatements typically rest their summaries of the state of the law in a particular field on a combination of court decisions, statutory reactions to those decisions, and academic commentary. Although the Third Restatement of Foreign Relations may have been somewhat unusual in occasionally fashioning doctrinal propositions that were not reflected in much case law, it has not been uncommon for the authors of Restatements to make suggestions, typically in the form of commentary, as to where they anticipate a particular doctrinal area may be heading.

In this vein, the Fourth Restatement can clearly be understood as signaling that although foreign affairs exceptionalism has not disappeared from cases and commentary, the broad support for it reflected in the Third Restatement can no longer be said to exist, and in some of its pivotal areas it might be said to be in jeopardy. A full comparison of the Third and Fourth Restatement is made difficult by

---

[109]  553 U.S. at 732–33.

[110]  Ganesh Sitaraman & Ingrid Wuerth, *The Normalization of Foreign Relations Law*, 128 Harv. L. Rev. 1897 (2015).

[111]  Curtis A. Bradley, *Foreign Relations Law and the Purported Shift Away from "Exceptionalism,"* 128 Harv. L. Rev. F. 294 (2015).

[112]  See *id.* at 298–301 (collecting cases).

the ALI's decision not to include a survey of recent treatments of customary international law in its coverage, nor to ask those involved with the preparation of the Fourth Restatement to address the general question of whether federal foreign relations powers can be understood as wholly preempting competing State law, even when those powers had not been exercised. But the Fourth Restatement's treatment of three areas, each of them integral to the Third Restatement's version of foreign relations exceptionalism, is suggestive.

Critical to the Court's decision in *Sabbatino* was its conclusion that the act of state doctrine, fashioned by American judges, had the status of federal common law that preempted inconsistent State law. It was not clear where that conclusion came from—the doctrine, as initially declared, only stated that acts of foreign nations would be given effect in U.S. courts—but understanding the act of state doctrine as preempting decisions of States helped resolve the allegedly delicate foreign relations issue posed in *Sabbatino*, where the Cuban government had chosen to confiscate the property of American nationals and a State court had refused to treat the seizure as valid.

*Sabbatino* described the act of state doctrine as requiring that "[t]he Judicial Branch will not examine the validity of a taking of property within its own territory by a foreign sovereign government . . . in the absence of a treaty or otherwise unambiguous agreement regarding controlling legal principles."[113] It was unclear what "will not examine" meant. It could have been the equivalent of judicial abstention, meaning that courts were not competent to pass on the validity of acts of foreign states because of the delicate foreign relations issues doing so might raise. Or it could simply have meant that courts would accept the acts of foreign states as presumptively valid and use them as rules for deciding cases. The Third Restatement adopted the former meaning, although qualifying it by suggesting that courts had some discretion as to whether to apply it.

In *Environmental Tectonics*, however, as we have seen, the Court sharply limited the reach of the act of state doctrine, stating that it "does not establish an exception for cases and controversies that may embarrass foreign governments, but merely that, in the course of deciding, the acts of foreign governments taken within their territories shall be deemed valid." "Courts in the United States," it added, "have the power, and ordinarily the obligation, to decide cases and controversies properly presented to them."[114] The Fourth Restatement emphasized this treatment, stopping short of suggesting that *Environmental Tectonics* had gutted the doctrine, but predicting that once it is no longer understood as a means of preventing embarrassments to foreign officials or other foreign

[113] 376 U.S. at 428.
[114] 403 U.S. at 409.

nationals, it leaves room for State and federal litigants to file claims against foreign actors that might have diplomatic reverberations.[115]

Another illustration of the Fourth Restatement's picking up on case-law developments that suggest movement away from the ambitions of foreign affairs exceptionalism comes in the area of subject matter jurisdiction under Article III. The Third Restatement's position was not only that the entire area of customary international law was federal common law within Article III jurisdiction, but that Section 1331 of Title 28 of the U.S. Code, which gives the federal district courts original jurisdiction over "all civil actions arising under the Constitution, laws, or treaties of the United States,"[116] ensured that any disputes involving applications of customary international law—a "'law' of the United States"— could be brought in the federal courts, even if the disputes did not satisfy other criteria for Article III subject matter jurisdiction.[117]

That position may have been myopic—did it make sense for the federal courts to be entertaining "foreign relations" cases where the Constitution, treaties or other federal laws were not at issue but customary international law doctrines were?—but it was in keeping with the Third Restatement's general confidence in the capacity of the federal courts to entertain international law disputes. A 2004 decision by the Supreme Court, *Sosa v. Alvarez-Machain*,[118] however, declined to conclude that customary international law cases were brought within Article III jurisdiction by Section 1331 and implied that customary international law rules would become "laws of the United States" only when statutes directly gave them that effect.[119] The Fourth Restatement did not endorse either of those implications of *Sosa*, possibly because the decision was an opaque one. But in the one area where some statutory support for U.S. federal courts entertaining claims based on customary international law existed—the so-called "Alien Tort Statute,"[120] which opened the district courts to claims by aliens against foreign defendants for violations of international human rights law—late twentieth- and early twenty-first-century decisions by the Supreme Court significantly undermined the Third Restatement's view that cases brought under the Alien Torts Statute satisfied Article III's subject matter requirements and thus could be brought in the federal courts even when they did not meet other jurisdictional requirements.[121]

---

[115] FOURTH RESTATEMENT § 441 (1).
[116] 28 U.S.C. § 1331, 62 Stat. 930 (1948).
[117] THIRD RESTATEMENT § 111 cmt. *e.*
[118] 542 U.S. 692 (2004).
[119] *Id.* at 724–25, 731 n.19.
[120] Judiciary Act of 1789, Sect. 9, 1 Stat. 73, 77 (1789).
[121] THIRD RESTATEMENT § 111 cmt. *f.*

Four Supreme Court decisions, taken together, would seem to negate the suggestion by the Third Restatement that the Alien Torts Statute (ATS) provides an independent basis for Article III jurisdiction over international human rights claims. The first, *Argentine Republic v. Amerada Hess Shipping Corp.*,[122] considered whether the ATS should be read as creating an exemption for claimants in cases where defendants would be protected by the Foreign Sovereign Immunities Act, designed to insulate foreign states and their corporations from being sued in the federal district courts, and concluded that it did not.[123] *Sosa* came next, holding that the ATS was only intended to incorporate a limited class of torts arising from violations of fundamental international legal rights into federal law, not to create general Article III subject matter jurisdiction for all torts based on international law. *Kiobel v. Royal Dutch Petroleum*[124] further narrowed the category of ATS-incorporated international tort claims, limiting it to those which "touch and concern the territory of the United States . . . .with sufficient force to displace the presumption against extraterritorial application."[125] And *Jesner v. Arab Bank, PLC*[126] ruled that under the *Sosa* test, claims against foreign corporations could not be included within the ATS.[127] In sum, the Third Restatement's expectation that the ATS might well provide an independent basis for bringing international law claims to the federal courts seems to have been largely unrealized.

A final suggestive area was the sort of "field preemption" of State laws and policies allegedly interfering with foreign relations that the Court considered in *Zschernig*. The Third Restatement had taken a strong position on the potential impact of *Zschernig*, proposing that the test for preemption of a competing State law or policy should be whether it "intruded" on the federal government's conduct of foreign relations, even when there was no direct conflict between the State action and an express position of the federal government. As the Third Restatement put it, "State law and policy must bow not only when inconsistent with federal law and policy but even when federal authority has shown a purpose, by 'preemption' or 'occupying the field,' to exclude even State activity that is not inconsistent with federal law or policy."[128]

That was an invitation to the federal courts to apply *Zschernig* across a range of cases, and possibly to give a broad definition of "intrusion." If that was the hope of those who participated in the Third Restatement, it was not realized,

---

[122]    488 U.S. 428 (1989).

[123]    *Id.* at 443. This was contrary to the Third Restatement's expectation: see THIRD RESTATEMENT §§ 454, 457.

[124]    569 U.S. 108 (2013).

[125]    *Id.* at 124–25.

[126]    138 S. Ct. 1386 (2018).

[127]    *Id.* at 1407.

[128]    THIRD RESTATEMENT § 1 reporters' note 5.

at least in Supreme Court decisions. In *Dames & Moore v. Regan*,[129] the Court, in concluding that a State policy was inconsistent with a federal one and thus preempted, based its conclusion on the fact that "Congress has implicitly approved the practice of claim settlement by executive agreement," and described that finding as "[c]rucial to our decision."[130] In *Barclays Bank*, we have seen, the Court found that executive branch "policy," as evinced by numerous complaints to the State Department from foreign nations about California's method for taxing international transactions and the State's Department's stated opposition to the practice, was insufficient to preempt the State's taxation scheme. And although, in *American Ins. Assn. v. Garamendi*, a 5–4 majority of the Court found that the federal government's negotiations with the German government and reliance on an international commission for Holocaust-era insurance claims to obtain compensation for the victims of Nazi confiscation of the policies preempted a California statute requiring insurance companies doing business in the State to disclose information about policies they sold between 1920 and 1945, it emphasized that there was a clear "conflict" between the federal and State policies and that the federal government's power to conduct the sort of diplomatic relations it had engaged in with Germany was clearly established. The dissent in *Garamendi* disagreed as to whether a "conflict" existed, noting that the federal government, in its dealings with Germany and the commission, had taken no position on the mandatory disclosure of information in insurance policies. Although the majority alluded to *Zschernig*, the dissent noted that the Court had "not relied on *Zschernig* since it was decided, and . . . would not resurrect that decision here." It pointed out that *Zschernig* involved a State policy that was critical of foreign governments, in effect "sitting in judgment" of them, and intimated that the decision should be confined to that situation.

The Fourth Restatement has something to say about foreign affairs preemption, but its comments are relatively muted. At one point it observes that the current Supreme Court "does not follow *Zschernig*,"[131] a comment that may mean "does not follow *Zschernig* as a charter for foreign affairs preemption." It stresses that the Court's recent decisions upholding foreign affairs preemption have focused on the inconsistency of State laws with enacted federal laws and policies rather than attempting to define "intrusion." It maintains that the Court's current approach "suggests that States may act within the areas of their traditional competence even if the action has foreign-policy implications, so long as no conflict with federal law exists."[132]

---

[129] 453 U.S. 654 (1981).
[130] *Id.* at 680.
[131] FOURTH RESTATEMENT § 403 reporters' note 5.
[132] *Id.*

One of the Coordinating Reporters of the Fourth Restatement has made it plain what he regards as the current legacy of its predecessor:

> Thirty years out from the Third Restatement's call for federalization of foreign relations law, the project seems endangered. The twin pillars of the nationalist position—insisting on the importance of a coherent and monolithic body of law to govern foreign relations and assigning this task to the federal courts—have eroded . . . The Supreme Court, generally unimpressed with arguments for increasing the lawmaking discretion of the federal courts, has not carved out an exception for foreign relations law. It has both resisted the federalization of the unwritten portion of public international law and ignored academic arguments for federalizing fields traditionally seen as part of private international law. The presence of a foreign-relations element in a controversy no longer results in field preemption that automatically invalidates State law.[133]

The Fourth Restatement might be said to operate in a jurisprudential space in which one set of attitudes affecting the law of foreign relations—the attitudes I have associated with foreign affairs exceptionalism—seem to be losing, but have not completely lost, their potency, and an alternative set of attitudes—those which can be identified with the critique of exceptionalism, including its historicization, have gained prominence but are not yet in a position of ascendancy. It may be that at some point in the future the Fourth Restatement's perspective will be identified as representing a transition between exceptionalist jurisprudence and a posture of greater tolerance on the part of the federal courts, including the Supreme Court, toward State policies with foreign relations dimensions, a more modest understanding of the act of state doctrine, and a limited conception of the body of customary international law that can serve as federal common law doctrines binding the States.

One might be inclined to predict the eventual ascendancy of such a posture simply because of the much greater involvement of American private actors, whether individuals or corporate enterprises, in the international arena. As the contacts between those actors and foreign nationals or governments widen, one might expect that many international transactions involving Americans, despite having "foreign relations" dimensions, would resemble private domestic transactions, traditionally the province of the States. If such transactions become increasingly the norm, one might wonder why the mere fact that they take place in an international setting should make them exercises in the conduct of foreign affairs. Where the federal government has not signaled, through some

---

[133] Paul B. Stephan, *The Waning of the Federal Common Law of Foreign Relations*, in this volume

enactment, a special interest in a particular class of transactions, one might wonder why the federal courts should be given the discretion, and the opportunity, to declare that States are not the appropriate institutions to address those transactions. This might particularly be so if one cannot summon up reasons to conclude that the federal courts are well suited to decide whether a given State policy "intrudes" on the federal government's conducting foreign affairs where that government has not expressed any views on the matter.

So one also might predict a jurisprudential future in which, as international contacts involving private American actors increase, the oversight of State policies affecting foreign relations recedes. That future was not the descriptive space extracted by the Fourth Restatement. Its mandate arguably prevented it from a bolder revisionist effort that would have included a reconsideration of both customary international law as federal common law and foreign affairs preemption that would have interred both *Sabbatino* and *Zschernig*. The legacy of both those decisions continues in the lower courts. So the American jurisprudence of foreign relations remains in what may well be a transition state, and the Fourth Restatement might be seen as something of a way station.

# PART II
# THE FOURTH RESTATEMENT AND THE LAW OF TREATIES

# 2

# Could the President Unilaterally Terminate All International Agreements?

## Questioning Section 313

*Harold Hongju Koh*

The completed sections of the Fourth Restatement resulted from an admirable effort by many committed international lawyers.[1] As a Counselor to that project, I applaud nearly all of it. But one section that still gives me pause is Section 313, regarding "Authority to Suspend, Terminate, or Withdraw from Treaties." That provision states that "*[a]ccording to established practice*, the President has the authority to act on behalf of the United States in suspending or terminating U.S. treaty commitments and in withdrawing the United States from treaties...."[2] While the reporters cautioned that this section currently applies only to Article II treaties, one of them recently wrote that "if presidents do have the legal authority to withdraw from Article II treaties, it is not clear why that authority would not extend to congressional-executive agreements" and presumably, other agreements as well.[3]

Donald Trump's tumultuous presidency has called this broad supposition into question. Since 2017, the Trump administration has announced its withdrawal from a host of bilateral and multilateral arrangements.[4] The obvious question is whether President Trump has legal authority—in a single tweet—unilaterally to

---

[1] This chapter derives from Harold Hongju Koh, *Presidential Power to Terminate International Agreements*, 128 YALE L.J. FORUM 432 (2018).

[2] See, e.g., FOURTH RESTATEMENT § 313.

[3] See Curtis A. Bradley, *Exiting Congressional-Executive Agreements*, 67 DUKE L.J. 1615, 1644 (2018) [hereinafter Bradley, *Exiting CEAs*].

[4] At this writing, these include the Paris Climate Agreement; the Joint Comprehensive Plan of Action with Iran; the United Nations Educational, Scientific, and Cultural Organization; the Global Compact on Migration; the U.N. Human Rights Council; the Trans-Pacific Partnership; the 1955 Treaty of Amity, Economic Relations and Consular Relations with Iran; the 1961 Optional Protocol to the Vienna Convention for Diplomatic Relations on Dispute Settlement; the Universal Postal Union Treaty, the Open Skies Treaty, and the Intermediate Nuclear Forces Treaty. President Trump has also hinted at his desire to withdraw from the North American Free Trade Agreement (NAFTA), the Korea-U.S. Free Trade Agreement, the World Trade Organization (WTO), and the North Atlantic Treaty Organization (NATO), the critical mutual defense alliance that the United States helped found more than seventy years ago.

Harold Hongju Koh, *Could the President Unilaterally Terminate All International Agreements?* In: *The Restatement and Beyond*. Edited by: Paul B. Stephan and Sarah H. Cleveland, Oxford University Press (2020). © Oxford University Press.
DOI: 10.1093/oso/9780197533154.003.0003

withdraw the United States from the United Nations, the International Monetary Fund, the World Bank, and other major long-standing treaties and international organizations that are foundational to the current world order. One could easily imagine this president and his lawyers misconstruing Section 313 as justifying a general power of the president to terminate, suspend or withdraw from any and all international agreements to which the United States is a party.[5]

This chapter argues that no such power exists. The U.S. Constitution does not confer upon the president a general unilateral power of treaty termination. Four decades ago, a D.C. Circuit judge warned against "an ambitious or unreasoned President disengaging the United States from crucial bilateral and multilateral treaties with the stroke of a pen."[6] Given that that scenario may have arrived, the time is ripe for both the academy and the courts to re-examine Section 313's conventional wisdom. Nor, this chapter argues, can such a general unilateral power be derived from constitutional text, structure, or Supreme Court precedent. Indeed, as the comment accompanying Section 313 clearly states, "[t]he Supreme Court has not resolved the constitutional authority to terminate a treaty."[7]

Section I describes the sole bases for Section 313's broad statement: so-called "functional considerations" and relatively recent historical practice following the Court's summary disposition nearly four decades ago in *Goldwater v. Carter*.[8] Yet more recent history has made clear that today such functional considerations cut against, not for, rapid unilateral agreement withdrawals. Section 313 of Fourth Restatement relied too uncritically on its predecessor provision, Section 339 of the Third Restatement, which seems to have been broadly influenced by the experience of its Chief Reporter, Louis Henkin, with the particular Taiwan treaty termination episode.[9] Yet on its face, *Goldwater* is a splintered nonjusticiability ruling, not a controlling precedent on the merits of this question. As section II explains, in the intervening four decades, the law on justiciability has substantially changed, and a court today could well decide on the merits a challenge to treaty termination.

In *Goldwater*, four Justices acknowledged "the fact that different termination procedures may be appropriate for different treaties."[10] That observation does not suggest a "one-size-fits-all" general rule authorizing unilateral presidential

---

[5] On the meaning of the term "international agreement" as well as distinctions between "withdrawal," "suspension," "abrogation," and "termination," see generally Vienna Convention on the Law of Treaties, pt. V.

[6] Goldwater v. Carter, 617 F.2d 697, 739 (D.C. Cir. 1979) (MacKinnon, J., dissenting in part and concurring in part).

[7] § 313 cmt. *b*.

[8] 444 U.S. 996 (1979).

[9] Professor Henkin served as a consultant for the Senate Foreign Relations Committee hearings and assisted in the presentation of the Senate's report on treaty termination. Louis Henkin, *Litigating the President's Power to Terminate Treaties*, 73 AM. J. INT'L L. 647, 654 n.35 (1979).

[10] 444 U.S. at 1003 (Rehnquist, J., joined by Burger, C.J., Stewart & Stevens, JJ., concurring).

termination for all agreements. If anything, it should demand consideration of a common-sense "mirror principle," which sections III and IV explain, has been applied both earlier in American history and in other constitutional democracies. Under that principle, absent exceptional circumstances, the degree of congressional participation constitutionally required to exit any particular agreement should mirror the degree of congressional participation that was required to enter that agreement in the first place.

In his foreword to the published Fourth Restatement extract governing treaties (including Section 313), the American Law Institute (ALI)'s executive director clarified that the "completed" sections of the as-yet unfinished comprehensive revision of the Fourth Restatement are not set in stone. "[I]n the not-too-distant future," he noted, when "we will undertake a new project designed to complete the Restatement Fourth . . . the sections published here will be incorporated into the full volume and updated *if intervening case law or practice makes that necessary.*"[11] Section V thus concludes by suggesting that as the Fourth Restatement expands to include discussion of agreements other than Article II "treaties," the black letter of Section 313 should be revised to accommodate a more nuanced constitutional typology governing different kinds of withdrawals.

## I. *Goldwater*, Historical Practice, and Functional Considerations

The claim that the Constitution authorizes unilateral presidential withdrawal from treaties is of surprisingly recent vintage. Article II, Section 2, Clause 2 of the Constitution empowers the president to "make Treaties, provided two thirds of the Senators present concur," but says nothing about which branch of government may unmake those treaties. As Curtis Bradley, one of the reporters of the Treaties Section of the Fourth Restatement, summarized after extensive historical review, "[w]hereas it was generally understood throughout the nineteenth century that the termination of treaties required congressional involvement, the consensus on this issue disappeared in the early parts of the twentieth century."[12] Yet "[a]t the end of the twentieth century," Louis Henkin, the Chief Reporter of the Third Restatement, concluded, "it is apparently accepted that the President has authority under the Constitution to denounce or otherwise terminate a treaty . . ."[13] That view was elaborated upon by Bradley, who wrote, "today

---

[11]   FOURTH RESTATEMENT intro. at xvii–xviii (emphasis added).

[12]   Curtis A. Bradley, *Treaty Termination and Historical Gloss*, 92 TEX. L. REV. 773, 773 (2014) [hereinafter Bradley, *Treaty Termination*].

[13]   LOUIS HENKIN, FOREIGN AFFAIRS AND THE US CONSTITUTION 214 (2d ed. 1996),

it is widely (although not uniformly) accepted that presidents have a unilateral power of treaty termination."[14]

How did this historical change occur? The breakdown of consensus favoring congressional involvement in treaty termination does not explain why the conventional wisdom should shift so dramatically in the opposite direction, to favor unilateral termination. That sea change was driven by the Supreme Court's 1979 ruling in *Goldwater v. Carter*, which dismissed a challenge by a group of senators, led by Barry Goldwater, to President Jimmy Carter's unilateral termination of the 1954 Taiwan Mutual Defense Treaty. Seven years later, Section 339 of the Third Restatement declared that "Under the law of the United States, the President has the power . . . to suspend or terminate an agreement in accordance with its terms."[15] Since *Goldwater*, the Fourth Restatement affirms, "the United States has terminated dozens of treaties, and almost all of the terminations have been accomplished by unilateral presidential action."[16] But closer study reveals that neither *Goldwater*, nor this recent historical practice, offer sufficient legal basis to support a blanket, unilateral presidential power to terminate all international agreements.

## A.  *Goldwater v. Carter*

On December 15, 1978, President Carter announced his intention both to recognize and establish diplomatic relations with the People's Republic of China and to terminate, as of January 1, 1980, the 1954 Mutual Defense Treaty between the United States and Taiwan. Seven U.S. senators and eight members of the House of Representatives sued the president and the secretary of state in the U.S. District Court for the District of Columbia. They sought an injunction and a declaration that the president's attempt to unilaterally terminate the treaty was "unconstitutional, illegal, null and void" unless "made by and with the full consultation of the entire Congress, and with either the advice and consent of the Senate, or the approval of both Houses of Congress."

A federal district court held that to be effective under the Constitution, the president's notice of termination needed the approval of either two-thirds of the Senate or a majority of both houses of Congress.[17] A fragmented D.C. Circuit,

---

[14] Bradley, *Treaty Termination, supra* note 12, at 73; see also Bradley, *Exiting CEAs, supra* note 3, at 1625 ("[I]t is generally accepted—although not entirely settled—that the president has the unilateral authority to act for the United States in withdrawing the country from a treaty. This authority stems in part from the president's power over diplomacy and role as head of state, as well as from long-standing historical practice.");

[15] THIRD RESTATEMENT § 339 (AM. LAW INST. 1986).

[16] FOURTH RESTATEMENT § 313 reporters' note 3.

[17] Goldwater v. Carter, 481 F. Supp. 949 (D.D.C. 1979).

sitting *en banc*, heard the case on an expedited basis and ruled for the president.[18] Declining to treat the matter as a political question, the circuit court instead held on the merits that the president had not exceeded his authority in terminating the bilateral treaty in accordance with its terms. Pressed to decide the case before the designated January 1, 1980, termination date, the Supreme Court issued no majority opinion. Instead, in a 6–3 per curiam decision, the Court dismissed the complaint as nonjusticiable, without plenary briefing or oral argument.

The Justices splintered around several rationales, with only one Justice reaching the merits. Four Justices—Chief Justice Burger and Justices Rehnquist, Stewart, and Stevens—found that the case raised a political question.[19] Justice Powell agreed that the case should be dismissed as not ripe and because it was unknown "whether there ever will be an actual confrontation between the Legislative and Executive branches" constituting a "constitutional impasse."[20] Justice Brennan voted on the merits to uphold the president's power to terminate the Taiwan treaty, based on the peculiar fact that the case involved derecognition of a foreign government, an issue over which he argued the president exercises textual plenary constitutional power.[21] Justice Marshall simply concurred in the dismissal without explaining why.[22] Only Justices Blackmun and White dissented, voting that the Court should "set the case for oral argument [to] give it the plenary consideration it so obviously deserves."[23]

Not surprisingly, *Goldwater* has been consistently overread, particularly by executive branch lawyers. *Goldwater* simply supports the *nonreviewability* of one attempted unilateral termination and, even then, on splintered grounds: four finding a political question and one finding nonripeness. Even at the time, *none* of the nine Justices embraced a rule favoring a general unilateral *transsubstantive* power of presidential termination. To the contrary, four Justices observed "that different termination procedures may be appropriate for different treaties," which logically should have led to consideration of a more context-dependent rule such as the mirror principle elaborated in section IV later.[24] Only one Justice opined that the president had the constitutional power to terminate even the particular treaty at issue in that case, and even then, only because the bilateral

[18] 617 F.2d 697, 697 (D.C. Cir. 1979) (en banc) (per curiam).
[19] *Id.* at 1002 (Rehnquist, J., joined by Burger, C.J., Stewart and Stevens, JJ., concurring).
[20] *Id.* at 997, 998 (Powell, J., concurring).
[21] See *id.* at 1006–107 (Brennan, J., dissenting).
[22] *Id.* at 996 (Marshall, J., concurring in the result).
[23] *Id.* at 1006 (Blackmun, J., dissenting) ("In my view, the time factor and its importance are illusory; if the President does not have the power to terminate the treaty (a substantial issue that we should address only after briefing and oral argument), the notice of intention to terminate surely has no legal effect. It is also indefensible, without further study, to pass on the issue of justiciability or on the issues of standing or ripeness.").
[24] *Id.* at 1003 (Rehnquist, J., concurring) (Burger, Stewart, and Stevens, JJ., joining in the concurrence).

treaty happened to have been unilaterally terminated both in accordance with international law *and* within the scope of the president's exclusive constitutional authority.[25]

Thus, *Goldwater* cannot be fairly read as a precedent supporting a general unilateral presidential power of treaty termination. As section V elaborates, *Goldwater* says nothing at all about three different factual scenarios: (1) terminations of or withdrawals from agreements that are not bilateral, but rather *multilateral*; (2) terminations or withdrawals that arguably are *not* implemented in accordance with the agreement's terms or that otherwise arguably violate international law; or (3) terminations or withdrawals that are carried out within the scope of concurrent legislative-executive authority or Congress's plenary authority, such as over international trade or foreign commerce, particularly when those agreements were initially adopted against a general background of congressional awareness and approval.

## B. Historical Practice

To be sure, since the 1930s, presidents have unilaterally terminated several international agreements, including "a few dozen" since *Goldwater*.[26] But as the Fourth Restatement's reporters correctly noted, "[m]ost of these terminations have not generated controversy in Congress."[27] The mere fact that the president may have unilaterally terminated agreements that Congress did not care about tells us little about what would happen if Congress were to actively *contest* a withdrawal. In fact, the appellate briefs in *Goldwater* debated whether there were genuinely more than three contested treaty withdrawals in all of American history.

Admittedly, the Supreme Court has at times recognized "historical practice" as a basis for normative reinterpretation of structural constitutional provisions. But as Justice Frankfurter's famous discussion of historical practice in *Youngstown* made plain, "systematic, unbroken, executive practice" places a historical "gloss on the 'executive power'" in Article II, only if—like adverse possession in property law—that practice has been "long pursued to the knowledge of the Congress and *never before questioned*. . . ."[28] Even four decades of

---

[25]  See *id.* at 1006–107 (Brennan, J., dissenting).

[26]  Curtis A. Bradley & Jack L. Goldsmith, *Presidential Control over International Law*, 131 HARV. L. REV. 1201, 1224 (2018).

[27]  FOURTH RESTATEMENT § 313 reporters' note 3. As the Chief Reporter of the Third Restatement, Louis Henkin, put it, "[c]ontroversy as to who has authority to terminate treaties has been infrequent, if only because the United States has not often been disposed to terminate treaties." HENKIN, *supra* note 13, at 213.

[28]  Youngstown Sheet & Tube Co. v. Sawyer, 343 U.S. 579, 610 (1952) (Frankfurter, J., concurring) (emphasis added).

consistent executive practice would not rise to the level of historical "gloss," unless the other affected branch of government affirmatively "acquiesced" in the legality of the executive acts. This plainly would not be the case with respect to important multilateral agreements that enjoy bipartisan congressional support, such as the North Atlantic Treaty Organization (NATO) agreement.

Even more glaring, no statutory provisions currently require the president even to notify Congress of an executive decision to terminate or withdraw from any treaty or international agreement. Nor is there any easily available listing of agreements or treaties that may have been unilaterally terminated. Although the State Department Legal Adviser's annual *Digests of United States Practice in International Law* voluntarily report on some terminations, there is no legal requirement that the Office of the Legal Adviser or the State Department do so, and the *Digests* are not published until after the incidents they describe. Finally, the 1972 Case-Zablocki Act, which ostensibly requires the executive branch to notify Congress of all foreign agreements, has prominently failed to ensure the complete reporting of all agreements and political commitments that presidents may actually make.

Yet even absent conclusive proof of acquiescence, Section 313 of the Fourth Restatement rests its acknowledgment of presidential authority almost exclusively on *historical practice*. But how "established," in fact, is that practice? Like *Goldwater* itself, Section 313's black letter comes with three significant limitations. First, whatever unilateral termination power may be recognized by historical practice, the Restatement does not recognize it as extending to unilateral acts by the president to suspend, terminate, or withdraw from treaties *not* in accordance with their terms or otherwise not in accordance with international law. Second, the Restatement nowhere "suggest[s] that Congress or the Senate lack the ability to limit suspension, termination, or withdrawal," for example, by the "No NATO Withdrawal Act" being considered by Congress. Third, the accompanying reporters' notes reaffirm that "[a]lthough historical practice supports a unilateral presidential power to suspend, terminate, or withdraw the United States from treaties, it does not establish that this is an *exclusive* presidential power."[29] Thus, if the president were to attempt a treaty termination within zones of either concurrent congressional-executive foreign affairs authority or exclusive legislative power—such as the foreign commerce power—the Senate could presumably limit executive discretion preemptively in its advice and consent to a particular treaty, as could Congress, by enacting a "no unilateral exit" statute with respect to that international agreement.

---

[29] *Id.* at reporters' note 6 (emphasis added).

## C. Functional Considerations

Apart from historical practice, the only other support offered for the Fourth Restatement's black letter is that "structural and functional considerations are consistent with the general ability of the President to act unilaterally, as it has been exercised in practice."[30] But looked at from a dynamic perspective, this statement no longer seems true. If anything, structural and functional considerations now cut the other way. As a matter of constitutional structure, the foreign affairs power is generally a power shared: Unilateral powers are the exception, not the rule, so whenever the Constitution's text does not explicitly assign a plenary power to one branch, the multiple, overlapping grants of foreign affairs authority should presumptively dictate that powers be shared between Congress and the executive.[31]

In support of a unilateral executive withdrawal power, some commentators have made a functional "quick divorce" argument: that foreign affairs exigencies may require the United States to exit entangling alliances that were entered deliberately, and with extensive congressional awareness and participation, over a much longer period of time. Under this functional theory, the president alone is best positioned to decide whether and when a quick divorce is necessary.[32] This theory argues that a constitutional rule that makes it harder to exit agreements will make future executives less keen to enter into them in the first place.

But as a functional matter, an overbroad unilateral executive power to withdraw from any and all international agreements would not only risk overly hasty, partisan, or parochial withdrawals by presidents, but would also tend to weaken systemic stability and the negotiating credibility and leverage of *all* presidents. The most prominent recent example is President Trump's abrupt withdrawal from the Iran Nuclear Deal (Joint Comprehensive Plan of Action or JCPOA) at the precise moment that he is attempting to negotiate a similar denuclearization deal with North Korea. Even if the short-term, first-order "functional" effect of more congressional involvement in the withdrawal process would be to constrain the executive, the second- and third-order functional effects would strengthen the executive's hand in future international negotiations. As recent

---

[30] FOURTH RESTATEMENT § 313 cmt. *d*. But in response to a lengthy history of enactment of legislative vetoes that were said to have a strong functional justification, the Supreme Court ruled that a law's efficiency, convenience, and usefulness had no bearing on its constitutionality in accordance with the defined powers of the separate branches. INS v. Chadha, 462 U.S. 919, 944–45 (1983).

[31] See HAROLD HONGJU KOH, THE NATIONAL SECURITY CONSTITUTION: SHARING POWER AFTER THE IRAN-CONTRA AFFAIR 69–71 (1990).

[32] The "quick divorce" rationale may apply with the greatest force in a historically rare setting like the Taiwan treaty termination, where quickly disentangling the country from a treaty must be done rapidly to effectuate the unilateral recognition of one regime and the concomitant derecognition of another.

denuclearization talks with North Korea and Iran show, the negotiating credibility of an executive who wishes to enter into a new agreement will be strengthened, not weakened, if such agreements are made harder to break by their successors, thereby giving their negotiating partners greater assurance regarding the continuity and stability of the proposed arrangement.

This concern has special force with respect to Article II treaties, which cannot be entered into on a whim. The constitutional barriers to entry into Article II treaties are enormous. The constitutional ratification requirement demands that two-thirds of the Senate consent, which entails a massive mobilization of executive branch and legislative resources. Allowing Article II treaties to be easily exited at the whim of the executive's pen could undermine legislative will to enter such treaties in the first place. Legislators could too easily conclude that their politically safest place is to never take a tough, visible vote, and stay on the sidelines with respect to all actions regarding international agreements, allowing the president unilaterally to make and unmake *all* international agreements through executive action. This would lead both to across-the-board diminution of both legislative participation in and accountability for international lawmaking, and establish a strong *de facto* bias against the United States' ability ever to participate in formal treaties.

Whatever functional sense a cross-cutting *Goldwater* approach—strong unilateral presidential termination rights coupled with minimal judicial review—might have made forty years ago, the world has plainly changed in ways that call into question its normative logic. As the United Kingdom has painfully learned since its June 2016 Brexit referendum vote, breaking up is hard to do. In the modern era, as a functional matter, international agreements are *not just transactional, but relational*. These agreements do not authorize sequential, one-off transactions so much as they create organic, evolving relationships that generate a deeply interconnected set of rights, duties, expectations, and reliance for all parties. Momentary lapses can be forgiven if a fundamental commitment to the enduring relationship has been demonstrated. But the disruptive act of termination engages the interests of all parties, both participating and represented, who accordingly should be as much involved in the decision to exit as they are in the initial decision to enter.

Particularly in legal systems where treaties are the supreme law of the land, they confer legal rights that have direct effect on domestic actors. Those treaties lay a foundation upon which, over time, sedimentary layers of legal acts, executing legislation, and court decisions build a deeply internalized framework of transnational law that embeds treaty membership strongly into the domestic fabric of political life.[33] Withdrawing abruptly from such an organic treaty

---

[33] Harold Hongju Koh, *Is There a "New" New Haven School of International Law?*, 32 YALE J. INT'L L. 559, 566 (2007).

framework becomes akin to trying to pull out only the red threads from a multicolored tapestry. Withdrawal rips the fabric of domestic law and disrupts all manner of domestic rights and expectations.

As proof, even as President Trump daily invokes a transactional approach to international affairs, condemning all manner of international agreements as "bad deals," his administration recently made the opposite, relational argument before the Supreme Court. In *Jam v. International Finance Corp.*, Solicitor General Noel Francisco responded to the Court's invitation to participate not by rejecting agreements as "bad deals," but by arguing that the "United States' participation in international organizations is a critical component of the Nation's foreign relations [that] reflects an understanding that robust multilateral engagement is a crucial tool in advancing national interests."[34]

Back when "politics stopped at the water's edge"—and a presumption of basic foreign policy continuity dominated whenever the White House changed hands—academics and justices might well have believed that their approach would *minimize* foreign policy conflict and make the United States *more* compliant overall with international norms. But the rise of a post–Cold War political era marked by radical foreign policy discontinuities from Presidents Clinton to Bush to Obama, and now to Trump, has dramatically undermined this assumption. As the current moment illustrates well, unless somehow blessed by Congress, unilateral presidential withdrawals based on individual presidential caprice are highly disruptive of both foreign and domestic policy. That very disruptiveness and unpredictability will, in turn, make it harder for future presidents and Congresses to negotiate valuable international agreements. And whether or not one president could unilaterally terminate an Article II treaty without Senate participation, an important unanswered constitutional question remains whether a future president could reinstate U.S. participation in that agreement without new advice and consent, on the ground that that the necessary legislative approval has already been obtained.

In sum, the best reading of historical practice is that *Goldwater* has functioned as a piece of "quasi-constitutional custom" that is "perennially subject to revision."[35] Much of the more recent historical practice of unilateral presidential termination since *Goldwater* can be attributed to path-dependence and conventional wisdom, as opposed to serious substantive review of the constitutional arguments on the merits. Any rule suggested by the most recent historical practice could be swiftly revised either by judicial decision or by altered interbranch

---

[34] See Brief of the United States as Amicus Curiae Supporting Reversal at 31, *Jam v. Int'l Fin. Corp.* No. 17-1011 (U.S. 2018).

[35] Koн, *supra* note 31, at 70–71.

practice going forward. In the modern era, an agreement-specific "mirror" principle—requiring parity of constitutional authority for entry and exit from an international agreement—represents a far better functional reading of the Constitution than a claimed general unilateral right of the president to terminate any and all international agreements.

To be workable, of course, a mirror principle would need to anticipate political exigencies, including the "quick divorce" scenario discussed earlier. To accommodate bona fide emergency situations, the U.S. Supreme Court could recognize the president's unilateral authority to suspend U.S. treaty obligations for a limited period, long enough for the president to make the case to Congress as to why withdrawal is warranted "for cause." But it would be wildly overbroad to allow a rare exception to swallow the rule. There is no reason to extrapolate from the narrow notion that, in a genuine emergency, a president may be best positioned to decide whether an exit from a treaty is urgently required, to the overbroad proposition that the Constitution authorizes any president, on impulse, to withdraw the United States from any and all bilateral and multilateral arrangements that it has joined over the centuries.

As Judge MacKinnon presciently warned in *Goldwater*: "In future years, a voracious President and Department of State may easily use this grant of absolute power [of unilateral termination] to the President to develop other excuses to feed upon congressional prerogatives that a Congress lacking in vigilance allows to lapse into desuetude."[36] Recognizing a very limited exception to the mirror principle for genuinely exceptional circumstances would acknowledge a decidedly narrower—and functionally, far better tailored—authority than according a single person a blanket unilateral power to terminate, withdraw, or suspend all treaties in all situations, emergency or otherwise.

## II. Would Treaty Withdrawal now be Justiciable?

An important background assumption underlying Section 313 may have been that, as a practical matter, no litigant could challenge a president's decision unilaterally to terminate or withdraw from international agreements. After *Goldwater*, the reporters may have assumed that few treaty terminations could be contested on the merits, because of the justiciability obstacles of standing, ripeness, and the political question doctrine. But in the four intervening decades, the law on the issue of justiciability has significantly changed. Because plaintiffs challenging

---

[36] *Goldwater*, 617 F.2d at 739 (MacKinnon, J., dissenting in part and concurring in part) (emphasis omitted)

treaty termination are now able to reach the merits, Section 313's background assumption must be revisited.

For example, Congress has recently introduced two bipartisan bills that would prevent President Trump from withdrawing the United States from NATO without congressional consent.[37] Should either of those bills receive a majority vote in both houses and not be vetoed, and should the president nevertheless attempt to withdraw the United States unilaterally from NATO, there can be little doubt that Congress, as a whole, would have properly challenged the president's action creating the kind of "constitutional impasse" between the political branches that Justice Powell envisioned as necessary for ripeness.

In the wake of *Goldwater*, several lower courts followed the lead of the *Goldwater* plurality by finding nonjusticiable suits challenging executive power to unilaterally withdraw from treaties.[38] But in an important recent case, *Zivotofsky v. Clinton* (*Zivotofsky I*), the Supreme Court declined to apply the political question doctrine to bar review of the president's power to recognize foreign states in the face of a contrary congressional statute.[39] Later, in *Zivotofsky v. Kerry* (*Zivotofsky II*), the Court held on the merits that the same statute was unenforceable because it was an unconstitutional intrusion on the president's exclusive power of recognition.[40]

---

[37] On July 26, 2018, Congressmen Jimmy Panetta (D-CA) and Steve Knight (R-CA) introduced the No NATO Withdrawal Act, H.R. 6530, 115th Cong., § 3 (2018) ("It is the sense of Congress that (1) the President shall not unilaterally withdraw the United States from NATO; and (2) the case Goldwater v. Carter is not controlling legal precedent with respect to the unilateral withdrawal of the United States from a treaty.") [hereinafter No NATO Withdrawal Act]. Just days later, Senators Lindsey Graham (R-SC), Bob Menendez (D-NJ), Cory Gardner (R-CO), Ben Cardin (D-MD), John McCain (R-AZ), and Jeanne Shaheen (D-NH) introduced the Defending American Security from Kremlin Aggression Act of 2018, S. 3336, 115th Cong. (2018) (specifying, inter alia, a requirement for two-thirds of the Senate to vote in favor in order to leave NATO); see also Karoun Demirjian, *Bipartisan Bill Would Prevent Trump from Exiting NATO Without Senate Consent*, WASH. POST (July 26, 2018), https://www.washingtonpost.com/powerpost/bipartisan-bill-would-prevent-trump-from-exiting-nato-without-senate-consent/2018/07/26/4ca1b206-9106-11e8-bcd5-9d911c784c38_story.html; Press Release, Senator Lindsey Graham; Graham, Menendez, Gardner, Cardin, McCain, Shaheen Introduce Hard-Hitting Russia Sanctions Package (Aug. 2, 2018), https://www.lgraham.senate.gov/public/index.cfm/press-releases?ID=E4AC5E4C-EFD0-4F25-9808-745E1737EF65.

[38] See, e.g., Kucinich v. Bush, 236 F. Supp. 2d 1 (D.D.C. 2002) (dismissing a challenge by thirty-two congressmen to President George W. Bush's decision to withdraw from the Anti-Ballistic Missile Treaty with Russia for raising a nonjusticiable political question); Beacon Products Corp. v. Reagan, 633 F. Supp. 1191, 1199 (D. Mass. 1986), *aff'd on other grounds*, 814 F.2d 1 (1st Cir. 1987) (holding with regards to President Ronald Reagan's unilateral termination of the United States' Treaty of Friendship, Commerce, and Navigation with Nicaragua that a "[constitutional] challenge to the President's power vis-a-vis treaty termination raise[s] a nonjusticiable political question").

[39] 566 U.S. 189 (2012).

[40] 135 S. Ct. 2076, 2091 (2015). Section 214 of the Foreign Relations Authorization Act, enacted in 2002, allowed passports issued by the U.S. State Department to list "Jerusalem" or "Jerusalem, Israel" as the place of birth. The parents of a boy born in Jerusalem sued Secretary of State Hillary Clinton, invoking § 214 to challenge the State Department's long-held policy that no country holds sovereignty over Jerusalem. In *Zivotofsky I*, the D.C. Circuit held that the case presented a nonjusticiable political question, but the Supreme Court disagreed and remanded. 566 U.S. at 201–202. The D.C. Circuit then held on the merits that the statute was an unconstitutional violation of the executive

Chief Justice Roberts's opinion for the *Zivotofsky I* Court called the political question doctrine a "narrow" exception to the general rule that the judiciary has the "responsibility to decide cases properly before it."[41] The opinion notably omitted mention of the six-factor political question test originally introduced in *Baker v. Carr*.[42] Instead, the Court narrowed that test to its first two "textual" elements, explaining that a political question exists only "[1] where there is 'a textually demonstrable constitutional commitment of the issue to a coordinate political department; or [2] a lack of judicially discoverable and manageable standards for resolving it.' "[43]

Under *Zivotofsky I*'s narrowed two-pronged political question test, treaty termination is not a political question. First, it is not a decision "textually committed" by the Constitution to a branch other than the judiciary. Article II, Section 2 of the Constitution authorizes the president to "make" treaties with the advice and consent of two-thirds of the senators present,[44] but no constitutional text expressly authorizes any branch to *unmake* such treaties, whether through suspension, termination, or withdrawal. Second, there is no "lack of judicially discoverable and manageable standards for resolving" the question. A court need only decide whether the president's action—standing alone—is legally sufficient to terminate an international treaty obligation. As Justice Powell noted in *Goldwater*, in such a case, "the Court would interpret the Constitution to decide whether congressional approval is necessary to give a Presidential decision on the validity of a treaty the force of law[,] an inquiry [that] demands no special competence or information beyond the reach of the Judiciary."[45]

In sum, neither *Goldwater*, historical practice, nor functional considerations offer strong precedent on the merits to support the legality of a contested

---

branch's exclusive recognition power, a ruling that Justice Kennedy, writing for the majority, went on to affirm in *Zivotofsky II*, 135 S. Ct. at 2091.

[41] *Zivotofsky I*, 566 U.S. at 194–95.

[42] 369 U.S. 186 (1962). The *Baker* Court famously introduced the following six-factor test for political question determinations:

> Prominent on the surface of any case held to involve a political question is found a textually demonstrable constitutional commitment of the issue to a coordinate political department; or a lack of judicially discoverable and manageable standards for resolving it; or the impossibility of deciding without an initial policy determination of a kind clearly for nonjudicial discretion; or the impossibility of a court's undertaking independent resolution without expressing lack of the respect due coordinate branches of government; or an unusual need for unquestioning adherence to a political decision already made; or the potentiality of embarrassment from multifarious pronouncements by various departments on one question.

*Id.* at 217.

[43] *Zivotofsky I*, 566 U.S. at 195 (quoting Nixon v. United States, 506 U.S. 224, 228 (1993)).

[44] U.S. Const. art. II, § 2.

[45] Goldwater v. Carter, 444 U.S. 996, 1000 (Powell, J., concurring).

presidential effort to terminate an important international agreement. Nor, today, would such an effort necessarily be insulated from judicial review.

## III. Comparative Constitutional Practice

Of course, the constitutional issue of treaty exit arises not just in the United States, but in every other country in the world. As Justice Breyer noted nearly two decades ago, the Supreme Court "has long considered as relevant and informative the way in which foreign courts have applied standards roughly comparable to our own constitutional standards in roughly comparable circumstances."[46] In *Printz v. United States*, he elaborated that the "experience [of other nations] may . . . cast an *empirical light* on the consequences of different solutions to a common legal problem."[47]

The recent foreign decision casting the most relevant empirical light on the termination of multilateral agreements whose provisions are deeply intertwined with domestic law is the United Kingdom's famous Brexit litigation, *R v. Secretary of State for Exiting the European Union*.[48] There, the Supreme Court of the United Kingdom held that the U.K. government may not use its executive prerogative powers but rather must seek parliamentary approval to trigger Article 50, the withdrawal provision of the Treaty of the European Union.[49] The court reasoned that prior parliamentary approval was required because Brexit would require fundamental constitutional changes, including the repeal of the 1972 European Communities Act, which expressly allowed for E.U. treaties to take effect within U.K. domestic law.[50] This is particularly the case, the court noted, because fundamental rights would undeniably be affected within the country once the treaty withdrawal was completed. As one commentator put it, "the years of [treaty] membership, the weaving of the [intertwined fabric of domestic and international legal rules], have constructed a reality that is hard to change."[51] Since the British executive would not have the power to effect the removal of the act unilaterally as a source of U.K. domestic law, the court reasoned, neither should the

---

[46] Knight v. Florida, 528 U.S. 990, 997 (1999) (Breyer, J., dissenting from denial of certiorari); see also STEPHEN BREYER, THE COURT AND THE WORLD: AMERICAN LAW AND THE NEW GLOBAL REALITIES (2015) (discussing the Supreme Court's increasing level of interaction with foreign affairs).

[47] 521 U.S. 898, 977 (1997) (Breyer, J., dissenting) (emphasis added) (citations omitted).

[48] [2017] UKSC 5, [36], [2017] 2 WLR 583 (appeal taken from England and Northern Ireland).

[49] *Id.* at [77].

[50] *Id.* at [78]–[93].

[51] Sam Knight, *Theresa May's Impossible Choice*, NEW YORKER (July 30, 2018), https://www.newyorker.com/magazine/2018/07/30/theresa-mays-impossible-choice.

prime minister have the power to unilaterally withdraw from the treaty without legislative participation.[52]

Similarly, in *Democratic Alliance v. Minister of International Relations and Cooperation*,[53] the High Court of South Africa for the Gauteng Division recently held that the executive branch could not unilaterally withdraw from the Rome Statute of the International Criminal Court without the parliamentary approval previously required for accession.[54]

The court's decision suggests a "mirror principle": the common-sense notion that there should be parity of legislative authority for entry and exit from an international agreement. Simply put, the degree of legislative participation necessary to exit an international agreement should mirror the degree of legislative participation that was involved when entering it in the first place. Relying on this mirror principle, the court held that South Africa could withdraw from the Rome Statute only on approval of parliament and after the repeal of the statute implementing the treaty.[55]

Similar mirror reasoning may be found in Canadian law.[56] A recent survey reports that parliamentary approval for withdrawal is required by organic laws in ten Eastern European countries and by constitutional or administrative interpretation or presidential decree in nine others.[57] The reasoning of these and

[52] [2017] UKSC 5 at [88]–[101].

[53] 2017 (3) SA 212 (GP) (S. Afr.).

[54] *Id.* at 247.

[55] Letter from the U.N. Sec'y Gen. to Treaty Servs. of Ministries of Foreign Affairs and Int'l Orgs. Concerned (Mar. 7, 2017), https://treaties.un.org/doc/Publication/CN/2017/CN.121.2017-Eng.pdf.

[56] Under Canadian law, unless the royal prerogative has been limited by legislation, the Canadian executive may make and unmake treaties without parliamentary involvement. Cf. *Turp v. Minister of Justice*, [2012] F.C. 893, ¶ 31 (Fed. Ct.) (allowing the executive to withdraw from the Kyoto Protocol because the Protocol's Implementation Act did not limit the royal prerogative). But where legislation does limit the prerogative, the prerogative power to withdraw from a treaty must be exercised in accordance with the legislated limits. Thus, where a Canadian treaty has been implemented internally with substantial legislative input, and the government seeks to withdraw from the treaty without securing the necessary legislative amendments, those laws would remain effective and in force until repealed by Parliament. See Maurice Copithorne, *National Treaty Law and Practice: Canada*, in NATIONAL TREATY LAW AND PRACTICE: CANADA, EGYPT, ISRAEL, MEXICO, RUSSIA, SOUTH AFRICA 1, 11–12 (Monroe Leigh, Merritt R. Blakeslee, & L. Benjamin Ederington eds., 2003); see also Hannah Woolaver, *From "Joining" to "Leaving": Domestic Law's Role in the International Legal Validity of Treaty Withdrawal*, 30 EUR. J. INT'L L. 73 (2019).

[57] Pierre-Hugues Verdier & Mila Versteeg, *Separation of Powers, Treaty-Making, and Treaty Withdrawal: A Global Survey*, in THE OXFORD HANDBOOK OF COMPARATIVE FOREIGN RELATIONS LAW 135, 139–41 (Curtis A. Bradley ed., 2019). Organic laws require parliamentary participation in withdrawal in ten Eastern European countries—Belarus, Bosnia and Herzegovina, Estonia, Latvia, Lithuania, Russia, Slovenia, Tajikistan, Turkmenistan, and Ukraine—and Mexico, *id.* at 16 n.47, and by constitutional or administrative interpretation or presidential decree in nine other countries: Austria, Czech Republic, Ethiopia, Hungary, Iran, Japan, Norway, Slovakia, and South Africa, *id.* at 16 n.48; see also *id.* ("In recent decades, several national legal systems have introduced constraints on that [executive] power, usually by requiring parliamentary approval of withdrawal from treaties whose conclusion required such approval."); *id.* at 15 (citing such provisions from Belgium, China, Denmark, and the Netherlands).

other foreign precedents cast "empirical light" on—and cut strongly against—the view that functional considerations should sanction a general unilateral termination rule. Instead, these cases suggest that U.S. withdrawal from a long-standing treaty or international organization—such as the United Nations or the World Trade Organization (WTO), whose rules have also been deeply internalized into U.S. law—should not become effective without congressional involvement, particularly since such a withdrawal or termination would similarly necessitate unwinding many domestic law statutes that the executive could not repeal alone.[58]

The constitutional issue raised by *Goldwater* may well be relitigated in the context of an attempted executive withdrawal from a multilateral treaty whose provisions are deeply internalized within U.S. domestic law. If so, we could expect the reasoning of these and other comparative law precedents—particularly the notion of a mirror principle requiring parallel legislative participation for entry and exit—to be prominently cited by both the litigants and Justices of the Supreme Court.

## IV.  An Alternative: The Mirror Principle

The notion that withdrawals from international agreements whose provisions have been deeply internalized into domestic law should be dictated by a "mirror principle" has long been acknowledged by U.S. constitutional jurisprudence.[59] As a constitutional matter, the mirror principle is simply a variant of the famous "last-in-time rule," first stated in the *Head Money Cases*[60] and *Whitney v. Robertson*.[61] Those cases long ago settled that, however made, a binding international agreement can only be superseded by an agreement or statute that is adopted with a comparable degree of legislative input. Because such a superseding legal enactment effectively exits the United States from a prior international commitment, for all practical purposes, the mirror principle was U.S. law long before *Goldwater* and remains so today. After all, self-executing treaties are the law of the land, no less than congressionally enacted statutes.[62] If the president cannot enact or repeal a statute alone, why should he be able to repeal the duly enacted law of the land—and its accompanying framework of deeply

---

[58] See Ellyn Ferguson, *Congress Can Stop Trump from Ditching WTO, Analysts Say*, ROLL CALL (July 5, 2018, 1:28 PM), https://www.rollcall.com/news/policy/congress-stop-trump-ditch-wto.

[59] Cf. *The Amiable Isabella*, 19 U.S. (6 Wheat.) 1, 75 (1821) (Story, J.) (the "obligations of [a] treaty could not be changed or varied but by the same formalities with which they were introduced, or at least by some act of as high an import, *and of as unequivocal an authority*.") (emphasis added).

[60] 112 U.S. 580, 599 (1884).

[61] 124 U.S. 190, 194 (1888).

[62] *Id.* at 194.

internalized domestic law—just because the initiating juridical act happened to be in treaty form?

Executive branch lawyers have tried to escape this reasoning by arguing—by analogy to executive appointments—that the president alone should be able to terminate a treaty that was made with the advice and consent of the Senate, because the president alone can fire a cabinet member appointed with the advice and consent of the Senate.[63] But the analogy to appointment of subordinates is inapposite, not least because it is a largely internal matter regarding control of the executive branch. The removal power also rests partially on the Article II Vesting Clause[64] and the Take Care Clause,[65] insofar as the president cannot properly discharge executive power or take care that the law be faithfully executed if he cannot use the threat of unilateral removal to hold subordinates accountable.[66] Treaty abrogation, by contrast, runs afoul of the Take Care Clause, because the president is unilaterally undoing, not enforcing, the law that has been made. Significantly, only one U.S. court—the en banc D.C. Circuit decision in *Goldwater*—has ever endorsed an unnuanced rule of unilateral presidential termination on the merits, and even then, for less than a month before that ruling was vacated by the U.S. Supreme Court.

If and when the Supreme Court finally considers this issue on the merits, I would argue, it should conclude that no single "transsubstantive" rule governs whether and how each and every international agreement may be terminated or withdrawn from as a matter of U.S. domestic law. Unlike an overbroad "unilateral presidential termination rule," the mirror principle does not mandate a "one-size-fits-all" mode of agreement termination. Instead, depending on substance and entry process, the mirror principle requires varying degrees of congressional and executive participation to exit from various kinds of international agreements.

I recently argued against simplistic application of the traditional transsubstantive "triptych" by which scholars have artificially divided the constitutional spectrum of U.S. international agreements into three categories: Article II treaties, congressional-executive agreements, and so-called sole executive

---

[63] See, e.g., Brief for the United States in Opposition to Certiorari at 17, Goldwater v. Carter, 444 U.S. 996 (1979) (No. 79-856); Memorandum from John C. Yoo, Deputy Assistant Att'y Gen., and Robert J. Delahunty, Special Counsel, to John Bellinger, III, Senior Assoc. Counsel to the President and Legal Adviser to the Nat'l Sec. Council (Nov. 15, 2001), http://www.justice.gov/olc/docs/memoabmtreaty11152001.pdf(concerning the authority of the president to suspend certain provisions of the ABM Treaty).

[64] U.S. CONST. art. II, § 1, cl. 1 ("The executive Power shall be vested in a President of the United States of America.").

[65] U.S. CONST. art. II, § 3 ("[The President] shall take Care that the Laws be faithfully executed, and shall Commission all the Officers of the United States.").

[66] Myers v. United States, 272 U.S. 52 (1926).

agreements, made solely pursuant to the president's constitutional powers.[67] If an agreement entails new, legally binding obligations, I argued, we should examine first, "the degree of congressional approval for the executive lawmaking," and second, "the constitutional allocation of institutional authority over the subject matter area at issue."[68] To be sure, the first factor—the *degree of congressional approval* legally required to enter an agreement—roughly maps onto the three *Youngstown* categories. But whether that degree of congressional approval is constitutionally mandated depends on a second factor as well: which branch of government has *substantive constitutional prerogatives* regarding that area of foreign policy. In the area of recognition, for example, the president's plenary power eliminates the need for congressional approval to enter an agreement; but in the area of foreign commerce, his discretion is limited and could even be barred by Congress's foreign commerce powers.[69]

Under the mirror principle, the degree of congressional and executive participation required to exit from an international agreement should turn on the same two factors: the *subject matter* of an agreement at issue and the *degree of congressional approval* involved in both the entry into and exit from it. Thus, as with entry into any particular international agreement, the degree of legislative participation required to exit that same agreement should be *substance-dependent*. Because the mirror principle requires for exit only the degree of legislative participation required for entry, it is flexible enough to vary according to the subject matter.

## V.  Updating the Fourth Restatement's Black Letter to Address a Typology of Withdrawals

Given the United States' admitted interests in international organizations and multilateral treaties, what constitutional test should govern the president's power to withdraw unilaterally from such arrangements? Applying a general unilateral rule of termination would potentially allow one man to disengage from most of our international commitments, devastating the post–World War II international order that these agreements have helped to construct. The current administration should not overgeneralize from the current wording of Section 313, for the simple reason that many of the international agreements that the United States may consider exiting simply do not fall within the purview of Section

---

[67] Harold Hongju Koh, *Triptych's End: A Better Framework to Evaluate 21st Century International Lawmaking*, 126 YALE L.J. F. 337 (2017).

[68] *Id.* at 344.

[69] See, e.g., United States v. Guy W. Capps, Inc., 204 F.2d 655, 658 (4th Cir. 1953), *aff'd on other grounds*, 348 U.S. 296 (1955).

313. As noted earlier, Fourth Restatement Section 313 regards only "Authority to Suspend, Terminate, or Withdraw from *Treaties*" and not other international agreements. If and when the Fourth Restatement drafting exercise resumes to address international agreements, a more accurate black-letter text (reflecting the words of the four-Justice plurality in *Goldwater*) would read:

> While recent historical practice recognizes that, in some circumstances, the President has the authority to act on behalf of the United States in suspending or terminating U.S. treaty commitments and in withdrawing the United States from treaties, in practice, courts may find that different termination procedures are appropriate for different agreements, depending on the degree of legislative input that went into their original entry.

How would this revised black-letter rule apply with respect to potential withdrawal from a broad range of global arrangements, including international organizations, international tribunals, mutual security organizations, and trade agreements? This section illustrates how the mirror principle would apply in four situations: (1) agreements lawfully concluded with *no* legislative input—so-called sole executive agreements; (2) agreements initially concluded with *considerable* legislative input, such as congressional-executive agreements and treaties; (3) agreements initiated by the executive with general congressional awareness and approval in a zone of congressional subject matter authority, such as the Paris Climate Agreement; and (4) agreements arguably terminated in violation of international law in an area of congressional subject matter authority, such as the Iran Nuclear Deal.

## A. Agreements Concluded with No Legislative Input: Sole Executive Agreements

There are undeniably subject matter areas where the president has plenary authority to make agreements acting alone. In those subject matter areas, the mirror principle would suggest that the president alone has the power to unmake those same agreements, so long as Congress has been silent on the matter. That said, historically, true "sole executive agreements"[70]—agreements based solely on the president's plenary constitutional authorities—have been extremely rare.

---

[70] See THIRD RESTATEMENT § 303 ("[T]he President, on his own authority, may make an international agreement dealing with any matter that falls within his independent powers under the Constitution."); HENKIN, *supra* note 13, at 219–24 (describing international agreements entered into solely by the executive).

Consider, for example, Franklin Delano Roosevelt's 1941 Destroyer-for-Bases deal with the United Kingdom[71] or the early twentieth-century agreements recognizing the new Soviet Union, upheld in *United States v. Belmont*[72] and *United States v. Pink*.[73]

In practice, however, few modern presidents ever claim to be making a controversial agreement based solely on their own plenary constitutional authority, particularly in cases where Congress has legislated extensively elsewhere regarding the same subject. As elaborated later, a recent accord like the Paris Climate Agreement is not a sole executive agreement in this narrow constitutional sense. Instead, it is what some call an "executive agreement plus," because it was not concluded solely within the zone of the president's exclusive constitutional authorities, but against a broad background of legislative support.[74] Thus, just because the president may appear to "make" an agreement alone does not necessarily mean that he is constitutionally empowered to break it alone. Moreover, an agreement like the Paris Accord was premised on a broader history of legislative authorization in a particular direction. During that period, Congress expressed no general approval for presidential actions disrupting or terminating climate change negotiations. Thus, for the president, acting alone, to terminate such an agreement would flout and disrupt congressional expectations and approbation in a way that a prior president's initial conclusion of the agreement did not.

## B.  Agreements Concluded with Considerable Legislative Input: Treaties and Congressional-Executive Agreements

Since World War II, the number of Article II treaties approved by two-thirds of the Senate has dropped dramatically, with a sharp attendant rise in congressional-executive agreements as "interchangeable instruments of national

---

[71] Arrangement between the United States of America and Great Britain Respecting Naval and Air Bases, Gr. Brit.–U.S., Sept. 2, 1940, 54 Stat. 2405.

[72] 301 U.S. 324, 330–33 (1937).

[73] 315 U.S. 203, 222–23 (1942).

[74] See Daniel Bodansky & Peter Spiro, *Executive Agreements+*, 49 VAND. J. TRANSNAT'L L. 885, 887 (2016). Under the Supreme Court's decision in *Dames & Moore v. Regan*, 453 U.S. 654 (1981), "executive agreements plus" represent forms of congressional-executive agreement made within the scope of Justice Jackson's *Youngstown* Category One: because "the President acts pursuant to an express or implied authorization of Congress, his authority is at its maximum, for it includes all that he possesses in his own right plus all that Congress can delegate." 343 U.S. 579, 635–38 (1952) (Jackson, J., concurring); see also Dames & Moore, 453 U.S. at 678–79 (so long as the executive acts consistently with "the general tenor of Congress's legislat[ive framework] in th[e]" particular issue area, and there is "a history of congressional acquiescence in conduct of the sort engaged in by the President" and "no contrary indication of legislative intent," Congress has effectively licensed a permissible space for executive action in that particular issue area).

policy" approved by a majority of both houses of Congress.[75] Both kinds of legal instruments require substantial legislative input for entry. The mirror principle would accordingly suggest that ordinarily, comparable legislative input should be required to exit the same agreements.

Applying Justice Jackson's *Youngstown* test to the termination of congressional-executive agreements could reflect three distinct political realities: congressional approval, disapproval, or ambivalence toward executive action. If Congress were to *approve* the president's termination, explicitly or implicitly, then the president's power is obviously at its zenith, and the president may terminate either a congressional-executive agreement or ratified treaty without controversy. But if Congress were expressly to *disapprove* of the president's attempted termination, the legal conclusiveness of the termination would become substance-dependent. That executive termination could only stand if the president were operating within a zone of exclusive presidential authority, such as state recognition, as illustrated by *Zivotofsky II*[76] or Justice Brennan's separate opinion in *Goldwater*.[77] Finally, if Congress were silent, or could not organize itself to make a collective statement, the president would be operating within what Justice Jackson famously referred to in *Youngstown* as the "twilight zone," where the president's power to terminate agreements unilaterally would depend on proof that Congress did more to approve that action than merely acquiesce.[78]

In *Goldwater* itself, for example, the president—in the face of collective congressional inaction—terminated the Taiwan Treaty, which as Justice Brennan noted, fell into the heart of the president's exclusive power of recognition.[79] Such a unilateral termination would invoke the president's exclusive and plenary constitutional power respecting recognition; *Zivotofsky II* later similarly invoked the exclusive recognition power to negate a contrary congressional statute. But it would be quite another matter if the president tried to act alone to terminate an agreement that was both made by and fell within the heart of Congress's concurrent or exclusive constitutional authority over a subject matter (for example, foreign commerce). For that reason, commentators have persuasively argued that President Trump's threat to terminate or withdraw from North American Free Trade Agreement (NAFTA) (which was later amended into the U.S.-Canada-Mexico Agreement) would be barred by Congress's Commerce Clause authority.[80] The same could be said for a treaty that affected Congress's exclusive

---

[75] Oona A. Hathaway, *Treaties' End: The Past, Present, and Future of International Lawmaking in the United States*, 117 YALE L.J. 1236, 1287 (2008).

[76] 135 S. Ct. 2076 (2015).

[77] 444 U.S. 996, 1007 (1979) (Brennan, J., dissenting).

[78] Youngstown Sheet & Tube Co. v. Sawyer, 343 U.S. 579, 637 (1952) (Jackson, J., concurring).

[79] *Goldwater*, 444 U.S. at 1007 (Brennan, J., dissenting).

[80] See, e.g., Julian Ku & John Yoo, *Trump Might Be Stuck with NAFTA*, L.A. TIMES (Nov. 29, 2016, 4:00 AM), https://www.latimes.com/opinion/op-ed/la-oe-yoo-ku-trump-nafta-20161129-story.html; Joel P. Trachtman, *Power to Terminate U.S. Trade Agreements: The Presidential Dormant*

power of the purse.[81] Again, the mirror principle should apply. If the president lacked the constitutional authority to make an agreement in a subject matter area without congressional approval, the president would lack authority unilaterally to *unmake* an agreement that Congress helped substantially to create in the same subject matter area.

## C.  "Executive Agreements Plus": Agreements Adopted Against a Background of Legislative Approval in a Zone of Congressional Power

A third category would include so-called executive agreements plus: international agreements adopted without an express congressional vote, but against a background of legislative approval in a zone of congressional power.[82] A paradigmatic example is the 2015 Paris Climate Change Agreement, a bundle of commitments made by executive initiative, but with general congressional awareness and approval in a zone of significant congressional power.[83] While there is considerable debate regarding the Paris Agreement's status under U.S. law, no one doubts that the agreement constitutes a "treaty" under international law, for purposes of the Vienna Convention on the Law of Treaties (VCLT). Some provisions of the Paris Agreement are legally binding under international law.[84] But they "are largely procedural in nature and in many instances are duplicative of existing U.S. obligations under the [UN Framework Convention on Climate Change], and, therefore, could be fully implemented based on existing U.S. law."[85] This feature allowed President Barack Obama to enter the Paris Agreement without submitting it for formal Senate approval, because he had sufficient domestic authority to implement any legal obligations assumed under the agreement merely by carrying out preexisting domestic legal obligations.

But exiting the same agreement is not so straightforward. International law makes clear that U.S. presidents cannot simply delete prior signatures from

---

*Commerce Clause Versus an Historical Gloss Half Empty* (Oct. 16, 2017), https://ssrn.com/abstract=3015981.

[81] See generally WILLIAM C. BANKS & PETER RAVEN-HANSEN, NATIONAL SECURITY LAW AND THE POWER OF THE PURSE (1994) (analyzing the scope of Congress's power of the purse in the sphere of national security).

[82] See *supra* note 74.

[83] The Paris Agreement was negotiated under the U.N. Framework Convention on Climate Change (UNFCCC), a treaty with 195 parties to which the Senate gave its advice and consent in 1992. Paris Agreement of the United Nations Framework Convention on Climate Change, Apr. 22, 2016, T.I.A.S. No. 16-1104 (entered into force Nov. 4, 2016) [hereinafter Paris Agreement].

[84] See Koh, *supra* note 67, at 351.

[85] *Id.* at 351.

treaties.[86] Nor under the VCLT can a single state party invalidate an entire multilateral agreement. Nevertheless, on June 1, 2017, President Trump announced his intent to withdraw from the Paris Agreement in more than two years' time.

Curiously, a recent *Harvard Law Review* article discussing presidential control over international law stated that "[t]here was significant controversy about the policy wisdom of this decision, *but no one questioned the President's legal authority to terminate in this context.*"[87] Putting to one side the factual inaccuracy of this statement,[88] even if true, it tells us little, for the simple reason that President Trump's announcement in June 2017 was thirty months premature. No one questioned the president's legal authority in that context because in June 2017, Trump neither terminated nor withdrew U.S. acceptance of the Paris Agreement, nor has he done so as of mid-2020. That announcement simply stated a future intent; it did not in any sense *legally* disengage the United States from the Paris Agreement. The Paris Agreement only recognizes withdrawal under the terms specified in its text, which plainly declares that a party cannot give notice of withdrawal to the U.N. Secretary General until "three years from the date on which this Agreement has entered into force."[89] Since the Paris Agreement entered into force on November 4, 2016, the earliest date that the United States could even give such legal notice would be November 4, 2019, the date when the Trump Administration in fact gave such notice.[90] That notification would then take another year to take legal effect. Thus, the earliest that the United States could legally withdraw from the Paris Agreement is November 4, 2020, the day *after* the next U.S. presidential election—and even that assumes that such an attempted unilateral withdrawal would be upheld following constitutional litigation. The obvious reason why no one questioned the president's legal authority "in this context" or launched any legal challenge against it simply because such a challenge was not yet remotely ripe for judicial examination. So at this writing the United States continues to participate in the Paris process, and will remain a state party until the day after the 2020 presidential election. The United States has only

[86] Harold Hongju Koh, *International Criminal Justice 5.0*, 38 YALE J. INT'L L. 525, 537 (2013).

[87] Bradley & Goldsmith, *supra* note 26, at 1225 (emphasis added).

[88] See, e.g., Koh, *supra* note 67, at 357; see also HAROLD HONGJU KOH, THE TRUMP ADMINISTRATION AND INTERNATIONAL LAW 48–51 (2019).

[89] Paris Agreement, *supra* note 83, at art. 28.1-28.2.

[90] Letter from Nikki R. Haley, U.S. Ambassador to the United Nations, to António Guterres, Sec'y Gen., United Nations (Aug. 8, 2017), https://treaties.un.org/doc/Publication/CN/2017/CN.464.2017-Eng.pdf (emphasis added). The State Department announcement, Press Release made clear that the United States would continue to participate in the UNFCCC through its Conference of Party (COP) meetings. On November 4, 2019, Secretary of State Pompeo announced that the United States had submitted formal notification of its withdrawal to the United Nations, to become effective one year thereafter. On the U.S. Withdrawal from the Paris Agreement, available at https://www.state.gov/on the u c withdrawal from the paris agreement/

"resign[ed] without leaving," thereby prematurely identifying itself as a lame duck.[91]

When, in November 2019, the administration finally carried through on its stated intent to give notice of its desire unilaterally to withdraw from the Paris Agreement in one year's time, those affected could argue that the notice is legally ineffective because the president lacks constitutional power to withdraw from the Paris Agreement without congressional participation. Only then would the broader constitutional question addressed here finally be joined.

At that time, the Trump administration would likely reply that the president possesses unilateral authority to withdraw from the Paris Agreement because—as fourteen senators argued in a 2016 letter to then-Secretary of State John Kerry—the Paris Agreement could be dissolved by the next president alone as a "'sole executive agreement[]' [which is] . . . one of the lowest forms of commitment the United States can make and still be considered a party to an [international] agreement."[92] But the senators' statement is legally inaccurate. In fact, the Paris Agreement is not a "sole executive agreement," adopted under the president's plenary constitutional powers, but rather was expressly preauthorized by a duly ratified Article II treaty, one negotiated within the scope of the Senate's original advice and consent to the 1992 UNFCCC.[93] In addition, the Paris Agreement followed a general statutory landscape that envisioned future efforts at international lawmaking to regulate climate change. Congress had expressed its support for climate change negotiations in: (1) the Global Climate Protection Act of 1987, which asserted the need for "international cooperation aimed at minimizing and responding to adverse climate change";[94] (2) the Clean Air Act, which the Supreme Court held in *Massachusetts v. EPA*[95] authorized the EPA to regulate carbon dioxide emissions from motor vehicles as a pollutant, thereby allowing the president to argue that he could negotiate international agreements as a necessary adjunct to regulating domestic emissions; and specifically in (3) Section 115 of the Clean Air Act, which authorizes federal action reciprocally with other nations to address "international air pollution," namely, transboundary pollution causing international damage;[96] and (4) in addition, the Byrd-Hagel Resolution, unanimously adopted by the Senate in 1997, envisioned

---

[91]   See generally Koh, *supra* note 86, at 39–70.

[92]   Letter from Senator James M. Inhofe et al. to Sec'y of State John Kerry (Nov. 3, 2016), https://www.epw.senate.gov/public/_cache/files/2/4/244c9583-e2ec-47cf-a329-28c7c9f64fe3/F973A463A1 0E2353E3D4F5C33A4045C6.letter-to-unfccc-re-paris-agreement-final.pdf.

[93]   See generally Koh, *supra* note 67, at 350–52.

[94]   Pub. L. No. 100-204, tit. XI, § 1102, 101 Stat. 1331, 1408 (1987).

[95]   See 549 U.S. 497, 528–32 (2007).

[96]   42 U.S.C. § 7415 (2018).

that the executive branch would enter into future climate change agreements like the Paris Agreement, which—as the U.S. government's lead climate lawyer put it—"reflects no doubts about the climate issue per se, and . . . implicitly appears to support an even-handed international climate agreement, [such as the Paris Accord] even one with legally binding targets."[97]

Simply put, the Paris Agreement was not a sole executive agreement in the traditional sense, but rather, an "executive agreement plus": an *agreement approved by Congress through both ex ante treaty and general legislative preauthorization.* Under the Supreme Court's decision in *Dames & Moore v. Regan,*[98] the Paris Agreement represents a form of congressional-executive agreement made within the scope of *Youngstown* Category One: because "the President acts pursuant to an express or implied authorization of Congress, his authority is at its maximum, for it includes all that he possesses in his own right plus all that Congress can delegate."[99] For the president to unilaterally break an agreement supported by such legislative approval at the time of entry would violate the mirror principle by undermining Congress's long-demonstrated intent and approval for agreement-making to mitigate the effects of climate change.

Under the mirror principle, the degree of congressional and executive participation required to exit from an international agreement turns on two factors: the *subject matter* of an agreement at issue and the *degree of congressional approval* involved in both the entry and exit from it. Because the Paris Agreement strongly implicates Congress's powers over commerce—here, the authority to regulate those activities that produce greenhouse gases—significant legislative input should also be required before the United States may constitutionally withdraw from it. Over time, the degree of legislative input into the making of the Paris Agreement was significantly higher than the degree of congressional input into a sole executive agreement. Moreover, Congress expressed no general approval for unilateral presidential actions that would disrupt future climate change negotiations. When an agreement is premised on a broad history of legislative authorization in a particular direction—here, *toward* climate change negotiation—unilateral presidential termination of such an agreement would flout congressional will and expectations in a way that the making of the agreement would not.

---

[97] Susan Biniaz, *What Happened to Byrd-Hagel: Its Curious Absence from Evaluations of the Paris Agreement* (Jan. 2018), http://columbiaclimatelaw.com/files/2018/01/Biniaz-2018-1-Byrd-Hagel-article-Working-Paper.pdf.

[98] 453 U.S. 654 (1981); see also *supra* note 75; Koh, *supra* note 67, at 344–45.

[99] Youngstown Sheet & Tube Co. v. Sawyer, 343 US 579, 635 (1952) (Jackson, J., concurring)

## D. The Iran Nuclear Deal: Terminating Agreements in Violation of International Law

For related reasons, it should not casually be assumed that the president has unilateral authority to withdraw from the Joint Comprehensive Plan of Action (JCPOA), commonly known as the Iran Nuclear Deal.[100] To be sure, under domestic and international law, the JCPOA is a politically, not legally, binding arrangement, that was made by the president acting alone.[101] But for two reasons, that fact alone does not dictate that the president should be able to terminate it unilaterally, without congressional participation.

First, under the Iran Nuclear Deal, the president exercises not his own constitutional powers, but *Congress's* delegated power to regulate foreign commerce by imposing or waiving economic sanctions. Congress is constitutionally entitled to review whether he is exercising that delegating sanctions power appropriately. Second, Iran has now argued before an international court that the president terminated the Iran Nuclear Deal in violation of international law without congressional approval, potentially subjecting the United States to international law liability. A decision in violation of international law plainly falls outside the scope of *Goldwater v. Carter*, will directly affect many constituents, and thus should engage Congress's institutional responsibility.

The JCPOA envisioned actions by Iran, the International Atomic Energy Agency (IAEA), and a group of states known as the P5+1.[102] After extended negotiations, Iran agreed to specified limits on its nuclear development program in exchange for the P5+1's joint undertaking to lift some domestic and international sanctions that had been imposed through the United Nations.[103] The JCPOA has been implemented on the U.S. side largely through executive orders that suspended nuclear-related sanctions, in exchange for Iran's dismantling of key elements of its nuclear program under the watchful eye of the IAEA.[104] Under the JCPOA, the United States and the European Union committed to removing their nuclear-related domestic sanctions and to proposing and voting for a new U.N. Security Council Resolution, which terminated and replaced past resolutions,[105] thereby changing the nature of the other countries'

---

[100] Joint Comprehensive Plan of Action, July 14, 2015, 55 I.L.M. 108 [hereinafter JCPOA].

[101] See Koh, *supra* note 67, at 351–55.

[102] The P5+1 includes the United States, the United Kingdom, France, China, and Russia, plus Germany, as a European Union representative.

[103] See generally JCPOA, *supra* note 100.

[104] See Letter from Denis McDonough, Assistant to the President and Chief of Staff, to the Honorable Bob Corker, Chairman, Senate Comm. on Foreign Relations (Mar. 14, 2015), https://www.pbs.org/newshour/world/read-disputed-letters-center-iran-nuclear-pact.

[105] S.C. Res. 2231, ¶ 2 (July 20, 2015), https://undocs.org/S/RES/2231 (2015).

legal obligations under Chapter VII of the U.N. Charter to provide sanctions relief to Iran.

The Iran Nuclear Deal derives from far more legislative input and support than is generally recognized. The Constitution plainly grants Congress subject matter authority over foreign commerce, and hence, economic sanctions. In turn, Congress delegated implementation of these authorities to the president. Congress also granted the president specific statutory authority to waive existing domestic law sanctions against Iran if he determines that it is in the national interest. Those laws gave President Obama ample statutory authority to enter a deal to waive the sanctions in question, as well as constitutional authority to make the nonbinding political commitment that the United States would not reimpose such sanctions under the terms of the JCPOA, so long as Iran kept its part of the bargain.[106] In addition to preexisting statutory sanctions authority, while the JCPOA was under consideration, Congress enacted the Iran Nuclear Agreement Review Act ("Corker-Cardin" bill), which did not undermine the president's legal authorities, and arguably added to them.[107] But significantly, nothing in the Corker-Cardin bill authorized a future president to violate the Iran Nuclear Deal in a manner inconsistent with international law.

On May 8, 2018, President Trump announced that the United States would withdraw from the JCPOA. In essence, Trump announced that he would no longer exercise his statutory option to waive U.S. statutory sanctions, "instituting the highest level of economic sanction" on Iran and "[a]ny nation that helps Iran in its quest for nuclear weapons."[108] But once again, the United States resigned without leaving: Trump's withdrawal alone has not killed the deal, nor has it eliminated the reasons for Congress to review the wisdom of the withdrawal.

The irony, of course, is that the entire structure of the JCPOA rested on the once-reasonable assumption that Iran, not the United States, would be the likely violator. But instead of immediately exiting the deal, Iran sued the Trump administration before the International Court of Justice (ICJ), which issued a provisional measures order that could lead to a final judgment that the United States violated international law by unilaterally abrogating the JCPOA.[109] Shortly after the court issued its order, the executive branch announced that it would terminate the 1955 Treaty of Amity with Iran in one year's time,[110] under the terms

---

[106] See Koh, *supra* note 67, at 351–55.

[107] Pub. L. No. 114-17, 129 Stat. 201 (2015) (codified as amended at 42 U.S.C. § 2160e).

[108] *Read the Full Transcript of Trump's Speech on the Iran Nuclear Deal*, N.Y. Times (May 8, 2018), https://www.nytimes.com/2018/05/08/us/politics/trump-speech-iran-deal.html.

[109] See Alleged Violations of the 1955 Treaty of Amity, Economic Relations, and Consular Rights (Iran v. U.S.), Order on Request for the Indication of Provisional Measures, 2018 I.C.J. Rep. 175 (Oct. 3).

[110] Michael R. Pompeo, Sec'y of State, Remarks to the Media, (Oct. 3, 2018), https://www.state.gov/remarks-to-the-media-3/.

of Article XXIII(3) of the treaty, and soon thereafter terminated the Optional Protocol on Dispute Settlement to the Vienna Convention on Diplomatic Relations.[111]

This history is doubly significant. First, historical practice, including *Goldwater*, does not recognize any right of the president unilaterally to breach an agreement in violation of international law. Even those who rely on recent historical practice only argue that it condones a president's power to unilaterally terminate an agreement *in accordance with its terms*. Congress has undeniable constitutional authority to implement and monitor the lawful implementation of treaty commitments, as illegal implementation or termination inevitably affects many constituents and many facets of the national interest. To be sure, Iran's legal claims before the ICJ against the United States have been challenged as weak and may well not ultimately prevail.[112] But as this episode illustrates, termination of a deal in a manner inconsistent with its terms can lead to cascading claims of international law violation and to termination of multiple other international agreements. One of the principal aims of the U.S. Constitution was undeniably to give the federal government authority to comply with its international legal commitments. Thus, even in cases where the president alone may have the power to make an agreement that binds the United States, the Constitution still requires that an attempted *termination* of that same agreement be subject to congressional review under circumstances where that termination could render the nation as a whole externally liable for an international law violation that would implicate many areas of congressional responsibility.

Under this reasoning, Congress would have a strong claim to challenge the president's authority to breach JCPOA unilaterally on the grounds that Iran, the other partner, had engaged in no such breach. Congress acquiesced in the adoption of the Iran Nuclear Deal through the delegated use of sanctions relief, but in so doing, anticipated that the president would grant or withhold the sanctions relief in accordance with the deal's terms. Even when a president makes an international agreement without congressional participation, if a subsequent president's disengagement from that same agreement would expose the United States as a nation to claims of international law violation, that disengagement should not be finalized without congressional participation and oversight.

Second, in the case of the JCPOA, the need for congressional participation is particularly strong, because the president is not exercising his own plenary

---

[111] *U.S. Withdrawing from Vienna Protocol on Dispute Resolution—Bolton*, REUTERS (Oct. 3, 2018), https://www.reuters.com/article/usa-diplomacy-treaty/us-withdrawing-from-vienna-protocol-on-dispute-resolution-bolton-idUSW1N1UJ00V.

[112] See John Bellinger, *Thoughts on the ICJ's Decision in Iran v United States and the Trump Administration's Treaty Withdrawals*, LAWFARE (Oct. 5, 2018), https://www.lawfareblog.com/thoughts-icjs-decision-iran-v-united-states-and-trump-administrations-treaty-withdrawals.

constitutional powers, but rather, exercising delegated congressional foreign commerce powers to adjust sanctions in a case where the agreement partner has apparently complied with its international commitments. Congress could undoubtedly revoke its delegation and use its foreign commerce power to decline to reimpose economic sanctions on Iran despite Trump's decision to withdraw, on the ground that it sees no basis for an executive claim of retaliatory breach.[113] Thus, citing the mirror principle, one or both houses of Congress could assert a constitutional right to review and participate in any final decision to withdraw from the Iran Nuclear Deal. If, as Trump claims, he wants a better deal with Iran, Congress could entirely withdraw his statutory rights to waive sanctions in this setting and require—as a condition of giving consent to any new agreement with respect to Iran—a presidential undertaking to terminate or withdraw from that same agreement only in accordance with congressionally prescribed procedures, which could include specified modes of congressional notification, consultation, and participation.

## VI.  Conclusion

In sum, it would be error for the president to overread Section 313 of the Fourth Restatement to claim an uncontested general unilateral power to terminate or withdraw from any and all international agreements. On its face, Section 313 does not claim a transsubstantive rule authorizing presidential withdrawal and termination from all international agreements, only Article II treaties. Nor does Section 313 argue that key multilateral treaties, such as the WTO, NAFTA, and IMF Articles of Agreement—which lie squarely within the zone of Congress's exclusive foreign commerce power—should be terminable by the president acting alone, when a high degree of congressional input was constitutionally required to create those obligations in the first place.

This chapter has argued that this issue is in fact governed by an agreement-specific "mirror" principle—reflected in early U.S. constitutional jurisprudence and the functional reasoning of parallel foreign decisions—that requires parity of constitutional authority for entry and exit. Absent exceptional circumstances, that mirror principle requires that the degree of congressional participation legally necessary to exit an agreement should mirror the degree of congressional and executive participation that was required to enter that agreement in the first

---

[113] On August 6, 2018, Trump issued an Executive Order "Reimposing Certain Sanctions with Respect to Iran." Exec. Order No. 13,846, 83 Fed. Reg. 38,949 (Aug. 7, 2018). See OFAC FAQs: Iran Sanctions, U.S. Dep't of the Treasury (Aug. 9, 2018, 1:12 PM), https://www.treasury.gov/resource-center/faqs/Sanctions/Pages/faq iran aspx

place. Section 313 should be revised accordingly, as suggested in the black-letter proposal in this chapter.

The president possesses no general unilateral power to terminate international agreements. Thus, neither Section 313 nor *Goldwater v. Carter* should be considered controlling with respect to many of the termination or withdrawal scenarios that may lie ahead. In future cases, the constitutional requirements for termination should be decided based on the type of agreement in question, the degree of congressional approval and subject matter in question, and Congress's effort to guide the termination and withdrawal process by framework legislation.[114] It would thus be a grievous error for the president or his lawyers to assume that the U.S. Constitution confides in him alone the power entirely to disengage the United States from the post–World War II legal order.

---

[114] For a description of better policy mechanisms—which better reflect both changing legal doctrine and shifting political realities—to guide America's process of agreement-unmaking in the future, see Koh, *supra* note 67, at 378–81.

# 3

# Taking Treaty-Implementing Statutes Seriously

*Samuel Estreicher*

Implementing legislation has been a critical aspect of the U.S. treaty-making process since the very beginning of the Republic. For example, James Madison, then in Congress, maintained that legislation was required to implement the Jay Treaty of 1794, touching off a significant debate within the founding generation.[1] Yet modern academic studies of U.S. foreign relations law too often neglect treaty-implementing statutes.[2] This conventional frame of reference—with the treaty at the center and implementing legislation essentially an afterthought— gets it wrong where our focus is the impact of the treaty on our domestic law and institutions. While the treaty spells out our international obligations, the implementing law is the domestic face of the treaty, except in the increasingly rare instances where the treaty is considered self-executing. Treaty-implementing legislation constitutes the operative law of the United States with respect to the treaty in question.[3]

This chapter seeks to rekindle interest in treaty implementation legislation. A renewed appreciation by the courts and politically accountable breaches (as well as academics) of, and focus on, the central role of the implementing statute

---

[1] James Madison, then in the House of Representatives, was of the view that the treaty itself could not authorize necessary funds for its implementation, the appropriations power was independent of the treaty power, and Congress controlled appropriations. See generally DAVID CURRIE, THE CONSTITUTION IN CONGRESS; THE FEDERALIST PERIOD 1789–1801, at 211–17 (1997).

[2] Even the expansive fifty-five-page essay by Oona Hathaway and colleagues exploring various means of enforcing non-self-executing treaties devotes less than a page to a brief description of a few treaty-implementing statutes. See Oona A. Hathaway, Sabria McElroy, & Gary A. Solow, *International Law at Home: Enforcing Treaties in U.S. Courts*, 37 YALE J. INTL. L. 51, 77 (2012). Neglect of implementing legislation has not always been the case. See JOHN NORTON MOORE, THE NATIONAL LAW OF TREATY IMPLEMENTATION (2001) (distillation of 1989 multivolume work); SAMUEL B. CRANDALL, TREATIES: THEIR MAKING AND ENFORCEMENT (2d ed. 1916). A prominent modern counterexample, which focuses on modes of enforcement, is David P. Stewart's excellent essay, *Recent Trends in U.S. Treaty Implementation*, in SUPREME LAW OF THE LAND? DEBATING THE CONTEMPORARY EFFECTS OF TREATIES WITHIN THE UNITED STATES LEGAL SYSTEM 228 (Gregory H. Fox, Paul R. Dubinsky, & Brad R. Roth eds., 2017).

[3] "[S]trictly, it is the implementing legislation, rather than the agreement itself, that is given effect as law in the United States. That is true even when a non-self-executing agreement is 'enacted' by, or incorporated in, implementing legislation." THIRD RESTATEMENT Section 111 cmt. h

Samuel Estreicher, *Taking Treaty-Implementing Statutes Seriously* In: *The Restatement and Beyond.* Edited by: Paul B. Stephan and Sarah H. Cleveland, Oxford University Press (2020). © Oxford University Press. DOI: 10.1093/oso/9780197533154.003.0004

in the case of non-self-executing treaties[4] is likely to yield several significant benefits for the development of U.S. foreign relations law. These include: (1) a better understanding of the precise U.S. law position on a particular issue (as, for example, discussed later on the question of corporate liability for financing terrorism); (2) avoiding the dangers of blanket incorporation of treaty language that fails to adjust for U.S. institutions and legal culture (as, for example, discussed later in the case of U.S. domestic-law treatment of the Chemical Weapons Convention); and (3) providing an opportunity for Congressional expansion of protection beyond the requirements of the treaty (as, for example, discussed later in the case of U.S. asylum legislation). This chapter also raises the question whether Congress, the president, and the courts are meeting the challenge in a post-*Medellín* world to address implementation issues regarding treaties we have entered into but do not, or are not properly read to, provide for automatic implementation in the domestic law of the United States.[5]

Despite the efforts of the newly minted Fourth Restatement, the Supreme Court's decision in *Medellín v. Texas*[6] is likely for the foreseeable future to be read as establishing a presumption that treaties are not self-executing, or at the very least dampening the willingness of courts to find that they are self-executing.[7] If so, non-self-executing treaties will be increasingly prevalent (where treaties are used) and will require implementing legislation to have domestic effect in U.S law.[8]

There is a certain resistance in the literature at least fully to come to terms with *Medellín*. Some have offered, with varying degrees of plausibility, avenues for enabling courts to enforce non-self-executing treaty provisions without legislative intervention, These include a reinvigorated role for the *Charming Betsy* canon, a

---

[4] Not all non-self-implementing treaties require implementing legislation because the Senate not infrequently declares that the United States satisfies the obligations of the treaty in question under existing law. This is an important theme of Professor Stewart's essay cited in the previous note.

[5] There has been a movement away from treaties towards greater reliance on executive agreements, whether entered into by the president without congressional authorization or pursuant to ex ante or ex post authorizing legislation. See Oona A. Hathaway, *Treaties' End: The Past, Present, and Future of International Lawmaking in the United States*, 117 YALE L.J. 1236 (2008). In some areas, such as trade and multilateral agreements (especially on human rights issues), treaties will continue to be the dominant vehicles for entering into binding obligations with other nations.

[6] 552 U.S. 491 (2008).

[7] For the Restatement's position, see FOURTH RESTATEMENT § 310 & cmt. *d* (indicating no-presumption approach). For support of the no-presumption view, see Curtis A. Bradley, *Intent, Presumptions, and Non-Self-Executing Treaties*, 102 AM. J. INT'L L. 540 (2008).Writing in 2012, Hathaway et al., *supra* note 2, find that post-*Medellín* lower courts "increasingly . . . adopt a strong presumption that treaties are neither self-executing nor protective of private rights, and thus do not give rise to a private right of action." *Id.* at 71.

[8] "The point of a non-self-executing treaty is that it 'addresses itself to the political, not the judicial department; and the legislature must execute the contract before it can become a rule for the Court.'" Medellín v. Texas, 552 U.S. at 516 (quoting Foster v. Nelson, 2 Pet. 253, 314 (1829) (emphasis omitted)).

generous conception of general statutes like 42 U.S.C. Section 1983 as providing a cause of action for violations of such provisions, and a willingness to empower the executive to assume authority to give some form of domestic effect to a non-self-executing treaty even in the absence of implementing legislation.[9]

These suggestions are not likely, however, to bear fruit because, with the possible exception of the *Charming Betsy* proposal, they are plainly foreclosed by Supreme Court precedent. Professor Bradley ably maintains, as of 2008, that *Medellín* could be read to hold only that non-self-enforcing treaties are not judicially enforceable, not that they are completely unenforceable domestic-law obligations.[10] But after *Medellín* there would seem only limited scope for recognizing such obligations. After all, the Court rejected President George W. Bush's claim that he had implied executive authority to implement the *Avena* judgment of the International Court of Justice (ICJ). The very reasons for finding a treaty non-self-executing, Chief Justice Roberts explained, "refute[] the notion that the ratifying parties vested the President with authority to unilaterally make treaty obligations binding on domestic courts, but also implicitly prohibit[] him from doing so."[11] It would seem that any invocation of a non-self-executing treaty as a basis for obligations binding on domestic courts would be problematic.[12]

---

[9] For use of *Charming Betsy* to overcome non-self-execution, see, e.g., Duncan B. Hollis, *Treaties—A Cinderella Story*, 102 AM. SOC'Y INT'L L. PROC. 412, 415 (2008) ("I am suggesting a theory of *Charming* Treaties. Unlike the current self-execution doctrine, a *Charming* Treaties model would accurately account for the role of all three branches in giving effect to treaties in U.S. law while accommodating more completely the compliance concerns that motivated those roles in the first place."). For a critique of this approach to the presumption, see Anthony J. Bellia Jr. & Bradford R. Clark, *Restating* The Charming Betsy *as a Canon of Avoidance*, in this volume.

For an exploration of whether Section 1983 can be used to enforce human rights treaties, see Penny M. Vanettis, *Making Human Rights Treaty Law Actionable in the United States: The Case for Universal Implementing Legislation*, 63 ALA. L. REV. 97 (2011). Use of § 1983 to enforce non-self-executing treaties is inconsistent with the Court's insistence in cases like *Gonzaga Univ. v. Doe*, 536 U.S. 273, 280 (2002), that private enforcement under § 1983 is available only with respect to "individually enforceable rights."

On the use of treaties as a basis of executive authority, see, e.g., Jean Galbraith, *Making Treaty Implementation More Like Statutory Implementation*, 115 MICH. L. REV. 1309 (2017).

[10] *Medellín* "leaves unclear . . . whether a non-self-executing treaty is simply judicially unenforceable, or whether it more broadly lacks the status of domestic law. . . . It is possible that the Court was not focused on the distinction, since from a judicial perspective, domestic law status largely comes down to judicial enforceability. Yet the distinction might matter it some contexts. It might matter, for example, if the executive branch seeks to take action to enforce a non-self-executing treaty and does not have an independent constitutional or statutory basis for doing so. [The Court] disallowed one type of executive branch action—the creation of a binding rule of decision for the courts—but did not rule out other possible actions. The distinction might also matter in debates within the executive branch over whether the president is obligated to comply with a non-self-executing treaty," Bradley, *supra* note 7, at 548–49 (emphasis omitted); see also *infra* note 16.

[11] 552 U.S. at 517.

[12] The merits of the *Charming Betsy* suggestion may be closer. While a D.C. Circuit judge, Justice Kavanaugh penned a concurring opinion in *Fund for Animals, Inc. v. Kempthorne*, 472 F.3d 877, 879 (D.C. Cir. 2006), stating that the doctrine does not apply at all to non-self-executing treaties. Judge Kavanaugh's view was based on a judgment that non-self-enforcing treaties have no "legal force" under domestic law and courts should defer to the decision of the president and the Senate to withhold domestic effect. Because the *Charming Betsy* canon applies only to ambiguous statues, however,

This again highlights the importance of looking to the implementing statute as the principal vehicle for giving effect to non-self-executing treaty obligations in U.S. law. As the Court stated back in 1888, "[w]hen the stipulations [of a treaty] are not self-executing, they can only be enforced pursuant to legislation to carry them into effect . . ."[13] More than commentators, the courts and the politically accountable branches have an obligation to take treaty implementing statues seriously.

## I. Focusing on the Treaty Implementing Statute as the Relevant Domestic Law

A good example of the need for litigants and courts to focus on the treaty implementing statute is the Supreme Court's decision in *Jesner v. Arab Bank*.[14] *Jesner* involved an action under the Alien Tort Statute (ATS)[15] brought by non-U.S. nationals against Arab Bank, a Jordanian entity, for transferring funds to terrorist groups in the Middle East. The Court held that foreign corporations were not suable under the ATS in part because corporate liability was not sufficiently well established as a matter of international law and in part because recognizing such a cause of action under the ATS would ignore limits Congress imposed in other statutes dealing with similar issues[16] and would generate considerable friction with other countries, thus undermining Congress's principal purpose in enacting the measure.[17] Justice Kennedy's opinion for the Court discusses the International Convention for the Suppression of the Financing of Terrorism, which requires each state party "to enable a legal entity located in [the territory of the state party] or organized under its law to be held liable when a person

adopting a reasonable alternative interpretation of the statute that avoids conflict with a treaty obligation, even if based on a non-self-executing instrument, would seem would be an instance of "respectful consideration" of treaties suggested in *Sanchez-llamas v. Oregon*, 548 U.S. 331, 352 (2006); *Breard v. Greene*, 523 U.S. 370, 375 (1998).

Since *Medellín* dealt with a presidential directive to State prison officials, it may not foreclose a directive to federal officials or the use of federal funds to encourage compliance with ICJ judgments or, more broadly, non-self-enforcing treaty obligations.

[13] Whitney v. Robertson, 124 U.S. 190, 194 (1888).
[14] 138 S. Ct. 1386 (2018).
[15] 28 U.S.C § 1350.
[16] See, e.g., Torture Victim Protection Act, Pub. L. 102-256, § 2, 106 Stat. 73.
[17] As a matter of strict holding, Justice Kennedy's opinion for the Court rests on the discretion prong of *Sosa v. Alvarez-Machain*, 542 U.S. 692 (2004), but the Court's reasoning is very much influenced by comity considerations—by the desire to avoid international friction in view of the fact that the requisite international consensus in support of corporate liability for international law violations had not been demonstrated. On comity considerations in international litigation, see Samuel Estreicher & Thomas H. Lee, *In Defense of International Comity*, 93 S. CAL. L. REV. 169 (2020).

responsible for management or control of the legal entity has, in that capacity, violated" the Convention.[18] The *Jesner* Court dismissed the relevance of the Convention, however, because it "imposes its obligations only on nation-states 'to enable' corporations to be liable in certain circumstances under domestic law."

Missing from both the Court's opinion and Justice Sotomayor's dissent, however, is a recognition that Congress in 2002 had *already* passed legislation, codified as 18 U.S.C. Section 2339C, to enforce U.S. obligations under the Convention.[19] This enactment created a civil penalty recoverable by the United States against "any entity located within the United States or organized under the laws of the United States, for the sum of at least $10,000 if a person responsible for the management or control of that legal entity in the U.S. has, in that capacity," violated the statutory prohibition against financing of terrorism. This provision, to be sure, authorizes only a civil penalty to be recovered by the U.S. government, not a private action for damages; moreover, it would likely not have provided a basis for assessing the civil penalty against the Arab Bank, which was not organized under U.S. law and had only a limited presence in this country.

But as the Court held in *Sosa v. Alvarez-Machain*,[20] whether the ATS provides a cause of action for certain international law violations involves a common law inquiry.[21] In that inquiry, Section 2339C certainly was relevant to the Court's consideration of the status of entity liability under U.S. and international law for terrorism-financing activities. It represented a recent instance in which both international law and U.S. law recognized a form of entity liability for funding terrorism. Just as the Court considered the absence of entity liability in the Torture Victim Protection Act as a reason for not reading the ATS as a basis for a cause of action against legal entities (in this case, foreign corporations), Section 2339C represented a factor cutting the other way even if it did not itself provide for private suits. The implementing statute for the Terrorism-Financing Convention also suggested an important limitation on when such liability might be appropriate. If the Court were inclined to interpret the ATS as a basis for a cause of action against corporations for financing terrorism, it might consider locating liability, as does Section 2339C, on the person or persons "responsible for management or control of the legal entity" who, "in that capacity," violated the

---

[18] International Convention for the Suppression of the Financing of Terrorism, Dec. 9, 1999, S. Treaty Doc. No. 106-49, 2178 U.N.T.S. 232.

[19] Pub. L. 107-97, tit. II, § 202(a), June 21, 2002, 116 Stat. 724; amended Pub. L. 107-273, div. B, tit. IV, § 4006, Nov. 2, 2002, 116 Stat. 1813; Pub. L. 108-458, tit. IV. 6604, Dec. 17, 2004, 118 Stat. 3764; Pub. L. 109-77, tit. IV, § 408, Mar. 9, 2006, 120 Stat. 245.

[20] 542 U.S. 692 (2004).

[21] *Id.* at 748 ("[A]lthough the ATS is a jurisdictional statute creating no new causes of action, the reasonable inference from the historical materials is that the statute was intended to have practical effect the moment it became law. The jurisdictional grant is best read as having been enacted on the understanding that the common law would provide a cause of action for the modest number of international law violations with a potential for personal liability at the time.").

financing prohibition. The Court's failure to deal with the statute implementing the Convention (likely due to the litigants' failure to bring it to the Court's attention) impoverished its discussion of the merits.

## II. Avoiding the Dangers of a Blanket Incorporation of Treaty Language that Fails to Adjust for U.S. Institutions and Legal Culture

In bilateral and perhaps also trilateral treaties, it is relatively easy for negotiators to keep track of treaty text and make sure needed amendments are made. In such circumstances, it is usually wise for Congress to pass an implementing law that fairly closely mirrors the text of the treaty. With respect to multilateral treaties, however, it is a good deal more difficult for potential treaty parties to insist on needed amendments—as any significant change would require all parties who previously had indicated their assent to agree to alter the framework document. Moreover, in order to secure a pact acceptable to a large number of states parties from varying legal cultures, the treaty instrument often contains ambiguous language and provisions that do not easily fit the U.S. legal culture. It is in part for this reason that the U.S. Senate often conditions its advice and consent on reservations, understandings, and declarations (RUDs). For the very same reason, it is important that lawmakers in Congress not fall to the temptation of simply inserting *in haec verba* the language of the treaty into the U.S. Code.[22]

*Bond v. United States*[23] illustrates the pitfalls involved in passing an implementation law that simply parrots the language of the treaty. In 1977, acting on the advice and consent of the Senate, the president ratified the Convention on the Prohibition of the Development, Production, Stockpiling and Use of Chemical Weapons and on Their Destruction (Convention, or CWC).[24] The CWC requires each state party, inter alia, to "undertake[] never under any circumstances . . . [t]o

---

[22] A situation where direct incorporation of treaty text in the U.S. Code has worked fairly well, in part because the treaty uses terms of reference not very dissimilar from U.S. law, is the U.N. Convention on the Recognition and Enforcement of Foreign Arbitral Awards of 1958 (known as the New York Convention), June 10, 1958, 21 U.S.T. 2517, 330 U.N.T.S. 38), which was enacted into federal law as Chapter Two of the Federal Arbitration Act (FAA), 9 U.S.C. §§ 201–208. Chapter Two of the FAA did not, of course, resolve all interpretive questions. See, e.g., G.E. Energy Power Conversion France SAS, Corp. v. Outokumpu Stainless USA, LLC, 140 S. Ct. 1637 (2020) (holding that the New York Convention, and hence Chapter Two of the FAA, permits a nonsignatory to an arbitration agreement to compel arbitration based on the doctrine of equitable estoppel.)

[23] 124 S. Ct. 2077 (2014).

[24] Convention on the Prohibition of the Development, Production, Stockpiling, and Use of Chemical Weapons and on Their Destruction, S. Treaty Doc. No. 103-21, 1974 U.N.T.S. 317.

use chemical weapons. . . ." "Chemical Weapons" are defined in relevant part as "[t]oxic chemicals and their precursors, except where intended for purposes not prohibited under this Convention, as long as the types and quantities are consistent with such purposes." "Toxic chemicals" are then defined to include all chemicals capable of causing death or harm to persons or animals, "regardless of their origin or of their method of production, and regardless of whether they are produced in facilities, in munitions, or elsewhere." Nonprohibited purposes are defined as "[i]ndustrial, agricultural, research, medical, pharmaceutical or other peaceful purposes." The Convention uses very broad language that is not in terms limited to what would seem to be the central purpose of the Convention—to prohibit the use of toxic chemical weapons in warfare or other armed conflict between nation states, between state and nonstate parties, or between militant groups within a state.

Even though the Convention as a purely textual matter appears to reach malicious use of toxic chemicals by private individuals engaged in personal disputes, and the legislators no doubt were aware of the possibility of such use, Congress in 1988 simply incorporated the treaty text in whole into the U.S. criminal code by enacting the Chemical Weapons Convention Implementation Act.[25] As one commentator has noted: "[Nothing in the testimony by State Department officials and other experts suggested that the Act could be used for purposes other than preventing chemical warfare and terrorism, much less prosecution of routine assaults."[26]

Because of the failure of Congress in the implementing statutes to do a better job of adjusting the obligations of the chemical weapons treaty to U.S. institutions and legal culture, a serious question of constitutional law was raised: whether Congress could enact legislation to enforce a treaty that it could not have enacted under its Article I authority. The case harkened back to Justice Holmes's opinion in *Missouri v. Holland*,[27] where the Court held that that the U.S. Constitution's treaty power extends beyond the sources of legislative authority in Article I and that Congress can enact legislation to enforce such treaties even if, in the absence of the treaty, it would lack authority to legislate.[28] Chief Justice Roberts'

[25] Pub. L. 105-277, div. I, title II, § 201(a), Oct. 2, 1988, 112 Stat. 6581, 2681–856, codified at 18 U.S.C. §§ 229, 229F (implementing Convention on the Prohibition of the Development, Production, Stockpiling, and Use of Chemical Weapons and on Their Destruction, S. Treaty Doc. No. 103-21, 1974 U.N.T.S. 317).

[26] Kevin L. Cope, *Lost in Translation: The Accidental Origins of Bond v. United States*, 112 MICH. L. REV. FIRST IMPRESSIONS 133, 137 (2014).

[27] 252 U.S. 416 (1920). The view of the *Holland* Court was anticipated in *Neely v. Henkel*, 180 U.S. 109 (1901).

[28] The constitutional basis for *Missouri v. Holland* relies in part on Article I, Section 8's Necessary and Proper Clause, which gives Congress power "to make all Laws which shall be necessary and proper for carrying into Execution the foregoing Powers" (i.e., Article I, Section 8), and "all other Powers vested by this Constitution in the Government of the United States, or in any Department or Officer thereof" (i.e., the president's authority "to make Treaties" under Article II, Section 2). It relies also in part on a conception of the President's "executive Power" under Article II's vesting clause

opinion for the Court in *Bond v. United States*[29] declined an opportunity to reconsider *Missouri v. Holland* but did apply a narrow reading of the implementing statute for the Chemical Weapons Convention[30] in order to obviate federalism concerns with the law's reaching purely local crimes. Three Justices in separate opinions concurred in the result while indicating agreement with the argument that Congress could not enact legislation beyond its Article I powers even if the statute sought to enforce a treaty that required such measures.[31]

The Court in *Bond* acted to mitigate the problem of overreach inhering in the text of the implementing statute through a judicial declaration that the statute does not reach traditionally local crimes. But judicial modification of legislation is not an ideal way to be translating treaty-based obligations into our domestic law. The *Bond* ruling supports recognizing a "clear statement" requirement before a treaty implementing law is read to reach local crimes.[32] But making sure that our domestic law is appropriately written, especially with respect to criminal offenses, is the principal responsibility of Congress, not the courts. And there is reason to believe that the Chemical Weapons Implementation Act is not an isolated instance of legislative oversight.[33]

## III. The Need for Implementing Legislation Provides an Opportunity for Congressional Elaboration of Protection beyond the Requirements of the Treaty

The very fact that congressional implementation is required before a treaty can have domestic effect serves to force the legislature squarely to confront

---

to act on behalf of the sovereign power of the United States as a whole. See generally United States v. Curtiss-Wright Corp., 299 U.S. 304 (1936). For the argument that Congress lacks this authority under the Necessary and Proper Clause, see Nicholas Rosencrantz, *Executing the Treaty Power*, 118 HARV. L. REV. 1867 (2005).

[29]  134 S. Ct. 2017 (2014).

[30]  See *supra* note 28.

[31]  Justice Scalia, joined by Justice Thomas and joined in part by Justice Alito, concurred in the judgment, arguing it was unconstitutional for Congress to exceed Article I, Section 8 limits by reaching purely local crimes even if it was acting to enforce a treaty that required that reach. Justice Thomas, joined by Justice Scalia and joined in part by Justice Alito, maintained that the treaty power was limited to truly international matters, not local crimes. Justice Alito concurred in the judgment on grounds similar to Justice Scalia.

[32]  See Curtis A. Bradley, Bond, *Clear Statement Requirements, and Political Process*, AJIL UNBOUND (June 5, 2014).

[33]  See, e.g., the Hostage Taking Act, 18 U.S.C. § 1203 (implementing International Convention Against the Taking of Hostages). This treaty has been interpreted to reach purely local kidnapping offenses. See United States v. Ferreria, 275 F.3d 1020 (11th Cir. 2001); United States v. Wang Kun Lue, 134 F.3d 79 (2d Cir. 1997), discussed in Curtis A. Bradley, *Federalism, Treaty Implementation, and Political Process: Bond v. United States*, 108 AM. J. INT'L L. 486, 493 n.46 (2014).

the requirements of the treaty and strive to implement the treaty in a manner consistent with U.S. legal institutions and culture. Such dialogic engagement can result in a stronger U.S. commitment to the treaty's objectives than if the Congress had no role other than senatorial advice and consent. A good example is the Refugee Act of 1980, which went beyond the requirements of the United Nations Protocol Relating to the Status of Refugees in "establish[ing] a second type of broader relief" than the Protocol's protection against deportation.[34] As the Court pointed out in *INS v. Cardoza-Fonseca*, the Protocol would protect an alien seeking asylum against deportation only when the alien "would be threatened" by persecution if he returned to his home country, effectively requiring that the alien show he "more likely than not [would] be subject to persecution."[35] But Congress in the 1980 act went beyond the strict requirements of the Protocol in enacting Section 208(a) to provide that asylum could be granted on a more subjective, less demanding showing that the alien is unable or unwilling to return to his home country "because of persecution or a well founded fear of persecution."[36] In effect, Congress implemented and made binding U.S. law a "precatory," that is, nonmandatory, provision of the Protocol.[37]

## IV. Worry about Delaying the Ratification Process Is Overstated

Noting that it had been the executive branch's practice generally to delay ratification until after treaty implementing legislation has been enacted,[38] some commentators worry that requiring implementing statutes and insisting, as this chapter does, they do a better job of tailoring requirements to U.S. institutions

[34] INS v. Cardozo-Fonseca, 480 U.S. 421, 423 (1987). See Refuge Act of 1980, Pub. L. No. 96-212, 94 Stat. 102, 120 (implementing Protocol Relating to the Status of Refugees, Jan. 31, 1967, 19 U.S.T. 6223, 606 U.N.T.S. 267; Convention Relating to the Status of Refugees, July 28, 1951, 189 U.N.T.S. 137).

[35] *Cardozo-Fonseca*, 480 U.S. at 430. The "more likely than not" interpretation of the "would be threated" language stems from *INS v. Stevic*, 467 U.S. 407, 429–30 (1984).

[36] 8 U.S.C. § 1158(a).

[37] See 480 U.S. at 441. By contrast, it has been suggested that one reason why the consular notification and access provisions of Article 36 of the 1963 Vienna Convention on Consular Relations have been honored largely in the breach in the U.S. is, paradoxically, the absence of implementation legislation due to its treatment as a self-executing treaty, see Stewart, *supra* note 2, at 263.

[38] See Jean Galbraith, *Congress's Treaty-Implementing Power in Historical Practice*, 56 Wm. & Mary L. Rev. 59, 76 (2014) (noting that "historically, U.S. practice sometimes required that the implementation of treaties occur prior to their ratification or entry into force," but that "today, '(i)n reality, the U.S. government has a policy and practice of not joining a treaty until it has determined U.S. law comports with whatever international law obligations the treaty imposes.'" (quoting Hollis, *supra* note 9, at 413).

and legal culture would worsen an already prolonged process of securing ratification of treaties to which the president has agreed.[39]

The point, while not without some merit, is overstated. The president decides whether and when he is ready to ratify a treaty on behalf of the United States after securing the Senate's advice and consent. Sometimes the president holds off ratification until Congress has passed implementing legislation. This would seem good practice, but is not always followed. We certainly have examples of implementing legislation coming *after* ratification. This was true of the Chemical Weapons Convention and the International Convention Against the Taking of Hostages, both of which were flawed, overbroad instruments. These examples indeed illustrate that sometimes it makes good policy sense to await the passage of implementing legislation before treaty ratification.

We should not assume, moreover, that just because there is an additional step to the process—here, passage of a treaty implementing statute—that there will be substantial additional delay in treaty ratification in most cases. If the president and the political branches support the treaty, the Senate's advice and consent and any implementation law will be readily forthcoming. Whether substantial delay occurs will depend on other factors—primarily, whether treaty's subject matter is considered at the moment to be too controversial by the legislators.

With a requirement of implementing legislation in the case of non-self-executing treaties, the House of Representatives is given a formal role in the treaty-making process (a point then-Representative James Madison stressed early on) and concerns senators express through RUDs are capable of being addressed in part by seeing in concrete detail what changes will be made in domestic law as a result of the treaty. In addition, from the standpoint of signaling compliance to our treaty partners,[40] a treaty that survives this gauntlet—ratification by the president, only after securing the Senate's advice and consent, and the enactment of implementing legislation specifying which enforcement measures will be available in U.S. courts and which will not (absent legislative change)—signals a fairly enduring commitment by the United States.

---

[39] Professor Damrosch, for example, notes the three-year delay in enactment of implementation legislation for the Genocide Convention. The Senate's consent expressly provided "[t]hat the President will not deposit the instrument of ratification until after the implementing legislation . . . has been enacted." See Lori F. Damrosch, *Role of the United States Senate Concerning Self-Executing and Non-Self-Executing Treaties—United States*, 67 CHI.-KENT L. REV. 515, 522 (1991) (quoting 130 Cong. Rec. S1377-78 (daily ed. Feb. 19, 1986)).

[40] Professor Bradley's chapter questions whether Article II treaties do perform a significant signaling function, suggesting they are likely used because of "internal rather than external considerations, in particular considerations relating to legal uncertainty, senatorial preferences, and bureaucratic tradition." Curtis A. Bradley, *Article II Treaties and Signaling Theory*, in this volume.

# V.  Conclusion

In a post-*Medellín* world, it is likely that most treaties that the United States enters into will be deemed non-self-executing treaties. Unless the treaty in question merely restates, and therefore requires no change in, existing law, there will be a need for treaty implementing legislation to help bring the United States into compliance with the obligations undertaken in the treaty. The importance of such legislation thus rises to the fore, as do the obligations of the courts and politically accountable branches to ensure that the law of the United States lines up with its treaty obligations. A judicially created cause of action to oversee this process is likely foreclosed by Supreme Court precedent, including *Medellín*. Courts can, however, make sure they are treating the implementation statute as the operative law of the United States in cases where the underlying treaty is in issue.

The significance of implementing legislation goes beyond judicial interpretation. The president should normally work closely with Congress to make sure that the Senate's reservations, understandings, and declarations do not undermine this country's ability to comply with the treaty obligations, and that appropriate implementing legislation is in place before the president ratifies the treaty. This may not always be possible, but it is the preferable approach. The president also may be able under existing authorities to encourage federal and State actors to change their practices in light of treaty provisions. Congress itself must take seriously the role of the treaty implementing statute, generally avoiding incorporation of the treaty text *in haec verba* so that the statute fits well U.S. institutions and legal culture. In appropriate cases, it might be appropriate to extend U.S. law beyond the obligations laid out in treaty as a means of ensuring an atmosphere conducive to compliance with the treaty.

# 4

# The Fourth Restatement's Treatment
# of International Law
# and Administrative Law

*Jean Galbraith*

The Fourth Restatement of Foreign Relations Law, or at least this first round of it, has focused on classic issues. Treaties, jurisdiction, and sovereign immunity—these are all topics that were familiar to the authors of the Third and Second Restatements and indeed would have been natural and familiar topics to international lawyers from the nineteenth century.

These topics have continuing vitality in the twenty-first century. But are they as important as they used to be? The Restatements put out by the American Law Institute matter not just because of what they say about specific issues of law but also because of how they conceptualize bodies of law. The First and Second Restatements of Contracts have helped to hold contracts law together—and the emerging Restatement of Consumer Contracts may fracture it. The characterization of a field is descriptive but inevitably it is analytic and normative as well.[1]

In the move from the Third to the Fourth Restatement, there is little overt acknowledgment that the boundaries of the field may have changed. Some discrete legal issues are of course treated differently.[2] But conversations about the field itself are either addressed tacitly or deferred, perhaps indefinitely. The very process by which the Fourth Restatement has unfolded, as I understand it, seems partly to have been designed to preclude these questions—to take on topics that everyone agreed were in the field, while leaving for another day the questions both of what else goes in the field and of how to resolve the knottiest matters that

---

[1] This claim is a premise and starting point for this chapter. For those interested in the ways meaning is constructed around fields more generally, a fairly recent discussion of Pierre Bourdieu's concept of fields can be found in Kim L. Scheppele, *Judges as Architects*, 24 YALE J.L. & HUM. 345, 350–57 (2012).

[2] For each section of the Fourth Restatement, the reporters' notes helpfully describe how the content tracks or differs from the Third Restatement. For identification of some key differences, see Jean Galbraith, *Contemporary Practice of the United States: American Law Institute Releases a Volume of the Restatement Fourth of the Foreign Relations Law of the United States, Partially Revising the Restatement Third*, 113 AM J. INT'L L. 396 (2019).

Jean Galbraith, *The Fourth Restatement's Treatment of International Law and Administrative Law* In: *The Restatement and Beyond*. Edited by: Paul B. Stephan and Sarah H. Cleveland, Oxford University Press (2020). © Oxford University Press.
DOI: 10.1093/oso/9780197533154.003.0005

everyone sees as in the field, such as the status of customary international law in domestic courts.

In this chapter, I argue that there is a disconnect between foreign relations law in practice and its portrayal in the Fourth Restatement. I begin by discussing two significant shifts in foreign relations law between the late 1980s and the present. The first shift is that there is now *more* distance between international law and U.S. domestic law. The second shift is that there is now *less* distance between foreign relations law and U.S. administrative law. I then turn to how these two shifts are or are not embodied in the Fourth Restatement. I show that the Fourth Restatement reflects the first change but overlooks the second one. The effect of this, I argue, is a distorted picture of the boundaries of foreign relations law. I then consider how further work on the Fourth Restatement could reduce or minimize this distortion.

Although I focus on two significant shifts in foreign relations law over time, I do not suggest that these are the only significant shifts. Nor do I mean to suggest that the only tension between the Fourth Restatement as it now stands and the practice of foreign relations law relates to its treatment of these shifts. There is plenty more to say about the first version of the Fourth Restatement, as other chapters in this book make clear. My purpose is to illustrate rather than to exhaust.

## I. From the Mid-1980s to the Present: Two Changes to Foreign Relations Law

The Third Restatement was completed in the mid-1980s. With the passage of over thirty years, it is appropriate to consider what has changed in the meantime about the field of foreign relations law. In what follows, I identify two significant changes. First, foreign relations law has become more separate as a field from international law. Second, foreign relations law has become more closely intertwined with administrative law. These developments have been gradual ones. To some extent they predate the Third Restatement, and I do not attempt to give them a precise timestamp. Whatever the exact timing, these developments are much more significant and evident now than they were at the time of the Third Restatement.

The first change—the rising distinction between foreign relations law and international law—reflects a normative and doctrinal shift. Leading scholars in foreign relations law today are more likely than in the past to have relatively light training in international law and to see domestic law as separate from international law. Curtis Bradley and Jack Goldsmith's 1997 article challenging the status of customary international law as federal common law is the iconic example of this phenomenon.[3] Interwoven within its specific legal argument was an underlying challenge to Louis Henkin, the Chief Reporter of the Third Restatement, and to the integration of foreign relations law with international law that Henkin had championed.[4] Bradley and Goldsmith have received considerable pushback in turn.[5] Whatever one thinks the right outcome is with respect to how international law is or is not incorporated into U.S. domestic law, however, there are more dualist voices in the field now than was true in the past.

This turn in the scholarship has been paralleled by doctrinal shifts by the increasingly conservative Supreme Court. Most notably, in its 2008 decision in *Medellín v. United States*, the Court established a more dualist approach to treaty implementation than the text of the Supremacy Clause suggests.[6] While *Medellín* has come in for strong criticism, it is now part of Supreme Court doctrine. The legal issues in the Bradley/Goldsmith article and the *Medellín* case are distinct—one involves customary international law and the other involves treaties. But both have the effect of creating more distance between international law and U.S. domestic law.

The second change is the rising role of administrative agencies and administrative law in foreign relations law. Internationally, we have more coordination than in the past between countries through formal international legal agreements or other arrangements, due presumably to some combination of the end of the Cold War, rising globalization, and the development of new technology. Networks, global administrative law, soft law—all of these terms lend themselves readily to foreign relations decision-making that is undertaken by national administrative bodies whose allegiance is not solely owed (and in some cases barely or not at all owed) to their head of state.[7] Much of this occurs in the context of regulatory coordination, where standards that will regulate private conduct are set cooperatively by a collection of national regulators.

For the United States, the rise of transnational cooperation has brought domestic statutory regimes and principles of domestic administrative law into

---

[3] Curtis A. Bradley & Jack L. Goldsmith, *Customary International Law as Federal Common Law: A Critique of the Modern Position*, 110 HARV. L. REV. 815 (1997).

[4] See, e.g., *id.* at 873–76 (suggesting as a "cautionary lesson[]" that judges might be relying too much on internationalist academics and referring in the footnotes to both the Third Restatement and to Professor Henkin as an example of such an academic).

[5] See generally, e.g., Harold Hongju Koh, *Is International Law Really State Law?*, 111 HARV. L. REV. 1824 (1998); Gerald L. Neuman, *Sense and Nonsense about Customary International Law: A Response to Professors Bradley and Goldsmith*, 66 FORDHAM L. REV. 371 (1997); Beth Stephens, *The Law of Our Land: Customary International Law as Federal Law After Erie*, 66 FORDHAM L. REV. 393 (1997).

[6] Medellín v. Texas, 552 U.S. 491, 525–26 (2008).

[7] E.g., ANNE-MARIE SLAUGHTER, A NEW WORLD ORDER (2004) (networks); Benedict Kingsbury, Nico Krisch, Richard B. Stewart, & Jonathan B. Wiener, *The Emergence of Global Administrative Law*, 68 LAW & CONTEMP. PROBS. 15 (Sum./Aut. 2005) (global administrative law); Jean Galbraith & David Zaring, *Soft Law as Foreign Relations Law*, 99 CORNELL L. REV. 735 (2014) (soft law).

the domain of foreign affairs. To give a modest example, when the Food and Drug Administration (FDA) participates in decision-making at the Codex Alimentarius, it has a statutory obligation to provide public notice about its negotiating objectives.[8] Domestic statutory schemes can shape even negotiations that are core presidential priorities. When the Obama administration negotiated the Paris Agreement, for example, the preexisting statutory delegations made to the Environmental Protection Agency (EPA) in the Clean Air Act were essential in framing what commitments the United States could make.[9] In negotiating the Iran deal, Obama administration officials needed to be aware of U.S. constitutional law regarding the kinds of international commitments that the president can make without congressional authorization. But perhaps even more than that, they needed to be aware of the ins and outs of preexisting congressional legislation regarding sanctions and the kinds of discretion these statutes granted to the executive branch.[10] While aspects of the Administrative Procedure Act are not applicable to agencies as they engage in foreign affairs decision-making,[11] administrative law principles nonetheless play a substantial role in their engagement in foreign affairs. To give a few examples: Domestic regulations that do go through notice and comment can have substantial impacts for foreign affairs (such as EPA regulations related to climate change); agencies often have internal rules and protocols that guide administrative decision-making; specific statutes can impose administrative requirements on agencies in relation to foreign affairs (as with the FDA requirement mentioned earlier); and agencies engaged in foreign affairs decision-making are accountable in various ways to Congress as well as to the president.[12]

Administrative agencies, domestic statutory schemes, and administrative law principles have become increasingly important not only where international cooperation is at stake but also when the president is pursuing noncooperative strategies. Consider two major foreign policy actions of the Trump administration—the "travel ban" on entry of citizens from several Muslim-majority countries into the United States and the imposition of tariffs on steel and aluminum imports. For both of these actions, courts and commentators

---

[8] Uruguay Round Agreements Act § 491, Pub. L. No. 103-465, 108 Stat 4809, 4970–71 (1994).

[9] Jean Galbraith, *From Treaties to International Commitments: The Changing Landscape of Foreign Relations Law*, 84 U. CHI. L. REV. 1675, 1731–44 (2017).

[10] For a description of the Iran deal, see Kristina Daugirdas & Julian Davis Mortenson, *Contemporary Practice of the United States, P5+1 and Iran Reach Agreement on Iranian Nuclear Program; Obama Administration Seeks Congressional Approval*, 109 AM. J. INT'L L. 649 (2015).

[11] E.g., 5 U.S.C. § 553(a)(1) (exempting regulations applicable to "a military or foreign affairs function of the United States" from the notice and comment requirement).

[12] See Galbraith, *supra* note 9, at 1691–97 (discussing in more detail how administrative law influences the making of international commitments by the United States).

considered the following questions: Is President Trump acting within his statutory authority in implementing these policies? Has the decision-making that went into these policies been sufficiently grounded in expertise and reasonableness, or does it instead reflect capricious and pretextual behavior? What kind of procedural steps were taken by Trump or executive branch agencies in order to promulgate these policies?[13] These kinds of questions are bread-and-butter to administrative law. And they are increasingly being asked in the foreign affairs context, even if courts remain exceptionally deferential to the executive branch in answering them.

## II. The Partial Incorporation of These Changes into the Fourth Restatement to Date

We have one version of the Fourth Restatement to date—a volume on treaties, jurisdiction, and sovereign immunity. This version took an enormous amount of work: six years, eight reporters, and many drafts. In subtle but noticeable ways, it also reflects the first change that I described earlier—the increased separation between foreign relations law and international law. But it does not reflect the second change that I described—the increased overlap between foreign relations law and administrative law. While this version of the Fourth Restatement is thus useful with respect to the particular legal issues that it covers, it would be a mistake to take it as framing the field.

As to the role of international law in foreign relations law, the Fourth Restatement does not overtly announce a general departure from the Third Restatement. Yet such the signs of such a departure emerge through a close read. Consider the difference in how the Third and Fourth Restatements describe foreign relations law. Section 1 of the Third Restatement provides:

---

[13] See Trump v. Hawaii, 138 S. Ct. 2392, 2407–15 (2018) (analyzing the scope of the president's statutory authority with respect to the travel ban and also stating, with respect to the basis and process of the president's reasoning, that "even assuming some form of review is appropriate, plaintiffs' attacks on the sufficiency of the Presidential findings cannot be sustained"); Severstal Export GMBH v. United States, 2018 WL 1705298 (Ct. Int'l Trade 2018) (finding that plaintiffs had a low likelihood of succeeding in their challenge to the tariffs in light of the breadth of the statutory language delegating authority to impose tariffs and further finding that the reasoning underlying these tariffs was "not wholly unrelated" to the statutory purposes). Both actions also raised constitutional questions—including, with respect to the travel ban, whether it was imposed due to prejudice against Muslims. Justice Sotomayor concluded in dissent that "[b]ased on the evidence in the record, a reasonable observer would conclude that the Proclamation was motivated by anti-Muslim animus" and that this "alone suffices to show that plaintiffs are likely to succeed on the merits of their Establishment Clause claim." 138 S. Ct. at 2343 (Sotomayor, J., dissenting).

The foreign relations law of the United States, as dealt with in this Restatement, consists of

(a) international law as it applies to the United States; and

(b) domestic law that has substantial significance for the foreign relations of the United States or has other substantial international consequences.[14]

International law here is given the pride of place, as the first of two components of foreign relations law. By contrast, the Fourth Restatement provides in its introduction:

The foreign relations law of the United States is drawn from different sources, including the Constitution, congressional legislation, judicial decisions, actions of the executive, customary international law, international agreements, and State law.[15]

Here, international law constitutes two of seven listed sources and is listed only after four other sources, including "actions of the executive." The two descriptions are formally compatible, yet there is an unmistakable difference in tone regarding international law.

Other aspects of the Fourth Restatement also signal a greater emphasis on domestic law and a lesser emphasis on international law. As one of the reporters for the section on jurisdiction has observed, "the Fourth Restatement contains greater coverage of U.S. domestic law than its predecessor, including domestic principles of statutory interpretation, the act of state doctrine and foreign state compulsion, rules of civil and criminal procedure, and rules concerning the recognition and enforcement of foreign judgments."[16] Even more generally, the very decision to start with treaties, jurisdiction, and sovereign immunity was a decision to select topics that engage heavily with domestic law. The American Law Institute could have chosen to revisit volume 2 of the Third Restatement—the volume that served mainly as a primer on international law, with sections on the law of the sea, international trade law, and the like. Instead, it chose to focus on topics that are strongly grounded in international law but where U.S. practice is quite distinctive and not always precisely in line with international law. I am not aware of much appetite to update volume 2 of the Third Restatement, whether because less importance is being placed on international law or because there is

---

[14] THIRD RESTATEMENT § 1.

[15] FOURTH RESTATEMENT intro. at 1.

[16] William S. Dodge, *Jurisdiction in the Fourth Restatement of the Foreign Relations Law*, 18 Y.B. PRIV. INT'L L. 143, 145 (2016).

now less need in light of other easily accessible sources that adequately describe international law.

While the Fourth Restatement signals a reduced focus on international law, it does so through decisions about emphasis rather than through doctrinal claims. Indeed, the Fourth Restatement does relatively little in terms of its black-letter law to support those who argue for a widening divide. The reporters' notes with respect to *Medellín*, for example, take pains to observe that:

> The unusual circumstances of *Medellín* . . . counsel against generalizing too much from the Court's finding there of non-self-execution, and make it difficult to derive from that decision any clear test for determining when treaty provisions should or should not be regarded as self-executing.[17]

The caution shown in the doctrinal sections makes clear that the degree of integration between international and domestic law remains an issue open for further contestation within the field.

The Fourth Restatement's treatment of the rising influence of administrative law in foreign relations law is starkly different from its treatment of the role of international law in foreign relations law. Where the shift on international law is noted and delicately finessed, the shift with respect to administrative law is utterly unrecognized. There are several understandable reasons for this gap, but the effect is to set the current version of the Fourth Restatement at a distance from some of the most interesting questions in foreign relations law.

One possible reason for the lack of treatment of administrative law is that Restatements are somehow inevitably more focused on substantive law than on procedural or structural law. The Third Restatement applied a light touch where the separation of powers was concerned. It did not take up war powers as a topic. Its nine parts were as follows: International Law and Its Relation to United States Law; Persons in International Law; International Agreements; Jurisdiction and Judgments; The Law of the Sea; The Law of the Environment; Protection of Persons; Selected Law of International Economic Relations; and Remedies for Violations of International Law.[18] Even looking back to the original proposal in 1977 calling for a Third Restatement, there was no push to have a part devoted to the distribution of powers between Congress and the president with respect to foreign affairs.[19] The distribution of power came up in particular parts, but it did

---

[17] FOURTH RESTATEMENT § 310 reporters' note 2.

[18] THIRD RESTATEMENT table of contents.

[19] R. Ammi Cutter & Herbert Wechsler, Proposed Revision and Expansion of the Restatement of the Foreign Relations Law of the United States: Background and Description of the Project & Annex A (Nov. 1977). The more expanded version of this proposal called for eight parts and looked fairly similar to the ultimate product, except that it did not propose a part on international economic law. See *id.*

not get taken up as its own topic. In part because of this, the Third Restatement itself was not a particularly good source for conceptualizing foreign relations law as a field.

Another reason why the first version of the Fourth Restatement omits discussion of administrative law may well be the topics that it covers. Administrative law principles come up more with respect to international agreements other than treaties than they do with respect to treaties. (I discuss this point more in the next section.) And administrative law principles come up more with respect to international environmental law and international economic law than they do with respect to jurisdiction and sovereign immunity. The former topics are inherently regulatory in nature, while the latter topics center around judicial doctrines. In picking treaties, jurisdiction, and sovereign immunity as the starting topics for the Fourth Restatement, the American Law Institute chose topics that to date have been at some distance from the growing overlap between administrative and foreign relations law.

Yet another reason may be that the field of foreign relations law does not yet fully recognize how saturated it is with administrative law. The relationship between foreign relations law and international law has long been at the heart of debates in the field. And no one doubts that foreign relations law is largely about constitutional law. Yet the role of administrative law—this other strand of public law—in foreign relations law has historically received less attention from scholars in the field. This is true even though administrative law is making a frequent appearance in high-profile issues like the Paris Agreement, the travel ban, and the trade sanctions and even though some of these issues have ended up in court. While scholarship in national security law and in foreign relations law is increasingly engaging with administrative law, it still has a long way to go.[20] Indeed, where administrative law is overtly invoked, this is often to advocate for reforms of foreign relations law rather than for the purpose of recognizing the administrative law roots of foreign relations law.[21]

All of these reasons can explain why the first version of the Fourth Restatement does little to engage with administrative law. The end result, however, is a volume that focuses on three topics that are important but discrete, and that cover only a sliver of the most important law-meets-foreign-policy issues of today. If a law

---

[20] For a discussion of how administrative law is being used more in these contexts, see Ganesh Sitaraman & Ingrid Wuerth, *The Normalization of Foreign Relations Law*, 128 HARV. L. REV. 1897, 1923–24, 1934, 1958–59 (2015).

[21] E.g., Oona Hathaway, *Presidential Power over International Law: Restoring the Balance*, 119 YALE L.J. 140, 241–68 (2009) (arguing that "[i]nternational lawmaking escaped the administrative law revolution of the 1940s" and calling for more administrative regulation of international agreements); Curtis A. Bradley & Jack L. Goldsmith, *Presidential Control over International Law*, 131 HARV. L. REV. 1201, 1270–96 (2018) (suggesting more transparency with respect to various exercises of executive foreign affairs powers).

student, judge, or practitioner were to look to the Fourth Restatement to try to understand what foreign relations law is, he or she would get a distorted vision. He or she would learn a great deal about treaties, jurisdiction, and sovereign immunity, but relatively little about the roles that principles of administrative law and public law more generally play in foreign relations law—principles like good faith, regularity, accountability, notice, and transparency.

The "selected topics" of the Fourth Restatement are thus aptly named—and should not be understood to be "representative topics." They are of very limited help in conceptualizing the field of foreign relations law. This is true both with respect to the subject matters that they cover and with respect to how they distribute their coverage between substance, structure, and procedure. Their limited scope may have benefits. It leaves for another day and another arena some of the most fundamental questions of foreign relations law. But it means that looking to the Fourth Restatement in conceptualizing the field would be like looking for the lost keys only under the lamplight.

## III. The Fourth Restatement and the Future

The first "selected topics" of the Fourth Restatement are done. It remains to be seen what else, if anything, will be taken on. The approach taken by the Third Restatement, combined with the particular delicacy with which the American Law Institute is approaching the Fourth Restatement, make it unlikely that it will include parts devoted specifically to structural concepts like the separation of powers or to procedural principles like regularity and transparency. To the extent these concepts and principles come up, it will likely be in relation to particular topics. In what follows, I focus on how the increasingly close connections between administrative law and foreign relations law could be addressed in a section on "international commitments other than treaties."

The "International Agreements" part of the Third Restatement covered both treaties (in the domestic constitutional sense of the word) and other international agreements entered into by the United States that were binding as a matter of international law. Given that the first version of the Fourth Restatement only covers treaties—and further given that international commitments other than treaties have become even more important to foreign relations law since the mid-1980s[22]—the topic of international commitments other than treaties seems

---

[22] See Curtis Bradley, Oona Hathaway, & Jack Goldsmith, *The Death of Article II Treaties?*, LAWFARE BLOG (Dec. 13, 2018), https://www.lawfareblog.com/death-article-ii-treaties (noting that "President Trump has submitted only one treaty to the Senate so far in his presidency" and that this is a "historic low"); Jean Galbraith, *Prospective Advice and Consent*, 37 YALE J. INT'L L. 247, 287 (2012) (discussing the Senate's reluctance to approve significant treaties where there is even a

a particularly good candidate for another round of "selected topics." This part could aptly portray the close connections between foreign relations law and administrative law by discussing the following three issues.

First, this part could include one or more sections on the creation of nonbinding commitments. Soft law agreements are a frequent and growing way through which the United States engages internationally. A section on this topic would need to engage with international law and how it distinguishes between commitments that are legally binding and that are not legally binding.[23] It could discuss the diversity of non-binding commitments. Nonbinding commitments can be used for major presidential initiatives like President Obama's Iran deal but also for much more mundane agency-to-agency cooperation across borders. These commitments can also be used by actors with considerable independence from the president, such as the federal reserve board and even—venturing outside the federal government—by the States. Some of these nonbinding commitments are negotiated in an ad hoc manner, while others are coordinated under the auspices of long-standing international bodies like the Basel Committee on Banking Supervision.[24]

After flagging the diversity of these soft law commitments, the section could also mention that the negotiation of these commitments is subject to a patchwork of regulatory control. For some commitments, congressional legislation spells out clear administrative requirements with respect to the process of their formation, as with the example of the FDA and the Codex Alimentarius mentioned earlier.[25] For other commitments, there is an ongoing tug of war between Congress and the executive branch with respect to the extent to which Congress can constitutionally impose procedural and substantive controls over negotiations undertaken by agency officials.[26] For still other commitments, the executive branch

---

touch of opposition); see generally Oona A. Hathaway, *Treaties' End: The Past, Present, and Future of International Lawmaking in the United States*, 117 YALE L.J. 1236 (2008) (charting the declining use of treaties and the rise of other forms of international agreements).

[23] For discussion, see ANTHONY AUST, MODERN TREATY LAW AND PRACTICE 14–54 (2018).

[24] For more discussion of the use of nonbinding commitments, see generally, e.g., Galbraith & Zaring, *supra* note 7; Duncan B. Hollis & Joshua J. Newcomer, *"Political" Commitments and the Constitution*, 49 VA. J. INT'L L. 507 (2009); Duncan B. Hollis, *Unpacking the Compact Clause*, 88 TEX. L. REV. 741 (2010).

[25] See *supra* note 8 and accompanying text.

[26] Consider, for example, the back-and-forth between Congress and the Trump administration over various statutory provisions related to international negotiations on standard-setting in the insurance industry. See, e.g., Economic Growth, Regulatory Relief, and Consumer Protection Act, Pub. L. 115-74, § 211, 132 Stat. 1296, 1316 (2018) (imposing reporting requirements related to international negotiations and finding that various executive branch agencies shall support transparency in international negotiations and "shall achieve consensus positions [in international negotiations] with State insurance regulators through the National Association of Insurance Commissioners"); Signing Statement by President Donald J. Trump on S. 2155 (May 24, 2018), available at https://www.whitehouse.gov/briefings-statements/statement-president-donald-j-trump-s-2155/ (objecting, in a

may have its own internal procedures that apply to their making. Most notably, Executive Order 13609 on Promoting International Regulatory Cooperation, issued in 2012, sets up procedures that agencies are to follow for certain kinds of significant international regulatory cooperation.[27] While the nuances of the regulation of soft law commitments are unlikely to be easily conveyable in a black-letter section, they could be set forth in the comments and the reporters' notes.

Second, a Fourth Restatement part devoted to international commitments other than treaties could have sections on the making of binding commitments through congressional-executive agreements and sole executive agreements. In addition to considering the constitutional parameters governing such agreements, these sections could engage with the procedural requirements for making such agreements that have been imposed by Congress and within the executive branch. The Case-Zablocki Act of 1972 requires that such agreements be reported to Congress shortly after their entry into force.[28] It also sets forth certain procedural requirements to be followed within the executive branch, including that "an international agreement may not be signed or otherwise concluded on behalf of the United States without prior consultation with the Secretary of State" and that "[t]he President shall, through the Secretary of State, promulgate such rules and regulations as may be necessary to carry out this section."[29] Consistent with this last provision and indeed predating it, the State Department has promulgated rules relating to the making of international agreements which are known collectively as the Circular 175 Procedure.[30] While these requirements existed at the time of the Third Restatement, they received very little attention in it.[31] Especially if the Fourth Restatement is now downplaying international

---

signing statement for this act, that Congress lacks the constitutional authority to order the agencies to pursue international transparency and to achieve consensus positions).

[27] Executive Order 13609 (May 1, 2012), available at https://www.govinfo.gov/content/pkg/CFR-2013-title3-vol1/pdf/CFR-2013-title3-vol1-eo13609.pdf. This executive order requires agencies to coordinate in specified ways through a Regulatory Working Group that is chaired by the head of the Office of Information and Regulatory Affairs (OIRA) within the White House. *Id.* OIRA in turn is a major player in administrative law, and its head "is often described as the nation's 'regulatory czar.'" Cass R. Sunstein, *The Office of Information and Regulatory Affairs: Myths and Realities*, 126 HARV. L. REV. 1838 (2013) (adding that "[w]hile it is an understatement to say that this term is an overstatement . . . it does give a sense of the range and responsibility of the office").

[28] 1 U.S.C. § 112b(a).

[29] *Id.* at (c) & (f).

[30] U.S. Dep't of State, 11 Foreign Affairs Manual §§ 720–27; see also 22 CFR § 181 (overlapping considerably with the FAM regulations).

[31] The Case-Zablocki Act is mentioned several times in the reporters' notes with respect to its requirement that agreements be transmitted to Congress but never with respect to its requirement that agreements go through the secretary of state or for the obligation of rulemaking that it imposes. THIRD RESTATEMENT § 301 reporters' note 4; § 303 reporters' note 12; § 312 reporters' note 5. The Circular 175 Procedure is mentioned briefly at several points in the reporters' notes. *Id.* § 303 reporters' note 8; § 311 reporters' note 3; § 312 reporters' note 8.

law and paying more attention to statutes and actions of the executive,[32] it would make sense to give more billing to these procedural requirements.

Such sections could also note the considerable heterogeneity that exists with respect to congressional authorizations for *ex ante* congressional-executive agreements. For these agreements, there is a widespread perspective that Congress authorized them in broad terms and retains no effective oversight powers.[33] This is true for many such agreements, but not for all. Some authorizations for *ex ante* congressional-executive agreements delegate power to particular agency heads, who in turn are more directly accountable to Congress than is the president.[34] Other authorizations impose considerable procedural as well as substantive constraints on the agreement-making process. A particularly powerful example can be found in the recent Clarifying Lawful Overseas Use of Data Act (CLOUD Act).[35] The CLOUD Act authorizes international agreements on data-sharing, but only subject to strong substantive and procedural limits, including extensive certification requirements, a 180-delay between the time Congress is given notice of the agreement and its entry into force, and a fast-track process by which Congress can pursue a joint resolution disapproving the agreement.[36] This is an example of how Congress can use some of the same kinds of robust controls used in administrative law to foreign relations law.

Third, a Fourth Restatement part devoted to international commitments other than treaties would presumably have one or more sections discussing the implementation of international commitments. It is here that adminis-trative agencies, statutory authorizations for domestic regulation, and the Administrative Procedure Act play particularly important roles. With the rise of international regulatory cooperation, the executive branch now frequently negotiates both hard and soft international commitments with the anticipation that these commitments will be implemented by agencies acting under their preexisting domestic authority. To give another environmental example besides the Paris Agreement, the Obama administration joined an important environ-mental convention on reducing mercury—the Minamata Convention—after determining that it could "implement Convention obligations under existing

---

[32] See *supra* notes 12–13 and accompanying text.
[33] This is the core of the argument made by Hathaway, *supra* note 21.
[34] Galbraith, *supra* note 9, at 1692–93 & n. 56.
[35] Pub. L. 115-41 Div. V.
[36] See generally *id.*; see also Jennifer Daskal, *Microsoft Ireland, the CLOUD Act, and International Lawmaking 2.0*, 71 STAN. L. REV. ONLINE 9, 13–15 (2018) (describing these provisions). Among other constraints, "[f]oreign governments are only eligible to enter into these agreements if the Attorney General, in conjunction with the Secretary of State, certifies in writing, and with an accompanying explanation, that the foreign government 'affords robust substantial and procedural protections for privacy and civil liberties' with respect to relevant data collection activities." *Id.* at 13–14 (quoting the CLOUD Act).

legislative and regulatory authority."[37] Because such implementation will likely be done through rule-making under the auspices of a domestic regulatory statute like the Clean Air Act, this implementation is subject to the usual administrative law procedures. As this becomes more common, courts will require more guidance on whether or not to accord extra deference to administrative agencies where they are implementing international commitments in the course of carrying out their delegated responsibilities under domestic law.[38] At the very least, the Fourth Restatement could flag these issues.

## IV. Conclusion

No flat map can fully reflect the globe—and no Restatement can perfectly model the field that it seeks to restate. Trade-offs are inevitable. To date, the Fourth Restatement has cut down on the role of international law, focused on three specialized areas, and left unaddressed the growing overlap between foreign relations law and administrative law. It remains to be seen what will be added by later versions of the Fourth Restatement. My hope is that any such versions will do considerably more with the relationship between foreign relations law and administrative law. This approach would make the Fourth Restatement a better representation of foreign relations law as it is practiced today.

---

[37] U.S. Dep't of State, United States Joins Minamata Convention on Mercury (Nov 6, 2013), archived at http://perma.cc/66VU-SNSJ.

[38] For a discussion of conditions under which added deference may be appropriate, see Galbraith & Zaring, *supra* note 7, at 773–75. In addition to whether added deference is appropriate as a matter of law, there may also be situations in which added deference is justified in light of the criteria that the agency is instructed to consider. Cf. Spector v. Norwegian Cruise Line Ltd., 545 U.S. 119, 135–37 (2005) (concluding in a case involving the physical access to cruise ships for disabled persons that the Department of Justice could consider the extent to which these accommodations were consistent with international law standards for ships in determining whether they met the statutory standard of being "readily achievable" accommodations).

# 5

# Article II Treaties and Signaling Theory

*Curtis A. Bradley*

Some scholars contend that, under modern law and practice, presidents can choose to conclude any international agreement by obtaining either ex ante authorization or ex post approval from a majority of Congress rather than obtaining the supermajority "advice and consent" of the Senate that is specified in Article II of the U.S. Constitution. If presidents in fact have this freedom of choice, there appears to be a puzzle: Why do they ever choose to use the Article II treaty process, which is more politically difficult than the executive agreement processes? To be sure, the use of the Article II process has been in decline, but the process is still used for some agreements, including in situations in which the process seems to make it more difficult for presidents to obtain approval of agreements that they support. A common answer to this puzzle is based on signaling theory: Using the Article II process, it is said, allows the president or the country to signal valuable information to potential treaty partners. This chapter argues that the signaling explanation is questionable and suggests that domestic legal and political factors better explain the continued (although recently much diminished) use of the Article II process. It also highlights a number of empirical questions relating to this issue that would benefit from further study.

## I. Treaties and Executive Agreements

The only process specified in the Constitution for making international agreements is the one set forth in Article II, which requires that presidents obtain the advice and consent of two-thirds of the Senate.[1] For many decades, however, presidents have concluded the vast majority of international agreements through some form of "executive agreement" process that does not involve obtaining two-thirds senatorial consent. Some scholars contend that, as a matter of U.S. constitutional law, presidents are never obligated to use the Article II process and can, whenever they choose, conclude any agreement with majority congressional consent, either given in advance of the agreement or after it is concluded. The

[1] See U.S. Const. art. II, § 2.

Curtis A. Bradley, *Article II Treaties and Signaling Theory* In: *The Restatement and Beyond.* Edited by: Paul B. Stephan and Sarah H. Cleveland, Oxford University Press (2020). © Oxford University Press. DOI: 10.1093/oso/9780197533154.003.0006

Third Restatement of the Foreign Relations Law of the United States, published in 1987, described such interchangeability between treaties and congressional-executive agreements as the "prevailing view."[2] (Because the Fourth Restatement of the Foreign Relations Law of the United States has not yet addressed the topic of executive agreements, it has not considered their potential interchangeability with Article II treaties.)

Of the various means of concluding international agreements, the Article II process is generally regarded as the most difficult politically for the president. This is because the president must obtain agreement from a supermajority in the Senate, which typically means that, even during times of unified government, the president will need the agreement of members of the opposing party and also the agreement of members far from the median in terms of partisanship and general support for international cooperation.[3] The difficulty of obtaining such agreement is compounded by the Senate's frequent reliance on unanimous consent procedures that allow individual Senators to block the consideration of treaties. The Senate has sometimes been dubbed the "graveyard" of treaties because of the difficulty of the advice and consent process. In recent decades, heightened political polarization has meant that it has been even more difficult to obtain the requisite senatorial consent for all but the most uncontroversial treaties.

Some scholars have argued that, in light of the choice that presidents purportedly have under modern law and practice between Article II treaties and congressional-executive agreements, it is normatively better for presidents to use congressional-executive agreements than Article II treaties.[4] The full Congress, they note, is more democratically representative than the Senate, and requiring only majority votes in each house of Congress would prevent a minority of

---

[2] THIRD RESTATEMENT § 303 cmt. *e*; see also, e.g., LOUIS HENKIN, FOREIGN AFFAIRS AND THE UNITED STATES CONSTITUTION 217 (2d ed. 1996) (noting that "it is now widely accepted that the Congressional-Executive agreement is available for wide use, even general use, and is a complete alternative to a treaty"); Bruce Ackerman & David Golove, *Is NAFTA Constitutional?*, 108 HARV. L. REV. 799, 802–803 (1995) (arguing that, "[d]uring and after [World War II], the President won the constitutional authority to substitute the agreement of both Houses [of Congress] for the traditional advice and consent of the Senate"); Harold Hongju Koh, *Twenty-First-Century International Lawmaking*, 101 GEO. L.J. 725, 727 (2013) (contending that "[t]he long-dominant view in the academy" is that "treaties and congressional-executive agreements are in fact interchangeable, legally available options for binding the United States in its international relations").

[3] Oona A. Hathaway, *Treaties' End: The Past, Present, and Future of International Lawmaking in the United States*, 117 YALE L.J. 1236, 1311 (2008); Lisa L. Martin, *The President and International Commitments: Treaties as Signaling Devices*, 35 PRES. STUD. Q. 440, 447 (2005). There are scenarios in which it might be more politically difficult for a president to obtain approval of an agreement by a majority of two houses of Congress rather than a supermajority of the Senate, but such scenarios are unusual in modern practice. Moreover, the vast majority of congressional-executive agreements are based on ex ante statutory authority and thus are never even presented to a majority of Congress after being concluded. By contrast, the Article II process is always ex post.

[4] See, in particular, Hathaway, *supra* note 3.

senators from blocking important agreements.[5] Moreover, the full Congress, un-like the Senate by itself, can pass legislation at the time of agreeing to a treaty, promoting better domestic implementation and potentially greater durability of the treaty commitment.

Nevertheless, presidents still sometimes use the Article II process. President George W. Bush, not known as an internationalist president, submitted over one hundred treaties to the Senate during his eight years in office.[6] The numbers dropped off sharply during the Obama presidency, with Barack Obama seeking senatorial advice and consent for only thirty-eight agreements.[7] President Donald Trump has largely failed to engage with the Article II treaty process to date, having submitted only two agreements to the Senate in his first three years in office.[8] But his administration may end up being an outlier in terms of inter-national cooperation.

Since World War II, Article II treaties have accounted for only about 6 per-cent of the international agreements concluded by presidents. But the percentage is significantly higher if one looks only at agreements coded along various dimensions as significant.[9] Moreover, modern presidents have seemed to view the Article II process as the only option for some agreements. This has led to the defeat or perpetual nonratification of certain treaties that presidents have said that they support. This was true even during the Obama administration, despite its low number of treaty submissions to the Senate and its controversial efforts to conclude some high-profile agreements unilaterally. For example, the Obama administration unsuccessfully sought Senate approval of both the Convention on the Rights of Persons with Disabilities and the Law of the Sea Convention. Moreover, despite its frustration when Senator Rand Paul was holding up

---

[5] To be sure, the Senate filibuster rules allow a minority of senators to block ex post congressional-executive agreements, but commentators have noted that it is significantly more difficult to obtain the sixty-seven votes in the Senate needed to approve an Article II treaty than to obtain the sixty votes needed to overcome a filibuster. See, e.g., Hathaway, *supra* note 3, at 1311–12. In any event, as noted, the vast majority of congressional-executive agreements are ex ante, not ex post, and even some ex post congressional-executive agreements have been statutorily exempted from the filibuster. See *id.* at 1304–05, 1311.

[6] See John Bellinger, *Senate Approves Two More Treaties, Bringing Obama Administration's Record to Fifteen*, LAWFARE (July 16, 2016), available at https://lawfareblog.com/senate-approves-two-more-treaties-bringing-obama-administration-treaty-record-fifteen (reporting that the Senate approved 163 treaties submitted by President Bush). The political scientist Jeff Peake reports that Bush sub-mitted 97 treaties to the Senate, see Jeffrey S. Peake, *The Decline of Treaties? Obama, Trump, and the Politics of International Agreements* (draft), but Peake appears to have counted groups of treaties that were bundled together as one treaty. See Curtis A. Bradley & Jack L. Goldsmith, *Presidential Control Over International Law*, 131 HARV. L. REV. 1201, 1211 n.22 (2018).

[7] See Bradley & Goldsmith, *supra* note 6, at 1210–11.

[8] See United States Senate, Treaties, available at https://www.senate.gov/legislative/trty_rcd.htm; Curtis Bradley, Oona Hathaway, & Jack Goldsmith, *The Death of Article II Treaties?*, LAWFARE (Dec. 13, 2018), available at https://www.lawfareblog.com/death-article-ii-treaties.

[9] See GLEN S. KRUTZ & JEFFREY S. PEAKE, TREATY POLITICS AND THE RISE OF EXECUTIVE AGREEMENTS 84, 88 (2009).

consideration of various tax treaties in the Senate, the Obama administration seemed to accept that it had to wait until the issue was resolved.[10]

If there is full interchangeability and the Article II process is the most difficult politically, there seems to be a puzzle: Why do presidents *ever* use the Article II process? A common answer is based on the economic concept of signaling. Signaling is a means by which one party in an interaction can credibly convey nonobvious information about themselves to another party.[11] In the context of contractual bargaining, the literature on signaling indicates that a commitment can be made more credible if accompanied by a costly action—in particular, an action that is more costly for a dishonest speaker to engage in than an honest one. Applied to the context of treaty negotiations, the relevant costly signal would be one indicating a commitment to ratify, comply with, or remain in the treaty if certain concessions are made, or perhaps a willingness to walk away from the negotiations if certain concessions are not made.[12] A number of scholars have suggested that one reason why presidents choose the Article II treaty process is in order to signal precisely such information to potential treaty partners. Although the literature is not entirely clear about the mechanisms of the signal, there appear to be two versions of the signaling story: one relating to the president's personal commitment to the treaty, and the other relating to the country's commitment to the treaty.

In the remainder of this chapter, I set forth some reasons to be skeptical of both versions of the signaling theory, and I suggest that domestic legal and political factors better explain why presidents sometimes still use the Article II process. In particular, I suggest that the continued use of the Article II process is best explained through some combination of legal uncertainty, senatorial preferences, and bureaucratic tradition, the result of which is that Article II treaties and congressional-executive agreements are not completely interchangeable. Without such interchangeability, there is no puzzle that needs to be solved through an external signaling account. To be clear, there may be circumstances in which involving *the legislature* in approving an agreement might send a more

---

[10] See Tax Treaties at Standstill in Senate over Privacy Issues, Roll Call (June 11, 2014), available at https://www.rollcall.com/news/tax_treaties_at_standstill_in_senate_over_privacy_issues-233761-1.html. In 2019, during the Trump administration, the Senate approved four tax treaties that had been submitted by President Obama and held up by Senator Rand Paul. See Jim Tankersley, *Senate Approves Tax Treaties for First Time in Decade*, N.Y. TIMES (July 17, 2019).

[11] See, e.g., ERIC A. POSNER, LAW AND SOCIAL NORMS 19–22 (2000); A. MICHAEL SPENCE, MARKET SIGNALING: INFORMATIONAL TRANSFER IN HIRING AND RELATED SCREENING PROCESSES (1974).

[12] If the president is obligated to use the Article II process, this obligation might impose a credible constraint on the president's ability to make concessions, which might sometimes benefit the United States in negotiations. This idea, known as the Schelling conjecture, is not a signaling theory and appears to assume that there is *not* full interchangeability between executive agreements and Article II treaties. See *infra* text accompanying notes 20–28.

credible indication of U.S. commitment than an agreement concluded solely by the president, a point that I will return to at the end of the chapter. My argument is simply that this point does little to explain the continued (although recently much diminished) use of the Article II treaty process.

## II. Signaling a President's Personal Commitment

One version of the signaling theory suggests that using the Article II process is a signal of the president's *personal commitment* to the treaty.[13] The idea is that it is costly for the president to use up political capital and Senate floor time in order to try to conclude an Article II treaty, and if presidents attempt to do so, it must mean that they are committed to the agreement. The high political cost, in other words, purportedly helps screen out presidents who are not genuinely committed.

There are a number of reasons to doubt this personal commitment version of the signaling theory. As an initial matter, going to the Senate cannot be serving as a signal that the United States is likely to become committed to the treaty relationship. Going to the Senate actually decreases that likelihood, given the difficulty of obtaining two-thirds senatorial consent. If the president is highly committed to obtaining an agreement, he or she should be using the process most likely to achieve that end. Indeed, sometimes the very act of *not* seeking senatorial advice and consent signals a high level of presidential commitment to an agreement, as was true, for example, of President Obama's decision to unilaterally conclude the Iran nuclear deal and the Paris Agreement on climate change.[14]

Moreover, it will usually be the case that a potential treaty partner can avoid incurring reliance costs until the United States actually ratifies the agreement and becomes legally bound by it. As a result, the treaty partner may not need particular assurance that the president is likely to ratify the agreement—it can simply observe whether he or she does so.[15] Furthermore, many modern international agreements (such as in the human rights area) are not built around bilateral reciprocity. For those agreements, the main goal of the other treaty parties

---

[13] See, e.g., Jack L. Goldsmith & Eric A. Posner, *International Agreements: A Rational Choice Approach*, 44 VA. J. INT'L L. 113, 124 (2003); Martin, *supra* note 3, at 460; see also Julian Nyarko, *Giving the Treaty a Purpose: Comparing the Durability of Treaties and Executive Agreements*, 113 AM. J. INT'L L. 54, 63 (2019) (describing the theory).

[14] See Bradley & Goldsmith, *supra* note 6, at 1217–20, 1248–49. His successor, President Trump, has different preferences and, as a result, has withdrawn the United States from the Iran nuclear deal and has indicated an intent to withdraw the United States from the Paris Agreement.

[15] But cf. John K. Setear, *The President's Rational Choice of a Treaty's Preratification Pathway: Article II, Congressional-Executive Agreement, or Executive Agreement?*, 31 J. LEG. STUD. S5, S14 (2002) ("A president who seeks legislative approval thereby provides a costly, and thus credible, signal of his own commitment to ratify the agreement in question.").

may simply be to get the United States into the agreement and potentially subject to international legal and institutional constraints.

Nor does this version of the signaling story make sense with respect to the parties' bargaining during negotiations. It will not ordinarily help a president in negotiations to indicate that he or she will be going to the Senate once the deal is concluded. It is well known that the Senate often refuses to consent to treaties and that, when it does consent, it often attaches reservations and other conditions to its consent. Moreover, even when the Senate does approve treaties, it often does so long after their negotiation—indeed, often in a later presidential administration.[16]

These known facts about the Senate lower the U.S. leverage rather than increase it. That is one reason presidents prefer to use a "fast track" congressional-agreement process for trade agreements (also called "trade promotion authority"): It gives them more negotiating leverage.[17] To take another example, in the Paris Agreement context, it would not have improved the U.S. negotiating position for President Obama to indicate that he would be seeking Senate approval, since the other parties would have thought (accurately) that this would mean that the United States would be unlikely to commit, and hence there would be little reason to give the United States concessions.

The treaty bargaining context may be distinguishable in this respect from some international relations situations in which playing a "game of chicken" can be advantageous. Consider, for example, threats to use force. In that context, a threatening country can potentially make their threat more credible by taking actions or making statements that render it difficult for them to back down—for example, by taking actions that increase the domestic audience costs of backing down.[18] In the treaty bargaining context, however, presidents do not make their commitment to join a treaty more credible by stating that they will take it to the Senate. If anything, they do the opposite. To be sure, it is conceivable that they could make a commitment to *walk away* from negotiations in the absence of certain concessions more credible by stating that they would be seeking approval from the Senate and suggesting that the Senate would demand such concessions. But there are easier and more direct ways for presidents to create audience costs

---

[16] See, e.g., Curtis A. Bradley, *Unratified Treaties, Domestic Politics, and the U.S. Constitution*, 48 HARV. INT'L L.J. 307, 309–10 (2007). The only treaties approved so far during the Trump administration have been treaties submitted by President Obama.

[17] Trade Promotion Authority (TPA): Frequently Asked Questions 1 (Cong. Res. Serv., June 21, 2019) (noting that trade promotion authority "afford[s] the President added leverage and credibility to negotiate trade agreements by giving trading partners assurance that final agreements can receive consideration by Congress in a timely manner and without amendments"), available at https://fas.org/sgp/crs/misc/R43491.pdf.

[18] See generally James D. Fearon, *Signaling Foreign Policy Interests: Tying Hands Versus Sinking Costs*, 41 J. CONFLICT RES. 69 (1997).

in this regard—namely, just by stating publicly that they will not accept a deal without certain concessions. To the extent that presidents think they benefit from having a "red line" in negotiations, it is difficult to see why they would want that line to be determined by a potentially unpredictable group of senators rather than by themselves.

Ultimately, the personal commitment version of the signaling theory must be positing that the costly action of seeking Senate approval is an indication that the president will comply with and stay in the treaty *after the United States joins the treaty*, assuming it does. But commentators have not explained or documented why this is so.

As an initial matter, even if seeking the Senate's advice and consent signals that a president has a significant desire to *obtain* an agreement, that would not necessarily be because the president intends to comply with it fully or stay in it. The president may desire the treaty because he or she thinks that the United States will be able to successfully cheat or reap short-term gains before withdrawing. As long as the benefits to the president of doing so are greater than the costs of using the Article II process, that process will not screen out opportunistic presidents. Indeed, treaty partners should be wary of a president who seems too eager to conclude an agreement, since this might suggest that the president thinks that the United States obtained an especially favorable deal to their disadvantage. Of course, knowing that this is what potential treaty partners might infer, a president will probably not want to signal that he or she is overly excited about the deal. So, if going to the Senate is a signal of a high desire to obtain an agreement (which, again, seems dubious), presidents should actually avoid the Senate.

Nor does presidential adherence to a treaty seem to follow merely from the fact that the president incurred political costs to obtain it. Once the agreement is ratified, those are merely sunk costs that should not by themselves affect decisions about compliance or withdrawal. Moreover, presidents serve limited terms and cannot credibly signal the personal commitment of their successors to a treaty, who will have just as much ability to undermine or terminate the agreement as they have.[19] As a result, the political costs associated with the Article II process are not a reliable signal of compliance going forward.

It might be argued that the president's willingness to go to the trouble of seeking the Senate's advice and consent signals that the president has a "low discount rate"—that is, that he or she will not act too impulsively in the treaty relationship. By analogy, an employer might prefer an applicant with a college degree even if the degree is not directly related to the job on the theory that the degree

---

[19] See Nyarko, *supra* note 13, at 64 ("It is unclear from the signaling model why negotiation partners should put much faith into promises made as treaties by one administration when future administrations can easily renege on the agreement.").

more generally suggests that the applicant is patient and hard-working. But there are many other, and better, indications of the president's general temperament, which will be evident from (for example) their backgrounds, the presidential election process, and how they handle other issues while in office. Even with respect to a specific agreement, there are likely to be better indicators of the degree to which the president is patient and values long-term gains, such as the extent to which he or she personally spends time on the negotiations. In any event, as noted, presidents serve limited terms and cannot signal the personal character traits of their successors.

## III. The Schelling Conjecture

Before turning to the second version of the signaling story, it is useful to address another argument in the literature about why presidents might use the Article II process. This is not a signaling account but is instead an account of how a constrained agent can sometimes obtain greater concessions in negotiations. This theory is traced to Thomas Schelling's 1960 book, *The Strategy of Conflict*, in which he argued:

> If the executive is free to negotiate the best arrangement it can, it may be unable to make any position stick and may end up conceding controversial points because its partners know, or believe obstinately, that the United States would rather concede than terminate the negotiations. But, if the executive branch negotiates under legislative authority, with its position constrained by law, and it is evident that Congress will not be reconvened to change the law within the necessary time period, then the executive branch has a firm position that is visible to its negotiating partners.[20]

This argument has been dubbed the "Schelling conjecture."[21]

It is difficult to see how the Schelling conjecture can explain presidential choice of the Article II treaty pathway. As an initial matter, the conjecture is not ultimately about presidential preferences. Rather, it is an argument about why *a nation* might want to structure its treaty negotiations in a way that limits the ability of its executive negotiator to make concessions, either through ex ante limitations or a requirement of ex post legislative agreement. In other words, it

---

[20] THOMAS C. SCHELLING, THE STRATEGY OF CONFLICT 28 (1960).

[21] See HELEN V. MILNER, INTERESTS, INSTITUTIONS, AND INFORMATION: DOMESTIC POLITICS AND INTERNATIONAL INSTITUTIONS 68 (1997).

is an argument about *lack* of presidential choice of pathway, which is contrary to the premise of the signaling literature.[22]

If presidents have a choice of pathway, as the signaling literature assumes, the Schelling conjecture cannot explain their choice of the Article II pathway. This is, after all, a pathway that is likely to make it substantially more difficult for presidents to conclude agreements, *even when they personally find the agreements beneficial*. One might argue that presidents might be able to obtain more concessions by announcing in advance that they are committed to seeking the Senate's advice and consent. If that announcement is credible (for example, if it makes it more politically difficult to choose a different pathway), presidents will in effect be tying their hands in a way that will demonstrate that they cannot accept anything that falls short of the Senate's preferences.[23]

The problem with this account is that, even if presidents could credibly tie their hands in this way, it is not clear why they would want to do so. If the president's preferences are the same as those of the Senate, the president can simply insist on those preferences in the negotiations. If, as is likely, the Senate's preferences are more demanding, then by committing to go to the Senate the president will risk losing deals that he or she wishes to have. As Jack Goldsmith and Eric Posner have observed, "[w]hatever one thinks about the [Schelling] argument, it cannot be (without further refinement) an explanation for why an executive would benefit from legislative participation in international agreements."[24]

It is also worth noting that, even from the perspective of *the nation* rather than the president, it is not clear how the Schelling conjecture supports a preference for Article II treaties as opposed to congressional-executive agreements. The Article II supermajority process is unusual among nations and, when followed, makes it especially difficult for the United States to make agreements.[25] Tellingly, the previous quotation from Schelling does not hypothesize an Article II treaty.

---

[22] Even considered in those principal-agent terms, there will be trade-offs to a nation, in terms of efficiency and flexibility, in restricting its agent's authority to negotiate. It is far from clear that the Article II process (assuming it actually restricts the president) is optimal in this regard. Indeed, it seems likely that one of the reasons that U.S. practice has drifted away from it is that it is not optimal.

[23] Cf. Robert D. Putnam, *Diplomacy and Domestic Politics: The Logic of Two-Level Games*, 42 INT'L ORG. 427, 440 (1988) (noting that "a small domestic win-set can be a bargaining advantage" and giving an example of President Carter telling Panama that the Panama Canal Treaty would need to be acceptable to the Senate).

[24] Goldsmith & Posner, *supra* note 13, at 125 n.29.

[25] See Hathaway, *supra* note 3, at 1271. Pierre-Hugues Verdier and Mila Versteeg have recently noted that, "while the United States' choice to require supermajority approval was long unpopular, a growing number of countries now require supermajority votes for certain categories of treaties," such as treaties shifting powers to international organizations. *Separation of Powers, Treaty-Making, and Treaty Withdrawal*, in THE OXFORD HANDBOOK OF COMPARATIVE FOREIGN RELATIONS LAW 141 (Curtis A. Bradley ed., 2019). But this adoption of supermajority consent is still relatively uncommon and, in any event, appears to be driven by a desire to make it more difficult to conclude certain types of agreements rather than a desire to increase the countries' bargaining power.

Rather, it hypothesizes a statute that imposes specific limitations on the nego-tiation position of the executive. As such, it is an argument for congressional-executive agreements, not Article II treaties.[26]

John Yoo has suggested that the Article II process might be more beneficial to the United States than congressional-executive agreements because the Article II process "allow[s] the United States to ratchet the constraints even higher."[27] But it cannot be the case that nations receive continuously upward benefits the more constraints that they impose on their ability to conclude international agreements. In particular, the cost of foregone agreements would have to be weighed against any negotiating advantages associated with legislative involve-ment. After all, a nation could ratchet its constraints up even higher than those set forth in Article II—by requiring unanimity of the legislature, for example—but the cost of foregone agreements would make such an arrangement unduly harmful to the national interest.[28] In any event, the key point here is that the Schelling conjecture cannot explain a presidential choice of the Article II treaty pathway.

## IV.  Signaling Country Support

The signaling theory becomes stronger when it shifts away from a story about the president's commitment to a story about *the country's* support.[29] This ver-sion of the signaling theory notes that getting at least sixty-seven votes in the Senate requires a high degree of bipartisan consensus in support of the agree-ment.[30] If there is this consensus, then, the argument goes, the country (and thus the executive and legislature) are less likely to undermine or withdraw from the agreement in the future. That in turn makes the agreement more valuable to the treaty partners, in which case it is in the president's interest to sometimes use that

---

[26] It is conceivable that, if the president could credibly commit to using the senatorial approval process *and* this process were more mysterious to potential treaty partners than the congressional-executive agreement process, the president might be able to leverage the uncertainty about this pro-cess (for example, about senatorial preferences) to obtain a better bargain. This is quite speculative, however, and it is difficult to think of examples in which this has occurred.

[27] John C. Yoo, *Rational Treaties: Article II, Congressional-Executive Agreements, and International Bargaining*, 97 CORNELL L. REV. 1, 43 (2011).

[28] Cf. Putnam, *supra* note 23, at 448 ("[T]he U.S. separation of powers imposes a tighter constraint on the American win-set than is true in many other countries. This increases the bargaining power of American negotiators, but it also reduces the scope for international cooperation."). Putnam is as-suming here the lack of presidential choice of the pathway, contrary to the signaling literature.

[29] See Nyarko, *supra* note 13, at 64 (describing this theory).

[30] See, e.g., Koh, *supra* note 2, at 728 ("Every time we enter into an Article II treaty, we also send the world a message. Securing a sixty-seven-vote Senate supermajority for a treaty is particularly hard work and requires a very high degree of bipartisanship.").

process in order to persuade other countries to make an agreement or to give the United States more concessions.

Although more plausible than the personal commitment signaling account, there are a number of reasons to question this country support version of the signaling theory. One reason is that, at least as a matter of practice, presidents are able to withdraw from Article II treaties without obtaining legislative consent.[31] So, if a country's commitment to the agreement depends on the president's preferences, which may change, it is not clear why senatorial consent is so reassuring to other treaty parties.[32] To be sure, it might be reassuring if, as a matter of domestic politics, the Senate tends to resist presidential withdrawals from, or undercompliance with, Article II treaties. But scholars have not to date presented evidence of such a constraint. There seems to be an assumption by those invoking this idea that if the president fails to comply with or withdraws from an Article II treaty, the Senate will perceive that its own commitment and reputation are being undermined and that it may suffer audience costs if it does not stand up for the agreement.[33] But it is not clear that the Senate understands treaties that way, and the U.S. electorate's general lack of interest in foreign policy makes the audience cost assumption questionable.

Recently, Julian Nyarko has presented evidence suggesting that Article II treaties might be more durable than executive agreements.[34] As he acknowledges, however, this could be true for a number of reasons other than the domestic political difficulty of exiting from them, including the nature of the agreements that get concluded as Article II treaties in the first place.[35] Relatedly, it may be that non–Article II processes are more likely to be used for agreements intended to have only a finite duration.[36] It is also worth noting that Nyarko does not take a

---

[31] See generally Curtis A. Bradley, *Treaty Termination and Historical Gloss*, 92 Tex. L. Rev. 773 (2014); Kristen E. Eichensehr, *Treaty Termination and the Separation of Powers*, 53 Va. J. Int'l L. 247, 299–300 (2013); see also Fourth Restatement § 313; Third Restatement § 339. But see Harold Hongju Koh, *Could the President Unilaterally Terminate All International Agreements? Questioning Section 313*, in this volume. President Trump has acted to withdraw the United States from a number of Article II treaties without first seeking congressional authorization.

[32] Yoo, *supra* note 27, at 35 ("By allowing presidential termination of treaties, constitutional practice has reduced their utility as a credible signal of commitment.").

[33] See, e.g., Lisa L. Martin, Democratic Commitments: Legislatures and International Cooperation 64 (2000) ("Once Senators have gone on record by ratifying a treaty, they will be more reluctant to allow a president to abrogate a treaty than if they had not gone through the formal ratification process."). An additional quibble here: Senators do not ratify treaties; rather, they provide their advice and consent, which allows the president to ratify the treaty.

[34] See Nyarko, *supra* note 13.

[35] See, e.g., *id.* at 83 ("[I]t is possible that, within a given subject matter, senatorial attention is selectively directed at certain types of agreements, such as those of particular importance, and that this selection is also correlated with durability.").

[36] See Barbara Koremenos, *Duration ≠ Seriousness of Commitment: An Empirical and Theoretical Critique of Nyarko's Treaties vs. Executive Agreements*, 113 AJIL Unbound 178 (2019). One of the factors considered by the State Department in deciding which process to be used for an agreement is its "proposed duration." 11 FAM 723.3(7), available at https://fam.state.gov/fam/11fam/11fam0720.html.

position on whether presidents in fact have complete freedom of choice between Article II treaties and executive agreements; if not, then even if Article II treaties are more durable, such durability might simply be a byproduct of factors other than presidential choice.

In addition, the ex post congressional-executive agreement process is likely a better vehicle than the Article II process for signaling the country's support for an agreement.[37] The ex post congressional-agreement process includes both houses of Congress (which might be controlled by different political parties), including the populist and thus more majoritarian House of Representatives. Moreover, there is actually more uncertainty about a president's legal authority to withdraw from ex post congressional-executive agreements than from Article II treaties.[38] This is in part due to the fact that, even if presidents have the authority to terminate international agreements, they are not thought to have the authority to terminate domestic legislation.[39] Ex post congressional-executive agreements not only take the form of statutes but are also more likely to include implementing legislation, which both helps with compliance and makes withdrawal more complicated.[40] Despite these advantages, presidents almost never use ex post congressional-executive agreements outside of the trade area. If this sort of legislative buy-in were so important to other treaty parties, one would expect to see presidents seek more of it, especially since it is often easier politically than going through the Article II process.

Another problem with the country support signaling theory is that it does not seem to match up well with the actual practice of Article II treaties. In recent presidencies, Article II treaties have often been used for fairly routine agreements, relating to matters such as international taxation, extradition, and mutual legal assistance. Yet those do not seem like the sort of agreements for which treaty partners need particular reassurance of commitment. While it is true that presidents also continue to submit some controversial and high-profile agreements to the Senate, such as human rights treaties, those are often multilateral instruments with numerous parties, and it is far from clear that the other parties need or demand assurances of the U.S. level of commitment; instead, they probably just want the United States to ratify in some capacity. Of course, the

[37] When comparing Article II treaties to executive agreements, the signaling literature often groups all types of executive agreements together and thus does not specifically compare Article II treaties with ex post congressional-executive agreements.
[38] Compare Curtis A. Bradley, *Exiting Congressional-Executive Agreements*, 67 DUKE L.J. 1615 (2018), with Joel Trachtman, *Power to Terminate U.S. Trade Agreements: The Presidential Dormant Commerce Clause Versus an Historical Gloss Half Empty*, 51 INT'L LAW. 445 (2018), and Koh, *supra* note 31.
[39] See Clinton v. New York, 524 U.S. 417, 438 (1998); INS v. Chadha, 462 U.S. 919, 954 (1983).
[40] See Hathaway, *supra* note 3, at 1322 (arguing for these and other reasons that "[a] congressional-executive agreement thus creates a more reliable commitment on behalf of the United States than does a treaty").

parties in those multilateral agreements might welcome it if presidents managed to obtain legislative buy-in, but it seems unlikely that they would insist on that or that it would affect their own willingness to make the agreement or the concessions they are willing to give in the agreement.

Probably the best example of a type of Article II treaty that might seem to implicate the country support signaling theory is an arms control agreement. Other parties to such agreements may have significant concerns about the extent to which the United States is committed to comply with and remain in the agreement, in part because they may take actions in reliance on the agreement and in part because monitoring compliance may be difficult. And proponents of this signaling theory sometimes offer various anecdotes about when potential treaty partners purportedly demanded the use of the Article II treaty process for such agreements. For example, Lisa Martin suggests that in 2002, Russia's president Vladimir Putin seemed to want an arms control agreement to be concluded as an Article II treaty.[41]

Even for this subject area, though, the country support signaling theory seems doubtful. As noted earlier, it is not at all clear that the Senate will restrain the president from failing to comply with or withdrawing from Article II treaties. And one might reasonably expect that the public and Congress will be fairly deferential to presidents when it comes to decisions to pull out of arms control and security agreements. Consider, for example, President George W. Bush's withdrawal of the United States from the Anti-Ballistic Missile (ABM) Treaty in 2002, and President Trump's withdrawal of the United States from the Intermediate-Range Nuclear Forces (INF) Treaty.[42] In both instances, presidents did not appear to incur any significant political cost for their actions, and the fact that those agreements had been concluded through the Article II process did not appear to trigger any additional constraint on withdrawal. It seems much more likely that in an arms control agreement the other party will want provisions designed to reduce cheating and opportunism, such as monitoring or long withdrawal periods, rather than senatorial consent. Moreover, while it is true that presidents have submitted most major arms control agreements to the Senate, when there has been a demand for that process it has generally come from *the Senate*,[43] not the other treaty parties. This appears to have been true even in the Putin example cited by proponents of the signaling theory.[44]

[41] See, e.g., Martin, *supra* note 3, at 448.

[42] See Terence Neilan, *Bush Pulls Out of ABM Treaty; Putin Calls Move a Mistake*, N.Y. TIMES (Dec. 13, 2001); U.S. Dep't of State, U.S. Withdrawal from the INF Treaty (Aug. 2, 2019), available at https://www.state.gov/u-s-withdrawal-from-the-inf-treaty-on-august-2-2019/.

[43] See CURTIS A. BRADLEY, ASHLEY S. DEEKS & JACK L. GOLDSMITH, FOREIGN RELATIONS LAW: CASES AND MATERIALS 394–95 (7th ed. 2020) (giving examples).

[44] See Edward T. Swaine, *Samsons or Methuselahs? The Potential Value of Article II Treaties*, 113 AJIL UNBOUND 175, 177 (2019). It appears that Putin was primarily just seeking to have the agreement take the form of a legally binding commitment rather than a "handshake agreement" as had

Finally, it should be kept in mind that, since World War II, the vast majority of agreements concluded by the executive branch have been ex ante congressional-executive agreements, which do not require any legislative participation once they are concluded. This practice has continued in the Trump administration.[45] Such ex ante congressional-executive agreements are concluded across a wide range of issue areas, they entail little political cost, and they are generally presumed to be subject to presidential exit. A central question for foreign relations law should be how this regime should best be regulated.[46] The regime is similar in some ways to the rise of the domestic regulatory state except that it lacks the overlay of any comprehensive administrative law.[47] The key point for present purposes is that this development is in substantial tension with signaling theory: If treaty partners valued the Article II process, or even ex post legislative buy-in more generally, we should be seeing more demands for it than we are seeing. So far, supporters of the signaling theory have offered only a few anecdotes, and even those anecdotes do not seem very supportive of the theory.[48]

## V. Other Explanations

There are other plausible explanations for why presidents sometimes still use the Article II process for concluding agreements. First, as a matter of U.S. constitutional law, it is not entirely clear that there is full interchangeability between Article II treaties and congressional-executive agreements.[49] Such full interchangeability would render the Article II Treaty Clause entirely voluntary, which seems problematic as a matter of constitutional interpretation, even if one accepts that the meaning of constitutional text can change over time. Moreover, one of the arguments for why Article II treaties are not subject to the same

---

originally been suggested by Bush. See Amy E. Woolf, *Nuclear Arms Control: The Strategic Offensive Reductions Treaty* 2 (Cong. Res. Serv. Feb. 7, 2011). The pressure to use the Article II treaty process came from the Senate. See *id.* at 4.

[45] See Curtis Bradley, Jack Goldsmith, & Oona Hathaway, *Executive Agreements: International Lawmaking without Accountability?*, LAWFARE (Jan. 9, 2019), available at https://www.lawfareblog.com/executive-agreements-international-lawmaking-without-accountability.

[46] See *id.*

[47] See Bradley & Goldsmith, *supra* note 6, at 1206.

[48] See also Swaine, *supra* note 44, at 177 ("Instances in which other states insisted on U.S. Senate approval, as against the congressional-executive form, seem rare. . . .").

[49] Some supporters of the signaling theory appear to assume that there is full legal interchangeability between *all* types of executive agreements (including sole executive agreements) and Article II treaties. See, e.g., Martin, *supra* note 3, at 443. But this assumption is inconsistent with prevailing legal understandings and has never been claimed even by the executive branch. Cf. THIRD RESTATEMENT § 303(4) (indicating that an agreement made solely by the President must "fall[] within his independent powers under the Constitution").

federalism constraints as domestic legislation is that they reflect the supermajority consent of the State-protective Senate, but this argument does not apply to executive agreements. Because of that, even some scholars who favor a general shift away from Article II treaties concede that there is not full interchangeability.[50] This federalism point may have particular relevance to prominent human rights treaties, which may regulate domestically in a way that sometimes exceeds Congress's normal legislative authority. Other legal scholars take an even more limited view of interchangeability. Based on text, structure, and historical practice, some scholars maintain that significant agreements in certain subject areas must constitutionally go to the Senate.[51]

So far courts have declined to decide the interchangeability issue.[52] But there is no Supreme Court decision holding that this issue lies beyond judicial cognizance, and the Court does not currently appear to have a robust conception of the political question doctrine.[53] Moreover, it is possible to imagine certain contexts in which judicial review of the issue would become more likely—for example, if the government attempted to extradite someone to another country based on an agreement that had not received Senate consent.[54] Once one relaxes the assumption of full interchangeability, the need for an external signaling model to explain why presidents use the Article II process is reduced.

In any event, constitutional interpretation is not limited to the courts, and executive branch lawyers, or the Senate, might be motivated in part by doubts

---

[50] See Hathaway, *supra* note 3, at 1349. Even the Third Restatement need not be read to suggest full interchangeability, given that its black-letter provisions assume plenary authority to conclude Article II treaties but state that a congressional-executive agreement can address "any matter that falls within the powers of Congress and of the President under the Constitution." THIRD RESTATEMENT § 303(2).

[51] See, e.g., Spiro, *supra* note 5, at 996–1002; Laurence H. Tribe, *Taking Text and Structure Seriously: Reflections on Free-Form Method in Constitutional Interpretation*, 108 HARV. L. REV. 1221 (1995); John C. Yoo, *Laws as Treaties?: The Constitutionality of Congressional-Executive Agreements*, 99 MICH. L. REV. 757 (2001); see also Curtis A. Bradley & Trevor W. Morrison, *Historical Gloss and the Separation of Powers*, 126 HARV. L. REV. 411, 476 (2012) (noting that "the historical practice suggests a constitutionally salient distinction between 'major' and 'minor' agreements (at least in certain subject areas)").

[52] See, e.g., Made in the USA Found. v. United States, 242 F.3d 1300, 1319–20 (11th Cir. 2001) (holding that "in the context of international commercial agreements such as NAFTA . . . the issue of what kinds of agreements require Senate ratification pursuant to the Art. II, § 2 procedures presents a nonjusticiable political question"). The court also noted, however: "In dismissing this case as a political question, we do not mean to suggest that the terms of the Treaty Clause effectively allow the political branches to exercise unfettered discretion in determining whether to subject a particular international agreement to the rigors of that Clause's procedural requirements; to state as much would be tantamount to rendering the terms of Art. II, § 2, cl. 2 a dead letter." *Id.* at 1319.

[53] See Zivotofsky v. Kerry, 566 U.S. 189, 194–95 (2012) (describing the political question doctrine as a "narrow exception" to the judiciary's responsibility decide cases properly before it). But cf. Rucho v. Common Cause, 139 S. Ct. 2484 (2019) (holding that the constitutionality of partisan gerrymandering is a political question).

[54] Cf. Ntakirutimana v. Reno, 184 F.3d 419, 427 (5th Cir. 1999) (concluding that it was constitutional for the executive branch to extradite an individual to an international tribunal based on a congressional-executive agreement)

about full legal interchangeability. Tellingly, the Justice Department's Office of Legal Counsel has not argued that congressional-executive agreements are fully interchangeable with Article II treaties. Instead, it is has merely argued that there are "many classes of agreements" that do not require use of the Article II process.[55] Nor does the State Department's internal Circular 175 process for deciding on an agreement's pathway appear to assume full interchangeability.[56] In any event, the executive branch may be wary of testing the legal boundaries for some agreements.

As noted earlier, most demands for the Article II process have come from the Senate, not from potential treaty partners. And the demands have sometimes been framed in constitutional terms.[57] Moreover, Congress at times has been concerned, on constitutional as well as policy grounds, about the widespread use of executive agreements. It was one of the reasons, for example, that Congress enacted the Case Act in 1972, which requires executive branch reporting of executive agreements, and it is a key reason that the Senate has not given its advice and consent to the Vienna Convention on the Law of Treaties (which, interestingly, the executive has not sought to have concluded outside of the Article II process). For all these reasons, presidents may sometimes use the Article II process, especially for certain high-profile agreements, because the law on full interchangeability is not certain.[58] Importantly, this phenomenon may not be observable merely by looking at general subject matter categorizations for agreements, as is common in the signaling literature, since such categorizations do not reflect the perceived political importance of particular agreements within the categories. Indeed, precisely because the dynamic here may involve some combination of uncertain legal norms and political bargaining, it may not produce a consistent empirical picture.

In addition, the executive may use the Article II process because of the Senate's preferences relating to its perceived prerogatives and institutional role (or the preferences of the Senate Foreign Relations Committee, which acts as a gatekeeper for Article II treaties), regardless of whether the Constitution is understood to require it.[59] It can be difficult to disentangle such political,

---

[55] Memorandum from Walter Dellinger, Assistant Attorney General, to Ambassador Michael Kantor, United States Trade Representative, Whether Uruguay Round Agreements Required Ratification as a Treaty, 18 Op. Off. L. Counsel 232, 234 (Nov. 22, 1994).

[56] One of the goals of the Circular 175 process is to ensure "[t]hat the making of treaties and other international agreements for the United States is carried out within constitutional and other appropriate limits." 11 FAM 722(1), available at https://fam.state.gov/fam/11fam/11fam0720.html.

[57] See, e.g., BRADLEY, DEEKS & GOLDSMITH, supra note 43, at 390 (quoting letter to the president from Senators Joseph Biden and Jesse Helms contending that "it is therefore clear that no Constitutional alternative exists to transmittal of the concluded agreement to the Senate").

[58] See, e.g., Goldsmith & Posner, supra note 13, at 125 ("One reason that the U.S. president asks for Senate consent is that there are constitutional norms that require him to do so.").

[59] See, e.g., CONG. RES. SERV., TREATIES AND OTHER INTERNATIONAL AGREEMENTS: THE ROLE OF THE UNITED STATES SENATE 26 (Comm. Print 2001) ("A perennial concern of Senators has been to

tradition-based preferences from legal understandings, and often such disentangling is not required in practice.[60] Senatorial preferences might relate to certain types of agreements, such as those relating to arms control and human rights, or to high-profile agreements in general. A president might also send some agreements to the Senate simply so that it does not perceive that it is entirely being left out of approving agreements, in order to avoid a general political backlash against executive agreements.[61] Just as the signaling literature tends to assume full legal interchangeability of executive agreements and Article II treaties, it also tends to assume full *domestic political* interchangeability, which is why it finds presidential use of the Article II process to present a puzzle that is potentially explained by external signaling. But this assumption of political interchangeability is even more doubtful than the assumption of legal interchangeability.[62]

Moreover, one should not underestimate the significance of bureaucratic tradition in large organizations, including in the executive branch. The executive branch processes hundreds of agreements each year and is likely influenced heavily by its own past practices, a factor that is expressly referenced in the State Department's Circular 175 guidelines.[63] This bureaucratic tradition in turn likely affects the expectations of the Senate, especially the Senate Foreign Relations Committee. None of this is to suggest, of course, that modern restrictions on treaty interchangeability reflect some sort of coherent national design, let alone one that is optimal for the United States. The point is simply that if the use of the Article II treaty pathway is a function of domestic legal, political, and

---

insure that the most important international commitments are made as treaties rather than executive agreements."); Koh, *supra* note 2, at 728 ("Congress has its own strong views on how certain types of agreements should be entered into and will fight for those outcomes as a matter of institutional and political prerogative."); see also 22 U.S.C. § 7401(a) ("The United States shall not become a party to the International Criminal Court except pursuant to a treaty made under Article II, section 2, clause 2 of the Constitution of the United States on or after November 29, 1999.").

[60] See generally Curtis A. Bradley & Trevor W. Morrison, *Presidential Power, Historical Practice, and Legal Constraint*, 113 COLUM. L. REV. 1097 (2013).

[61] Lisa Martin has found that the Article II process is more likely to be used for agreements when they are multilateral rather than bilateral and when they are with a wealthy treaty partner. See Martin, *supra* note 3, at 459. Martin suggests that this may be because, when an agreement is deemed more valuable by a president, he or she is more likely to want to send the costly signal of the Article II process to the other treaty parties. But, again, what Martin has observed could equally be the result of internal legal or political factors that make it more likely that the Article II process will be used for multilateral agreements and agreements with certain countries.

[62] See also KRUTZ & PEAKE, *supra* note 9, at 81 ("The president's decisions to classify agreements as treaties or executive agreements are not politically interchangeable."). A senatorial preferences account might also help explain the recent drop-off in the use of the Article II process. Factors such as heightened partisanship and a reduction in the prestige or influence of the Senate Foreign Relations Committee may mean that, as an institution, the Senate is now less likely to assert itself politically in this domain.

[63] See 11 FAM 723.3(4) (listing as a factor "[p]ast U.S. practice as to similar agreements"), available at https://fam.state.gov/fam/11fam/11fam0720.html.

bureaucratic factors, there is less need to try to explain the choice of that pathway through other theories such as external signaling.

It is nevertheless worth emphasizing something noted at the outset of this chapter: Even if the signaling account is not persuasive, there may be other reasons why potential treaty partners will sometimes want the United States to involve its legislature in the treaty process. First, involving the legislature may require presidents to disclose additional information about their understandings relating to the treaty and their plans relating to compliance with it.[64] Second, it might help to reveal the extent to which there is domestic political opposition to the agreement (beyond what might be apparent from media coverage), which can be useful because there are a variety of ways that an unsupportive Congress could undermine an agreement after it is ratified.[65] Importantly, ex post congressional-executive agreements probably serve these goals even better than Article II treaties, given that they will involve deliberation in both chambers of Congress. Furthermore, although it might seem trivial, treaty partners, uncertain about the complicated U.S. agreement-making practice, might sometimes prefer a process that uses the same term ("treaty") as is used in international law and that is actually specified in the text of the Constitution, out of an understandable risk-aversion. If so, such a preference would not be the "costly commitment" preference typically posited by the signaling theories.

# VI.  Conclusion

It is possible that the Article II process is dying. If not, it might seem puzzling that presidents still use that process given how difficult it is politically. The answers to that puzzle likely stem more from internal rather than external considerations, in particular considerations relating to legal uncertainty, senatorial preferences, and bureaucratic tradition. That said, there are empirical questions relevant to signaling theory that could usefully be explored, in particular the extent to which it is politically more difficult for presidents to violate or withdraw from Article II treaties as compared with other agreements. It might also be useful to do more qualitative research about why the Article II process is still sometimes used and about potential changes in recent years in the interbranch dynamics between

---

[64] See Yoo, *supra* note 27, at 26 ("Executive branch testimony and Senate consideration provides important private information that can be seen as part of the negotiating process itself, since it occurs after the President has signed the treaty, but before it is approved and ratified.").

[65] See MARTIN, *supra* note 33, at 63 ("More open, formal ratification mechanisms, particularly those that involve a vote in the legislature, send more information about the preferences and intentions of those who will be responsible for implementing the agreement"); Goldsmith & Posner, *supra* note 13, at 123 ("This process reveals information about the policy preferences of the legislature and thus (in a reasonably democratic state) of the public and/or the elite.").

the executive branch and the Senate concerning treaties. Relatedly, it would be useful to know more about potential changes in recent years in the operations and influence of the Senate Foreign Relations Committee.

Even if the Article II process does not serve signaling functions, it might be justified on other grounds. There are, of course, formal legal arguments in support of this process, given that it is the only one set forth in the constitutional text. In addition, "historical gloss" on the Constitution may support some use of this process, if one concludes (as I tend to) that U.S. practice does not reflect full interchangeability between Article II treaties and congressional-executive agreements.[66] The Article II process might also do a better job than congressional-executive agreements (especially ex ante congressional-executive agreements) of protecting federalism interests, something that may be especially relevant to treaties that address matters that potentially fall outside the scope of Congress's domestic legislative authority.[67] This chapter critiques only the signaling justifications for the use of the Article II process.

Of course, if the Article II process is dying, debates about the value of this process may be rendered moot. There would still be important questions to explore, however, about the choices that presidents (and the executive branch more generally) make among the other agreement pathways, which range from nonbinding political commitments, to binding sole executive agreements, to ex ante congressional-executive agreements, to ex post congressional-executive agreements.[68] It seems plausible that potential treaty partners will sometimes have a preference among those options. For example, potential partners may sometimes prefer an agreement that is binding under international law, on the assumption that it is more difficult for the United States to violate or terminate such an agreement. This may describe the Putin example discussed earlier. It is also possible, as previously noted, that agreements approved by the legislature are stickier than those concluded solely by the president, although more empirical work is needed in order to establish this point.

---

[66] See Bradley & Morrison, *supra* note 51, at 468–76.

[67] See, e.g., David Sloss, *International Agreements and the Political Safeguards of Federalism*, 55 STAN. L. REV. 1963 (2003). One factor listed in the State Department's Circular 175 guidelines is "[w]hether the agreement is intended to affect state laws." 11 FAM 723.3(2), available at https://fam. state.gov/fam/11fam/ 11fam0720.html.

[68] See Bradley & Goldsmith, *supra* note 6, at 1207–108.

PART III

# THE FOURTH RESTATEMENT, INTERNATIONAL LAW, AND DOMESTIC COURTS

# 6

# International Law in American Courts

*Gary Born*

The current treatment of international law in American courts is gravely flawed. Both the status and content of public and private international law in the United States are uncertain, frequently governed by contradictory or parochial rules of State law; the resulting body of international law that is applied by U.S. courts is unpredictable and incoherent. Over the past fifty years, U.S. federal courts have also increasingly marginalized both international law and the role of American courts in resolving international disputes. This treatment of international law threatens serious damage to historic U.S. values and frustrates vitally important national policies.

At the same time, the current treatment of international law in American courts is contrary to the U.S. Constitution's allocation of authority over the nation's foreign relations and international trade, which vests the federal government with both plenary and exclusive authority over U.S. foreign relations and commerce, while, exceptionally, forbidding State involvement in either field. The current treatment of international law in U.S. courts also conflicts with vital national interests and policies in both fields, frustrating long-standing national interests in the nation's compliance with international law and development of the international legal system.

This Chapter proposes a body of federal common law rules that would govern all issues of international law in American courts. Among other things, these rules would govern all private international law issues of judicial jurisdiction over foreign parties, international forum selection agreements, *forum non conveniens*, antisuit injunctions against foreign proceedings, act of state, choice of foreign law, and recognition of foreign judgments. The proposed body of federal law would also govern all issues of public international law, including treaty interpretation and validity and application of customary international law in American courts. These rules would apply even in the absence of federal legislative action, but, like other rules of federal common law, would be subject to contrary direction by the federal political branches.

Gary Born, *International Law in American Courts* In: *The Restatement and Beyond*. Edited by: Paul B. Stephan and Sarah H. Cleveland, Oxford University Press (2020). © Oxford University Press.
DOI: 10.1093/oso/9780197533154.003.0007

# I. Marginalizing International Law

International law in the United States is currently subject to a confused patchwork of federal and State law characterized by uncertainty and incoherence. Issues of international law in American courts are governed by a bewildering assortment of State and federal law rules, derived from an equally bewildering assortment of constitutional, statutory, procedural, and other sources. At the same time, over the past fifty years, U.S. federal courts have progressively marginalized both the role of international law in American courts and the role of those courts in resolving international disputes. These developments are inconsistent with historic American values and contemporary national interests, and with the Constitution's allocation of authority over the Nation's foreign affairs and international commerce.

## A. Public and Private International Law

Preliminarily, beginning in the late nineteenth century, many commentators and some U.S. courts began to distinguish between "public" and "private" international law.[1] The category of "public international law" was typically defined to include those rules governing the conduct of states toward, and their relations with, other states, as well as limited categories of rules governing relations between states and nonstate actors.[2] This includes the law of treaties, recognition of states, state succession, limits on state jurisdiction, sovereign immunity, diplomatic and consular immunities, the law of the sea, international environmental law, human rights, law of war, and law of international organizations.[3] These categories of "public" international law were often distinguished from "private" international law, also termed "conflict of laws," which is typically defined as those rules governing the treatment and status of foreign law, judicial proceedings, judgments, and conduct in U.S. courts, including issues of judicial jurisdiction,

---

[1] See ALEX MILLS, THE CONFLUENCE OF PUBLIC AND PRIVATE INTERNATIONAL LAW—JUSTICE, PLURALISM AND SUBSIDIARITY IN THE INTERNATIONAL CONSTITUTIONAL ORDERING OF PRIVATE LAW 1–2 (2010); Edward Dickinson, *The Law of Nations as Part of the National Law of the United States*, 101 U. PA. L. REV. 26, 26–34 (1952); see also United States v. Bank of New York & Tr. Co., 77 F.2d 866, 875–76 (2d Cir. 1935) ("we invoke, in a truer and broader sense, the application of principles of public and private international law which must be made to coexist and to co-operate toward the adoption of a policy of substantial justice."); Neely v. Club Med Mgmt. Servs., Inc., 63 F.3d 166, n.15 (3d Cir. 1995).

[2] See THIRD RESTATEMENT § 101 ("rules and principles of general application dealing with the conduct of states and of international organizations and with their relations inter se, as well as with some of their relations with persons").

[3] *Id.* Parts II–VII; FOURTH RESTATEMENT (law of treaties, jurisdiction, and state immunity).

forum selection, choice of law, recognition of foreign judgments, and international judicial assistance.[4]

In recent years, critics have mounted compelling challenges to the distinction between public and private international law. They have cited the significant overlaps and close relationships between the categories of public and private international law, including the application of "public" international law rules of foreign sovereign immunity, treaty interpretation, and judicial and legislative jurisdiction in "private" international disputes.[5] They have also pointed out that rules of "public" international law frequently and increasingly apply to "private" parties, including with regard to the rights of foreign investors and, following the Nuremburg trials, the obligations of individuals under international law.[6] Most fundamentally, critics observe that both public and private international law rules serve the same basic purpose, of allocating and regulating the jurisdictional authority of sovereign states.[7]

More generally, critics have observed that the various subjects now treated separately as matters of public and private international law were historically all regarded as aspects of the "Law of Nations,"[8] which drew no distinction between public and private international law; that was true during both the century before and the century after ratification of the Constitution.[9] As Blackstone authoritatively explained, in the 1760s:

> The law of nations is a system of rules, deducible by natural reason, and established by universal consent among the civilized inhabitants of the world . . . to insure the observance of justice and good faith, in *that intercourse which must*

---

[4] THIRD RESTATEMENT §101 cmt. *c*; RESTATEMENT (SECOND) OF CONFLICT OF LAWS § 2 cmt. *a* (Am. Law Inst. 1971).

[5] See, e.g., MILLS, *supra* note 1, at 2, 74–112 ("challeng[ing] this conventional distinction on both descriptive and normative grounds"); Andreas Lowenfeld, *Public Law in the International Arena: Conflict of Laws, International Law, and Some Suggestions for Their Interaction*, 163 HAGUE RECUEIL DES COURS 311, 321–29 (1979).

[6] See, e.g., Mark W. Janis, *Individuals as Subjects of International Law*, 17 CORNELL INT'L L.J. 61, 64–65 (1984); PHILIP JESSUP, A MODERN LAW OF NATIONS 1–2 (1952); Lea Brilmayer, *International Law in American Courts: A Modest Proposal*, 100 YALE L.J. 2277, 2279–80 (1991).

[7] See, e.g., MILLS, *supra* note 1, at 74–112; Lowenfeld, *supra* note 5, at 321–29; Joel P. Trachtman, *Conflict of Laws and Accuracy in the Allocation of Government Responsibility*, 26 VAND. J. TRANSNAT'L L. 975, 985 ("all conflict of laws rules allocate power to government").

[8] RANDALL BRIDWELL & RALPH U. WHITTEN, THE CONSTITUTION AND THE COMMON LAW 51 (1977) (conflict of laws "was a constituent part of a more comprehensive jurisprudence known as the law of nations"); Stewart Jay, *The Status of the Law of Nations in Early American Law*, 42 VAND. L. REV. 819, 821–28 (1989); Edward Dickinson, *The Law of Nations as Part of the National Law of the United States*, 101 U. PA. L. REV. 26, 26–34 (1952) ("the Law of Nations in the eighteenth century embraced a good deal more than the body of practice and agreement which came later to be called public international law").

[9] Joel Paul, *The Isolation of Private International Law*, 7 WISC. INT'L L.J. 149, 155–64 (1988) ("As late as the nineteenth century scholars like Justice Story conceptualized a unified field of international law"); Mark Janis, *Individuals as Subjects of International Law*, 17 CORNELL INT'L L.J. 61 (1988)

*frequently occur between two or more independent states, and the individuals belonging to each.*[10]

It is clear from these and similar authorities that the law of nations was understood throughout the eighteenth and nineteenth centuries as encompassing what would later become rules of "private" international law, applicable to relations among parties from different states, as well as rules of "public" international law, applicable to relations among states.[11]

Despite these criticisms, and the historical treatment of international law, many contemporary U.S. (and other) authorities have continued to distinguish between public and private international law. As discussed later, however, the treatment of both categories of international law in U.S. courts has followed similar paths over the past fifty years and now suffers from very similar, and equally serious, flaws. In both categories, international law is subject to an incoherent patchwork of federal and State law, prescribing uncertain and inconsistent substantive rules, drawn from disparate and often inapposite sources; in part as a consequence, U.S. courts have, over the same time period, increasingly marginalized the role of international law and, conversely, the role of U.S. courts in resolving international disputes. Considering the treatment of both public and private international law together is useful in understanding, illustrating, and remedying these flaws in both contexts.

## B. Public International Law in American Courts

Over the past century, the federal political branches have prescribed rules of federal law addressing a substantial range of important issues of both public and private international law, including by treaty, international agreement, federal legislation, and federal regulation. These instruments govern a significant proportion of the issues of public and private international law that arise in U.S. courts. Nonetheless, in a number of other important areas of international law, the federal political branches have not adopted either international agreements or legislation—leaving American courts to interpret and apply rules of international law with only limited legislative direction.

In the absence of either a treaty or federal legislation, U.S. courts and commentators have reached widely differing conclusions regarding the status and sources of public international law in U.S. courts. Applying Article VI's

---

[10]  4 WILLIAM BLACKSTONE, COMMENTARIES ON THE LAWS OF ENGLAND *66 (1765–70).

[11]  Arthur Nussbaum, *Rise and Decline of Law-of-Nations Doctrine in the Conflict of Laws*, 42 COLUM. L. REV. 189 (1942).

Supremacy Clause, all U.S. authorities treat "self-executing" U.S. treaties and other international agreements of the United States as federal law, directly applicable in U.S. courts.[12] In contrast, "non-self-executing" treaties and other international agreements are treated differently, with most authorities holding that they are neither federal law nor directly applicable in U.S. courts.[13]

The distinction between self-executing and non-self-executing treaties has been difficult to apply in practice,[14] with courts frequently reaching contradictory results, sometimes treating the same treaty or treaty provision as both self-executing and non-self-executing. More generally, U.S. courts have moved away from applying a presumption that treaties are self-executing, as prescribed by the Third Restatement,[15] to apparently applying no presumption regarding self-executing status,[16] or, arguably, applying a presumption that treaties are non-self-executing.[17]

Unsurprisingly, the result has been a pronounced trend toward treating treaties and other U.S. international agreements as non-self-executing.[18] At the same time, U.S. courts have also fashioned a number of other doctrines that further limit the effects of treaties in U.S. courts, including requirements for private causes of action, standing, and the like.[19] Applying these rules, U.S. courts have increasingly denied treaty provisions direct domestic effect, leaving State (or foreign) law applicable to issues governed by U.S. treaties and exposing the United States to violations of its international law obligations.

The treatment of customary international law, in the absence of federal legislation, is even less consistent and predictable than that of U.S. treaties, with

[12] Foster v. Nielson, 27 U.S. (2 Pet.) 253, 314 (1829).

[13] See THIRD RESTATEMENT § 111; FOURTH RESTATEMENT § 310 cmt. *a*; Medellín v. Texas, 552 U.S. 491, 504 (2008).

[14] See Carlos M. Vázquez, *The Four Doctrines of Self-Executing Treaties*, 89 AM. J. INT'L L. 695, 695 (1995); Tim Wu, *Treaties' Domains*, 93 VA. L. REV. 571, 572, 579 (2007) ("judicial treaty enforcement is widely seen as unpredictable, erratic, and confusing"; "recipe for chaos in judicial clothing"); Duncan B. Hollis & Carlos M. Vázquez, *Treaty Self-Execution as "Foreign" Foreign Relations Law*, in THE OXFORD HANDBOOK OF COMPARATIVE FOREIGN RELATIONS LAW 467, 468 (Curtis A. Bradley ed., 2018) ("few doctrines of U.S. foreign relations law have confounded U.S. courts and commentators as thoroughly").

[15] THIRD RESTATEMENT § 111 reporters' note 5 ("strong presumption" that "political branches" consider treaties self-executing).

[16] *Medellín*, 552 U.S. at 512–14; FOURTH RESTATEMENT § 310 reporters' note 3 ("[C]ase law has not established a presumption for or against self-execution."). But see Samuel Estreicher, *Taking Treaty-Implementing Statutes Seriously*, in this volume.

[17] ESAB Grp., Inc. v. Zurich Ins. PLC, 685 F.3d 376, 387 (4th Cir. 2012) ("[T]here is an emerging presumption against finding treaties to be self-executing.") (citing Safety Nat'l Cas. Corp. v. Certain Underwriters, 587 F.3d 714, 737 (5th Cir. 2009) (Clement, J., concurring)).

[18] DAVID SLOSS, THE DEATH OF TREATY SUPREMACY 85–86, 90, 105, 145, 149, 258–61 (2016); Carlos M. Vázquez, *Laughing at Treaties*, 99 COLUM. L. REV. 2154 (1999).

[19] See, e.g., Roger P. Alford, *Judicial Barriers to the Enforcement of Treaties*, in SUPREME LAW OF THE LAND? DEBATING THE CONTEMPORARY EFFECTS OF TREATIES WITHIN THE UNITED STATES LEGAL SYSTEM 333, 351, 355–56 (Gregory Fox, Paul Dubinsky, & Brad Roth eds., 2017).

U.S. federal courts adopting inconsistent approaches to the topic while progressively limiting the application of customary international law rules.[20] On the one hand, a sizeable body of U.S. authority has held that most rules of customary international law have the status of federal, rather than State, law, even in the absence of federal legislation or treaty.[21] On the other hand, a number of U.S. courts and commentators have concluded that, absent a treaty, other international agreement, or federal statute, most issues of customary international law have the status of State, not federal, law.[22]

Judicial decisions have generally mirrored the uncertainty resulting from the modernist and revisionist treatments of customary international law, with different lower courts adopting different positions on the topic.[23] The Supreme Court has addressed the issue on two occasions, but in doing so has left the status of customary international law in U.S. courts both uncertain and precarious. In *Sosa v. Alvarez-Machain*,[24] the Court held that the Alien Tort Statute[25] granted federal courts subject matter jurisdiction over cases involving alleged violations of the law of nations and, in addition, authorized federal courts to identify and apply a limited set of customary international law rules as rules of federal common law.[26] More recently, in *Jesner v. Arab Bank*,[27] the Court held that the rights asserted by the plaintiffs had not achieved sufficient recognition as rules of international law to provide the basis for a claim under the Alien Tort Statute. The Court again acknowledged the possibility of federal common law rules of customary international law, but held that such rules would only rarely provide the basis for a private cause of action in U.S. courts.[28] Moreover, the tenor of the Court's opinion, and of two concurring opinions, suggested that future

---

[20]  See Ernest A. Young, *Sorting Out the Debate Over Customary International Law*, 42 VA. J. INT'L L. 365 (2002); Gary Born, *Customary International Law in United States Courts*, 92 WASH. L. REV. 1641 (2017).

[21]  Gerald L. Neuman, *Sense and Nonsense About Customary International Law: A Response to Professors Bradley and Goldsmith*, 66 FORDHAM L. REV. 371, 383 (1997); Harold Hongju Koh, *Is International Law Really State Law?*, 111 HARV. L. REV. 1824, 1825 (1998).

[22]  See Curtis Bradley & Jack Goldsmith, *Customary International Law as Federal Common Law: A Critique of the Modern Position*, 110 HARV. L. REV. 815, 849 (1997); Curtis A. Bradley & Jack L. Goldsmith, *Federal Courts and the Incorporation of International Law*, 111 HARV. L. REV. 2260 (1998).

[23]  Compare Kadic v. Karadžić, 70 F.3d 232, 246 (2d Cir. 1995), and In re Estate of Marcos Human Rights Litig., 978 F.2d 493, 502 (9th Cir. 1992), and Filártiga v. Peña-Irala, 630 F.2d 876, 887 n.20 (2d Cir. 1980) ("international law has an existence in the federal courts independent of acts of Congress"), with Ghaleb Nassar Al-Bihani v. Obama, 619 F.3d 1, 13 (D.C. Cir. 2010) (Kavanaugh, J., concurring).

[24]  542 U.S. 692 (2004).

[25]  28 U.S.C. § 1350 (2016).

[26]  542 U.S. at 732.

[27]  138 S. Ct. 1386 (2018).

[28]  *Id.* at 1402.

majorities would be even less willing to apply international law as a rule of federal common law.[29]

As with treaties, the clear trend of U.S. judicial decisions over recent years has been toward denying customary international law effect in U.S. courts. That has occurred in *Sosa, Jesner,* and other decisions under the Alien Tort Statute, very significantly limiting the scope of international law claims under the statute. Again paralleling the treatment of treaties, this trend has also been evident in other respects, including decisions by U.S. courts that international law provides no private right of action,[30] imposes exhaustion requirements,[31] or otherwise creates prudential bars to international law claims.[32] The result of these various developments has, over the past two decades, been a significant reduction in the role and importance of customary international law in American courts— instead leaving State (or other) law to govern many international disputes in U.S. courts.

## C.  Private International Law in American Courts

As with public international law, the treatment of private international law in U.S. courts over the past fifty years has been inconsistent and unpredictable. Federal legislation and U.S. treaties have addressed a variety of private international law topics (including judicial assistance and international arbitration), sometimes directly prescribing rules of federal law applicable in U.S. courts, and generally producing satisfactory results.[33] Many other topics of private international law are not, however, governed by U.S. treaties or federal legislation, and the results in these fields have been neither consistent nor satisfactory.

Paralleling their treatment of public international law, U.S. courts have increasingly marginalized their role in resolving international disputes over the past half century, largely through devising limitations on U.S. judicial and legislative jurisdiction. Among other things, U.S. federal courts have imposed increasingly stringent due process limits on U.S. judicial jurisdiction,[34] significantly expanded

---

[29] *Id.* at 1380–90; 1402–03, 1408–12 (Alito, J., concurring); 1412–20 (Gorsuch, J., concurring); see also Kiobel v. Royal Dutch Petroleum Co., 569 U.S. 108, 114, 124–25 (2013) (ATS directed principally to conduct on U.S. territory).

[30] See, e.g., *Jesner*, 138 S. Ct. at 1403; Herero People's Reparations Corp. v. Deutsche Bank, 2003 WL 26119014, at *8 (D.C.C. 2003); Stutts v. De Dietrich Group, 2006 WL 1867060, at *6–*10 (E.D.N.Y. 2006).

[31] See, e.g., Fischer v. Magyar Államvasutak Zrt., 777 F.3d 847, 857 (7th Cir. 2015).

[32] See, e.g., *Sarei*, 550 F.3d 822; Abelesz v. Magyar Nemzeti Bank, 692 F.3d 661, 678–85 (7th Cir. 2012).

[33] See GARY BORN & PETER B. RUTLEDGE, INTERNATIONAL CIVIL LITIGATION IN UNITED STATES COURTS: COMMENTARY AND MATERIALS 861–1220 (6th ed. 2018).

[34] See J. McIntyre Machinery v. Nicastro, 564 U.S. 873, 886 (2011); Goodyear Dunlop Tires Operations, S.A. v. Brown, 564 U.S. 915 (2011); Daimler AG v. Bauman, 134 S. Ct. 746, 763 (2014);

the *forum non conveniens* and *lis pendens* doctrines,[35] formulated constitutional limits on U.S. legislative jurisdiction[36] and revived (and substantially extended) a rigorous presumption against the extraterritorial application of U.S. law,[37] used new applications of the international comity doctrine to limit access to U.S. judicial remedies.[38] As with the treatment of treaties and customary international law, these developments have increasingly marginalized the role of U.S. courts in international disputes—turning the United States from what had been termed a "magnet forum"[39] into one now characterized by "litigation isolationism."[40]

At the same time, U.S. courts and commentators have reached widely divergent conclusions regarding both the status and content of numerous categories of private international law rules. Some issues of private international law—such as judicial jurisdiction[41] and, to a lesser extent, legislative jurisdiction[42]—are governed principally by judge-made federal constitutional limits (derived

---

FOURTH RESTATEMENT § 422; see also Linda Silberman, *Goodyear and Nicastro: Observations from a Transnational and Comparative Perspective*, 63 S.C. L. REV. 591, 598 (2012); Alan Trammell, *A Tale of Two Jurisdictions*, 68 VAND. L. REV. 501, 522 (2015); William Dorsaneo, *Pennoyer Strikes Back: Personal Jurisdiction in a Global Age*, 3 TEX. A. & M. L. REV. 1, 18 (2015).

[35] See FOURTH RESTATEMENT § 424; Kevin Clermont & Theodore Eisenberg, *Exorcising the Evil of Forum-Shopping*, 80 CORNELL L. REV. 1507, 1508 (1995); Donald Earl Childress III, *Forum Conveniens: The Search for a Convenient Forum in Transnational Cases*, 53 VA. J. INT'L L. 157, 169 (2012); Austen Parrish, *Duplicative Foreign Litigation*, 78 GEO. WASH. L. REV. 237 (2010); Christopher Whytock, *The Evolving Forum Shopping System*, 96 CORNELL L. REV. 481, 486–89 (2011).

[36] See, e.g., United States v. Empskamp, 832 F.3d 154, 168–69 (2d Cir. 2016); United States v. Murillo, 826 F.3d 152, 157 (4th Cir. 2016); United States v. Rojas, 812 F. 3d 382, 393 (5th Cir. 2016); FOURTH RESTATEMENT § 403; see also Lea Brilmayer & Charles Norchi, *Extraterritoriality and Fifth Amendment Due Process*, 105 HARV. L. REV. 1217 (1992).

[37] See, e.g., EEOC v. Arabian Am. Oil Co. (Aramco), 499 U.S. 244, 248 (1991); Morrison v. National Australia Bank Ltd., 561 U.S. 247 (2010); *Kiobel*, 569 U.S. at 118, 124; RJR Nabisco, Inc. v. European Cmty., 136 S. Ct. 2090, 2100–201 (2016); FOURTH RESTATEMENT § 404; George Rutherglen, *Territoriality and Its Troubles*, in this volume; see also Gary Born, *A Reappraisal of the Extraterritorial Reach of U.S. Law*, 24 L. & POL'Y INT'L BUS. 1 (1992); Zachary Clopton, *Replacing the Presumption against Extraterritoriality*, 94 B.U. L. REV. 1, 2–4 (2014).

[38] See als, e.g., Donald Earl Childress III, *Comity as Conflict: Resituating International Comity as Conflict of Laws*, 44 U.C. DAVIS L. REV. 11, 51, 59 (2010); William S. Dodge, *International Comity in American Law*, 115 COLUM. L. REV. 2071 (2015); Michael Ramsey, *Escaping "International Comity,"* 83 IOWA L. REV. 893, 893 (1998).

[39] Childress, *supra* note 35, at 162 ("United States is frequently viewed as a 'magnet forum' for transnational cases"); Cassandra Burke Robertson, *Transnational Litigation and Institutional Choice*, 51 BOSTON COLL. L. REV. 1081, 1087 (2010) ("United States as a Magnet Forum").

[40] Pamela Bookman, *Litigation Isolationism*, 67 STAN. L. REV. 1081, 1085 (2015).

[41] See, e.g., Asahi Metal Indus. Co. v. Superior Court of Cal., 480 U.S. 102, 115 (1987); see also Gary Born, *Reflections on Judicial Jurisdiction in International Cases*, 17 GA. J. INT'L & COMP. L. 1, 5–6 (1987); Arthur von Mehren, *Theory and Practice of Adjudicatory Authority in Private International Law: A Comparative Study of the Doctrine, Policies and Practices of Common—And Civil-Law Systems*, 295 RECUEIL DES COURTS 9, 95 (2002); Ralf Michaels, *Two Paradigms of Jurisdiction*, 27 MICH. J. INT'L L. 1003, 1009, 1021 (2006).

[42] See authorities cited *supra* note 36.

from the Due Process Clause); other issues—such as *forum non conveniens*,[43] *lis pendens*,[44] and, less clearly, the validity and enforceability of forum selection clauses[45]—are governed by various formulations of federal procedural law; a few issues—such as the act of state doctrine—are governed by federal common law.[46] In contrast, most other issues of private international law—such as rules governing choice of law[47] and recognition of foreign judgments[48]—are generally treated as matters of State law.

Likewise, the content of many rules of private international law in the United States is varied and uncertain, with the substance of such rules differing from State to State, and between federal and State courts. That includes choice-of-law rules (where widely divergent conflicts rules apply in different States),[49] recognition of judgments (where divergent rules apply in different States),[50] *forum non*

---

[43] Compare DTEX, LLC v. BBVA Bancomer, S.A., 508 F.3d 785, 793 (5th Cir. 2007) (*forum non conveniens* is federal procedural rule applicable in federal courts); Esfeld v. Costa Crociere, S.P.A., 289 F.3d 1300, 1308 (11th Cir. 2002) (same), with Rothluebbers v. Obee, 668 N.W.2d 313, 317 (S.D. 2003) (applying federal common law to *forum non conveniens* analysis in State court); Hall v. Maritek Corp., 170 A.3d 149, 158 (Del. Super. Ct. 2017) (same); FOURTH RESTATEMENT § 424 cmt. *b* (federal procedural law not binding on States); Paul B. Stephan, *The Waning of the Federal Common Law of Foreign Relations*, in this volume (federal procedural law); see BORN & RUTLEDGE, *supra* note 33, at 356–93, 437–43.

[44] Compare *Royal & Sun*, 466 F.3d at 94; *AAR Int'l*, 250 F.3d at 518; and Neuchatel Swiss Gen. Ins. Co. v. Lufthansa Airlines, 925 F.2d 1193, 1194 (9th Cir. 1991) (applying federal common law), with Innes v. Carrascosa, 391 N.J. Super. 453, 492 (App. Div. 2007), and Kingsland Holdings Inc. v. Fulvio Bracco, 1996 WL 422340, at *1 (Del. Ch. July 22, 1996) (applying State common law); FOURTH RESTATEMENT § 424 reporters' note 2 (listing cases applying State law in State courts).

[45] See Atlantic Marine Constr. Co. v. U.S. District Court for Western District of Texas, 134 S. Ct. 568, 580 (2013) ("because both § 1404(a) and the *forum non conveniens* doctrine from which it derives entail the same balancing-of-interests standard, courts should evaluate a forum-selection clause pointing to a nonfederal forum in the same way that they evaluate a forum-selection clause pointing to a federal forum").

[46] See, e.g., Banco Nacional de Cuba v. Sabbatino, 376 U.S. 398, 421–22, 421 n.22, 427 (1964); FOURTH RESTATEMENT § 441; BORN & RUTLEDGE, *supra* note 33, at 793–853; Stephan, *supra* note 43.

[47] See, e.g., Day & Zimmermann, Inc. v. Challoner, 423 U.S. 3, 4–5 (1975); RESTATEMENT (SECOND) OF THE CONFLICT OF LAWS § 6 (Am. Law Inst. 1971); Stephan, *supra* note 43.

[48] See, e.g., THIRD RESTATEMENT § 481 cmt. *a* ("recognition and enforcement of foreign country judgments is a matter of State law"); FOURTH RESTATEMENT § 481 cmt. *a* (same); RESTATEMENT (SECOND) OF THE CONFLICT OF LAWS § 98 cmt. *c*; Phillips USA, Inc. v. Allflex USA, Inc., 77 F.3d 354, 359 (10th Cir. 1996); Choi v. Kim, 50 F. 3d 244, 248 n.7 (3d Cir. 1995)

[49] See Symeon C. Symeonides, *Choice of Law in the American Courts in 2013: Twenty-Seventh Annual Survey*, 62 AM. J. COMP. L. 223, 282 (2014) (summarizing choice-of-law rules in U.S. States); Stephan, *supra* note 43; see also Lea Brilmayer, *Methods and Objectives in the Conflict of Laws: A Challenge*, 35 MERCER L. REV. 555, 555 (1984) ("methodologically bankrupt"); Joel P. Trachtman, *Conflict of Laws and Accuracy in the Allocation of Government Responsibility*, 26 VAND. J. TRANSNAT'L L. 975, 978 ("Conflict of laws is a source of constant embarrassment to lawyers, judges and scholars"); Andrew T. Guzman, *Choice of Law: New Foundations*, 90 GEO. L.J. 883, 890 (2002).

[50] See Ronald A. Brand, *The Continuing Evolution of U.S. Judgments Recognition Law*, 55 COLUM. J. TRANSNAT'L L. 277, 277 (2017) (UFMJRA "has not brought about true uniformity, and significant discrepancies exist among the states"; "significant substantive law differences from state to state"); Melinda Luthin, *U.S. Enforcement of Foreign Money Judgments and the Need for Reform*, 14 U.C. DAVIS J. INT'L L. & POL'Y 111, 120 (2007) ("Although most states have adopted some form of the '62 Recognition Act, the laws are still not *uniform*").

*conveniens* and *lis pendens* (where, again, materially different standards apply in different forums),[51] and enforcement of forum selection clauses.[52] The resulting uncertainty is heightened by the fact that a number of rules of American private international law have been regarded as matters of trial court discretion, largely insulated from appellate review.[53]

Relatedly, the development of private international law rules in the United States has produced anomalous results, which are impossible to reconcile with the nation's interests. Among other things, the current treatment of the validity of international forum selection clauses under the laws of many States (which subjects such clauses to uncertain and restrictive limitations) contradicts the needs of U.S. business and the policies of the federal government (favoring party autonomy). Similarly, existing State law allows recognition and enforcement of foreign judgments more liberally than any other jurisdiction in the world.[54] That is generally true even where serious doubts exist regarding the competence, integrity, and fairness of foreign judicial proceedings,[55] and even without any requirement of reciprocity;[56] existing U.S. law also applies an unusually generous

[51] Compare Inv'rs Equity Life Holding Co. v. Schmidt, 233 Cal. App. 4th 1363, 1368 (Ct. App. 2015), with Huani v. Donziger, 129 A.D.3d 523, 523 (N.Y. App. Div. 2015) and Mar-Land Indus. Contractors, Inc. v. Caribbean Petroleum Ref., L.P., 777 A.2d 774, 778 (Del. 2001); see also Ronald A. Brand, *Challenges to Forum Non Conveniens*, 45 N.Y.U. J. INT'L L. & POL. 1003, 1017 (2013) ("the law of the various states tends to both move away from, and back to, the federal standard").

[52] Compare Guest Assocs., Inc. v. Cyclone Aviation Prod., Ltd., 30 F. Supp. 3d 1278, 1282 (N.D. Ala. 2014) ("the validity of a forum-selection clause must first be determined under general contract law."), and Union Elec. Co. v. Energy Ins. Mut. Ltd., 2014 WL 4450467, at *4 (E.D. Mo. Sep. 10, 2014) (same), with Black Hills Truck & Trailer, Inc. v. MAC Trailer Mfg., Inc., 2014 WL 5782452, at *5 (D.S.D. Nov. 6, 2014) (applying reasonableness requirement), and Red Barn Motors, Inc. v. Nextgear Capital, Inc., 2014 WL 4986674, at *2 (M.D. La. Sept. 29, 2014) (same); see also BORN & RUTLEDGE, *supra* note 33, at 511–28.

[53] Sinochem Int'l Co. v. Malaysia Int'l Shipping Corp., 549 U.S. 422, 425 (2007); see Cassandra Robertson, *Forum Non Conveniens on Appeal: The Case for Interlocutory Review*, 18 Sw. J. INT'L L. 445, 472 (2012) ("Judges possess largely unreviewable discretion in ruling on forum non conveniens motions, and courts often come to inconsistent decisions on very similar facts.").

[54] See, e.g., ANDREAS F. LOWENFELD, INTERNATIONAL LITIGATION AND ARBITRATION 368 (1993) ("[T]he United States . . . appears to be the most receptive of any major country to recognition and enforcement of foreign judgments . . . "); Statement of Professor Linda J. Silberman before the Subcommittee on Commercial and Administrative Law of the U.S. House of Representatives, Committee on the Judiciary, February 12, 2009, at 5 ("recognition and enforcement of foreign country judgments has tended to be much more generous than the treatment given by foreign courts to U.S. judgments"); Montre D. Carodine, *Political Judging: When Due Process Goes International*, 48 WM. & MARY L. REV. 1159, 1162 (2007) ("Blind deference to foreign courts is becoming the norm in the area of judgment recognition").

[55] E.g., UFMJRA, § 4(a)(1); *Ashenden*, 233 F.3d at 476–77 ("The statute, with its reference to 'system,' does not support such a retail approach"); The Society of Lloyd's v. Turner, 303 F.3d 325 (5th Cir. 2002); FOURTH RESTATEMENT § 483 cmts. *b–d*; see Niklaus Meier, *Undue Due Process: Why the Application of Jurisdictional Due Process Requirements to the Recognition of Foreign-Country Judgments Is Inappropriate*, 18 OR. REV. INT'L L. 51 (2016).

[56] FOURTH RESTATEMENT § 484 cmt. *k*; see RECOGNITION AND ENFORCEMENT OF FOREIGN JUDGMENTS ACT: ANALYSIS & PROPOSED FEDERAL STATUTE §11 reporters' note 1, at 133 (Am. Law Inst. 2005); Franklin O. Ballard, *Turnabout Is Fair Play: Why a Reciprocity Requirement Should Be Included in the American Law Institute's Proposed Federal Statute*, 28 HOUS. J. INT'L L. 199, 211 (2006).

"mirror-image" approach to foreign judicial jurisdiction, again making the United States uniquely liberal in recognizing foreign judgments.[57] None of these various developments is the result of federal policy, and, on the contrary, both they and other existing American private international law rules conflict with substantial national objectives and interests.

Finally, there is no coherent national objective underlying the current treatment of international law in American courts. Instead, international law in the United States has been the product of a variety of disparate domestic sources— including the Constitution, federal and State statutes, common law rulings, procedural rules, and inherent judicial authority. The application of these various sources has proceeded with no effort to achieve any central purpose, and has instead been the result of individual doctrines or rules, applied by multiple judiciaries, and often transposed with little or no reflection from domestic to international settings. Unsurprisingly, this process has produced a confused patchwork of uncertain rules, lacking any central unifying purpose, which are often in tension with one another.

Relatedly, many of these rules are also the judge-made products of U.S. courts (principally federal courts), acting without direction from American political branches. Indeed, in those areas of international law where the federal political branches have acted in recent decades, they have almost always expanded, rather than restricted, the role of U.S. courts and U.S. law in international matters.[58] Conversely, no federal policy has supported the current treatment of foreign judgments, which is inconsistent with U.S. foreign relations initiatives (including the negotiation of international agreements for the recognition of foreign judgments). More generally, the marginalization of international law in U.S. courts, and the role of U.S. courts in the development of international law, conflicts with long-standing national interests, dating from the beginning of the Republic, in complying with international law and developing the international legal system.

These developments, and the current treatment of international law by American courts, are fundamentally at odds with historic American conceptions

---

[57] FOURTH RESTATEMENT § 483 cmt. *e*; see, e.g., UFCMJRA, § 5(1), (2); UFMJRA § 5(a), (b); see Silberman, *supra* note 54, at 351, 353 (United States has "mirror image" standard to evaluating foreign courts' judicial jurisdiction in recognition context, in contrast other states); Meier, *supra* note 55, at 54–55.

[58] See, e.g., FED. R. CIV. PRO. RULE 4(k)(2) (national contacts in federal question cases); Clayton Act, 15 U.S.C. §25 (nationwide jurisdiction); Foreign Sovereign Immunities Act, 28 U.S.C. §§ 1601–11 (granting federal courts broad judicial jurisdiction over foreign states and determinations of foreign sovereign immunity); Alien Venue Act, 28 U.S.C. § 1391(d) ("An alien may be sued in any district"); Civil Rights Act of 1991, Pub. L. No. 102-166, § 109(a), 105 Stat. 1071, 1077 (codified at 42 U.S.C. §§ 2000e(f), 2000e-1 (2006) (modifying *Aramco*); Dodd-Frank Wall Street Reform and Consumer Protection Act, Pub. L. No. 111-203, § 929P(b)(2), § 27(b), 124 Stat. 1376, 1862 (2010) (modifying *Morrison*)).

of international law and the role of U.S. courts in the development of international law. The United States has a long-standing and substantial commitment to compliance with both international law and principles of international comity; the unilateral judicial marginalization of international law in American courts betrays that commitment. Likewise, the United States has vital interests in a stable, fair, and effective international legal system and in facilitating the nation's international commerce. The withdrawal of American courts from consideration of issues of international law and resolution of international disputes contradicts these U.S. interests, producing serious damage to the nation and its policies.

## II. Federalizing International Law

The contemporary treatment of public and private international law in U.S. courts is not only seriously flawed. The current treatment of international law by American courts is also contrary to the Constitution's allocation of authority over the nation's foreign relations and international trade. That allocation of constitutional authority mandates treating all rules of public and private international law as matters of federal common law, subject to uniform rules of federal law in both federal and State courts.

## A. Federal Common Law

The standards governing the application of federal common law rules are familiar, if imprecise. It is well settled that recognition of a federal common law rule requires that the rule arise in an area of "uniquely federal interests"[59] or an area in which the "interstate or international nature of the controversy makes it inappropriate for state law to control."[60] As the Supreme Court's most thorough discussion of the issue explained:

> a few areas, involving "uniquely federal interests," are so committed by the Constitution and laws of the United States to federal control that state law is preempted and replaced, where necessary, by federal law of a content prescribed (absent explicit statutory directive) by the courts—so-called "federal common law."[61]

---

[59] *Sabbatino*, 376 U. S. at 426.

[60] Texas Indus. v. Radcliff Materials, 451 U.S. 630, 641 (1981); see United States v. Kimbell Foods, Inc., 440 U. S. 715, 726–29 (1979); United States v. Little Lake Misere Land Co., 412 U.S. 589, 592–94 (1973).

[61] Boyle v. United Technologies Corp., 487 U.S. 500, 504 (1988).

Assuming that an issue arises in area involving compelling federal interests, inquiry then turns on whether "a 'significant conflict' exists between an identifiable federal policy or interest and the operation of state law."[62] Where such a conflict exists, then federal courts are authorized, and arguably required, to formulate and apply rules of federal common law.[63]

## B. Federal Authority over Foreign Relations and Commerce

The recognition and application of rules of international law fall squarely within the scope of federal authority over the nation's foreign relations and international commerce.[64] The grants of federal authority over U.S. foreign affairs in Articles I, II, and III of the Constitution are uniquely expansive.[65] Conversely, State powers relating to foreign relations and the making of international law are not only limited, but, exceptionally, forbidden by Article I, Section 10 of the Constitution—confirming the exclusivity of federal authority.[66]

Federal authority over the nation's foreign commerce is nearly as expansive, while State power in the field is again, exceptionally, limited by Article I, Section 8 of the Constitution.[67] As the Court's decisions interpreting the Foreign Commerce Clause have observed, "[t]he commerce of the United States with foreign nations, is that of the whole United States,"[68] is "exclusive and plenary,"[69] "exclusive and absolute,"[70] and, more recently, "pre-eminently a matter of national concern."[71]

---

[62] *Id.*

[63] *Id.*; *Texas Indus.*, 451 U.S. at 640; *Kimbell Foods*, 440 U.S. at 728–29.

[64] See, e.g., *Sabbatino*, 376 U.S. at 425–27 & n.25; *Texas Indus.*, 451 U.S. at 641.

[65] This includes the power to raise armies and declare war, U.S. CONST. art. I, § 8, cls. 11, 14, regulate foreign commerce, *id.* art. I, § 8, cl. 3, "define and punish . . . Offenses against the Law of Nations," *id.* art. I, § 8, cl. 10, issue letters of marque, *id.* art. I, § 8, cl. 11, regulate immigration and naturalization, *id.* art. I, § 8, cl. 4, regulate the value of "foreign Coin," *id.* art. I, § 8, cl. 5. It also includes the power to appoint and receive ambassadors, *id.* art. II, § 3, cl. 1, negotiate and make treaties, *id.* art. II, § 2, cl. 2, and exercise both "Executive" powers and authority as commander-in-chief, *id.* art. II, § 1, cl. 1, § 2, cl. 1; see MICHAEL D. RAMSEY, THE CONSTITUTION'S TEXT IN FOREIGN RELATIONS 51–73, 74–90, 115–31 (2007); Saikrishna Prakash & Michael Ramsey, *The Executive Power over Foreign Affairs*, 111 YALE L.J. 231 (2001). Finally, Article III provided the federal courts with grants of jurisdiction over multiple categories of cases which were deliberately drafted to encompass, collectively, all disputes that might affect the Nation's foreign relations or involve application of the law of nations. U.S. Constitution, art. III, § 2, cl. 1 (alienage), § 2, cl. 1 (admiralty), § 2, cl. 1 (prize), § 2, cl. 2 (treaties), and § 2, cl. 1 (foreign ambassadors and ministers).

[66] U.S. CONST. art. I, § 10, cls. 1, 3 ("No State shall enter into any Treaty, Alliance, or Confederation, [or] grant Letters of Marque and Reprisal. . . . No State shall, without the Consent of Congress, lay any Duty of Tonnage, . . . enter into any Agreement or Compact with another State, or with a foreign Power. . . .").

[67] U.S. CONST. art. I, § 8, cl. 10.

[68] Gibbons v. Ogden, 22 U.S. (9 Wheat.) 1, 193–95 (1824).

[69] Bd. of Trustees of Univ. of Ill. v. United States, 289 U.S. 48, 56, 59 (1933).

[70] Buttfield v. Stranahan, 192 U.S. 470, 492–93 (1904).

[71] Japan Line, Ltd. v. County of Los Angeles, 441 U.S. 434, 448 (1979)

This allocation of federal and State authority over the nation's foreign relations was designed to serve fundamentally important national objectives—namely, to ensure that national organs, representing national interests and responsible to foreign states, have sole responsibility for the nation's international relations with foreign states. In Madison's words, "[i]f we are to be one nation in any respect, it clearly ought to be in respect to other nations."[72] As Hamilton elaborated, in his classic explanation:

> [T]he peace of the WHOLE ought not to be left at the disposal of a PART. The Union will undoubtedly be answerable to foreign powers for the conduct of its members. And the responsibility for an injury ought ever to be accompanied with the faculty of preventing it.[73]

The Constitution's grants of federal foreign relations and commerce authority are particularly extensive with respect to actions implicating the nation's international legal obligations, whether through the conclusion of "treaties," or other international agreements, or development of the "law of nations" and customary international law. Thus, the Constitution grants the federal government the power to make treaties and other international agreements (Article II, Section 2), to define rules of customary international law (Article I, Section 8), to issue declarations of war and letters of marque (Article I, Section 8), to recognize and conduct diplomatic intercourse with foreign states (Article II, Section 1), and to exercise an expansive "Executive" power, which encompassed a wide range of activities implicating the nation's international legal obligations (Article II, Section 1). These provisions give effect, in multiple respects, to plenary federal authority over the central aspects of the nation's international legal obligations.

The Constitution's grants of federal authority over issues that are now categorized as private international law are no less extensive than those over public international law. That is hardly surprising, given that the framers did not recognize any distinction between the "public" and "private" aspects of the eighteenth-century and early nineteenth-century law of nations, instead understanding the "law of nations" to include all issues of what are today categorized as public and private international law. Thus, the power to make "Treaties" is directed no less to issues of private international law than issues of public international law,[74] and most judicial decisions applying the law of nations in the eighteenth and early

---

[72] THE FEDERALIST No. 42, at 264 (Madison) (Clinton Rossiter ed., 1961).

[73] Id. No. 80, at 476; see also id. No. 44, at 249 (Madison) (urging "immediate responsibility to the nation in all those for whose conduct the nation itself is to be responsible").

[74] A number of the United States' most successful treaties concern private international law matters, including the New York Convention, the ICSID Convention, the Warsaw Convention, and the Hague Evidence and Service Conventions.

nineteenth centuries involved private international law issues.[75] Indeed, it is fair to say that the principal focus of the law of nations in U.S. courts between 1780 and 1800 was what are today categorized as rules of private international law, rather than what is now often characterized as public international law rules.[76]

## C. Federal Interests and Policies Relating to International Law and Comity

Issues of public and private international law do not merely arise in fields that are uniquely, and exclusively, federal in character. Issues of international law also implicate a number of related, vitally important national interests and federal policies, all of which are frustrated by treating rules of public and private international law as matters of State law. In particular, the United States has vital, long-standing national policies regarding compliance with international law,[77] developing the international legal system,[78] furthering international comity,[79] and promoting the nation's international trade and investment.[80]

[75] See, e.g., The Nereide, 13 U.S. (9 Cranch) 388 (1815) (choice of law); The Schooner Exchange v. M'Faddon, 11 U.S. (7 Cranch) 116 (1812) (foreign sovereign immunity); Rose v. Himely, 8 U.S. (4 Cranch) 241 (1808) (judicial jurisdiction; recognition of foreign judgments).

[76] Jay, *supra* note 8, at 822; Dickinson, *supra* note 8, at 26–27.

[77] Violations of U.S. treaty obligations and the law of nations by individual States were one of the principal reasons for adoption of the Constitution, and for the Constitution's grants of exclusive federal authority over foreign relations and commerce and inclusion of treaties in Article VI's Supremacy Clause. David Golove & Daniel Hulsebosch, *A Civilized Nation: The Early American Constitution, the Law of Nations, and the Pursuit of International Recognition*, 85 N.Y.U. L. Rev. 932, 935 (2010); Anthony Bellia Jr. & Bradford Clark, *Why Federal Courts Apply the Law of Nations Even Though It Is Not the Supreme Law of the Land*, 106 Geo. L.J. 1915, 1923 (2018) ("A central reason the Founders established a new Constitution was to enable the United States as a whole to uphold the law of nations and avoid hostilities with other nations."); see also The Federalist No. 3, at 43 (Jay) ("observe the *law of nations*"; "treaties and articles of treaties, as well as the *law of nations*") (emphasis added); *id.* 80, at 439 ("the denial or perversion of justice by the sentences of courts . . . is 'with reason classed among the just causes of war'"); *id.* ("an unjust sentence against a foreigner, . . . if unredressed, be an aggression upon his sovereign, as well as one which violated the stipulations in a treaty or the general *laws of nations*") (emphasis added); James Kent, Commentaries on American Law 1–2 (1826) ("When the United States ceased to be a part of the British empire, and assumed the character of an independent nation, they became subject to that system of rules which reason, morality, and custom had established among the civilized nations of Europe, as their public law. . . . The faithful observance of this law is essential to national character, and to the happiness of mankind.").

[78] See Peter Onuf & Nicholas Onuf, Federal Union, Modern World: The Law of Nations in an Age of Revolutions, 1776–814, at 97–98 (1993); Golove & Hulsebosch, *supra* note 77, at 935 ("core purpose of American constitution-making was to facilitate the admission of the United States into the European-based system of sovereign states governed by the law of nations"); Douglas Sylvester, *International Law as Sword or Shield? Early American Foreign Policy and the Law of Nations*, 32 N.Y.U. J. Int'l L. & Pol'y 1 (1999).

[79] Childress, *supra* note 38, at 59; Dodge, *supra* note 38, at 2072 ("Comity has long served as the basis for the conflicts of laws and enforcement of foreign judgments in the United States.").

[80] Onuf & Onuf, *supra* note 78, at 117–22, 123–34 (1993); Albert Abel, *The Commerce Clause in the Constitutional Convention and in Contemporary Comment*, 25 Minn. L. Rev. 432 (1941), Daniel

All of these policies require that the United States speak with a single, unified voice and act with a single, unified purpose. That is evident from the Constitution's grants of plenary, and exclusive, authority to the federal government over the nation's foreign relations and international commerce, particularly as the United States' international legal rights and obligations and regulatory authority were concerned. That view was adopted in the Supreme Court's earliest considerations of the subject:

> The United States had, by taking a place among the nations of the earth, become amendable to the law of nations; and it was their interest as well as their duty to provide, that those laws should be respected and obeyed; in their national character and capacity, the United States were responsible to foreign nations for the conduct of each State, relative to the laws of nations, and the performance of treaties; and there the inexpediency of referring all such questions to State Courts, and particularly to the Courts of delinquent States became apparent.[81]

As a consequence, the Court continued, in cases involving "the joint [interests] of nations, whose right and privileges relative thereto, are regulated by the law of nations and treaties, such cases necessarily belong to national jurisdiction" and "*all questions touching the justice due to foreign nations . . . depend on national authority.*"[82] In the language of Article VI, the law of nations, as it affected the nation's relations with foreign states, was the supreme Law of the Land, to be applied by federal courts.

The application of State law to issues of international law—both public and private—conflicts significantly with each of the related federal interests and policies outlined earlier. As Jay reasoned in the Federalist Papers, it was of "high importance" that the United States "observe the law of nations towards all [foreign] Powers," while it was "evident" that this "will be more perfectly and punctually done by one national government, than it could be either by thirteen separate States, or by three or four distinct confederacies."[83] Likewise, as Hamilton wrote, the Articles of Confederation were almost universally regarded as inadequate principally because they left the law of nations "liable to the infractions of thirteen different legislatures, and as many different courts of final jurisdiction," and

---

Hulsebosch, *From Imperial to International Law: Protecting Foreign Expectations in the Early United States*, 65 UCLA L. REV. DISC. 142, 146–48 (2018).

[81]  Chisholm v. Georgia, 2 U.S. (2 Dall.) 419, 474 (1793).

[82]  *Id.* at 475–76 (emphasis added).

[83]  THE FEDERALIST No. 3, at 43 (Jay); see *id.* at 44 ("either designed or accidental violations of treaties and of the law of nations [less likely] under one general government than under several lesser ones").

therefore "[t]he faith, the reputation, the peace of the whole Union [were] continually at the mercy of the prejudices, the passions, and the interests of every member of which it was composed."[84]

It is clear, as the framers' generation emphasized, that treating international law as State law would materially increase the risk that the United States would be placed in violation of its international obligations. If international law were a matter of State law (in the absence of a treaty or federal statute), the Queen of England and the President of China would be subject to different customary international law rules of immunity, fashioned by different State courts, in Massachusetts, Michigan, and Texas, as would Japanese and Mexican state officials and consuls and diplomats from a number of foreign states. The same result would generally apply to many other issues of international law—attribution of state responsibility, state succession, treatment of aliens, limits on extraterritorial jurisdiction, validity of U.S. (and non-U.S.) treaties, law of the sea, and international environmental issues—where no U.S. treaty prescribes the rules of international governing U.S. conduct.

As a consequence, if customary international law were not a matter of federal law, a foreign head of state or other senior official could be immune from suit in New York, but not New Jersey; a foreign state could be liable for actions of its agents in California, but not Arizona; a foreign (or U.S.) investor could be entitled compensation under one State's view of international law, but not another State's; and a treaty could be effective or applicable in one State, and not in another State. Indeed, not only State courts would be permitted to apply divergent rules of customary international law, in the foregoing and other cases; in addition, federal courts would be required, by the Rules of Decision Act and otherwise, to apply those contradictory rules—without the possibility of Supreme Court review.[85] All of these results squarely contradict vital U.S. interests and national policies, requiring the formulation of rules of federal common law in the field.

The same analysis applies to rules of private international law and applications of international comity (as the treatment of the act of state doctrine and other rules of private international law as federal common law confirms). As discussed earlier, applying State law to (some) issues of judicial jurisdiction, *forum non conveniens*, forum selection, legislative jurisdiction, choice of law, and recognition of foreign judgments has proven deeply dysfunctional—producing uncertain and unpredictable results, violating principles of international law and comity, inviting retaliation against U.S. parties, and undermining national

---

[84] *Id.* No. 22, at 119 (Hamilton).
[85] Born, *supra* note 20, at 1655–72.

interests in a fair and effective international legal system. Again, these results require the formulation of federal common law rules of private international law.

## D. Federalism and Separation of Powers

These proposed federal common law rules are entirely consistent with, and compelled by, both the Constitution's federal structure and Article VI's Supremacy
Clause. Formulation and application of these rules is not contradicted by the
observation that federal common law rules of international law, in contrast
to U.S. treaties, are not included among the categories of law listed in Article
VI as the "supreme Law of the Land."[86] The same observation about the text of
the Supremacy Clause applies with equal force to all other categories of federal common law,[87] congressional-executive agreements,[88] sole executive
agreements,[89] and federal administrative regulations[90]—all of which are directly
applicable in U.S. courts as federal law, but which are also omitted from Article
VI's text. The Supremacy Clause's reference to the "Laws of the United States"
readily encompasses federal common law rules of international law, just as it
encompasses other forms of federal law other than Acts of Congress.

That conclusion is confirmed by the Supreme Court's holding in *Banco
Nacional de Cuba v. Sabbatino*, where the Court's various opinions unanimously
endorsed Professor Jessup's conclusion that "rules of international law should
not be left to divergent and perhaps parochial state interpretations,"[91] and went
out of its way to declare that this "basic rationale is *equally* applicable to the act of
state doctrine."[92] The Court observed that it could avoid addressing the issue,[93]
but nonetheless announced, in expansive language, that it was

---

[86] U.S. CONST. art. VI, cl. 2 ("This Constitution, and the Laws of the United States which shall be
made in Pursuance thereof; and all Treaties made, or which shall be made, under the Authority of
the United States, shall be the supreme Law of the Land; and the Judges in every State shall be bound
thereby, any Thing in the Constitution or Laws of any State to the Contrary notwithstanding.").

[87] Illinois v. City of Milwaukee, 406 U.S. 91, 100 (1972) (federal common law is "law" for purposes
of statutory arising under jurisdiction; "laws" include "claims founded upon federal common law
as well as those of a statutory origin"); see Henry P. Monaghan, *Supremacy Clause Textualism*, 110
COLUM. L. REV. 731, 756–65 (2010).

[88] See Dames & Moore v. Regan, 453 U.S. 654 (1981).

[89] See United States v. Pink, 315 U.S. 203 (1942); United States v. Belmont, 301 U.S. 324 (1937).

[90] See Monaghan, *supra* note 87, at 756–65.

[91] *Sabbatino*, 376 U.S. at 425.

[92] *Id.* (emphasis added). Justice White's dissenting opinion agreed that rules of international law
were federal law. *Id.* at 451 & n.2 (White, J., dissenting) (international law intended by framers to be
"administered uniformly in the federal courts").

[93] *Id.* at 425.

constrained to make it clear that an issue concerned with a basic choice regarding the competence and function of the Judiciary and the National
Executive in ordering our relationships with other members of the international community must be treated exclusively as an aspect of federal law.[94]

Subsequent Supreme Court decisions confirmed *Sabbatino*'s treatment of rules
of international law as matters of federal common law. In *First National City
Bank v. Banco Para el Comercio Exterior de Cuba*,[95] for example, the Supreme
Court adopted a rule of corporate attribution for companies owned by foreign
states, refusing to apply State (or foreign) law and instead formulating principles "common to both international law and federal common law."[96] More recently, the Court made clear in *Sosa v. Alvarez-Machain* and *Jesner v. Arab Bank*
that the content of the international law claims that were authorized under the
Alien Tort Statute were issues of federal law.[97] As Justice Souter put it in *Sosa*,
citing *Sabbatino* and other federal common law authorities, "*Erie* did not in
terms bar any judicial recognition of new substantive rules, no matter what the
circumstances, and post-*Erie* understanding has identified limited enclaves in
which federal courts may derive some substantive law in a common law way."[98]
Notably, in each of these cases, the relevant rule of international law that was
governed by federal common law, not State law, was a rule of so-called private international law, not public international law—including the act of state doctrine,
the attribution of corporate liability, and private rights of action for damages.

Textually, Article VI's reference to the "Laws of the United States" which "shall
be made" pursuant to the Constitution also readily encompasses rules of international law which have been made a part of the nation's laws by actions undertaken by the federal political branches pursuant to their plenary (and exclusive)
authority under the Constitution; those rules of international law are therefore,
as provided by Article VI, supreme over contrary State law. There is no serious
doubt that the term "Laws" encompasses the "Law" of Nations,[99] nor that the

[94] *Id.* at 426.
[95] 462 U.S. 611 (1983).
[96] *Id.* at 623.
[97] Sosa v. Alvarez-Machain, 542 U.S. 692, 730 (2004); *Jesner*, 138 S. Ct. at 1405–08.
[98] *Id.* at 729–30 (citing Texas Industries, Inc. v. Radcliff Materials, Inc., 451 U.S. 630, 641 (1981));
see also *Sosa*, 542 U.S. at 723, 730.
[99] That conclusion is supported by the breadth of the term "Laws," an expansive term that includes
all categories of "law," not just statutory enactments. Contemporary dictionaries defined "law" as
including "[a] decree, edit, statute, or custom, publicly established," "judicial process" and "[a]n established or constant mode of process," Dictionary by Samuel Johnson 18 (1792), and "a particular
form or mode of judging; as law martial, law mercantile." Dictionary of Samuel Johnson 423 (1828).
That is confirmed by the fact that, as discussed elsewhere, the law of nations was commonly referred
to in the late eighteenth and early nineteenth century as the "law of the land," or "part of the law of
the land," reflecting its obvious status as "law." The Nereide, 13 U.S. (9 Cranch) 388, 423 (1815) ("the
Court is bound by the law of nations, which is part of the law of the land"); Henfield's Case, 11 F. Cas.
1099, 1120 n.6 (C.C.D. Pa. 1793) (prosecution's argument (unchallenged by defendant): "the law of

framers so understood the term.[100] Moreover, Article VI's reference to "Laws" was intentionally adopted instead of earlier proposals that would have limited the Supremacy Clause to "Acts" of Congress.[101] Rather, as finally adopted, Article VI was drafted expansively to encompass all forms of U.S. "Law," including forms of U.S. law other than Acts of Congress, provided only that these forms of law be made pursuant to the Constitution.

Likewise, it is clear that Article VI's reference to the "Laws *of the United States*" includes the law of nations when that law comes to be applied by American courts. That conclusion follows inevitably from the inescapable, and universally acknowledged, fact that the law of nations was binding on the United States: As such, it would make neither logical nor practical sense to treat the law of nations as only a matter of State law. That is precisely the way that the framers' generation, and subsequent American authorities, referred to the law of nations. In particular, the law of nations was routinely referred to by the framers, and in subsequent decades, as the "law of the United States,"[102] the "law of the nation,"[103] "national law,"[104] or "American law."[105] These references are impossible to interpret as anything other than expressing an understanding that the law of nations was the "law of the United States." In contrast, there are virtually no instances in which someone, during the framers' generation, said that the law of nations was *not* the law of the United States.

There were frequent references, during and after the framers' generation, to the law of nations being part of the laws of individual States.[106] These references

nations, being the common law of the civilized world, may be said, indeed, to be a part of the law of every civilized nation").

[100] As the Supreme Court emphasized in the first years of the Republic, "[t]he United States had, by taking a place among the nations of the earth, become amendable to the law of nations; and it was their interest as well as their duty to provide, that those laws should be respected and obeyed." Chisholm v. Georgia, 2 U.S. (2 Dall.) 419, 474 (1793).

[101] See Peter L. Strauss, *The Perils of Theory*, 83 NOTRE DAME L. REV. 1567, 1568–71 (2008) (initial drafts of Article VI applied to "Acts," but were revised to refer to "Laws"); see also John C. Harrison, *International Law in U.S. Courts within the Limits of the Constitution*, in this volume.

[102] See, e.g., Henfield's Case, 11 F. Cas. 1099, 1102–104 (C.C.D. Pa. 1793) (No. 6,360); United States v. Ravara, 2 U.S. (2 Dall.) 299, 299 n.* (C.C.D. Pa. 1793); United States v. The Ariadne, 24 F. Cas. 851, 856 (D.C.D. Pa. 1812) (No. 14,465); *John Jay's Charge to the Grand Jury of the Circuit Court for the District of Virginia (May 22, 1793)*, 2 THE DOCUMENTARY HISTORY OF THE SUPREME COURT, 1789–1800 at 381, 382 (Maeva Marcus et al. eds., 1988); *id.* at 360; *James Wilson's Charge to the Grand Jury of a Special Session of the Circuit Court for the District of Pennsylvania (July 22, 1793) id.* at 414.

[103] *John Jay's Charge to the Grand Jury of the Circuit Court for the District of New York (April 12, 1790)*, 2 *id.* at 29; John Jay's 1793 Virginia Charge, *id.* at 380.

[104] See, e.g., *Henfield's Case*, 11 F. Cas. at 1117.

[105] See, e.g., Woodworth v. Fulton, 1 Cal. 295, 306 (1850).

[106] See, e.g., Respublica v. De Longchamps, 1 U.S. (1 Dall.) 111, 114, 116 (Pa. O. & T. 1784) (This case "must be determined on the principles of the laws of nations, which form a part of the municipal law of Pennsylvania. . . . The first crime in the indictment is an infraction of the law of Nations. This law, in its full extent, is part of the law of this State. . . ."); Wilcocks v. Union Ins. Co., 2 Binn. 574, 1809 1427 (Pa. 1809); Taylor v. Sumner, 4 Mass. 56, 108 WL 1039 (1808).

have been cited for the proposition that the law of nations was not regarded as U.S. law, because it was considered part of the laws of the several States.[107] That logic is flawed: It ignores the fact that the law of nations was part of the law of *both* the United States and individual States. As the Supreme Court later observed, "[i]nternational law is a part of our law *and as such is the law of all States of the Union.*"[108] Indeed, it is precisely because the law of nations was regarded as "national" or "United States" law that it was also regarded as part of the law of all the several States (not just some, or most of them). In this respect, the law of nations was no different from other types of United States law, which were also regarded (as Article VI mandates) as part of the law of each of the several States.[109]

It is also clear that the rules of the law of nations that are applied in American courts are among Article VI's "Laws of the United States which shall be made in pursuance" of the Constitution. Some commentators have argued that, even if the law of nations was U.S. law, it was not considered to be law that was "made in pursuance of" the Constitution.[110] The rationale for this conclusion is that the law of nations was not "made" by individual nations, but was instead the joint product of multiple nations or a branch of the law of nature—neither involving lawmaking under the U.S. Constitution.[111] That analysis is flawed.

The framers chose expansive language ("Laws" of the United States that are "made" in pursuance of the Constitution), rather than narrower language (Legislation "enacted," Acts "adopted" or Bills "passed" pursuant to Article I of the Constitution). The term "made" had a very broad meaning in the framers' generation, including create, form, arrive at, compose, produce, establish, and constitute.[112] Article VI's text readily allows a conclusion that the law of nations was "made" applicable in American courts, thus comprising part of the Law of the United States, when, "in pursuance of" the Constitution, the nation was formed and asserted rights under international law, thereby subjecting it to that law, and when the nation's international legal rights (and obligations) were acted upon by the federal political branches.[113]

---

[107] Bellia & Clark, *supra* note 77, at 1919.

[108] Skiriotes v. Florida, 313 U.S. 69, 72–73 (1941) (emphasis added).

[109] See, e.g., Claflin v. Houseman, 93 U.S. 130, 136 (1876) ("The laws of the United States are laws in the several States, and just as much binding on the citizens and courts thereof as the State laws are."); *Pacificus No. 1*, 15 THE PAPERS OF ALEXANDER HAMILTON 34 (Harold C. Syrett ed., 1973) ("the laws of the land (of which the law of Nations is a part)").

[110] RAMSEY, *supra* note 65, at 348–49; Bellia & Clark, *supra* note 77, at 1931 ("the law of nations was not 'made in Pursuance' of the Constitution"); Curtis Bradley, *The Alien Tort Statute and Article III*, 42 VA. J. INT'L L. 587 (2002).

[111] Andrew Kent, *Congress's Under-Appreciated Power to Define and Punish Offenses Against the Law of Nations*, 85 TEX. L. REV. 843, 938, n.420 (2007).

[112] Dictionary by Samuel Johnson 35 (1792).

[113] But see John Harrison, *The Constitution and the Law of Nations*, 106 GEO. L.J. 1659, 1671–80 (2018).

This was exactly the formulation employed by contemporary authorities in explaining why the law of nations was applicable to, and in, the United States.[114] As Alexander Hamilton explained why the law of nations was applicable to the United States: "we have taken our station among nations[,] have claimed the benefits of the laws which regulate them, and must in our turn be bound by the same laws."[115] Other authorities described the reception of international law in the United States in the same manner: "The United States had, by taking a place among the nations of the earth, become amenable to the law of nations; and it was their interest as well as their duty to provide, that those laws should be respected and obeyed."[116]

Thus, the law of nations was not, in its international form, law made by the United States, pursuant to the Constitution; instead, the law of nations was law made by the community of nations. In that sense, the law of nations was not U.S. law, made pursuant to the Constitution. Critically, however, both the framers and subsequent generations understood that the various rules of the law of nations needed to be accepted by the United States before it would either be binding on the United States or applicable as the law of the land in the United States. Equally critically, in the eyes of the framers, the United States' acceptance of the

---

[114] See, e.g., Bentzon v. Boyle, 9 Cranch 191, 198 (1815) ("The law of nations is the great source from which we derive those rules respecting belligerent and neutral rights which are recognized by all civilized and commercial states throughout Europe and America. . . . The United States having, at one time, formed a component part of the British Empire, their prize law was our prize law. When we separated it continued to be our prize law, so far as it was adapted to our circumstances, and was not varied by the power which was capable of changing it."); KENT, *supra* note 77, at 1–2 ("When the United States ceased to be a part of the British empire, and assumed the character of an independent nation, the became subject to that system of rules which reason, morality, and custom had established among the civilized nations of Europe, as their public law. . . . The faithful observance of this law is essential to national character, and to the happiness of mankind.").

[115] *Second Letter from Phocian to the Considerate Citizens of New York* (Apr. 1784), in 3 THE PAPERS OF ALEXANDER HAMILTON, *supra* note 109, at 550.

[116] Chisholm v. Georgia, 2 U.S. (2 Dall.) 419, 474 (1793); see also *The Rutgers Briefs, Brief No. 6*, in 1 THE LAW PRACTICE OF ALEXANDER HAMILTON: DOCUMENTS AND COMMENTARY 331, 367 (Julius Goebel Jr. ed., 1964) (United States, by their "public acts . . . claim[ing] the sanction of the law of Nations . . . formally assented to that law"); *id.* at 341–42 ("we have appealed to and acted upon the modern law of Nations as understood in Europe. Various resolutions of Congress during our revolution—the correspondencies of Executive officers—the decisions of our Courts of Admiralty, all recognised this standard"); *Pacificus No. 1*, 15 THE PAPERS OF ALEXANDER HAMILTON, *supra* note 109, at 40 ("The Executive is charged with the execution of all laws, the laws of Nations as well as the Municipal law, which recognizes and adopts those laws."); John Jay's Charge to the Grand Jury of the Circuit Court for the District of New York (April 12, 1790) (in 2 THE DOCUMENTARY HISTORY OF THE SUPREME COURT, *supra* note 102, at 29 ("the Laws of Nations make Part of the Laws of this, and every other civilized Nation"); *id* at 27 ("We had become a Nation—as such we were responsible to others for the observance of the Laws of Nations; and as our national Concerns were to be regulated by national Laws, national Tribunals became necessary for the Interpretation & Execution of them both"); cf. Miller v. United States, 78 U.S. (11 Wall.) 268, 315–16 (1870) (Field, J., dissenting) ("When the United States became an independent nation, they became . . . 'subject to that system of rules which reason, morality, and custom had established among the civilized nations of Europe as their public law.' ").

law of nations came pursuant to the Constitution, when the newly formed nation, through the federal political branches acting pursuant to the Constitution, first accepted and then subsequently relied upon the law of nations.

## E.  Separation of Powers

Separation of powers concerns also argue for, not against, the proposed body of federal law. Consistent with the historic role of American courts in developing rules of public and private international law in multiple different fields, U.S. courts would formulate and apply specific legal rules to govern particular issues, rather than apply open-ended balancing analyses which purported to weigh U.S. foreign policy interests on an ad hoc basis in individual disputes. These rules would provide predictable, uniform standards governing issues of international law in U.S. courts, without intruding on the authority of the federal political branches to conduct U.S. foreign relations. Under the proposal made here, this body of federal common law would be directly applicable in U.S. courts, like self-executing treaties, only when the federal political branches so intended. This body of federal common law would entail materially less risk of judicial interference in the political branches' conduct of U.S. foreign relations and regulation of international commerce than does the treatment of rules of international law as matters of State law.[117]

Moreover, the rules of public and private international law comprising this body of federal common law would be directly applicable in U.S. courts, like self-executing treaties, only when the federal political branches so intended. In many instances, particularly with respect to "new" rules of public international law, such as human rights or environmental protections, evidence of such intentions would be lacking. Similarly, rules of public international law directed toward interstate conduct or relations, such as the laws of war, would also typically not be directly applicable in U.S. courts.

In contrast, most rules of private international law would be directly applicable in U.S. courts, consistent with the historic character of such rules. The judicial branch, whether state or federal, has historically played the leading, and often exclusive, role in formulating rules governing international forum selection, *forum non conveniens*, antisuit injunctions against foreign proceedings, international *lis pendens*, act of state, choice of foreign law, foreign state and related immunities, and recognition of foreign judgments. These rules are also generally

---

[117] Some commentators suggest that federal courts lack the capacity to realize this goal. See Stephan, *supra* note 43. That misses the essential point, which is that a single, federal judiciary is better able than fifty state judiciaries to minimize interference with federal interests and policies.

well suited for judicial, rather than legislative, action: All are focused on the litigation process, rather than primary commercial or other conduct by primary parties. Judicial formulation of common law rules regarding these issues, applicable principally in commercial and other civil litigation between private parties, does not intrude significantly upon historic federal legislative and executive prerogatives.

## III.  Federalized International Law

Under the analysis outlined in the previous section, all rules of international law must be rules of federal common law. The federalization of international law is compelled by the Constitution's exclusive grants of plenary authority over the nation's foreign relations and foreign commerce to the federal government and by federal policies and interests relating to international law and comity. Divergent State court decisions (or legislative enactments) addressing issues of international law, both public and private, conflict with long-established federal policies regarding international law, the international legal system, international comity, and the nation's foreign commerce. These policies require treating all issues of public and private international law as matters of federal common law— in the manner discussed in the following section.

Preliminarily, the proposed body of federal common law would apply only to rules of international law. In particular, as detailed in the following, the proposed body of law would apply to rules that define the rights and obligations of states under public international law, as well as rules of private international law that define the extent of U.S. judicial and legislative jurisdiction over foreign parties and conduct, and the effects of foreign laws, judgments, and judicial proceedings in U.S. courts.

This body of federal law would include only those rules that are addressed specifically to the treatment of foreign states, parties, laws, judicial proceedings, and judgments, historically categorized as issues of public or private international law, or the "law of nations." None of these various rules of international law is directed toward domestic conduct; instead, all of these rules are specifically and exclusively addressed to foreign and international matters, involving the rights and obligations of the United States under international law and the treatment of foreign states, laws, parties, conduct, judicial proceedings, and judgments in U.S. courts. The proposed body of federal law would also not extend more broadly, to rules of substantive contract, tort, or property law, whether in international or domestic settings, or to other issues, merely because their application might affect or implicate U.S. "foreign relations" or "foreign policy."

The existence and content of rules of international law in these areas would be derived in significant part by the positions and statement of the federal political branches. International law rules would not be matters of State law, and would instead be ascertained by reference to the interests of the United States, as formulated by Congress, the Senate, and the president. The federal political branches' constitutional responsibility for matters of international law, and the constitutional requirement that the Nation speak with one voice about matters of international law, require looking to the policies and actions of those branches, and not the several States, to determine what rules of customary international law the United States has accepted and what their content is.

The rules of federal common law summarized in the following discussion are neither exhaustive (because a number of rules of international law are not addressed) nor definitive (because different substantive rules of international law are plausible). Rather, the rules outlined in this section are representative and illustrate how the proposed body of federal common law could address significant issues of international law; international rules with different content might well be preferred, for example, regarding limitations on judicial or legislative jurisdiction, choice-of-law rules or *forum non conveniens* rules. Nonetheless, the rules outlined in the following discussion illustrate how the proposed body of federal common law would function, the relative ease with which these rules could be formulated and the advantages that federalized rules of international law would provide.

## A.  Public International Law

Under the proposed approach to international law, the existence and content of all rules of customary international law would be matters of federal law. This would include jurisdictional limitations imposed by international law (on judicial, legislative, and enforcement jurisdiction); jurisdictional immunities (for heads of state, diplomats, consular officials, and otherwise); rules of treaty validity and interpretation; laws of war and humanitarian law; law of the sea; international human rights law; rules of attribution and liability; international environmental law; and international investment law. In all of these areas, the existence of rules of customary international law and the content of any such rules would be matters of federal law, not the law of individual States.

Importantly, despite the character of international law as federal law, not all rules of customary international law are directly applicable, or self-executing, in U.S. courts. This parallels the treatment of U.S. treaties and other international agreements, only some of which are self-executing. Only where the federal political branches have either expressly or impliedly approved of direct application of a rule of customary international law would the rule apply in U.S. courts.[118] The same consideration of the content, character, and surrounding context of particular international law rules is required in the case of rules of customary international law as with treaties and other international agreements.

Applying this analysis, some rules of customary international law would be directly applicable in U.S. courts, without further authorization by the political branches, while others would not be. U.S. courts have historically been hesitant to conclude that the federal political branches have impliedly authorized the direct application of rules of public international law addressing relations between a state and its citizens.[119] That reluctance is particularly acute where the asserted rules of international law are aspirational, emergent, or ambiguous—as the Supreme Court has emphasized in *Sabbatino, Sosa,* and elsewhere.[120] As a consequence, as a matter of federal law, many rules of international law addressing issues of human rights, humanitarian law, and the law of war would, as a matter of federal law, presumptively not be directly applicable in U.S. courts.

On the other hand, some rules of customary international law would generally be directly applicable in U.S. courts. Jurisdictional immunities are a prime example of international law rules directed specifically to national courts, which would be presumptively applicable in American courts. International law limitations on judicial and legislative jurisdiction would also be presumptively applicable—again being directed to national courts.[121]

## B.  Private International Law

Under the proposed approach to international law, the existence and content of all rules of private international law would also be matters of federal law. The proposed body of federal common law would include substantive rules governing judicial jurisdiction, *forum non conveniens, lis pendens,* antisuit injunctions, forum selection agreements, legislative jurisdiction, choice of law, act of state doctrine, and recognition of foreign judgments. At the same time, this body of federal law would leave intact substantial elements of existing American private international law. In a number of fields, federal common law rules of private

---

[118] Born, *supra* note 20, at 1701–11.

[119] *Id.* at 1713–15.

[120] *Sabbatino,* 376 U.S. 398, 427–37 (holding that in the absence of a treaty or other express agreement, federal courts do not have jurisdiction over disputes between the United States and a foreign country over a taking); *Sosa,* 542 U.S. 692, 738 (holding that the proposed "aspiration[al]" rule of customary international law was too vague to give rise to an independent federal cause of action); and *Jesner,* 138 S. Ct. 1386, 1403 ("the separation-of-powers concerns that counsel against courts creating private rights of action apply with particular force in the context of the [Alien Torts Act]").

[121] Born, *supra* note 20, at 1717–18.

international law would be based in substantial part on those rules which are currently followed by a majority of U.S. courts. Adopting federal common law rules would build on existing U.S. private international law developments, while remedying the significant defects in the current treatment of the subject.

Preliminarily, in contrast to a number of public international law rules (which would not be directly applicable in U.S. courts), most rules that are traditionally categorized as matters of private international law would apply directly in U.S. courts. Private international law rules governing issues of judicial jurisdiction, forum selection, choice of law, recognition of judgments, and similar matters are all by their nature addressed specifically to courts (prescribing the jurisdiction of courts, the law applicable in courts, and the recognition by courts of other judicial decisions) and clearly intended for direct judicial application. Unsurprisingly, all of these topics were governed principally by common law rules, formulated by courts, rather than legislatures, when the Constitution was drafted.[122]

Most rules of private international law have also continued to be principally the subject of common law rules since 1789. Joseph Story's *Commentaries* addressed issues of judicial and legislative jurisdiction, forum selection, choice of law, and recognition of foreign judgments, treating them as common law subjects, with virtually no reference to statutory or similar legislative sources.[123] Similarly, beginning with *Rose v. Himely*[124] and *Schooner Exchange*[125] and continuing from *Pennoyer v. Neff*[126] to *Daimler AG v. Baumann*,[127] the limits on the judicial jurisdiction of U.S. courts have been primarily the subject of common law, judge-made rules. Choice-of-law rules are no less subjects of common law treatment today[128] than they were when the first edition of Story's *Commentaries* was published in 1834. Rules governing the recognition of foreign judgments were judge-made before *Rose v. Himely* and *Hilton v. Guyot*,[129] and, even today, they generally remain matters of common law in most U.S. States, either formally or effectively.[130] *Forum non conveniens, lis pendens,* and other matters of forum

---

[122] See Symeon C. Symeonides, *Choice-of-Law Revolution Fifty Years after Currie: An End and a Beginning,* 2015 U. ILL. L. REV. 1847, 1850, 1863; Robert Leflar, *Choice-of-Law Statutes,* 44 TENN. L. REV. 951, 951 (1976); Willis L.M. Reese, *Statutes in Choice of Law,* 35 AM. J. COMP. L. 395, 395, 403 (1987).

[123] JOSEPH STORY, COMMENTARIES ON THE CONFLICT OF LAWS (1st ed. 1834).

[124] 8 U.S. 241 (1808).

[125] 11 U.S. 116 (1812).

[126] 95 U.S. 714 (1878).

[127] 571 U.S. 117 (2014).

[128] Symeonides, *supra* note 122, at 1917.

[129] See *Hilton,* 159 U.S. at 163 ("But when, as is the case here, there is no written law upon the subject, the duty rests upon the judicial tribunals of ascertaining and declaring what the law is. . . ."); *Rose,* 8 U.S. at 269.

[130] Even in those States that have adopted the UFMJRA, the provisions of the act are based squarely on *Hilton*'s common law rules, and the application of those provisions remains a matter of common law interpretation.

selection have also been developed as common law rules, and remain quintessentially common law in character.

It is also unsurprising that issues of private international law have historically been treated as matters of common law. Almost all private international law subjects involve the conduct of the litigation process; issues of judicial jurisdiction, forum selection (including *forum non conveniens* and *lis pendens*), choice of law, recognition of judgments, and judicial assistance do not involve the prescription of substantive standards for primary conduct, but instead involve aspects of the adjudicative process itself.[131] These types of issues have historically been primarily the subject of judge-made common law rules in the United States.

For more than two centuries, the federal political branches have acknowledged and accommodated the application of these common law rules—which have been fashioned and applied almost entirely by federal or State courts—with virtually no legislative interference. Both the nature and content of these rules, as well as their historical context, confirm the authority of U.S. courts (whether state or federal) to apply them, without further authorization by the federal political branches. Thus, where the rule of international law provides foreign states, heads of state, and foreign consuls with immunity in national court proceedings, limits the scope of judicial jurisdiction of U.S. courts, requires judicial abstention or restraint, determines issues of forum selection, or addresses the appropriate extent of international judicial assistance, the terms and content of those rules themselves evidence the intentions of the political branches that the rules apply directly in U.S. courts (because, by their terms, those rules are addressed to the judiciary and because, historically, those rules have routinely been developed and applied by U.S. courts).

## C. Renewing International Law in American Courts

The proposed federal common law rules would provide a number of important advantages, correcting the serious defects that exist in the current treatment of both public and private international law in U.S. courts. These advantages are structural and would exist regardless of the specific rules of international law that were adopted on particular topics.

First, the proposed approach would treat all rules of international law as rules of federal common law. The existing patchwork of State laws (and, in some instances, federal constitutional or federal procedural law) applicable to most private international law rules, and, potentially, customary international

---

[131] See SYMEON C. SYMEONIDES, AMERICAN PRIVATE INTERNATIONAL LAW 15, 16 (2008).

law rules, would be replaced with a single, uniform set of federal common law rules. With respect to private international law, the proposed federal rules would eliminate the current uncertainties and anomalies resulting from the disparate treatment of foreign judgments, laws, and judicial proceedings in different U.S. States: Foreign judgments or laws, that would be recognized in one U.S. State, are not recognized in others, and vice versa. The proposed body of federal common law would eliminate these uncertainties and anomalies, instead providing a uniform set of American private international law rules in all U.S. States. In doing so, these federal common law rules would better achieve the objectives of private international law rules and better serve the nation's interests, in the development of the international legal system, application of international comity and regulation of foreign trade.

Similarly, the proposed body of federal law would also provide for uniform treatment of customary international law in U.S. courts, as well as both uniformity and clarity in determining when U.S. treaties and other international agreements are self-executing. Under existing U.S. law, the status of customary international law, treaties, and other agreements is often unclear, with uncertain standards addressing when treaties and other agreements are self-executing. This approach creates material risks of U.S. noncompliance with both international law and treaty obligations (as evidenced by the current treatment of those obligations by the federal government).[132] Customary international law cannot, consistent with U.S. compliance with its international obligations, be a matter of either uncertainty or of State law. Likewise, the status of treaties should not be subject to uncertainty, which leaves it unclear whether Congress must enact legislation to implement the treaty domestically or, alternatively, whether the treaty is self-executing. The better rule would make it clear, for the political branches and otherwise, what the status of a U.S. treaty is.

Second, the proposed approach would permit international law to be developed in American courts as a coherent body of law, rather than as separate and largely disconnected rules based on disparate sources, often derived from State law, with no guiding purpose. Issues of jurisdiction, *forum non conveniens, lis pendens*, and antisuit injunctions, as well as rules of customary international law, could be developed in a single, comprehensive manner, rather than as unrelated rules. Rather than patching together disparate, sometimes contradictory rules, based on different legal sources (e.g., Due Process Clause, inherent judicial authority over dockets, State law), the proposed body of federal common law would permit development of a single, comprehensive body of international law consciously designed to advance the nation's interests, based upon the directions

---

[132] See, e.g., Medellín v. Texas, 552 U.S. 491 (2008) (refusing to give effect to ICJ judgment).

and policies of the federal political branches. Moreover, in contrast to the current judicial treatment of international law, the proposed body of federal common law would be based upon the directions of the federal political branches—rather than disparate judicial views about State legislative enactments or procedural rules, nineteenth-century territoriality principles, or the convenience of individual judges.

The proposed approach would also fill in the interstices of what has become, albeit in a haphazard and erratic manner, an increasingly federalized treatment of international law in the United States. As discussed earlier, either treaties (or other international agreements) or federal legislation governs broad areas of international law in U.S. courts. Federal legislation addressing issues of foreign sovereign immunity, judicial assistance, and forum selection,[133] and U.S. treaties addressing issues of judicial assistance, recognition of international arbitration agreements and awards, sale of goods, air transport, and investment protection,[134] illustrate the detailed, far-ranging character of federal law in the field. The (judicially formulated) federal constitutional limitations on U.S. judicial and legislative jurisdiction add further reach and detail to the body of federal law addressing international issues. As a consequence, the existing treatment of international law in U.S. courts produces anomalies, such as the application of federal law to international arbitration agreements and awards, and State law to forum selection agreements and foreign court judgments.[135] The application of rules of federal common law to fill in the interstices, and connect different bodies, of existing treaties and legislation would eliminate these anomalies, while completing, in a reasoned manner, the partial federalization of international law that has already occurred.

Third, the proposed body of federal common law would entail American courts more assiduously considering and expressly giving effect to national policies and interests, formulated by the federal political branches, than the current treatment of international law. The rules of federal common law governing issues of international law would be based upon articulated federal policies and national interests (including compliance with international law, development of the international legal system, and facilitation of U.S international commerce), rather than the various, inconsistent policies underlying State laws, federal constitutional and procedural law, and the like. As a consequence, American private

---

[133] BORN & Rutledge, *supra* note 33, at 218–19 (foreign sovereign immunity), 863–67, 959–62, and 1154–65 (judicial assistance), 513–15 (forum selection).

[134] *Id.* at. 1019–25 (Hague Evidence Convention); 905–907 (Hague Service Convention), 1152–55 (New York Convention).

[135] See BORN & Rutledge, *supra* note 33, at 1152–62 (international arbitration agreements), 511–16 (forum selection agreements), 1069–71 (foreign court judgments).

international law rules would be materially more reflective of, and responsive to, the policies and actions of the federal political branches.

This would be particularly true with respect to those aspects of U.S. private international law which have been constitutionalized. Judicial applications of the Due Process Clause have largely removed issues of U.S. judicial and legislative jurisdiction from the reach of the federal political branches—notwithstanding the increasing importance of these subjects to the United States. The proposed approach would replace these constitutional limitations with federal common law rules that would be both more responsive to the federal political branches and subject to legislative revision by Congress or to being superseded by a U.S. treaty. This would materially advance the nation's interests, and be materially more consistent with the Constitution's allocation of authority, particularly given the political branches' primary responsibility for the nation's foreign relations and commerce.

Fourth, the proposed approach would also moderate the marginalization of international law that has occurred over the past fifty years. Among other things, constitutional restrictions on U.S. judicial jurisdiction over foreign parties, based on nineteenth-century concepts of interstate sovereignty, would be replaced by federal common law limitations that give greater weight to the policies of the federal political branches and to contemporary rules of international law. This would allow broader assertions of U.S. judicial jurisdiction than currently permitted, paralleling those in many foreign states, while presumptively prohibiting bases of jurisdiction that are rejected internationally. It would also permit jurisdiction over foreign defendants based on national contacts, rather than requiring contacts with a single U.S. State. Similarly, current approaches to the doctrines of *forum non conveniens* and *lis pendens* would be replaced by federal common law rules providing for greater consistency and heightened consideration of national regulatory policies. As a consequence, U.S. judicial jurisdiction in international cases would be exercised more broadly, with greater attention to U.S. regulatory interests and limitations of international law.[136]

Similarly, existing due process and other constitutional limits on U.S. legislative jurisdiction would be replaced by federal common law limits based on international law. At the same time, the existing presumption against the extraterritorial application of U.S. law, and State choice-of-law rules based on the First Restatement of the Conflict of Laws, would be replaced by contemporary international law and choice-of-law approaches, which give greater weight to U.S. regulatory requirements.[137] This approach would simultaneously give greater effect

---

[136] *Id.* at 49–57, 79–89, 127–303, & 532–36.
[137] *Id.* at 629–35.

to federal legislative protections and policies, while ensuring that the exercise of U.S. legislative jurisdiction was consistent with international law.

These changes in existing American private international law rules would moderate the marginalization of international law that has occurred in U.S. courts over the past fifty years. The proposed body of federal common law would accord contemporary rules of customary international law materially more significance than existing American practice (which is instead focused principally on nineteenth-century conceptions of territoriality or considerations of local convenience). The proposed federal common law rules would also moderate the trend toward judicial isolationism in American courts, instead according U.S. courts a more significant role in resolving international disputes and applying international law—as the framers and most subsequent generations contemplated.

Fifth, the scope of the proposed body of federal common law is well defined and clearly demarcated from other fields. As noted earlier, the proposed body of federal common law would apply only to rules of international law—rules that are addressed specifically to the international rights and obligations of the United States and the treatment of foreign states, parties, laws, judicial proceedings, and judgments in American courts—historically categorized as issues of public or private international law, or the "law of nations." None of these various rules of public and private international law is directed toward domestic (intrastate or interstate) conduct; instead, all of these rules are specifically and exclusively addressed to international matters, involving the rights and obligations of the United States under international law and the treatment of foreign states, laws, parties, conduct, judicial proceedings, and judgments in U.S. courts.

The proposed federal common law rules would not extend more broadly, to issues of substantive contract or tort law, but would instead be limited to issues of public and private international law. Moreover, the proposed body of federal common law would not include issues merely because they implicate or touch upon U.S. foreign relations in particular cases. It also would not require courts to attempt to assess the impact of decisions in particular cases on the nation's foreign relations or to engage in the balancing of foreign policy considerations. Rather, the proposed body of federal common law would only involve the traditional judicial functions of formulating and applying specific rules of law regarding particular issues of public and private international law. Indeed, precisely such rules are already applied in numerous fields (such as *forum non conveniens* in federal courts, forum selection clauses in admiralty cases, choice of law in admiralty and federal question cases, and recognition of judgments in federal question cases).[138]

---

[138] *Id.* at 349–57, 511–15, 1067–76.

Finally, the proposed approach to private international law would also rationalize U.S. rules regarding judicial jurisdiction and forum selection, on the one hand, and the recognition of judgments, on the other. That approach would apply a reciprocity requirement to the recognition of foreign judgments (paralleling federal treatment of arbitral awards), moderate the "mirror-image" approach to foreign court jurisdiction, permit enhanced scrutiny of the procedural fairness and integrity of foreign proceedings, and allow a degree of choice-of-law scrutiny of foreign judgments. These changes would ensure that foreign judgments would not be enforced in U.S. courts without scrutiny necessary to safeguard both national interests and private (mostly U.S.) parties from foreign judgments based on procedurally or substantively unacceptable proceedings. The treatment of international law in American courts is gravely flawed. Both the status and content of international law in the United States are unpredictable and incoherent, inevitably producing results that compromise long-standing national interests. Over the past half century, U.S. federal courts have also increasingly marginalized both international law and the role of American courts in resolving international disputes. This treatment of international law has caused serious damage to historic U.S. values and frustrates vitally important national policies.

The current treatment of international law in American courts is also contrary to the Constitution's allocation of authority over the nation's foreign relations and international commerce. That allocation mandates that all rules of both public and private international law be matters of federal common law. Treating international law as federal, not state, law will remedy the existing defects in the application of international law by American courts—permitting the development of a uniform body of international law, formulated on the basis of U.S. interests and policies, which better ensures compliance with the nation's international obligations and effectuation of the nation's policies.

# 7

# The Waning of the Federal Common Law of Foreign Relations

*Paul B. Stephan*

The nationalist position, occasionally endorsed by the Supreme Court and widely embraced by foreign relations scholars, maintains that the United States must speak with one voice when dealing with the rest of the world, and that principle justifies the federal judiciary's stewardship of foreign relations law.[1] The premise seems compelling, but the implication is not. This chapter argues that concentrating authority in the federal judiciary to make foreign relations law in the absence of congressional enactments (either statutes or treaties) both ignores the capacity of the States to promote encounters with foreign actors and the tendency of the federal courts toward entropy, rather than coherence.

The 1987 Third Restatement of the Foreign Relations Law of the United States largely endorsed the nationalist position. Its most ambitious claim was that all international law qualifies as the law of the United States for purposes of the Supremacy Clause and the "arising under" prong of federal court subject matter jurisdiction.[2] In the absence of enacted federal law, it maintained, the federal courts must make rules that oust State law so as to fulfill the international legal obligations of the United States. As to other, nonobligatory bodies of law that might affect foreign relations, the Third Restatement asserted that courts must be vigilant to ensure that the States not adopt law in a way that intrudes into foreign relations.[3]

After initially inspiring courts and scholars alike to pursue the one-voice idea, the Third Restatement later faced a revisionist critique.[4] The Supreme Court

---

[1] See Martin S. Flaherty, Restoring the Global Judiciary: Why the Supreme Court Should Rule in U.S. Foreign Affairs (2019); Gary Born, *International Law in American Courts*, in this volume.

[2] Third Restatement §§ 111(1)–(3), 112(2); but see *id.* § 111(3)–(4) (noting exception for non-self-executing treaties).

[3] *Id.* § 1 reporters' note 5; cf. § 481 cmt. *a* (State law normally governs recognition and enforcement of foreign court judgments, unless that law intrudes into foreign relations of United States).

[4] The most influential statement of the revisionist position was Curtis A. Bradley & Jack L. Goldsmith, *Customary International Law as Federal Common Law: A Critique of the Modern Position*, 110 Harv. L. Rev. 815 (1997).

Paul B. Stephan, *The Waning of the Federal Common Law of Foreign Relations* In: *The Restatement and Beyond*. Edited by: Paul B. Stephan and Sarah H. Cleveland, Oxford University Press (2020). © Oxford University Press.
DOI: 10.1093/oso/9780197533154.003.0008

began to limit the federal common law of foreign relations as it reined in more generally the lawmaking powers of the lower federal courts. The new Fourth Restatement follows that lead. It confirms that many important legal doctrines that affect the foreign-relations interests of the United States rest on State law, unless and until the federal political branches enact something else. According to the Fourth Restatement, the existence of *plenary* federal power over foreign relations does not automatically translate into *exclusive* federal authority.

This chapter argues that the Fourth Restatement not only captures the temper of the times but that good functional arguments support its position. The growth of international commerce and connectivity since the 1980s has greatly increased pressure on the States to adopt laws that promote foreign contacts and business. Moreover, it has become apparent that a sprawling and diverse federal judiciary cannot pursue nationally uniform law except under stringent conditions that limit, rather than expand, judicial discretion to make law. The Supreme Court accordingly sees its task as inducing lawmaking by Congress and the executive. It pursues this goal by barring the lower courts from adopting stopgaps. As a result, the federal common law of foreign relations has shrunk and may disappear.[5]

## I. The Possibilities of a Federal Common Law of Foreign Relations

This section sketches the nationalist position that the Third Restatement largely, but not entirely, expressed, as well as the efforts of courts and scholars in its immediate wake to extend that position even further. It then describes the revisionist response, led principally by the Supreme Court. It looks at seven doctrinal pockets where the Third Restatement pushed for a one-voice outcome and then compares the Fourth's treatment of these issues. It depicts the revisionist position as ascending but not yet triumphant.

## A. The Nationalist Position

Earlier intimations notwithstanding, full articulation of the one-voice position came only in the waning days of dual federalism in the 1930s.[6] Underlying the

---

[5] This chapter draws on an article that develops these arguments in greater detail and with fuller citation of the literature. Paul B. Stephan, *One Voice in Foreign Relations and Federal Common Law*, 60 VA. J. INT'L L. 1 (2019).

[6] United States v. Curtiss-Wright Corp., 299 U.S. 304, 316–17 (1936); Belmont v. United States, 301 U.S. 324, 331 (1937); see G. Edward White, *From the Third to the Fourth Restatement of Foreign Relations: The Rise and Potential Fall of Foreign Affairs Exceptionalism*, in this volume.

Court's historical and constitutional claims were functional arguments. Not only had the framers intended the national government to have exclusive power in foreign relations, but they were wise to do so. Relations with other states require a single actor to engage with foreign states. Choices made with respect to the outside world affect the nation as a whole and have to be made by an authority that is accountable to the whole nation. Local interests cannot not be allowed to sabotage the general interest of the United States.[7]

The reporters for the Third Restatement added another layer to the nationalist position by stressing the special role of the judiciary in maintaining foreign affairs exceptionalism under the nationalist position.[8] By federalizing international law and bolstering foreign-relations preemption, the Third Restatement enlarged the scope of the Supremacy Clause's ouster of State law. Extending constitutional protection to overseas aliens further ensured a central role for the courts, as constitutional enforcers, in supervising the outward-facing acts of the political branches.[9]

The Third Restatement did not embrace the most ambitious version of the nationalist position, and the Fourth Restatement does not adopt the revisionist position in all respects. The Third Restatement proposed to discipline private international law through situational preemption, rather than federalizing the field; the Fourth Restatement does not address some of the Third's more ambitious proposals, such as the federalization of customary international law. A careful comparison of how the two Restatements treated specific subjects, however, reveals movement away from what an ambitious conception of one voice would require.

---

[7] E.g., Japan Line, Ltd. v. Los Angeles County, 441 U.S. 434, 453 (1979):

> California's tax thus creates an asymmetry in international maritime taxation operating to Japan's disadvantage. The risk of retaliation by Japan, under these circumstances, is acute, and such retaliation of necessity would be felt by the Nation as a whole. . . . California, by its unilateral act, cannot be permitted to place these impediments before this Nation's conduct of its foreign relations and its foreign trade.

[8] It observed:

> In recent years, principally as a result of reinterpretations by the Supreme Court and adjustments by Congress, there has been some redistribution of power among the three branches of government, and some increased protection of the rights of the individual, in matters relating to foreign relations as well as in other matters.

THIRD RESTATEMENT intro. at 4.

[9] Id. at § 721.

## B. The Response of the Fourth Restatement

### 1. Act of State Doctrine

Perhaps no doctrine in foreign relations law generates greater confusion than act of state. *Banco Nacional de Cuba v. Sabbatino* contains the canonical statement of the doctrine:

> [T]he Judicial Branch will not examine the validity of a taking of property within its own territory by a foreign sovereign government, extant and recognized by this country at the time of suit, in the absence of a treaty or other unambiguous agreement regarding controlling legal principles, even if the complaint alleges that the taking violates customary international law.[10]

The Court further declared that the doctrine functions as federal law that overrides State law, even in the absence of any clear conflict between the Court's position and State law.[11]

In assessing the scope and effect of the doctrine, the operative words are "will not examine the validity." Two different ideas are implicit in this phrase. To say that a court will not examine something is to suggest that a court will abstain from deciding a matter because of its delicacy and a lack of judicial competence. To say that a court will not question the validity of a foreign official act, however, indicates something else. It means that a court will treat the official act as binding because that act provides a rule of decision for resolving a dispute that the court is competent to adjudicate. The distinction matters for purposes of assessing the doctrine's status as federal common law. To the extent it permits a practice of abstention, it implies a general incapacity and potentially widespread application. To the extent it provides a rule of decision, it has clearer limits, and its federal status seems less consequential.

Both the Second Restatement, finalized shortly after *Sabbatino* came down, and the Third, promulgated two decades later, emphasized the first prong. Each tracked precisely the *Sabbatino* language on refraining from examining validity, thus preserving its suggestion of discretionary abstention.[12] Each also contained qualifications and elaborations that suggested that, like other abstention doctrines, act of state could be adjusted to reflect competing policy concerns.[13]

---

[10] Banco Nacional de Cuba v. Sabbatino, 376 U.S. 398, 428 (1964).

[11] *Id.* at 423–25.

[12] RESTATEMENT (SECOND) OF THE FOREIGN RELATIONS LAW OF THE UNITED STATES § 41 (Am. Law Inst. 1965) [hereinafter SECOND RESTATEMENT]; THIRD RESTATEMENT § 443.

[13] E.g., SECOND RESTATEMENT, *supra* note 12, § 41 cmt. *c*; THIRD RESTATEMENT § 443 cmt. *a* (emphasizing judicial restraint).

In the interval between the Third and Fourth Restatements, the Supreme Court handed down *W.S. Kirkpatrick & Co., Inc. v. Environmental Tectonics, Int'l.*[14] The opinion said nothing about the status of the doctrine as federal common law, but did clarify the doctrine's scope and squeezed out most, if not all, judicial discretion. Act of state, the Court explained, is simply a rule of decision that applies only where the outcome of a case turns on the application of an official act of a foreign state:

> The act of state doctrine does not establish an exception for cases and controversies that may embarrass foreign governments, but merely that, in the course of deciding, the acts of foreign sovereigns taken within their own jurisdictions shall be deemed valid.[15]

Where the issue before a court might impugn the integrity of foreign officials, but not the validity of their acts, the doctrine does not apply.[16]

In response to the Court's change in emphasis, the Fourth Restatement offered a new description of the doctrine: "In the absence of a treaty or other unambiguous agreement regarding controlling legal principles, courts in the United States will assume the validity of an official act of a foreign sovereign performed within its own territory."[17] The word "refrain" disappeared from the text.

The shift from a soft rule of abstention to a hard rule of decision has implications for arguments about a federal common law of foreign relations. Allowing State courts to develop their own tests would undermine the national government's "pursuit of goals both for itself and for the community of nations as a whole in the international sphere."[18] Accordingly, *Sabbatino* held that

> an issue concerned with a basic choice regarding the competence and function of the Judiciary and the National Executive in ordering our relationships with other members of the international community must be treated exclusively as an aspect of federal law.[19]

The narrower and less discretionary doctrine that *Kirkpatrick* articulated and the Fourth Restatement embraces suggests limits more than expansion. Were act of state about avoiding embarrassments to foreign officials that might interfere with

[14]  493 U.S. 400 (1990).
[15]  *Id.* at 409.
[16]  *Id.* at 409–10 (determination that a party paid a bribe to induce foreign officials to enter into a contract did not require a determination of the contract's validity under local law).
[17]  FOURTH RESTATEMENT § 441(1).
[18]  376 U.S. at 423.
[19]  *Id.* at 425.

foreign relations, one might expect it to extend to, for example, State-law tort claims based on fraud or similar misconduct. *Kirkpatrick* seems to foreclose that possibility. The validity constraint leaves States as well as federal litigants with considerable room to harass foreign actors in ways that might impair federal foreign policy.[20]

## 2. Federal Court Subject Matter Jurisdiction

Article III, Section 2 of the U.S. Constitution authorizes the exercise of the federal judicial power over cases "arising under this Constitution, the Laws of the United States, and Treaties made, or which shall be made, under their Authority."[21] A provision of federal law traceable to an 1875 enactment implements, but does not precisely track, the constitutional provision.[22] The Third Restatement asserted that customary international law is part of U.S. law and therefore counts as part of the "Laws of the United States" for purposes of Article III.[23] It further concluded that Section 1331 comprises cases based on customary international law.[24] This position would give federal courts the power to hear disputes that do not fit within the other categories of federal court subject matter jurisdiction— mostly party diversity and admiralty—even where the law in dispute is not based on the Constitution, any positive enactment of Congress, or a treaty to which the United States is a party.

Case law in support of this position was scant at the time of the Third Restatement and has become scarcer since. *Sosa v. Alvarez-Machain*, a 2004 decision, indicated that Section 1331 does not pick up cases based on customary international law.[25] The decision also implied that customary international law becomes the law of the United States for Article III purposes only when Congress, either expressly or implicitly, adopts a statute incorporating that law.[26]

The Fourth Restatement takes no position on these issues. It notes that cases arising under treaties satisfy Article III and observes that the Supreme Court has interpreted the statutory prong of "arising under" subject matter jurisdiction more narrowly than it has the corresponding language of Article III.[27] It avoids the question of whether customary international law is federal law and thus draws no conclusions from the indications of *Sosa*.

---

[20] The law of state immunity, which is statutory and clearly preempts State law, removes one category of lawsuits that might agitate foreign relations. FOURTH RESTATEMENT §§ 451–64. But state immunity provides only limited protection to state-owned enterprises and none at all to private actors who transact with foreign states.

[21] U.S. CONST. art. III, § 2.

[22] 28 U.S.C. § 1331.

[23] *Supra* note 2 and accompanying text.

[24] THIRD RESTATEMENT § 111 cmt. *e*.

[25] 542 U.S. 692, 731 n.19 (2004).

[26] *Id.* at 724–25.

[27] FOURTH RESTATEMENT §§ 301(2); 421 cmt. *d*.

The Fourth Restatement nonetheless indirectly limits the Third's claims by its narrower approach to what rules count as international law. A confusion of international comity and international law permeated the Third Restatement, as well as much of the scholarship asserting the federal common law claim. Examples abound, but I will discuss two here. As to the international law governing prescriptive jurisdiction, the Third Restatement declared that a state otherwise having a legitimate basis to regulate "may not exercise jurisdiction to prescribe law with respect to a person or activity having connections with another state when the exercise of such jurisdiction is unreasonable."[28] As to the exercise of in personam jurisdiction to adjudicate disputes, it declared that "'[t]ag' jurisdiction, i.e., jurisdiction based on service of process on a person only transitorily in the territory of the state, is not generally acceptable under international law."[29]

Each of these claims about what international law forbids was controversial at the time and provoked significant criticism, especially by foreign observers. No one disputed that exercises of prescriptive jurisdiction that fail to give due regard to foreign regulatory interests contribute to international disharmony or that tag jurisdiction puts defendants at a disadvantage and justifies a refusal to recognize judgments that emanate out of judicial proceedings that commenced in that manner. What the critics believed was missing, however, was evidence that these common-sense policies were mandated by international law.[30]

Accordingly, the Fourth Restatement embraces the wisdom of these policies but rejects the assertion that they rest on an international legal obligation.[31] It rejects the argument of commentators such as Lea Brilmayer that private international law, also being international law, should be treated the same as customary international law.[32] Although it does not provide a general definition of what constitutes international law, it generally focuses on state practice rather than scholarly commentary and distinguishes between rules that carry a duty to comply, on the one hand, and menus for cooperation, on the other.

Courts and scholars also have argued that, even in the absence of public or private international law, the presence of a foreign-relations element in a case might count as raising a federal question justifying federal court jurisdiction.

[28] THIRD RESTATEMENT § 403(1).

[29] Id. § 421 cmt. e.

[30] William S. Dodge, International Comity in the Fourth Restatement, in this volume. For a rebuttal, see Austen Parrish, Adjudicatory Jurisdiction and Public International Law: The Fourth Restatement's New Approach, id.

[31] FOURTH RESTATEMENT §§ 405 reporters' note 6; 407 reporters' notes 3 & 6; 422 reporters' notes 5 & 11; 484 reporters' note 7. This conclusion itself has been controversial. Compare Hannah Buxbaum & Ralf Michaels, Reasonableness as a Limitation on the Extraterritorial Application of U.S. Law: From 403 to 405 (via 404), in this volume, with Dodge, supra note 30.

[32] Compare Lea Brilmayer, Federalism, State Authority, and the Preemptive Power of International Law, 1994 SUP. CT. REV. 295, 315–22, with FOURTH RESTATEMENT §§ 401 reporters' note 2; 407 reporters' note 5; 441 reporters' note 9; 481 cmt. a; 489 reporters' note 3.

The argument asserts that any issue that implicates "important foreign policy concerns" requires federal common law and thus triggers the "arising under" prong of federal court jurisdiction. The Third Restatement endorsed this extension of federal judicial power.[33] But the federal courts have not invoked foreign relations arising-under jurisdiction in recent decades.[34] Although it is too early to declare the concept definitively rejected, the Fourth Restatement suggests that the one-voice principle is deflated, if not yet empty.

### 3. Forum Non Conveniens

The doctrine of *forum non conveniens* permits a court to stay or dismiss a suit in favor of another forum. The doctrine applies not only to motions to defer to another U.S. forum but also to foreign courts.[35] The decision to defer or not to a foreign jurisdiction implicates the foreign relations of the United States, inasmuch as the doctrine requires a U.S. court to determine the adequacy of the alternate forum. A failing grade might provoke irritation and even retaliation by the foreign nation whose courts have been attacked.

*Piper Aircraft*, the first Supreme Court decision to apply the doctrine in an international context, avoided the issue by leaving the question open.[36] It indicated that, if the doctrine involves a forum's internal housekeeping rather that a substantive rule of decision, *Erie* would be irrelevant. Thirteen years later, *American Dredging Co. v. Miller*, an admiralty case, held that a State court could refuse to apply the doctrine in spite of the federal nature of admiralty law.[37] Critical to the Court's decision was that the *forum non conveniens* issue is one of procedure rather than substance.[38]

Because *American Dredging* involved a domestic, rather than a foreign, alternative forum, one cannot read it as definitively excluding the possibility that the doctrine might preempt State procedural law in instances where the interests of a foreign sovereign might be at stake. No case, however, has held that a State court must apply the federal *forum non conveniens* doctrine in these circumstances, and State courts have asserted their right to disregard that doctrine in international cases.[39] The Fourth Restatement accordingly recognizes that States may

---

[33] THIRD RESTATEMENT § 111 reporters' note 4.

[34] Ingrid Wuerth, *The Future of the Federal Common Law of Foreign Relations*, 106 GEO. L.J. 1825, 1851 (2018).

[35] Piper Aircraft Co. v. Reyno, 454 U.S. 233 (1981); see also Donald Earl Childress III, Forum Non Conveniens *in the Fourth Restatement*, in this volume.

[36] *Id.* at 248–49 n.13.

[37] 510 U.S. 443 (1994).

[38] *Id.* at 453–54.

[39] E.g., Exxon Corp. v. Choo, 881 S.W.2d 301 (Tex. 1994); Stier v. Reading & Bates Corp., 992 S.W.2d 423 (1999); Tananta v. Cruise Ships Catering and Services Int'l, N.V., 909 So.2d 874 (Fl. 3d Dist. Ct. App. 2004); Coto v. J. Ray McDermott, S.A., 709 So.2d 1023 (La. 4th Cir. Ct. App. 1998).

apply their own conception of the doctrine (including, in some jurisdictions, its abolition) even where the alternative forum is foreign.[40]

### 4. Choice of Law

Under the Full Faith and Credit Clause of the U.S. Constitution and related legislation, the States must recognize and enforce the judgments of the courts of the other States.[41] As to the application of another State's law to a case over which its courts have jurisdiction, however, a State enjoys a wide, even if not limitless, range of discretion as to which conflicts rules to apply.[42] There is no clear evidence that involvement of the law of a foreign state, rather than of a sister State, materially affects that range.[43]

One may contrast this laissez-faire approach under national law with the evolving view of the Restatements as to the requirements of international law. The Third Restatement saw in international law an obligation for U.S. courts to defer to foreign rules in circumstances where the exercise of U.S. prescriptive jurisdiction was unreasonable.[44] The Fourth Restatement, in contrast, characterizes the reasonableness-in-prescriptive-jurisdiction principle as a rule of interpretation of federal statutes based on prescriptive comity, not as an obligation of international law.[45] It further concludes that State exercises of prescriptive jurisdiction face no international law limits that do not also apply to the national government.[46] The Fourth Restatement avoids the question whether the customary rules of international conflicts of law might function as federal common law binding on the States by denying that this field qualifies as international law.

### 5. Choice of Forum

Contractual choices of forum may elect either a foreign court or an arbitral tribunal. Under U.S. law, agreements to arbitrate disputes with an international dimension come under a treaty (the Convention on the Recognition and Enforcement of Foreign Arbitral Awards) and a statute (Chapter Two of the

---

[40] FOURTH RESTATEMENT § 424 cmt. *b* & reporters' note 2.

[41] U.S. CONST. art. IV, § 1; 28 U.S.C. § 1738. An exception to this rule allows one State to refuse to honor another State's judgment where the first State lacked jurisdiction to issue its judgment. Williams v. North Carolina, 325 U.S. 226 (1945).

[42] FOURTH RESTATEMENT § 403 reporters' note 4; Paul B. Stephan, *Competing Sovereignty and Laws' Domains*, 45 PEPP. L. REV. 239, 292–95 (2018).

[43] See Restatement (Third) of the Law of Conflicts § 1.04 cmt. *d* (Tentative Draft No. 1, Am. Law Inst. 2020) (enumerating factors that might lead to differential treatment).

[44] THIRD RESTATEMENT § 403. For an earlier and less sweeping statement, see SECOND RESTATEMENT, *supra* note 12, § 9 cmt. *a*.

[45] FOURTH RESTATEMENT § 405; Dodge, *supra* note 30.

[46] FOURTH RESTATEMENT §§ 404 reporters' note 5, 406 reporters' note 4. Unlike the Third Restatement, the Fourth Restatement does indicate that the Constitution imposes distinct limits on the extraterritorial application of prescriptive jurisdiction by the States. *Id.* § 402 reporters' note 4.

Federal Arbitration Act).[47] Both these instruments are uncontroversially federal and thus preempt State law.[48] The United States has signed, but not yet ratified, a treaty that would do the same for choice-of-forum contracts relating to international civil or commercial matters.[49] A dispute over the manner of its implementation, and in particular whether to leave to the States the right to adopt necessary laws or instead to displace State law with federal rules, has held up its ratification.[50]

The courts seem to accept fully that there is no general federal common law governing the interpretation and enforcement of contractual clauses choosing a foreign court as a forum. The Supreme Court's leading case, *The Bremen*, applied admiralty law, which in the last century has been regarded as federal law, to uphold such a contract.[51] Cases extending *The Bremen* outside of admiralty mostly have looked to the law of the forum to determine the validity of such clauses.[52] No court has held that there exists a federal common law governing the validity of choice-of-forum contracts that binds State courts.

The Third Restatement noted the shift in U.S. law in favor of enforcement but did not indicate the source of law bringing about that result.[53] The Fourth Restatement, in contrast, declares that, "[i]n State court, the enforceability of a clause choosing a foreign court is governed by State law."[54] Moreover, in disputes over the interpretation, rather than the validity, of such a clause, the Restatement indicates that the law governing the contract, which almost never would be federal law, applies.

## 6. Recognition and Enforcement of Foreign Judgments

The treatment of the status of foreign judgments in the United States by the Third and Fourth Restatements illustrates the shift away from federalizing private law rules with foreign relations implications. As a general matter, State law governs

---

[47] Convention on the Recognition and Enforcement of Foreign Arbitral Awards, June 10, 1958, 21 U.S.T. 2517, 330 U.N.T.S. 38; 9 U.S.C. §§ 201–208.

[48] A dispute does exist as to the self-executing status of the New York Convention. If it is not self-executing, then there would be no preemption. Restatement of the U.S. Law of International Commercial and Investment Arbitration §§ 1-1, reporters' note k, 1-6, reporters' note a(iv) (Am. Law Inst. Proposed Final Draft, Apr. 24, 2019); Gary Born, *The New York Convention: A Self-Executing Treaty*, 40 MICH. J. INT'L L. 115 (2018).

[49] Hague Convention on Choice of Court Agreements, June 30, 2005.

[50] Peter D. Trooboff, *Implementing Legislation for the Hague Choice of Courts Convention*, in FOREIGN COURT JUDGMENTS IN THE UNITED STATES LEGAL SYSTEM 131 (Paul B. Stephan ed., 2014); David P. Stewart, *Implementing the Hague Choice of Court Convention: The Argument in Favor of "Cooperative Federalism,"* in *id.* at 147.

[51] M/S Bremen v. Zapata Off-Shore Co., 407 U.S. 1 (1972).

[52] E.g., Albemarle Corp. v. AstraZeneca UK Ltd., 628 F.3d 643, 650 (4th Cir. 2010) (treating issue as procedural under *Erie*). But cf. Abbott Laboratories v. Takeda Pharmaceutical Co. Ltd., 476 F.3d 421, 423 (7th Cir. 2007) (clause governed by the law governing the rest of the contract).

[53] THIRD RESTATEMENT §§ 421 reporters' note 6, 482 reporters' note 5.

[54] FOURTH RESTATEMENT § 424 reporters' note 6.

the recognition and enforcement of money judgments issued by foreign courts.[55] The Third Restatement did not reject this allocation of authority, but proposed a limitation. It maintained:

> Ordinarily, a decision of a State court granting or denying recognition to a foreign judgment is not subject to review by the United States Supreme Court, unless the decision raises questions under the United States Constitution, for example, intrusion into the foreign affairs of the United States, . . .[56]

As a result, even entrenched rules in areas traditionally regarded as exclusive State enclaves, such as intestate succession or recognition of foreign judgments, could be ousted where smooth foreign relations demanded.

The Fourth Restatement, while not repudiating the Third, sets a different tone. In the interval Congress had enacted a law, the SPEECH Act, that federalized a narrow slice of the law governing foreign judgments.[57] The Fourth Restatement observes that the "recognition and enforcement of foreign judgments in the United States are generally governed by State law."[58] A reporters' note elaborates:

> [I]t has been accepted that, in the absence of a federal statute or treaty, State law governs the enforcement of foreign-country judgments. . . . There are two principal exceptions to the general rule that the recognition and enforcement of foreign judgments are governed by State law. First, the federal SPEECH Act, 28 U.S.C. §§ 4101–4105, governs the recognition and enforcement of foreign defamation judgments in both federal and State courts . . . Second, the preclusive effect of foreign judgments with respect to federal-law claims is governed by federal law . . . The United States is not party to any treaty requiring the recognition and enforcement of civil judgments . . . Customary international law imposes no obligation on states to give effect to the judgments of other states.[59]

The Fourth Restatement gives no indication that a simple "intrusion" of a State rule in foreign relations might bring about its invalidity. As with private international law, the Fourth Restatement's treatment of foreign judgments avoids the international-law-as-federal-law issue by finding no international law.

---

[55] Recognition and enforcement of foreign arbitral awards, by contrast, are governed by the New York Convention and the Federal Arbitration Act.

[56] THIRD RESTATEMENT § 481 cmt. *a*. The comment cited § 1 reporters' note 5 of that Restatement, which in turn advanced *Zschernig v. Miller*, 389 U.S. 429, 432 (1968), as authority that State law that "intrudes" in foreign relations is unconstitutional.

[57] 28 U.S.C. §§ 4101–405.

[58] FOURTH RESTATEMENT § 481 cmt. *a*.

[59] *Id.* reporters' note 1.

## 7. General Preemption

Defending the "one voice" of the United States in foreign relations requires more than mobilizing the resources of the national government, the federal judiciary in particular, to enforce international law. It also requires suppressing aspects of State law that add noise to the signal that the national government seeks to send to the rest of the world. This logic would support a robust preemption doctrine that invalidates State law not only when it contradicts federal law but also when it complicates foreign relations in the absence of positive federal law.

Supreme Court doctrine has invoked various kinds of preemption, including express legislative provision, direct conflict with federal law, overcoming obstacles to the achievement of the purposes of federal law, and occupation of a field by federal law.[60] The kind of preemption on which the Third Restatement focused, and the extension of which most foreign relations scholars have advocated, instead posits a field of law that, independent of the presence of any federal enactment, drives out State law. The preeminent case imposing foreign-affairs field preemption (and the only instance of the Supreme Court relying on this doctrine in more than fifty years) is *Zschernig v. Miller*.[61] The majority interpreted the State law as an effort to take part in the Cold War and thus an impermissible interference with the federal government's exclusive authority over foreign relations.[62]

The Third Restatement broadly embraced the idea that any State law that interfered with foreign relations was subject to field preemption, citing *Zschernig* repeatedly as a template to be employed and extended. As part of its depiction of the modest role of States in the field of foreign relations law, it proclaimed:

> Supremacy implies that State law and policy must bow not only when inconsistent with federal law or policy but even when federal authority has shown a purpose, by "preemption" or "occupying the field," to exclude even State activity that is not inconsistent with federal law or policy.[63]

The reference to "policy" ensured that issues touching on matters in which the national executive might be engaged, even in the absence of any positive law, would come within field preemption. The Restatement said little about what counted as impermissible intrusion into this field, but invited the federal courts to do much.

---

[60] *Id.* § 308 cmt. *c.*

[61] 389 U.S. 429, 432 (1968).

[62] *Id.* at 440–41.

[63] THIRD RESTATEMENT § 1 reporters' note 5 (citing *Zschernig*). Other references to *Zschernig* can be found in *id.* §§ 208 reporters' note 4; 302 cmt. *d*; 326 reporters' note 1; 402 reporters' note 5.

The Fourth Restatement does not propose any general approach to federal preemption of State law. Its passing references to the doctrine, however, suggest a more modest scope. It notes that the more recent decisions of the Court have based preemption on inconsistency with positive federal enactments, rather than with intrusion as such. It observes that the emerging doctrine "suggests that States may act within the areas of their traditional competence even if the action has foreign-policy implications, as long as no conflict with federal law exists."[64] It recognizes the validity of preemption when a federal enactment expresses an intent to occupy a particular field, but does not depict foreign relations law as such as broadly ousting State law.[65] In particular, it rejects any presumption regarding the preemptive effect of self-executing treaties.[66]

## 8. Summary: The Decline of One Voice as a Basis for Judicial Power

Thirty years out from the Third Restatement's call for federalization of foreign relations law, the project seems endangered. The Supreme Court, generally unimpressed with arguments for increasing the lawmaking discretion of the federal courts, has not treated foreign relations law as different. It has both resisted the federalization of the unwritten portion of public international law and ignored academic arguments for federalizing areas traditionally seen as part of private international law. The presence of a foreign-relations element in a controversy no longer produces field preemption that automatically invalidates State law.

## II. Law in the Era of Globalization: Centralized versus Distributed Lawmaking

Underlying the debate between the nationalist and revisionist positions in foreign relations law are profoundly different assumptions about how lawmaking works. To begin with, the nationalists imagine a welter of State and local actors that seek to exploit the network of global economic and political connections for parochial gains.[67] The revisionist position does not deny that State and local lawmakers are selfish and have the potential to threaten national interests. It posits, however, broader economic and political forces that can rein in their potential for mischief.

If State interference with foreign relations is a problem, we should expect to see both instances of States laws burdening transnational transactions and federal

---

[64] FOURTH RESTATEMENT § 403 reporters' note 5 (indicating that the contemporary Supreme Court does not follow *Zschernig*).
[65] *Id.* § 308 cmt. *c.*
[66] *Id.* reporters' note 2.
[67] These views are summarized in Born, *supra* note 1.

efforts to suppress such conduct. A review of actual legal practice, however, does not show such behavior. Congress occasionally adopts laws that exclude States from acting in particular areas, but more commonly it only prohibits discrimination against foreign nationals. Instances of State hostility to foreigners are rare, while efforts to adopt uniform legal standards to encourage more transactions with foreigners, both business and personal, are common.

Legislation that expressly ousts the States from regulating categories of transnational transactions is unusual. An important instance of such ouster is Chapter 2 of the Federal Arbitration Act, which implements U.S. obligations under the New York Convention on the Recognition and Enforcement of Foreign Arbitral Awards.[68] More commonly, federal enactments instead employ a nondiscrimination rule. For example, many U.S. treaties dealing with trade, commerce, and investment contain a rule of national treatment.[69] This norm sets no minimum standard for the legal rights of aliens, but rather requires that the same rules apply to nationals of the obligated (or host) state and nationals of the other states protected by the treaty. Such provisions bind the national government to a rule that, under the dormant foreign commerce clause, already applies to the States.

An emerging pattern in some U.S. private-international-law treaties is encouragement of cooperative federalism.[70] Some invite States to adopt a conforming law that meets certain requirements, with a federal template serving as a backstop in the absence of a State enactment. Instances of this approach include U.S. implementation of the UNCITRAL Model Law on Electronic Commerce and the Hague Convention on the International Recovery of Child Support and Other Forms of Family Maintenance.[71] Implementation of the Hague Convention on Choice of Court Agreements, a treaty that the United State has signed but not ratified, might follow a similar path.[72]

Finally, some private-international-law treaties defer to State lawmaking by making it easy to escape the treaty regime. The most prominent example is the

---

[68]  9 U.S.C. §§ 201–208.

[69]  John F. Coyle, *The Treaty of Friendship, Commerce and Navigation in the Modern Era*, 51 COLUM. J. TRANS. L. 302, 318–21, 353–56 (2013).

[70]  See Jean Galbraith, *Cooperative and Uncooperative Federalism*, 130 HARV. L. REV. 2131 (2017). In other instances, Congress has relied on express preemption. E.g., Hague Securities Convention, Senate Treaty Doc. 112-6 at VIII (2012); Resolution of Ratification, § 2; 162 Cong. Rec. S6195 (Sept. 28, 2016).

[71]  Model Law on Electronic Commerce, G.A. Res. 51/162, U.N. Doc. A/RES/51/162 (Jan. 30, 1997), implemented by Electronic Signatures in Global and National Commerce Act, Pub. L. No. 106-229, 114 Stat. 464, codified at 15 U.S.C. § 102(a) (allowing reverse preemption by Uniform Electronic Transactions Act); Hague Convention on the International Recovery of Child Support and Other Forms of Family Maintenance, Nov. 23, 2007, implemented by Preventing Sex Trafficking and Strengthening Families Act, P.L. 113-183, § 301, 128 Stat. 1919, codified at 42 U.S.C. § 664 (allowing reverse preemption by Uniform Interstate Family Support Act).

[72]  Stewart, *supra* note 50, at 155–58.

Convention on the International Sale of Goods, a multilateral instrument that displaces portions of domestic sales law.[73] By its terms, the Convention allows the parties to opt out of its application.[74] U.S. parties almost always do this, and fail only by inadvertence.[75]

Even more significant than the occasional expressions of federal deference to State lawmaking are State choices to make law that meets the needs of transnational actors. Some of these efforts entail adoption of uniform laws to promote harmonized law. Others involve cooperation with private entities to support standardized contracts that dominate particular business sectors.

An important example is the recognition and enforcement of foreign judicial judgments. A majority of States have adopted model laws to regulate parts of this field, namely, the 1962 Uniform Foreign Money-Judgments Recognition Act, supplemented by the 2005 Uniform Foreign-Country Money Judgments Recognition Act.[76] The American Law Institute promulgated a proposed federal statute in 2006 that would have displaced State law in this field.[77] Some scholars have argued that the courts should go further by adopting a body of federal common law that would preempt these statutes even in the absence of congressional action.[78] Congress, however, has let State law continue to apply, except in the case of foreign defamation judgments.[79]

In areas where there are no uniform laws, States have adopted either piecemeal enactments or common law to stabilize the law affecting foreign transactions. It is remarkable how much international finance and commerce relies on the laws of U.S. States. This begins with the Uniform Commercial Code, which every State has adopted (only Louisiana omitting the chapters on sale of goods, leases, and bulk sales). Moreover, every State gives effect to the standardized contractual terms that prevail in important international transactions such as sales of goods (the Incoterms), letters of credit (the Uniform Customs and Practice for Documentary Credits), and derivatives and swaps (the ISDA master

---

[73] Convention on Contracts for the International Sale of Goods, Apr. 10, 1980, U.N. Doc. A/Conf./97/18, reprinted in 52 Fed. Reg. 6264 (1987).

[74] *Id.* art. 6.

[75] John F. Coyle, *The Role of the CISG in U.S. Contract Practice: An Empirical Study*, 38 U. PA. J. INT'L L. 195, 214–31, 234–38 (2016).

[76] FOURTH RESTATEMENT ch. 8, intro. note. These statutes apply only to money judgments, but State law governs the impact in U.S. courts of nonmoney judgments as well. *Id.* § 481 cmt. *a* & reporters' note 1.

[77] RECOGNITION AND ENFORCEMENT OF FOREIGN JUDGMENTS: ANALYSIS AND PROPOSED FEDERAL STATUTE (Am. Law Inst. 2006).

[78] Ronald A. Brand, *Enforcement of Foreign Money-Judgments in the United States: In Search of Uniformity and International Acceptance*, 67 NOTRE DAME L. REV. 253, 257 (1991); Brilmayer, *supra* note 32, at 319–20; John N. Moore, *Federalism and Foreign Relations*, 1965 DUKE L.J. 248, 262–63.

[79] SPEECH Act, 28 U.S.C. §§ 4101–405; FOURTH RESTATEMENT § 483(c) & cmt. *g*

agreements). Goods and services worth trillions of dollars a year cross the U.S. border in transactions that rely almost entirely on State, and not federal, law.

Perhaps even more significantly, the mix of functions lumped together as "the internet"—email transmission, the World Wide Web, cloud storage, and the like—depends mostly on State law for those transactions that have a nexus with the United States. The Internet Corporation for Assigned Names and Numbers, the entity that regulates the domain name registry and other aspects of internet governance, is chartered under California charitable corporation law. Whether one thinks of the cyberworld as a force for good or evil in the contemporary world, its presence and operations have taken on the force that they have without resort to uniform federal law.


## III. Federal Common Law: The Path to Entropy

The nationalist position rests not only on assumptions about the inadequacies of State law but also about the virtues of the federal judiciary. The federal judiciary, it maintains, expresses a common commitment to reasoned application of unifying principles and a devotion to the rule of law. The Supreme Court serves as the repository of these principles and a guardian of the commitments. It monitors subordinate courts, both federal and State, to detect defections as well as to resolve good-faith disagreements over how these ideals cash out in particular cases. It imposes order through its decisions, which function as commands both in the particular—its disposition of cases—and the general—its announcement of rules and reasons that bind lower courts.

But a single voice in foreign relations would not make much sense if that voice were incoherent. In this section I explore the structural features of federal common-law making that frustrate coherence and make entropy a more likely outcome. I then illustrate that argument with examples of failures by the federal courts to advance the development of a useful federal common law of foreign relations.

Consider first the structural features of federal courts and federal litigation. The system as a whole promotes the entrenchment of the policy commitments of judges appointed at different times and with heterogeneous preferences. The mix of preferences of lower-court judges are unlikely to match those of the Supreme Court. The Supreme Court in turn is likely to reach outcomes that reflect the process of cycling, that is, moving back and forth among outcomes based on irrelevant factors, rather than consistent expressions of policy commitments. The combination of lower-court diversity and highest-court cycling is more likely to produce entropy than consistent outcomes and clear intellectual leadership.

. A focus on the policy commitments of judges, as distinguished from other credentials such as professional status and position in élite institutions, has unquestionably shaped the selection process in the last several decades.[80] High-profile and deeply politicized debates over Supreme Court nominations, from Haynsworth and Bork to Thomas and Kavanaugh, have increased the salience of judicial nominations generally. The battles over judicial nominations have extended to the lower courts. Both parties face pressure to choose younger and more reliable (in the policy sense) nominees, bringing about an arms race in which each justifies its choices as a reaction to the other's.

Part of what this process produces is segmentation of the lower federal courts based on somewhat predictable policy preferences that affect judicial decision-making. Litigants will seek out those judges whose preferences align with their preferred outcomes, skewing the distribution of outcomes somewhat in the direction of the preferences of those who can select to the forum. As the number of judges in the lower courts grows, the potential for segmentation correspondingly increase.[81] This increase in the rolls of the lower-court judiciary during a period when the political salience of nominations increased has reinforced the policy-preference heterogeneity of those who produce federal common law.

Firm supervision of the federal judiciary by the Supreme Court might address this problem. But persuasive theoretical and practical reasons explain why it is unlikely that the Supreme Court can provide this kind of guidance. Professor Frank Easterbrook provided the basic insight nearly forty years ago: Supreme Court voting satisfies the conditions for the application of the Arrow Impossibility Theorem.[82] He observed that, where the decision of cases implicate more than two options and Justices do not agree among themselves as to the order of preference for those options, a majority of the Court will not be able to arrive at consistent outcomes absent rigid adherence by a stable majority to a rule of complete deference to precedent.[83] When cases present multiple outcomes about which the individual Justices have inconsistent and nontransitive preferences, the Court is condemned to some combination of cycling (transparent inconsistency in outcomes), path dependency (excessive deference to undesirable precedents),

---

[80] For a review of the literature on the observability of the policy preferences of individual judges, see Joshua B. Fischman, *Reuniting "Is" and "Ought" in Empirical Legal Scholarship*, 162 U. PA. L. REV. 117 (2013).

[81] In 1969, the year that the Court delivered *Zschernig*, the federal judiciary contained 76 appellate judges and 320 district court judges. The numbers include senior judges but not retired judges or Article III judges serving on specialized first-instance courts. At the beginning of 2019, the corresponding numbers were 166 and 545.

[82] Frank H. Easterbrook, *Ways of Criticizing the Court*, 95 VA. L. REV. 802 (1982). For the source of the theorem, for which Arrow won a Nobel Prize, see KENNETH J. ARROW, SOCIAL CHOICE AND INDIVIDUAL VALUES 92–120 (2d ed. 1963), and *A Difficulty in the Concept of Social Welfare*, 58 J. POL. ECON. 328 (1950).

[83] Easterbrook, *supra* note 82, at 814–23,

and strategic voting that will exacerbate the prior two tendencies.[84] Incoherence is the inevitable consequence.

Empirical evidence indicates that individual Justices sort themselves out along at least two axes, substantive and methodological.[85] They vary along both an axis that reflects the values of particular interest groups (such as pro-business versus pro-consumer) and one that reflects methodology (such as formalist versus purposive interpretation).[86] The methodological commitments need not, and as observed do not, work as proxies for substantive preferences.[87]

Absent a sea change in the current political context surrounding Supreme Court appointments, then, one should expect inconsistent outcomes of cases that engage significant substantive and methodological commitments. Much of the federal common law of foreign relations meets this description. First, the context is fraught. Foreign relations by definition requires a decision maker to imagine the impact of rules and outcomes on persons who are in some sense strangers and free from the decision maker's control. The impulse to build discretion into these rules in the face of this uncertainty is powerful. And discretion begets legal rules that lend themselves to bending and shading in light of the actor's policy preferences.

Case histories support the theoretical prediction. I consider here two episodes where the Supreme Court sought to dispel confusion in the lower courts over questions of significant practical importance to the foreign relations of the United States. One involves the development of a federal common law of compensation for injuries caused by violations of international law, the other the development of the choice-of-law rules applicable to financial instruments issued by international banks. Both stories give cold comfort to those who envision the Court as promoting the making of coherent foreign relations law.

As discussed earlier, civil suits based on egregious violations of international human rights law burst on the scene in the United States at the end of the Carter presidency, cementing the legacy of an administration that had promised to put human rights at the center of U.S. foreign policy.[88] The idea that U.S. law provided a tort remedy to anyone who suffered from a violation of international law, in particular unwritten customary international law, flourished in the lower

---

[84] *Id.*

[85] Joshua B. Fischman, *Do the Justices Vote Like Policy Makers? Evidence from Scaling the Supreme Court with Interest Groups*, 44 J. LEGAL STUD. S269 (2015); Joshua B. Fischman & Tonja Jacobi, *The Second Dimension of the Supreme Court*, 57 WM. & MARY L. REV. 1671 (2016).

[86] Fischman, *supra* note 85, at S271–73; Fischman & Jacobi, *supra* note 85, at 1689–97.

[87] Fischman, *supra* note 85, at S282–87; Fischman & Jacobi, *supra* note 85, at 1699–1708.

[88] Filártiga v. Peña-Irala, 630 F.2d 876 (2d Cir. 1980) (recognizing federal cause of action); SAMUEL MOYN, THE LAST UTOPIA: HUMAN RIGHTS IN HISTORY 150–61 (2012) (human rights and Carter administration).

courts over the next two decades.[89] The Court has responded with four decisions to date, each made by a more badly divided court than its predecessor.[90]

*Argentine Republic v. Amerada Hess Shipping Corp.*, a dispute over state immunity, produced a unanimous opinion.[91] *Sosa v. Alvarez-Machain*,[92] the first case to address the substance of the federal law of international torts, revealed a 6–3 split. *Kiobel v. Royal Dutch Petroleum Co.*,[93] decided nine years later, resulted in a 4–1–4 split, with Justice Kennedy's tiebreaking decision leaving most questions open.[94] *Jesner v. Arab Bank PLC*,[95] Justice Kennedy's final contribution, produced an even more fragmented outcome with no majority agreeing on the reasons for dismissing a claim against a foreign bank operating in the United States.[96]

In these cases one can find support for (1) a formalist argument that federal tort claims should rest on a clear statutory basis; (2) a purposivist argument that federal courts should look to international law to develop a system of remedies for atrocities; (3) a substantive argument that the federal common law of international torts should not extend beyond events for which the United States as a nation bears some responsibility; (4) a substantive argument that corporations should not be subject to accountability for international torts in the absence of clear international law; and (5) and (6), the reverse of arguments (3) and (4). No majority has emerged in support of any of these six positions, leaving it to the shifting composition of the Court, rather than principled reasons, to determine the outcome of future cases. Aware of this indeterminacy, the lower courts have seen themselves free to embrace any of the six possible outcomes, recognizing that reversal is a possibility but by no means assured.

The Court has shown similar inability with respect to private international law. *Citibank, N.A. v. Wells Fargo Asia Ltd.*[97] involved a question on which

---

[89] Paul B. Stephan, *Privatizing International Law*, 97 Va. L. Rev. 1573, 1613, 1636–37 (2011) (describing litigation).

[90] The Third Restatement welcomed this development and did not anticipate the Court's skepticism. Third Restatement § 111 cmt. f.

[91] 488 U.S. 428, 435–38 (1989) (holding that Foreign Sovereign Immunities Act contains no implied exception for human rights cases). Justice Blackmun, joined by Justice Marshall, did not join that portion of the majority's opinion holding that none of the act's express exceptions applied to the case. *Id.* at 443–44.

[92] 542 U.S. 692 (2004).

[93] 569 U.S. 109 (2013).

[94] Fourth Restatement § 404 reporters' note 3.

[95] 138 S. Ct. 1386 (2018).

[96] Justice Kennedy took the position that the applicability of international law to corporations was insufficiently established to justify a federal common law rule of liability. *Id.* at 1399–1402. Chief Justice Roberts and Justice Thomas concurred, although Justice Thomas wrote separately to express his skepticism about this federal common law more generally. *Id.* at 1408 (Thomas, J., concurring). Justices Alito and Gorsuch wrote separate opinions explaining why they were inclined not to recognize this body of federal common law, although they indicated different methodological grounds for doing so. *Id.* at 1408–12 (Alito, J., concurring in part and concurring in the judgment); *id.* at 1412–19 (Gorsuch, J., concurring in part and concurring in the judgment). The four *Kiobel* dissenters again opposed the Court's shutting down of this body of law. *Id.* at 1419–37 (Sotomayor, J., dissenting).

[97] 495 U.S. 660 (1990).

billions of dollars of liability turned, namely, the choice of law governing dollar-denominated certificates of deposit issued by foreign banks. These accounts took off in the 1960s and attracted enormous sums.[98] Because these transactions typically occur in large volumes on the basis of terse electronic communications, few express terms accompany them, and in particular, the choice of law was left open.

During the so-called Third World debt crisis of the early 1980s, many countries adopted currency controls that barred or discouraged local banks from exporting dollars. Depositors sued, forcing courts to decide whether, in the absence of express contractual provisions on point, the law of the local bank or the law of place where the transaction cleared applied and determined whether a breach had occurred. In practice this meant either the law of place of the debtor bank or that of New York, where the clearance of dollar-denominated banking transactions takes place.

Seeking legal clarity that could apply globally, the banks sought an answer from the Supreme Court.[99] Faced with the most consequential private international law question presented to it in the postwar era, the Court failed utterly. Rather than choosing the law to apply or articulating a choice-of-law methodology, *Citibank, N.A. v. Wells Fargo Asia Ltd.*[100] remanded the case to the lower court for further findings.[101] Only Justice Stevens, in dissent, proposed a rule to resolve the case, although his brief opinion did not identify the choice-of-law process on which he relied.[102] The Second Circuit, taking its cue from the Court, issued a one-off decision that focused on the peculiar facts of the case and declined to choose a rule that might apply under any other circumstances.[103]

This story had a happy ending, but only because of the federal judiciary's failure to resolve the issue and the focused concern of a powerful interest group. Responding to pressure from the banks, Congress adopted a statute allocating liability for nonperformance due to foreign currency controls.[104] But this denouement underscores the inability of the Court to rise to the challenge of developing a workable federal common law of choice of law.

---

[98] Peter S. Smedresman & Andreas F. Lowenfeld, *Eurodollars, Multinational Banks, and National Laws*, 64 N.Y.U. L. Rev. 733 (1989).

[99] *Id.* at 765–66.

[100] 495 U.S. 660 (1990).

[101] *Id.* at 673–74 (ordering the lower court to determine which law applies as well as its content).

[102] *Id.* at 674–75 (Stevens, J., dissenting).

[103] Wells Fargo Asia Ltd. v. Citibank, N.A., 936 F.2d 723 (2d Cir. 1991), *cert. denied*, 505 U.S. 1204 (1992) (as Philippine Central Bank had authorized some dispersals of dollars, the question of whether a currency control regulation would excuse nonperformance did not arise in the case).

[104] Riegle Community Development and Regulatory Improvement Act of 1994, Pub. L. 103-325, § 326(a), 108 Stat. 2160, 2229 (codified as 12 U.S.C. § 633 (2012)) (freeing parent from foreign subsidiary's liability due to foreign government's regulatory actions "unless the member bank has expressly agreed in writing to repay the deposit under those circumstances").

## IV.  Doctrinal Implications

What might foreign relations law look like in the absence of federal common law? This section speculates about the future of the nationalist position in foreign relations law. It also looks at positions that the Fourth Restatement might take, were the American Law Institute to extend the mandate of the project.

## A.  Public International Law as Federal Common Law

Let us suppose that the Third Restatement was wrong about the status of customary international law as the law of the United States. Suppose that an extension of the current Fourth Restatement were to adopt this conclusion.[105] What this would mean is that the obligatory rules of general international law—the rules that bind states and that do not depend only on treaties for their existence—might apply in any given case, but not automatically and not in the presence of an otherwise applicable rule of State law. International law would be part of our law in the sense that it would be on the menu of possible rules that could apply if a prior choice-of-law rule so required, but they would not come under the particular choice-of-law rule imposed by the Supremacy Clause.

Note what this conclusion does not entail. A court might still refer to these rules as an interpretive mechanism, so as to better divine a lawmaker's intent as well as to avoid putting the United States in violation of its international obligations.[106] But because international law does not generally require states to vindicate the interests of victims, as distinguished from the obligation of states not themselves to violate the rules of international law, a court would not have to rectify injuries traceable to international law violations, absent an express treaty requirement or a domestic command to do so. A court could refer to international law to determine the authorities that a U.S. official might possess or the limitations that a federal statute might impose on private actors, but international law on its own would not empower a court to compensate those injured because of its violation.

To focus on a long-standing statutory question on which the Third Restatement took a strong position, the courts might end up completing their drift away from *Sosa* and conclude that there is no federal common law of international torts. Three Justices on the Supreme Court already have expressed

---

[105] The terms of references of the Fourth Restatement did not include addressing this question, but the American Law Institute has left open the possibility of the project's extension. See FOURTH RESTATEMENT intro. at xvii.

[106] FOURTH RESTATEMENT § 406 (compliance with international law as a rule of interpretation)

their preference for this outcome, and it would not be inconsistent with other positions taken by Chief Justice Roberts and Justice Kavanaugh to anticipate that they might go along. Whether a thin majority might stabilize into an entrenched position will depend on many factors. It is not unreasonable, however, to expect Congress to prefer a definitive closing down of litigation to continuance of the present confused status quo. It seems especially unlikely that Congress long will tolerate a rule that imposes liability only on domestic corporations.[107]

It is not true, however, that shutting down the federal common law of international torts will be a complete loss for victims of abuse. Perhaps surprisingly, not according international law the status of binding federal common law might leave open some litigation opportunities that international law would close. At present, U.S. statutory law limits suits against foreign states, but not against foreign officials.[108] The Court has suggested that federal common law might fill that gap. If international law were understood as supplying immunity from suit even for claims based on grave violations of human rights law—a proposition that enjoys some support from international authorities—then a federal court might be obligated to dismiss human-rights suits.[109] If international law does not constitute federal law, it becomes easier to keep these suits alive.

## B. The Act of State Doctrine as Federal Common Law

The Fourth Restatement did not challenge *Sabbatino*'s determination that the act of state doctrine enjoys the status of federal law.[110] Although *Kirkpatrick* narrowed the doctrine's scope, it did not revisit the federal-law question.[111] If the Court were to reconsider the nationalist position across the board, however, it is not clear that this holding can survive. The problem is that *Sabbatino*'s arguments for federalizing the doctrine largely track the claims of the one-voice principle.

Would downgrading its status as federal law radically undermine the doctrine? The answer is far from clear. Congress reversed the case's specific holding

---

[107] *Jesner* by its terms applies only to foreign corporations. 138 S. Ct. at 1413 n.1 (Alito, J., concurring). A case now before the Court might address the liability of U.S. corporations. Nestlé USA, Inc. v. Doe, 140 S. Ct. 912 (2020) (calling for the views of the Solicitor General on a petition for certiorari raising this issue).

[108] Yousuf v. Samantar, 560 U.S. 305 (2010) (Foreign Sovereign Immunities Act does not apply to natural persons).

[109] Jurisdictional Immunities of the State (Ger. v. It.: Greece intervening), Judgment, 2012 I.C.J. Rep. 99 (Feb. 3) (immunities extend to claims based on grave violations of international humanitarian law); Jones v. Ministry of Interior of Saudi Arabia, [2006] UKHL 26 (same as to torture when defendants include officials). One U.S. Court has rejected this conclusion. Yousuf v. Samantar, 699 F.3d 763 (4th Cir. 2012) (no immunity as to jus cogens claims).

[110] FOURTH RESTATEMENT § 441 cmt. *b*.

[111] See *supra* notes 14–16 and accompanying text.

as to expropriations of property within days of the decision.[112] Moreover, the *Sabbatino* opinion acknowledged that the States had shown no signs of rejecting its pre-*Erie* decisions, whatever their legal basis.[113] One might recast the doctrine as imposing a general rule of decision in cases that turn on the validity of foreign official acts. This rule could operate without requiring the federal judiciary to serve as its exclusive expounder and enforcer.[114]

## C.  Foreign Relations as a Basis for Categorical Preemption

What might be the fate of *Zschernig* as a tool of policing State law to suppress interference with foreign relations? The Court has expressed some reservations about the opinion but has not yet repudiated it. Instead, it has sought to anchor preemption of State law to particular acts or policies adopted by the federal government. Were disenchantment with the one-voice premise to prevail, one might anticipate an express repudiation of the "intrusion" test. What may replace it, however, is uncertain.

Even if *Zschernig* were to be interred, the courts still would have to decide whether only an enactment involving Congress can invalidate State law, or whether interference with legitimate foreign policy initiatives of the executive suffices to trigger preemption.[115] This question blends issues of federalism with those of separation of powers. A critic of executive power logically could embrace a strong preemption doctrine but insist on a link to an act of Congress; a friend of the executive could endorse a limited doctrine but still invalidate State law that obstructs legitimate executive acts. This is, in short, a multidimensional problem of the sort that the Supreme Court will find difficult to address consistently.

Other questions would include what counts as interference and how much is too much. At the end of the day, what the demise of the one-voice premise might do is motivate the courts to decide these cases with less suspicion of the potential of State law for mischief. Other considerations undoubtedly will apply in particular cases, and context may dominate general principles. But removing one

---

[112] Second Hickenlooper Amendment, 22 U.S.C. § 2370(e)(2); see FOURTH RESTATEMENT § 441 cmt. *h* & reporters' note 12.

[113] *Sabbatino*, 376 U.S. at 423–25.

[114] For more on this point, see John C. Harrison, *International Law in U.S. Courts within the Limits of the Constitution*, in this volume.

[115] Compare American Ins. Assn. v. Garamendi, 539 U.S. 396, 424 (2003) (executive branch policy in core foreign relations area sufficient to preempt State law), with Barclays Bank PLC v. Franchise Tax Bd. of California, 512 U.S. 298 (1994) (executive branch policy insufficient to preempt State law regarding taxation of international transactions). Cf. Dames & Moore v. Regan, 453 U.S. 654, 680 (1981) ("Crucial to our decision today is the conclusion that Congress has implicitly approved the practice of claim settlement by executive agreement.").

confounding factor from the equation should count as progress, even if solutions remain less than perfect.

## V.  Conclusion

The idea that a state should organize its conduct of foreign relations in such a way as to maximize its influence with the rest of the world and to minimize the possibility of misunderstanding and friction seems compelling. Certainly the framers of the U.S. Constitution, recognizing the uncertain legitimacy of their republican project in the eyes of European monarchs and the range of hostile forces arrayed against their new nation, would have pursued these goals. What this chapter questions is not this principle as such, but rather the inference that it justifies wide-ranging lawmaking powers in the federal judiciary.

The premise of this chapter is that lawmaking by the federal courts is different from lawmaking by the States or interventions by Congress and the executive. Both the States and the federal political branches might make unwise decisions and complicate foreign relations. But they also both face incentives not to do so and have the capacity to quickly correct their mistakes. The federal judiciary, seen as a complex and divided system, lacks both the ability to combat tendencies toward incoherence and the capacity to respond quickly to the challenges of a complex and dangerous world.

# 8

# Restating *The Charming Betsy*
# as a Canon of Avoidance

*Anthony J. Bellia Jr. & Bradford R. Clark*

The Supreme Court recognized the *Charming Betsy* canon more than two centuries ago, and it has since become a well-known tool of statutory construction. As formulated in 1804, the canon instructed that a federal statute "ought never to be construed to violate the law of nations if any other possible construction remains."[1] In 1987, the Third Restatement restated the canon as follows: "Where fairly possible, a United States statute is to be construed so as not to conflict with international law or with an international agreement of the United States."[2] Although the goal may have been merely to restate the *Charming Betsy* canon in modern terminology, the Restatement arguably expanded the domain of the canon beyond its original formulation and actual use by the Supreme Court. At the time *The Charming Betsy* was decided, the canon functioned as a canon of avoidance. It ensured that courts did not usurp the constitutional authority of the political branches over the conduct of war and foreign relations by violating the rights of foreign nations without clear authorization to do so. The Supreme Court's use of the canon has continued to serve this function.

The Supreme Court did not adopt the *Charming Betsy* canon to enforce international law in and of itself. When *The Charming Betsy* was decided in 1804, the law of nations consisted of three main branches—the law merchant, the law maritime, and the law of state-state relations.[3] At that time, the United States could "violate" the law of nations only by failing to respect the rights of foreign nations under the law of state-state relations, such as the right to neutral use of the high seas at issue in *The Charming Betsy*. The law of state-state relations governed the rights and obligations of nations vis-à-vis one another. Thus, at the time of *The Charming Betsy*, the canon required the judiciary to construe federal statutes,

---

[1]  Murray v. The Schooner Charming Betsy, 6 U.S. (2 Cranch) 64, 118 (1804).
[2]  THIRD RESTATEMENT § 114.
[3]  See ANTHONY J. BELLIA JR. & BRADFORD R. CLARK, THE LAW OF NATIONS AND THE UNITED STATES CONSTITUTION (2017).

Anthony J. Bellia Jr. & Bradford R. Clark, *Restating* The Charming Betsy *as a Canon of Avoidance* In: *The Restatement and Beyond.* Edited by: Paul B. Stephan and Sarah H. Cleveland, Oxford University Press (2020). © Oxford University Press.
DOI: 10.1093/oso/9780197533154.003.0009

whenever possible, not to violate the rights of foreign nations under the law of state-state relations.

Understood in this light, the canon served to ensure that courts upheld the U.S. Constitution's allocation of powers over war and foreign relations. The Constitution grants Congress and the president—the political branches of the federal government—exclusive authority to conduct relations with foreign nations. In 1804, if one nation violated another nation's rights under the law of state-state relations, the aggrieved nation had just cause to retaliate against the other nation, including by waging war. Thus, one nation's decision to violate another nation's rights was a major foreign policy decision with potentially grave consequences. If Congress and the president authorized courts to violate such rights, any resulting judicial action implementing their decision would not encroach on the constitutional prerogatives of the political branches. On the other hand, if courts violated the rights of foreign nations without such authorization, they would usurp the exclusive constitutional authority of the political branches to decide whether to violate another nation's rights and risk triggering hostilities. The *Charming Betsy* canon avoided judicial violations of the Constitution's allocation of powers by requiring courts to construe federal statutes not to violate the rights of foreign nations whenever possible. For this reason, the canon appears to have been the first canon of constitutional avoidance recognized by the Supreme Court.

The Supreme Court has continued to apply the *Charming Betsy* canon as a canon of avoidance since its adoption. In each case in which the Court has applied the canon—from *The Charming Betsy* until today—it has upheld the traditional rights of foreign nations under the law of state-state relations, including their rights to govern within their own territory and on vessels flying their flag. This use of the canon preserves the Constitution's allocation of war and foreign relations powers exclusively to the political branches. Specifically, it ensures that Congress and the president—rather than the courts—will decide whether the United States will violate the rights of foreign nations under the law of state-state relations, and thereby risk triggering conflict or even war with the aggrieved nations. Under the Constitution, the decision to risk such consequences belongs solely to the political branches. For this reason, courts have long construed federal statutes not to violate the traditional sovereign rights of foreign nations unless the statute makes its intent to do so unmistakably clear.

The Third Restatement formulation does not adequately capture the essential role of *the Charming Betsy* canon as a canon of constitutional avoidance. By instructing courts to construe statutes "so as not to conflict with international law," the Third Restatement arguably goes beyond avoiding U.S. violations of another nation's rights under the law of state-state relations. For example, the Third Restatement could be read to require courts to construe statutes to enforce international law against other nations. It also could be read to require courts to construe federal (and State) statutes to avoid violations of modern customary international law rules that restrict how nations treat their own citizens within their own territory. These uses of the canon would not avoid constitutional difficulties but could actually generate them. Thus, it is not surprising that the Supreme Court has never used the canon in these ways.

The Fourth Restatement does not include a general restatement of the *Charming Betsy* canon, but Section 406 restates an important application of the canon to avoid conflicts with international law governing jurisdiction to prescribe.[4] Like the original *Charming Betsy* canon, Section 406 serves as a canon of constitutional avoidance by preventing courts from usurping the political branches' constitutional authority to decide whether the United States should violate other nations' rights under international law—in this case, jurisdiction to prescribe. While Section 406 is a significant step in the right direction, the American Law Institute should undertake to restate the broader *Charming Betsy* canon in terms that reflect its role as a canon of constitutional avoidance.

In this chapter, we propose a new restatement of the *Charming Betsy* canon that tracks its actual use by the Supreme Court as a canon of avoidance, and excludes potential misuses that might contradict, rather than uphold, the Constitution's allocation of powers. First, we explain the origins of the canon in early Supreme Court cases. Next, we describe how the Court has used the canon over time. Finally, we set forth a proposed restatement of the canon that more accurately depicts its original function and continued use as a canon of constitutional avoidance.

## I. The Origins of the *Charming Betsy* Canon

To understand the original function of the *Charming Betsy* canon as a canon of avoidance, it is useful to appreciate that *The Charming Betsy* itself was one of a broader group of early Supreme Court decisions that prevented federal courts from usurping the constitutional authority of Congress and the president over war and foreign relations.[5] In addition to *The Charming Betsy*, these decisions

---

[4] FOURTH RESTATEMENT § 406 (2017) ("Where fairly possible, courts in the United States construe federal statutes to avoid conflict with international law governing jurisdiction to prescribe.").

[5] As William Dodge has observed, "[a]lthough *The Charming Betsy* has come to be seen as a landmark for international law in the United States, it is really just a representative example of the age in which it was decided." William S. Dodge, The Charming Betsy *and* The Paquete Habana *(1804 and 1900)* 1, 12, in LANDMARK CASES IN PUBLIC INTERNATIONAL LAW (Eirik Bjorge & Cameron Miles eds., 2017). Although we disagree with Dodge's position that *The Charming Betsy* reflected the view that U.S. law automatically incorporated international law as supreme federal law, see BELLIA & CLARK, *supra* note 3; Anthony J. Bellia Jr. & Bradford R. Clark, *Why Federal Courts Apply the Law of Nations Even Though It Is Not the Supreme Law of the Land*, 106 GEO. L.J. 1915 (2018), we agree

include *United States v. Peters* and *The Schooner Exchange v. M'Faddon*. In all three cases, the Court narrowly construed acts of Congress to avoid generating conflict or even war with foreign nations by violating their rights under the law of nations. When understood in the broader context of these cases, the *Charming Betsy* canon functioned as a canon of constitutional avoidance. Not surprisingly, the Supreme Court has since repeatedly described the broader canon of constitutional avoidance as having its "roots" in *The Charming Betsy*.[6]

*United States v. Peters*[7] was an important precursor to the *Charming Betsy* decision, and underscores the correlation between judicial respect for the sovereign rights of foreign nations and the Constitution's allocation of powers between the judiciary and the political branches. *Peters* considered whether a U.S. district court could exercise its admiralty jurisdiction to adjudicate the legality of a capture by the *Cassius*, a French ship authorized to seize enemy vessels. James Yard, a Philadelphia merchant, filed a libel in federal court against the *Cassius* while the vessel was at port in Philadelphia, alleging that it had improperly captured his neutral U.S. vessel on the high seas in violation of U.S. rights under the law of nations. After capturing Yard's vessel, the *Cassius* took it to France, where a French court condemned it as a lawful prize. Yard disputed the legality of this determination and initiated an *in rem* action against the *Cassius* in Philadelphia in order to obtain redress. As part of this action, the district court took possession of the *Cassius* pending adjudication of Yard's claim.

The Supreme Court granted a request for a writ of prohibition by the owners of the *Cassius*, thereby preventing the district court from exercising jurisdiction over the ship. The Court stated that the district court's adjudication of the legality of the capture would violate France's right to make binding prize determinations in its own courts:

> [B]y the laws of nations, the vessels of war of belligerent powers, duly by them authorized, to cruize against their enemies, and to make prize of their ships and goods, may, in time of war, arrest and seize the vessels belonging to the subjects or citizens of neutral nations, and bring them into the ports of the sovereign under whose commission and authority they act, there to answer for any breaches of the laws of nations, concerning the navigation of neutral ships, in time of war; and the said vessels of war, their commanders, officers and crews,

that the canon represented an important principle of interpretation in early Supreme Court cases involving the law of nations.

[6] *See infra* notes 68–70, and accompanying text.
[7] 3 U.S. (3 Dall.) 121 (1795).

are not amenable before the tribunals of neutral powers for their conduct therein. . . .[8]

In the eighteenth and early nineteenth centuries, the law of nations recognized prize determinations by one nation's courts as authoritative acts of state, and prohibited the courts of other nations from contradicting them. Thus, had the Supreme Court permitted the district court to adjudicate Yard's claim, it would have violated France's rights under the law of state-state relations, and given France just cause to retaliate against the United States, including by waging war. This background explains why the *Peters* opinion characterized Yard's suit as "contriving and intending to disturb the peace and harmony subsisting between the United States and the French Republic."[9]

This background also explains why the *Peters* opinion characterized the district court proceedings as "in contempt of the government of the United States, against the laws of nations, and the treaties subsisting between the United States and the French Republic, and against the laws and customs of the United States."[10] A decision by the district court contradicting France's right to make prize determinations would have been "in contempt of the government of the United States" because that government—through treaties and the exchange of ambassadors—recognized France as an independent nation with all of the rights that accompanied that status under the law of nations, including the right to make binding prize determinations within its territory. A judicial decision contradicting France's prize determination would have been inconsistent with this recognition. Such a decision also would have intruded upon the political branches' powers over war and peace by giving France just cause for war against the United States.

The Supreme Court's disposition in *Peters* reflects the Constitution's allocation of exclusive authority to the political branches to decide whether, when, and how to hold foreign nations accountable for their alleged violations of U.S. rights under the law of nations. Although U.S. courts refrained from reviewing foreign prize determinations, an aggrieved party remained free to seek assistance from the political branches in various ways. First, an aggrieved party could ask the executive branch to take up its cause through the practice of espousal. Historically, a nation's espousal of a claim against a foreign state "rendered it a public claim on the international plane, and the [claimant's] sovereign could lawfully wage war to vindicate the espoused claim."[11] Thus, espousal often triggered negotiations

---

[8] *Peters*, 3 U.S. at 129–30.
[9] *Id.* at 130.
[10] *Id.* at 131 (emphasis omitted).
[11] Thomas H. Lee, *The Supreme Court of the United States as Quasi-International Tribunal: Reclaiming the Court's Original and Exclusive Jurisdiction over Treaty-Based Suits by Foreign States Against States*, 104 COLUM. L. REV. 1765, 1856 (2004) (citations omitted); *see also* Ingrid Brunk

between nations resulting in some form of compensation.[12] Second, the victim of an erroneous prize determination could ask Congress to provide redress by authorizing reprisals or captures against the offending nation, its nationals, or their property—including the offending vessel. As illustrated by the Quasi-War with France, congressional action of this kind could lead to an escalation of hostilities or even war. Third, Congress could specifically authorize U.S. courts to adjudicate claims like Yard's, knowing that such action could trigger conflict with foreign nations. The important point is that all of these methods of obtaining redress enabled the political branches—rather than the courts—to decide whether, when, and how to respond to a foreign nation's alleged violation of U.S. rights.

Although it did not come out and say so, the *Peters* Court implicitly applied a clear statement requirement to construe Congress's general grant of admiralty jurisdiction narrowly to avoid jurisdiction in that case. Section 9 of the Judiciary Act of 1789 gave the district courts "exclusive original cognizance of all civil causes of admiralty and maritime jurisdiction."[13] This grant of jurisdiction allowed federal district courts to exercise *in rem* jurisdiction over foreign ships found within U.S. ports to adjudicate and redress claims that a ship improperly impeded the operations of U.S. vessels on the high seas. In *Peters*, however, the Supreme Court prohibited the district court from using this jurisdiction to adjudicate Yard's claim against the *Cassius*, notwithstanding the general authorization set forth in Section 9. In other words, the Court presumed that—in the absence of clearer and more precise statutory language—Congress would not authorize federal courts to violate the rights of France under the law of nations and thereby "disturb the peace and harmony subsisting between the United States and the French Republic."[14]

The Supreme Court made this presumption explicit in *Murray v. The Schooner Charming Betsy*.[15] *The Charming Betsy* involved interpretation of the Non-Intercourse Act of 1800, a federal statute enacted during the Quasi-War with France. The act prohibited commercial intercourse between residents of the

---

Wuerth, *The Dangers of Deference: International Claim Settlement by the President*, 44 HARV. INT'L L.J. 1, 20 (2003) ("Historically, claims settlement by the executive branch has been closely tied to the doctrines of espousal and state responsibility.").

[12] See Bradford R. Clark, *Domesticating Sole Executive Agreements*, 93 VA. L. REV. 1573, 1626–29 (2007).

[13] An Act to Establish the Judicial Courts of the United States, ch. 20, 1 Stat. 73, 77.

[14] *Peters*, 3 U.S. at 130.

[15] 6 U.S. (2 Cranch) 64 (1804). In fact, the Court endorsed a similar canon of construction three years earlier in *Talbot v. Seeman*, 5 U.S. (1 Cranch) 1 (1801). There, the Court accepted the suggestion "that the laws of the United States ought not, if it be avoidable, so to be construed as to infract the common principles and usages of nations, or the general doctrines of national law." *Id.* at 43. We focus here on *The Charming Betsy* decision because it is the more prominent case for which the canon is named.

United States and residents of any French territory.[16] The *Jane*, a vessel owned and operated by Americans, traveled from Baltimore to the Caribbean Islands with instructions to sell the ship and her cargo. After disposing of the cargo, the American Captain proceeded to St. Thomas, where he sold the ship to Jared Shattuck, a Danish burgher.[17] Shattuck renamed the ship the *Charming Betsy* and sent her to the French island of Guadalupe as a Danish vessel carrying a cargo of American produce.[18]

During her voyage, the ship was first captured by French privateers, and then recaptured by the USS *Constellation*, a Navy frigate deployed during the Quasi-War with France.[19] Alexander Murray, the *Constellation's* captain, believed that the vessel violated the Non-Intercourse Act either because its new owner (Shattuck) was an American citizen, or because the ship had been sold to Shattuck for the purpose of evading the act. Accordingly, Murray brought the vessel to Philadelphia where he initiated a libel action in federal court seeking to condemn the ship and its cargo under the act.[20] The consul of Denmark maintained that the ship and its cargo were the bona fide property of a Danish subject (Shattuck), and thus beyond the reach of the act.

Upon review, the Supreme Court ruled that the Non-Intercourse Act should not be construed to authorize the seizure and condemnation of the ship and its cargo. Chief Justice Marshall's opinion began by reciting the principle that a federal statute "ought never to be construed to violate the law of nations if any other possible construction remains, and consequently can never be construed to violate neutral rights, or to affect neutral commerce, further than is warranted by the law of nations as understood in this country."[21] The Court believed this principle "to be correct," and that it "ought to be kept in view in construing" the Non-Intercourse Act.[22]

To determine whether the *Charming Betsy's* trade with France violated the act, the Supreme Court had to address two questions. First, the Court considered whether Shattuck was—within the meaning of the statute—a "person . . . resident within the *United States* or under their protection,"[23] or a "citizen thereof residing elsewhere."[24] Shattuck was born in Connecticut prior to the Declaration of Independence, and then moved to St. Thomas as an infant.[25] In 1797, he

---

[16]  Federal Non-intercourse Act, ch. 10, § 1, 2 Stat. 7, 8 (1800) (expired 1801).
[17]  *Charming Betsy*, 6 U.S. (2 Cranch) at 115.
[18]  *Id.* at 116.
[19]  *Id.*
[20]  *Id.*
[21]  *Id.* at 118.
[22]  *Id.*
[23]  *Id.*
[24]  *Id.*
[25]  *Id.* at 116.

took an oath of allegiance to Denmark.[26] The Court declined to decide whether Shattuck was a U.S. citizen or could "divest himself absolutely" of this status "otherwise than in such manner as may be prescribed by law."[27] Instead, the Court simply concluded that he was outside the general terms of the act because he was neither a resident of the United States nor under their protection. The Court reasoned that having "made himself the subject of a foreign power" and having acquired in a foreign country "the commercial privileges attached to his domicil,"[28] Shattuck was "not a person within the protection of the *United States*" as required by the act.[29] The Court thus concluded "that the *Charming Betsy*, with her cargo, being at the time of her recapture the *bona fide* property of a *Danish* burgher, is not forfeitable in consequence of her being employed in carrying on trade and commerce with a *French* island."[30]

To reach this conclusion, the Court had to construe the Non-Intercourse Act narrowly and arguably ignore part of the statute. By its terms, the act applied not only to "any person or persons resident within the United States or under their protection,"[31] but also to "any ship or vessel, owned, hired, or employed wholly or in part by any person or persons resident within the United States, *or any citizen or citizens thereof resident elsewhere*."[32] The *Jane* arguably fell within this second category if Shattuck had become a U.S. citizen before moving to St. Thomas and had retained this status under U.S. law (notwithstanding his declaration of allegiance to Denmark). Rather than confronting and deciding this question, the Court found it sufficient that Shattuck—whatever his citizenship—was not under the protection of the United States at the time of the relevant events. In reaching this conclusion, the Court arguably collapsed two separate statutory prohibitions into one in order to avoid the application of the act.

The second question under the act was whether the sale of the *Jane* to Shattuck was made "for the purpose that [it] may proceed" to a French port and thereby evade the act.[33] Again, Chief Justice Marshall avoided the question by effectively reading the prohibition on evasive sales out of the statute. According to the Court, "[i]f it was intended that any American vessel sold to a neutral should, in the possession of that neutral, be liable to the commercial disabilities imposed on her while she belonged to citizens of the United States, such extraordinary intent ought to have been plainly expressed."[34] A prohibition on evasive sales to

---

[26] *Id.*
[27] *Id.* at 120.
[28] *Id.*
[29] *Id.*
[30] *Id.* at 120–21.
[31] 2 Stat. at 8.
[32] *Id.* (emphasis added).
[33] *Charming Betsy*, 6 U.S. (2 Cranch) at 119.
[34] *Id.*

neutral citizens would have been "extraordinary" because it would have violated the rights of neutral nations—such as Denmark—under the law of state-state relations.

The right to neutral use of the high seas was one of the most important rights nations possessed vis-à-vis one another under the law of state-state relations. In fact, it was one of a handful of "perfect" rights, the violation of which gave the offended nation just cause for war.[35] Thus, *The Charming Betsy* Court had good reason to uphold the neutral rights of Denmark in the absence of unmistakably clear instructions from Congress to the contrary. This approach ensured that courts would not usurp the political branches' constitutional authority to make the momentous decision whether to violate another nation's neutral rights.

The Constitution's allocation of powers accounts for why the Supreme Court articulated and applied such a strong canon of avoidance in *The Charming Betsy*. As we have explained elsewhere, the Constitution's exclusive allocation of war and foreign relations powers to Congress and the president required courts to uphold the rights of foreign nations under the law of state-state relations.[36] First, judicial violations of such rights would contradict the political branches' recognition of the nation in question as an independent sovereign entitled to all of the rights that accompanied that status under the law of nations.[37] Second, judicial violation of such rights would give the aggrieved nation just cause to retaliate against the United States, including by waging war, in contravention of the political branches' exclusive authority to initiate war with other nations.[38] Because the Constitution vested decisions relating to war and peace exclusively in the political branches, courts refrained from redressing the misconduct of foreign nations without clear authorization from the political branches to do so.[39]

The *Charming Betsy* canon guarded against this precise danger. By requiring courts, whenever possible, to construe federal statutes not to violate other nations' rights under the law of nations, the canon ensured that Congress and the president—rather than the courts—would make the crucial decision to risk hostilities with foreign nations by violating such rights. In short, the canon upheld the Constitution's allocation of war and foreign relations powers to the political branches by requiring courts to err on the side of upholding—rather than violating—the rights of foreign sovereigns in the absence of unmistakably clear statutory instructions from the political branches to disregard them.

---

[35] See Anthony J. Bellia Jr. & Bradford R. Clark, *The Federal Common Law of Nations*, 109 COLUM. L. REV. 1, 16–19 (2009); see also 2 EMMERICH DE VATTEL, THE LAW OF NATIONS bk. III, §§ 111–12, at 40 (1759) (recognizing the perfect right of neutral nations to engage in neutral trade).

[36] BELLIA & CLARK, *supra* note 3, at 41–112.

[37] *Id.* at 53–57.

[38] *Id.* at 57–67.

[39] *Id.* at 73–112.

Seen in this light, the *Charming Betsy* canon appears to have been the first canon of constitutional avoidance employed by the Supreme Court. Construing federal statutes not to violate the law of state-state relations avoided judicial usurpation of the political branches' exclusive constitutional authority to decide whether, when, and how to override a foreign nation's rights and risk conflict with that nation.[40] Both *Peters* and *The Charming Betsy* illustrate the point. If Yard's allegations in *Peters* were true, then France violated U.S. rights by allowing the *Cassius* to capture his neutral vessel and erroneously finding it to be a lawful prize of war. Congress could have exercised its exclusive power to authorize reprisals or captures in response but had not done so in clear and unmistakable terms. Thus, a unilateral judicial "reprisal" against the *Cassius* in the form of seizure and damages would have usurped Congress's constitutional authority. Similarly, in *The Charming Betsy*, the Non-Intercourse Act sought to curtail trade with France but did not expressly authorize U.S. courts to interfere with the neutral rights of third countries in the process. In both cases, the Supreme Court essentially employed a canon of constitutional avoidance to prevent the lower courts from usurping the constitutional prerogatives of Congress and the president to manage U.S. relations with foreign nations.

Eight years after *The Charming Betsy*, the Supreme Court applied a similar canon of constitutional avoidance in *The Schooner Exchange v. M'Faddon*.[41] There, the Court construed the Judiciary Act of 1789 not to confer admiralty jurisdiction over a former American ship alleged to have been "violently and forcibly taken" by French nationals on the high seas and refitted as a French warship "in violation of the rights of the [original owners], and of the law of nations."[42] The Judiciary Act appeared to authorize the district court to hear the case by giving it general cognizance over "all civil causes of admiralty and maritime jurisdiction."[43] The Court, however, employed a clear statement rule and concluded that the act should not be read to confer jurisdiction over foreign warships in the absence of clear and express statutory language to that effect. As the Court put it, "until [the sovereign] power be exerted *in a manner not to be misunderstood*, the sovereign cannot be considered as having imparted to the ordinary tribunals a jurisdiction, which it would be a breach of faith to exercise."[44] The Supreme Court's use of a clear statement rule in *The Schooner Exchange* confirms the original function of the *Charming Betsy* canon as a canon of constitutional

[40] See Amy C. Barrett, *Substantive Canons and Faithful Agency*, 90 B.U. L. REV. 109, 119 (2010) (describing the origins of the *Charming Betsy* canon and acknowledging that it not only respects international law but also protects "the political branches' authority over foreign affairs").

[41] 11 U.S. (7 Cranch) 116 (1812).

[42] *Id.* at 117.

[43] An Act to Establish the Judicial Courts of the United States, ch. 20, 1 Stat. 73, 77.

[44] *The Schooner Exch.*, 11 U.S. (7 Cranch) at 146 (emphasis added).

avoidance. As in *Peters*, the Supreme Court construed the Judiciary Act narrowly to deny district court jurisdiction to adjudicate a claim that could have usurped political branch authority and triggered significant foreign policy repercussions.

In one respect, however, the allocation of powers rationale in *The Schooner Exchange* was even clearer than in *Peters*. In *The Schooner Exchange*, the original American owners of a French warship (temporarily located in the port of Philadelphia to make repairs) brought an action to recover the vessel on the ground that French nationals had "violently and forcibly taken" the ship from them on the high seas "in violation of the rights of the libellants, and of the law of nations."[45] Unlike *Peters*, however, "no sentence or decree of condemnation had been pronounced against [the ship], by any [French] court of competent jurisdiction."[46] Thus, judicial review of the legality of the capture could have vindicated U.S. rights under the law of state-state relations without violating France's right to make binding prize determinations in its own courts. Nonetheless, in order to avoid usurping the powers of the political branches over foreign relations, the Court employed a canon of avoidance to prevent U.S. courts from adjudicating the claim.

The question presented in *The Schooner Exchange* was "whether an American citizen can assert, in an American court, a title to an armed national vessel [of another country], found within the waters of the United States."[47] The Court began its analysis by explaining that the immunity of foreign warships in the United States could not derive its "validity from an external source" because the "jurisdiction of the nation within its own territory is necessarily exclusive and absolute."[48] Accordingly, the Court explained,

> all exemptions from territorial jurisdiction, must be derived from the consent of the sovereign of the territory, that this consent may be implied or expressed, and that when implied, its extent must be regulated by the nature of the case, and the views under which the parties requiring and conceding it must be supposed to act.[49]

On this view, any applicable immunity "must be traced up to the consent of the nation itself" in conformity with "those principles of national and municipal law by which it ought to be regulated."[50]

---

[45] *Id.* at 117.
[46] *Id.* at 117, 146–47.
[47] *Id.* at 135.
[48] *Id.* at 136.
[49] *Id.* at 143.
[50] *Id.* at 135–36.

In determining whether the United States had consented to an immunity for foreign warships found within its ports, the Supreme Court considered the Constitution's allocation of powers to the political branches. Some background is helpful in assessing the Court's analysis. In response to the plaintiff's libel action against the ship, the U.S. Attorney "(at the instance of the executive department of the government of the United States, as it is understood,) filed a *suggestion*" of immunity with the court.[51] The district court accepted this suggestion and dismissed the case on the ground that "a public armed vessel of a foreign sovereign, in amity with our government, is not subject to the ordinary judicial tribunals of the country."[52] The circuit court, however, reversed and allowed the plaintiffs' claim to proceed. Because the Supreme Court considered the case to involve "the political relations between the United States and France," the Court agreed to expedite its review of the case.[53]

In his presentation before the Supreme Court, the U.S. Attorney argued that "[i]f the courts of the United States should exercise such a jurisdiction[,] it will amount to a judicial declaration of war."[54] Indeed, he went so far as to argue that the judiciary's exercise of jurisdiction in a case of this nature "will absorb all the functions of government, and leave nothing for the legislative or executive departments to perform."[55] The Court apparently found these arguments persuasive and upheld France's claim of immunity just one week after oral argument.[56]

The Supreme Court concluded that the United States' consent to immunity for foreign warships could be inferred from the practice of nations, and that this "implication" could be destroyed only by "the sovereign power of the nation."[57] The Court's reference to the "sovereign power of the nation" appears to have been a reference to the constitutional authority of the political branches over war and reprisals. A judicial decision seizing a French warship in response to France's violation of U.S. rights almost certainly would have triggered fresh hostilities with France. The Court's refusal to allow judicial intervention in the dispute indicates that it understood the political branches to possess exclusive constitutional power to decide whether, when, and how to retaliate against France for its misconduct. France would have regarded any form of retaliation against its warship—whether by U.S. courts or by the political branches—to be a hostile act. The Court understood the Constitution to vest the political branches alone with

---

[51] *Id.* at 117–18.
[52] *Id.* at 119–20.
[53] *Id.* at 116, 120.
[54] *Id.* at 126.
[55] *Id.*
[56] *Id.* at 135.
[57] *Id.* at 146.

the "sovereign power" to authorize such retaliation and thereby risk triggering hostilities.

In the course of this analysis, Chief Justice Marshall emphasized that, "[w]ithout doubt, the sovereign of the place is capable of destroying" the immunity suggested by the practice of nations.[58] "He may claim and exercise jurisdiction either by employing force, or by subjecting such vessels to the ordinary tribunals."[59] Because the political branches had not *clearly* taken either course, the Court ruled that courts must treat "national ships of war, entering the port of a friendly power open for their reception, . . . as exempted by the consent of [the sovereign] power from its jurisdiction."[60] The Court also rejected counsel's argument that courts could take it upon themselves to deny immunity on the ground that France's initial seizure of the vessel violated the United States' right to neutral use of the high seas. Chief Justice Marshall found "great weight" in the argument

> that the sovereign power of the nation is alone competent to avenge wrongs committed by a sovereign, that the questions to which such wrongs give birth are rather questions of policy than of law, [and] that they are for diplomatic, rather than legal discussion.[61]

Although *The Schooner Exchange* is not typically cited for its reliance on a clear statement requirement to avoid constitutional concerns, the canon of avoidance played a pivotal role in the decision. As in *Peters*, the general grant of admiralty jurisdiction in the Judiciary Act of 1789 arguably authorized the district court to hear this case. The *Schooner Exchange* Court, however, refused to interpret the act to permit jurisdiction. According to the Court, "until [the sovereign] power be exerted *in a manner not to be misunderstood*, the sovereign cannot be considered as having imparted to the ordinary tribunals a jurisdiction, which it would be a breach of faith to exercise."[62] In other words, *The Schooner Exchange* Court construed the statute not to authorize jurisdiction in order to prevent courts from violating the Constitution's allocation of powers to the political branches.

In the context of these contemporaneous decisions, the *Charming Betsy* canon is best understood as a canon of constitutional avoidance. The canon ensured that courts would not commit unauthorized violations of foreign nations' rights under the law of state-state relations, and thus prevented the judiciary from usurping the exclusive constitutional authority of the political branches over war

---

[58] *Id.*
[59] *Id.*
[60] *Id.* at 145–46.
[61] *Id.*; see also The Nereide, 13 U.S. (9 Cranch) 388 (1815).
[62] *The Schooner Exch.*, 11 U.S. (7 Cranch) at 146 (emphasis added),

and foreign relations. In keeping with this conception of the canon, the Court has subsequently used it solely to uphold the sovereign rights of foreign nations. The Court has never applied the canon to hold other nations accountable for their alleged violations of international law. As *The Schooner Exchange* demonstrates, to use the canon in that way would usurp rather than uphold the political branches' exclusive constitutional authority to decide whether, when, and how the United States will respond to such violations. As section II explains, the Supreme Court has applied the *Charming Betsy* canon—from its adoption through today—solely to uphold the traditional rights of foreign nations under the law of nations and thus avoid violations of the Constitution's allocation of powers.

## II. The Canon in the Supreme Court

*The Charming Betsy* has been cited in Supreme Court opinions on numerous occasions. Before the 1920s, Justices cited the case for propositions unrelated to the canon, namely, for the substantive questions of law that the case addressed.[63] Since the 1920s, however, Justices have cited the case in support of two propositions: first, where fairly possible, courts should interpret federal statutes to avoid constitutional questions (the canon of constitutional avoidance); and second, courts should not interpret acts of Congress to apply either extraterritorially (the presumption against extraterritoriality) or to the internal affairs of foreign ships (the internal affairs presumption) unless the act in question clearly and expressly applies in these circumstances.[64]

Upon analysis, however, these two propositions are closely related. The presumption against extraterritoriality and the internal affairs presumption are specific applications of the broader canon of constitutional avoidance. If courts were to apply U.S. law extraterritorially or to govern the internal affairs of foreign ships, they would be enforcing U.S. law in an area within the prescriptive jurisdiction

---

[63] See, e.g., The Panama, 176 U.S. 535, 547 (1900); United States v. Wong Kim Ark, 169 U.S. 649, 658–59 (1898); The Scotland, 105 U.S. 24, 35–36 (1881); Shanks v. Dupont, 28 U.S. 242, 267 (1830); Manro v. Almeida, 23 U.S. 473, 486–87 (1825); Sands v. Knox, 7 U.S. 499 (1806); Maley v. Shattuck, 7 U.S. 458, 489 (1806); see also Dodge, *supra* note 5, at 16 (describing these matters of prize law). The Court did, however, sometimes apply related canons of construction during this period without citing *The Charming Betsy*. See, e.g., United States v. Klintock, 18 U.S. 44, 151–52 (1820) (stating that "the words of [a statute] ought to be restricted to offences committed by persons who, at the time of committing them, were within the ordinary jurisdiction of the United States").

[64] Paul Stephan has observed that the Supreme Court has invoked the *Charming Betsy* canon on a limited basis since the end of World War II, mostly in cases dealing with prescriptive jurisdiction and as support for the canon of constitutional avoidance. Paul Stephan, *Privatizing International Law*, 97 Va. L. Rev. 1573, 1646 & n.177 (2011). As explained, the Fourth Restatement dealt with this important category of cases by restating the application of the canon to statutes implicating the international law governing jurisdiction to prescribe. See *supra* note 4 and accompanying text.

of another nation in violation of the traditional sovereign rights of that nation under the law of state-state relations. When Congress has clearly expressed its intent to override such rights, courts must implement the statute's directive. But when Congress has not clearly expressed an intent to regulate within the territory or on the vessels of another nation, courts risk violating the Constitution's allocation of powers by extending federal law to such places. As explained, the Constitution assigns the decision whether to violate another nation's traditional rights under the law of nations exclusively to the political branches. If courts violated such rights without political branch authorization, they would usurp the exclusive constitutional authority of the political branches over war and foreign relations. For this reason, judicial use of the *Charming Betsy* canon to avoid extraterritorial application of U.S. law (or to avoid any other violation of the traditional sovereign rights of foreign nations) is simply one application of the canon of constitutional avoidance.

This section describes the Supreme Court's reliance on *The Charming Betsy* as support for the canon of constitutional avoidance and the presumption against the extraterritorial application of U.S. law. It then explains why the presumption against extraterritoriality (like the broader presumption against violating the sovereign rights of foreign nations) is best understood as a specific application of the canon of constitutional avoidance.

## A. Canon of Constitutional Avoidance

Under the canon of constitutional avoidance, courts construe statutes to avoid constitutional difficulties whenever such a construction is fairly possible. "[W]here an otherwise acceptable construction of a statute would raise serious constitutional problems, the Court will construe the statute to avoid such problems unless such construction is plainly contrary to the intent of Congress."[65] In other words, "[w]hen 'a serious doubt' is raised about the constitutionality of an act of Congress, 'it is a cardinal principle that this Court will first ascertain whether a construction of the statute is fairly possible by which the question may be avoided.'"[66] The canon of constitutional avoidance "comes into play only when, after the application of ordinary textual analysis, the statute is found to be susceptible of more than one construction."[67]

---

[65] *DeBartolo*, 485 U.S. at 575.

[66] Jennings v. Rodriguez, 138 S. Ct. 830, 842 (2018) (quoting Crowell v. Benson, 285 U.S. 22, 62 (1932)).

[67] *Id.* (quoting Clark v. Martinez, 543 U.S. 371, 385 (2005)).

The Supreme Court has described the canon of constitutional avoidance as having its roots in *The Charming Betsy* decision. In 1979, the Court explained that "[i]n a number of cases [it] has heeded the essence of Mr. Chief Justice Marshall's admonition in *Murray v. The Charming Betsy* by holding that an Act of Congress ought not be construed to violate the Constitution if any other possible construction remains available."[68] A few years later, the Court described the canon of avoidance as a "cardinal principle" that "has its roots in Chief Justice Marshall's opinion for the Court in *Murray v. The Charming Betsy*, and has for so long been applied by this Court that it is beyond debate."[69] In short, the Justices have invoked *The Charming Betsy* in numerous opinions in support of the general canon of constitutional avoidance.[70]

## B.  Avoiding Interference with Other Nations

In addition to citing *The Charming Betsy* to support the general canon of constitutional avoidance, the Supreme Court has invoked the case to avoid the extraterritorial application of U.S. law—in other words, to avoid the application of U.S. law to territories and vessels subject to the prescriptive jurisdiction of another nation. The Fourth Restatement sets forth the presumption against extraterritoriality as follows: "Courts in the United States interpret federal statutory provisions to apply only within the territorial jurisdiction of the United States unless there is a clear indication of congressional intent to the contrary."[71] As the reporter's note explains, "the presumption against extraterritoriality has its roots in the [*Charming Betsy*] canon."[72] Significantly, the Court has justified its use of the *Charming Betsy* canon to avoid extraterritorial application of U.S. law on the grounds that the canon serves both to uphold exclusive constitutional authority of Congress over war and foreign relations, and to implement presumed congressional intent on these matters.

---

[68]  NLRB v. Catholic Bishop of Chicago, 440 U.S. 490, 500–501 (1979).

[69]  Edward J. DeBartolo Corp. v. Florida Gulf Coast Building & Constr. Trades Council, 485 U.S. 568, 575 (1988) (citation omitted); see also Skilling v. United States, 561 U.S. 358, 406 n.40 (2010) (same).

[70]  See McConnell v. FEC, 540 U.S. 93, 192–93 (2004) (citing *The Charming Betsy* to support the canon of constitutional avoidance); INS v. St. Cyr, 533 U.S. 289, 299–300 (2001) (same); Steel Co. v. Citizens for a Better Env't, 523 U.S. 83, 133 (1998) (Stevens, J., concurring) (same); United States v. IBM, 517 U.S. 843, 868 (1996) (Kennedy, J., dissenting) (same); Concrete Pipe and Prods. v. Constr. Laborers Pension Trust, 508 U.S. 602, 629 (1993) (same); Metropolitan Wash. Airports Auth. v. Citizens for Abatement of Aircraft Noise, 501 U.S. 252, 280–81 (White, dissenting) (same); Dalia v. United States, 441 U.S. 238, 265 n.7 (1979) (Stevens, J., dissenting) (same).

[71]  FOURTH RESTATEMENT § 404.

[72]  *Id.* § 404 reporters' note 1.

For example, in *Lauritzen v. Larsen*, the Supreme Court cited *The Charming Betsy* in support of the rule that a federal maritime law does not reach acts committed on foreign ships on the high seas unless Congress makes clear that such law applies.[73] The Court explained:

> This doctrine of construction is in accord with the long-heeded admonition of Mr. Chief Justice Marshall that "an Act of Congress ought never to be construed to violate the law of nations if any other possible construction remains." *The Charming Betsy*, 2 Cranch 64, 118. And it has long been accepted in maritime jurisprudence that "if any construction otherwise be possible, an Act will not be construed as applying to foreigners in respect to acts done by them outside the dominions of the sovereign power enacting. That is a rule based on international law, by which one sovereign power is bound to respect the subjects and the rights of all other sovereign powers outside its own territory." Lord Russell of Killowen in *The Queen v. Jameson* (1896), 2 Q.B. 425, 430. This is not, as sometimes is implied, any impairment of our own sovereignty, or limitation of the power of Congress. "The law of the sea", we have had occasion to observe, "is in a peculiar sense an international law, but application of its specific rules depends upon acceptance by the United States." *Farrell v. United States*, 336 U.S. 511, 517. On the contrary, we are simply dealing with a problem of statutory construction rather commonplace in a federal system by which courts often have to decide whether "any" or "every" reaches to the limits of the enacting authority's usual scope or is to be applied to foreign events or transactions.[74]

In other words, the *Lauritzen* Court determined that, in the absence of a clear statement from Congress, U.S. courts should not apply federal statutes to govern the internal affairs of foreign ships on the high seas. The reason, the Court explained, was not that international law itself could prevent Congress from extending its laws to such matters. Rather, the rationale was that the Court would

---

[73]  345 U.S. 571, 578 (1953).

[74]  *Id.* at 578–79 (internal citations omitted). The Court relied on a similar analysis a few years later in *Romero v. Int'l Terminal Oper. Co.*, 358 U.S. 354 (1959). In that case, the Court faced the question whether it could apply the Jones Act and general federal maritime law to injuries sustained by a foreign crew member upon a foreign ship while the vessel was temporarily in U.S. waters. Because the injury occurred in U.S. waters, the presumption against extraterritoriality did not apply. Nonetheless, the Court refused to apply U.S. law (the Jones Act and federal common law) to the claim for the same reasons it did not apply U.S. law in *Loritzen*. "Due regard for the relevant factors we there enumerated, and the weight we indicated to be given to each, preclude application of American law to the claims here asserted." *Id.* at 383. Of paramount importance to the Court were the interests of foreign nations in regulating their own ships and their own nationals: "Although the place of injury has often been deemed determinative of the choice of law in municipal conflict of laws, such a rule does not fit the accommodations that become relevant in fair and prudent regard for the interests of foreign nations in the regulation of their own ships and their own nationals, and the effect upon our interests of our treatment of the legitimate interests of foreign nations." *Id.* at 384.

not impute to Congress a desire to regulate the vessels of another nation unless Congress made that intent unmistakably clear in the text of the statute. This approach upheld the Constitution's allocation of powers by ensuring that courts would not usurp Congress's exclusive power to decide whether to risk conflict with another nation by applying federal law to its vessels.

In subsequent cases, the Supreme Court expressly invoked the Constitution's allocation of powers to justify its use of the *Charming Betsy* canon to avoid applying U.S. law to foreign vessels. In *McCulloch v. Sociedad Nacional de Marineros de Honduras*,[75] the Court considered whether the National Labor Relations Act applied to a foreign-flagged ship employing alien crew members. The act defined "commerce" broadly to include "trade, traffic, commerce, transportation, or communication . . . between any foreign country and any State."[76] In addition, the act defined "affecting commerce" to include anything "having led or tending to lead to a labor dispute burdening or obstructing commerce or the free flow of commerce."[77] The National Labor Relations Board ruled that the act applied to the foreign crew of a foreign vessel flying a foreign flag engaged in the transportation of products to the United States. The Supreme Court disagreed because application of the act to such vessels would contradict the recognition afforded them by Congress and the executive branch and invite retaliation by other nations. In the Court's view, a decision to apply U.S. law to matters within the prescriptive jurisdiction of another nation was for Congress rather than the courts to make.[78]

The *McCulloch* Court began by acknowledging that "Congress has constitutional power to apply the National Labor Relations Act to the crews working foreign-flag ships."[79] The question for the Court was "whether Congress exercised that power."[80] In examining the statute, the Court found "no basis for a construction which would exert United States jurisdiction over and apply its laws to the internal management and affairs of the vessels here flying the Honduran flag, contrary to the recognition long afforded them not only by our State Department but also by the Congress."[81] The Court observed that it was a "well-established rule of international law that the law of the flag state ordinarily governs the internal affairs of a ship."[82] Thus, application of the act to alien crews working on foreign-flagged ships would generate a strong "possibility of international discord" and potentially "invite retaliatory action."[83] Under "such highly

---

[75]   372 U.S. 10 (1963).
[76]   29 U.S.C. § 152(6).
[77]   29 U.S.C. § 152(7).
[78]   372 U.S. at 20–22.
[79]   *Id.* at 17.
[80]   *Id.*
[81]   *Id.* at 20–21.
[82]   *Id.* at 21.
[83]   *Id.*

charged international circumstances," the Court invoked "the admonition of Mr. Chief Justice Marshall in *The Charming Betsy* that 'an act of congress ought never to be construed to violate the law of nations if any other possible construction remains.' "[84] Accordingly, the Court concluded "that for us to sanction the exercise of local sovereignty under such conditions in this 'delicate field of international relations there must be present the affirmative intention of the Congress clearly expressed.' "[85] Because the act contained "no such clear expression," the Court rejected its application to the foreign-flagged vessel.[86]

Significantly, the Supreme Court invoked the Constitution's allocation of powers to Congress in support of this conclusion. Quoting *Lauritzen*, the Court explained that its decision not to apply the National Labor Relations Act to foreign vessels did not imply " 'any impairment of our own sovereignty, or limitation of the power of Congress' in this field."[87] Rather, because Congress " 'alone has the facilities necessary to make fairly such an important policy decision,' . . . the arguments should be directed to the Congress rather than to us."[88]

The Supreme Court has relied on *McCulloch* in several cases to support application of the presumptions against extraterritoriality and against the application of U.S. law to the internal affairs of foreign vessels.[89] For example, in *EEOC v. Arabian American Oil Co.*,[90] the Court employed the presumption against extraterritoriality to conclude that Title VII does not apply to the employment practices of U.S. companies who employ U.S. citizens in foreign countries. Although the Court did not invoke the *Charming Betsy* canon directly, it did rely on the "longstanding principle of American law 'that legislation of Congress, unless a contrary intent appears, is meant to apply only within the territorial jurisdiction of the United States.' "[91] Citing *McCulloch*, the Court explained that this principle "serves to protect against unintended clashes between our laws and those of other nations which could result in international discord."[92] *McCulloch*,

---

[84]  *Id.* (quoting Murray v. The Schooner Charming Betsy, 6 U.S. (2 Cranch) 64, 118 (1804)).

[85]  *Id.* at 21–22 (quoting Benz v. Compania Naviera Hidalgo, 353 U.S. 138, 147 (1957)).

[86]  *Id.* at 22.

[87]  *Id.* (quoting *Lauritzen*, 345 U.S. at 578).

[88]  *Id.* (quoting *Benz*, 353 U.S. at 147).

[89]  See Spector v. Norwegian Cruise Line, 545 U.S. 119, 131 (2005) (citing *McCulloch* to support the "the presumption against applying general statutes to foreign vessels' internal affairs"); EEOC v. Arabian Am. Oil Co., 499 U.S. 244, 264–65 (1991) (holding that Title VII does not apply to employment practices of U.S. employers who employ U.S. citizens extraterritorially); Weinberger v. Rossi, 456 U.S. 25, 30–32 (1982) (citing *McCulloch* to support application of the *Charming Betsy* canon to determine the application of U.S. law "on United States enclaves outside of the territorial limits of this country"); Hellenic Lines v. Rhoditis, 398 U.S. 306, 311–12 (1970) (Harlan, J., dissenting) (relying on *McCulloch* and *Lauritzen*, and citing *The Charming Betsy*, in arguing against the application of the Jones Act to a foreign vessel in American waters).

[90]  499 U.S. 244 (1991).

[91]  *Id.* at 248 (quoting *Foley Bros.*, 336 U.S. at 285).

[92]  *Id.* (citing *McCulloch*, 372 U.S. at 20–22)

in turn, had expressly relied on the *Charming Betsy* canon to reject the extraterritorial application of U.S. law to a foreign-flag vessel, as discussed.[93]

Similarly, in *Hoffman-LaRoche v. Empagran*,[94] the Supreme Court relied on *McCulloch* in applying the *Charming Betsy* canon to interpret the Foreign Trade Antitrust Improvements Act of 1982. The question in *Hoffman-LaRoche* was whether the act applied to certain conduct causing harm in foreign nations. The Court read the act in accord with Congress's presumed intent not to violate the rights of foreign nations. The Court began its analysis by stating that it "ordinarily construes ambiguous statutes to avoid unreasonable interference with the sovereign authority of other nations."[95] Citing *The Charming Betsy*, the Court explained that "[t]his rule of construction reflects principles of customary international law—law that (we must assume) Congress ordinarily seeks to follow."[96] The Court justified the canon as a means of preventing courts from contradicting Congress's presumed intent to respect the sovereign rights of other nations:

> This rule of statutory construction cautions courts to assume that legislators take account of the legitimate sovereign interests of other nations when they write American laws. It thereby helps the potentially conflicting laws of different nations work together in harmony—a harmony particularly needed in today's highly interdependent world.[97]

---

[93] More recently, the Supreme Court has strongly reaffirmed the presumption against extraterritorial application of U.S. law. See Kiobel v. Royal Dutch Petroleum Co., 569 U.S. 108 (2013); Morrison v. National Australia Bank, 561 U.S. 247 (2010). In the examples discussed in this section, the Court cited the *Charming Betsy* canon as support for the presumption against extraterritorial application of U.S. law or against the application of U.S. law to a foreign-flagged vessel. It is worth noting that in two dissenting opinions, Justices attempted to disaggregate the *Charming Betsy* canon from the presumption against extraterritoriality. First, in *Arabian American Oil Co.*, Justice Marshall, dissenting, described the *Charming Betsy* canon as a rule of construction "wholly independent" of the presumption against extraterritoriality. 499 U.S. at 264 (Marshall, J., dissenting). Second, in *Hartford Fire Ins. Co. v. California*, 509 U.S. 764, 814–15 (1993), Justice Scalia's dissent described the presumption against extraterritoriality and the *Charming Betsy* canon as two separate canons of construction. In describing the *Charming Betsy* canon, Justice Scalia wrote: "Though it clearly has constitutional authority to do so, Congress is generally presumed not to have exceeded those customary international-law limits on jurisdiction to prescribe." *Id.* at 815 (Scalia, J., dissenting). Thus, "even where the presumption against extraterritoriality does not apply, statutes should not be interpreted to regulate foreign persons or conduct if that regulation would conflict with principles of international law." *Id.* As we explain here, the presumption against extraterritoriality is better understood as simply one application of the *Charming Betsy* canon rather than a wholly independent canon of construction.

[94] 542 U.S. 155 (2004).

[95] *Id.* at 164.

[96] *Id.*

[97] *Id.* at 164–65. The Court has long presumed, as it did in *Hoffman-LaRoche*, that Congress takes account of "the legitimate sovereign interest of other nations." In *Talbot v. Seeman*, decided a few years before *The Charming Betsy*, the Court employed a similar canon and explained that by construing an act of Congress to respect neutral rights under the law of nations, the act "will never violate those principles which we believe, and which it is our duty to believe, the legislature of the United States will always hold sacred." 5 U.S. (1 Cranch) 1, 44 (1801). Of course, the *Talbot* Court was referring to principles of the law of state-state relations as they then existed. A judicial presumption that Congress does not mean to violate neutral rights of foreign sovereigns under the law of

Although the Supreme Court has applied the *Charming Betsy* canon to avoid U.S. violations of other nations' rights under international law, it has declined to use the canon to construe federal statutes to hold foreign nations accountable for their own violations of U.S. rights or international law more generally. The Court's 1989 decision in *Argentine Republic v. Amerada Hess Shipping Corp.*[98] is illustrative. In that case, Liberian corporations brought suit against the Argentine Republic in a federal district court under the Alien Tort Statute seeking redress for an alleged tort in violation of international law committed by Argentine armed forces in international waters.[99] A key question in the case was whether the Argentine Republic had immunity from suit under the Foreign Sovereign Immunities Act (FSIA).[100]

Although the District Court found the Argentine Republic to be immune under the act, the Second Circuit reversed and made novel use of the *Charming Betsy* canon as a sword rather than a shield. Rather than use the canon to prevent courts from violating the rights of Argentina, the Second Circuit applied the canon to permit courts to hold that nation accountable for its alleged violations of international law. The court began its analysis by explaining that it was reviewing "the FSIA mindful of the [*Restatement*'s] tenet of statutory construction that '[w]here fairly possible, a United States statute is to be construed so as not to bring it into conflict with international law.' "[101] The court stated that under modern customary international law, "sovereigns are not immune from suit for their violations of international law."[102] Because "international law would deny immunity in these circumstances," the court would "construe the FSIA to grant immunity only if Congress clearly expressed such an intent."[103]

The Second Circuit's approach was in tension with both the FSIA and the Supreme Court's traditional use of the *Charming Betsy* canon as a canon of avoidance. The FSIA grants foreign nations broad sovereign immunity subject only to

---

state-state relations ensures that courts will not violate the rights of other nations in the absence of clear instructions from Congress to do so in the exercise of its exclusive powers over war and foreign relations. Cf. Paul Stephan, Bond v. United States *and Information-Forcing Defaults: The Work that Presumptions Do*, 90 NOTRE DAME L. REV. 1465, 1495 (2015) ("Attributing to Congress an inclination to avoid conflicts with these competing sovereigns, even where the constitutional rule would allow Congress to prevail, seems a plausible majoritarian default based on a reasonable assumption about the legislature's preferences.").

[98]   488 U.S. 428 (1989).
[99]   *Id.* at 431.
[100]  Foreign Sovereign Immunities Act of 1976, Pub. L. No. 94-583, 90 Stat. 2891, codified at 28 U.S.C.A. §§ 1330, 1332(a)(4), 1391(f), 1441(d), 1602–611.
[101]  Amerada Hess Shipping Corp. v. Argentine Rep., 830 F.2d 421, 426 (1987) (quoting Restatement of Foreign Relations Law of the United States (Revised) § 134 (Tent. Draft No. 6, 1985), and citing Murray v. The Schooner Charming Betsy, 6 U.S. (2 Cranch) 137, 143 (1804)).
[102]  *Id.* at 425.
[103]  *Id.* at 426.

several specific exceptions set forth in the act. These exceptions did not include an open-ended exemption for violations of international law. Instead of applying the act and its exceptions as written to uphold immunity, the Second Circuit invoked the *Charming Betsy* canon to conclude that Congress did not intend the FSIA to grant foreign nations sovereign immunity for violations of international law. This use of the canon narrowed immunity under the statute in order to bring it into conformity with the more limited immunity recognized by modern customary international law.[104] Having interpreted the FSIA to deny immunity to the Argentine Republic, the Second Circuit allowed the suit against it to proceed.

The Supreme Court reversed and held that the Argentine Republic enjoyed immunity under the FSIA. Specifically, the Court rejected the Second Circuit's conclusion that the FSIA does not grant immunity to foreign sovereigns sued for violations of international law. The Court concluded that "the text and structure of the FSIA demonstrate Congress' intention that the FSIA be the sole basis for obtaining jurisdiction over a foreign state in our courts."[105] Unlike the Second Circuit, the Court did not invoke the *Charming Betsy* canon to hold another nation accountable for violating international law. Instead, the Court applied the presumption against extraterritoriality to avoid construing the FSIA to permit the suit against the Argentine Republic to proceed.

The Supreme Court began by reciting the act's general directive that " 'a foreign state shall be immune from the jurisdiction of the courts of the United States and of the States except as provided in' " the other provisions of the act.[106] It then determined that none of the statutory exceptions applied to this case. Because Congress chose to deny immunity for some—but not all—violations of international law, the Court drew "the plain implication that immunity is granted in those cases involving alleged violations of international law that do not come within one of the FSIA's exceptions."[107] By rejecting the Second Circuit's construction of the FSIA, the Court necessarily rejected that court's novel attempt to use the *Charming Betsy* canon to bring the act into conformity with more limited rules of immunity under customary international law.

The Supreme Court's decision to use the presumption against extraterritoriality to reject an expansive interpretation of the FSIA's exceptions was just as significant as the Court's refusal to use the *Charming Betsy* canon to narrow the scope of immunity conferred by the act. Upon reviewing the act's exceptions, the Court concluded that none of them allowed the suit to proceed. The plaintiffs claimed that the exception for noncommercial torts was the one "most in

---

[104] *Id.* at 427.
[105] 488 U.S. at 435.
[106] *Id.* at 434 (quoting 28 U.S.C. § 1604).
[107] *Id.* at 436.

point."[108] This exception, however, withdrew immunity only for certain torts causing injury or damage "in the United States."[109] In this case, the damage occurred on the high seas, but the plaintiffs argued that the exception should apply because the high seas "is within the admiralty jurisdiction of the United States."[110] The Court rejected this argument in deference to congressional authority. "When it desires to do so," the Court explained, "Congress knows how to place the high seas within the jurisdictional reach of a statute. We thus apply '[t]he canon of construction which teaches that legislation of Congress, unless contrary intent appears, is meant to apply only within the territorial jurisdiction of the United States.'"[111]

The Supreme Court's decision in *Amerada Hess* was a continuation of its uniform practice of using the *Charming Betsy* canon solely to avoid violations of the traditional sovereign rights of foreign nations. Accordingly, the Court rejected the Second Circuit's attempt to use the canon to narrow the scope of foreign sovereign immunity under the FSIA. At the same time, the Court employed the presumption against extraterritoriality to reject an expansive interpretation of the FSIA's *exceptions*. In other words, the Court rejected the Second Circuit's attempt to use the *Charming Betsy* canon to hold another nation accountable for violating international law; instead, the Court used the presumption against extraterritorial application of U.S. law to ensure that the political branches—rather than the courts—made the crucial decision to override the territorial sovereignty of another nation. Both aspects of the Court's decision upheld Argentina's foreign sovereign immunity notwithstanding the allegation that it had violated international law. The Constitution assigns power to the political branches to decide both when U.S. law will apply extraterritorially and whether and how the United States will hold other nations accountable for violating international law.[112] The Court's construction of the FSIA to uphold foreign sovereign immunity avoided a potential violation of the Constitution's allocation of powers by ensuring that the political branches, rather than the courts, made any decision to apply U.S. law extraterritorially to hold the Argentine Republic accountable for its alleged violations of international law.

---

[108] *Id.* at 439.

[109] *Id.* (quoting 28 U.S.C. § 1605(a)(5)).

[110] *Id.* at 440.

[111] *Id.* (quoting Foley Brothers v. Filardo, 336 U.S. 281, 285 (1949); and citing Weinberger v. Rossi, 456 U.S. 25, 32 (1982)) (internal footnote omitted). This reading of the FSIA was consistent with the traditional rule of interpretation that a legal instrument should not be interpreted to divest a sovereign of its rights under the law of nations unless it did so clearly and expressly. *See* 1 VATTEL, THE LAW OF NATIONS, *supra* note 35, bk. II, § 307, at 233–35 (explaining that treaties or other legal instruments that divested a nation's rights under the law of nations was "odious" and that ambiguous terms should be interpreted to avoid such consequences).

[112] *See* BELLIA & CLARK, *supra* note 3, at 193–211.

## III.  Restating the Canon

From its inception to the present day, the *Charming Betsy* canon has served to implement the Constitution's allocation of powers by ensuring that the political branches, rather than the courts, decide whether, when, and how the United States will violate another nation's rights under international law.[113] When an Act of Congress is unclear as to whether it violates such rights, respect for the Constitution's allocation of powers has led the Supreme Court to construe the act to avoid the violation and preserve the constitutional prerogatives of the political branches. This long-standing use of the canon avoids constitutional difficulties by preventing courts from usurping the exclusive constitutional authority of the political branches to decide whether to violate the rights of foreign nations under international law.

When the American Law Institute next undertakes a general restatement of the *Charming Betsy* canon, it should adopt a formulation that better captures the canon's original function and actual use as a canon of constitutional avoidance— one that prevents courts from usurping the constitutional authority of the political branches over war and foreign relations. Rather than generally instructing courts to construe federal statutes "not to conflict with international law" (as the Third Restatement does), any future Restatement should instruct them to construe federal statutes "not to violate the jurisdiction, rights, or immunities of another nation under international law." Under this formulation, the canon

---

[113] Curt Bradley has endorsed a similar view of the *Charming Betsy* canon, which he calls "the separation of powers conception." See Curtis A. Bradley, *The* Charming Betsy *Canon and Separation of Powers: Rethinking the Interpretive Role of International Law*, 86 GEO. L.J. 479, 524 (1997). This conception of the canon "rests on the belief that, for formal and functional reasons, the political branches should determine when and how the United States violates international law." *Id.* at 526. At the same time, however, Professor Bradley believes that use of the *Charming Betsy* canon creates its own separation-of-powers concerns because the judiciary is "making judgments relating to this country's interpretation of and relationship with international law." *Id.* at 532. Although he considers it to be a "close question," Bradley nonetheless concludes that the "separation of powers benefits" outweigh the "separation of powers costs." *Id.* Our proposed restatement of the canon mitigates the costs he identifies. By limiting the use of the canon to prevent courts from violating "the jurisdiction, rights, or immunities of another nation under international law," our proposal would reduce the need for courts to interpret new and contested norms of customary international law.

Roger Alford also favors a view of the canon rooted in separation of powers. As he explains, "[t]he most recent pronouncements by the Supreme Court confirm that *Charming Betsy* is a constitutional avoidance doctrine premised on a concern for separation of powers." Roger P. Alford, *Foreign Relations Law as a Matter of Interpretation: The Use and Abuse of* Charming Betsy, 67 OHIO ST. L.J. 1339, 1352 (2006). "Consistent with separation of powers concerns, [the canon] reflects a desire to interpret statutes to avoid inter-branch usurpations of power and carefully husbands the complex relationship of the federal branches in the international context." *Id.* In our view, the Constitution's specific allocation of war and foreign relations powers to the political branches obligates courts to avoid reading statutes to violate the jurisdiction, rights, or immunities of other nations, but it does not license courts to read statutes to enforce international law against other nations or to limit how the United States regulates its own citizens within its own territory. Using the canon in the latter ways might generate constitutional difficulties rather than avoid them.

would continue to serve its historic function of ensuring that Congress and the president—rather than the courts—make the crucial decision to override such rights and risk triggering conflict with foreign nations. In other words, this formulation would avoid violations of the Constitution's allocation of powers by preventing courts from usurping the constitutional prerogatives of the political branches.

Section 406 of the Fourth Restatement, applying the *Charming Betsy* canon to avoid conflicts with jurisdiction to prescribe, is consistent with this approach: "Where fairly possible, courts in the United States construe federal statutes to avoid conflict with international law governing jurisdiction to prescribe."[114] This provision upholds the Constitution's allocation of powers by minimizing judicial interference with another nation's jurisdiction to prescribe, including "jurisdiction to prescribe law with respect to persons, property, and conduct within its territory."[115] At the same time, Section 406 makes clear that courts must apply statutes that unavoidably conflict with international law on this subject: "If a federal statute cannot be so construed, the federal statute is controlling as a matter of federal law."[116] This language upholds the Constitution's allocation of powers by recognizing that the political branches—rather than the courts—have the ultimate responsibility to decide whether to override another nation's jurisdiction to prescribe. Thus, Section 406 is an important first step in the process of accurately restating the broader *Charming Betsy* canon.

Any future restatement of the *Charming Betsy* canon should require U.S. courts to avoid violations of the rights, immunities, and jurisdiction of foreign nations under international law—rather than "international law" in general. Of course, such rights, immunities, and jurisdiction would encompass not only jurisdiction to prescribe but also other rights traditionally enjoyed by nations under the law of state-state relations. In *The Charming Betsy* itself, the Court construed the Non-Intercourse Act not to violate Denmark's traditional right to neutral use of the high seas. The Court's statement of the canon—that a federal statute "ought never to be construed *to violate* the law of nations if any other possible construction remains"[117]—required this construction. In the modern era, the Court has relied on the canon to prevent the extraterritorial application of federal statutes to matters within the territory of a foreign nation or to the internal affairs of a foreign vessel. These uses of the canon avoid violations of the Constitution's allocation of powers by preventing courts from violating the territorial rights of foreign nations without clear statutory authority to do so. This rationale for the

---

[114] FOURTH RESTATEMENT § 406 (2017).
[115] *Id.* § 408.
[116] *Id.* § 406.
[117] *The Charming Betsy*, 6 U.S. (2 Cranch) at 118 (emphasis added).

canon also requires courts to interpret federal statutes, where possible, to avoid violating other rights of foreign nations, such as consular immunity and head-of-state immunity. In those situations, the *Charming Betsy* canon also serves as a canon of constitutional avoidance because it prevents courts from usurping the exclusive constitutional authority of the political branches to decide whether to violate such rights and risk international conflict.

For these reasons, the following proposal provides a more accurate re-statement of the general *Charming Betsy* canon than the Third Restatement formulation:

> Where fairly possible, a United States statute is to be construed so as not to violate the jurisdiction, rights, or immunities of another nation under interna-tional law or under an international agreement with the United States.

This proposal describes how the Supreme Court actually used the canon in *The Charming Betsy* and other early cases, and has continued to use it to the present day. Although our proposed restatement of the canon does not explicitly char-acterize it as a canon of constitutional avoidance, the reporter's notes should ex-plain that the canon's focus on preventing violations of the traditional rights of foreign nations ensures that it will avoid—rather than generate—violations of the Constitution's allocation of powers over war and foreign relations for all of the reasons discussed in this chapter.

Our proposed restatement of the *Charming Betsy* canon has two primary advantages over the Third Restatement formulation. First, it conforms much more closely to the Supreme Court's original formulation and actual use of the canon. As discussed, the *Charming Betsy* canon required U.S. courts to construe acts of Congress not "to violate" other nations' rights under the law of nations. The Supreme Court's actual use of the canon has been limited to avoiding such violations.

Second, our proposal would prevent potential misuse of the *Charming Betsy* canon in ways that could generate—rather than avoid—constitutional concerns. As discussed, the Supreme Court has used the canon solely to uphold the tra-ditional rights of foreign nations under international law. The Court has never used the canon to hold a foreign nation accountable for its violations of interna-tional law. Such use would raise—rather than avoid—constitutional concerns by usurping the exclusive constitutional authority of the political branches to decide whether, when, and how to hold foreign nations accountable for their miscon-duct.[118] As explained in the previous section, the Supreme Court's decision in

---

[118] See BELLIA & CLARK, *supra* note 3, at 193–211.

*Amerada Hess* both rejected the Second Circuit's reliance on the canon to narrow foreign sovereign immunity under the FSIA and applied a presumption derived from the canon—the presumption against extraterritoriality—to prevent the unwarranted expansion of the FSIA's exceptions to narrow such immunity. Both features of the Court's decision ensured that the political branches, rather than courts, would make any decision to hold the Argentine Republic accountable for its alleged violations of international law. In so doing, the Court's approach avoided judicial usurpation of the political branches' exclusive constitutional authority over war and foreign relations.

The Third Restatement formulation of the *Charming Betsy* canon might also be misread to suggest that courts could use the canon to restrict the way in which the United States regulates its own citizens within its own territory. At the founding, the law of nations did not limit the authority of a nation over its own citizens within its own territory. To the contrary, it protected such authority from interference by other nations. By the twentieth century, customary international law evolved to impose certain limits on how nations can treat their own citizens, and is now widely acknowledged to include prohibitions on genocide, torture, and extrajudicial killing.[119] Although the Constitution, laws, and treaties of the United States independently prohibit such governmental misconduct, customary international law continues to evolve.[120] Some scholars have urged courts to apply the *Charming Betsy* canon to ensure that federal statutes do not violate new and emerging norms of international law.[121] Such use of the canon, however, would depart from its original function as a canon of avoidance and generate rather than avoid constitutional concerns. The Constitution provides specific, finely wrought procedures for the enactment of federal law. Construing such law to conform to modern rules of customary international law would raise constitutional concerns by allowing courts to circumvent the political and procedural safeguards of federalism built into the constitutional structure to govern

---

[119] See *id.* at 139–48.

[120] It has been argued, for example, that customary international law includes, or should include, a range of rights that citizens may assert against their governments. "[P]otential candidates for rights recognized under customary international law" include "the right to free choice of employment; the right to form and join trade unions; and the right to free primary education, subject to a state's available resources." Comm. on the Enf't of Human Rights Law, Int'l Law Ass'n, *Final Report on the Status of the Universal Declaration of Human Rights in National and International Law*, in INTERNATIONAL LAW ASSOCIATION, REPORT OF THE SIXTY-SIXTH CONFERENCE 525, 548 (1994) (footnotes omitted). Other proposed rights under customary international law include the right to healthy environment, see John Lee, *The Underlying Theory to Support a Well-Defined Human Right to a Healthy Environment as a Principle of Customary International Law*, 25 COLUM. J. ENVTL. L. 283, 332, 339 (2000); and the right of juvenile offenders to avoid life imprisonment without parole. See Molly C. Quinn, Comment, *Life Without Parole for Juvenile Offenders: A Violation of Customary International Law*, 52 ST. LOUIS U. L.J. 283, 284–85, 294 (2007).

[121] See, e.g., Ralph G. Steinhardt, *The Role of International Law as a Canon of Domestic Statutory Construction*, 43 VAND. L. REV. 1103 (1990).

federal lawmaking.[122] Thus, it is not surprising that the Supreme Court has never endorsed such use of the *Charming Betsy* canon, and the Restatement should reflect the Court's actual practice.

## IV. Conclusion

The *Charming Betsy* canon is best understood as a canon of constitutional avoidance. From the earliest to the most recent cases applying the canon, the Supreme Court has read federal statutes, whenever possible, to avoid violating the traditional rights of foreign sovereigns under the law of nations. By reading statutes not to violate such rights, the Court has avoided usurping the exclusive constitutional authority of Congress and the president over war and foreign relations. The Court has never applied the canon to construe a vague or ambiguous federal statute to hold a foreign nation accountable in U.S. courts for violating international law, nor has it applied the canon to limit the domestic application of U.S. laws to conform to modern customary international law limits on how the United States may treat its own citizens. If courts were to apply the canon in these novel ways, they would generate rather than avoid constitutional concerns. Accordingly, when the American Law Institute next undertakes a general restatement of the *Charming Betsy* canon, it should make clear that the canon requires courts to construe federal laws, where fairly possible, "not to violate the jurisdiction, rights, or immunities of another nation under international law." By returning to *The Charming Betsy*'s original admonition that courts should avoid *violating* other nations' rights, this formulation would not only more accurately reflect the Supreme Court's use of the canon but also avoid the constitutional concerns that would arise from its expansion.

---

[122] See Bradford R. Clark, *Process-Based Preemption*, in PREEMPTION CHOICE: THE THEORY, LAW AND REALITY OF FEDERALISM'S CORE QUESTION 192–213 (William W. Buzbee ed., 2009); Bradford R. Clark, *Separation of Powers as a Safeguard of Federalism*, 79 TEX. L. REV. 1321 (2001).

# 9

# Personal Jurisdiction and Fifth Amendment Due Process Revisited

*Chimène I. Keitner*

The role of U.S. courts in adjudicating disputes with foreign elements remains contested. As a matter of domestic law, the Due Process Clauses in the U.S. Constitution constrain the scope of adjudicatory jurisdiction that legislatures can confer on State and federal courts. The Fourth Restatement restates the U.S. law of personal jurisdiction in civil proceedings as requiring that "sufficient contacts" exist between the defendant and the forum, "and that the exercise of jurisdiction be reasonable."[1] These criteria limit the reach of U.S. courts' personal jurisdiction. This chapter explores these limits and Congress's ability to extend them.

The Restatement distinguishes among a State's jurisdiction to *prescribe* (i.e., to create law that governs conduct), jurisdiction to *adjudicate* (i.e., to apply law to a party's conduct, especially in deciding a legal claim or dispute), and jurisdiction to *enforce* (i.e., to impose measures of constraint).[2] The distinction between jurisdiction to adjudicate and jurisdiction to prescribe often underlies problems that we think of under the rubric of conflicts of law or private international law. For example, State A might have jurisdiction to adjudicate a dispute between two parties, perhaps because they both live in State A. However, State B's substantive, conduct-regulating rules might govern the outcome of that dispute, perhaps because the claim involves conduct that occurred in State B. Conversely, just because State B has jurisdiction to prescribe rules of conduct does not necessarily mean it has jurisdiction to adjudicate every alleged violation of those rules.[3] The

---

[1] FOURTH RESTATEMENT § 422. Unlike constraints on subject matter jurisdiction, constraints on a court's personal jurisdiction may be waived by the defendant. *Id.* § 422 cmt. *b.* As Donald Childress notes in his chapter, other doctrines, such as *forum non conveniens*, speak to the "appropriateness" of courts exercising jurisdiction in a particular case, rather than limits on their adjudicatory authority. See Donald Earl Childress III, Forum Non Conveniens *in the Fourth Restatement*, in this volume.

[2] FOURTH RESTATEMENT § 401 (distinguishing between jurisdiction to prescribe, "i.e., the authority of a state to make law applicable to persons, property, or conduct," jurisdiction to adjudicate, "i.e., the authority of a state to apply law to persons or things, in particular through the processes of its courts or administrative tribunals," and jurisdiction to enforce, "i.e., the authority of a state to exercise its power to compel compliance with the law").

[3] The Fourth Restatement recognizes these possible gaps between prescriptive and adjudicatory jurisdiction. For example, in the criminal context, "[a] state may exercise jurisdiction to prescribe

Chimène I. Keitner, *Personal Jurisdiction and Fifth Amendment Due Process Revisited* In: *The Restatement and Beyond.* Edited by: Paul B. Stephan and Sarah H. Cleveland, Oxford University Press (2020). © Oxford University Press. DOI: 10.1093/oso/9780197533154.003.0010

distinction between prescriptive and adjudicatory jurisdiction explains why, as the Restatement indicates, "[a] state may exercise jurisdiction to adjudicate in a civil case if it has personal jurisdiction over the defendant, . . . and may apply the substantive law of another state under choice-of-law principles, even if the adjudicating state lacks jurisdiction to prescribe with respect to the defendant. . . ."[4] These examples illustrate that a country's prescriptive jurisdiction and its adjudicatory jurisdiction are not necessarily congruent.

U.S. lawmakers have occasionally conflated prescriptive and adjudicatory jurisdiction, leading to perplexing results. For example, Congress apparently enacted Section 929P(b) of the Dodd-Frank Act for the purpose of enabling certain types of U.S. Securities and Exchange Commission and Department of Justice enforcement actions involving extraterritorial conduct to be brought in U.S. courts.[5] Congress did this shortly after the Supreme Court held that Section 10(b) of the Securities Exchange Act did not overcome the presumption against extraterritorial application of statutes.[6] However, the language in Section 929P(b) only purports to expand courts' adjudicatory jurisdiction and does not, on its face, extend the prescriptive reach of Section 10(b). If the drafters of this provision had better understood the distinction between prescriptive and adjudicatory jurisdiction, they could have avoided the debates that have ensued.

As indicated, Restatement Section 422 restates the U.S. law of personal jurisdiction in civil proceedings as requiring that "sufficient contacts" exist between the defendant and the forum "and that the exercise of jurisdiction be reasonable."[7] This creates a potential gap between Congress's authority, on the one

rules of criminal law for its own nationals acting anywhere in the world, . . . even if it could not arrest its nationals found in another state without that other state's consent, . . . or try such persons unless they were present in its territory. . . ." *Id.* § 401 cmt. *d* (internal cross-references omitted).

[4] *Id.* As the Restatement notes, the Alien Tort Statute of 1789 creates a federal forum for adjudicating certain disputes that were originally viewed as governed by the law of nations. *Id.* § 402 reporters' note 10 (suggesting that, "[i]n cases involving no specific connection with the United States, the recognition of a cause of action under the ATS might have been viewed as an exercise of jurisdiction to prescribe on the basis of universal jurisdiction"); see also *id.* § 311 reporters' note 5 (indicating that "[t]he Supreme Court has construed the Alien Tort Statute as authorizing the federal courts to develop federal common-law causes of action to support a limited number of 'law of nations' claims brought under the statute by foreign plaintiffs"). Among the many relevant analyses by contributors to this volume, see Chimène I. Keitner, *Conceptualizing Complicity in Alien Tort Cases,* 60 HASTINGS L.J. 61 (2008) (analyzing choice-of-law issues under the ATS).
[5] This question was raised in *Scoville v. Securities and Exchange Commission* (No. 18-1566), *cert. denied,* 140 S. Ct. 483 (2019).
[6] Richard W. Painter, *The Dodd-Frank Extraterritorial Jurisdiction Provision: Was It Effective, Needed or Sufficient?* 1 HARV. BUS. L. REV. 195, 199 (2011) (indicating that "Congress was not careful in the language it used"); see Morrison v. National Australia Bank, 561 U.S. 247 (2010).
[7] FOURTH RESTATEMENT § 422; but cf. Burnham v. Superior Court, 495 U.S. 604 (1990) (upholding in-state personal service on an individual defendant as constitutionally sufficient to establish general personal jurisdiction, even over a transient defendant). Unlike constraints on subject matter jurisdiction, constraints on a court's personal jurisdiction may be waived by the defendant. *Id.* § 422 cmt. *b.* When it comes to potential limits under international law, the Fourth Restatement takes

hand, to prescribe rules that apply to extraterritorial conduct on the basis of the victim's nationality (for example, by creating tort remedies for certain acts that harm U.S. nationals abroad) or because the offense is of universal concern (for example, because it amounts to torture under color of foreign law) and a federal court's authority, on the other hand, to exercise civil adjudicative jurisdiction over alleged violations—or violators—of those rules. Whether Congress has the power to bridge this gap through legislation depends on the proper interpretation of the limits on personal jurisdiction that flow from the requirements of due process.

Most judicial opinions curbing the assertion of personal jurisdiction based on the lack of "sufficient contacts" have involved Fourteenth Amendment due process limits on the reach of State long-arm statutes.[8] Fewer have considered Fifth Amendment due process limits on the assertion of personal jurisdiction in federal question cases. The Supreme Court has yet to consider whether the Fifth Amendment's guarantee of "due process of law" in the context of personal jurisdiction carries the same meaning as the Fourteenth Amendment's due process guarantee.[9] Moreover, in cases arising to date, it has explicitly declined to articulate "the utmost reach of Congress' power."[10] This question may become increasingly difficult for the Court to avoid, as Congress adopts expansive views of U.S. adjudicatory jurisdiction in statutes such as the Anti-Terrorism Clarification

---

the position that "[w]ith the significant exception of various forms of immunity, modern customary international law generally does not impose limits on jurisdiction to adjudicate." *Id.* pt. IV, ch. 2, intro. note; see also *id.* § 422 reporters' note 1.

[8]  As Lea Brilmayer and Matthew Smith have observed, even under the Fourteenth Amendment, "[w]e do not have a clear answer to the question of whether interstate cases and international cases should be treated the same for constitutional purposes." Lea Brilmayer & Matthew Smith, *The (Theoretical) Future of Personal Jurisdiction: Issues Left Open by* Goodyear Dunlop Tires v. Brown *and* J. McIntyre Machinery v. Nicastro, 63 S.C. L. REV. 617, 632 (2012).

[9]  See Asahi Metal Indus. v. Superior Court of Cal., Solano Cnty., 480 U.S. 102, 113 n.* (1987) (O'Connor, J., plurality opinion) (indicating that "[w]e have no occasion here to determine whether Congress could, consistent with the Due Process Clause of the Fifth Amendment, authorize federal court personal jurisdiction over alien defendants based on the aggregate of *national* contacts, rather than on the contacts between the defendant and the State in which the federal court sits"); Omni Capital Int'l v. Rudolf Wolff & Co., 484 U.S. 97, 102 n.5 (1987) (noting the appellant's theory that "a federal court could exercise personal jurisdiction, consistent with the Fifth Amendment, based on an aggregation of the defendant's contacts with the Nation as a whole, rather than on its contacts with the State in which the federal court sits"). See generally Jonathan R. Nash, *National Personal Jurisdiction*, 68 EMORY L.J. 509, 561 (2019) (concluding that "Congress has the power to introduce national personal jurisdiction to all claims that fall within or could fall within federal court jurisdiction"); Gary B. Born, *Reflections on Judicial Jurisdiction in International Cases*, 17 GA. J. INT'L & COMP. L. 1, 40 (1987) (asserting that the "United States territory as a whole should be the relevant geographical unit for purposes of assessing minimum contacts by foreigners in federal question cases").

[10]  United States v. Scophony Corp., 33 U.S. 795, 804 n.13 (1948); see also *id.* at 804 (noting, in a case involving civil antitrust proceedings against a British corporation, that there was no "question of the exercise of Congress' power to its farthest limit. The issue is simply how far Congress meant to go . . .").

Act of 2018 (ATCA).[11] The rest of this chapter uses the ATCA to ground a discussion of limits on federal adjudicatory jurisdiction in transnational cases.

Congress passed the ATCA as an antidote to circuit-level judgments that found the Palestinian Authority beyond the scope of U.S. personal jurisdiction in cases seeking damages for certain acts of international terrorism. This chapter uses the ATCA's passage as an opportunity to revisit the history and jurisprudence of Fifth Amendment due process limits on personal jurisdiction. In particular, although the terms of the ATCA are not as broad as the assertions in the House Report that accompanied it, this chapter evaluates Congress's assertion that, as a constitutional matter, "carrying out or assisting an act of international terrorism that injures or kills American citizens abroad should be, in and of itself, sufficient to establish [specific] personal jurisdiction in U.S. courts."[12] This assertion rests, in turn, on the broader proposition that Congress can confer adjudicatory authority on U.S. courts that is at least commensurate with the reach of its prescriptive jurisdiction—a proposition that I argue conflicts with prevailing understandings of the constraining role of constitutional due process.

The analysis of Fifth Amendment due process proceeds in four sections. Section I provides a brief sketch of the roots of due process in the Anglo-American legal tradition, and their role in the Supreme Court's decision in *Pennoyer v. Neff*.[13] Section II looks at the contemporary doctrinal framework for analyzing due process limits on personal jurisdiction. Section III details the debate over these limits in the context of litigation under the Anti-Terrorism Act (ATA). Section IV concludes that limiting the exercise of personal jurisdiction in cases involving a foreign defendant's overseas conduct to those cases in which a defendant has intentionally targeted U.S. nationals or U.S. interests best reflects prevailing judicial understandings of constitutional constraints on adjudicatory jurisdiction. Although the nature of the required links might vary with the nature of the conduct, the federal government does not have unlimited authority

---

[11]  Antiterrorism Clarification Act of 2018 (ATCA), Pub. L. No. 115-253, 132 Stat. 3183, amending 18 U.S.C. §§ 2331, 2333–34. The ATA was further amended by the Promoting Security and Justice for Victims of Terrorism Act of 2019 (PSJVTA), Pub. L. No. 116-94, div. J, tit. IX, § 903, 133 Stat. 3082, amending 18 U.S.C. § 2334.

[12]  H.R. Rep. No. 115-858 at 6 (2018). In an amicus brief submitted in the post-ATCA proceedings in *Klieman*, the United States took the position that the ATCA's factual predicates were not satisfied in the instant case, but that the ATCA's provisions regarding constructive consent are constitutional because "[a]s long as a defendant's consent is 'knowing and voluntary,' the court's exercise of jurisdiction is consistent with due process." See Brief for United States as Amicus Curiae, Kleiman v. Palestinian Authority (Mar. 13, 2019), 2019 WL 1200589 at *10. As the United States explained, defendants are "*sui generis* foreign entities" whose "right to operate in the United States and their receipt of foreign assistance is dependent on the coordinated judgments of the political branches," including the imposition of conditions motivated by concerns about support for acts of terrorism. *Id.* at *12–*13. That said, the brief indicated that the court need not, and should not, reach the constitutional question given that the factual predicates were not satisfied. *Id.* at *1.

[13]  Pennoyer v. Neff, 95 U.S. 714 (1878).

to endow itself with worldwide adjudicatory jurisdiction. This is so, even though the United States can exercise extraterritorial prescriptive jurisdiction on the basis of more attenuated links as a matter of both domestic and international law.

## I. The Historical Origins of Due Process

While Article III of the Constitution authorizes Congress to create federal courts, limits on personal jurisdiction are rooted in the Due Process Clauses of the Fifth and Fourteenth Amendments. The Supreme Court established a constitutional basis for such limits in *Pennoyer v. Neff*, when it held that an Oregon statute authorizing service by publication on an absent, nonresident defendant violated the Fourteenth Amendment's due process guarantee.[14] The *Pennoyer* Court cited classic treatises by Joseph Story and Henry Wheaton for the proposition that "no State can exercise direct jurisdiction and authority over persons or property without its territory."[15] *Pennoyer's* understanding that regard for the prerogatives of other sovereigns mandates a certain degree of jurisdictional self-restraint continues to animate strands of contemporary due process doctrine.[16]

The original concept of "due process" in Anglo-American law can be traced at least as far back as Sir Edward Coke's *Commentary on Magna Carta*, which was published posthumously in 1642. Coke's *Commentary* includes a discussion of the phrase "but by the law of the land" (*nisi per Legem terrae*) found in chapter 39 of Magna Carta, which is commonly understood as the precursor to constitutional due process guarantees.[17] Although scholars of due process have debated whether or not the "law of the land" and "due process of law" should be

---

[14] Pennoyer, 95 U.S. at 733 (holding that, since the adoption of the Fourteenth Amendment, judgments may be challenged on the grounds that "proceedings in a court of justice to determine the personal rights and obligations of parties over whom that court has no jurisdiction do not constitute due process of law").

[15] *Id.* at 722. Under this strictly territorial understanding of personal jurisdiction, a State or federal court could exercise jurisdiction to determine the personal rights and obligations of a party who was personally served with process within the forum state, even if the dispute arose outside the state's borders. See, e.g., Chimène I. Keitner, *State Courts and Transitory Torts in Transnational Human Rights Cases*, 1 U.C. IRVINE L. REV. 81, 83–87 (2013) (discussing early cases involving suits against foreign defendants who were served with process in the United States).

[16] See *Pennoyer*, 95 U.S. at 722–23.

[17] See Robert E. Riggs, *Substantive Due Process in 1791*, 1990 WIS. L. REV. 941, 958; W.J. Brockelbank, *Role of Due Process in American Constitutional Law*, 39 CORNELL L.Q. 561, 562 (1954) (indicating that the "save by . . . the law of the land" clause of Magna Carta and the "without being brought in Answer by due Process of Law" clause of the confirmation of Magna Carta by Edward III bore fruit "in the Fifth Amendment to the Constitution of the United States and in the Constitutions of all the states except five," while noting that the search for the original meaning of these words "will not yield much fruit"); see also Riggs, *supra*, at 963 (noting that "[b]y the end of the seventeenth century, most of the English colonies had attempted, in one form or another, to include the Great Charter's due process guarantees in their fundamental laws").

interpreted as synonymous, they agree that the late seventeenth-century concep-tion of due process entailed, at a minimum, "the right of being brought to answer by due course (or process) of law, meaning, presumably, the service of proper process as prescribed by the common law."[18] Due process therefore mandated compliance with common-law requirements for haling a defendant into court.

In addition to the United States' inherited common-law tradition, late eighteenth-century American thought also embraced the idea that certain fun-damental laws limit the scope of government action.[19] Congress proposed the first ten amendments to the U.S. Constitution against this intellectual backdrop.[20] The Fifth Amendment, as drafted and ratified, focuses largely on criminal pro-cedure, but it also includes the guarantee that "no person shall [ . . . ] be deprived of life, liberty, or property, without due process of law."[21] Even though the con-cept of judicial review was still "in an embryonic stage and a subject of contro-versy" in the antebellum United States,[22] the idea that due process "entailed some legal norms beyond the reach of the legislature gained ground with American courts"[23] during this time.

When the Supreme Court first considered the meaning of Fifth Amendment due process in the mid-nineteenth century, it emphasized that "[i]t is manifest that it was not left to the legislative power to enact any process which might be devised," and that the article "cannot be so construed as to leave Congress free to make any process 'due process of law,' by its mere will."[24] Reducing due process

---

[18] Riggs, *supra* note 17, at 965. Coke construed the phrase "but by the law of the land," and its later rendering by Edward III as "without due process of law," as a guarantee "that no man be taken, im-prisoned, or put out of his free-hold without proces [*sic*] of the law" and "[w]ithout being brought in to answere [*sic*] but by due Process of the Common law." E. COKE, 2 INSTITUTES OF THE LAWES OF ENGLAND 50 (1797) (Garland ed., 1979), *quoted in* Riggs, *supra* note 17, at 959.

[19] *Id.* at 984; see also James W. Ely Jr., *The Oxymoron Reconsidered: Myth and Reality in the Origins of Substantive Due Process*, 16 CONST. COMM. 315, 324 (1999) (indicating that "[t]he newly inde-pendent Americans emphatically rejected the English notion of legislative supremacy" and "adhered to the older tradition, exemplified by Magna Carta, that legitimate government was restrained by re-spect for fundamental rights"); Thomas C. Grey, *Origins of the Unwritten Constitution: Fundamental Law in American Revolutionary Thought*, 30 STAN. L. REV. 843 (1978). In the words of legal histo-rian James Ely Jr., "[t]he newly independent Americans emphatically rejected the English notion of legislative supremacy" and "adhered to the older tradition, exemplified by Magna Carta, that legit-imate government was restrained by respect for fundamental rights." Ely Jr., *supra*, at 324. The idea of "fundamental law" as a check on the exercise of royal power in France also played a significant role in the decades leading up to the French Revolution. See CHIMÈNE I. KEITNER, THE PARADOXES OF NATIONALISM: THE FRENCH REVOLUTION AND ITS MEANING FOR CONTEMPORARY NATION BUILDING 49–51 (2007).

[20] Unfortunately for scholars and jurists, "existing records offer no evidence of any debate on the due process clause in the Congress . . . or in the state legislatures that ratified" the Bill of Rights. Riggs, *supra* note 17, at 987; see also Ely Jr., *supra* note 19, at 325 (characterizing "[t]he history of framing and debating the Bill of Rights" as "remarkably skimpy").

[21] U.S. CONST. amend. V.

[22] Ely, *supra* note 19, at 328.

[23] *Id.* at 331.

[24] Murray's Lessee v. Hoboken Land & Improvement Co., 59 U.S. (18 How.) 272, 276 (1856); see also *id.* (observing that "[t]he words, 'due process of law' were undoubtedly intended to convey the

to treatment in accordance with duly enacted legislation would run counter to the idea of fundamental law as a constraint on the exercise of government power. This historical background pushes against the idea that Congress can define what process is "due" simply by enacting a statute and that it can therefore legislate personal jurisdiction in certain contexts without regard to constitutional limits that lie beyond its own power to define.

## II. Contemporary Due Process Doctrine

Despite the historical pedigree of the Due Process Clause, it might not seem self-evident that the U.S. Constitution constrains the exercise of personal jurisdiction by federal courts in cases involving non-U.S. citizens, or that it limits Congress's ability to confer such authority on the federal courts. Yet, as indicated earlier, the idea of territorial limits on the exercise of adjudicatory jurisdiction has long been rooted in deference to other territorial sovereigns. In fact, the Supreme Court has remarked that the "transnational context" of a dispute can warrant a more restrictive, rather than a more expansive, approach to personal jurisdiction.[25]

The specific question of Fifth Amendment due process in the personal jurisdiction context has largely avoided sustained scrutiny. Recent judicial analysis of the extraterritorial reach of federal jurisdiction has focused primarily on questions of statutory interpretation, which may combine elements of prescriptive and adjudicatory jurisdiction.[26] The Supreme Court's extraterritoriality cases have thus focused less on whether it is constitutional to hale a particular defendant into U.S. court, and more on whether Congress intended to permit a certain category of defendants to be haled into court for claims relating to certain

---

same meaning as the words 'by the law of the land,' in Magna Carta"). The Court went on to define due process as, first, process that is not in conflict with any provisions in the Constitution itself, and second, process that does not conflict with "those settled usages and modes of proceeding existing in the common and statute law of England. . . ." *Id.* at 277. As noted by Ryan Williams, the Court "soon backed away from the historically defined standard described in *Murray's Lessee*, and this interpretation has not played a significant role in the subsequent development of procedural due process." Ryan C. Williams, *The One and Only Substantive Due Process Clause*, 120 YALE L.J. 408, 422 (2010) (citing Hurtado v. California, 110 U.S. 516, 528 (1884)).

[25] See Daimler AG v. Bauman, 571 U.S. 117, 140 (2014); see also Asahi Metal Indus. v. Superior Court of Cal., Solano Cnty., 480 U.S. 102, 114 (1987) (O'Connor, J., plurality opinion) (indicating that "the unique burdens placed upon one who must defend oneself in a foreign legal system should have significant weight in assessing the reasonableness of stretching the long arm of personal jurisdiction over national borders").

[26] Recent cases include Jesner v. Arab Bank, 138 S. Ct. 1386 (2018) (Alien Tort Statute); RJR Nabisco v. European Community, 136 S. Ct. 2090 (2016) (Racketeer Influenced and Corrupt Organizations Act); Kiobel v. Royal Dutch Petroleum Co., 569 U.S. 108 (2013) (Alien Tort Statute); Morrison v. National Australia Bank, 561 U.S. 247 (2010) (Securities Exchange Act §10(b)); see also Fourth Restatement § 404.

types of conduct. Scholars have explored the geographic limits of the United States' prescriptive jurisdiction, as well as certain limits on its adjudicatory jurisdiction.[27] Some have posited that nonresident aliens do not have constitutional due process rights, including in the personal jurisdiction context.[28] This does not, however, appear to be the prevailing approach, as courts continue to conduct constitutional due process analyses in cases involving assertions of personal jurisdiction over nonresident alien defendants.[29]

To be sure, not all exercises of extraterritorial government authority are viewed as implicating provisions of the Constitution. That said, whether or not an individual or entity can invoke certain constitutional rights in one context does not necessarily dictate whether the same individual or entity can invoke other constitutional rights in a different context. The idea that aliens abroad are outside of our constitutional system has a long pedigree; yet so does the idea that the Constitution governs the exercise of governmental authority within the United States.[30] In the foundational case *United States v. Verdugo-Urquidez*, the majority reasoned that constitutional violations of the right against self-incrimination

---

[27]  See, e.g., Anthony J. Colangelo, *Constitutional Limits on Extraterritorial Jurisdiction: Terrorism and the Intersection of National and International Law*, 48 HARV. INT'L L.J. 121 (2007) (focusing on prescriptive jurisdiction); Lea Brilmayer & Charles Norchi, *Extraterritoriality and Fifth Amendment Due Process*, 105 HARV. L. REV. 1217 (1992) (focusing primarily on potential constitutional limits on the extraterritorial application of federal law, or what they call "excesses of legislative jurisdiction"). Scholarly contributions on adjudicatory jurisdiction include: Robin J. Effron, *Solving the Nonresident Alien Due Process Paradox in Personal Jurisdiction*, 116 MICH. L. REV. ONLINE 123 (2018); Steven R. Swanson, *Fifth Amendment Due Process Foreign Shipowners, and International Law*, 36 TUL. MAR. L.J. 123, 154 (2011); Wendy Perdue, *Aliens, the Internet, and Purposeful Availment: A Reassessment of Fifth Amendment Limits on Personal Jurisdiction*, 98 NW. U. L. REV. 455 (2004). Bill Dodge and Scott Dodson have proposed applying "a national-contacts test for personal jurisdiction to aliens for all claims, state or federal, and in all courts, state or federal," but they do not address the questions posed in this contribution. William S. Dodge & Scott Dodson, *Personal Jurisdiction and Aliens*, 116 MICH. L. REV. 1205, 1235 (2018).

[28]  Austen L. Parrish, *Sovereignty, Not Due Process: Personal Jurisdiction Over Nonresident Alien Defendants*, 41 WAKE FOREST L. REV. 1, 33 (2006) (arguing for treaty-based limits on personal jurisdiction over nonresident aliens); cf. Austen Parrish, *Adjudicatory Jurisdiction and Public International Law: The Fourth Restatement's New Approach* in this volume; A. Mark Weisburd, *Due Process Limits on Federal Extraterritorial Legislation?*, 35 COLUM. J. TRANSNAT'L L. 379 (1997) (focusing on legislative jurisdiction, and on whether "aliens acting abroad are among the persons protected by the Fifth Amendment"); Gary A. Haugen, *Personal Jurisdiction and Due Process Rights for Alien Defendants*, 11 B.U. INT'L L.J. 109, 130 (1993) (arguing that "there seems to be no constitutional limitation that an alien may assert against the jurisdictional reach of a U.S. court"); Paul B. Stephan III, *Constitutional Limits on the Struggle Against International Terrorism: Revisiting the Rights of Overseas Aliens*, 19 CONN. L. REV. 831 (1987) (arguing that "overseas aliens" enjoy no U.S. constitutional protections from the overseas actions of U.S. officials).

[29]  See Republic of Argentina v. Weltover, 504 U.S. 607, 619 (1992) (assuming but not deciding that foreign states are "persons" under the Due Process Clause); Livnat v. Palestinian Authority, 851 F.3d 45, 52 (D.C. Cir. 2017), *cert. denied*, 139 S. Ct. 373 (2018) (applying personal jurisdiction protections under the Due Process Clause to the Palestinian Authority as a "non-sovereign foreign government"); Waldman v. Palestine Liberation Organization, 855 F.3d 317, 329 (2d Cir. 2016) (holding that "[b]ecause neither defendant is a [foreign] state, the defendants have due process rights"), *cert. denied sub nom*, Sokolow v. Palestine Liberation Organization, 138 S. Ct. 1438 (2018).

[30]  See generally Chimène I. Keitner, *Rights Beyond Borders*, 36 YALE J. INT'L L. 55 (2011).

occur at trial in the United States, not at the time of interrogation.[31] As a result, "any violation of the privilege against self-incrimination occurs, not at the moment law enforcement officials coerce statements through custodial interrogation, but when a defendant's involuntary statements are actually used against him at an American criminal proceeding."[32] For this reason, as the Second Circuit has explained, "it naturally follows that, regardless of the origin—i.e., domestic or foreign—of a statement, it cannot be admitted at trial in the United States if the statement was 'compelled.' Similarly, it does not matter whether the defendant is a U.S. citizen or a foreign national: 'no person' tried in the civilian courts of the United States can be compelled 'to be a witness against himself.' "[33] By analogy, it makes the most sense to think of the exercise of civil adjudicatory jurisdiction as happening within a U.S. courtroom.[34] The Fifth Amendment's due process protections thus apply to any "person" haled into a U.S. court.[35]

Restatement Section 422 restates the U.S. law of personal jurisdiction in civil proceedings as requiring that "sufficient contacts" exist between the defendant and the forum "and that the exercise of jurisdiction be reasonable."[36] The Federal Rules of Civil Procedure direct courts to look to the Constitution to delineate the outer bounds of personal jurisdiction. For example, Federal Rule of Civil Procedure 4(k)(1)(C) indicates simply that "[s]erving a summons or filing a waiver of service establishes personal jurisdiction over a defendant when authorized by a federal statute." Yet, as one district court put it, this provision does not "override the controlling constitutional limitations on [a] Court's exercise of general or specific personal jurisdiction imposed by the Fifth Amendment's Due Process Clause."[37] Rule 4(k)(2) provides that "[f]or a claim that arises under federal law, serving a summons or filing a waiver of service establishes personal jurisdiction over a defendant" if two conditions are met. First, the defendant must not be "subject to jurisdiction in any state's courts of general jurisdiction." Second, exercising jurisdiction must be "consistent with the United States Constitution and laws."[38] The Advisory Committee's Notes to the 1993

[31] United States v. Verdugo-Urquidez, 494 U.S. 259, 264 (1990).
[32] United States v. Bin Laden, 132 F. Supp. 2d 168, 181 (2d Cir. 2001).
[33] *In re* Terrorist Bombings of U.S. Embassies in East Africa, 552 F.3d 177, 199 (2d Cir. 2008) (quoting U.S. Const. amend. V).
[34] William Dodge and Scott Dodson have similarly observed that "an American court exercising adjudicatory authority over an alien in violation of one of the Constitution's Due Process Clauses is by definition violating the Constitution within the United States." See Dodge & Dodson, *supra* note 27, at 1222.
[35] The threshold questions of whether foreign states or foreign nonsovereign entities are "persons" for due process purposes fall outside the scope of this chapter.
[36] FOURTH RESTATEMENT § 422. Unlike constraints on subject matter jurisdiction, constraints on a court's personal jurisdiction may be waived by the defendant. *Id.* § 422 cmt. *b.*
[37] Siswanto v. Airbus, 153 F. Supp. 3d 1024, 1027 (N.D. Ill. 2015); see Fed. R. Civ. P. 4(k)(1)(C).
[38] Fed. R. Civ. P. 4(k)(2).

amendment to Rule 4 specifies that, even if an individual defendant is served with summons within a judicial district of the United States under Rule 4(e), "[s]ervice of the summons under this subdivision does not conclusively establish the jurisdiction of the court over the person of the defendant," and that "[a] defendant may assert the territorial limits of the court's reach set forth in subdivision (k), including the constitutional limitations that may be imposed by the Due Process Clause of the Fifth Amendment."[39] Moreover, the amended rule, while designed to "facilitate the use of federal long-arm law in actions brought to enforce the federal law against defendants who cannot be served under any state law," was intended only to extend to those "who can be constitutionally subjected to the jurisdiction of the federal court."[40] The notes to Rule 4(k)(2) similarly emphasize that the rule was intended to "correct a gap in the enforcement of federal law," but that "[t]here remain constitutional limitations on the exercise of territorial jurisdiction by federal courts over persons outside the United States."[41] In particular, in the view of the Advisory Committee, "[t]he Fifth Amendment requires that any defendant have affiliating contacts with the United States sufficient to justify the exercise of personal jurisdiction over that party."[42]

As noted earlier, the question of constitutional limits on the exercise of personal jurisdiction has arisen most frequently in the context of the assertion of State, rather than federal, adjudicatory authority.[43] Perhaps as a result, lower courts have generally imported Fourteenth Amendment due process standards into their Fifth Amendment analyses of limits on personal jurisdiction, although they have looked at a defendant's nationwide, as opposed to State-specific, contacts. As the D.C. Circuit Court of Appeals observed in *Livnat v. Palestinian Authority*, "[n]o court has ever held that the Fifth Amendment permits personal jurisdiction without the same 'minimum contacts' with the United States as the Fourteenth Amendment requires with respect to States."[44] That said, the circuit court also acknowledged that "neither this court nor the Supreme Court has expressly analyzed whether the Fifth and Fourteenth Amendment standards differ."[45] As recently

[39] Fed. R. Civ. P. Advisory Committee Notes—1993 Amendment.
[40] *Id.*
[41] *Id.*
[42] *Id.*
[43] Federal courts exercising personal jurisdiction under Fed. R. Civ. P. 4(1)(k)(A) are constrained by the Fourteenth Amendment limits applicable to State long-arm statutes.
[44] Livnat v. Palestinian Authority, 851 F.3d 45, 54 (D.C. Cir. 2017), *cert. denied*, 139 S. Ct. 373 (2018).
[45] Livnat, 851 F.3d at 54; cf. Waldman v. Palestine Liberation Organization, 855 F.3d 317, 331 (2d Cir. 2016), *cert. denied sub nom*, Sokolow v. Palestine Liberation Organization, 138 S. Ct. 1438 (2018) (concluding that "the minimum contacts and fairness analysis is the same under the Fifth Amendment and the Fourteenth Amendment in civil cases"); see also THIRD RESTATEMENT § 721 reporters' note 6 (1987) (observing that "[t]he meaning and scope of due process have developed largely in the application of the clause of the Fourteenth Amendment governing action by the States, but it is established that due process has essentially the same meaning and scope in the Fifth Amendment as applied to the Federal Government").

as 2017, the Supreme Court explicitly confirmed that it has left this question open.[46]

Current Fourteenth Amendment doctrine generally requires that a defendant be "at home" within a State in order to be subject to that State's exercise of general personal jurisdiction over any claim[47] and that a nonresident defendant's "suit-related conduct . . . create a substantial connection with the forum State" in order to subject the defendant to the State's exercise of specific personal jurisdiction over a particular claim.[48] Some ambiguity persists regarding what types of "suit-related conduct" will provide the requisite connection.[49]

State long-arm statutes often explicitly authorize personal jurisdiction over out-of-state defendants to the limits of Fourteenth Amendment due process.[50] This language begs the question of where such constitutional limits lie, which Rule 4(k)(2) also leaves unanswered. The Supreme Court has cautioned against approaches to due process that are "simply mechanical or quantitative,"[51] although the rationales underlying its limit-drawing have varied over the years.[52]

---

[46] Bristol-Myers Squibb v. Superior Court, 137 S. Ct. 1773, 1784 (2017) (leaving open "the question whether the Fifth Amendment imposes the same restrictions on the exercise of personal jurisdiction by a federal court" as the Fourteenth Amendment does on the exercise of specific jurisdiction by a State).

[47] Daimler AG v. Bauman, 571 U.S. 117, 122 (2014), citing Goodyear Dunlop Tires, S.A. v. Brown, 564 U.S. 915, 919 (2011) (holding that "[a] court may assert general jurisdiction over foreign (sister-state or foreign-country) corporations to hear any and all claims against them when their affiliations with the State are so 'continuous and systematic' as to render them essentially at home in the forum State"); but cf. Burnham v. Superior Court, 495 U.S. 604 (1990) (upholding in-state personal service on an individual defendant as constitutionally sufficient to establish general personal jurisdiction, even over a transient defendant).

[48] Walden v. Fiore, 571 U.S. 277 (2014) (addressing the "minimum contacts" required to create specific jurisdiction); see id. at 283 n.6 (citing Goodyear for the proposition that "'specific' or 'case-linked' jurisdiction 'depends on an 'affiliatio[n] between the forum and the underlying controversy' (i.e. an 'activity or occurrence that takes place in the forum State and is therefore subject to the State's regulation')"). Applying this standard, a defendant cannot be haled into court in a forum State "based on the 'random, fortuitous, or attenuated' contacts he makes by interacting with other persons affiliated with the State." Id. at 286, citing Burger King Corp. v. Rudzewicz, 471 U.S. 462, 475 (1985).

[49] Compare Calder v. Jones, 465 U.S. 783, 789 (1984) (finding specific personal jurisdiction in California over Florida defendants on the grounds that California was "the focal point both of the [allegedly libelous] story and of the harm suffered"), with Walden, 571 U.S. at 285 (indicating that "our 'minimum contacts' analysis looks to the defendant's contacts with the forum State itself, not the defendant's contacts with persons who reside there"); see generally Patrick J. Borchers, Extending Federal Rule of Civil Procedure 4(k)(2): A Way to (Partially) Clean Up the Personal Jurisdiction Mess, 67 AM. U. L. REV. 413, 426 (2017) (arguing that although the Supreme Court "tried mightily," its decision in Walden is "hard to square" with its prior jurisprudence basing specific personal jurisdiction on the predictable effects of intentional torts committed by out-of-state defendants).

[50] See, e.g., Cal. Civ. Pro. Code § 410.10 (providing that "[a] court of this state may exercise jurisdiction on any basis not inconsistent with the Constitution of this state or of the United States").

[51] International Shoe Co. v. State of Wash., 326 U.S. 310, 319 (1945).

[52] See, e.g., Wendy C. Perdue, What's Sovereignty Got to Do with It? Due Process, Personal Jurisdiction, and the Supreme Court, 63 S.C. L. REV. 729, 739 (2012) (noting that "the core inquiry in personal jurisdiction is no longer a state-centered inquiry that focuses on the nature of state sovereignty, but rather a defendant-centered inquiry"); see also Pamela J. Stephens, The Federal Court Across the Street: Constitutional Limits on Federal Court Assertions of Personal Jurisdiction, 18 U.

Congress, meanwhile, has bristled at perceived judicial curtailment of certain aspects of its legislative agenda on due process grounds, as illustrated by its reaction to cases finding a lack of personal jurisdiction in the Anti-Terrorism Act cases described in the following section.[53]

## III. Litigation over the Reach of the Anti-Terrorism Act

Having canvased the historical origins and doctrinal framework of due process limits on personal jurisdiction, I now turn to a recent example of conflicting views of Congress's power to confer adjudicatory jurisdiction on the federal courts. Congress enacted the ATA to provide a cause of action in U.S. federal court for "[a]ny national of the United States injured in his or her person, property or business by reason of an act of international terrorism," and to provide treble damages for victims.[54] Anticipating potential procedural hurdles, Section 2334 provides for venue in "any district where any plaintiff resides or where any defendant resides or is served, or has an agent," and it limits the availability of common-law *forum non conveniens* as a basis for dismissing a suit brought under the ATA.[55] The Anti-Terrorism Clarification Act of 2018 added Section 2334(e), which specifies conditions in which a defendant "shall be deemed to have consented to personal jurisdiction" in a civil action brought under the ATA.[56] This subsection was adopted specifically to create personal jurisdiction over the Palestinian Authority (PA) and the Palestine Liberation Organization (PLO), which previously accepted foreign assistance under specified sections of the Foreign Assistance Act of 1961,[57] and which also previously benefited

RICH. L. REV. 697, 700 (1984) (characterizing *International Shoe* as "redefin[ing] the theoretical basis of state court personal jurisdiction").

[53] See, e.g., ZOA Lobbied for and Praises Enactment of the Anti-Terrorism Clarification Act of 2018 (Oct. 4, 2018), available at https://zoa.org/2018/10/10378585-zoa-lobbied-for-and-praises-enactment-of-the-anti-terrorism-clarification-act/ (indicating that the co-directors of the organization's government relations department "met with lawmakers to discuss this important bipartisan legislation and seek their support for it"); McGuire Woods Consulting Helps Secure Passage of New Anti-Terrorism Clarification Act, Helping Victims of Foreign Terror Attacks Pursue Financial Recoveries (Oct. 12, 2018), available at https://www.mwcllc.com/ideas/news/2018/10/mcguirewoods-consulting-helps-secure-passage-new-anti-terrorism-clarification-act.aspx (indicating that one of the firm's senior advisors "helped lead a multi-pronged lobbying team that collaborated to pass the Act").

[54] Federal Courts Administration Act of 1992, Pub. L. 102-572, § 1003, 106 Stat. 4506, 4521–24, codified at 18 U.S.C. §§ 2331–38.

[55] 18 U.S.C. § 2334(d).

[56] ATCA, *supra* note 11, § 4, 132 Stat. 3183, 3184, codified at 18 U.S.C. § 2334(e).

[57] The ATCA resulted in the PA's renunciation of the designated sources of U.S. foreign aid on the grounds that, although "U.S. assistance has . . . supported peace and stability for Palestine and its neighbors," the ATCA "purports to alter the rules of jurisdiction over the Government of Palestine in the U.S. legal proceedings if it continues to accept such aid." The PA disclaimed the ability of the

from a designated waiver under the ATA.[58] The PSJVTA of 2019 modified these conditions, and explicitly provides that the PA and PLO will be deemed to have consented to jurisdiction if they make payments to "individuals imprisoned for terrorist acts against Americans or to families of individuals who died while committing terrorist acts against Americans."[59]

Prior to the ATCA's enactment, the Second Circuit found that the PA and PLO are not subject to general jurisdiction in U.S. courts because they are not "at home" in the United States, and that they were not subject to specific jurisdiction for their alleged involvement in a series of enumerated terrorist attacks because "these actions, as heinous as they were, were not sufficiently connected to the United States to provide specific personal jurisdiction in the United States."[60] In the Second Circuit's view, the fact that U.S. citizens were "victims of indiscriminate violence that occurred abroad" was insufficient to support specific jurisdiction under applicable Supreme Court precedent.[61] Although the Second Circuit had previously upheld the exercise of specific personal jurisdiction over a foreign bank on the grounds that the defendant's conduct outside of the United States was "expressly aimed" at the United States, it did not deem that standard to have been met here.[62] Instead, absent any "evidence that these indiscriminate terrorist attacks were specifically targeted against United States citizens," the court of appeals held that "the mere knowledge that United States citizens might be wronged in a foreign country goes beyond the jurisdictional limit set forth [by the Supreme Court] in *Walden*."[63] Moreover, "[u]nlike [the Supreme Court's

---

ATCA to "support an exercise of the general jurisdiction of the U.S. courts over the Palestinian National Authority and its agencies," but nonetheless felt itself "constrained" to renounce such aid given the ATCA's "conver[sion of] these constitutional issues into political ones." Letter from Prime Minister Rami Hamdallah to Secretary of State Michael Pompeo (Dec. 26, 2018), available at https://twitter.com/DanielEstrin/status/1086253205640699904. Ironically, some of the strongest opposition to the ATCA's provision specifying that acceptance of certain types of U.S. aid would be deemed consent to general personal jurisdiction came from Israel, which benefits from U.S. funding that supports its security cooperation with the PA. See Michael Bachner, *Israel Said Pushing US to Amend Law That Threatens Security Coordination with PA*, TIMES OF ISRAEL (Jan. 24, 2019), https://www.timesofisrael.com/israel-said-pushing-us-to-amend-law-that-threatens-security-coordination-with-pa/.

[58] The Trump administration announced in September 2018 that the PLO Office in Washington, which had been permitted to conduct operations under a waiver, would be closed. See Press Statement, Closure of the PLO Office in Washington (Sept. 10, 2018), available at https://www.state.gov/closure-of-the-plo-office-in-washington/ (criticizing PLO leadership for "condemn[ing] a U.S. peace plan they have not yet seen" and indicating that the closure "is also consistent with Administration and Congressional concerns with Palestinian attempts to prompt an investigation of Israel by the International Criminal Court").

[59] 18 U.S.C. § 2334(e)(1)(A).

[60] *Waldman*, 835 F. 3d at 337.

[61] *Id.* (citing *Walden* and *Goodyear*).

[62] *Id.* (citing Licci ex rel. Licci v. Lebanese Canadian Bank, SAL, 732 F.3d 161, 173 (2d Cir. 2013)).

[63] *Id.* at 338 (citing Walden v. Fiore, 571 U.S. 277 (2014)); see also *id.* at 338–39 (distinguishing facts in *Mwani v. Bin Laden*, 417 F.3d 1 (D.C. Cir. 2005), which found specific jurisdiction over Osama Bin Laden and al Qaeda for allegedly orchestrating the bombing of the American embassy in Nairobi, and distinguishing *In re Terrorist Attacks on September 11, 2001* ("*O'Neill*"), 714 F.3d 659

decision] in *Calder*, it cannot be said that the United States is the focal point of the torts alleged in this litigation. In this case, the United States is not the nucleus of the harm—Israel is."[64]

The House Report accompanying the Anti-Terrorism Clarification Act objects strenuously to this "flawed Second Circuit decision" for "severely limit[ing] the extraterritorial scope of the ATA," and asserts that "[c]arrying out or assisting an act of international terrorism that injures or kills American citizens abroad should be, in and of itself, sufficient to establish personal jurisdiction in U.S. courts."[65] Although the D.C. Circuit also found that the PA and PLO were not subject to general or specific personal jurisdiction,[66] the Second Circuit's decision garnered more attention because it vacated a $218.5 million jury verdict, which had been trebled under the ATA to $655.5 million.[67] In attempt to restore the jury's award and enable future similar awards, the ATCA relies on a fiction of constructive consent to general personal jurisdiction based on the defendant's acceptance of certain categories of foreign aid or maintenance of a particular type of U.S. office pursuant to a designated waiver.[68] The ATCA and the PSJVTA provide potent examples of Congress's proactive stance in creating judicial remedies for certain types of harm caused by foreign actors.[69]

---

(2d Cir. 2013), which held that the foreseeability of harm in the forum is insufficient to establish specific personal jurisdiction, but that jurisdictional discovery was warranted with respect to twelve defendants whose support for designated foreign terrorist organizations might have been "expressly aimed" at the United States).

[64] *Id.* at 340 (citing Calder v. Jones, 465 U.S. 783 (1984)).

[65] H.R. Rep. No. 115-858 at 6 (2018). Aaron Simowitz has argued that Congress's implicit interpretation of constitutional due process in the ATA merits judicial deference, and that a statutory amendment (such as the ATCA) should suffice to create personal jurisdiction to avoid rendering the ATA and other federal statutes "largely inoperative." See Aaron D. Simowitz, *Legislating Transnational Jurisdiction*, 57 VA. J. INT'L L. 325, 369–70 (2018).

[66] Livnat v. Palestinian Authority, 851 F.3d 45, 52 (D.C. Cir. 2017), *cert. denied*, 139 S. Ct. 373 (2018).

[67] Sokolow v. Palestine Liberation Organization, 2015 WL 10852003 (S.D.N.Y. Oct. 1, 2015) (Judgment).

[68] Subsequent decisions held that the ATCA's jurisdictional provisions do not permit courts to reopen closed cases, and that the PA and PLO do not meet the ATCA's statutory criteria for deemed consent to general jurisdiction. See Waldman v. Palestine Liberation Organization, 925 F.3d 570 (2d Cir. 2019) (denying motion to recall the mandate vacating the district court's original judgment in favor of the plaintiffs); Estate of Kleiman v. Palestinian Authority, 923 F.3d 1115 (D.C. Cir. 2019) (finding that the factual predicates for applying the ATCA were not satisfied, and declining to reach defendants' constitutional objections to the ATCA). On April 27, 2020, the Supreme Court granted petitions to review both of these decisions, vacated the judgments, and remanded the cases "for further consideration in light of the Promoting Security and Justice for Victims of Terrorism Act of 2019." Estate of Kleinman v. Palestinian Authority, 140 S. Ct __ (2020); Sokolow v. Palestinian Liberation Organization, 140 S.Ct. __ (2020).

[69] Beth Stephens's contribution in this volume explores another example of this phenomenon: the state sponsors of terrorism exception to the Foreign Sovereign Immunities Act. See Beth Stephens, *The Fourth Restatement, International Law, and the "Terrorism" Exception to the Foreign Sovereign Immunities Act*, in this volume; see also Kristina Daugirdas, *The Restatements and the Rule of Law*, in this volume (also considering the state-sponsors-of-terrorism exception).

Even before the ATCA was enacted, the briefing at the cert petition stage in *Sokolow* crystallized certain core arguments regarding Fifth Amendment due process limits on personal jurisdiction. The petitioners in *Sokolow* sought review of the Second Circuit's holding that the Fifth and Fourteenth Amendment due process analyses are the same in civil cases, and that the assertion of personal jurisdiction over the PA and PLO did not comport with established Fourteenth Amendment limits. The Second Circuit explained:

> The plaintiffs and amici argue that the Fourteenth Amendment . . . imposes stricter limits on the personal jurisdiction that courts can exercise because that Amendment, grounded in concepts of federalism, was intended to referee jurisdictional conflicts among the sovereign States. The Fifth Amendment, by contrast, imposes more lenient restrictions because it contemplates disputes with foreign nations, which, unlike States, do not follow reciprocal rules and are not subject to our constitutional system.[70]

The Second Circuit found this argument unpersuasive, and the Supreme Court declined review.

Petitioners subsequently expanded upon this argument, building on the United States' observation in another case that Congress can "provide for the exercise of federal judicial power *in ways that have no analogue at the state level.*"[71] Petitioners received support from the U.S. House of Representatives as amicus curiae, which argued that "the decision below impermissibly intrudes upon Congress's constitutional authority to legislate extraterritorially . . ."[72] An amicus curiae brief on behalf of U.S. Senators argued that U.S. courts should be able to exercise adjudicatory jurisdiction over ATA claims if the terrorist attacks at issue "implicate vital U.S. interests."[73] The brief further argued that existing case law

---

[70]  Waldman v. Palestine Liberation Organization, 855 F.3d 317, 329–30 (2d Cir. 2016).

[71]  Supplemental Brief for Petitioners, Sokolow v. Palestine Liberation Organization, No. 16-1071 at 10 (Mar. 2018), citing CVSG Brief for United States, BNSF Ry. Co. v. Tyrrell, No. 16-405 at *32 (Mar. 2017) (emphasis added in supplemental brief). Interestingly, in an amicus brief filed in subsequent litigation involving the ATCA, the United States articulated one concrete way in which the Fifth and Fourteenth Amendment constraints differ:

> In the foreign affairs context, in contrast to the limited and mutually exclusive sovereignty of the several states, Congress may deem certain actions of defendants like the Palestinian Authority and the Palestine Liberation Organization to be consent to personal jurisdiction in the United States, even if a State cannot enact similar legislation.

See Brief for United States as Amicus Curiae, Klieman v. Palestinian Authority (Mar. 13, 2019), 2019 WL 1200589 at *15. Litigation over the PSJVTA's deemed consent provisions will likely test this premise.

[72]  Brief for the U.S. House of Representatives as *Amicus Curiae* Supporting Certiorari, Sokolow v. Palestine Liberation Organization, No. 16-1071 at 12 (Apr. 2017).

[73]  Brief of United States Senators Charles E. Grassley et al. as *Amici Curiae* Supporting Certiorari, Sokolow v. Palestine Liberation Organization, No. 16-1071 at 4 (Apr. 2017).

supports the exercise of personal jurisdiction over the PA and PLO for "acts of international terrorism harming U.S. persons" because "[t]he interests underlying the ATA's application to attacks abroad" establish the constitutionally " 'requisite relationship' " between the defendants and a U.S. forum.[74]

The concern that restrictive interpretations of personal jurisdiction could hamper Congress's antiterrorism efforts also animated other briefs. For example, an amicus curiae brief on behalf of former federal officials objected:

> Restricting the jurisdiction of federal courts over terrorists and those that provide them material support by incorporating the Fourteenth Amendment's federalism-based limits into the Fifth Amendment would impose a unilateral constraint on United States Courts, even when, as with the ATA, the political branches of government have concluded that extraterritorial jurisdiction is in the national interest.[75]

Yet, even if Fourteenth Amendment standards are not directly applicable, the Fifth Amendment does not necessarily permit the unilateral exercise of adjudicatory jurisdiction solely on the basis of "national interests." The rationales animating Fourteenth Amendment limits on personal jurisdiction, which include consideration of a defendant's reasonable expectations and respect for other territorial sovereigns, are also present in the Fifth Amendment context.

The respondents in *Sokolow* argued that limits on adjudicatory jurisdiction do not impermissibly infringe on prescriptive and enforcement jurisdiction. They contended that recognizing due process limits on personal jurisdiction over defendants in ATA cases "does not encroach on Legislative Branch jurisdiction to prescribe laws, or on Executive Branch authority to enforce the Nation's antiterrorism laws and policies."[76] They noted that "[d]ue process has always constrained jurisdiction to adjudicate claims against specific defendants in specific cases, and has always limited the case-specific application of Congress's jurisdiction to prescribe laws that apply extraterritorially."[77] They further argued that "[t]he Executive Branch has a robust arsenal of antiterrorism tools unconstrained by traditional due process limits on jurisdiction in ATA civil cases, including criminal prosecutions, asset freezes, export controls, and even the 'use of force,' which the legislative sponsors of the ATA acknowledged."[78] It remains

---

[74] *Id.* at 12, quoting J. McIntyre Machinery, Ltd. v. Nicastro, 564 U.S. 873, 884 (2011).

[75] Brief of Former Federal Officials as *Amici Curiae* in Support of Petitioners, Sokolow v. Palestine Liberation Organization, No. 16-1071 at 18 (Apr. 2017).

[76] Brief in Opposition, Sokolow v. Palestine Liberation Organization, No. 16-1071 at 27 (May 2017).

[77] *Id.* at 28.

[78] *Id.* at 31 (citing Brief of United States Senators, *supra* note 73). Although some of these tools are not completely "unconstrained" by due process limits, the "traditional" due process analysis referenced here applies only in civil suits.

unclear whether the prospect of civil damages judgments, as opposed to the use of these other tools, can credibly be said to deter or prevent terrorist attacks.

The United States as amicus took the position in *Sokolow* that "[r]eview of petitioners' broad Fifth Amendment arguments would be premature," and that "the contours and implications of petitioners' jurisdictional theory—which turns on whether a defendant's conduct 'interfered with U.S. sovereign interests as set out in a federal statute,'—are not themselves well developed."[79] Consequently, the United States recommended that the Supreme Court allow "further development in the lower courts" before it "addresses arguments that the federal courts may, in particular circumstances, exercise personal jurisdiction over civil cases without regard to the principles of specific and general jurisdiction developed under the Fourteenth Amendment."[80] Because the ATCA's sponsors presumably thought deemed consent would be more likely to survive constitutional challenge than an open-ended provision, the ATCA will not prompt such "further development" in the lower courts, thus leaving the broader question open.[81]

## IV. The Role of Fifth Amendment Due Process

Although due process jurisprudence in the personal jurisdiction context has evolved since *Pennoyer*, the Supreme Court's core holding that "[d]ue process requires that a judgment be rendered by a court of competent jurisdiction"[82] remains valid. The current Fourteenth Amendment dividing line—that a court has specific personal jurisdiction over an absent, nonresident defendant who has targeted or aimed its conduct at the forum State, including by targeting the forum State's nationals abroad, but not over an absent, nonresident defendant whose conduct has foreseeably, but not intentionally, harmed the forum State's nationals abroad—requires an element of intentional association with the forum.[83] This intentionality provides the constitutionally required link between

---

[79] Brief for the United States as *Amicus Curiae*, Sokolow v. Palestine Liberation Organization, No. 16-1071 at 17 (Feb. 2018), quoting Petitioners' Reply Brief 11.

[80] *Id.*

[81] If a court finds that the PA/PLO satisfies the deemed consent provisions added by the PSJVTA, then the Fifth Amendment due process question could work its way back up to the U.S. Supreme Court for potential review.

[82] Perdue, *supra* note 52, at 732; cf. Lea Brilmayer, *Consent, Contract & Territory*, 74 MINN. L. REV. 1, 8 (1989) (observing that "[a]n inference of consent typically involves the application of a legal rule establishing that certain conduct constitutes consent. The application of such a legal rule is itself an exercise of political sovereignty.").

[83] See *supra* note 63 and accompanying text. In *Freeman v. HSBC Holdings PLC*, the district court found personal jurisdiction over Iranian Bank Saderat at the pleading stage based on plaintiffs' allegations that the bank "engaged in affirmative acts aimed at New York, directing its co-conspirators to illegally clear and settle dollar-denominated transactions through correspondent accounts in New York." Freeman v. HSBC Holdings PLC, 2019 WL 4452364 (E.D.N.Y., Sept. 16, 2019), at 7.

the defendant and the forum, such that the forum can adjudicate the defendant's rights and obligations for the purposes of determining civil liability.[84] There are sound reasons for courts to require similar connecting links under the Fifth Amendment, although the concept of intentional harm to the United States or its nationals might be interpreted in a somewhat more elastic fashion.

Even thought it might be appropriate to require a lesser degree of intentional targeting of U.S. nationals or U.S. interests when it comes to conduct that is universally proscribed, the impact on the United States cannot be simply fortuitous or happenstance in order for the defendant's conduct to create a constitutionally sufficient link. Whether a particular terrorist attack meets the required threshold will turn largely on evidence of the defendant's intent. As in domestic cases, ascertaining intent could require a certain amount of jurisdictional discovery, in addition to publicly available circumstantial evidence and inferences that can be drawn from the nature of the attack. Conditioning the existence of personal jurisdiction on the defendant's aims poses challenges that are difficult to avoid unless one adopts a pure "effects" test for personal jurisdiction that includes incidental, and even unintended, effects. However, predicating personal jurisdiction on such an attenuated connection between a defendant and the forum seems inconsistent with the Supreme Court's admonition in *Murray's Lessee* that "it was not left to the legislative power to enact any process which might be devised" and that the principle of due process "cannot be so construed as to leave Congress free to make any process 'due process of law,' by its mere will."[85] A recognition of this principle likely inspired the ATCA's and the PSJVTA's drafters to rely on somewhat contrived proxies for deemed consent, rather than on pure congressional fiat, as the basis for personal jurisdiction in ATA cases involving attacks that did not intentionally target U.S. nationals or U.S. interests.

Even without external constraints on adjudicative jurisdiction imposed by international law, internal constraints embedded in the Constitution can circumscribe the authority of U.S. courts to adjudicate civil disputes. These constraints also inform the allocation of adjudicatory authority between the United States

---

[84] The *Sokolow* court acknowledged that the Second Circuit uses a "more expansive due process test in criminal cases," but it found that this "more expansive" test does not apply to civil actions. Waldman v. Palestine Liberation Organization, 855 F.3d 317, 341 (2d Cir. 2016); see also United States v. Murillo, 826 F.3d 152, 156 (4th Cir. 2016), citing United States v. Brehm, 691 F.3d 547, 552 (4th Cir. 2012) (indicating that the enforcement of an extraterritorial criminal statute "in a particular instance must comport with due process," and that there must be "a sufficient nexus between the defendant and the United States" so that applying the statute to the accused "would not be arbitrary or fundamentally unfair"). It is also worth noting that U.S. criminal trials, unlike civil proceedings, require the physical presence of the defendant. See FOURTH RESTATEMENT § 427.

[85] Murray's Lessee v. Hoboken Land & Improvement Co., 59 U.S. (18 How.) 272, 276 (1856).

and other countries. Although there might be a strong temptation to allow the unilateral extension of civil adjudicatory jurisdiction in all cases involving an asserted U.S. interest, the international system relies on a certain degree of mutual self-restraint. Under U.S. domestic law, judicial interpretation and application of the Due Process Clauses helps perform this restraining function by delineating the boundaries of personal jurisdiction in civil disputes.

# 10

# Customary International Law and U.S. Judicial Power

## From the Third to the Fourth Restatements

*Thomas H. Lee*

One notable difference between the Third and Fourth Restatements of the Foreign Relations Law of the United States is their divergent treatment of customary international law and how the U.S. federal courts should engage with it. The Third Restatement, adopted in 1987, envisioned U.S. courts fluent in and engaged with international law, deploying a U.S. foreign relations jurisprudence in dialogue with international law and lawyers. Customary international law was a central feature of this vision because it was the prime pathway for human rights litigation in federal courts when U.S. treaty-based human-rights initiatives had stalled.

Appearing thirty years later, the Fourth Restatement exhibits a fundamentally different orientation toward customary international law. Customary international law is no longer embraced as it was in the Third Restatement as an opportunity to play offense, to advance the international law of human rights. The Third Restatement's vision inspired a reaction among some U.S. legal scholars who questioned the U.S. federal law status of customary international law and the legitimacy of U.S. judges advancing the customary international law of human rights. The Fourth Restatement seeks a middle ground by defending against this revision of customary international law's status and role in the United States, concerned that the revisionist view might encourage and provide cover for U.S. courts to dismiss cases and claims with foreign policy ramifications that they should be adjudicating. The new Restatement, by contrast to the Third, strongly implies that federal courts have little discretion in foreign affairs, whether to recognize the customary international law of human rights or to invoke it as a ground for dismissing cases. The Fourth Restatement disavows customary international law-based judicial discretion where the Third Restatement embraced it.

This chapter has three aims. The first is to identify and describe specific points of divergence between the Third and Fourth Restatements, specifically regarding how U.S. courts should engage with customary international law. The second

Thomas H. Lee, *Customary International Law and U.S. Judicial Power* In: *The Restatement and Beyond.* Edited by: Paul B. Stephan and Sarah H. Cleveland, Oxford University Press (2020). © Oxford University Press.
DOI: 10.1093/oso/9780197533154.003.0011

aim is to explain the causes for the differences, both doctrinal-legal, and extra-legal and contextual. Third, I offer a brief assessment of the relative merits and demerits of the two different approaches toward customary international law presented by the two Restatements. In short, the Third Restatement went over-board in encouraging the use of U.S. judicial power to advance the customary international law of human rights, but the Fourth Restatement has overcorrected by seeking to constrain customary international law as a basis for U.S. courts to dismiss cases with foreign policy implications. Both approaches have contrib-uted to the disengagement of U.S. judges from customary international law to the detriment of U.S. conduct of foreign policy and contrary to the original con-stitutional specification of the "judicial Power of the United States" as reflected in Article III, the Judiciary Act of 1789 that established the federal courts, and early historical practice.

# I. Customary International Law and U.S. Courts

## A. The Traditional View of Customary International Law

Customary international law—state practices done out of a sense of legal ob-ligation (*opinio juris*)—was historically the main category of international law norms. Until the twentieth century, treaties were mostly bilateral and did not purport to frame rules binding on all states. Rather, they bound only the states that ratified them. Custom, instead, was the main font of the generally applicable rules of the European-led international legal order.

Defining what counts as custom has always been a somewhat subjective en-terprise, particularly given the absence of a centralized, hierarchical system of lawmaking or adjudication at the international level. But the ambiguity inherent in identifying binding custom did not matter so much when jurists, statesmen, and scholars understood international law to be limited in scope to interactions between "civilized" nation-states and saw it as a pseudo-science of identifying norms that existed between these states independent of social, political, and eco-nomic contexts. Morality, too, although closely linked to international law's me-dieval origins,[1] was stripped away from international law during the eighteenth and nineteenth centuries, although it re-emerged in the twentieth century. Faith in transcendent objectivity was a distinct feature of all of law's then-identity as an autonomous discipline. In the field of international law, the broad acceptance of treatises like Emer de Vattel's *Law of Nations* (1758), Henry Wheaton's *Elements*

---

[1] RICHARD TUCK, THE RIGHTS OF WAR AND PEACE: POLITICAL THOUGHT AND THE INTERNATIONAL ORDER FROM GROTIUS TO KANT (2001).

*of International Law* (1836), and Lassa Oppenheim's *International Law: A Treatise* (1905) as authoritative statements of custom by lawyers and judges as well as academics,[2] confirmed this vision of law as an objective and scientific discipline with principles as universal as Isaac Newton's principles of mechanics.

The general jurisprudential belief in law's separateness, transcendence, and universality was eroded by legal positivism (law as the command of a sovereign) and its progeny, legal realism (the view that law cannot be separated from larger political, social, economic forces). International law was not immune from these intellectual developments. Oppenheim's classic treatise, for instance, attempted a justification of international law from a positivist viewpoint. He characterized customary international law as the rules of the community of civilized states enforceable by self-help and the aid of other states as against rule breakers.[3] As such, he believed that customary international law met the three conditions of law: a community, agreed-upon rules, and external means of enforcement. The third element diverged most obviously from domestic or municipal law, which had a more reliable enforcement capacity in the existence of the sovereign. But Oppenheim, writing before the World Wars, believed self-help and balancing against potential rule breakers to suffice.

If you were to ask a U.S. federal judge in 1905 what customary international law (also called the "law of nations" then) was and where to find it, the judge would likely have pointed in one of two directions. First, the judge might have directed you to the "law of peace" parts of the canonical treatises—Vattel, Wheaton, or perhaps Oppenheim, if he stayed abreast of the most current work. These treatises followed a standard formula: definitions and scope of the law of nations; the state and its rights and responsibilities; and relations between states, including treaties and alliances. Or, the judge might have directed you to the law of the sea, whether its peacetime half (admiralty), or its wartime and quasi-wartime variants (the law of prize and maritime captures). If so, there was a well-developed body of British and U.S. judicial decisions as well as centuries of treatises. Henry Wheaton, for instance, the leading American international-law treatise writer of the nineteenth century, was renowned for both his 1836 *Elements of International Law* and his earlier 1815 work, *A Digest of the Law of Maritime Captures and Prizes.*[4] The iconic 1900 U.S. Supreme Court decision in *Paquete Habana*,[5] was of course a prize case, and its holding, which cited

---

[2] EMER DE VATTEL, THE LAW OF NATIONS, OR PRINCIPLES OF THE LAW OF NATURE, APPLIED TO THE CONDUCT AND AFFAIRS OF NATIONS AND SOVEREIGNS (Béla Kapossy & Richard Whatmore eds., 1797 English trans., 2008) (1758); HENRY WHEATON, ELEMENTS OF INTERNATIONAL LAW: WITH A SKETCH OF THE HISTORY OF THE SCIENCE (1836); LASSA OPPENHEIM, INTERNATIONAL LAW: A TREATISE 10–13 (1905).

[3] OPPENHEIM, *supra* note 2, at 10–13.

[4] HENRY WHEATON, A DIGEST OF THE LAW OF MARITIME CAPTURES AND PRIZES (1815).

[5] 175 U.S. 677 (1900).

Wheaton's 1815 treatise prominently, is redolent of U.S. judges' understanding of customary international law at the time:

> This review of the precedents and authorities on the subject appears to us abundantly to demonstrate that at the present day, by the consent of the civilized nations of the world, and independently of any express treaty or other public act, it is an established rule of international law, founded on considerations of humanity to a poor and industrious order of men, and of mutual convenience of belligerent States, that coast fishing vessels, with their implements and supplies, cargoes and crews, unarmed, and honestly pursuing their peaceful calling of catching and bringing in fresh fish, are exempt from capture as prize of war.[6]

The modern debate about whether customary international law is federal law or State law or something else would have been incomprehensible to the early twentieth-century U.S. jurist. If pressed to answer, the judge would have likely replied that State law could not possibly give answers to questions such as whether the U.S. Navy could seize Spanish coastal fishing vessels as prize, whether U.S. merchants could seize the cargo of an Italian public steamship, or whether the Colombian consul in Boston was entitled to immunity from a trespass action filed in federal district court. Instead, the judge would have looked to "precedents and authorities" just as the Supreme Court did in *Paquete Habana*—U.S. Supreme Court decisions if available or British precedents if not, and esteemed treatises like Vattel or Wheaton. *Paquete Habana*'s formula was in no sense original: it was part of an unbroken Anglo-American legal tradition that preceded the American founding. William Blackstone himself had observed in 1769 that with respect to "disputes relating to prize," "there is no other rule of decision but this great universal law, collected from history and usage, and such writers of all nations and languages as are generally approved and allowed of."[7]

## B. Customary International Law after *Filártiga*

After the twentieth-century World Wars, consensus developed among world leaders and their lawyers that the international legal order required a fundamental transformation to prevent the catastrophic wars and mass human atrocities that modern technologies had enabled. To be sure, the humanizing instinct had significant antecedents. For instance, the late nineteenth and early twentieth centuries had witnessed several multilateral law-of-war treaties to mitigate

---

[6] *Id.* at 708.
[7] 4 WILLIAM BLACKSTONE, COMMENTARIES *67 (Oxford, Clarendon Press 1769).

modern warfare's toll on humanity, such as the 1864 Geneva Convention for the Wounded and the Sick, and the 1899 and 1907 Hague Conventions restricting various ends and means of warfare on land and at sea. But the years immediately after World War II ended were the critical period: The Charter of the United Nations was forged in 1945, the Universal Declaration of Human Right was adopted by the U.N. General Assembly in 1948, and the four current Geneva Conventions regulating *jus in bello* were open for signatures in 1949.

Thus, the core of universal international law shifted from custom to treaty. Domestically within the United States, Congress started passing statutes in the twentieth century to regulate much of the subject matter that had formerly been regulated by customary international law as interpreted and applied by the federal courts. For example, the Jones Act, Section 27 of the Merchant Marine Act of 1920, displaced federal judicial lawmaking in maritime commerce.[8] And the Foreign Sovereign Immunities Act of 1976 codified state immunity rules that the federal courts had for centuries derived from customary international law, albeit with substantial deference to the State Department after 1952.[9]

The upshot was that the prominent space that customary international law had occupied from the time of the American founding in 1787 until 1900 when *Paquete Habana* was decided had evaporated by the time the Third Restatement appeared in 1987. Relatedly, federal judges were no longer fluent and experienced in accessing customary international law for rules of decision in cases before them. True, the federal common law enclave of admiralty law weathered the *Erie* revolution, but statutes like the Jones Act had moved into the field.[10] And where the U.S. Code did not supply a rule of decision, there were ample Supreme Court precedents on point or nearly on point by this time, obviating the need to peruse treatises or survey the decisions of foreign courts. As such, it was easy to forget that admiralty law (the peacetime branch of international maritime law) was a part of the law of nations or customary international law, and not a homegrown flavor of federal common law. More fundamentally, the technology of the shipping industry (and insurance) had evolved to the point that federal judicial interventions were not as frequent as they had been in the ages of sail and of steam.

The 1980 decision of the U.S. Court of Appeals for the Second Circuit in *Filártiga v. Peña-Irala* paved a new and different path for customary international law in U.S. federal courts.[11] *Filártiga* involved claims under the Alien Tort

---

[8] Pub. L. 66-261 (1920), 41 Stat. 988, codified at 46 U.S.C. § 50101 *et seq.*

[9] Foreign Sovereign Immunities Act of 1976, Pub. L. No. 94-583, 90 Stat. 2891, codified at 28 U.S.C. §§ 1330, 1332(a)(4), 1391(f), 1441(d), 1602–1611.

[10] Pope & Talbot v. Hawn, 346 U.S. 406, 410 (1953) (suits within the federal courts' admiralty jurisdiction not subject to the rule of Erie Railroad Co. v. Tompkins, 304 U.S. 64 (1938)); Levinson v. Deupree, 345. U.S. 648, 651 (1953) (same).

[11] 630 F.2d 876 (2d Cir. 1980).

Statute (ATS), which provides that a U.S. district court has original jurisdiction of a suit brought by an "alien . . . for a tort only . . . in violation of the law of nations or a treaty of the United States."[12] Paraguayan nationals brought the suit against a Paraguayan national in New York for the alleged torture killing of their relative in Paraguay. The Second Circuit affirmed jurisdiction under the ATS's law-of-nations prong. As I have argued elsewhere, *Filártiga* converted a national security statute originally enacted in 1789 to allow foreigners to obtain damages in federal court for noncontract injuries to their persons or property for which the United States bore responsibility under contemporaneous international law into an international human rights statute.[13] But the conversion quickly gained traction.

*Filártiga* launched a wave of human rights litigation in U.S. courts. Many of the lawsuits were "foreign-cubed" actions: lawsuits brought by foreigners against foreigners for torts committed in foreign countries. The standard modus operandi for ATS plaintiffs after *Filártiga* was to plead provisions in human rights treaties that the United States had *not* ratified by arguing that they had become customary international law by virtue of general state practice and *opinio juris*. In other words, the law-of-nations prong of the ATS provided a pathway for accessing U.S. federal courts to bring international human rights litigation based on treaty norms that the United States has not explicitly ratified. Moreover, it was imaginable that those customary international norms could be "backdoored" into the U.S. domestic law of rights as to U.S. persons.

Step back for a moment and consider how fundamentally different the job of engaging customary international law would be for a federal judge in an ATS suit brought in 1981, the year after *Filártiga* was decided, as compared to a federal judge in 1901 deciding a prize case the year after *Paquete Habana* was handed down. The primary sources the 1981 judge is asked to consult for finding the law are not U.S. Supreme Court or British admiralty court precedents or universally respected treatises. Rather, the primary sources are treaties that the United States has not ratified. Not only was the method different, so was the basic function. In 1901, customary international law supplied rules of decision for federal judges to decide whether or not to convey title to a foreign ship and its cargo to the U.S. Navy; or to hold a French public steamer liable in a collision; or to decide if a foreign consul could be prosecuted for murder. After *Filártiga*, customary

---

[12] 28 U.S.C. § 1350 (2006). The original version in the Judiciary Act of 1789 provided that the district courts "shall also have cognizance, concurrent with the courts of the several States, or the circuit courts, as the case may be, of all causes where an alien sues for a tort only in violation of the law of nations or a treaty of the United States." An Act to Establish the Judicial Courts of the United States, ch. 20, § 9, 1 Stat. 73, 77 (1789).

[13] See Thomas H. Lee, *The Safe-Conduct Theory of the Alien Tort Statute*, 106 COLUM. L. REV. 830, 900 (2006) ("The ultimate aims of the enactment were national security and commerce; the specific foreign policy of concern was injury to British creditors and merchants within the United States.").

international law would arise as a body of law a federal judge was asked to apply to vindicate the human rights claims of a foreigner in a foreign land.

## II. From the Third to the Fourth Restatements

### A. Changed Circumstances

Thus, when the Third Restatement was finalized in 1986, customary international law—uncodified and therefore amenable to diverse and potentially expansive formulations—provided a promising canvas for creatively wielding U.S. federal judicial power in the service of individual rights. It was also a way to bring the United States judiciary branch into the human rights movement, even as the executive branch and the Senate had balked in ratifying human rights treaties. The vision of the institutional role of the U.S. federal judge in foreign affairs as a human rights commissioner that *Filártiga* baptized and the Third Restatement blessed was dynamic and individual rights oriented. It was a counterweight to the Reagan administration's Cold War turn to *realpolitik* and the political branches' concomitant adoption of a muscular foreign policy that tended to subordinate individual rights abroad to U.S. national interests and to marginalize international legal obligations.[14]

When the Fourth Restatement took its final form thirty years later in 2017–2018, its framers' attitudes toward the judiciary branch's role in the nation's foreign affairs had undergone great change, in line with changes in the views of the U.S. federal judiciary itself. The dominant view now is that the political branches have primary responsibility over foreign affairs and that the federal courts should generally keep out. The vindication of international human rights law, in particular, is no longer a priority. Indeed, customary international law's status as federal law, at least in the field of human rights, is under attack.[15]

The underlying reason for the shift was the transformed world order. The Cold War had been won; the likelihood of nuclear Armageddon in the era of superpower tension had eased considerably. More recently, the value of American military power has been diluted by the rise of Chinese economic power and the nonstate, unconventional threats posed by militant Islamic terrorism. At the same time, the Thermidorean reaction to individual rights-based judicial activism on the domestic front, merely embryonic during the Burger and early

---

[14] Cf. Paul Stephan, *Courts, the Constitution, and Customary International Law: The Intellectual Origins of the Restatement (Third) of the Foreign Relations Law of the United States*, 44 Va. J. Int'l L. 33, 55–57 (2003).

[15] Compare Gary Born, *International Law in American Courts*, in this volume, with Paul B. Stephan, *The Waning of the Federal Common Law of Foreign Relations*, in this volume.

Rehnquist Courts when the Third Restatement was framed, had fully flowered. Today, even rights-based activists are more doubtful about the prudence and prospects for using the courts for public rights litigation.

On the foreign affairs front, ATS litigation is again a telling canary in the coal mine marking these geopolitical developments. It took the Supreme Court twenty-four years after *Filártiga* to decide an ATS case, but then it issued three increasingly narrowing decisions in the span of just fourteen years: (1) *Sosa v. Alvarez-Machain* (2004)[16] signaled cautious endorsement of *Filártiga*, tempered by a warning for judicial moderation; (2) *Kiobel v. Royal Dutch Petroleum* (2013)[17] grafted on a U.S. touch-and-concern requirement, effecting a death knell for the idea of the ATS as a case study in universal jurisdiction;[18] and (3) *Jesner v. Arab Bank* (2018)[19] foreclosed foreign corporate liability, and likely U.S. corporate liability too.

## B. Black-Letter Divergences

To preview the analysis that follows, recall my claim that the Third Restatement was an *offensive* document—a manifesto for federal judges to make them comfortable about engaging with customary international law and recognizing international rights abroad. The Fourth Restatement, by contrast, is a *defensive* document—distancing itself from *Filártiga*-style activism, but, at the same time, seeking to constrain U.S. federal judges inclined to kick out cases with important foreign policy ramifications. Relatedly, the Third Restatement frames prescriptive jurisdiction—the power to make rules of decision—as constrained and informed by customary international law, while the Fourth Restatement pitches it as a doctrine cabined to U.S. domestic law. Some examples may help illustrate the point.

First, the Third Restatement's definition of prescriptive jurisdiction explicitly envisioned the possibility that judges were prescribers, too. The Fourth Restatement black letter, by contrast, refers generally to "the authority of a state" and makes no explicit mention that this authority might be exercised by courts. Implicitly, the new phrasing makes "prescriptive" seem like a synonym for "legislative" jurisdiction. Furthermore, and perhaps most importantly, the Third

---

[16]  542 U.S. 692 (2004).

[17]  569 U.S. 108 (2013).

[18]  The Fourth Restatement's continuing reference to ATS as a universal jurisdiction statute is somewhat puzzling in this respect. See FOURTH RESTATEMENT Section 402(1)(f) and accompanying comments and reporters' notes. Indeed, Reporter's Note 10 explicitly observes that "[b]ecause ATS cases after *Kiobel* must have some connection to the United States, the recognition of a cause of action in such cases will not depend on universal jurisdiction."

[19]  138 S. Ct. 1386 (2018).

Restatement indicated that international law supplied a limit on prescriptive power, a constraint the Fourth Restatement's black letter notably removes:

Restatement (Third) Section 401 Categories of Jurisdiction

*Under international law*, a state is subject to limitations on

(a) jurisdiction to prescribe, *i.e.*, to make its law applicable to the activities, relations, or status of persons, or the interests of persons in things, whether by legislation, by executive act or order, by administrative rule or regulation, *or by determination of a court*.

Restatement (Fourth) Section 401 Categories of Jurisdiction

The foreign relations law of the United States divides jurisdiction into three categories:

(a) Jurisdiction to prescribe, i.e., the *authority of a state* to make law applicable to persons, property or conduct....

Second, the Third Restatement speaks of "bases" of jurisdiction to prescribe in Section 402, whereas Section 402 of the Fourth Restatement refers to "United States practice" with respect to jurisdiction to prescribe.[20] In one sense, this may indicate humility: the framers are effectively saying "we can only speak for what we do." But, at the same time, they are disavowing any claim to shared universal practices and implying that U.S. foreign relations law is a self-contained legal order. Additionally, it is Comment *a* to Section 402, not Section 401 black letter, that explains: "Legislative bodies exercise jurisdiction to prescribe when they enact statutes, but so does the executive branch when it makes generally applicable orders or regulations, and so do courts when they make generally applicable common law."[21] From the last phrase, it is unclear whether this is a broad, anodyne statement about courts in common law jurisdictions generally, or a more specific, contested assertion about U.S. judicial power to make federal common law derived from customary international law in foreign affairs enclaves, for example, prize law in *Paquete Habana*. If I am right in my central claim about the shift from the Third to the Fourth Restatements, then the latter may be the more accurate characterization.

Third, Section 403 of the Third Restatement, "Limitations on Jurisdiction to Prescribe," begins with the general direction that a state should not exercise jurisdiction to prescribe when it overlaps with another state's prescriptive jurisdiction and would be "unreasonable." It then offers a list of eight factors to consider

---

[20] The Fourth Restatement does contain provisions describing the international law of prescriptive jurisdiction, including universal jurisdiction. FOURTH RESTATEMENT, pt. IV, ch. 1, subch. B. But this portion of the Restatement does not indicate clearly how this body of international law either limits or empowers exercises of U.S. prescriptive jurisdiction.

[21] *Id.* at § 402 cmt. *a*.

in performing the unreasonableness analysis and counsels deferring to another state "if that state's interest is clearly greater." The Reporter's Notes indicate that the analysis is culled from U.S. and foreign case law and statutes, suggestive of general state practice or embryonic customary international law.

Section 403 of the Fourth Restatement, by contrast, is entitled "Federal Constitutional Limits" and states: "An exercise of prescriptive jurisdiction by the federal government, any State, or any component thereof may not exceed the limits set on the authority of those governments by the Constitution." The shift in emphasis is stark and clear. And if it wasn't clear enough, Section 402, "United States Practice with Respect to Jurisdiction to Prescribe," begins by stating "[s]ubject to the constitutional limits set forth in § 403."[22] Of course, the framers of the Third Restatement would surely have agreed with their successors that the federal Constitution applied, but they did not feel the need to emphasize it (twice), choosing instead to imply the relevance of customary international law.

Fourth, universal jurisdiction is demoted and "war crimes" are deleted in the new Restatement. In the Third Restatement, "Universal Jurisdiction to Define and Punish Certain Offenses" warranted its own section—Section 404. In the Fourth Restatement, it is subpart (f) of Section 402(1), which means that it is "[s]ubject to the constitutional limits set forth in Section 403."[23] Moreover, "certain offenses recognized by the community of nations as of universal concern"—a relic of Oppenheim's customary international law framework, is replaced by "certain offenses of universal concern." Reporter's Note 10 explains that the deletion of "war crimes" was because "the federal war-crimes statute is limited to war crimes committed by or against U.S. nationals and members of the U.S. armed forces" and that the "United States has not exercised universal jurisdiction to the full extent permitted by customary international law."[24]

Fifth, independent judicial discretion is subtly diminished by focusing on "prescriptive comity" but not "adjudicative comity" and by characterizing what had formerly been framed as judicial prescription or lawmaking as interpretation. As the reference to "prescriptive comity" in Fourth Restatement Section 402 indicates, the judicial role is subtly demoted in the black letter from the power to prescribe itself to the role of interpreting the statutes the legislature has passed to prescribe. Moreover, as William Dodge has argued, the notion of "*adjudicative* comity" is channeled into existing doctrines like *forum non conveniens*, rather than allowed purchase as an independent ground for abstaining in cases touching upon foreign affairs subject to a multifactor reasonableness enquiry,

---

[22] *Id.* at § 402.
[23] *Id.* § 402(1)(f).
[24] *Id.* reporters' note 10.

as many lower courts have done.[25] Section 424 Comment *i*, for example, begins with the overbroad but oft-cited dictum from *Colorado River* that "Federal courts have a 'virtually unflagging obligation' to exercise jurisdiction."[26] And the Restatement continues: "Although the Supreme Court has recognized abstention doctrines allowing dismissal in favor of other federal courts in in favor of State courts, *forum non conveniens* is the only doctrine under which the Supreme Court has approved dismissal in favor of foreign courts. Lower federal courts have developed other abstention doctrines allowing dismissal in favor of foreign courts, but the status of these doctrines remains uncertain."[27]

The comment is factually accurate. But its tone plainly suggests disproval of what the lower courts are doing. I suspect that this attitude is based on the views of Fourth Restatement's framers that lower courts will use a freestanding and manipulable doctrine of adjudicative comity abstention to shirk cases that they should be deciding. In other words, the framers are again playing defense, not offense. But the view that federal judges should not be dismissing cases over which they have jurisdiction because of international comity without a basis in settled doctrines, however well-intentioned, flies in the face of history. "[J]udicial discretion to manage international comity as a federal common law matter was the original position and historical practice for centuries, not an aberration or a new development."[28]

Sixth, the Fourth Restatement characterizes the question of whether a court should recognize U.S. prescriptive power in a particular case as statutory interpretation, not a common-lawish reasonableness enquiry grounded in customary international law.[29] Recall that Third Restatement Section 403, "Limitations on Jurisdiction to Prescribe," provides that "even when one of the bases for jurisdiction under Section 402 is present, a state may not exercise jurisdiction to prescribe law with respect to a person or activity having connections with another state when the exercise of such jurisdiction is unreasonable."[30] The Fourth Restatement, by contrast, talks about "Reasonableness in Interpretation" in Section 405: "As a matter of prescriptive comity, courts in the United States may

[25] William S. Dodge, *International Comity in American Law*, 115 COLUM. L. REV. 2071, 2079 (2015); see, e.g., Timberlane Lumber Co. v. Bank of Am., N.T. & S.A., 549 F.2d 597(9th Cir. 1976).

[26] Colo. Riv. Water Conserv. Dist. v. United States, 424 U.S. 800, 817 (1976).

[27] FOURTH RESTATEMENT § 424 cmt. *i*; see also *id.* reporters' note 9.

[28] Samuel Estreicher & Thomas H. Lee, *In Defense of International Comity*, 93 SO CAL. L.REV. 169, 191 (2020).

[29] Hannah Buxbaum and Ralf Michaels lament the deletion of the multiple factor reasonableness enquiry. Hannah Buxbaum & Ralf Michaels, *Reasonableness as a Limitation on the Extraterritorial Application of U.S. Law: From 403 to 405 (via 404)*, in this volume. One compromise possibility was to keep the reasonableness enquiry as a matter of federal common law, untethered from customary international law, along the lines of the Supreme Court's decision on act-of-state doctrine in *Banco Nacional de Cuba v. Sabbatino*, 376 U.S. 398 (1964).

[30] THIRD RESTATEMENT § 403(1).

interpret federal statutory provisions to include other limitations on their applicability."[31] Again, the net result is that judicial forays into foreign affairs are subordinated to the political branches by being framed as statutory interpretation. Federal common law, by definition, is a judicial rule of decision that cannot be traced to an explicit constitutional, treaty, or statutory provision by conventional methods of interpretation.[32]

## III.  Assessment

To sum up, I have tried to show how the Fourth Restatement frames a more modest judicial role and seeks to cabin judicial discretion by comparison to the Third Restatement and to take a guess at why. The Third Restatement arrived at a moment when *Filártiga* had ignited both the hope and the opportunity to enlist U.S. judicial power in the international human rights movement, using customary international law as the engine. That moment has now passed. Customary international law today is not what it was at Founding or at the start of the twentieth century. Nor is the federal judiciary. Today's federal judges have little to no experience in foreign affairs or diplomacy, in contrast to figures like Chief Justices John Jay (chief negotiator of the 1783 Treaty of Paris and the country's first foreign minister), William Howard Taft (president of the United States, commissioner of the Philippines, secretary of war), and Charles Evans Hughes (secretary of state, convener of the Washington Naval Conference). The idea that the Chief Justice of the United States should have significant foreign policy experience seems utterly foreign today.

Relatedly, the Fourth Restatement frames U.S. foreign relations law as an autonomous domestic legal order operating independent of customary international law. The Third Restatement, by contrast, presumed a much greater degree of dialogue and exchange. With specific respect to the law of jurisdiction, the view of the Fourth Restatement seems to be that customary international law may inform the domestic law but does not meaningfully constrain it, outside the enclave of state immunity. A jurisdictional norm adopted by other leading countries may be relevant in a comparative law sense, but it is not an obligatory international law norm. The Third Restatement, by contrast, cast international law as an outer envelope within which domestic jurisdictional norms—whether prescriptive, adjudicative, or enforcement—operated.

---

[31] FOURTH RESTATEMENT § 404.

[32] See RICHARD H. FALLON JR., JOHN F. MANNING, DANIEL J. MELTZER, & DAVID L. SHAPIRO, HART & WECHSLER'S THE FEDERAL COURTS AND THE FEDERAL SYSTEM 635 (7th ed. 2015) (Federal common law "loosely . . . refer[s] to federal rules of decision whose content cannot be traced directly by traditional methods of interpretation to federal statutory or constitutional commands.").

Which approach is right and what is to be done? It is hard to imagine that we can return to federal judges engaging proficiently with customary international law like Justice Gray's maestro disquisition on the international law of maritime captures and prizes in *Paquete Habana*. It seems to me not dissimilar to the difficulty modern U.S. judges would have in engaging with iconic English common law decisions, like Sir Edward Coke's decision in *Calvin's Case*.[33] But as someone who respects the original constitutional settlement in constitutional interpretation, I can also appreciate the importance of ensuring that the federal judiciary is engaging with customary international law as founding Americans ordained in the Constitution. On the other hand, the customary international law engagement under the aegis of the ATS that *Filártiga* launched and the Third Restatement endorsed was unduly normative and rights advocacy oriented. Anchored in a 1789 statute and forced to navigate a series of winding precedents, the customary international law of human rights as articulated in U.S. ATS jurisprudence must seem strange and Galapagos-like in its eccentric insularity to non-U.S. human rights lawyers and international jurists.

A very distinguished and able federal appellate judge once confided in me that she (the pronoun is used without regard to actual gender) had very little idea of what customary international law was or where to look for it. Of course, she knew the well-worn "state practice and *opinio juris*" formula, but where could she look up the rules to apply to specific cases? Surely, she could not be expected to replicate Justice Gray and do her own research into treatises and survey what the leading "civilized" nations had been up to. Her only experience in ascertaining customary international law had been in ATS cases, where plaintiffs' lawyers typically cited treaties the United States had not ratified, nongovernmental and international organization reports, law review articles, and international and foreign court decisions. When I explained to her that foreign state immunity and maritime law had been two key aspects of customary international law now regulated by statutes, a light bulb turned on for her. She only then comprehended how integral customary international law had been to the development of the U.S. legal order and the country itself. The reality is that, from the founding of the nation, the judicial power of the United States was inextricably engaged with customary international law, then viewed as part of the law of nations. "The law of nations was the original federal common law."[34] This judicial mission was essential to the security of a young and fragile nation with an immense coastline. Accordingly, although federal judges did not have the same common-law making power as their state judge colleagues as a general matter,

---

[33] Calvin v. Smith, 77 Eng. Rep. 377 (K.B. 1608).
[34] Thomas H. Lee, *The Law of Nations and the Judicial Branch*, 106 Geo. L.J. 1707, 1709 (2010).

customary international law was the exception. The disengagement of the two that the Fourth Restatement exhibits may faithfully reflect the reality on the ground today, but it is plainly a departure from the original constitutional settlement and early historical practice. Consequently, the disconnect should trouble nationally-minded originalists as much as it troubles internationally-oriented presentists.

# 11

# International Law in U.S. Courts within the Limits of the Constitution

*John C. Harrison*

What can be done to facilitate the expert, impartial, and uniform ascertainment, development, and application of customary international law by U.S. courts, State and federal?

One class of answers to that question works by expanding the scope of substantive federal law, the kind that displaces State law and is binding in State and federal courts. The Third Restatement proposed one such answer, and pointed toward another, which has some supporters. I will suggest an answer that falls into a different category, one that works through the rules that govern the decision-making processes of the federal courts. Answers that work through federal law that has preemptive effect are highly controversial, and I think rightly so. The proposal I will set out also rests on controversial assumptions, but I think they are less so than those that underlie the solution based on preemption.

In order to facilitate the expert, impartial, and uniform ascertainment, development, and application of customary international law in U.S. courts, the Supreme Court of the United States should return to treating customary international law as neither State nor federal but general law. The federal courts should ascertain the content of that body of law for themselves, treating State-court precedents on that subject with respect but not as binding on them. Although I will not propose applying this approach to all of conflict of laws (private international law), I will suggest that the federal courts apply general principles of conflicts to decide when and whether the substantive law of a State of the Union applies to transactions outside the United States.

This chapter will begin by describing two aggressive means of pursuing the goal I have posited, one of which was endorsed and the other of which was suggested by the Third Restatement. Both, I will explain, are highly controversial and, in my view, incorrect. The chapter will then turn to the less bold but still controversial solution I propose.

John C. Harrison, *International Law in U.S. Courts within the Limits of the Constitution* In: *The Restatement and Beyond*. Edited by: Paul B. Stephan and Sarah H. Cleveland, Oxford University Press (2020). © Oxford University Press.
DOI: 10.1093/oso/9780197533154.003.0012

# I. Uniformity and Customary International Law

Customary international law from time to time figures in the decision of cases in U.S. courts, State and federal. It comes in, for example, when an official of a foreign government is sued for damages arising out of conduct under color of office and asserts official immunity.[1] The category from the time of the framing that corresponds to customary international law today, the law of nations, also included the law of admiralty, which continues to form an important component of the federal courts' jurisdiction.[2] Some of the most hotly contested cases with an international connection in recent decades have involved international human rights law.[3]

The goals of expertise, uniformity, and impartiality in ascertaining and applying customary international law are sufficiently self-recommending that I will comment only on uniformity, which might be thought not to be. Federal systems like that of the United States cultivate substantial diversity, not uniformity, in law and policy. There are good reasons to allow the law of Ohio and that of Connecticut to differ substantially. The law of Ohio, however, is the law of Ohio, and variation in its application cannot be justified on the grounds that support a different law for Connecticut. Customary international law, elusive as it sometimes is, in principle is one system of jurisprudence for the entire world. Even courts that vary from its current formulation in the interests of developing it seek to contribute to a new and again uniform version of that one law.[4] Parts of customary international law that are not subjects of that kind of experimentation should be implemented in the same way throughout every legal system and if possible throughout the world.

In the United States, two main paths to uniformity are available. One is strong coordination among coordinate legal and judicial systems, as manifest, for example, in the Uniform Commercial Code and as encouraged by the Restatements. The difficulties in achieving uniformity in judicial interpretation are seen, for example, in State variation in readings of the UCC: Even when legislatures adopt a policy of uniformity, courts may disagree with one another and so be unable fully to implement that policy.

---

[1]  See, e.g., Samantar v. Yousuf, 560 U.S. 305 (2010) (immunity of a foreign official is governed by customary international law, not the Foreign Sovereign Immunities Act).

[2]  ANTHONY J. BELLIA JR. & BRADFORD R. CLARK, THE LAW OF NATIONS AND THE UNITED STATES CONSTITUTION 3–4 (2017) (maritime law was part of the law of nations at the time of the framing).

[3]  See, e.g., Kiobel v. Royal Dutch Shell Petroleum Co., 569 U.S. 108 (2013) (Alien Tort Statute, 28 U.S.C. 1350, has only limited application outside U.S. territory).

[4]  As this stress on the intrinsic uniformity of customary international law suggests, that body of norms is by no means identical to the law that affects international affairs or relations. Different sovereigns have different laws about trade and banking, for example, and thereby affect one another and their mutual relations. When I refer to customary international law, I mean a single system, albeit a system the content of which is unclear and disputed.

The other main path to judicial uniformity runs through the Supreme Court of the United States. In principle, judicial doctrine about the federal Constitution is a single body of case law developed by the Court. In practice, matters are much more complicated than that. Any lawyer advising a client about, for example, the application of the First Amendment to public education, would want to know which State or federal courts might be involved in potential litigation, and what those courts' cases say. Federal courts of appeals have adumbrated the Supreme Court's principles concerning limited public forums in many factual configurations that the Court has never addressed and probably never will. The Court's cases nevertheless create a doctrinal framework within which other courts operate, and its appellate jurisdiction enables it to reverse decisions that represent serious departures from the principles it has announced.

One leading peculiarity of the American legal system, however, is that the Supreme Court of the United States provides authoritative precedent only with respect to federal law. If the highest courts of New York and Delaware disagree on an important point of English contract law, any views the Supreme Court of the United States may have expressed on the issue will be only persuasive authority.[5]

The Court's role with respect to federal law is a premise for the Third Restatement's proposed solution to the problem I have posed. That solution, which is quite bold, holds that customary international law is law of the United States for purposes of Articles III and VI of the Constitution.[6] Because it is law of the United States under Article VI, customary international law displaces any contrary State law rule. Because it is law of the United States under Article III, it supports federal question jurisdiction.[7]

Another bold answer, which the Third Restatement endorsed, begins not with the federal judicial power but with the federal legislative power. Matters respecting the foreign relations of the United States, including the application of customary international law in U.S. courts, are within Congress's legislative power. Therefore Congress may adopt federal law that has the content of

---

[5] As the example shows, disagreement between American jurisdictions about the content of a foreign jurisdiction's law is not just a possibility that illustrates a point. New York and Delaware are important business-law jurisdictions, and many large business contracts call for English law to apply in their interpretation.

[6] THIRD RESTATEMENT §§ 111, 112 (1987) (international law is supreme law in the United States; questions of international law support federal-question jurisdiction).

[7] The most important statutes giving jurisdiction based on federal questions are 28 U.S.C. § 1331, respecting the original jurisdiction of the district courts, and 28 U.S.C. § 1257, respecting the appellate jurisdiction of the Supreme Court of the United States over the State courts. The Supreme Court's appellate jurisdiction over the federal courts of appeals, 28 U.S.C. § 1254, is not limited to federal-question cases, but includes appeals from the courts of appeals in cases based on a federal question, like those arising under Section 1331. The Supreme Court's appellate jurisdiction enables it to set precedents that are treated as binding in all American courts, State and federal, and to reverse any lower court that fails to follow those precedents.

customary international law. Whatever the status of customary international law in the U.S legal system in the absence of congressional action might be, statutes adopted pursuant to Congress's legislative power unquestionably are law of the United States under Articles III and VI.

An even bolder variant of the answer based on congressional power, which the Third Restatement may not have fully endorsed but which it seems to have favored, holds that Congress's plenary legislative authority concerning foreign affairs has so-called dormant preemptive effect. That is, the existence of the power nullifies any State laws that are within the power's scope, unless Congress affirmatively legislates to the contrary. That principle would foster the uniform development of customary international law in the U.S. legal system insofar as it generally would exclude State law on matters covered by customary international law, all or nearly all of which affect the foreign relations of the United States. If State law cannot operate on some issue, unwritten federal law may fill the resulting legal gap.

Each of those solutions is subject to serious objection, and in my view those objections are sound. The Third Restatement's position concerning the status of customary international law has long been controversial. The most sweeping objection, to which I subscribe, is that the laws of the United States referred to in Articles III and VI consist entirely of Acts of Congress. They have no unwritten component. That is not to say that the American legal system has no unwritten law. Many of the most important rules in that system are unwritten, like most of the private law of most of the States. The principle that Articles III and VI refer only to written law as laws of the United States does mean, however, that customary international law as such does not override contrary State law and does not support federal-question jurisdiction under Article III. The Third Restatement is explicitly to the contrary.[8]

Although the claim that no unwritten law is law of the United States and the Third Restatement's position that customary international law as such is law of the United States cannot both be right, they can both be wrong. A less radical objection to the Third Restatement's position accepts that some law of the United States under Articles III and VI is unwritten, but holds that the Restatement substantially overstates the extent to which customary international law is federal law. One leading alternative to the Restatement's wholesale position is that

---

[8] The Supreme Court's doctrine is also explicitly to the contrary of the reading of the Constitution I espouse, which is not to say that the Court has endorsed the Third Restatement's position, which it has not. The Court does take the position that some unwritten law, like the act of state doctrine, is federal law that displaces State law. Banco Nacional de Cuba v. Sabbatino 376 U.S. 398, 425–26 (1964). The Court in *Sabbatino* did not attribute the act of state doctrine to international law, *id.* at 421, but rather to the structure of the U.S. government, in particular the relation between the courts and the executive, *id.* at 427–28.

customary international law becomes law of the United States on a more retail basis, when it is brought into the U.S. legal system by the federal political branches acting pursuant to their constitutional powers.[9] The Third Restatement's wholesale position remains a matter of serious controversy.

The same is true about the assertion that Congress has general authority to legislate in matters affecting foreign relations. Congress clearly has substantial legislative authority concerning foreign relations and the operation of customary international law in the U.S. legal system. Whether its legislative power reaches to all issues that affect foreign relations, however, is not clear. One theory in favor of plenary congressional power in this connection is that because the United States as such is a sovereign under international law, its legislature can make laws on all topics that affect that sovereignty. The principle that the national government has only the powers given by the Constitution, goes the reasoning, applies only in the domestic context, not when foreign relations are concerned.[10] General congressional foreign-affairs power is a matter of controversy. It has been subject to substantial academic criticism, and the Supreme Court today probably would not regard its precedents as establishing the power's existence.[11]

General foreign-relations power, if Congress has it, by itself operates only when Congress acts. In order to support ouster of State law in the absence of legislation, congressional power would have to have a dormant aspect, so that its mere existence restricts the States. The structure in which non-use of federal power can have legal effects is familiar from the Commerce Clause, and for many

---

[9] That is Professors Bradley and Goldsmith's position. "[I]n the absence of federal political branch authorization, [customary international law] is not a source of federal law." Curtis A. Bradley & Jack L. Goldsmith, *Customary International Law as Federal Common Law: A Critique of the Modern Position*, 110 HARV. L. REV. 815, 870 (1997)

[10] The classic Supreme Court statement of that principle is in *United States v. Curtiss-Wright Export Co.*, 299 U.S. 304 (1936). The reporters of the Third Restatement apparently endorsed that view. Citing *Curtiss-Wright*, they wrote, "Congress, moreover, has an unexpressed power to legislate in foreign affairs, a legislative component of powers of the United States that inhere in its sovereignty and nationhood." THIRD RESTATEMENT § 1 reporters' note 1; see also G. Edward White, *From the Third to the Fourth Restatement of Foreign Relations: The Rise and Potential Fall of Foreign Affairs Exceptionalism*, in this volume.

[11] Professor Michael Ramsey is a leading academic critic. See, e.g., Michael D. Ramsey, *The Myth of Extraconstitutional Foreign Affairs Power*, 42 WM. & MARY L. REV. 379 (2000). The Court recently rejected the argument that under *Curtiss-Wright*, the president has "unbounded" power in foreign affairs. Zivotofsky v. Kerry, 135 S. Ct. 2076, 2089 (2015). As the Court pointed out, statements about broad presidential power were unnecessary to the holding of *Curtiss-Wright*: The President in that case was acting pursuant to an explicit grant of power, so the extent of presidential power in the absence of congressional authorization was not an issue. *Id.* at 2090. The statute at issue in *Curtiss-Wright* was a ban on arms exports, and thus an exercise of the enumerated power over foreign commerce. Just as the case did not present an issue of purely constitutionally based presidential power, it did not present an issue of inherent, nontextual, or unenumerated congressional power. *Zivotofsky II* thus indicates that the current Court would regard statements in *Curtiss-Wright* about general congressional power over foreign affairs as dicta.

decades the dormant commerce principle was central to American federalism.[12] The Supreme Court case that most plausibly can be said to have relied on a dormant foreign affairs power, *Zschernig v. Miller*,[13] has not given rise to a robust doctrine and has been criticized on the Court itself.[14]

The current Supreme Court's reluctance to embrace dormant foreign-affairs preemption may reflect a recognition that each of the two main lines of reasoning that lead to preemption based on power that has not been exercised encounters serious difficulties. One familiar route to dormant effect is the principle that the congressional power at issue is implicitly or explicitly exclusive of State power.[15] If exclusive federal power is relatively broad, the States are disabled from regulating a great deal of conduct otherwise within their authority.[16] One standard solution to the difficulty involving State power is to conclude that Congress may affirmatively restore it. That solution, however, is subject to challenge on the grounds that it allows Congress to give federal power to the States.[17] The problem of ousting State power is less severe if Congress's power is interpreted more narrowly, and indeed the presumed dormant effect of federal power for decades underlay Supreme Court cases taking a restrictive view of it.[18] That approach is not available when the premise concerning federal power is that it is plenary.

---

[12] As Professor Barry Cushman explains, "in the late nineteenth and early twentieth centuries, the central question in constitutional federalism was not the extent to which the Commerce Clause empowered Congress to regulate local activities," but instead "the degree to which the 'negative implications' of that clause limited the regulatory authority of state and local governments." Barry Cushman, *Formalism and Realism in Commerce Clause Jurisprudence*, 67 U. CHI. L. REV. 1089, 1101 (2000). During that period, "the Court began a conscious and increasingly aggressive campaign to break down local barriers to interstate trade through a 'free-trade' construction of the dormant Commerce Clause." *Id.*

[13] 389 U.S. 429 (1968).

[14] "We have not relied on *Zschernig* since it was decided, and I would not resurrect that decision here." American Insurance Association v. Garamendi, 539 U.S. 396, 439 (2003) (Ginsburg, J., dissenting). The majority in *Garamendi* based its decision on a presidential policy, not on wholly unexercised federal power, and so did not rely on *Zschernig* by way of applying its doctrine.

*Zschernig* has also faced substantial academic criticism. See, e.g., Jack L. Goldsmith, *Federal Courts, Foreign Affairs, and Federalism*, 83 VA. L. REV. 1617, 1642 (1997) (states have concurrent power in foreign affairs matters except where they are subject to an affirmative prohibition by the Constitution); see also Paul B. Stephan, *The Waning of the Federal Common Law of Foreign Relations*, in this volume.

[15] Chief Justice Marshall discussed that possibility without endorsing it in *Gibbons v. Ogden*, 22 U.S. 1 (1824).

[16] As Cushman explains, because late nineteenth- and early twentieth-century dormant commerce clause doctrine was mainly predicated on the principle that federal commerce power was exclusive, the Court had to find a way to protect the national market without completely eliminating State regulatory authority by taking a somewhat narrow view of the affirmative commerce power and using categories like the distinction between direct and indirect effects to do so. See Cushman, *supra* note 12, at 1108–114.

[17] The Supreme Court found that Congress could not lift the preemptive effect of the law of admiralty, which it held to be federal and preemptive even though unwritten in *Southern Pacific Co. v. Jensen*, 244 U.S. 205 (1917), because "Congress cannot transfer its legislative power to the States— by nature this is non-delegable." Knickerbocker Ice Co. v. Stewart, 253 U.S. 149, 164 (1920).

[18] See *supra* note 16.

The other main route to a dormant effect of congressional power goes through congressional intent, but that route too is rocky. Congress's failure to regulate a field as to which it has power can be construed as a substantive decision in favor of nonregulation, and hence against State regulation too.[19] Whether congressional inaction reflects any such policy will of course be highly debatable in any policy context. Moreover, attributing binding force to congressional inaction is controversial, and the Court has done so in some cases while rejecting arguments based on inaction in others.[20]

## II. Customary International Law as General Law

Having pointed out the controversy surrounding possible solutions to the problem with which this chapter is concerned, I will propose another. The Supreme Court should return to regarding customary international law as general law and should determine its content independently of any views of the State courts. The lower federal courts should follow both the Supreme Court's approach to customary international law and any principles thereof that it announces. The Court should encourage the State courts to follow its precedents on issues of customary international law, while recognizing that issues concerning it are not federal questions within the Court's appellate jurisdiction. The Court should take the same approach to private international law when a conflicts question concerns the extraterritorial application of the law of a State of the Union.

As part of this program, the Supreme Court should also adjust its certiorari policy. To serve as the balance wheel for customary international law, the Court will have to decide cases that turn on it. If customary international law is regarded as general and not federal law, the Court will have to return to its practice of deciding a substantial number of cases coming from the lower federal courts that arise from the trial courts' diversity jurisdiction and that do not turn on federal law. Some questions of customary international law will arise in cases that otherwise qualify for the federal-question jurisdiction under Section 1331 of Title 28, but many will not. The Court today hardly ever grants certiorari in a diversity case that has no federal question, but if it adopts my suggestion it will need to do so in a significant number of cases.

---

[19] For a discussion of the two theories, their inconsistency with one another, and the Court's difficulties in settling on one, see Henry W. Bikle, *The Silence of Congress*, 41 HARV. L. REV. 200 (1927).

[20] A leading case relying on congressional inaction to endorse judicial precedent is *Flood v. Kuhn*, 407 U.S. 258 (1972). A standard example of a case rejecting that approach is *Helvering v. Hallock*, 309 U.S. 106 (1940).

This proposal is in large measure a return to the approach to customary international law that the Constitution itself assumed. The drafters of the Constitution almost certainly did not think that the law of nations was law of the United States as they used that term.[21] Yet they did envision a central role for the federal courts in cases implicating the country's foreign affairs, a category notably including but just as notably not limited to cases turning on the law of nations. Their primary tool to give the courts that role was not substantive federal law but jurisdiction.[22]

Perhaps most important in this respect was the alien diversity jurisdiction.[23] Cases involving aliens were especially likely to bring the United States into conflict with other sovereigns, many of which were much more powerful at the time. Indeed, much of the impetus for the Constitution, and not just the new federal judiciary, came from the framers' belief that State courts were refusing to allow foreign creditors to collect debts from American citizens, very much to the detriment of the country's commerce and its standing with other countries. Alien diversity cases often would turn on the general law merchant, which was part of the law of nations at the time of the framing, but often they would not. Many would be simple debt-collection suits, governed by local American law.[24]

Admiralty jurisdiction was another way to put cases affecting foreign relations and turning on the law of nations into national tribunals. Admiralty and maritime law, like the general law merchant, was in principle uniform across trading nations (and hence of course was supposed to be applied uniformly within every national jurisdiction).[25] Admiralty included a category of cases that

---

[21] See John Harrison, *The Constitution and the Law of Nations*, 106 GEO. L.J. 1659, 1671–80 (2018).

[22] As a result, the copious statements from the founding era about the law of nations serving as law to be applied by U.S. courts, e.g., Born, *International Law in American Courts*, in this volume (summarizing and citing), are beside the point. The framers recognized that U.S. courts could and would apply the law of nations, but not because international law was part of "the Laws of the United States" referred to by Article III, § 2 or Article VI of the Constitution.

[23] Foreign-state diversity jurisdiction was also important in this respect, but probably was expected to involve far fewer cases, even if the cases themselves might be quite significant.

[24] In *The Federalist No. 80*, Hamilton argued that cases involving the maintenance of peace should come within federal jurisdiction, and that cases involving aliens met that description. "The union will undoubtedly be answerable to foreign powers for the conduct of its members. . . . As the denial or perversion of justice by the sentences of courts, is with reason classed among the just causes of war, it will follow, that the federal judiciary ought to have cognizance of all causes in which the citizens of other countries are concerned." THE FEDERALIST, NO. 80, at 536 (Alexander Hamilton) (Jacob E. Cooke ed., 1961). Hamilton then rejected the argument that federal jurisdiction should be confined to cases "arising upon treaties and the law of nations" and not extend to "those which may stand merely upon the footing of the municipal law." *Id.* Cases with no international law component but an alien party could create friction between the United States and another sovereign. "But it is at least problematical, whether an unjust sentence against a foreigner, where the subject was wholly relative to the *lex loci*, would not, if unredressed, be an aggression upon his sovereign, as well as one which violated the stipulations of a treaty or the general law of nations." *Id.*

[25] "The most bigoted idolizers of state authority have thus far not shewn a disposition to deny the national judiciary the cognizance of maritime cases. These so generally depend on the laws of nations, and so commonly affect the rights of foreigners, that they fall within the considerations that are relative to the public peace." *Id.* at 538.

were especially likely to implicate foreign interests: prize.[26] During the turbulent 1790s, with the Wars of the French Revolution fought at sea throughout the globe, prize was an especially important part of the Supreme Court's docket.[27] In the Judiciary Act of 1789, Congress not only conferred admiralty jurisdiction with no amount-in-controversy minimum but made the admiralty jurisdiction of the federal courts exclusive of the State courts.[28] The Constitution's answer to the foreign-relations dangers posed by admiralty cases, implemented by Congress from the very beginning, used jurisdiction and not substance. Admiralty law's now-familiar status as preemptive federal law is a product, not even of the nineteenth but of the twentieth century.[29]

Perhaps the clearest indication that the Constitution's strategy for a federal judicial role in foreign-relations cases turns on jurisdiction and not substance comes from a small but very delicate class of cases: those involving foreign personnel, especially foreign diplomats. The Supreme Court itself has trial jurisdiction in cases affecting ambassadors, other public ministers (meaning other diplomats), and consuls.[30] The Constitution provides jurisdiction based on the identity of the parties and says nothing about the applicable law. That law might well come from a State of the Union; for example, a public minister or consul might sue about a lease. The framers apparently believed that the strong federal interest in the impartial and expert resolution of a case like that would be served by the federal tribunal, which would apply whatever law was appropriate.

One leading goal of Article III was to put cases with important foreign-relations implications in the federal courts. The Constitution does not, however, provide that the judicial power shall extend to cases with important foreign-relations implications. Rather, it implements that goal with rules that are more concrete and determinate than the goal, just as it implements the goal of judicial independence with specific rules like tenure on good behavior. Rules sometimes do not fully match their rationales, and there are some cases that might affect U.S. foreign relations that do not appear on the Article III list. For example, some cases between two aliens that involve no federal law no doubt meet that description,

---

[26] Professor William Casto argues that prize cases were a leading reason to give the federal courts admiralty jurisdiction. William R. Casto, *The Origins of Federal Admiralty Jurisdiction in an Age of Privateers, Smugglers, and Pirates*, 37 AM J. LEG. HIST. 117, 118 (1997).

[27] "[P]rize cases arising from the wars following the French Revolution utterly dominated the Supreme Court's appellate jurisdiction over maritime cases." *Id.* at 150.

[28] An Act to Establish the Judicial Courts of the United States, ch. 20, § 9, 1 Stat. 73, 77 (district courts given "exclusive original cognizance of all civil causes of admiralty and maritime jurisdiction" saving to suitors "the right to a common law remedy, where the common law is competent to give it").

[29] Southern Pacific Co. v. Jensen, 244 U.S. 205 (1917) (admiralty law is federal and displaces State law).

[30] U.S. CONST., art. III, § 2, ¶ 2.

but Article III does not reach them.[31] Rule-like norms have weaknesses, as do norms that seek to make their goal the operative rule by incorporating it.

The proposal I offer would return the federal courts to the approach to customary international law that the Constitution's drafters almost certainly contemplated and that prevailed for many decades.[32] The main innovation I suggest is an explicit call by the Supreme Court to the State courts to follow its lead where they are not required to do so. This approach would avoid the controversy that comes with the Third Restatement's assertion that customary international law is as such law of the United States.[33]

This suggestion would also give the federal courts a larger role in a class of cases that can affect U.S. foreign relations: those involving extraterritorial application of the law of a State. Although I do not suggest that the federal courts decide all conflicts questions for themselves, I do propose that, in cases otherwise in their jurisdiction (mainly diversity cases), they do so when a party argues that the law of a State applies in a foreign country. One notable category of such cases involves passive-personality jurisdiction: States sometimes apply their own law, including their own tort law, to injuries suffered by their residents outside of the United States. Contemporary international law sometimes accepts that form of jurisdiction to prescribe, but it can raise delicate issues.[34] If any choice-of-law questions are suited for independent resolution by the federal courts, those in which a subnational actor seeks to exercise sovereign power outside of the United States certainly are.[35]

---

[31] Hodgson v. Bowerbank, 9 U.S. 303 (1809) (Article III diversity jurisdiction does not include suits between two aliens).

[32] As to the understanding that prevailed at the time of the framing, see Harrison, *supra* note 21. As Bradley and Goldsmith explain, the view that "the law of nations, which included what we today call [customary international law], had the legal status of general common law" prevailed in the period up to *Erie*. Bradley & Goldsmith, *supra* note 9, at 824.

[33] Although my own view is that no unwritten law is law of the United States under Article III or VI, the Court has held to the contrary. See *supra* note 8 (some unwritten law, including act of state doctrine, has status of federal law). The Court is quite unlikely to eliminate the category of unwritten federal law. The version of my suggestion that is consistent with the existence of some unwritten federal law is that the Court should reject the Third Restatement's principle, should keep the category of unwritten federal law based on customary international law narrow, and should regard questions of customary international law that are not federal law (which should be most such questions) as questions of general law that the federal courts resolve for themselves, not bound by the precedents of the State courts.

[34] For example, in consolidated lawsuits by U.S. domiciliaries against Libya growing out of an alleged terrorist bombing of an aircraft in flight over Africa that crashed in Niger, the district court applied the tort law of the plaintiffs' place of domicile, including Virginia, Georgia, and Texas. Pugh v. Socialist People's Libyan Arab Jamahiriya, 530 F. Supp. 216 (D.D.C. 2008). That application of passive-personality jurisdiction was in a grey zone of customary international law. According to a comment to the Fourth Restatement, "[p]assive-personality jurisdiction historically has been more controversial than jurisdiction based on territory or active personality. Despite this, states increasingly have exercised this form of prescriptive jurisdiction, particularly with respect to terrorist offenses." FOURTH RESTATEMENT § 411 cmt. *a*.

[35] The suggestion that federal courts independently decide choice-of-law questions when possible conflicts with foreign law are at issue has been made before. See, e.g., Donald Earl Childress III, *When*

The choice-of-law solution that I suggest may seem like an ersatz form of federal preemption: If the application of State law outside a State's territory embarrasses the foreign relations of the United States, the Constitution should displace it. In fact, in this context, preemption is an ersatz form of choice of law. Choice-of-law rules based on territorial sovereignty are founded on concerns about the allocation of authority among sovereigns, not concerns about the substance of the law. Choice-of-law principles and cases contain the resources needed to decide when and whether States of the Union may operate outside their own territory.

The main supposed ground of federal preemption—exclusive federal authority over foreign relations—raises serious problems in this connection. Foreign-affairs preemption is of the dormant kind: It comes from federal power, not from an affirmative restriction on the States. To say, for example, that dormant foreign affairs power restricts the extraterritorial reach of the States is to say that federal power does have that reach. For example, sovereigns have some authority to regulate the conduct of their nationals outside their borders, though because they are extraterritorial, those regulations can create tensions with the territorial sovereign. If dormant federal foreign-affairs power debars States from imposing such regulations, that is because it empowers Congress to do so. Congress, on this theory, is able to impose criminal sanctions on U.S. citizens for conduct outside the United States, without regard to the domestic allocation of power between the State and national governments.[36] For similar reasons, if States may not apply their law of torts to harms to their own residents outside the United States, then Congress has power to enact ordinary tort law, insofar as it applies to harms to U.S. nationals outside of the United States.

Limits on State extraterritoriality derived from dormant federal power thus have significant implications for active federal power. No such implications arise when the extraterritorial reach of State regulation is assessed on the basis of conflict of laws principles. Under conflicts analysis, the question is one of the allocation of jurisdiction between States and foreign countries, not of the peculiar

Erie *Goes International*, 105 Nw. L. Rev. 1531 (2011) (recommending that *Klaxon* as applied to international choice-of-law cases be replaced in federal court with a specialized federal common law of conflicts).

[36] Courts have wrestled with the constitutionality of 18 U.S.C. § 2423(c), which punishes U.S. citizens who travel in foreign commerce and engage in certain illicit sexual relations. The main focus of those cases has been Congress's foreign commerce power. E.g., United States v. Clark, 435 F. 3d 1100 (9th Cir., 2006) (prohibition is within Congress's foreign commerce power); FOURTH RESTATEMENT § 403 reporters' note 1. If Congress can exercise all the extraterritorial authority that international law allows the United States to exercise, then its enumerated powers are irrelevant to extraterritorial regulation.

American federal system with its many perplexities. When foreign sovereigns are involved, general principles of jurisdiction should be controlling.

Extending independent federal-court decision concerning choice of law is a manifestation of the larger theme of my proposal and, I think, the Constitution: Functions that today are thought to be performed by substantive law and Article VI preemption are properly performed by jurisdictional principles. Both the authority of the federal courts and the norms of choice of law fall into the jurisdictional category, which is where problems of this kind belong.

The choice-of-law component of my proposal, however, may seem to underline the point that the change I suggest would trade a frying pan for a fire. *Erie Railroad v. Tompkins*,[37] the reasoning goes, rejected the category of general law, and *Klaxon v. Stentor Elec. Mfg. Co.*[38] held that choice-of-law questions are generally governed by State law.

If *Erie* held that customary international law does not exist, it should be overruled, but of course it did not. Nor did it hold that federal courts are for some reason institutionally incapable of treating customary international law as what it is—a body of unwritten norms found in the practice of states that is followed because it is seen as obligatory—and must treat it as the law of either a State or the United States. As Professor Caleb Nelson has shown, *Erie* addresses a question unrelated to legal metaphysics: How should federal courts go about identifying the content of State law, in cases in which it applies? The answer in *Erie* is that they should give absolute deference to the cases of the highest court of the State involved.[39] As Professor Nelson also explains, that principle is itself a piece of federal common law: an unwritten norm that governs federal courts.[40] That principle is not objectionable for those who believe that no unwritten law is law of the United States under Article III or Article VI, because it need not qualify as either in order to function. The *Erie* rule governs the decisional processes of federal courts, and State courts are not called on to follow it, so it need have no preemptive force under Article VI. It operates in cases that are otherwise within federal jurisdiction, and so need itself not support jurisdiction under Article III.[41]

---

[37] 304 U.S. 64 (1938).

[38] 313 U.S. 487 (1941).

[39] Caleb Nelson, *A Critical Guide to* Erie Railroad *v.* Tompkins, 54 WM. & MARY L. REV. 921, 950 (2013) (*Erie* instructs federal courts to defer to State courts on issues within the States' legislative competence).

[40] Nelson reaches the "ironic conclusion" that "the *Erie* doctrine might best be characterized as what modern lawyers call 'federal common law.'" *Id.* at 985–86.

[41] Customary international law's continued vitality obviates any need to decide whether American courts can decide according to any other forms of general law as that category was understood in the eighteenth and nineteenth centuries. Bellia and Clark argue, for example, that the States have replaced the general law merchant with local law, so federal courts cannot properly look to it in cases within the States' prescriptive jurisdiction. BELLIA JR., & CLARK, *supra* note 2, at 170, 251. That may well be correct. If customary international law did not exist, the Third Restatement would be

The proposal I offer probably does call for a modification of *Klaxon*, which directs the lower federal courts to follow the choice-of-law principles of the State in which they sit. *Klaxon* has long been subject to strong criticism.[42] Whether the Court's opinion attributes the result to the Constitution is hard to say.[43] Whatever *Klaxon* may mean on this point, its rule cannot reasonably be attributed to the Constitution. As one venerable criticism points out, nothing in the Constitution requires that the jurisdiction of federal trial courts track State boundaries; Congress can create a federal trial court that is incapable of applying the rule of *Klaxon* because there is no one State in which it sits.[44] Moreover, the Constitution itself creates a trial court that has not sat in any State since the federal government left Philadelphia for the District of Columbia.[45] Like *Erie*, *Klaxon* can be reasonably understood as resting only on a principle of unwritten federal law about the choice-of-law rules in federal court.[46]

As such a doctrine, the rule of *Klaxon* is ripe for reconsideration. As its critics have long pointed out, the case for independent federal-court decision

incoherent in attributing to it the status of law of the United States. If it can exist only as law of the United States, other countries' courts will be somewhat surprised to learn how often they have been applying another country's law.

[42] See, e.g., Henry M. Hart Jr., *The Relations Between State and Federal Law*, 54 COLUM. L. REV. 489, 513–15 (1954) (federal courts as impartial tribunals are well suited to develop principles that choose among State jurisdictions).

[43] The Court pointed to the danger that independent federal determination of choice-of-law issues would "disturb equal administration of justice" within a State, 313 U.S. at 496, which may allude to a constitutional principle, but also could point to a consideration of policy. The Court also explained that any nonuniformity among the States is "attributable to our federal system, which leaves to a state, within the limits permitted by the Constitution, the right to pursue local policies diverging from those of its neighbors," *id.* The Constitution to some extent secures to the States the right to pursue their own policies, with no general obligation of uniformity, so again the Court may have relied on the Constitution. On the other hand, the Court did not explicitly state that any other rule would be unconstitutional.

[44] See Alfred Hill, *The Erie Doctrine and the Constitution*, 53 Nw. U. L. REV. 541, 558 (1958). Subsequent to Professor Hill's article, Congress created a trial court with nationwide jurisdiction. The Court of International Trade has offices in New York City, 28 U.S.C. 251(b), but its jurisdiction is described by kinds of cases, not geography, 28 U.S.C. § 1581, and it may conduct trials or hearings at any port or place within the United States, 28 U.S.C. § 256(a). There is no one State in which the Court of International Trade sits.

[45] The Supreme Court's original jurisdiction, U.S. CONST., art. III, § 2, ¶ 2, makes it a trial court.

[46] In a contribution to a book about a Restatement, no higher authority can be found than the American Law Institute, and the ALI has taken the position that Congress may and should enact choice-of-law rules for the federal courts to apply in certain cases in which the applicable substantive law is that of a State (or more than one State). AMERICAN LAW INSTITUTE, COMPLEX LITIGATION: STATUTORY RECOMMENDATIONS AND ANALYSIS §§ 6.01–6.04 (1994). The Institute's position entails that *Klaxon* is not constitutionally mandated, because Congress cannot override the Constitution any more than the common law can. The comments argue that *Erie* and *Klaxon* do not bar statutory choice-of-law rules because those cases "address the capacity of the federal courts to utilize their common law powers to create federal choice of law rules; they do not deal with the power of Congress to do so." *Id.*, § 6.01 cmt. *b*. I understand those cases as founded, not on a constraint on the courts' "common law powers," but on an exercise of them—that is to say, a determination of the content of the common law.

is especially strong with respect to choice of law.[47] State tribunals will have incentives to formulate choice-of-law principles that favor their own residents, with respect to both other States of the Union and foreign states. Federal courts are supposed to be impartial among the States and to reflect the national government's concerns with good relations with other sovereigns. Federal court jurisdiction in cases affecting foreigners is especially important because the costs of ill-treatment of foreign interests will be felt by the country as a whole, not just by a State whose courts might favor their own. One of the main purposes of choice-of-law rules is uniformity among jurisdictions, so that parties can predict the law that will apply to any disputes they may find themselves in. Uniformity within the United States is a necessary condition for its participation in an international uniform system of private law.

The case for modifying or simply abandoning *Klaxon* is thus quite strong. It is especially strong where foreign interests are concerned, because foreign states can create kinds of trouble for the United States that the States of the Union cannot or will not create for one another. My proposal is therefore limited to choice of law when a federal court is called on possibly to apply the law of a State outside the territory of the United States. I also recommend a wholesale reconsideration of *Klaxon*, but this is the sort of reform that can usefully be pursued piecemeal. Once the Supreme Court has discovered that today's judges can apply the general law of conflicts as their predecessors did, the Court may and I hope will reconsider *Klaxon* altogether.

Part of this proposal is unusual, not in its boldness but in its modesty. Some cases in which customary international law figures do not appear on the Article III menu; the framers did not perfectly implement the goal of putting such cases in federal court. Perhaps they simply did not think about cases involving aliens on both sides, for example. Or perhaps they omitted alien-alien cases because they regarded extensions of federal jurisdiction as costly to the role of State courts and thought that State courts would have no incentive to be biased when no State citizen was a party. As to case not on the Article III list, I recommend that the Supreme Court ask the State courts to follow its lead, even though they do not have to.

The Court is not accustomed to making such requests; for all its statements of respect for State courts, today it either leaves them wholly alone or commands them in the name of federal law, written or unwritten. State courts might find an invitation to cooperate in a combined effort so refreshing, not to say shocking, that they might accept it. The Supreme Court could further encourage cooperation by actually taking seriously State courts' views on customary international

---

[47]  See, e.g., Hart, *supra* note 42.

law. Were the Court to endorse Professor Nelson's characterization of *Erie* as resting on federal common law, it could further point out to the State courts that the federal courts follow State cases, not because the Constitution requires them to but in pursuit of a harmonious allocation of decisional responsibility between the courts of State and nation. Reminded that they are given respect by a federal judge-made rule of deference, State courts might reciprocate with State judge-made rules of deference. They might embrace their role as part of a system of courts that "are not foreign to one another, nor to be regarded by one another as such, but [as] courts of the same country, exercising jurisdiction partly different and partly concurrent," and further to pursue Justice Bradley's words, they might take their part in creating "one system of jurisprudence which constitutes the law of the land" for States and Union alike.[48]

If State courts decline that role, Article III limits the disharmony they can produce, by putting the most important foreign-relations cases in federal court. Federal legislative jurisdiction also provides a substantial solution for possibly disharmonious State legislation that purports to operate extraterritorially. Behind the federal courts is another federal institution that has substantial if not unlimited authority in matters affecting foreign relations: Congress. Together, the resources that the Constitution unquestionably provides are more than capable of securing the expert, impartial, and uniform ascertainment, development, and application of customary international law in the courts of this country.

[48] Claflin v. Houseman, 93 U.S. 130, 137 (1876) (Bradley, J.).

# PART IV

# THE RESTATEMENT AND INTERNATIONAL LAW'S LIMITS ON DOMESTIC JURISDICTION

# 12

# Reasonableness as a Limitation on the Extraterritorial Application of U.S. Law

## From 403 to 405 (via 404)

*Hannah L. Buxbaum & Ralf Michaels*

According to Section 405 of the Fourth Restatement of Foreign Relations Law, "courts in the United States may interpret federal statutory provisions to include other limitations on their applicability." This rather vague ("other") and non-committal ("may") phrase is found in a provision entitled "Reasonableness in Interpretation." The reference to reasonableness suggests continuity with the Third Restatement of Foreign Relations Law, in particular its Section 403, which prohibited the "unreasonable" exercise of prescriptive jurisdiction. However, those provisions differ quite significantly with respect to the source, content, and operation of that limitation. In particular, the Fourth Restatement rejects the idea that courts are required to determine the reasonableness of extraterritorial application of law on a case-by-case basis.

The new Section 405 is already progress compared to early drafts of the Fourth Restatement, which included no provision on reasonableness at all. Still, the new Section 405 is no more than a compromise between those who wanted to abolish a provision like this altogether (as had indeed been the intention of the reporters in earlier drafts) and those (including the authors of this chapter) who advocated that Section 403 simply be updated—and it curtails the role of reasonableness quite significantly. While we applaud the reporters' decision ultimately to restore a reasonableness provision, we continue to believe that preserving a reasonableness requirement along the lines of Section 403 would have been the better step.

This chapter begins with a description of Section 405's genealogy, as well as a more detailed comparison between the old Section 403 and the new Section 405. We then make two main arguments, one empirical and one normative. Empirically, a reasonableness requirement is part of existing case law, even though it appears under a range of different doctrinal headings. Normatively, such a requirement is necessary to achieve an adequate balance between under- and overregulation in a world of overlapping regulatory claims. Experience teaches that neither the international law of jurisdiction nor the presumption

Hannah L. Buxbaum & Ralf Michaels, *Reasonableness as a Limitation on the Extraterritorial Application of U.S. Law* In: *The Restatement and Beyond*. Edited by: Paul B. Stephan and Sarah H. Cleveland, Oxford University Press (2020).
© Oxford University Press. DOI: 10.1093/oso/9780197533154.003.0013

against extraterritoriality alone can produce that balance. Therefore, the question is not *whether* there should be a "reasonableness requirement," but rather what the *content* of that requirement is. In our view, instead of its vague general reference to "other limitations," the Fourth Restatement ought to have maintained a case-by-case reasonableness test, and listed the criteria that courts actually use in ascertaining the applicability of U.S. law in cases with foreign elements.

## I.  Genealogy and Comparison

Section 405 of the Fourth Restatement was written against the experience with the Third Restatement, so it makes sense to look at developments both before and after that earlier Restatement. Although its Section 403 has often been described as an invention lacking sufficient empirical evidence, the provision, at the moment when it was written, had support. And although it is sometimes said that Section 403 was abandoned by the courts, the truth is more complicated.

## A.  Before the Third Restatement

The reasonableness requirement in Section 403 of the Third Restatement was a novelty when introduced, but the provision was not written on a blank slate. Instead, it arose from decades of development of U.S. law regarding the extraterritorial application of federal statutes. That development was most clearly visible in the area of antitrust law, but was present in other areas as well.

In antitrust law, the well-known path of the case law from *American Banana* via *Alcoa* to *Mannington Mills* shows a clear development from strict territoriality through unbounded extraterritoriality to a middle way—from a concern about underregulation through a concern about overregulation to an attempt to reach just the right level. In *American Banana* (1909), the Supreme Court denied the applicability of U.S. antitrust law to anticompetitive conduct in the Dominican Republic on the basis of the law's territorial boundaries, even though the conduct, by a U.S. corporation, was directed almost exclusively at the U.S. market.[1] The unfortunate consequence was that U.S. law was unable to deter anticompetitive conduct whenever that conduct remained outside the United States, a clearly unattractive level of underregulation. In response to such criticism, voiced forcefully by administrative agencies, the Court of Appeals for the Second Circuit, filling in for the U.S. Supreme Court, switched course in its 1945 *Alcoa*

---

[1]  American Banana Co. v. United Fruit Co., 213 U.S. 347 (1909).

decision.[2] There, the court determined that U.S. law could be applied to actions taken outside of U.S. territory if those actions were intended to and did affect the U.S. market.[3] This decision countered the concern about underregulation emerging from *American Banana*, but led to the opposite concern, namely, overregulation. Foreign nations, many of which had no antitrust laws similar to those in the United States, protested against what they considered an inappropriate assertion of U.S. regulatory power.

This realization that strict territoriality leads to underregulation and unmitigated extraterritoriality to overregulation[4] led the courts, as well as scholars, to look for intermediate ways. The U.S. Supreme Court developed a more nuanced multifactor test with regard to the Jones Act, a test that influenced both the drafters of the Restatement (Second) of Conflict of Laws and federal courts considering statutes in other substantive areas.[5] In antitrust law, several lower courts developed detailed multifactor tests as case-specific constraints on the application of U.S. federal law in situations of conflict with foreign laws.[6] The hope behind such projects was to enable courts to find just the right level of regulating extraterritoriality, a decision to be made in light of the specific facts and conditions of each case. This was in line with several general developments in the law at the time. The field of choice of law had left behind the traditional formal territorial rules and replaced them with case-specific approaches.[7] A realist/post-realist theory of law viewed statutes as representing regulatory and ideological policies, and suggested that analysis of these policies should guide matters of their interpretation. Finally, great trust was put in the ability of courts to make complicated judgments in a legitimate way.

## B. The Third Restatement

It is against these developments that Andreas Lowenfeld, one of the reporters for the Third Restatement of Foreign Relations Law, drafted its Section 403.[8]

---

[2] U.S. v. Aluminum Co. of America, 148 F.2d 416 (2d Cir. 1945).

[3] *Id.* at 444.

[4] For a clear statement on this point, see Andrew Guzman, *Choice of Law—New Foundations*, 90 GEO. L. REV. 883, 906–13 (2002).

[5] Lauritzen v. Larsen, 345 U.S. 571 (1953); RESTATEMENT (SECOND) OF THE CONFLICT OF LAWS § 6 (Am. Law Inst. 1971).

[6] See, e.g., Timberlane Lumber Co. v. Bank of America, 549 F.2d 597 (9th Cir. 1976); Mannington Mills, Inc. v. Congoleum Corp., 595 F.2d 1287 (3d Cir. 1979); Montreal Trading Ltd. v. Amax Inc., 661 F.2d 864 (10th Cir. 1981).

[7] Cf. RESTATEMENT (SECOND) OF THE CONFLICT OF LAWS, *supra* note 5, § 6(2).

[8] That article provides:

   (1) Even when one of the bases for jurisdiction under s 402 is present, a state may not exercise jurisdiction to prescribe law with respect to a person or activity having connections with another state when the exercise of such jurisdiction is unreasonable.

Lowenfeld claimed that international law required states to limit the exercise of prescriptive jurisdiction in view of other states' regulatory interests. And he drafted something like an entire little choice-of-law code to lay out the relevant approach. Indeed, Section 403 was strongly influenced by the list of factors in Section 6(2) of the Restatement (Second) of Conflict of Laws, which as noted earlier had itself found inspiration in the federal courts' case law on extraterritoriality.

The provision's fate was mixed. On the one hand, many courts applied it.[9] And both in the United States and elsewhere, Section 403 was widely considered to be a valuable restatement of international practice, although (or perhaps because) its open-ended structure allowed for widely varying results. On the other hand, the provision was criticized along several lines. One line of criticism concerned the proclaimed *status* of the section as international law. It was said that the reporter had not demonstrated its status as binding customary international law and that indeed there was insufficient evidence to support such a conclusion. A second line of criticism concerned the *form* of the rule. It was considered too open-ended, too complicated, and to leave too much discretion to judges in the application. A final line of criticism was directed against the *content* of the rule. Comity (or reasonableness) was considered an inappropriate restraint on U.S. regulatory power and interest.

(2) Whether exercise of jurisdiction over a person or activity is unreasonable is determined by evaluating all relevant factors, including, where appropriate:
  (a) the link of the activity to the territory of the regulating state, i.e., the extent to which the activity takes place within the territory, or has substantial, direct, and foreseeable effect upon or in the territory;
  (b) the connections, such as nationality, residence, or economic activity, between the regulating state and the person principally responsible for the activity to be regulated, or between that state and those whom the regulation is designed to protect;
  (c) the character of the activity to be regulated, the importance of regulation to the regulating state, the extent to which other states regulate such activities, and the degree to which the desirability of such regulation is generally accepted.
  (d) the existence of justified expectations that might be protected or hurt by the regulation;
  (e) the importance of the regulation to the international political, legal, or economic system;
  (f) the extent to which the regulation is consistent with the traditions of the international system;
  (g) the extent to which another state may have an interest in regulating the activity; and
  (h) the likelihood of conflict with regulation by another state.
(3) When it would not be unreasonable for each of two states to exercise jurisdiction over a person or activity, but the prescriptions by the two states are in conflict, each state has an obligation to evaluate its own as well as the other state's interest in exercising jurisdiction, in light of all the relevant factors, including those set out in Subsection (2); a state should defer to the other state if that state's interest is clearly greater.

THIRD RESTATEMENT § 403.

[9] A Westlaw search in May 2020 shows over 150 cases that cite the provision itself. As discussed later, because courts incorporate Section 403's reasonableness analysis under a variety of different doctrinal headings, this is not a full reflection of its importance.

It was, presumably, a mix of all three criticisms that led to the slow (though by far not complete) demise of the provision. Stripped of its presumed status of international law, the provision seemed optional and discretionary. Its multifactor form ran against a renewed interest, promoted especially by conservatives, in legal formalism and simple rules that judges could apply without much discretion. Its content on the other hand concerned progressives, who sought more aggressive unilateral application of U.S. law and feared that judges might undermine the regulatory force of that law. The result was an apparent bipartisan opposition to the provision. Moreover, as discussed later, the U.S. Supreme Court seemed to move away from Section 403, relying increasingly on a different doctrinal basis, namely, the presumption against extraterritoriality, as the source of limitations on the geographic reach of federal law.

## C. The Fourth Restatement

Such were the considerations that led the reporters for the Fourth Restatement to abolish Section 403 altogether, at least in earlier drafts. The Fourth Restatement separates into different subchapters the provisions addressing international law governing jurisdiction to prescribe and those addressing U.S. law and practice. With respect to international law, it explicitly rejects the position of the Third Restatement, stating that "state practice does not support a requirement of case-by-case balancing to establish reasonableness as a matter of international law."[10] Rather, "reasonableness" in the exercise of legislative jurisdiction is satisfied as long as there is a genuine connection between the subject of the regulation and the state seeking to regulate—generally in the form of a connection with the regulating state's territory, such as conduct or effects, that is commonly recognized as an acceptable basis of jurisdiction.[11]

In their treatment of U.S. law and practice, too, the reporters for the Fourth Restatement deviated from their predecessors in a significant way. On the one hand, they included, in what has now become Section 404, a provision on the presumption against extraterritoriality. This rule of statutory construction appeared in the Restatement (Second)[12] but had been omitted from the Third Restatement. The decision to include the presumption is in accordance with the increased importance given to the presumption in more recent Supreme Court case law.[13]

---

[10]  FOURTH RESTATEMENT § 407 reporters' note 3.
[11]  *Id.* cmt. *c.*
[12]  RESTATEMENT (SECOND), *supra* note 5, at § 38.
[13]  FOURTH RESTATEMENT § 404 reporters' note 1; see also William S. Dodge, *The New Presumption Against Extraterritoriality*, 133 HARV. L. REV. 1582 (2020).

On the other hand, the reporters originally planned to omit entirely a reasonableness provision like Section 403. Preliminary Draft No. 2 concluded not only that international law does not require a case-by-case reasonableness assessment, but also that U.S. courts have not adopted a case-by-case approach to assess the reasonableness of prescriptive jurisdiction.[14] Accordingly, the draft did not include a reasonableness requirement along the lines of Section 403. Further, while the reporters' notes recognized that states and courts often restrict or limit their jurisdiction to prescribe on the basis of international comity,[15] the draft also did not include a section on comity—or any other similar limitation mechanism. As a consequence, absent specific legislative provisions, geographic limits on the application of federal law would have been determined entirely by the presumption against extraterritoriality.

This decision spurred protests. At the November 2014 meeting of the Advisory Board, several advisers urged the reinstatement of an additional reasonableness requirement along the lines of the old Section 403. Nonetheless, although the subsequent draft (Preliminary Draft No. 3) was changed in its structure and addressed the question of reasonableness at greater length in its comments and reporters' notes,[16] in substance it remained essentially unchanged from the previous draft on this point. In particular, although the draft now conceded that "[i]n construing the geographic scope of U.S. law, U.S. courts follow a principle of reasonableness," it took all potential bite out of this concession through an extensive definition of reasonableness that included the international law requirement of a genuine connection and the presumption against extraterritoriality, leaving no room for additional limitations.[17]

Further discussions, and a detailed memo laying out existing case law applying Section 403 or comparable doctrines,[18] finally led the reporters to change their approach and add a reasonableness provision back into the draft.[19] That provision's wording, originally modeled closely on the Supreme Court's

---

[14] See Restatement of the Law Fourth, The Foreign Relations Law of the United States: Jurisdiction § 204 reporters' note 4 (Preliminary Draft No. 2, Sept. 13, 2013).

[15] See *id.* reporters' notes 2, 4.

[16] See Restatement of the Law Fourth, The Foreign Relations Law of the United States: Jurisdiction § 201 reporters' notes 11, 12 (Preliminary Draft No. 3, Sept. 15, 2015).

[17] See William S. Dodge, *Reasonableness in the Restatement (Fourth) of Foreign Relations Law*, 55 WILLAMETTE L. REV. 521 (2019).

[18] Hannah Buxbaum & Ralf Michaels, Memorandum to Reporters re: Reasonableness in the exercise of prescriptive jurisdiction (Sept. 30, 2015) (providing empirical evidence of court practice as well as normative considerations in favor of maintaining a provision on reasonableness).

[19] Restatement of the Law Fourth, The Foreign Relations Law of the United States: Jurisdiction § 204 (Council Draft No. 2, Dec. 11, 2015):

> To avoid unreasonable interference with the legitimate sovereign authority of other states, courts in the United States may interpret statutory provisions to include additional limitations on their applicability as a matter of prescriptive comity. These limitations help the potentially conflicting laws of different states work together in harmony.

opinion in *Empagran*,[20] was later revised in the final version, dropping in particular a reference to "unreasonable interference with the legitimate sovereign authority of other states"[21] and the rather lofty concept of "help[ing] the potentially conflicting laws of different states work together in harmony."[22] Section 405 now provides as follows: "As a matter of prescriptive comity, courts in the United States may interpret federal statutory provisions to include other limitations on their applicability."

## D. Comparison

Section 405 of the Fourth Restatement is comparable to Section 403 of the Third Restatement in one way: It permits the consideration of comity.[23] However, the Fourth Restatement significantly diminishes the importance and function of reasonableness analysis in several respects:[24]

- Whereas the old Section 403 claimed the reasonableness limitation was a requirement of international law, the new Section 405 derives it merely from the practice of U.S. courts.
- Third Restatement Section 403 required courts to assess the reasonableness of an exercise of prescriptive jurisdiction even when a basis for jurisdiction was present, making unreasonable exercise "unlawful." Fourth Restatement Section 405 does not make this inquiry mandatory, instead characterizing any additional reasonableness considerations as a matter of "prescriptive comity."
- Whereas the old Section 403 specifically defined the doctrinal test to prevent the unreasonable exercise of jurisdiction in cases connected with another state, the new Section 405 simply uses the word "reasonableness" in the heading and otherwise contains no more than an open-ended reference to "other limitations"; the idea of avoiding "unreasonable interference with the sovereign authority of other states" has moved to the comments.
- Whereas the old Section 403 required a case-by-case analysis of the requirements of reasonableness in view of concrete conflict with foreign law, the Fourth Restatement operates only "provision by provision" and not "case by case."

[20] F. Hoffmann-LaRoche Ltd. v. Empagran S.A., 542 U.S. 155 (2004).

[21] Cf. *Empagran*, 542 U.S. at 164 ("unreasonable interference with the sovereign authority of other nations").

[22] Cf. *id.* at 164–65 ("help[ing] the potentially conflicting laws of different nations work together in harmony"). Justice Breyer used this language earlier in *Howe v. Goldcorp Invs., Ltd.*, 946 F.2d 944, 950 (1st Cir. 1991).

[23] See FOURTH RESTATEMENT § 405 reporters' note 6 ("This Restatement continues to recognize a principle of reasonableness and acknowledges that lower courts have imposed comity limitations under particular statutes.").

[24] See also Dodge, *Reasonableness, supra* note 17, at 530–33.

– Unlike the old Section 403, the new Section 405 does not provide a list of factors to be considered in reasonableness analysis, either in the rule or in the comments and reporters' notes.

## II. Empirics: Case Law

### A. U.S. Supreme Court

One of the reporters' main justifications for rejecting a case-by-case reasonableness requirement in drafts prior to the final Restatement was their conclusion that the Supreme Court had rejected Section 403. In particular, one of the reporters who worked on the sections on jurisdiction had suggested that the Court had all but abandoned the principle of reasonableness in favor of a tool of statutory interpretation, the presumption against extraterritoriality.[25] The reporters cited only two opinions—both in the area of antitrust law—as evidence of that shift. In *Hartford Fire*, the majority held that a reasonableness test would come into play only in the (rare) case in which a party could not comply with U.S. law without violating a foreign law.[26] And in *Empagran*, the Court characterized a multifactor test as "too complex to prove workable."[27]

We do not believe that these opinions can be read as general rejections of a case-by-case reasonableness limitation. First, both decisions concerned specific circumstances. *Hartford Fire* rested on the confusion of Section 403 with the doctrine of foreign sovereign compulsion, and the statement in question has been followed only inconsistently by lower courts.[28] And although the Court in *Empagran* (which does not cite *Hartford Fire* on this point) certainly criticized multifactor reasonableness analysis, the case must be read in light of the particular facts presented. The Court there assumed that *no* U.S. interest in the application of U.S. law was present, thereby making application of U.S. law ipso facto unreasonable without the need for further analysis. The decision therefore has

---

[25] William S. Dodge, *International Comity in American Law*, 115 COLUM. L. REV. 2071, 2104 (2015) ("Going forward, it seems likely that prescriptive comity will continue to operate as a principle of restraint in American law, but primarily through the presumption against extraterritoriality, which the Supreme Court in Morrison instructed lower courts to apply 'in all cases.'") (footnote omitted). See also § 201, reporters' note 11 ("But the Supreme Court has not adopted the case-by-case approach to evaluating reasonableness set forth in § 403 ... Instead, the Supreme Court has found the application of U.S. law to be reasonable if it rests on a recognized basis for jurisdiction to prescribe and the case has a genuine connection to the United States.").

[26] Hartford Fire Ins. Co. v. California, 509 U.S. 764, 799 (1993).

[27] F. Hoffmann-La Roche Ltd. v. Empagran S.A., 542 U.S. 155, 168 (2004).

[28] See, e.g., Mujica v. Airscan, Inc., 771 F.3d 580, 600 (9th Cir. 2014) ("We think that *Hartford Fire* does *not* require proof of a 'true conflict' as a prerequisite for invoking the doctrine of comity, at least in a case involving adjudicatory comity"). We return to this point later.

little bearing on cases in which such an interest exists; it does not, contrary to what the reporters assume, easily lend itself to generalizations.

It is worth pointing out that neither of the two Supreme Court Justices most responsible for the rise of the presumption against extraterritoriality and the decline of reasonableness analysis, Justices Scalia and Breyer, ruled out a case-by-case reasonableness test. Justice Scalia's opinion in *Morrison* was crucial in re-establishing the presumption against extraterritoriality—but it does not even mention, let alone reject, his analysis thirteen years earlier in *Hartford Fire*, where in a dissenting opinion he had admonished the majority for not paying proper attention to Section 403. In *Hartford Fire*, he found that the presumption against extraterritoriality had been overcome, making resort to Section 403 necessary.[29] In *Morrison*, by contrast, he was able to dispense of the case through application of the presumption, so he had no need to address additional limitations. And Justice Breyer, on whose opinion in *Empagran* the Fourth Restatement relies heavily, does not seem to read the decision as having rejected a multifactor analysis, as evidenced by his own writings.[30]

Second, even if one were to read these decisions broadly, it seems questionable that the approach laid out in *Hartford Fire* and *Empagran* can be easily extended to other areas of law. Both cases addressed the scope of antitrust law, where a clear conflicts rule (the effects doctrine) has long existed and has been enshrined in statutory law through the Foreign Trade Antitrust Improvements Act.[31] Where Congress has spoken as to the extraterritorial applicability of a statute, there is a strong argument that its statement should not be undermined by means of comity considerations.[32] It is not at all clear, however, that this approach should be extrapolated to areas of law in which Congress's intent is not expressed in a rule but is merely hypothesized on the basis of the presumption against extraterritoriality.

Now, it is true that in more recent cases, the Court has emphasized the presumption against extraterritoriality as the predominant means to restrict the scope of U.S. regulatory law.[33] In the course of doing so, the Court has put

---

[29] 509 U.S. at 814 (Scalia, J., dissenting).

[30] See STEPHEN BREYER, THE COURT AND THE WORLD: AMERICAN LAW AND THE NEW GLOBAL REALITIES 100, 103–104 (2015) (discussing strengths and weaknesses of a multifactor test without taking an ultimate position; reporting on the multifactor test in § 403 of the Third Restatement without taking an explicit position on whether or not it underlies the court's opinion).

[31] Foreign Trade Antitrust Improvements Act, 15 U.S.C. § 6a.

[32] Cf. FOURTH RESTATEMENT § 405 cmt. *a*, reporters' notes 1, 2.

[33] Morrison v. National Australia Bank, 561 U.S. 247 (2010) (applying the presumption to foreclose application of U.S. securities antifraud law to claims arising out of foreign transactions); Kiobel v. Royal Dutch Petroleum Co., 569 U.S. 108 (2013) (applying the presumption to foreclose claims under the Alien Tort Statute related to acts occurring within the territory of foreign sovereigns); RJR Nabisco, Inc. v. European Community, 136 S. Ct. 2090 (2016) (suggesting, in the context of RICO, the need to apply the presumption specifically for each provision); WesternGeco LLC v. ION Geophysical Corporation, 138 S. Ct. 2129 (2018) (applying the presumption to a right but not a remedy with regard to the Patent Act).

relatively less emphasis on the question of reasonableness. This means little, however. Consideration of the presumption against extraterritoriality is logically antecedent to application of a reasonableness test. If application of the presumption already results in inapplicability of the statute, the Court simply has no occasion to engage with the additional question of a reasonableness limitation.[34]

The Court does not seem to think that these two tools are interchangeable. Seemingly, a passage in *Morrison* could be read this way. Justice Scalia, for the Court, criticized that the "Second Circuit had excised the presumption against extraterritoriality from the jurisprudence of Section 10(b) and replaced it with the inquiry whether it would be reasonable (and hence what Congress would have wanted) to apply the statute to a given situation."[35] This does not, however, imply that a reasonableness inquiry is never suitable—merely that it should not replace a prior application of the presumption against extraterritoriality. Whether reasonableness should limit the application of the Securities Exchange Act was a question the Court never reached. The same is true for *Kiobel v. Royal Dutch Petroleum Co.*, where the Court went further and applied the presumption to the Alien Tort Statute (ATS), even though the ATS was clearly passed with international concerns in mind and although it is a jurisdictional statute.[36] The reasonableness test advocated by Justice Breyer's concurring opinion did not carry the day.[37] Again, however, rejection of this position meant only that reasonableness should not supplant the presumption, not that it should be altogether unavailable.

If anything, case law suggests the opposite: that the Court assumes the continued existence of both the presumption against extraterritoriality and a separate reasonableness requirement. True, in *Morrison*, the Court suggests "[i]f Section 10(b) did apply abroad, we would not need to determine which transnational frauds it applied to; it would apply to all of them," suggesting that an additional choice-of-law approach is not available.[38] This could be read as excluding a second reasonableness inquiry. But the Court immediately continues with a caveat: "barring some other limitation."[39] Is reasonableness such a limitation? Subsequently, in *RJR Nabisco*, the Court reads *Empagran* to establish a rule separate from (though "related" to) the presumption: the rule "that we construe statutes to avoid unreasonable interference with other nations' sovereign authority where possible."[40] Here it cites Justice Scalia's dissent in *Hartford Fire* discussing "the two canons."

---

[34]  See Al Shimari v. Caci Premier Technology, Inc., 758 F.3d 416, 527 (4th Cir. 2014) (noting that the Court in *Kiobel* did not need to reach the question of defining its "touch and concern" standard, since all of the conduct in that case occurred abroad).

[35]  *Morrison*, 561 U.S. at 257.

[36]  569 U.S. 108 (2013).

[37]  *Id.* at 132 (Breyer, J., concurring in the judgment).

[38]  *Morrison*, 561 U.S. at 267 n.9.

[39]  *Id.*

[40]  *RJR Nabisco*, 136 S. Ct. at 2107 n.9.

The only case that can be read to suggest that the presumption against extraterritoriality had replaced the reasonableness approach is *WesternGeco LLC v. ION Geophysical Corporation*.[41] Here, for the first time since reinvigorating the presumption against extraterritoriality in *Morrison*, the Court found that a statute, in this case Section 284 of the Patent Act, remained applicable despite the presumption of extraterritoriality. Disagreement existed only with regard to the remedy, in particular whether lost foreign profits could be considered in the calculation of damages. Justice Gorsuch's dissent on this point did not rest specifically on Section 403, but did invoke general comity considerations: "principles of comity counsel against an interpretation of our patent laws that would interfere so dramatically with the rights of other nations to regulate their own economies. While Congress may seek to extend U.S. patent rights beyond our borders if it chooses, cf. Section 105 (addressing inventions made, used, and sold in outer space), nothing in the Patent Act fairly suggests that it has taken that step here."[42] The majority would have none of this, suggesting that the dissent "wrongly conflates legal injury with the damages arising from that injury."[43] The majority left room for the limitation or preclusion of damages based on "other doctrines, such as proximate cause."[44] Whether this would include reasonableness is unclear. But it also seems that not too much can be read into such a narrowly focused decision regarding the general status of a reasonableness test.

## B. Lower Court Case Law

Many lower courts have considered explicitly the connection between the presumption against extraterritoriality and case-by-case reasonableness analysis. Some directly support the conclusion of the previous section that the Supreme Court has not in fact ruled out a role for reasonableness analysis.[45] Others do

---

[41]   138 S. Ct. 2129 (2018).

[42]   *Id.* at 2143 (Gorsuch, J., dissenting).

[43]   *Id.* at 2138.

[44]   *Id.* at 2139 n.3.

[45]   See, e.g., *Al Shimari, supra* 34, at 528 ("[T]he clear implication of the Court's 'touch and concern' language is that courts should not assume that the presumption categorically bars cases that manifest a close connection to United States territory . . . a fact-based analysis is required in such cases to determine whether courts may exercise jurisdiction . . ."); Parkcentral Global Hub v. Porsche Automobile Holdings, 763 F.3d 198 (2d Cir. 2014) (analyzing the holding in *Morrison* and concluding that the fact that a domestic transaction was *necessary* for the application of U.S. law did not compel the conclusion that a domestic transaction was *sufficient* for the application of U.S. law—in other words, that *Morrison* did not preclude a multifactor reasonableness test); see also Judge Leval's concurring opinion in that case ("*Morrison* cannot be understood as intending to prohibit the use of flexible, multi-factor tests to guard against extraterritorial application of § 10(b). Most important, the Supreme Court itself in *Kiobel* . . . has construed *Morrison* and its presumption against extraterritoriality in a manner that calls for employment of a flexible, multi-factor analysis"); United States v. Ali, 718 F.3d 929, 935 (D.C. Cir. 2013); see also Mastafa v. Chevron Corp., 770 F.3d 170, 183 (2d Cir.

not mention the Supreme Court jurisprudence, but reach the same result, stating that reasonableness analysis remains available. Indeed, with respect to a wide range of federal statutes, reasonableness analysis continues to play a prominent role in the lower courts. That practice is not uniform. Some lower courts have critiqued or explicitly rejected case-by-case reasonableness analysis in interpreting particular statutes.[46] Others have adopted the majority's approach in *Hartford Fire*, restricting reasonableness to cases in which a "true conflict," as there defined, exists, that is, a case in which a party cannot comply with two laws at the same time.[47] But many continue to apply a reasonableness analysis similar to that laid out in the Third Restatement. Many courts—including in cases decided after *Empagran*—continue to apply Section 403 directly, sometimes identifying the Restatement as authority,[48] sometimes not.[49] Others adopt similar or comparable approaches under other headings, including jurisdictional rule of reason,[50] comity,[51] and due process.[52]

2014); Doe v. Nestle USA, Inc., 766 F.3d 1013 (9th Cir.2014); Doe v. Drummond Co., Inc., 782 F.3d 576, 585 (11th Cir. 2015); Mujica v. AirScan Inc., 771 F.3d 580, 594 (9th Cir. 2014).

[46] See, e.g., Ofori-Tenkorang v. American Intern. Group, Inc., 460 F.3d 296, 305 (2006) (declining to adopt a "center of gravity test" or a "balancing of contacts analysis" in interpreting the Civil Rights Act of 1871); Bell v. Honeywell Tech. Solutions, Inc., 2010 WL 3211045 (S.D. Ind. 2010) (accord).

[47] See, e.g., In re Maxwell Communication Corp. plc, 93 F.3d 1036, 1046–48 (2d Cir 1996) (applying *Hartford Fire* only once the court determined there was a true conflict between U.S. and U.K. insolvency laws); Chavez v. Carranza, 559 F.3d 486, 494–95 (6th Cir. 2009) ("in order for an issue of comity to arise, there must be an actual conflict between domestic and foreign law.")

[48] See, e.g., United States v. Vasquez-Velasco, 15 F.3d 833, 840 (9th Cir. 1994); In re French, 440 F.3d 145 (4th Cir. 2006); United States v. Daniels, 2010 WL 2557506, at *7 (N.D. Cal. 2010); United States v. Hijazi, 845 F. Supp. 2d 874, 884–85 (C.D. Ill. 2011).

[49] See, e.g., Baloco v. Drummond Co., Inc. (*Baloco II*), 767 F.3d 1229, 1235 (11th Cir. 2014) ("consideration of all facts weighs against a finding that Plaintiffs' claims touch and concern the territory of the United States with sufficient force to displace the presumption against extraterritorial application.")

[50] See, e.g., Gallup, Inc. v. Business Research Bureau, 688 F.Supp.2d 915, 925 (N.D. Cal. 2010) (applying a *Timberlane* analysis as a "jurisdictional rule of reason" to preclude the application of the Lanham Act in a trademark infringement case); U.S. v. Lloyds TSB Bank, 639 F. Supp. 2d 314, 326–26 (S.D.N.Y. 2009) (concluding that "even if [the money laundering statute] could be read to extend subject matter jurisdiction over the claims . . . in this case, that exercise in extraterritorial jurisdiction is unreasonable, and hence impermissible in law," and referring to the "rule of jurisdictional reasonableness").

[51] See, e.g., Mujica v. Airscan, Inc., 771 F.3d 580, 598 (9th Cir. 2014) (applying international comity as "a doctrine of prudential abstention"); In re French, 440 F.3d 145 (4th Cir. 2006) ("[a]pplying [§ 403 reasonableness factors], we can only conclude that the doctrine of international comity does not require that we forego application of the United States Bankruptcy Code . . . ."); Doe I v. State of Israel, 400 F. Supp. 2d 86, 116 (D.D.C. 2005) ("[n]otions of comity further support the conclusion that asserting extraterritorial jurisdiction in this particular case would be unreasonable"); Ungaro-Benages v. Dresdner Bank AG, 379 F.3d 1227, 1238–39 (11th Cir. 2004).

[52] See, e.g., United States v. Hijazi, 845 F. Supp. 2d 874, 884–85 (C.D. Ill. 2011) ("In addition to meeting a basis for jurisdiction pursuant to § 402, in order for Hijazi's prosecution to comport with international law it must also be 'reasonable.' Third Restatement of Foreign Relations § 403(1). Whether jurisdiction is reasonable is a context specific inquiry, however § 403(2) of the Restatement provides some relevant factors to consider").

The role of reasonableness analysis varies. In some areas, a Section 403–style test is used to determine the geographic scope of U.S. law (that is, it *is* the test of extraterritorial reach). This is true in trademark law, where one of the leading tests involves a consideration of foreign as well as domestic regulatory interests. As a recent case explains:

> Congress directed that the Lanham Act applies to "all commerce which may lawfully be regulated by Congress." Whether this provision sweeps foreign activities into the Act's proscriptive reach depends on a three-part test we originally applied to the Sherman Act in *Timberlane Lumber Co. v. Bank of America National Trust & Savings Ass'n*, 549 F.2d 597 (9th Cir. 1976). . . . [T]the Lanham Act applies extraterritorially if: "(1) the alleged violations . . . create some effect on American foreign commerce; (2) the effect [is] sufficiently great to present a cognizable injury to the plaintiffs under the Lanham Act; and (3) the interests of and links to American foreign commerce [are] sufficiently strong in relation to those of other nations to justify an assertion of extraterritorial authority."[53]

In other areas, case-by-case reasonableness is used to mitigate the conflicts that would otherwise result from the application of a statute interpreted to have broad extraterritorial reach. This is the case in insolvency. The Bankruptcy Code explicitly provides that a bankruptcy estate encompasses all of the debtor's legal and equitable interests in property "wherever located." As a result, other sections of the bankruptcy code (for instance, the provision permitting avoidance of fraudulent transfers) are often interpreted to have extraterritorial effect. In order to avoid conflict with foreign bankruptcy laws, U.S. courts routinely turn to case-by-case reasonableness analysis to limit the application of domestic bankruptcy law. As one leading case puts it, framing this as a comity analysis, "at base comity involves the recognition that there are circumstances in which the application of foreign law may be more appropriate than the application of our own law."[54]

Finally, case-by-case reasonableness analysis may be used to mitigate the conflicts that might arise even from the "territorial" application of U.S. law in cases with significant foreign elements. This is the case both in securities regulation and in commodities regulation (as we discuss in more detail later).

All of this suggests that the practice of reasonableness analysis has wide application in the lower courts.

[53] Trader Joe's Company v. Hallatt, 835 F.3d 960, 969 (9th Cir. 2016) (quoting Love v. Associated Newspapers, Ltd., 611 F.3d 601, 613 (9th Cir. 2010)).
[54] In re French, 440 F.3d 145, 153 (4th Cir. 2006); see also Securities Investor Protection Corp. v. Madoff Investment Securities LLC, 513 B.R. 222 (S.D.N.Y. 2014) (similarly discussing the role of comity in bankruptcy cases); In re Picard, 917 F.3d 85, 100–105 (2d Cir. 2019).

## III. Normative Arguments

So much for empirics. But maybe the Fourth Restatement is correct that the presumption against extraterritoriality included in the new Section 404 performs the same function that reasonableness did in the old Section 403, only more effectively? What purpose would an additional case-by-case reasonableness inquiry serve? Is it not redundant, next to a presumption against extraterritoriality?

## A. The Functional Difference

It may seem that reasonableness and the presumption both serve the same purpose, and that therefore a shift from the old Section 403 to the new Section 404 is merely a shift to a sounder doctrinal basis. The Supreme Court has suggested that "considerations relevant to one rule are often relevant to the other."[55] And Bill Dodge, the reporter mainly responsible for drafting the sections on jurisdiction, suggests that the presumption against extraterritoriality is, just like the new Section 405, an expression of a principle of reasonableness that permeates the rules on jurisdiction.[56] Indeed, when the Court suggests, in *Kiobel*, that the presumption " 'serves to protect against unintended clashes between our laws and those of other nations which could result in international discord,' "[57] it invokes language that it had earlier linked with an analysis along the lines of Section 403. In this sense, one might argue that having both Section 403 and the reinvigorated presumption against extraterritoriality would be needlessly duplicative. Moreover, requiring a Section 403–style analysis might run the risk that the interests of foreign states are counted twice, once in each step, a danger that the Restatement explicitly warns against in one of the comments to new Section 405.[58]

But the presumption against extraterritoriality and the reasonableness requirement perform quite different functions. The presumption against extraterritoriality is today regularly justified with the assertion that Congress can be presumed to legislate with domestic concerns in mind. It is, in other words, based on domestic concerns.[59] Stated otherwise, it is a *scope* rule.[60] In terms of

---

[55]   *RJR Nabisco*, 136 S. Ct. at 2107 n.9.

[56]   Dodge, *Reasonableness, supra* note 17, at 522.

[57]   Kiobel v. Royal Dutch Petroleum Co., 569 U.S. 108, 115, citing EEOC v. Arabian American Oil Co., 499 U. S. 244, 248 (1991).

[58]   FOURTH RESTATEMENT § 405 cmt. *c* & reporter's note 4; see also Dodge, *Reasonableness, supra* note 17, at 531–2 (discussing *Parkcentral*).

[59]   William S. Dodge, Understanding the Presumption Against Extraterritoriality, 16 Berkeley J. Int'l L. 85, 113 (1998). Dodge, *The New Presumption, supra* note 13, at 1594–5, 1645.

[60]   For the difference between scope rules and priority rules, see Hannah L. Buxbaum, *Determining the Territorial Scope of State Law in Interstate and International Conflicts*, 27 DUKE J. COMP. & INT'L L. 381, 381–82 (2017).

the purpose of such a rule, minimization of conflicts with other states is at best a mere byproduct of its application. And indeed, analysis under new Section 404 does not include whether such a conflict exists in the concrete case or even whether a particular statutory interpretation is more or less likely to create such conflicts in the abstract. The presumption is supposed to come into play "regardless of whether there is a risk of conflict between the American statute and a foreign law."[61]

The reasonableness limitation, by contrast, serves the quite different purpose of minimizing conflicts with foreign states. It is, in this sense, a *priority* rule. The list of factors in the old Section 403 allowed courts to assess, case by case, whether application of the relevant statute, though possible on its face, should nonetheless be constrained not in the abstract but instead in light of the actual regulatory interests of specific other states in the specific case. In the special circumstance in which the United States has no regulatory interest at all in the application of its own law—as was true in *Empagran*—it may be possible to make such a judgment as a general matter. In all other situations, it requires a case-specific analysis.

A case in the area of securities regulation, *Parkcentral Global Hub Ltd. v. Porsche Auto. Holdings SE*,[62] provides an excellent illustration of the functional difference between the presumption against extraterritoriality and reasonableness analysis. The plaintiffs in that case had entered into securities-based swap agreements that referenced the stock of Volkswagen, a German company. The defendant was another German company, Porsche Automobil Holdings, that was not a counterparty to or otherwise involved in the swap agreements. The claims alleged that Porsche had made fraudulent statements (largely in Germany) that adversely affected the price of Volkswagen's stock, thereby diminishing the value of the plaintiffs' investments.[63] The swaps had been executed in the United States, and the claims therefore were not barred by the presumption against extraterritoriality—under the second prong of the *Morrison* test, the application of U.S. antifraud law would be considered "permissibly territorial." In light of the "predominantly foreign" nature of the claims, however, the Second Circuit proceeded to a second analytical step. It noted that Porsche was not a party to the transactions in question (indeed, may have been "completely unaware" of them), and that the fraudulent conduct in question concerned "securities in a foreign company, traded entirely on foreign exchanges."[64] Under these circumstances,

---

[61]  *RJR Nabisco*, 136 S. Ct. 2090, 2100 (quoting *Morrison*, 561 U.S. at 255); FOURTH RESTATEMENT §
405 reporter's note 2.
[62]  Parkcentral Global Hub Ltd. v. Porsche Auto. Holdings SE, 763 F.3d 198 (2d Cir. 2014).
[63]  *Id.* at 201.
[64]  *Id.* at 215–16.

the court concluded, the application of U.S. law would create unnecessary and unreasonable conflict with a foreign regulatory system. As a result, it held, Section 10(b) did not apply to the claims in question.

What the Second Circuit identified here was "the problem with treating the location of a transaction as the definitive factor in the extraterritoriality inquiry."[65] That problem is the consequence of relying solely on the presumption against extraterritoriality. The court recognized that it is important to consider not only the U.S. interest at stake but also the likelihood that the particular combination of foreign and domestic elements in a given case may create the risk of unreasonable conflict with another system.

In one of the notes following Section 405, the reporters cite this decision and somewhat grudgingly concede that "in rare cases," in interpreting statutes that lack extraterritorial reach, courts may "supplement the statutory test developed by applying the presumption with other limitations." But it is not at all clear why these cases are or will be rare. Indeed, the Second Circuit has already extended this two-step approach to the Commodities Exchange Act (CEA). The leading case applying the presumption against extraterritoriality to the CEA concluded that the statute applies only to claims arising from U.S.-based commodities transactions.[66] In a number of cases, however, courts have considered U.S.-based claims involving significant foreign elements—and have insisted upon a second analytical step intended to assess the risk of unreasonable interference with foreign regulatory systems.[67]

Such a two-step process involving both scope and priority rules is common in the law. It underlies the current project developing a new Restatement for the Conflict of Laws. It can also be found in the combination between rules on adjudicatory jurisdiction and "jurisdictional equilibration" mechanisms like *forum non conveniens*, antisuit injunctions, and *lis pendens*.[68] In all of these areas, there is a recognition of the different purposes to be served. The law of extraterritorial application of federal law is no different.

---

[65] *Id.* at 215.

[66] Loginovskaya v. Batratchenko, 764 F.3d 266 (2d Cir. 2014).

[67] Prime International Trading, Ltd. v. BP P.L.C., 2019 WL 4062219 (2d. Cir. 2019) (formally extending the *Parkcentral* "rule" to CEA claims). See also In re London Silver Fixing, Ltd., Antitrust Litigation, 332 F. Supp. 3d 885 (S.D.N.Y. 2018) ("the extraterritoriality analysis under the CEA has two parts: at step one the Court must determine whether the plaintiff's claim involves a 'domestic transaction.' Assuming this requirement is satisfied, the Court *must proceed to step two* and consider whether the claims are 'so predominantly foreign as to be impermissibly extraterritorial' " (emphasis added) (quoting *Parkcentral*, 763 F.3d at 216).

[68] See Ralf Michaels, *Two Paradigms of Jurisdiction*, 27 MICH. J. INT'L L. 1003, 1017–20 (2006). For the term "jurisdictional equilibration" in this context, see *id.* at 1061.

## B. The Risks of Over- and Underregulation through the Presumption

The fact that the presumption against extraterritoriality operates without a view to actual conflicts can have unfortunate consequences in practice. One possible consequence is *overregulation*, as evidenced in the *Parkcentral* case discussed in the previous section. Another possible consequence is *underregulation*. Because the Court aims only at the avoidance of "potential" conflict with the regulatory interests of other states,[69] a statute may remain inapplicable even though there is no actual conflict with another state's policies—either because no other state has an interest in regulation or because another state's policy coincides with that of the U.S. statute. This was Justice Stevens's concern in his concurrence in *Morrison*.[70]

For many proponents of a second-step reasonableness requirement, the main concern is to counter overregulation. But those concerned about underregulation—about the possibility that the regulatory interests embodied in federal law will not be fully implemented—should also be wary of a system that relies exclusively on the presumption against extraterritoriality to avoid conflicts with foreign states. This is perhaps not intuitive. How would a second analytical step allowing for additional limitation in fact increase the application of U.S. law? The answer lies in the interaction of the presumption and case-specific reasonableness analysis. A reasonableness requirement would take weight off the presumption. If no additional backstop exists to prevent an actual conflict, courts interested in avoiding such conflicts will likely err on the side of underenforcement, just to be on the safe side. If they have a second tool at hand, they do not have to do this.[71]

Consider *Morrison* in light of this interaction. The lower courts had determined that the United States had a regulatory interest in applying its law to the facts. Under the old approach, this would have meant that the conduct in question fell within the scope of U.S. law. A second step, a reasonableness step, would have enabled the courts to determine whether those interests should yield to those of other regulators. One might well have thought that they should not. The Supreme Court, through its adoption of the presumption against extraterritoriality as the

---

[69] *Empagran*, 542 U.S. at 164; FOURTH RESTATEMENT § 405.

[70] See *Morrison*, 561 U.S. 285 (Stevens, J., concurring). The rule adopted in *Morrison*, on the basis of the presumption against extraterritoriality, forecloses the application of U.S. law to claims based on foreign transactions. As Stevens notes, this rule will operate to withdraw the protection of the anti-fraud rules even in cases where the injury in question was suffered by U.S. investors—a circumstance in which regulation by any other state would be unlikely.

[71] See Hannah L. Buxbaum, *Extraterritoriality in the Public and Private Enforcement of U.S. Regulatory Law*, in PRIVATE INTERNATIONAL LAW: CONTEMPORARY CHALLENGES AND CONTINUING RELEVANCE (F. Ferrari & D. Fernández-Arroyo eds., forthcoming 2020).

main tool for determining the applicability of U.S. law, made such considerations impossible. And if a reasonableness limitation were not available, courts would need to rely exclusively on the presumption.

These risks of under- and overregulation can only be countered through a two-step process, in which a relatively robust determination of the scope of U.S. law (at the first step) can then be limited with a view to the specifics of the case (at the second step).[72] Notably, a reasonableness limitation does not at all mean that courts must defer to foreign regulatory interests, not even if those interests are, in the abstract, more significant than those of the United States. All it requires is that those foreign interests are taken into account in the concrete case.

## C. The Role of Courts

One concern with case-by-case analysis as in the old Section 403 has always been the fear that it would give excessive discretion to courts.[73] That concern has two aspects—one having to do with separation of powers, the other with certainty and predictability.

As for the first aspect, the suggestion here is that it should be up to Congress, not the courts, to determine the scope of application of a federal statute. This argument, although frequently voiced, is surprisingly weak. First, the problem is that Congress regularly fails to speak to the question of territorial scope, at least explicitly. In such situations it is unavoidable (and also frequently in line with what Congress intends) that courts must determine the scope of application of the relevant statute.[74] The only question is what considerations they should use as the basis for this determination—interpretation (including the presumption against extraterritoriality), assessment of reasonableness factors, or both. Second, even if determination of the scope is ideally left to the legislator, it is not at all clear that the relevant criteria can be clearly derived from the substantive rules themselves. The policies underlying a statute may be relevant in establishing a scope rule but are of only limited relevance in establishing priority rules addressing the resolution of conflicts with the laws of other states. Third, legislators are unable to predict, or to formulate in the necessarily general terms of legislation, all the diverse fact patterns that may arise under a particular statute.[75] Notably, that

---

[72] An alternative two-step process would be to apply a state's law only domestically in principle, but permit its application also extraterritorially where to do so would be reasonable. This possibility has no basis in U.S. law and therefore falls outside the scope of this analysis.

[73] See *Morrison*, 561 U.S. at 258–61; Dodge, *Reasonableness, supra* note 17, at 535–37.

[74] See also *Morrison*, 561 U.S. at 276 n.3 (Stevens, J., concurring).

[75] See *Parkcentral*, 763 F.3d 198, 217. "In a world of easy and rapid transnational communication and financial innovation, transactions in novel financial instruments . . . can come in innumerable

diversity increases exponentially once more than one legal system is involved. Legislators can provide some guidance for such cases, by laying down explicit rules on scope or explicit choice-of-law rules. Even then, fine-tuning is a typical task for judges—a matter of concrete application, not of abstract formulation of a rule. There is nothing arbitrary about such application, contrary to what the Restatement suggests.[76] The assessment of whether conflicts exist, and, if so, how to resolve them has for centuries been a task for judges, and a task that they have, by and large, been able to perform reasonably well. There is no convincing reason to believe they are not capable of this in the international realm.

The second aspect of this concern relates to certainty and predictability. A case-by-case analysis, so it is argued, leads to uncertainty, all the more so if it rests on the assessment of multiple factors.[77] Again, this is not a particularly strong argument. First, experience with post-*Morrison* case law suggests that a provision-by-provision analysis, as espoused by the Restatement, does not provide much predictability, at least for provisions for which no case law exists yet. Moreover, application of the presumption against extraterritoriality is not easy either. In *Morrison*, the Court first expresses the need for a clear-cut rule in order to provide certainty and predictability, and then spends page after page applying its allegedly easy rule to the facts. Second, even if the presumption were indeed a clearer rule, that alone would not avoid uncertainty and unpredictability because transnational situations are by nature less certain and predictable than purely domestic ones. Actors on the transnational plane area already always confronted with multiple potentially applicable laws; it is not clear whether a reasonableness requirement enhances or reduces predictability. Third, greater certainty and predictability always comes at a cost, as is well known from the discipline of conflict of laws. The cost, in this case, is the risk of both over- and underregulation, as shown earlier.

## IV. Conclusion

Our conclusion follows quite naturally from the argument outlined in this chapter. On the one hand, we think that the reporters were right to add a provision dealing with reasonableness (Section 405) in addition to the presumption

---

forms of which we are unaware and which we cannot possibly foresee. . . . We believe courts must carefully make their way with careful attention to the facts of each case and to combinations of facts that have proved determinative in prior cases . . ."

[76] FOURTH RESTATEMENT § 405 cmt. *a*; see also Dodge, *The New Presumption, supra* note 13, at 1627 (criticizing the "unbridled discretion of a case-by-case approach").

[77] *Empagran*, 542 U.S. at 168–69; Dodge, *Reasonableness, supra* note 17, at 532.

against extraterritoriality (Section 404). This is in accordance with both existing case law and normative considerations. On the other hand, the new Section 405, added belatedly, is incomplete in several ways. The Fourth Restatement presents reasonableness considerations as matters of statutory interpretation, and thereby attributes to Congress and its hypothetical intent what is in reality a judicial task. As a consequence, the functional difference between the presumption and the reasonableness limitation is obscured: The reasonableness requirement appears as no more than an appendix to the presumption against extraterritoriality, not as a separate tool. The Restatement accounts for the wealth of existing practices only with a general observation that "[i]n rare cases, a court may supplement the statutory test developed by applying the presumption with other limitations, if consistent with the text, history, and purpose of the statutory provision in question."[78] It fails to provide a firm doctrinal basis for the consideration of reasonableness, leaving untouched the plethora of doctrinal bases that exist in the case law. And it fails to catalog and prescribe the factors that should be relevant for the application of reasonableness limitations. In our view, the prevalence of reasonableness analysis in the lower courts—and the diversity of the ways in which it is applied—required more recognition and better guidance for courts.

The main blame for this lies not with the reporters but with the Supreme Court. The Court's decision to deploy the presumption against extraterritoriality to bear the brunt of what are effectively choice-of-law problems was and is deeply problematic. If we had a more sophisticated choice-of-law regime for federal law, the need for a case-by-case reasonableness inquiry would be greatly reduced (though it would likely not disappear). Professor Dodge suggests, perhaps too optimistically, that the new presumption against extraterritoriality is both more nuanced and more flexible than the old one,[79] which might suggest that perhaps a new choice-of-law regime can be derived from it. Maybe, then, there is hope for the development of a comprehensive choice-of-law regime including both scope and priority rules. The current Restatement does not yet achieve this goal.

---

[78] Fourth Restatement § 405 reporters' note 4.
[79] Dodge, *Reasonableness, supra* note 17, at 529–30; Dodge, *supra* note 13, at 1630–32.

# 13

# Adjudicatory Jurisdiction and Public International Law

## The Fourth Restatement's New Approach

*Austen Parrish*

In late 2018, the American Law Institute published its Fourth Restatement of the Foreign Relations Law of the United States. It's an important work that, like its predecessor, should be influential. One question, however—common after the publication of any Restatement—is whether it restates existing law, or whether it attempts to effect change. While much of the Fourth Restatement recites settled understandings and reflects the law's evolution over the last three decades, in at least one area it charts a new, unexpected path.

In the context of adjudicatory jurisdiction, the Fourth Restatement breaks with common understandings to find that personal jurisdiction is not a concern of international law. It indicates that "[w]ith the significant exception of various forms of immunity, modern customary international law generally does not impose limits on jurisdiction to adjudicate."[1] One of the reporters of the section on jurisdiction, William Dodge, has asserted that the issue is so well settled that concerns over international law's constraints on adjudicatory jurisdiction can be "easily dismissed,"[2] as even exorbitant assertions of adjudicatory jurisdiction are only constrained as a matter of comity. According to Professor Dodge, state practice and *opinio juris* reveal no limitations on jurisdiction to adjudicate outside the area of immunity.[3]

---

[1] FOURTH RESTATEMENT ch. 2, intro. note.

[2] William S. Dodge & Scott Dodson, *Personal Jurisdiction and Aliens*, 116 MICH. L. REV. 1205, 1234 (2018).

[3] William S. Dodge, *International Comity in the Fourth Restatement*, in this volume (asserting, using one example, that "state practice seems inconsistent with the proposition that exorbitant bases of personal jurisdiction violate customary international law"); see also William S. Dodge, *The Customary International Law of Jurisdiction in the Restatement (Fourth) of Foreign Relations Law*, OPINIO JURIS (Aug. 3, 2018), http://opiniojuris.org/2018/03/08/the-customary-international-law-of-jurisdiction-in-the-restatement-fourth-of-foreign-relations-law/ (arguing that "an honest look at state practice and opinio juris today reveals no limitations on jurisdiction to adjudicate outside the area of immunity").

Austen Parrish, *Adjudicatory Jurisdiction and Public International Law* In: *The Restatement and Beyond*. Edited by: Paul B. Stephan and Sarah H. Cleveland, Oxford University Press (2020). © Oxford University Press. DOI: 10.1093/oso/9780197533154.003.0014

The Fourth Restatement's new view that international law does not limit state judicial power to adjudicate is tendentious. It represents a break both from the ALI's prior understandings and from the view of most, although admittedly not all, international law scholars. Public international law imposes limits on the judicial branch exerting power over another state's citizens with which it has no connection. While the precise contours of those limits may be amorphous, state power exercised through the judiciary in civil litigation is not uniquely exempt from public international law's purview. And even if one disagrees, the Fourth Restatement should have been explicit that it was staking a contested position,[4] if not one departing from the most common understanding.

The Fourth Restatement's discussion of adjudicatory jurisdiction also appears to premise its conclusion on two unorthodox approaches to international law. First, it implies that fundamental structural limits of the international legal system can disappear unless states are vigilant in protesting illegal activity of other states. But states aren't required to persistently protest illegal activity, and it's far from clear that the absence of protests can nullify long-standing principles of sovereignty. Second, the Restatement appears to assume that states have unfettered authority absent a limiting customary rule. Yet international legal practice hasn't traditionally addressed jurisdictional questions that way. To reach the Fourth Restatement's conclusion, proof of widespread state practice and *opinio juris* supporting a customary rule authorizing universal civil jurisdiction would be required. State practice, however, points in the opposite direction.

This chapter critiques the Fourth Restatement's new approach to adjudicatory jurisdiction. It begins with a brief description of public international law's limits on adjudicatory jurisdiction before addressing responses to the critique. It ends with a description of the broader implications for the Fourth Restatement's position that public international law no longer constrains state power in civil judicial proceedings.

---

[4] Pamela K. Bookman, *Toward the Fifth Restatement of U.S. Foreign Relations Law: The Future of Adjudicative Jurisdiction under Public International Law*, in this volume (describing the debate that exists, but noting "[t]here is some global consensus that adjudicative jurisdiction should be based on some connection between the defendant, the controversy, and the forum state."); Hannah Buxbaum & Ralf Michaels, *Reasonableness as a Limitation on the Extraterritorial Application of U.S. Law: From 403 to 405 (via 404)*, in this volume (describing the Fourth Restatement's discarding of a case-by-case reasonableness test as a limitation on jurisdiction and whether reasonableness is a limitation imposed by international law, at least in the prescriptive jurisdiction context).

# I. Public International Law's Limits
## on Adjudicatory Jurisdiction

Public international law limits a state's authority over persons with which it has no connection.[5] This is a fundamental structural feature of an international system designed to reduce conflict, and a necessary component to the principles of self-determination, sovereign equality, and nonintervention. As a result, international rules on jurisdiction have long been understood to be a manifestation of international law's limits on state sovereignty. And while those limits may evolve over time—a wide array of scholarship has addressed the changing scope of extraterritorial regulation as the dominance of territoriality-based jurisdiction wanes—previously few have argued that public international law exempts state power exercised through the judiciary from its purview.

To be clear, this is not to argue that the limits on a state's exercise of jurisdiction in particular contexts—prescriptive, enforcement, and adjudicatory jurisdiction, as the terms are used in the Fourth Restatement—are always the same. Nor does it contest that comity may also play a role in a court declining jurisdiction authorized under law. But public international law provides a floor and sets the outer boundary for any exercise of jurisdiction, requiring at minimum some nexus or connection between the state and the person or conduct. Said differently, a state may not unilaterally regulate or assert power over noncitizens living in foreign countries with which the state has no genuine connection or link, at least absent consent (and putting aside possible contexts involving egregious international law and human rights violations, the one area where universal jurisdiction may have some resonance).

This basic understanding is a long-standing one. Canonical treatises of public international law—from Oppenheim's, to Brownlie's, to Lowe's—are uniform in their agreement that some link between the state and the defendant is needed to justify a court's exercise of jurisdiction.[6] In a well-cited *Harvard Law Review* article from the 1920s, Joseph Beale described the established rule that no state "can confer legal jurisdiction on [its] courts or [its] legislature, when [the state] has no jurisdiction under international law."[7] F.A. Mann in his famous lectures at the Hague Academy of International Law underscored how public international law limits court jurisdiction in civil cases.[8] In the early 1990s, Oscar Schachter

---

[5] IAN BROWNLIE, PRINCIPLES OF PUBLIC INTERNATIONAL LAW 298, 306–308 (4th ed. 1990) (describing the necessity of a sufficient nexus between the subject matter and the state for a state's assertion of jurisdiction); LASSA OPPENHEIM, OPPENHEIM'S INTERNATIONAL LAW §§ 136–37, at 456 (9th ed. 1992) (describing how international law limits a state's jurisdictional authority); VAUGHAN LOWE, JURISDICTION IN INTERNATIONAL LAW 342 (Malcolm D. Evans ed., 2d ed. 2006) (same).

[6] *Id.*

[7] Joseph H. Beale, *The Jurisdiction of a Sovereign State*, 36 HARV. L. REV. 241, 243 (1923).

[8] F.A. Mann, *The Doctrine of Jurisdiction in International Law*, 111 RECUIEL DES COURS 1, 14, 17, 73–81 (1964).

emphasized that "[t[here is no dissent from the general proposition that public international law sets limits on the authority of States to legislate, adjudicate and enforce its domestic law."[9] The International Law Commission reached the same conclusion too.[10] In 2002, the High Court of Australia explained in the adjudicatory jurisdiction context that principles of public international law require "a substantial and bona fide connection between the subject matter and the source of jurisdiction" and concluded that "no country's legal system can ignore the influence of public international law."[11] Similarly, in 2007, the Canadian Supreme Court described how customary international law sets the outer boundaries to judicial jurisdiction.[12]

These aren't isolated pronouncements. Most international law experts reach the same conclusion,[13] and the ALI once agreed too. Both the Second and Third Restatements found that international law limits a state's power to adjudicate cases against persons or entities with which the state has no connection.[14] And states followed these norms. Just over a decade ago, the ALI and UNIDROIT in their *Principles of Transnational Civil Procedure* concluded that a "substantial connection" was the generally accepted standard for personal jurisdiction in international cases.[15]

These long-standing understandings continue today. For example, two chapters published in 2017 in the *Encyclopedia of Private International Law*—one by Donald E. Childress III and one by Ralf Michaels—while noting that international law's limits are not universally accepted and are "open to debate," explain the generally accepted view that public international law sets the outer boundaries of adjudicatory jurisdiction.[16] Or as Gary Born and Peter (Bo) Rutledge

---

[9] OSCAR SCHACHTER, INTERNATIONAL LAW IN THEORY AND PRACTICE 250 (1991). For other examples, see Campbell McLachlan, *The Influence of International Law on Civil Jurisdiction*, 6 HAGUE Y.B. INT'L L. 125, 128 (1993) (describing international law's limits on civil jurisdiction).

[10] International Law Commission, Draft Articles on Jurisdictional Immunities of States and their Property, art. 6, cmt. 3, published in Report of the International Law Commission to the General Assembly, U.N. GAOR, 43d Session, Supp. No. 10, U.N. Doc. A/46/10 (1991) ("The first prerequisite to any question involving jurisdictional immunity is therefore the existence of a valid 'jurisdiction,' primarily under internal law rules of a State, and, in the ultimate analysis, the assumption and exercise of such jurisdiction not conflicting with any basic norms of public international law.").

[11] Regie Nationale des Usines Renault SA v. Zhang (2002), 210 CLR 491, 528–29 (Austl.) (Kirby, J.).

[12] R v. Hape, 2007 SCC 26 (explaining that "[w]hile extraterritorial jurisdiction—prescriptive, enforcement or adjudicative—exists under international law, it is subject to strict limits under international law that are based on sovereign equality, non-intervention and the territoriality principle").

[13] For a list of sources, see Austen Parrish, *Personal Jurisdiction: The Transnational Difference*, 59 VA. J. INT'L L. 97, 125–30 nn.171–76 (2019).

[14] RESTATEMENT (SECOND) OF THE FOREIGN RELATIONS LAW OF THE UNITED STATES § 20 (Am. Law Inst. 1965); THIRD RESTATEMENT § 403.

[15] ALI/UNIDROIT, PRINCIPLES OF TRANSNATIONAL CIVIL PROCEDURE 18, at 104 (2006).

[16] Donald Earl Childress III, *Jurisdiction: Limits under International Law*, in 2 ENCYCLOPEDIA OF PRIVATE INTERNATIONAL LAW 1041, 1052–53 (2017) (describing international law's limits, but noting that the view that international law imposes restraints is not uniformly accepted); Ralf Michaels, *Jurisdiction: Foundations*, in 2 ENCYCLOPEDIA OF PRIVATE INTERNATIONAL LAW 1042, 1043 (2017) (describing how international law sets the outer boundaries of jurisdiction).

underscore in the Sixth Edition of their influential casebook on international litigation published last year: "the weight of authority agrees with the Third Restatement in supporting the existence of some international law limits on national assertions of judicial jurisdiction."[17] Or as the British scholar Alex Mills recently confirmed: "there is little in practice or policy to support the idea that an assertion of jurisdiction . . . in civil proceedings is anything other than an exercise of state regulatory power," which is "restricted by public international rules on jurisdiction."[18] Or, as he wrote for the *Oxford Handbook on Jurisdiction in International Law* after surveying statements by the European Commission and other European states, the "starting premise [is] that the exercise of jurisdiction by states in matters of private law is regulated by the same general constraints which apply in matters of public law—the need, absent exceptional circumstances, for a recognized connection (such as a territorial or nationality-based link) to justify the exercise of jurisdiction."[19]

It's not just international law and foreign relations scholars who believe international law constrains adjudicatory jurisdiction. Civil procedure scholars within the United States have the same understanding. Domestic personal jurisdiction law in the United States, while dictated by the U.S. Constitution, was derived from international law's limits. That was true both at the time personal jurisdiction became first tethered to the Fourteenth Amendment and later as *International Shoe*'s minimum contacts test became the core of modern doctrine.[20] The key debate among civil procedure scholars in the U.S. for decades has been how much sovereignty individual States retained under the U.S. Constitution, and how much domestic doctrine has moved away from international law's constraints to focus more on individual liberty concerns.[21] Periodically scholars have urged the U.S. Supreme Court to pay more attention

---

[17] GARY B. BORN & PETER B. RUTLEDGE, INTERNATIONAL CIVIL LITIGATION IN UNITED STATES COURTS 101 (6th ed. 2018).

[18] Alex Mills, *Rethinking Jurisdiction in International Law*, 84 BRIT. Y.B. INT'L L. 187, 201 (2014).

[19] Alex Mills, *Private Interests and Private Law Regulation in Public International Law*, in OXFORD HANDBOOK ON JURISDICTION IN INTERNATIONAL LAW 331, 337 n.28 (Stephen Allen, Daniel Costelloe, Malgosia Mitzmaurice, Paul Gragl, & Edward Guntrip eds., 2019). For another recent discussion, see RESEARCH HANDBOOK ON INTERNATIONAL LAW AND CYBERSPACE 31–33 (Nicholas Tsagourias & Russell Buchan eds., 2014) (noting argument that public international law does not impose limits on civil cases, but finding it "perverse" for international law to govern criminal but not civil actions, and that a division between criminal and civil jurisdiction would "seem artificial").

[20] Patrick J. Borchers, *Comparing Personal Jurisdiction in the United States and the European Community: Lessons for American Reform*, 40 AM. J. COMP. L. 121, 123 (1992); Roger H. Trangsrud, *The Federal Common Law of Personal Jurisdiction*, 57 GEO. WASH. L. REV. 849, 871–76 (1989); Max Rheinstein, *The Constitutional Bases of Jurisdiction*, 22 U. CHI. L. REV. 775, 796–808 (1955).

[21] For a recent description, see Stephan E. Sachs, *Pennoyer Was Right*, 95 TEX. L. REV. 1249, 1255, 1270–73 (2017) (arguing for a return to jurisdiction's "general- and international-law origins" in U.S. personal jurisdiction).

to these international law limits when deciding cases under the Fourteenth Amendment's Due Process Clause.[22]

This view is neither outdated nor based on older authority. Sarah Cleveland, writing in 2010 about the international law of jurisdiction, explained that "U.S. domestic principles regarding personal jurisdiction have evolved mostly (although not entirely) consistently with modern international law."[23] The "doctrine of minimum contacts [itself] originated in international law."[24] And this is how other nations interpret international law too, often finding that international law informs domestic personal jurisdiction doctrine.[25]

The Fourth Restatement's approach is concerning for another reason. The American Law Institute indicates that the Fourth Restatement intended to set out settled and established law and to steer clear of an upheaval of existing law. The reporters themselves emphasized the caution by which they approached their task.[26] Given that context, even if doubt exists as to whether fundamental structural principles of public international law remain applicable, the best approach would have been to acknowledge the existing majority position. Proclaiming that public international law no longer constrains adjudicatory jurisdiction, without acknowledging the significant literature to the contrary,[27] is out of step with the Fourth Restatement's cautious approach. At the very least, as the ALI

---

[22] Andrew L. Strauss, *Beyond National Law: The Neglected Role of the International Law of Personal Jurisdiction in Domestic Courts*, 36 HARV. INT'L L.J. 373 (1995); cf. Ronan E. Degnan & Mary Kay Kane, *The Exercise of Jurisdiction Over and Enforcement Against Alien Defendants*, 39 HASTINGS L.J. 799, 814–15 (1988) (describing how as "a principle of international law" that sovereignty and territoriality limit jurisdiction internationally).

[23] Sarah H. Cleveland, *Embedded International Law and the Constitution Abroad*, 110 COLUM. L. REV. 225, 246 (2010).

[24] Graham C. Lilly, *Jurisdiction Over Domestic and Alien Defendants*, 69 VA. L. REV. 85, 124 (1998).

[25] For example, Canadian courts may assert jurisdiction over foreign defendants only when a real and substantial connection exists between the forum and the defendant or the subject matter of the dispute. The real and substantial connection test is derived from customary international law. See Club Resorts Ltd v. Van Breda, 2012 SCC 17 (describing the real and substantial connection test as a requirement of private international law); R v. Hape, 2007 SCC 26 (describing how "international law—and in particular the overarching customary principle of sovereign equality—sets the limits of state jurisdiction [including judicial jurisdiction]"); see generally Steve Coughlan, Robert Currie, Hugh Kindred, & Teresa Scassa, *Global Reach, Local Grasp: Constructing Extraterritorial Jurisdiction in the Age of Globalization*, 6 CAN. J.L. & TECH. 29 (2006) (initially prepared as a Report to the Law Commission of Canada) (describing the real and substantial connection test as derived from international law on civil adjudicatory jurisdiction).

[26] Sarah H. Cleveland & Paul B. Stephan, *Introduction: The Roles of the Restatements in U.S. Foreign Relations Law*, in this volume ("Restatements are not meant to be speculative or groundbreaking, but rather distillations of the best of contemporary legal practice in a particular area.").

[27] The literature is evidence of international law and should be addressed for that reason too. See ICJ Statute, art. 38(1)(d) (describing the writing of scholars as a subsidiary means for determining international law); see also The Paquete Habana, 175 U.S. 677, 700 (1900) (looking to scholarly works to determine customary international law).

ADJUDICATORY JURISDICTION AND PUBLIC INTERNATIONAL LAW 309

Council explains: "if a Restatement declines to follow the majority rule, it should say so explicitly and explain why."[28]

## II. The Reporters' Response

While not directly addressing the contrary authority, the reporters to the Fourth Restatement's section on jurisdiction make two principal assertions. First, they push back on the suggestion that the Fourth Restatement is a departure from the ALI's prior understandings. According to the reporters, the Third Restatement's "position was more ambiguous than is commonly appreciated," the Second Restatement didn't address adjudicatory jurisdiction, and the *Principles of Transnational Civil Procedure* are "not on point" because they don't purport to set out international law.[29] Second, and their primary argument, the reporters argue that the Fourth Restatement "fairly reflects customary international law today."[30] According to the reporters, states do not protest the assertion of jurisdiction, and when states confine their court's adjudicatory jurisdictional reaches, they do so without a sense of legal obligation. In many ways, the reporters echo the minority position famously advocated by Michael Akehurst in the early 1970s that "when one examines the practice of states . . . one finds that states claim jurisdiction over all sorts of cases and parties having no real connection with them and that this practice has seldom if ever given rise to diplomatic protests. . . ."[31]

On the first point, the reporters' position of continuity rather than change is difficult to square with the Second and Third Restatements. Andreas Lowenfeld, the key architect of the jurisdictional sections of the Third Restatement, explicitly rejected the idea that the limits of adjudicatory jurisdiction are imposed only as a matter of comity, rather than law.[32] Indeed, one of the purposes of separating out adjudicatory authority from prescriptive and enforcement jurisdiction in the Third Restatement was to better understand international law's limits. It's true that Professor Lowenfeld's approach to determining those limits—using reasonableness as the touchstone for legality—was contested and may no longer

---

[28] AMERICAN LAW INSTITUTE, CAPTURING THE VOICE OF THE AMERICAN LAW INSTITUTE: A HANDBOOK FOR ALI REPORTERS AND THOSE WHO REVIEW THEIR WORK 6 (2015).

[29] William S. Dodge, Anthea Roberts, & Paul Stephan, *Jurisdiction to Adjudicate Under Customary International Law*, OPINIO JURIS (Sept. 11, 2018), available at http://opiniojuris.org/2018/09/11/33646/.

[30] *Id.*

[31] Michael Akehurst, *Jurisdiction in International Law*, 46 BRIT. Y.B. INT'L L. 145, 170 (1973).

[32] ANDREAS F. LOWENFELD, INTERNATIONAL LITIGATION AND THE QUEST FOR REASONABLENESS 47, 80 (1996) (noting that "the subject of judicial jurisdiction is best understood within a framework of international law").

be regarded as the applicable standard.[33] But he did not view reasonableness as mere comity, and the basic premise that public international law constrained state judicial power was unquestioned. As the then-legal adviser of the U.S. State Department explained at the time: "[i]f there is a universally recognized prohibitive rule, it's that a state may not exercise jurisdiction over events or persons unless the state has some genuine link with those persons or events."[34] The reporters themselves acknowledge that the Third Restatement identified at least one practice (tag jurisdiction) as not generally acceptable under international law.[35]

The Second Restatement and the *Principles of Transnational Civil Procedure* also do not support the Fourth Restatement's position. While admittedly the Second Restatement only expressly addressed prescriptive and enforcement jurisdiction, adjudicatory jurisdiction was understood to be encapsulated within and subsidiary to these other forms of jurisdiction. For the Second Restatement, jurisdiction to prescribe referred to the lawmaking process, regardless of whether that process occurred in connection with power exercised by the legislative, executive, or judicial branch. Indeed, many public international law scholars, particularly outside the United States, continue to view adjudicatory jurisdiction as a component of prescriptive or enforcement jurisdiction under public international law. In any case, the Second Restatement did not take the affirmative position, now taken by the Fourth, that adjudicatory jurisdiction is unconstrained and exempt from international law's limits. And while it's true that the *Principles of Transnational Civil Procedure* is not a restatement of international law, those principles set out internationally accepted standards, underscoring that a substantial connection is the generally accepted jurisdictional requirement for international civil legal disputes.[36] The *Principles* are on point because they provide evidence of state practice.

[33] See David B. Massey, *How the American Law Institute Influences Customary International Law: The Reasonableness Requirement of the Restatement of Foreign Relations Law*, 22 YALE J. INT'L L. 419, 423, 428–37 (1997) (noting "numerous commentators" who argue that the reasonableness requirement of the Third Restatement did not reflect customary international law); Cecil J. Olmstead, *Jurisdiction*, 14 YALE J. INT'L L. 468, 472 (1989) (disputing that reasonableness is an international law requirement). For an argument that case-by-case reasonableness analysis is still required, see Buxbaum & Michaels, *supra* note 4, in this volume.

[34] Davis R. Robinson, Speech Before the Association of the Bar of the City of New York (Feb. 14, 1984), in 1981–1988 2 CUMULATIVE DIGEST OF UNITED STATES PRACTICE IN INTERNATIONAL LAW ch. 6, §1 at 1330; see also David H. Small, *Managing Extraterritorial Jurisdictional Problems: The United States Government Approach*, 50 LAW & CONTEMP. PROBS. 283, 292 (1987) (noting that "U.S. government spokesmen identified only one firmly established international law limit—a threshold requirement that a state have a sufficient nexus with the matter to justify an assertion of jurisdiction.").

[35] Dodge et al. *supra* note 29 ("The Restatement (Third) did identify one particular state practice, the exercise of 'tag' jurisdiction based on the service of process to a person with only a transitory presence in the jurisdiction, as 'not generally acceptable under international law.'").

[36] ALI/UNIDROIT, PRINCIPLES OF TRANSNATIONAL CIVIL PROCEDURE, *supra* note 15.

It's their second assertion focused on state practice, however, on which the reporters most rely. Yet the evidence is not as clear as the reporters suggest and certainly not so settled to find that international law concerns can be easily dismissed. As an initial matter, as described earlier, the ALI and UNIDROIT in their *Principles of Transnational Civil Procedure* read state practice differently. So too do the Canadian and Australian courts.[37] Even ignoring this, the selective evidence offered by the reporters—the European Union may have ignored international law's limits in one context, or that states disagree as to whether all exorbitant assertions are violations of international law—show that the limits of international law and its contours are at best contested. It does not prove that no limits exist.[38] Just because some exorbitant bases of jurisdiction may not violate international law, does not mean that all exorbitant bases are lawful.

The reporters' reliance on two purported examples of noncompliance (the Brussels I Regulation and the U.S. use of jurisdiction based on transient presence) is problematic for other reasons. Noncompliance with international law is generally evidence of a violation of law, not evidence of a new custom.[39] When the U.S. Supreme Court found that transient jurisdiction was consistent with U.S. constitutional due process, most found the United States to have adopted a rule in violation of international norms, not that suddenly international law's constraints had disappeared.[40] The reporters also provide no authority for the idea that two examples of noncompliance are sufficient to overturn settled and long-standing structural principles of the international legal system. Nor do they explain how these two examples trump other examples of state practice, such as the Australian and Canadian pronouncements described earlier. There's also reason to believe the European Union would not permit the Brussels I Regulation (Recast) to be interpreted in a way that would violate public international law's

---

[37] *Supra* notes 11–12, 25.

[38] Ralf Michaels, *Is Adjudicatory Jurisdiction a Category of Public International Law?*, OPINIO JURIS (Sept. 20, 2018), available at http://opiniojuris.org/2018/09/20/is-adjudicatory-jurisdiction-a-category-of-public-international-law/.

[39] Military and Paramilitary Activities in and Against Nicaragua (Nicar. v. U.S.), Merits, 1986 ICJ 14, 98, ¶ 186 (June 27) (noting "instances of State conduct inconsistent with a given rule should generally have been treated as breaches of that rule, not as indications of the recognition of a new rule") (https://www.icj-cij.org/files/case-related/70/070-19860627-JUD-01-00-EN.pdf). And even occasional breaches do not necessarily nullify customary international rules. Anthea E. Roberts, *Traditional and Modern Approaches to Customary International Law: A Reconciliation*, 95 AM. J. INT'L L. 757, 789–90 (2001).

[40] Russell J. Weintraub, *An Objective Basis for Rejecting Transient Jurisdiction*, 22 RUTGERS L.J. 611 (1991) (sketching the "relevant civil law, European Economic Community, and international law rejections of transient jurisdiction" over foreigners without other connections); THIRD RESTATEMENT § 421 & reporters' note 5 (1987) ("Jurisdiction based on service of process on one only transitorily present in a state is no longer acceptable under international law if that is the only basis for jurisdiction and the action is question is unrelated to that state")

limits on jurisdiction (i.e., to permit jurisdiction over foreigners absent some genuine connection or link).[41]

The reliance on the lack of recent protests also isn't convincing. There are pragmatic reasons why a state might not lodge protests, even if the state believes a violation of international law has occurred. This is particularly true when readily available alternative arguments exist under national law or under rules regulating prescriptive jurisdiction, when the contours of international law's limits are contested, and when the international law violation can be accounted for at the enforcement stage. Usually a basis for states to refuse to enforce a foreign judgment is when the assertion of jurisdiction by the rendering court violated international law. Also, while relatively rare, states do protest against exorbitant assertions of personal jurisdiction as violating international law.[42] And it's not entirely clear that the numerous foreign state protests over U.S. extraterritorial civil jurisdiction is limited to the prescriptive jurisdiction context.[43] Those protests are perhaps best read as rejecting assertions of state power over people and matters with which the United States has little connection regardless of the form in which that purported overreach takes. Finally, while formal protests may be evidence of *opinio juris*, it's unclear how the absence of protests over another state's possible illegal action can cause long-standing, fundamental structural principles limiting state power—to which there is widespread agreement—to disappear.[44]

The reporters also underscore a problem of a different nature with their approach. In defending their position, the reporters say their review of state

---

[41] Recently, the Court of Justice of the European Union held that the "Right to be Forgotten" under EU law does not require search engines to delist search results on a global basis despite the law having no territorial limits in part because of "the principles of courtesy and non-interference recognised by public international law." Google v. Commission nationale de l'informatique et des libertés (CNIL), Case C-507/17, Sept. 24, 2019, at ¶ 32.

[42] *Id.* ("It may be true that diplomatic protests against the exercise of adjudicatory jurisdiction are rare . . . But they are not nonexistent"); see also BORN & RUTLEDGE, *supra* note 17.

[43] Michaels, *supra* note 38 ("And one might also query whether the numerous protests that have been voiced against judicial proceedings in areas of criminal law, antitrust law, etc., are really neatly confined to the aspect of prescriptive jurisdiction."). For a good example, see Supplemental Brief of the Governments of the Kingdom of the Netherlands and the United Kingdom of Great Britain and Northern Ireland as Amici Curiae in Support of Neither Party at 11–13, Kiobel v. Royal Dutch Petroleum Co., 133 S. Ct. 1659 (2013) (No. 10-1491) (asserting that international law requires "a sufficiently close factual nexus" for any assertion of extraterritorial civil jurisdiction).

[44] Michaels, *supra* note 38 ("But the absence of protest proves only, at best, that existing law complies with limits, not that such limits do not exist."). The International Court of Justice has used the principle of the sovereign equality of states to ascertain customary international law. See, e.g., Military and Paramilitary Activities in and Against Nicaragua (Nicar. v. U.S.), Merits, 1986 I.C.J. Rep. 106, ¶ 202 (June 27) (deducing the principle of nonintervention from the principle of the sovereign equality of states); Jurisdictional Immunities of the State (Ger. v. It.: Greece Intervening), Judgment, 2012 I.C.J. Rep. 99, ¶ 57 (Feb. 3) (finding the right to immunity derived from principles of sovereign equality and "the principle of territorial sovereignty and the jurisdiction which flows from it.").

practice reveals no evidence of "a limit" on adjudicatory authority.[45] That approach to jurisdictional questions, however, is itself controversial. For most public international lawyers, states are not authorized to exercise jurisdiction unless a customary international norm permits it. Cedric Ryngaert has explained the consensus view, which "reflects customary international law" and "has been taken by most States and the majority of doctrine":

> Under this approach, States are *not* authorized to exercise their jurisdiction, unless they can rely on such permissive principles as the territoriality, personality, protective, and universality principles.[46]

Indeed, this is how the Fourth Restatement handles the limits on state power in the prescriptive jurisdiction context.[47]

Accordingly, to reach the Fourth Restatement's conclusion, evidence of state practice and *opinio juris* would be necessary to demonstrate an affirmative permissive rule for states to exercise universal civil jurisdiction. But outside the narrow context of certain recognized international crimes and human rights violations, states do not take the position that universal civil jurisdiction is permitted. Universal civil jurisdiction under international law, to the extent it exists, is limited to a narrow category of cases where "heinous conduct, such as genocide, torture, and crimes against humanity" is implicated.[48] As Ralf Michaels recently noted: "the fact that every existing jurisdictional provision appears to rest on some kind of connection to the forum, however detached, might be more plausibly interpreted as evidence for a state practice and *opinio juris* in favor of some kind of genuine link."[49] Or as Alex Mills also explains:

> The Restatement approach appears to be premised on the outdated assumption that the exercise of jurisdiction is permitted unless a specific prohibition can be identified. . . . It might instead have been asked: is there state practice and *opinio juris* to support the claim that states can exercise adjudicative jurisdiction in the absence of any connection to the dispute. . . .[50]

The Fourth Restatement also represents a step back from the major trends in modern international law. Over the last several decades, international law moved

---

[45] Dodge et al., *supra* note 29.
[46] CEDRIC RYNGAERT, JURISDICTION IN INTERNATIONAL LAW 5, 29 (2d ed. 2015).
[47] FOURTH RESTATEMENT §§ 408–13.
[48] Donald Francis Donovan & Anthea Roberts, *The Emerging Recognition of Universal Civil Jurisdiction*, 100 AM. J. INT'L L. 142 (2006).
[49] Michaels, *supra* note 38.
[50] Mills, *supra* note 19, at 338 n.31.

beyond the old Westphalian notion of near impermeable sovereign power, to focus on the individual and on human rights.[51] That evolution sought for the rule of law to further limit state power: to avoid having sovereignty used as a shield and to constrain aggressive tendencies. Rejecting colonial practices, international law recognized even more sharply the right of states and their citizenry—so long as human rights norms were respected—to be free from foreign oversight or hegemonic expansion.[52] In this context, it's hard to understand how international law permits states to universally adjudicate garden-variety public and private law claims of citizens of other states without limit. At the very least, if the fundamental structural limits of the international system no longer exist, then some explanation much be proffered for why principles of national sovereignty, self-determination, and noninterference no longer apply. The Fourth Restatement provides no explanation for the anomalous result.

Finally, more pragmatic foreign policy considerations render the Fourth Restatement's new approach puzzling. The U.S. Constitution provides separate, more restrictive limitations on judicial power. As a result, the Fourth Restatement's new position is unlikely to change the scope of U.S. courts' adjudicatory authority. But the Fourth Restatement could be influential abroad. Absent self-imposed domestic law limitations, the Fourth Restatement suggests that foreign courts can lawfully exercise jurisdiction over U.S. citizens in all manner of civil cases when no connection to the U.S. defendant exists. This should be concerning if, as many have observed, the legal profession continues to globalize, the competition for forums heats up, and foreign courts become increasingly attractive to litigants.[53]

---

[51] See W. Michael Reisman, *Editorial Comment: Sovereignty and Human Rights in Contemporary International Law*, 84 AM. J. INT'L L. 866, 872 (1990) (describing how human rights shifted international law's focus from protection of sovereigns to protection of people); see also RUTI TEITEL, HUMANITY'S LAW (2011) (describing how the normative foundations of the international legal order has shifted from an emphasis on state security to the security of persons and peoples).

[52] Nico Krisch, *International Law in Times of Hegemony: Unequal Power and the Shaping of the International Legal Order*, 16 EUR. J. INT'L L. 369, 400–404 (2005) (describing the U.S. use of domestic law as a form of hegemonic expansion and withdrawal from international law).

[53] Pamela K. Bookman, *Litigation Isolationism*, 67 STAN. L. REV. 1081, 1108–19 (2015) (describing the growing potential of foreign courts to attract transnational litigation); Donald E. Childress III, *Escaping Federal Law in Transnational Cases: The Brave New World of Transnational Litigation*, 93 N.C. L. REV. 995 (2015) (describing forum competition in transnational cases); Jens Dammann & Henry Hansmann, *Globalizing Commercial Litigation*, 94 CORNELL L. REV. 1, 3 (2008) (encouraging the filing of cases in foreign courts).

## III. Broader Implications

For those not toiling in the details of jurisdiction or international law, one might be tempted to see the Fourth Restatement's new approach as a technicality: a change with only modest impacts. But the Fourth Restatement's pronouncements have far-reaching implications.

First, adjudicatory jurisdiction is likely to take on increased importance as the amount of transnational litigation continues to grow. The limits on state judicial power become particularly important in cases governed by foreign or international law because in those cases international law's constraints on prescriptive jurisdiction, which is focused on legislative action, generally do not apply.[54] In these contexts, adjudicatory jurisdiction becomes the key and possibly only significant limitation on state power. The same is true for cases involving unilateral extraterritorial civil discovery orders. In those cases, adjudicatory jurisdiction is often the only limitation on state power.[55] Also, as the U.S. Supreme Court has read almost no limits into Congress's authority to regulate extraterritorially— so long as it says so clearly—adjudicatory jurisdiction becomes a safeguard to prevent the United States from exceeding enforcement limits imposed by public international law.

Second, the Fourth Restatement's approach is significant for how much it privileges politics over law. Contestation over the limits of jurisdiction previously occurred within a claim of legality. Debates centered on international law's contours with disagreement over what links in different contexts would be necessary for a state to claim jurisdictional competency. So, for example, those urging universal jurisdiction for violation of egregious human rights do not claim that human rights enforcement exists outside of law (that legal limits are inapplicable), but rather that international law has evolved to recognize a jurisdictional assertion less tethered to territoriality in a narrow set of cases. In that context, the debate has been over whether there exists sufficient international consensus on the undesirability of certain activities (and whether the procedural differences between states can be managed), so that states should be lawfully empowered to intervene in the affairs of others to advance global justice goals.[56]

The Fourth Restatement's approach to adjudicatory jurisdiction is fundamentally different. Because it claims that international law imposes no constraint on

---

[54] Prescriptive jurisdiction under the Restatement limits legislative action. THIRD RESTATEMENT § 403(a). On why adjudicatory jurisdiction is the critical limitation when the law that's being applied is derived from international law, see Anthony Colangelo, Kiobel: *Muddling the Distinction Between Prescriptive and Adjudicative Jurisdiction*, 28 MD. J. INT'L L. 65, 68–70 (2013).

[55] See BORN & RUTLEDGE, *supra* note 17, at 968, 997 (describing how U.S. courts are often willing to order broad discovery of evidence located abroad if the court has personal jurisdiction).

[56] For a discussion, see Cedric Ryngaert, *Jurisdiction*, in CONCEPTS FOR INTERNATIONAL LAW 577, 582–84 (Jean d'Aspremont & Sahib Singh eds., 2019).

state power in civil proceedings, it attempts to move judicial exercises of state power entirely outside the realm of law, into the realm of politics. Since international law's purpose is to define the powers of states, the claim that international law says nothing about judicial jurisdiction (outside the issue of immunity) is an attack on the very foundations of that law. It's a stunning change because it doesn't tether what it purports to be a change in the law to substantive global justice goals, but rather tries to exempt an entire form of state power from international law's concern. If adhered to, the Fourth Restatement's approach also leads to a bizarre anomaly. Adjudicatory authority in universal criminal jurisdiction cases involving flagrant human rights abuses—where the claim to universality is presumably the strongest—is constrained under international law with various exhaustion and other limitations, while civil adjudicatory jurisdiction, if the Fourth Restatement is to be believed, would have no limits of any kind.[57]

Finally, the Fourth Restatement's treatment of adjudicatory jurisdiction also reveals a fairly radical view of customary international law and law's evolution. Previously, those advocating for a stricter, more positivistic understanding of *opinio juris* and state practice have done so out of worry that hastily declared custom might only serve the interests of powerful states and undermine international law's legitimacy. Other scholars have sought to detail how custom is a source of law that can respond to global challenges.[58] Both these visions are law-reinforcing. The Fourth Restatement on this front is different because it seeks to use a positivistic approach to customary international law as a way to sidestep long-standing and established legal principles and to remove a key limit on state sovereignty from international law's purview. It may be the first time that purported custom is being used as a way to abdicate law.

## IV.  Conclusion

International law's limits have been amorphous in the adjudicatory jurisdiction area. Regrettably, however, the Fourth Restatement has adopted a position that neither restates existing law nor acknowledges where contestation exists. Its position is not only in tension with fundamental structural principles of our

[57] Anthony Colangelo, *The Legal Limits of Universal Jurisdiction*, 47 VA. J. INT'L L. 149 (2006) (discussing universal adjudicative jurisdiction under international law for a limited set of heinous crimes); PRINCETON UNIV. PROGRAM IN LAW & PUB. AFFAIRS, THE PRINCETON PRINCIPLES ON UNIVERSAL JURISDICTION, princ. 8, pp. 32 & 53 (2001) (Even for universal criminal jurisdiction, the preference is for states with significant links to the acts to adjudicate the matter, when that state is able to provide an effective remedy.).

[58] For an overview, see Roberts, *supra* note 39, at 758–60; see also David P. Fidler, *Challenging the Classical Concept of Custom: Perspectives on the Future of Customary International Law*, 39 GERMAN Y.B. INT'L L. 198 (1996).

international system (principles of nonintervention, sovereign equality, and self-determination, among others), but seems designed to partly eliminate public international law's role in limiting state power to interfere with the affairs of other states.

Engagement over the contours of public international law and how those contours have evolved within the confines of the structural limits of the international system is important. Questions remain on how best to determine the scope of international law's limits in the face of a changing world. The Fourth Restatement's position, however, risks foreclosing that conversation and engagement. The likelihood of it doing so is greater because it carries the ALI's imprimatur, which—as the reporters have asserted elsewhere—seemingly becomes itself an independent reason why the Fourth Restatement must be right.[59] The worry is that judges and scholars alike will cite to it without realizing its heterodoxy. And in that way it becomes a self-fulfilling prophesy. Other nations don't bother objecting to jurisdictional overreach because they realize doing so is futile, and judges, government officials, and practitioners in the United States, who rely on the Fourth Restatement, are led into error. This abstention and practice then serve only to further justify the once novel approach, and public international law is further eroded.[60]

---

[59] Dodge et al., *supra* note 29 (The Fourth Restatement "does not simply reflect the views of the reporters about the content of customary international law governing jurisdiction. It reflects the best judgment of the American Law Institute based on an evaluation of state practice and opinio juris today.").

[60] Pamela Bookman's contribution makes a similar observation. Bookman, *supra* note 4, in this volume ("In the end, I must acknowledge a variation on the Observer Effect: The fact that the Restatement (Fourth) holds that adjudicative jurisdiction is not governed by public international law may itself affect the likelihood of future developments in perceptions of international law limits on adjudicative jurisdiction."); see also Kristina Daugirdas, *The Restatements and the Rule of Law*, in this volume (explaining how the Restatement may influence customary international law). Gary Born describes the broader trend as a marginalization of public and private international law. Gary Born, *International Law in American Courts*, in this volume.

# 14

# International Comity in the Fourth Restatement

## William S. Dodge

In the United States, international comity is the foundation for most doctrines that mediate between the U.S. legal system and those of other nations.[1] Some of these doctrines recognize foreign laws, foreign judgments, and foreign governments as plaintiffs.[2] Others restrain the reach of U.S. law, the jurisdiction of U.S. courts, and in particular the jurisdiction of U.S. courts over foreign governments as defendants.[3]

There have been many definitions of international comity. In *Hilton v. Guyot*, the U.S. Supreme Court unhelpfully characterized comity as "neither a matter of absolute obligation, on the one hand, nor of mere courtesy and good will, upon the other."[4] The Fourth Restatement of Foreign Relations Law more clearly defines international comity in distinction to international law: "International comity reflects deference to foreign states that international law does not mandate."[5] This definition of comity is also consistent with the International Court of Justice's use of the term.[6]

---

[1] See generally William S. Dodge, *International Comity in American Law*, 115 COLUM. L. REV. 2071 (2015).

[2] See, e.g., Banco Nacional de Cuba v. Sabbatino, 376 U.S. 398, 408–09 (1964) ("Under principles of comity governing this country's relations with other nations, sovereign states are allowed to sue in the courts of the United States."); Hilton v. Guyot, 159 U.S. 113, 163 (1895) (noting that enforcement of a "judicial decree . . . depends upon what our greatest jurists have been content to call 'the comity of nations'"); Bank of Augusta v. Earle, 38 U.S. (13 Pet.) 519, 589 (1839) ("[T]he laws of the one [country], will, by the comity of nations, be recognised and executed in another. . . .").

[3] F. Hoffmann-La Roche Ltd. v. Empagran S.A., 542 U.S. 155, 169 (2004) (concluding that "principles of prescriptive comity" limit the geographic scope of U.S. antitrust law); Republic of Austria v. Altmann, 541 U.S. 677, 696 (2004) (characterizing foreign sovereign immunity as a "gesture of comity"); Société Nationale Industrielle Aérospatiale v. U.S. Dist. Court for S. Dist. of Iowa, 482 U.S. 522, 543–44 (1987) (noting that the "concept of international comity" requires "particularized analysis" of discovery requests).

[4] *Hilton*, 159 U.S. at 163–64; see also Dodge, *supra* note 1, at 2074–75 (criticizing *Hilton*'s definition of comity).

[5] FOURTH RESTATEMENT § 401 cmt. *a*.

[6] See Jurisdictional Immunities of the State (Ger. v. It.: Greece intervening), Judgment, 2012 I.C.J. Rep. 99, ¶ 53 (Feb. 3) ("both Parties agree that immunity is governed by international law and is not a mere matter of comity"); see also Arrest Warrant of 11 April 2000 (Dem. Rep. Congo v. Bel.), Judgment, 2002 I.C.J. Rep. 3, 137, ¶ 23 (Feb. 14) (dissenting opinion by Van Den Wyngaert, J.) ("Belgium may have acted contrary to international comity, but has not infringed international

William S. Dodge, *International Comity in the Fourth Restatement* In: *The Restatement and Beyond*. Edited by: Paul B. Stephan and Sarah H. Cleveland, Oxford University Press (2020). © Oxford University Press.
DOI: 10.1093/oso/9780197533154.003.0015

International comity played a minor role in the Third Restatement of Foreign Relations Law, and the distinction between international comity and international law helps to explain why.[7] The Third Restatement recognized comity as the basis for U.S. rules governing the recognition and enforcement of foreign judgments,[8] but generally it attempted to show that rules originating in comity had developed into customary international law. Some of these attempts were criticized as unsupported by state practice and *opinio juris*. The Fourth Restatement takes a more restrained approach to restating rules of customary international law and correspondingly embraces international comity as a way of distinguishing limits on jurisdiction that are required by international law from limits on jurisdiction that are required only by domestic law.

This chapter compares the treatment of international comity in the Third and Fourth Restatements. Section I describes the Third Restatement's emphasis on international law over international comity. Section II describes the Fourth Restatement's more cautious approach to international law and its use of comity to characterize rules of U.S. domestic law that international law does not require. Section III considers some of the implications of looking at doctrines of foreign relations law through an international-comity lens.

## I. Comity in the Third Restatement

The Third Restatement defined "the foreign relations law of the United States" to include both "international law as it applies to the United States" and also "domestic law that has substantial significance for the foreign relations of the United States or has other substantial international consequences."[9] But its emphasis was on restating international law. Indeed, the Third Restatement adopted a stylistic convention that "normative statements in this Restatement set forth rules or principles of international law" unless specifically designated "Law of the United States."[10] This emphasis on restating international law combined with a willingness to characterize rules as customary international law even when they did not meet the Third Restatement's own test of state practice and *opinio juris*.[11]

---

law."); Fisheries Jurisdiction (U.K. v. Ice.), Judgment, 1974 I.C.J. Rep. 3, 53, 58 (July 25) (separate opinion of Dillard, J.) ("[I]n practice States accord deference to the 12-mile limit as a matter of legal obligation and not merely as a matter of reciprocal tolerance or comity.").

[7] The Third Restatement also recognized this distinction. See THIRD RESTATEMENT § 101 cmt. *e*.
[8] *Id.* § 481 reporters' note 1 (quoting *Hilton*).
[9] *Id.* § 1.
[10] *Id.* introduction.
[11] *Id.* § 102(2) ("Customary international law results from a general and consistent practice of states followed by them from a sense of legal obligation.").

As former State Department Legal Adviser Monroe Leigh observed at the time, the Third Restatement was "a bit too prone . . . to finding new customary international law."[12]

The most famous example was Section 403, which called for case-by-case determination of whether the exercise of jurisdiction to prescribe was reasonable.[13] The Third Restatement specifically noted that, while some courts in the United States had "applied the principle of reasonableness as a requirement of comity," Section 403 "states the principle of reasonableness as a rule of international law."[14] But the Restatement cited little state practice to support this rule beyond the practice of U.S. courts, which it acknowledged had sought to restrain the extraterritorial application of U.S. law as a matter of comity rather than legal obligation. As one observer noted, "it seems implausible that section 403 rises to the level of . . . having 'emerged as a principle of international law.' "[15]

Much the same thing happened with jurisdiction to adjudicate, which the Third Restatement recognized as a category separate from jurisdiction to prescribe and jurisdiction to enforce.[16] It asserted that "[t]he exercise of jurisdiction by courts of one state that affects interests of other states is now generally considered as coming within the domain of customary international law and international agreement."[17] But again, almost all the state practice cited was that of U.S. courts, and there was no discussion of *opinio juris*.[18] The bases for personal jurisdiction listed in Section 421(2) looked remarkably like a summary of the U.S. Supreme Court's due process decisions.[19] The Third Restatement also addressed service of process and the discovery of evidence, focusing on the rules set forth in the relevant Hague Conventions and appending discussion of U.S. domestic rules as "Law of the United States."[20] But topics of adjudicative jurisdiction for

---

[12] *The Restatement of Foreign Relations Law of the United States, Revised: How Were the Controversies Resolved?* 81 AM. SOC. INT'L L. PROC. 180, 192 (1987) (remarks of Monroe Leigh).

[13] THIRD RESTATEMENT § 403.

[14] *Id.* § 403 cmt. *a*; see also *id.* pt. IV, intro. note ("Increasingly, . . . these [jurisdictional] rules, notably the principle of reasonableness (§§ 403, 421, 431), have been followed by other states and their courts and by international tribunals, and have emerged as principles of customary law.").

[15] Cecil J. Olmstead, *Jurisdiction*, 14 YALE J. INT'L L. 468, 472 (1989) (quoting THIRD RESTATEMENT § 403 cmt. *a*); see also Davis R. Robinson, *Conflicts of Jurisdiction and the Draft Restatement*, 15 LAW & POL'Y INT'L BUS. 1147 (1983) ("Section 403, as currently drafted, does not accurately reflect the state of international law.").

[16] See THIRD RESTATEMENT § 401 (identifying three categories of jurisdiction).

[17] *Id.* pt. IV, ch. 2, intro. note.

[18] See *id.* § 421 reporters' note 1 (additionally citing U.K. law and the Brussels Convention).

[19] The Third Restatement observed that "[t]he modern concepts of jurisdiction to adjudicate under international law are similar to those developed under the due process clause of the United States Constitution." *Id.*

[20] See *id.* § 471 (discussing Hague Service Convention); *id.* § 472 (discussing U.S. rules of service); *id.* § 473 (discussing Hague Evidence Convention); *id.* § 474 (discussing U.S. rules of discovery).

which the U.S. rule had no international-law counterpart—like subject matter jurisdiction and *forum non conveniens*—tended to be ignored.[21]

The Third Restatement's chapter on foreign-state immunity began with a restatement of the restrictive theory under customary international law.[22] The sections discussing the various kinds of suits that are permitted against foreign states each began with a statement of customary international law, followed by the details of U.S. law codified in the Foreign Sovereign Immunities Act.[23] With respect to the act of state doctrine, the Restatement acknowledged *Sabbatino's* statement that the doctrine was not required by international law[24] but still observed that it "is related in spirit to the rules of international law that accord to foreign sovereigns large immunity from adjudication in domestic courts."[25] The *Restatement* also set forth the doctrine of foreign-state compulsion as a rule of international law, giving preference to the law of the state in which the act in question was to be carried out.[26] All of the state practice cited in support of the rule on foreign-state compulsion came from the United States, however, and nowhere did the Restatement discuss whether U.S. courts had deferred to foreign law out of a sense of legal obligation.[27]

The Third Restatement's focus on international law left little room for international comity, which it expressly distinguished from international law.[28] Comity was cited as the basis for the Restatement's rules only in the chapter on foreign judgments,[29] where it acknowledged that there were no rules of customary international law to apply.[30]

---

[21] An exception was Section 422(2), which restated the U.S. constitutional requirement that a criminal defendant be present at the time his trial begins.

[22] See THIRD RESTATEMENT § 451 ("Under international law, a state or state instrumentality is immune from the jurisdiction of the courts of another state, except with respect to claims arising out of activities of the kind that may be carried on by private persons.").

[23] See, e.g., *id.* § 453 (commercial activities); *id.* § 454 (torts); see also *id.* pt. IV, ch. 5, intro. note ("Each section contains first a statement of the international law rule, then more specific rules applicable by statute or case law in the United States.").

[24] *Id.* § 443 cmt. *a*; see Banco Nacional de Cuba v. Sabbatino, 376 U.S. 398, 421 (1964) ("That international law does not require application of the doctrine is evidenced by the practice of nations.").

[25] THIRD RESTATEMENT § 443 cmt. *a*.

[26] *Id.* § 441; see also *id.* pt. IV, ch. 4, intro. note ("Exercises of jurisdiction by more than one state sometimes result in conflicting mandates to the same person, so that the regulation of one state compels the person to violate the mandate of another state. International law has developed principles to reduce the severity of the dilemma for affected persons."). A separate section restated the U.S. law on compulsion in the context of discovery orders. See *id.* § 442.

[27] See *id.* § 441 reporters' notes 1–5.

[28] See *id.* § 101 cmt. *e*.

[29] See *id.* § 481 reporters' note 1 (noting that *Hilton* "treated the enforceability of foreign country judgments as a matter of the 'comity of nations'").

[30] See *id.* pt. IV, ch. 8, intro. note ("[T]here are no agreed principles governing recognition and enforcement of foreign judgments, except that no state recognizes or enforces the judgment of another state rendered without jurisdiction over the judgment debtor.").

The Third Restatement's avoidance of comity seems to have reflected not just its emphasis of international law but also the sense of its reporters that comity was the antithesis of legal obligation. Professor Andreas Lowenfeld, the associate reporter responsible for the Third Restatement's provisions on jurisdiction, later explained: "The Restatement avoids the word 'comity' except for cross-references, because the reporters believed that comity carries too much of the idea of discretion or even political judgment, as contrasted with the principle of reasonableness, which is conceived of in terms of legal obligation."[31] It is true, of course, that rules based on international comity do not reflect an *international* legal obligation. But such rules certainly may reflect a *domestic* legal obligation. International comity is not synonymous with discretion and may serve as the basis for binding rules of domestic law.

The Third Restatement's emphasis of international law at the expense of international comity did not fare well in the courts of the United States. The Supreme Court refused to apply Section 403's reasonableness analysis in *Hartford Fire*,[32] and subsequently rejected case-by-case balancing in *Empagran* on the ground that it was "too complex to prove workable."[33] To determine the geographic scope of federal statutes, the Supreme Court instead relied primarily on a canon of statutory interpretation known as the presumption against extraterritoriality,[34] which the Third Restatement had not addressed.[35] Moreover, the Court repeatedly discussed questions of geographic scope in terms of comity rather than international law.[36]

---

[31] Andreas F. Lowenfeld, *Conflict, Balancing of Interests, and the Exercise of Jurisdiction to Prescribe: Reflections on the Insurance Antitrust Case*, 89 AM. J. INT'L L. 42, 52 n.50 (1995); see also Andreas F. Lowenfeld, *Antitrust, Interest Analysis, and the New Conflict of Laws*, 95 HARV. L. REV. 1976, 1984 (1982) (reviewing JAMES R. ATWOOD & KINGMAN BREWSTER, ANTITRUST AND AMERICAN BUSINESS ABROAD (2d ed. 1981) ("I think the authors' reliance on comity hurts the effort to build on *Timberlane, Mannington Mills*, and the two Restatements in order to persuade the legal profession both in the United States and abroad that the values that the authors share with these sources are the stuff of obligation.").
[32] See Hartford Fire Ins. Co. v. California, 509 U.S. 764, 797–99 (1993) (refusing to dismiss in the absence of a "true conflict" between U.S. and foreign law).
[33] F. Hoffman-La Roche Ltd. v. Empagran S.A., 542 U.S. 155, 168 (2004).
[34] See, e.g., RJR Nabisco, Inc. v. European Community, 136 S. Ct. 2090 (2016); Morrison v. National Australia Bank Ltd., 561 U.S. 247 (2010); EEOC v. Arabian American Oil Co. (Aramco), 499 U.S. 244 (1991).
[35] It made sense for the Third Restatement not to restate the presumption against extraterritoriality in 1986, since the Supreme Court had not applied the presumption since *Foley Bros. v. Filardo*, 336 U.S. 281 (1949). For an account of the presumption's history, see William S. Dodge, *The New Presumption Against Extraterritoriality*, 133 HARV. L. REV. 1582 (2020).
[36] See, e.g., *Empagran*, 542 U.S. at 169 (relying on "principles of prescriptive comity" to limit the reach of U.S. antitrust law); *Hartford Fire*, 509 U.S. at 797–99 (considering whether to dismiss antitrust claims "on grounds of international comity"). Dissenting in *Hartford Fire*, Justice Scalia argued that the Sherman Act should be interpreted in light of customary international law and relied on Section 403 for the relevant principles. See *Hartford Fire*, 509 U.S. at 818–19 (Scalia, J., dissenting). Justice Scalia later backed away from his uncharacteristic embrace of balancing in *Hartford Fire*, arguing that "fine tuning" the extraterritorial reach of statues "through the process of case by case

In the area of personal jurisdiction, the Supreme Court unsurprisingly did not abandon its reliance on due process and embrace international law in its stead.[37] But when the Court in *Daimler* decided to limit general jurisdiction to the forum of the defendant's domicile, it did turn to "international comity" to reinforce that decision.[38] In the area of state immunity, the Supreme Court has made occasional references to international law.[39] But it has repeatedly characterized foreign sovereign immunity as a "gesture of comity."[40] The Court has invoked international comity in other contexts as well—from the interpretation of foreign laws for use in U.S. courts[41] to the discovery of evidence in the United States for use in foreign courts.[42]

## II. Comity in the Fourth Restatement

The Fourth Restatement applies essentially the same test for customary international law that the Third Restatement had adopted.[43] But the Fourth Restatement

---

adjudication is a recipe for endless litigation and confusion." Spector v. Norwegian Cruise Ship Line Ltd., 545 U.S. 119, 158 (2005) (Scalia, J., dissenting).

[37] Three of the five significant personal jurisdiction cases the Supreme Court has decided since 2011 have involved foreign defendants. See William S. Dodge & Scott Dodson, *Personal Jurisdiction and Aliens*, 116 MICH. L. REV. 1205, 1212–20 (2018) (discussing cases).

[38] Daimler AG v. Bauman, 571 U.S. 117, 141 (2014).

[39] See, e.g., Bolivarian Republic of Venezuela v. Helmerich & Payne Int'l Drilling Co., 137 S. Ct. 1312, 1319 (2017) ("The [Foreign Sovereign Immunities] Act for the most part embodies basic principles of international law long followed both in the United States and elsewhere."); Permanent Mission of India to the United Nations v. City of New York, 551 U.S. 193, 199 (2007) (noting that one of the Foreign Sovereign Immunity Act's purposes was the "codification of international law at the time of the FSIA's enactment").

[40] Dole Food Co. v. Patrickson, 538 U.S. 468, 479 (2003); see also Republic of Argentina v. NML Capital, Ltd., 573 U.S. 134, 140 (2014) ("Foreign sovereign immunity is and always has been, 'a matter of grace and comity on the part of the United States . . . .'" (quoting Verlinden B.V. v. Central Bank of Nigeria, 461 U.S. 480, 486 (1983))); Republic of the Philippines v. Pimentel, 553 U.S. 851, 866 (2008) ("Giving full effect to sovereign immunity promotes the comity interests that have contributed to the development of the immunity doctrine."); Republic of Austria v. Altmann, 541 U.S. 677, 696 (2004) ("[Foreign sovereign] immunity reflects current political realities and relationships, and aims to give foreign states and their instrumentalities some present 'protection from the inconvenience of suit as a gesture of comity.'" (quoting Dole Food, 538 U.S. at 479)).

[41] See Animal Sci. Products, Inc. v. Hebei Welcome Pharm. Co. Ltd., 138 S. Ct. 1865, 1873 (2018) ("In the spirit of 'international comity,' a federal court should carefully consider a foreign states views about the meaning of its own laws." (quoting Société Nationale Industrielle Aérospatiale v. U.S. Dist. Court for S. Dist. of Iowa, 482 U.S. 522, 543 (1987))).

[42] Intel Corp. v. Advanced Micro Devices, Inc., 542 U.S. 241, 261 (2004) (noting that "comity and parity concerns may be important as touchstones for a district court's exercise of discretion" under 28 U.S.C. § 1782).

[43] Compare FOURTH RESTATEMENT § 402 cmt. *b* ("Customary international law results from a general and consistent practice of states followed out of a sense of legal right or obligation."), with THIRD RESTATEMENT § 102(2) ("Customary international law results from a general and consistent practice of states followed by them from a sense of legal obligation.").

does not characterize a rule as required by customary international law unless that rule is supported by state practice and *opinio juris*. As a result, the balance in the Fourth Restatement shifted significantly toward restating U.S. domestic law. International comity became useful way to describe domestic rules of restraint and recognition that international law did not require. As the Fourth Restatement explains, "International comity reflects deference to foreign states that international law does not mandate."[44]

The Fourth Restatement does restate the customary international law governing jurisdiction to prescribe at some length. Section 407 states the basic requirement of a "genuine connection" between the subject of the regulation and the state seeking to regulate,[45] while Sections 408–413 cover the traditional bases of territory, effects, active personality, passive personality, the protective principle, and universal jurisdiction.[46] The sections on active personality, passive personality, and universal jurisdiction each use international comity to describe limits on the exercise of prescriptive jurisdiction that are commonly observed but understood not to be required by customary international law.[47]

On the question of concurrent prescriptive jurisdiction, the Fourth Restatement notes that "[i]nternational law recognizes no hierarchy of bases of prescriptive jurisdiction and contains no rules for assigning priority to competing jurisdictional claims."[48] With respect to old Section 403, the new Restatement concludes that "state practice does not support a requirement of case-by-case balancing to establish reasonableness as a matter of international law," citing three cases decided after 1987—two by the U.S. Supreme Court and one by the Court of Justice of the European Union.[49] Instead, the Fourth Restatement notes, "[s]tates have developed domestic-law rules for reducing the likelihood of actual or potential instances of concurrent prescriptive jurisdiction as a matter of international comity."[50]

The new Restatement's section discussing U.S. practice with respect to prescriptive jurisdiction notes that "the United States takes account of the legitimate

---

[44] FOURTH RESTATEMENT § 401 cmt. *a*.

[45] *Id.* § 407.

[46] See *id.* §§ 408–413.

[47] See *id.* § 410 cmt. *d* & reporters' note 4 (noting common limits on active personality jurisdiction); *id.* § 411 cmt. *b* & reporters' note 2 (noting common limits on passive personality jurisdiction); *id.* § 413 cmt. *e* & reporters' note 5 (noting common limits on universal jurisdiction); see also *id.* § 407 cmt. *e* ("States often adopt such limits to promote international comity, but international law does not require them to do so.").

[48] *Id.* § 407 cmt. *d*.

[49] *Id.* § 407 reporters' note 3. Professors Hannah Buxbaum and Ralf Michaels argue that the Fourth Restatement should have included a case-by-case reasonableness test, but they do not argue that such a test is required by customary international law. See Hannah Buxbaum & Ralf Michaels, *Reasonableness as a Limitation on the Extraterritorial Application of U.S. Law: From 403 to 405 (via 404)*, in this volume.

[50] *Id.* § 407 reporters' note 4.

interests of other nations as a matter of prescriptive comity."[51] The reporters' notes give examples of prescriptive comity by Congress, the executive branch, and the courts.[52] Three doctrine of prescriptive comity deserve particular mention. First, the Fourth Restatement addresses the presumption against extraterritoriality, which has been the Supreme Court's primary tool for determining the geographic scope of federal statutes since 1991.[53] Second, the Restatement articulates a principle of reasonableness based on the *Empagran* decision that allows courts to supplement the presumption with other limitations "[a]s a matter of prescriptive comity."[54] Third, the Restatement sets forth a doctrine of foreign-state compulsion that allows courts in some instances to excuse violations of U.S. law if the violations are compelled by foreign law.[55] The new Restatement specifically departs from its predecessor by noting that the doctrine of foreign-state compulsion is not required by international law but instead "reflects the practice of states in the interests of comity."[56]

The Fourth Restatement also differs from the Third Restatement in its treatment of jurisdiction to adjudicate. The old Restatement had asserted that adjudicative jurisdiction "is now generally considered as coming within the domain of customary international law."[57] But the new Restatement concludes that, "[w]ith the significant exception of various forms of immunity, modern customary international law generally does not impose limits on jurisdiction to adjudicate."[58]

---

[51] *Id.* § 402(2).

[52] *Id.* § 402 reporters' note 3.

[53] *Id.* § 404.

[54] *Id.* § 405. The principle is a limited one and should not be confused with the reasonableness analysis of old Section 403. As the comments explain, "[r]easonableness is a principle of statutory interpretation and not a discretionary judicial authority to decline to apply federal law." *Id.* § 405 cmt. *a.* The new Restatement's principle of reasonableness thus operates provision by provision, not case by case. See William S. Dodge, *Reasonableness in the Restatement (Fourth) of Foreign Relations Law*, 55 WILLAMETTE L. REV. 521 (2019); see also Buxbaum & Michaels, *supra* note 49, at 288 ("Whereas the old § 403 required a case-by-case analysis of the requirements of reasonableness in view of concrete conflict with foreign law, the Fourth Restatement operates only 'provision by provision' and not 'case by case.'").

Professors Buxbaum and Michaels argue that U.S. cases support a case-by-case approach to reasonableness. While acknowledging contrary language in the Supreme Court's decisions, they contend that the Court has not rejected case-by-case reasonableness as a general matter, and they point to lower court decisions continuing to follow a case-by-case approach, principally in the areas of trademark law, bankruptcy, and securities regulation. See *id.* The Fourth Restatement acknowledges lower court decisions in each of these areas. See FOURTH RESTATEMENT § 405 reporters' note 4. But it concludes that these decisions do not support a case-by-case reasonableness test that is applicable to all statutes. See *id.* § 405 cmt. *d* ("Courts have construed statutory provisions to include a variety of other comity limitations depending on the text, history, and purpose of the particular provision.").

[55] FOURTH RESTATEMENT § 442. The comments explain that the doctrine is a rule of statutory interpretation and that the scope of a court's discretion depends "on the text, structure, and history of the law in question." *Id.* § 442 cmt. *d.*

[56] *Id.* § 442 reporters' note 10.

[57] THIRD RESTATEMENT pt. IV, ch. 2, intro. note.

[58] FOURTH RESTATEMENT pt. IV, ch. 2, intro. note. Dean Austen Parrish disagrees with this conclusion. See Austen Parrish, *Adjudicatory Jurisdiction and Public International Law: The Fourth Restatement's New Approach*, in this volume. The reporters for the jurisdictional provisions of the

Both volumes note that certain bases of personal jurisdiction are considered exorbitant.[59] But the Fourth Restatement observes that the refusal to enforce a foreign judgment rendered on such a basis of personal jurisdiction "is not necessarily evidence that the exercise of personal jurisdiction violates customary international law."[60] Specifically, it notes that although the European Union has prohibited its member states from exercising personal jurisdiction on exorbitant bases over defendants from other member states, it has expressly authorized the exercise of personal jurisdiction on the same bases over defendants from third countries.[61] Such state practice seems inconsistent with the proposition that exorbitant bases of personal jurisdiction violate customary international law.[62]

Without customary international law to restate, the Fourth Restatement's provisions on jurisdiction to adjudicate in civil cases focus on rules of U.S. domestic law governing subject matter jurisdiction, personal jurisdiction, service of process, *forum non conveniens*, antisuit injunctions, and discovery of evidence, while also incorporating treaties like the Hague Service Convention and the Hague Evidence Convention where appropriate.[63] Some of these rules—like subject matter jurisdiction and *forum non conveniens*—are highly relevant to international litigation but were not covered in the Third Restatement.[64] Some of the Fourth Restatement's provisions on adjudicative jurisdiction expressly mention international comity.[65] But the new Restatement had less need to refer to

Fourth Restatement responded to an earlier version of this critique. See William S. Dodge, Anthea Roberts, & Paul B. Stephan, *Jurisdiction to Adjudicate Under Customary International Law*, Opinio Juris (Sept. 11, 2018), available at http://opiniojuris.org/2018/09/11/33646/. We noted there that "[t]he rules of customary international law depend on state practice and *opinio juris* with respect to each category of jurisdiction." *Id.* What is still missing from Dean Parrish's analysis is an explanation of how state practice and *opinio juris* support limits on jurisdiction to adjudicate as a matter of customary international law.

[59]  See Fourth Restatement § 422 reporters' note 1; Third Restatement pt. IV, ch. 2, intro. note.
[60]  Fourth Restatement § 422 reporters' note 1.
[61]  See *id.*; see also Regulation (EU) No. 1215/2012 of the European Parliament and of the Council of 12 December 2012 on Jurisdiction and the Recognition and Enforcement of Judgments in Civil and Commercial Matters (Recast) art. 5(2), 2012 O.J. (L 351) 1 (prohibiting exorbitant bases of personal jurisdiction with respect to defendants from other member states); *id.* art. 6(2) (authorizing exorbitant bases of personal jurisdiction with respect to defendants from other countries).
[62]  Professor Pamela Bookman considers what future developments might shape the customary international law governing jurisdiction to adjudicate. See Pamela K. Bookman, *Toward the Fifth Restatement of U.S. Foreign Relations Law: The Future of Adjudicative Jurisdiction under Public International Law*, in this volume. She rightly notes that state objections to future exercises of adjudicative jurisdiction "will not be sufficient if they do not tie themselves to an objection on the basis of international law." *Id.* at 353.
[63]  See Fourth Restatement §§ 421–426.
[64]  See *supra* note 21 and accompanying text.
[65]  See Fourth Restatement § 425 reporters' note 3 ("Courts in the United States have admonished judges considering whether to issue an antisuit injunction to use the remedy sparingly and to exercise great care and restraint in light of principles of comity."); *id.* § 426 cmt. *a* ("Decisions about the scope and scale of production orders are entrusted to the court's discretion, which should

comity in the context of jurisdiction to adjudicate simply because it had less need to distinguish international comity from international law.

The one area in which customary international law clearly does limit jurisdiction to adjudicate is the immunity of certain defendants from suit in the courts of third countries.[66] The Fourth Restatement's chapter on state immunity begins with the statement that "[u]nder international law and the law of the United States, a state is immune from the jurisdiction of the courts of another state, subject to certain exceptions."[67] But the new Restatement's emphasis is clearly on the domestic law of the United States.[68] As the chapter on state immunity explains, the Foreign Sovereign Immunities Act (FSIA) "governs the immunity of foreign states from the jurisdiction of State and federal courts in the United States," and "customary international law on the jurisdictional immunity of foreign states is therefore not directly applicable in courts in the United States."[69] Although the new Restatement's chapter on state immunity rarely mention comity directly,[70] it does note that "[a] state may choose to confer more extensive immunity than is required" under international law.[71] U.S. rules of state immunity that go beyond what international law requires obviously meet the Restatement's definition of international comity.[72]

As just discussed, the Fourth Restatement addresses many rules of U.S. domestic law in which international comity operates as a principle of restraint, restraining the reach of U.S. laws, the jurisdiction of U.S. courts, and in particular the jurisdiction of U.S. courts over foreign states as defendants.[73] But the new Restatement also restates rules of U.S. domestic law in which international

---

be exercised in light of proportionality and international comity when the information is located abroad.").

[66] See, e.g., Jurisdictional Immunities of the State (Ger. v. It.: Greece intervening), Judgment, 2012 I.C.J. Rep. 99, ¶ 78 (Feb. 3) (concluding that customary international law "require[s] that a State be accorded immunity in proceedings for torts allegedly committed on the territory of another State by its armed forces and other organs of the State in the course of conducting an armed conflict").

[67] FOURTH RESTATEMENT § 451.

[68] See id. pt. IV, ch. 5, intro. note ("Except as specifically noted, the Sections in this Chapter restate the domestic law of the United States governing state immunity rather than international law."). A few of the sections expressly restate customary international law. See id. § 453(6) (waiver of immunity); id. § 454(3) (commercial activities); id. § 457(2) (noncommercial tort).

[69] Id. § 451 cmt. c.

[70] But see id. § 462 ("Trial courts exercise their discretion over discovery to protect the interests of foreign sovereigns and to promote international comity.").

[71] Id. § 451 cmt. a; see also Jurisdictional Immunities of the State (Ger. v. It.: Greece intervening), Judgment, 2012 I.C.J. Rep. 99, ¶ 55 (Feb. 3) (noting that "States sometimes decide to accord an immunity more extensive than that required by international law" but cautioning that "the grant of immunity in such a case is not accompanied by the requisite opinio juris and therefore sheds no light upon [customary international law]").

[72] See id. § 401 cmt. a ("International comity reflects deference to foreign states that international law does not mandate.").

[73] See supra notes 47–72 and accompanying text.

comity operates as a principle of recognition.[74] Section 441 restates the act of state doctrine, requiring courts in the United States to recognize "an official act of a foreign sovereign performed within its own territory."[75] Whereas the Third Restatement had noted the act of state doctrine's status as U.S. domestic law,[76] the Fourth Restatement expressly characterizes it as a doctrine of "prescriptive comity."[77] Finally, the new Restatement sets forth rules for the recognition and enforcement of foreign judgments.[78] Because "[c]ustomary international law imposes no obligation on states to give effect to the judgments of other states," the Restatement notes that the United States "recognizes and enforces foreign judgments out of comity rather than because of an international legal obligation to do so."[79]

The prominence of international comity in the Fourth Restatement reflects its caution in restating rules of international law and its corresponding emphasis on restating rules of U.S. domestic law. The reporters of the new Restatement relied on the concept of international comity to distinguish rules that are not required by international law from rules that are.

## III.  Foreign Relations Law through a Comity Lens

The reporters of the Third Restatement worried that the concept of comity inevitably carried with it the idea of discretion and political judgment.[80] But a review of the international-comity doctrines covered by the Fourth Restatement shows that such concern is misplaced.

Certainly some comity doctrines, like *forum non conveniens*, give U.S. courts considerable discretion.[81] But others operate as more clear-cut rules. The act of state doctrine does not give courts discretion to dismiss any case that may embarrass a foreign government.[82] Rather it "directs a court in the United States to

---

[74] See Dodge, *supra* note 1, at 2078–79 (explaining the distinction between restraint and recognition).

[75] FOURTH RESTATEMENT § 441.

[76] See *supra* note 24 and accompanying text.

[77] FOURTH RESTATEMENT pt. IV, ch. 4, intro. note; see also *id.* § 441 cmt. *a* (noting that the "act of state doctrine . . . reflect[s] considerations of international comity").

[78] See *id.* §§ 481–490. The recognition and enforcement of foreign judgments in the United States are generally governed by State law. *Id.* § 481 cmt. *a*. The Fourth Restatement generally tracks the provisions of two Uniform Acts that have been adopted in the majority of States.

[79] *Id.* pt. IV, ch. 8, intro. note (citing Hilton v. Guyot, 159 U.S. 113 (1895)).

[80] See *supra* note 31.

[81] See Piper Aircraft Co. v. Reyno, 454 U.S. 235, 257 (1981) ("The *forum non conveniens* determination is committed to the sound discretion of the trial court."); FOURTH RESTATEMENT § 424 cmt. *h* (discussing the discretion of the trial court).

[82] The Supreme Court expressly rejected such a version of the doctrine in *W.S. Kirkpatrick & Co. v. Envtl. Tectonics Corp., Int'l*, 493 U.S. 400, 409 (1990); see also FOURTH RESTATEMENT § 441 reporters' note 1 (discussing *Kirkpatrick*).

treat an official act of a foreign sovereign as conclusive," and it "bars a court from questioning the validity of the foreign act on the ground that it did not comply with that sovereign's own legal requirements, international law, or U.S. law or policy."[83] The rules codified in the FSIA establish a "comprehensive framework" for state immunity determinations, and U.S. courts lack discretion to grant immunity not conferred by the act.[84] Similarly, the rules laid down in the two Uniform Acts that most U.S. States have adopted to govern the recognition and enforcement of foreign judgments leave little room for judicial discretion.[85] As the Fourth Restatement notes, even those grounds for nonrecognition that are commonly called "discretionary" are treated as mandatory in practice.[86]

In fact, the comity-based interpretive rules that the Fourth Restatement sets forth for determining the geographic scope of federal statutes give courts considerably less discretion than the case-by-case reasonableness approach of the Third Restatement. The presumption against extraterritoriality grants courts some flexibility in determining when the presumption has been rebutted[87] and whether the application of a statute should be considered domestic or extraterritorial.[88] But once the geographic scope of a provision has been determined and a test has been developed, courts lack case-by-case discretion to refuse to apply U.S. law based on other factors. The principle of reasonableness in interpretation allows courts to supplement the presumption with additional limitations "as a matter of "prescriptive comity."[89] But the Restatement emphasizes that "[r]easonableness is a principle of statutory interpretation and not a discretionary judicial authority to decline to apply federal law."[90] Under these interpretive rules, courts

---

[83] FOURTH RESTATEMENT § 441 cmt. a.

[84] Republic of Argentina v. NML Capital, Ltd., 573 U.S. 134, 141 (2014); see also FOURTH RESTATEMENT § 455 reporters' note 11 (criticizing lower court decisions that imposed an exhaustion requirement for expropriation claims brought under the FSIA).

[85] Uniform Foreign-Country Money Judgments Recognition Act (2005); Uniform Foreign Money-Judgments Recognition Act (1962).

[86] FOURTH RESTATEMENT § 484 cmt. b ("When one of the grounds stated in § 484(a)–(h) clearly applies, however, a court in the United States will refuse to recognize the foreign judgment, unless it finds that the problem should have been corrected in the foreign proceeding.").

[87] See id. § 404 cmt. b ("The presumption is not a clear-statement rule, and a court will examine all evidence of congressional intent to determine if the presumption has been overcome."); see, e.g., RJR Nabisco, Inc. v. European Community, 136 S. Ct. 2090, 2103 (2016) (finding presumption rebutted by the structure of the statute).

[88] FOURTH RESTATEMENT § 404 cmt. c ("If the presumption against extraterritoriality has not been rebutted, a court will determine if application of the provision would be domestic or extraterritorial by looking to the focus of the provision, for example, on conduct, transactions, or injuries. If whatever is the focus of the provision occurred in the United States, then application of the provision is considered domestic and is permitted."); see, e.g., Morrison v. Nat'l Australia Bank Ltd., 561 U.S. 247, 266 (2010) (finding that the focus of Exchange Act is on the transaction not the fraud). The current presumption against extraterritoriality is more flexible than the one the Supreme Court applied prior to 2010. Dodge, supra note 35, at 1613.

[89] FOURTH RESTATEMENT § 405.

[90] Id. § 405 cmt. a.

have the authority to tailor the geographic scope of federal statutes provision by provision, but not case by case.[91]

Nor do most of the doctrines of international comity found in the Fourth Restatement grant case-by-case discretion to the executive branch. Many of these doctrines—like *forum non conveniens* and the recognition of foreign judgments—are considered inherently judicial, leaving no role for political judgment.[92] There are two possible exceptions. First, the Second Circuit has held that the executive has authority to waive the act of state doctrine in particular cases under the so-called *Bernstein* exception.[93] The Fourth Restatement does not take a position on this question, simply noting that the Supreme Court has not resolved it.[94] Second, in the Supreme Court suggested in *Altmann* that, in cases raising state immunity, if the State Department were to express an opinion on the foreign relations implications of exercising jurisdiction in a particular case, "that opinion might well be entitled to deference as the considered judgment of the Executive on a particular question of foreign policy."[95] But *Altmann*'s suggestion has not been included in the Fourth Restatement's chapter on state immunity.

Describing a doctrine of foreign relations law as based on international comity does not, therefore, carry any necessary implication of case-by-case discretion either by the courts or by the executive branch. But describing a doctrine as based on international comity does necessarily imply discretion vested in each *nation* to shape the doctrine as it thinks best. This is simply because doctrines of international comity are by definition doctrines that are not required by international law.[96]

Other nations also have rules for determining the geographic scope of their laws, the jurisdiction of their courts, the recognition foreign acts of state, and the recognition and enforcement of foreign judgments. Those rules often differ from those in the United States. Whereas the U.S. presumption against

---

[91] Professors Buxbaum and Michaels argue that a case-by-case approach is normatively desirable to prevent both over- and underregulation. See Buxbaum & Michaels, *supra* note 49. It is important to remember, however, that not every instance of jurisdictional overlap constitutes overregulation. Their argument that case-by-case analysis can prevent underregulation by "tak[ing] weight off the presumption" and permitting "a relatively robust determination of the scope of U.S. law," *id.* at 297–98, seems to assume a presumption against extraterritoriality different from the one that the Supreme Court has adopted. Finally, the more factors judges are asked to evaluate, the more likely they are to make decisions based on instinct rather than analysis. See Dodge, *supra* note 54; see also Maggie Gardner, *Parochial Procedure*, 69 STAN. L. REV. 941, 959–60 (2017).

[92] For discussion, see Dodge, *supra* note 1, at 2132.

[93] See Bernstein v. N.V. Nederlandsche-Amerikaansche Stoomvaart-Maatschappij, 210 F.2d 375, 376 (2d Cir. 1954).

[94] FOURTH RESTATEMENT § 441 reporters' note 13 (citing W.S. Kirkpatrick & Co., Inc. v. Envtl. Tectonics, Int'l, 493 U.S. 400, 405 (1990)).

[95] Republic of Austria v. Altmann, 541 U.S. 677, 702 (2004).

[96] See FOURTH RESTATEMENT § 401 cmt. *a* ("International comity reflects deference to foreign states that international law does not mandate."),

extraterritoriality considers the application of a provision domestic if the focus of the provision is found in the United States,[97] the New Zealand presumption against extraterritoriality considers the application of a provision domestic only if the person being regulated is in New Zealand.[98] Whereas the United States allows its courts to dismiss cases over which they have jurisdiction under the doctrine of *forum non conveniens*,[99] the European Union prohibits its courts from doing so.[100] Whereas the U.S. act of state doctrine is limited to official acts fully performed within a foreign sovereign's own territory,[101] one strand of the U.K. act of state doctrine is not.[102] Whereas U.S. courts will generally recognize foreign judgments without any showing of reciprocity,[103] Chinese courts will not.[104] Identifying these doctrines as doctrines of international comity, rather than doctrines of international law, emphasizes the freedom that each nation enjoys to shape the doctrines as it sees fit.[105]

Identifying such doctrines as doctrines of international comity also highlights that they are part of a single toolkit that courts use to address problems in transnational cases. The problem of multiple proceedings arising from the same dispute can be addressed by limiting the potential places where a suit can be brought through rules of personal jurisdiction,[106] by dismissing on grounds of *forum non conveniens* in favor of a foreign court[107] or enjoining litigation in a foreign court,[108] or by allowing all the suits to continue and using the rules on the recognition and enforcement of foreign judgments to sort out the results.[109]

---

[97] See *id.* § 404 cmt. *c* ("If whatever is the focus of the provision occurred in the United States, then application of the provision is considered domestic and is permitted.").

[98] See Poynter v. Commerce Comm'n [2010] NZSC 38 at [36]–[45] (N.Z.).

[99] See FOURTH RESTATEMENT § 424.

[100] See Case C-281/02, Owusu v. Jackson, 2005 ECR I-1383.

[101] See FOURTH RESTATEMENT § 441 cmt. *e* ("The doctrine applies only to an act of state performed with respect to persons, property, or other legal interests within the foreign sovereign's territory.").

[102] See Buttes Gas and Oil Co. v. Hammer (No. 3) [1982] AC 888; see also William S. Dodge, *The UK Supreme Court's Landmark Judgment Belhaj v. Straw: A View from the United States*, JUST SECURITY (Jan. 19, 2017), https://www.justsecurity.org/36507/uk-supreme-courts-landmark-judgment-belhaj-v-straw-view-united-states (discussing differences).

[103] See FOURTH RESTATEMENT § 484 cmt. *k* ("Most U.S. States today will recognize a foreign judgment even if the issuing forum would not accord the same treatment to a similar U.S. judgment, but a few States make reciprocity a mandatory or discretionary ground for recognition.").

[104] Civil Procedure Law of the People's Republic of China (promulgated by the Nat'l People's Cong., Apr. 9, 1991, effective Apr. 9, 1991, last amended June 27, 2017) art. 282 (China) (providing for recognition of foreign judgments "in accordance with an international treaty concluded or acceded to by the People's Republic of China or under the principle of reciprocity").

[105] Continental European states tend to view these doctrines as doctrines of domestic law but do not tie them explicitly to international comity. See William S. Dodge, *International Comity in Comparative Perspective*, in THE OXFORD HANDBOOK OF COMPARATIVE FOREIGN RELATIONS LAW 701, 706–08 (Curtis A. Bradley ed., 2019) (discussing the historical reasons for the difference in characterization).

[106] See FOURTH RESTATEMENT § 422.

[107] See *id.* § 424.

[108] See *id.* § 425.

[109] See *id.* §§ 481–490.

No single doctrine provides the best solution in every case, but taken together the doctrines of adjudicative comity provide adequate tools to address most problems that arise. The problem of overlapping regulations can be addressed by limiting the geographic scope of domestic laws through interpretation,[110] by assuming the validity of foreign acts of state fully performed within another nation's territory,[111] or by recognizing foreign compulsion as a valid defense when a party has tried in good faith to avoid the conflict.[112] Again, no single doctrine answers every case, but the doctrines of prescriptive comity give courts multiple options for handling regulatory conflicts.

Sometimes the question will be whether the best tool is one of prescriptive comity or adjudicative comity. In *RJR Nabisco, Inc. v. European Community*,[113] the Supreme Court applied the presumption against extraterritoriality to limit the private cause of action under the Racketeer Influenced and Corrupt Organizations Act (RICO) to cases involving injury to business or property in the United States.[114] Justice Ginsburg dissented. "To the extent extraterritorial application of RICO could give rise to comity concerns not present in this case," she wrote, "those concerns can be met through doctrines that serve to block litigation in U.S. courts of cases more appropriately brought elsewhere," citing *forum non conveniens* and due process constraints on the exercise of personal jurisdiction as two such doctrines.[115]

Nor is the international-comity toolkit closed. New tools may be added, and existing ones refashioned. The U.S. Supreme Court substantially narrowed the act of state doctrine in 1990.[116] The Court articulated a new version of the presumption against extraterritoriality in 2010.[117] Congress amended the FSIA to permit certain suits involving terrorism to be brought against foreign states in 1996 and again in 2016.[118] In 2005, the Uniform Law Commission revised the Uniform Act governing the recognition and enforcement of foreign judgments, adding two new grounds for nonrecognition.[119] Some lower courts have tried to add new doctrines of adjudicative comity to the toolkit, like "international comity

---

[110] See *id.* §§ 404–405.

[111] See *id.* § 441.

[112] See *id.* § 442.

[113] 136 S. Ct. 2090 (2016).

[114] *Id.* at 2111.

[115] *Id.* at 2115 (Ginsburg, J., dissenting).

[116] W.S. Kirkpatrick & Co. v. Envtl. Tectonics Corp., Int'l, 493 U.S. 400 (1990); see also FOURTH RESTATEMENT § 441 reporters' note 6 (discussing *Kirkpatrick*).

[117] Morrison v. National Australia Bank Ltd., 561 U.S. 247 (2010); see also Dodge, *supra* note 35, at 1603–14 (describing the new presumption).

[118] 28 U.S.C. §§ 1605A & 1605B; see also FOURTH RESTATEMENT § 460 & reporters' note 9 (discussing terrorism exceptions).

[119] Uniform Foreign-Country Money Judgments Recognition Act § 4(b)(7)–(8) (2005) (adding exceptions for substantial doubt about the integrity of the rendering court and for lack of due process in the specific proceeding).

abstention"[120] and "prudential exhaustion."[121] The fact that the international-comity toolkit is open to change does not lead back to unbridled case-by-case discretion. Each existing doctrine of international comity has its "ground rules," and it is reversible error for a court not to follow them.[122] New doctrines of international comity must also be consistent with general principles that the Supreme Court has articulated, like "the virtually unflagging obligation of the federal courts to exercise the jurisdiction given them."[123]

The Fourth Restatement of Foreign Relations Law describes the toolkit available to U.S. courts for handling problems in international litigation as of 2018. That toolkit will inevitably change. At some point, another Restatement will be needed. The reporters and advisers who labored over the Fourth Restatement for nearly six years might greet that prospect with a sigh. But the ability to change is a strength not a weakness. One of the contributions that the Fourth Restatement makes to the field of foreign relations law is to facilitate its ability to change by recognizing that many of its doctrines are founded on international comity rather than on international law.

---

[120] See, e.g., Royal & Sun Alliance Ins. Co. of Canada v. Century Int'l Arms, Inc., 466 F.3d 88, 92–97 (2d Cir. 2006); see also FOURTH RESTATEMENT § 424 reporters' note 9 (discussing international comity abstention cases).

[121] Compare Fischer v. Magyar Allamvasutak Zrt., 777 F.3d 847, 856–59 (7th Cir. 2015) (recognizing prudential exhaustion in expropriation cases under the FSIA), with Philipp v. Federal Republic of Germany, 894 F.3d 406, 414–16 (D.C. Cir. 2018) (refusing to recognize prudential exhaustion in expropriation cases under the FSIA); see also FOURTH RESTATEMENT § 424 reporters' note 10. The Fourth Restatement does not endorse either international comity abstention or prudential exhaustion, and it notes that "forum non conveniens is the only doctrine under which the Supreme Court has approved dismissal in favor of foreign courts." Id. § 424 cmt. i.

[122] Simon v. Republic of Hungary, 911 F.3d 1172, 1182 (D.C. Cir. 2018) (reversing district court's dismissal on ground of forum non conveniens).

[123] Colorado River Water Conservation District v. United States, 424 U.S. 800, 817 (1976); see also W.S. Kirkpatrick & Co. v. Envtl. Tectonics Corp., Int'l, 493 U.S. 400, 409 (1990) ("Courts in the United States have the power, and ordinarily the obligation, to decide cases and controversies properly presented to them.").

# 15

# Toward the Fifth Restatement of U.S. Foreign Relations Law

## The Future of Adjudicative Jurisdiction under Public International Law

*Pamela K. Bookman*

The Fourth Restatement of Foreign Relations Law has received considerable attention for its conclusion that adjudicative jurisdiction is not a concern of public international law. But exercises of adjudicative jurisdiction around the world are not static. Innovations and expansions of international adjudication in courts around the world are in process and looming on the horizon. This chapter surveys these developments and considers whether they could lead the next Restatement to alter its position on adjudicative jurisdiction.

Engaging in this thought experiment provides an opportunity to survey current cutting-edge developments in courts' use of power around the world and helps in understanding what is at stake in this debate. It raises questions about the foreign-relations implications of private international law and the overlap between public and private international law. These questions also implicate the influence of the Restatement itself. In the end, I must acknowledge a variation on the Observer Effect: The fact that the Fourth Restatement holds that adjudicative jurisdiction is not governed by public international law may itself affect the likelihood of future developments in perceptions of international law limits on adjudicative jurisdiction. This influence is particularly likely within the United States, but evolution in the view of international law limits is unlikely here in any event. The new frontier of expansions in adjudicative jurisdiction is mostly likely to be found outside of U.S. courts, and future objections to such jurisdiction may come from states, parties, and courts outside of the United States.

How might changes in adjudicative jurisdiction alter future Restatement reporters' perspective on this issue? It is possible that courts' self-imposed restraint could reflect state practice recognizing international law limits on adjudicative jurisdiction. But this chapter's central claim is that change that will push the Restatement to alter its position is more likely to follow from *breaches* of commonly understood limits on such jurisdiction. While U.S. courts historically

Pamela K. Bookman, *Toward the Fifth Restatement of U.S. Foreign Relations Law* In: *The Restatement and Beyond.*
Edited by: Paul B. Stephan and Sarah H. Cleveland, Oxford University Press (2020). © Oxford University Press.
DOI: 10.1093/oso/9780197533154.003.0016

have been notorious offenders on this front, future breaches are most likely to come from courts outside the United States.

There would be three steps that could affect such change: First, some courts would start asserting adjudicative jurisdiction more aggressively. Recent developments around the world suggest such aggressive assertions of jurisdiction are beginning to appear and more may be imminent. For example, global forum shopping has led courts to find creative ways to exert adjudicative jurisdiction over foreign parties in the context of international human rights cases and global securities settlements. In addition, new international commercial courts around the world may extend their jurisdiction even to parties who have not consented, for example in the context of joining noncontracting third parties to a contract dispute between two consenting parties.

Alone, such jurisdictional power grabs would be insufficient to change public international law. The reporters cite a lack of both *opinio juris* (the belief that public international law governs adjudicative jurisdiction) and state practice (states' restraining their exercise of adjudicative jurisdiction to obey that public international law). Thus, the second step would be other countries or foreign nationals objecting to expansive exertions of adjudicatory power because they violate international law. Third, something must be done about it. Foreign courts would have to refuse to enforce judgments that exceeded international law limits on adjudicative jurisdiction *for that reason*. As even better evidence, the rendering court might circumscribe its jurisdiction in response to those objections.

The chapter first briefly describes the debate that the Restatement has sparked regarding the status of adjudicative jurisdiction under public international law. Second, it considers current developments in adjudicative jurisdiction. Third, it discusses how those developments could translate into state practice and expressions of *opinio juris* that might affect the international law status of adjudicative jurisdiction. A brief fourth section raises questions for the future and concludes.

## I. The Restatement Sparks a Debate

The Fourth Restatement declares that "[w]ith the significant exception of various forms of immunity, modern customary international law generally does not impose limits on jurisdiction to adjudicate."[1] There is some global consensus that adjudicative jurisdiction should be based on some connection between the defendant, the controversy, and the forum state. But many states, including the

---

[1] FOURTH RESTATEMENT § 401.

United States, exercise adjudicative jurisdiction on bases that are widely criticized as "exorbitant" because they provide an insufficient link among these elements. For example, the common law tradition allows "tag jurisdiction" based on serving the defendant while briefly present in the forum state. Article 14 of the French Civil Code permits jurisdiction over cases based on the plaintiff's French nationality. Both bases for asserting jurisdiction are often considered unfair by other nations.[2] But although these other nations may object to judgments based on exorbitant jurisdiction, they do not object *because* such jurisdiction violates international law. And while some nations confine their own exercise of adjudicative jurisdiction to recognized bases, there is little evidence that they do so out of a sense of legal obligation.

Some critics of the Restatement's position point to other courts' refusals to recognize and enforce judgments on the basis of exorbitant jurisdiction, or the rarity of exorbitant jurisdiction, or the connections that even exorbitant jurisdiction relies on (such as service of process within the state), as evidence that states believe in and follow international law limits on adjudicative jurisdiction. Objectors also question the Restatement's limited view of sources of international law, pointing to widespread agreement in scholarship and treatises that universal civil jurisdiction (i.e., the exercise of adjudicative jurisdiction without any connection between the forum state and the defendant or the case) would violate international law. But the Restatement defends its conclusion by explaining that even if a second country refuses to recognize and enforce the judgment of a first country that exercised personal jurisdiction on a basis thought to be exorbitant, "such a refusal is not necessarily evidence that the exercise of personal jurisdiction violates customary international law."[3] Indeed, as William Dodge, one of the Restatement's reporters, has explained, the Brussels I Regulation (Recast) prohibits the exercise of exorbitant jurisdiction over defendants from EU member states but expressly allows such jurisdiction over defendants from elsewhere. Dodge concludes that "[i]f states do not refrain from exercising jurisdiction on exorbitant bases of jurisdiction out of a sense of legal obligation, there can be no rule of customary international law prohibiting their use."[4] What is missing, Paul Stephan reminds us in this volume, is "evidence that these common-sense policies were mandated by international law."[5]

---

[2] Donald Earl Childress III, *Jurisdiction, Limits Under International Law*, in ENCYCLOPEDIA OF PRIVATE INTERNATIONAL LAW 1052, 1054–55 (Jürgen Basedow, Giesela Rühl, Franco Ferrari, & Pedro de Miguel Asensio eds., 2017).

[3] FOURTH RESTATEMENT § 422 reporters' note 1.

[4] William S. Dodge, *The Customary International Law of Jurisdiction in the Restatement (Fourth) of Foreign Relations Law*, OPINIO JURIS (Aug. 3, 2018), http://www.opiniojuris.org/2018/03/08/The-Customary-International-Law-of-Jurisdiction-in-the-Restatement--Fourth--of-Foreign-Relations-Law/.

[5] Paul B. Stephan, *The Waning of the Federal Common Law of Foreign Relations*, in this volume at 185.

Austen Parrish's chapter in this volume questions the Fourth Restatement's conclusion. Parrish accuses the Restatement of "break[ing] with common understandings" that public international law limits adjudicative jurisdiction, just like it limits any other sovereign exercise of power. He also disputes the starting point for the Fourth Restatement's analysis of international law. Whereas the Restatement asserts that a state's jurisdiction is unconstrained absent evidence of a specific limit under customary international law, Parrish contends instead that to reach the Restatement's conclusion, there would need to be affirmative evidence of state practice and *opinio juris* establishing the acceptance of universal civil jurisdiction (which the Restatement does not have). Parrish expresses concern that declaring adjudicative jurisdiction free of public international law constraints will "become[] a self-fulfilling prophesy," influencing judges, government officials, and practitioners in the United States and perhaps even around the globe, who will not recognize international law restraints in the future.[6] He notes that such a result "may be particularly concerning" if "foreign courts become increasingly attractive to litigants."[7]

Ralf Michaels has articulated a middle approach. He suggests that the "the question of public international law limits on adjudicative jurisdiction remains open."[8] Michaels has posed two conceptual questions. First, he asks whether adjudicatory, prescriptive, and enforcement jurisdiction are truly (and always) separate and separable, which is necessary to properly assess state practice. There is plenty of evidence of objections to abuses of prescriptive and enforcement jurisdiction on the basis of international law, some of which are hard to separate from objections to the exercise of adjudicative jurisdiction. Second, he questions the starting position of the assessment of state practice. He offers that "the absence of protest proves only, at best, that existing law complies with limits, not that such limits do not exist."[9] Perhaps the nonrecognition of foreign judgments rendered on the basis of exorbitant jurisdiction is the foreign state opposition that we should be looking for. Michael Akehurst has found one nineteenth-century example of nonrecognition *because* a rendering court's exercise of exorbitant jurisdiction violated the law of nations.[10] Modern examples or diplomatic

---

[6] Austen Parrish, *Adjudicatory Jurisdiction and Public International Law: The Fourth Restatement's New Approach*, in this volume.

[7] *Id.* at 6.

[8] Ralf Michaels, *Is Adjudicative Jurisdiction a Category of Public International Law?*, OPINIO JURIS (Sept. 20, 2018), http://opiniojuris.org/2018/09/20/is-adjudicatory-jurisdiction-a-category-of-public-international-law/.

[9] *Id.*

[10] Michael Akehurst, *Jurisdiction in International Law*, 46 BRIT. Y.B. INT'L L. 145, 173 n.11 (1973) (describing nineteenth-century Italian decision refusing to enforce French judgment based on Article 14 jurisdiction for this reason).

protests objecting to the use of adjudicative jurisdiction, however, appear to be unheard of.[11]

In sum, there is little overt evidence of state practice or *opinio juris* affirmatively proving the existence of public international law limits on adjudicative jurisdiction the way there is for prescriptive jurisdiction (assuming the two are separable). On the other hand, there is little evidence proving states can exercise jurisdiction in the absence of *any* connection to the dispute.[12] The status quo could be interpreted as demonstrating a background acceptance of international law limits and overwhelming adherence to them. Or it could be interpreted, as the Restatement sees it, as a lack of international law limits at all. Perhaps other factors are creating this status quo.

Rather than taking sides in this debate among such esteemed scholars, this chapter engages a different angle: Taking the current Restatement's position as a starting point, what future developments could occur to provide that affirmative evidence that the reporters went looking for, but thus far have not found? The possibility of such developments in the near future is not as fanciful as it may seem. U.S. courts seem to be on a trajectory of constraining the scope of their adjudicative jurisdiction (for reasons mostly unrelated to international law). But a number of foreign courts are leading a vanguard of innovation in international dispute resolution. They are experimenting with several innovative aspects of procedure and jurisdiction—with results that are as yet unknown.

## II. The Future of Adjudicative Jurisdiction: Possible Expansions of "Exorbitant" Jurisdiction

Recent developments in international adjudication provide opportunities to consider what kind of court action could prompt a change in states' conceptions of and reactions to uses of adjudicative jurisdiction. If there are international law limits on adjudicative jurisdiction, evidence of those limits may first come from someone breaching them. An expansive assertion of adjudicative jurisdiction is thus a first step toward a recognition of international law limits on such jurisdiction. This section first explains why such expansion is unlikely to happen in U.S. courts. It then discusses two areas of such expansion in courts around the world: global forum shopping and international commercial courts.

---

[11] *Id.*; see also, e.g., Childress, *supra* note 2, at 1055 ("[I]t is far too soon to conclude that international law places meaningful limits on judicial jurisdiction and assertions of exorbitant jurisdiction.").

[12] Alex Mills, *Private Interests and Private Law Regulation in Public International Law*, in OXFORD HANDBOOK ON JURISDICTION IN INTERNATIONAL LAW 338 n.31 (Stephen Allen, Daniel Costelloe, Malgosia Mitzmaurice, Paul Gragl, & Edward Guntrip eds., 2019).

These developments are necessary to rebut the Restatement's position in the future, but alone they are not sufficient: Expressions of state practice and *opinio juris* opposing these assertions of jurisdiction are also necessary. Those are discussed in section III.

## A. Developments in the United States

The outer boundaries of the scope of extraterritorial jurisdiction—whether adjudicatory, prescriptive, or enforcement jurisdiction—have long been set and stretched by U.S. practice. But one should no longer expect the United States to be the country challenging the outer boundaries of limits on adjudicative jurisdiction.

In the 1980s, 1990s, and early 2000s, litigation under the Alien Tort Statute (ATS) and other federal statutes led to U.S. courts' reputation as "judicial imperialists."[13] That is, U.S. courts stretched their influence extraterritorially in ways that offended or were said to offend foreign nations and their sovereignty. In that era, U.S. courts regularly applied federal laws, like the ATS and U.S. antitrust laws, to foreign persons and foreign conduct in cases that had little connection with the United States. These efforts were sometimes met with objections that such efforts violated public international law limits on prescriptive jurisdiction.[14]

But the United States was also in the vanguard of extending adjudicative jurisdiction, including in some of these same cases. For example, many controversial ATS lawsuits were based on exorbitant bases of adjudicative jurisdiction.[15] Until recently, U.S. courts had an expansive conception of personal jurisdiction over foreign companies "doing business" in the United States.[16] Sufficient business transactions were thought to establish general "all-purpose" jurisdiction over suits relating to conduct anywhere in the world. In *Daimler v. Bauman* in

---

[13] See, e.g., Hannah L. Buxbaum, *Foreign Governments as Plaintiffs in U.S. Courts and the Case Against "Judicial Imperialism,"* 73 WASH. & LEE L. REV. 653, 657 (2016) (defining judicial imperialism as the idea that U.S. courts' engagement "in the global arena . . . interfere[s] with the sovereign authority of other countries"); Robert H. Bork, *Judicial Imperialism,* WALL ST. JOURNAL (July 12, 2004), https://www.wsj.com/articles/SB108958310422660738.

[14] See Kristen E. Eichensehr, *Foreign Sovereigns as Friends of the Court,* 102 VA. L. REV. 289, 316 (2016) (describing foreign sovereign amicus briefs in these cases).

[15] *Filártiga v. Peña-Irala,* the Second Circuit case that resurrected the Alien Tort Statute for use in international human rights litigation, asserted personal jurisdiction over the Paraguayan defendant based on tag jurisdiction. The defendant was served "at the Brooklyn Navy Yard, where he was being held pending deportation." Filártiga v. Peña-Irala, 630 F.2d 876, 879 (2d Cir. 1980). *Daimler AG v. Bauman* is another prime example. Personal jurisdiction in that case was based on an expansive reading of "doing business" general jurisdiction, which the Supreme Court ultimately found unconstitutional because it subjected the defendant to general jurisdiction in a state where it was not "at home." Daimler AG v. Bauman, 571 U.S. 117 (2014).

[16] See Alan Trammell, *A Tale of Two Jurisdictions,* 68 VAND. L. REV. 501, 512 (2015).

2014, the Supreme Court brought U.S. adjudicative jurisdiction back into step with global opinion by limiting general jurisdiction to fora where the defendant is "at home." For corporate defendants, that was no longer wherever they did significant business, but instead, their *principal* place of business and place of incorporation. In cabining adjudicative jurisdiction, the Court cited comity—but not international law—concerns. It explained that overbroad concepts of general jurisdiction created "risks to international comity," noting that "[o]ther nations do not share" such an approach, that this disagreement has impeded U.S. negotiations of international agreements, and that the approach "has led to 'international friction.'"[17]

In short, over the past fifteen years, the U.S. Supreme Court has reversed course on pursuing anything resembling "judicial imperialism" and instead has embarked on a road of what I have called "litigation isolationism"—the practice of limiting access to U.S. courts for cases involving foreign parties or foreign conduct.[18] Since I documented the phenomenon in 2015, the Supreme Court has mostly continued the trend.[19] As a result, the Court has made the United States one of the most "jurisdictionally stingy" in the world.[20]

The Fourth Restatement, concluding that there are no public international law limits on adjudicative jurisdiction, "restates rules of personal jurisdiction exclusively as domestic law of the United States."[21] It seems likely that these rules of personal jurisdiction are on a trajectory to become, if anything, more limited. Given the Supreme Court's control over personal jurisdiction and the unlikelihood of it expressly relying on international law to guide its personal jurisdiction decisions, it seems highly unlikely that U.S. practice of exercising adjudicative jurisdiction will prompt any changes in the perceived international law status of such jurisdiction.

As discussed in the following sections, however, other countries are pushing the envelope. It is possible that this change in global political dynamics could affect the likelihood of other nations objecting to adjudicative jurisdiction on the basis of international law.

[17] Daimler AG v. Bauman, 571 U.S. 117, 141–42 (2014); Pamela K. Bookman, *Litigation Isolationism*, 67 STAN. L. REV. 1081, 1103–104 (2015).

[18] Bookman, *supra* note 17, at 1085.

[19] See, e.g., Pamela K. Bookman, *Doubling Down on Litigation Isolationism*, 110 AJIL UNBOUND 57 (2016); Jesner v. Arab Bank, PLC, 138 S. Ct. 1386 (2018); OBB Personenverkehr AG v. Sachs, 136 S. Ct. 390 (2015). But see WesternGeco LLC v. ION Geophysical Corp., 138 S. Ct. 2129 (2018). Some of the Supreme Court's domestic cases also may have the effect of promoting litigation isolationism. See, e.g., Bristol-Myers Squibb Co. v. Superior Court of California, 137 S. Ct. 1773 (2017); Pamela Bookman, *Supreme Court Decision on Specific Personal Jurisdiction a "SomethingBurger,"* THE TEMPLE 10-Q (Aug. 14, 2017), https://www2.law.temple.edu/10q/supreme-court-decision-specific-personal-jurisdiction-somethingburger/.

[20] Aaron D. Simowitz, *Legislating Transnational Jurisdiction*, 57 VA. J. INT'L L. 325, 328 (2018).

[21] FOURTH RESTATEMENT § 422 reporters' note 11.

## B. Global Forum Shopping

Plaintiffs' search for a friendly forum to resolve global tort and regulatory disputes has yielded developments that expand exorbitant exercises of adjudicative jurisdiction. In addition to the well-recognized bases of exorbitant jurisdiction often discussed in debates about adjudicative jurisdiction like tag jurisdiction and plaintiff-personality-based jurisdiction, this section will highlight two recent developments. First, there have been recent innovations in exercises of exorbitant jurisdiction through the long arm of joinder principles. Second, developments in aggregate dispute resolution have led to an innovative procedure in the Netherlands that converts a global securities settlement into a judgment binding all class members unless they opt out. Both of these are examples of adjudicative jurisdiction developments that could be a recipe for international-law-based objections in the future.

First, potential plaintiffs who might once have thought to bring suit in the United States under the ATS for corporate human rights abuses are seeking out other possible fora. A pending case, *Vedanta Resources v. Lungowe*,[22] involves claims against a U.K. holding company and its Zambian subsidiary. Plaintiffs, Zambian residents, allege that they were harmed by toxic emissions from a Zambian mine owned and operated by the Zambian subsidiary. From the United Kingdom's perspective, the case could be defined as "foreign-cubed": The plaintiffs were from Zambia, the defendants that were alleged to have done most of the harm were Zambian, and the alleged injury and damage took place in Zambia.[23]

The presence of Vedanta, the U.K. company defendant, in the case was hotly contested. The plaintiffs assert that Vedanta breached a duty of care to supervise its Zambian subsidiary, but Vedanta contested the existence of such a duty of care under the common law. Adjudicative jurisdiction over the U.K. defendant, however, was uncontroversial. The reverse was true of the Zambian subsidiary, which was plainly the proper defendant from a liability perspective, but had virtually no contacts with the United Kingdom to support adjudicative jurisdiction.

The U.K. Supreme Court's recent decision allowing the case to proceed addressed only the jurisdictional issue. The Court approved of jurisdiction over the Zambian subsidiary on the basis of the "necessary and proper party gateway."[24] In the course of the complicated jurisdictional analysis, the U.K.

---

[22] Vedanta Resources v. Lungowe, [2019] UKSC 20.

[23] See Bryan Cave Leighton Paisner, Nicole Bigby, & Aidan Thomson, *Supreme Court Affirms in* Vedanta *a General Principles Path to Hear Zambian Environmental Claims*, JD SUPRA (May 24, 2019), https://www.jdsupra.com/legalnews/supreme-court-affirms-in-vedanta-a-43279/.

[24] Julianne Hughes-Jennett & Peter Hood, Vedanta: *UK Supreme Court Takes the "Straitjacket" Off Claims against Parent Companies in the English Courts*, HOGAN LOVELLS: FOCUS ON REGULATION (Apr. 11, 2019), https://www.hlregulation.com/2019/04/11/vedanta-uk-supreme-court-takes-

Supreme Court concluded that although Zambia would ordinarily be the forum for the litigation, the risk that the claimants would be denied access to justice in Zambia was too high and, therefore, English courts could nonetheless exercise jurisdiction over the foreign defendant.[25] The court reached this conclusion over the protests of the attorney general of Zambia, who argued that English jurisdiction violated international comity.[26]

Opt-out class actions and class settlements provide another testing ground for adjudicative jurisdiction.[27] In perhaps the most intriguing example, the Netherlands adopted a collective settlement mechanism, known as the WCAM, which allows parties to petition the Amsterdam Court of Appeals to make a global settlement binding on all class members who do not opt out.[28] Although developed to address product liability arising out of the use of an anti-miscarriage drug, the mechanism has been used in several global securities settlements.[29] For example, in 2018, the Amsterdam Court of Appeals approved a whopping $1.5 billion settlement of shareholder claims against the Belgian financial company Fortis.[30]

The WCAM tests a number of assumptions about jurisdiction.[31] The only required connection to the Netherlands is that at least one claimant must be Dutch.[32] The settlement agreement must be concluded between the liable parties

the-straitjacket-off-claims-against-parent-companies-in-the-english-courts/ ("Jurisdiction over a foreign domiciled defendant (for example a non-EU subsidiary of the anchor defendant) who the claimants seek to join to the proceedings against the anchor defendant is more controversial and it is in this area that the *Vedanta* judgment is most significant.").

[25] Vedanta Resources v. Lungowe, [2019] UKSC 20; Hughes-Jennett & Hood, *supra* note 24. For an explanation of how this analysis maps onto the doctrine of *forum non conveniens*, see Gabrielle Holley, Vedanta v. Lungowe *Symposium: A Non Conveniens Revival—The Supreme Court's Approach to Jurisdiction in* Vedanta, OPINIO JURIS (Apr. 24, 2019), https://opiniojuris.org/2019/04/24/vedanta-v-lungowe-symposium-a-non-conveniens-revival-the-supreme-courts-approach-to-jurisdiction-in-vedanta%EF%BB%BF/.

[26] See Hughes-Jennett & Hood, *supra* note 24.

[27] See Bookman, *supra* note 17, at 1111–12 (discussing other countries that have adopted class action mechanisms); Christopher Young et al., *Manufacturers Face the Rise of Global Class Actions*, LAW360 (Jan. 2, 2019), https://www.law360.com/articles/1113871/manufacturers-face-the-rise-of-global-class-actions.

[28] See Pamela K. Bookman, *The Unsung Virtues of Global Forum Shopping*, 92 NOTRE DAME L. REV. 579, 627 (2016).

[29] See Pamela K. Bookman & David L. Noll, Ad Hoc *Procedure*, 92 N.Y.U. L. REV. 767, 811–14 (2017).

[30] Fortis shareholders had sued the company for misconduct following the 2008 financial crisis. The settlement sought to resolve those claims. Jonathan E. Richman, *Dutch Court Approves Collective Settlement of Fortis Shareholders' Claims*, THE NATIONAL LAW REVIEW (July 14, 2018), https://www.natlawreview.com/article/dutch-court-approves-collective-settlement-fortis-shareholders-claims.

[31] Ruud Hermans & Jan de Bie Leuveling Tjeenk, *Netherlands: International Class Action Settlements in the Netherlands Since Converium*, MONDAQ (Jan. 3, 2013), http://www.mondaq.com/x/213872/Class+Actions/The+International+Comparative+Legal+Guide+to ("From an international perspective, one of the most important issues in [WCAM settlements] is the question of whether the Court had jurisdiction.").

[32] *Id.*

and a foundation or association representing potential plaintiffs, but it covers all plaintiffs who do not opt out. Once these requirements are satisfied, these global settlements are theoretically enforceable on the same terms as any other Dutch judgment.

These European experiments can be seen as efforts to fill in access-to-justice gaps once filled by the United States in the field of international human rights litigation and international securities litigation. These courts experiment with different variations on expansive adjudicative jurisdiction—but they maintain *some* modicum of connection to the forum. In the United Kingdom, even if parent company liability becomes well established, there will need to be a domestic parent company as the "anchor defendant" to establish the initial jurisdiction over the case and thus over foreign subsidiaries. In the Netherlands, the global settlement authority depends on there being at least one affected Dutch investor in the claimant class.[33] These are slender reeds on which to base jurisdiction, but they are not nonexistent. It is difficult to say whether those tenuous connections are maintained out of a respect for international law, or perhaps whether these minimal requirements will give way in the future to situations where courts may exercise jurisdiction even without them.

To date, the adjudicative jurisdiction of these kinds of experiments has raised many eyebrows but has not been contested. But these kinds of cases also have not yet faced the hurdle of being recognized and enforced by foreign courts, which is one context in which judges could express international-law-based objections to the rendering courts' jurisdiction.

The testing ground over time may depend on who stands to lose the most from these judgments. Perhaps the "losers" will be potential plaintiffs who did not want to be bound to a global securities settlement to which they were not a party. Perhaps they will be a subsidiary hauled into a faraway foreign court for alleged misconduct unrelated to the forum country. These entities may object to jurisdiction in the first instance; they may lobby their home countries to object to jurisdiction on the basis of international law in addition to comity; they may seek to block enforcement of any resulting judgment. Such objections could open opportunities for the development of an international law on adjudicative jurisdiction.

---

[33] By contrast, the new Dutch class action *litigation* statute requires a closer connection for adjudicative jurisdiction. Wet Afwikkeling Massaschade in een Collectieve Actie, Stb. 2019, 130. The case will be admissible "if any of the following conditions are met: [i] if the majority of the individuals on behalf of whom the collective action is initiated reside in the Netherlands; [ii] if the defendant resides in the Netherlands; or [iii] if the circumstance(s) on which the collective action is based took place in the Netherlands." Bas Keizers & Carlijn Van Rest, *Hogan Lovells, A Collective Action for Damages in the Netherlands Is a Fact!*, JD SUPRA (Apr. 2, 2019), https://www.jdsupra.com/legalnews/a-collective-action-for-damages-in-the-73587/.

## C. International Commercial Courts

There has also been considerable experimentation in the world of commercial disputes. In the past fifteen years, English-language-friendly international commercial courts have been established in China (2018), Singapore (2015), Qatar (2009), Dubai (2004), the Netherlands (2019), Germany (2018), France (2010), and beyond. These courts or chambers limit their jurisdiction to "international" "commercial" disputes. New business courts in tax havens such as Bermuda, the British Virgin Islands, and the Cayman Islands also welcome transnational litigation, typically involving companies incorporated in those locations.[34] The cases heard in those offshore courts may relate not only to disputes over those localities' internal business law but also contract disputes, insurance disputes, investment disputes, and insolvency claims.[35]

International commercial courts are an interesting case study for the status of adjudicative jurisdiction internationally because commercial litigation can isolate the adjudicative jurisdiction question. As the Restatement notes, the three kinds of jurisdiction are separable.[36] This is the paradigm of international commercial courts. The Singapore International Commercial Court (SICC) could hear a case between a Malaysian party and an Indonesian party in a controversy over a contract governed by English law and yield a judgment that may be enforced in Australia. That case would implicate Singapore's adjudicatory authority, but not its prescriptive or enforcement authority.

In the short term, it seems likely that these courts will exercise jurisdiction judiciously. The courts' paradigm basis for adjudicative jurisdiction is consent, a basis that has inherent appeal and legitimacy even though its accepted validity is relatively recent. These courts will be seeking out business; that is, they will try to make themselves attractive venues for plaintiffs to bring suits and for parties to designate as their chosen forum in their international contracts.[37] As such, they should seek to build their reputation for legitimacy, efficiency, and fairness. Early exorbitant exercises of jurisdiction might compromise those efforts.

But as they gain power and influence, some of these courts may become judicial imperialists themselves. Several of these courts, including the popular SICC and the new Netherlands Commercial Court (NCC) do not require parties to have a connection to the locality in order to select to have their private disputes

---

[34] William J. Moon, *Delaware's New Competition*, 114 Nw. L. Rev. 1403 (2020).

[35] *Id.*

[36] Fourth Restatement § 401 cmt. *d* ("A state may exercise jurisdiction to adjudicate ... and may apply the substantive law of another state under choice-of-law principles, even if the adjudicating state lacks jurisdiction to prescribe with respect to the defendant ... or the defendant has no assets within the adjudicating state against which a judgment may be enforced.").

[37] See Daniel Klerman & Greg Reilly, *Forum Selling*, 89 S. Cal. L. Rev. 241, 244 (2016).

litigated there. And the courts are not *limited* to consent-based jurisdiction. For example, they liberally allow joinder of nonparties.[38]

It is of course possible that the growth of these courts could have no effect on the current landscape of adjudicative jurisdiction under public international law. They could end up with small dockets and little influence. Alternatively, they could prove popular, but nonetheless constrain themselves exclusively to exercising consent-based jurisdiction. If both parties before the court have agreed to subject themselves to that court, there will be no strain on our understanding of the possible public international law constraints on adjudicative jurisdiction. Jurisdiction would go undisputed by the parties and their home states.

Two aspects of these courts should be watched for their possible effect on international law of adjudicative jurisdiction: institutional design and exercises of exorbitant jurisdiction.

### 1. Institutional Design

First, with respect to institutional design, the proliferation of new courts and judicial chambers presents opportunities for states and localities to experiment with the scope of their jurisdiction. New courts from the Netherlands to Dubai to China exemplify this kind of experimentation. They experiment with procedures, judges, and technologies.[39] They also experiment with jurisdiction. For example, several have cast aside any requirement of a connection with the territory where the court is found if the parties agree pre- or postdispute.[40] They also allow broad joinder of additional parties who may not have consented to jurisdiction.[41] Some exclude investor-state disputes, but they may be confronted by cases that require innovative articulations of the dividing line between commercial and investor-state disputes.[42]

In designing the scope of a court's jurisdiction, a state could specify that it is restricting jurisdiction in light of international law limits. The state would need to be explicit about any such restraints. For example, the courts all recognize that to join a third party defendant, there must be some nexus between the *case* and the party.[43] But the scope of these limits are unclear. Moreover, they do not

---

[38] See, e.g., Sing. R. Ct. O 110, r. 9; Johannes Landbrecht, *The Singapore International Commercial Court (SICC)—An Alternative to International Arbitration?*, 34 ASA BULL. 112, 118 (2016).

[39] See generally Pamela K. Bookman, *The Adjudication Business*, 45 YALE J. INT'L L. (forthcoming 2020).

[40] See *id.* (identifying courts or proposed courts in Dubai, Qatar, Brussels, and the Netherlands that would not require a connection with the territory to exercise jurisdiction).

[41] See, e.g., Rules of Dubai Court (RDC) pt. 20, available at https://www.difccourts.ae/court-rules/part-20-addition-and-substitution-of-parties/; Rules of Court, O 110, r 9 (SICC).

[42] See Stratos Pahis, *Investment Misconceived: The Impact and Fallacy of the Investment-Commerce Distinction in ICSID Arbitration*, YALE J. INT'L L. 69 (2020).

[43] See, e.g., art. 107 Rv (Neth.); SICC Procedural Guide 7.1 (Rules of Joinder), https://www.sicc.gov.sg/docs/default-source/legislation-rules-pd/sicc_procedural_guide.pdf; Singapore ROC O. 15 r. 4, https://sso.agc.gov.sg/SL/SCJA1969-R5#PO15-pr4-; Al Tamimi & Company, *The DIFC Court of*

expressly reflect international law restraints. Without such expressions, the fact that new courts are established within these limits would not necessarily *prove* to the Restatement reporters that international law constrained the courts' jurisdictional design. An easier explanation could be that the courts are cabining their reach to promote legitimacy or popularity. That would yield the impression that the new courts were following the status quo: courts abiding by popular conceptions of the limits on adjudicative jurisdiction as common sense policies rather than a reflection of international law mandates.

Thus, one area to watch for evidence of international law's limits on adjudicative jurisdiction is not only the end product, that is, the scope of courts' jurisdiction, but also the process by which the courts' jurisdiction is established. This involves paying attention to court decisions, legislative hearings, and public debates about establishing new courts and new chambers. It also may involve conversations behind closed doors. But if a tree falls in the forest with no one around to hear it, perhaps no one can raise an international-law-based objection to felling it.

## 2. The New Exorbitant Jurisdiction

Second, these new courts provide opportunities for courts to innovate with exorbitant jurisdiction. That innovation may involve pushing accepted norms and boundaries, and possibly triggering state objections.

As noted, the paradigm basis for jurisdiction in these courts is consent, whether based on commercial contracts or incorporation in a particular nation. In many ways, these courts are competing with arbitration for adjudication business, and as such, they follow arbitration's model for jurisdiction.[44] But in their competition with arbitration, these courts also seek to offer what arbitration cannot—including jurisdiction over third parties and the power to order interim measures and injunctive relief, such as global asset seizures.

This jurisdiction over third parties may prove to be a testing ground for the limits of adjudicative jurisdiction in the context of joinder. The issue is similar to the *Vedanta* question of whether the U.K. courts had jurisdiction over Vedanta's Zambian subsidiary. The court may have adjudicative jurisdiction over the dispute generally based on the contracting parties' consent, but not over a third

*Appeal Confirms the DIFC Courts' "Necessary or Proper Party" Jurisdiction,* LEXOLOGY (May 6, 2019), https://www.lexology.com/library/detail.aspx?g=a719dccd-a836-4c00-9485-8fa9f6f5ff0a (discussing "necessary or proper party" jurisdiction in DIFC Courts); DIFC Courts, RDC pt. 20.7 ("The Court may order a person to be added as a new party if: (1) it is desirable to add the new party so that the Court can resolve all the matters in dispute in the proceedings; or (2) there is an issue involving the new party and an existing party which is connected to the matters in dispute in the proceedings, and it is desirable to add the new party so that the Court can resolve that issue.").

[44] See Bookman, *supra* note 39; cf. Moon, *supra* note 34.

party that the contracting parties wish to include in the suit. In U.S. court, the suit against that third party would be dismissed for lack of personal jurisdiction. But it is unclear how international commercial courts will treat the problem. The following might be a typical example: Imagine a Belt and Road Initiative contract dispute between an Italian company and a Chinese state-owned enterprise arising out of a contract that designated the Chinese International Commercial Court (CICC) as its chosen forum. In the course of the dispute, the Italian company blames its alleged breach on a German entity's tortious interference with the contract. The CICC allows joinder of the German party and subsequent judgment against it. In such proceedings, the German party contests the Chinese court's jurisdiction. Might it protest that the court is exceeding its powers under international law?

Even if a court's jurisdiction is primarily based on consent and involves only the contracting parties, it is possible that the definition of *consent* as a part of adjudicative jurisdiction will come under closer scrutiny. While "jurisdiction based on consent is widely accepted," the idea of consent itself is circumscribed by principles of general contract law.[45] New international commercial courts may stretch the idea of consent beyond the bounds of those principles in objectionable ways.

Moreover, basing extraterritorial adjudicative jurisdiction on consent raises questions about parties' authority to exercise autonomy over forum selection. In the United States, the issue of personal jurisdiction is theorized as an individual right, and therefore one that parties can waive.[46] But such waiver theory cannot justify jurisdiction over a third party to the contract. The public international law justification for party control over forum choices relies not on principles of individual freedom and autonomy but on states' indulgence of those choices.[47] This theory could be tested depending on how much stress a court puts on the concept of choice, for example, finding that parties selected the forum court notwithstanding evidence that such a choice was not freely made.

There may also be stress on these ideas if courts assert jurisdiction in the face of forum selection clauses opting for alternative fora. If parties have complete reign over forum choice, that could reinforce the Fourth Restatement's conclusion that public international law does not constrain adjudicative jurisdiction; perhaps it would even suggest that sovereignty does not constrain it. But new international commercial courts may be protective of their own jurisdiction. For example, the Dubai International Financial Center (DIFC) Courts have exercised jurisdiction

---

[45] Ralf Michaels, *Jurisdiction, Foundations*, in ENCYCLOPEDIA OF PRIVATE INTERNATIONAL LAW, *supra* note 2, at 1042, 1049.

[46] See FOURTH RESTATEMENT §422 reporters' note 3 (on "waiver and consent").

[47] Alex Mills, *Rethinking Jurisdiction in International Law*, 84 BRIT. Y.B. INT'L L. 187, 231 (2014).

over a case involving a DIFC entity even though a dispute resolution clause in a freely negotiated contract chose Swiss courts.[48] Decisions of this nature could test the international law foundations of recognizing party autonomy.

The Chinese International Commercial Court (CICC), established in 2018, provides another interesting forum to watch for possible developments.[49] The CICC encompasses two new Chinese international commercial tribunals. Its purpose, according to its website, is "to try international commercial cases fairly and timely in accordance with the law, protect the lawful rights and interests of the Chinese and foreign parties equally, and create a stable, fair, transparent, and convenient rule of law international business environment."[50] The CICC is intended to "streamline and control" the flow of disputes arising out of China's Belt and Road Initiative (BRI).[51]

These courts "mark[] the first time [China] is creating legal institutions for the world."[52] The CICC's jurisdiction is limited to international commercial disputes, defined as involving one or more foreign parties or relevant foreign "objects" or "legal facts."[53] It purports to lack jurisdiction over investor-state disputes, although it is unclear how it will differentiate between investor-state disputes and other kinds of disputes arising out of the BRI.[54] The CICC has jurisdiction to hear

---

[48] Latham & Watkins, *New Dispute Resolution Options in the DIFC Courts*, CLIENT ALERT 2–3 (Oct. 21, 2012), https://www.lw.com/thoughtLeadership/dispute-resolution-options-difc-courts (discussing Al-Khorafi v. Sarasin).

[49] Matthew Erie, *The China International Commercial Court: Prospects for Dispute Resolution for the "Belt and Road Initiative,"* 22(11) AMER. SOC. INT'L. L. (Aug. 31, 2018), https://www.asil.org/insights/volume/22/issue/11/china-international-commercial-court-prospects-dispute-resolution-belt; CICC, A Brief Introduction of China International Commercial Court, China International Commercial Court (June 28, 2018), http://cicc.court.gov.cn/html/1/219/193/195/index.html. This section focuses on the CICC, but it should be understood in the broader context of China's development of free-trade zones and courts for transnational disputes, often in the shadow of regional competition within China. Shenzhen, for example, contains a "Hong Kong Modern Services Cooperative District" based in a free-trade zone that has special courts for transnational disputes, including the Shenzhen Qianhai Cooperative District People's Court with jurisdiction over transnational disputes, Hong Kong jurors, and English-language proceedings. See Matthew Erie, *The New Legal Hubs: The Emergent Landscape of International Commercial Dispute Resolution*, 59 VA. J. INT'L L. (forthcoming).

[50] CICC, *supra* note 49.

[51] Erie, *supra* note 49; Freshfields Bruckhaus Deringer, *China Establishes International Commercial Courts to Handle Belt and Road Initiative Disputes*, OXFORD BUSINESS LAW BLOG (Aug. 17, 2018), https://www.law.ox.ac.uk/business-law-blog/blog/2018/08/china-establishes-international-commercial-courts-handle-belt-and.

[52] Erie, *supra* note 49.

[53] The Regulations define "international commercial disputes" as those whereby:

   i. one or both parties are foreign,
   ii. the domicile of one or both parties lies outside the PRC,
   iii. the object of the dispute lies outside the PRC, or
   iv. legal facts producing, changing, or destroying commercial relations in dispute occur outside the PRC.

*Id.* (footnotes omitted).

[54] *Id.*

five categories of disputes: (1) international commercial cases where the amount in dispute is of at least RMB 300 million (approximately $44 million) and the parties selected the SPC as their forum of choice;[55] (2) first-impression international commercial cases that fall under a High People's Court jurisdiction, that are then moved to the SPC, who suggest a transfer to the CICC; (3) international commercial cases that have a "nationwide significant impact"; (4) applications for preservation measures in aid of arbitration, or applications for revocation or enforcement of an arbitral award; and (5) other international commercial cases that the SPC transfers to the CICC.[56]

Notably, this is not an entirely consent-based system of jurisdiction. The fact that the caseload is limited to commercial cases does not prevent the possibility that defendants who did not sign a forum-selection clause selecting a Chinese court may find themselves before this tribunal. Chinese civil procedure rules in any Chinese court, including the CICC, requires that disputes have some connection with China.[57] But it is unclear how the CICC will interpret these requirements over time, or whether (or why) the requirements will remain.

Even consent-based jurisdiction may take on a different valence if China exercises its considerable bargaining power in Belt-and-Road-related projects to effectively require parties to designate the CICC for resolution of disputes arising out of those contracts. As *The Economist* recently noted, reporting on the CICC's first hearings, "[t]oo many belt-and-road contracts are secretive, unequal[,] and reward local power-brokers in opaque ways, reflecting deep cynicism about global norms."[58] Indeed, the CICC is not alone in its uncertain approach to transparency in its courts. International commercial courts tend to be open to the public by default but allow requests for confidentiality based on varying metrics. Confidentiality may hamper states' ability to see what excesses may be going on in these courts, but also may be a fertile breeding ground for those excesses, which, if brought to light, could lead to diplomatic strains.

There is also the question if China may have aspirations to resemble American judges, for example, in their ability to issue injunctions to seize assets in foreign countries.[59] *The Economist* further commented that "[t]hough Chinese officials

---

[55] But cf. Zihao Zhou et al., *Survey Results: Rules on China's International Commercial Courts*, 3 CHINA L. CONNECT (Dec. 2018), https://cgc.law.stanford.edu/commentaries/clc-3-201812-26-zhou-harpainter-cao/ (suggesting that the rules are unclear as to whether the value of the contract or the value of the dispute should exceed RMB 300 million).

[56] *Id.* at art. 2; see also Erie, *supra* note 49 (summarizing provisions).

[57] See, e.g., Chinese Rule of Civil Procedure, rule 34.

[58] *A Belt-and-Road Court Dreams of Rivalling the West's Tribunals*, THE ECONOMIST (June 6, 2019), https://www.economist.com/china/2019/06/06/a-belt-and-road-court-dreams-of-rivalling-the-wests-tribunals.

[59] These new courts like the CICC may also challenge the asserted separation between adjudicatory, prescriptive, and enforcement jurisdiction. If a rendering court imposes a global asset freeze, for example, public international law limits on enforcement jurisdiction may constrain adjudicative jurisdiction. If a rendering court imposes a global asset freeze, for example, that can lead to public

denounce America as a bully with a long reach, some scholars wonder whether China might one day begin issuing more extraterritorial judgments of its own."[60]

Over time, these courts are likely to expand their jurisdiction. The DIFC Court in Dubai, one of the oldest of this new spate of international commercial courts, offers an illustration.[61] The DIFC opened in 2004 to be "a hub for institutional finance and . . . a regional express way for capital and investment."[62] The DIFC establishes a business-friendly legal jurisdiction for international investment. DIFC law, a common-law-based system that applies within the free-trade zone, protects foreign companies from the local shari'a law that would otherwise govern commerce in that country. The DIFC has its own court system as well as an arbitration center; the courts operate in English (rather than Arabic).

When it was first established, the DIFC Court limited its bases for jurisdiction to cases with a territorial link to Dubai. In 2011, however, the DIFC removed that requirement.[63] The DIFC Court now has jurisdiction over, inter alia, all "civil or commercial claims and actions to which the DIFC or any DIFC Body, DIFC Establishment or Licensed DIFC Establishment is a party."[64] This party-based jurisdiction, if applied when only the claimant is a DIFC entity, can be akin to the exorbitant Article 14 jurisdiction in France. The DIFC Court also has liberal joinder rules, allowing any number of claimants or defendants to be joined on the Court's initiative or upon a party's motion.[65] The DIFC Court's enthusiasm for exerting jurisdiction can also be seen in cases where they have disregarded

international law limits on enforcement jurisdiction having a constraining effect on adjudicative jurisdiction. Likewise, if a court applies mandatory rules in derogation of the substantive law that should otherwise apply to a dispute under choice-of-law rules, that application would amount to an exercise of prescriptive jurisdiction, again subject to international law limits on prescriptive jurisdiction. This point is already accounted for in the Restatement, however, which recognizes restraints on prescriptive and enforcement jurisdiction.

[60]  *A Belt-and-Road Court, supra* note 58.

[61]  See, e.g., Latham & Watkins, *supra* note 48, at 4 (discussing how "the DIFC Courts have become increasingly assertive in their jurisdictional claims").

[62]  Zain Sharar & Mohammed Al Khulaifi, *The Courts in Qatar Financial Centre and Dubai International Financial Centre: A Comparative Analysis,* 46 H.K. L.J. 530, 536 (2016); see also Erie, *supra* note 49, at 35 (describing Dubai's efforts to "repatriate Middle Eastern money," "secure FDI and encourage international banks to lend in Dubai," including opening the DIFC Courts).

[63]  Marta Requejo, International Commercial Courts in the Litigation Market 6-7 (MPILux Research Paper 2019 (2)), https://papers.ssrn.com/sol3/papers.cfm?abstract_id=3327166; Jayanth K. Krishnan, The Story of the Dubai International Financial Centre Courts: A Retrospective 40 (Indiana Legal Studies Research Paper No. 404, 2018), https://papers.ssrn.com/sol3/papers.cfm?abstract_id=3280883.

[64]  Law No. (16) of 2011 Amending Certain Provisions of Law No. (12) of 2004 Concerning Dubai International Financial Centre Courts, https://www.difccourts.ae/2011/10/31/law-no-16-of-2011-amending-certain-provisions-of-law-no-12-of-2004-concerning-dubai-international-financial-centre-courts/.

[65]  DIFC Courts, RDC pt. 20; Al Tamimi & Company, *supra* note 43 (noting expansion of "necessary or proper party" jurisdiction over a third party over which the court would not otherwise have had jurisdiction).

forum-selection clauses choosing other courts and nevertheless asserted DIFC Court jurisdiction.[66]

The DIFC Court also offers parties the ability to bring a court-rendered money judgment to arbitration at the DIFC-LCIA Arbitration Centre (or any other arbitration center).[67] This unusual process would allow a prevailing party to convert its court money judgment into an arbitral award, which can be easier to enforce in a broader number of countries under the New York Convention.[68] The DIFC Court's reliance on consent, shunning of geographical connection requirements, and blurring of the distinction between court judgments and arbitral awards could also raise questions about the interaction between party autonomy, adjudicative jurisdiction, and international law limits.

It should be recalled that the widespread emergence and acceptance of party autonomy—that is, parties' ability to choose which court will hear their disputes and which law will govern them—is a relatively new innovation itself. While it was once considered anathema that parties could decide for themselves which courts would hear their disputes and which law would govern their relations, those principles today are widely accepted.[69] The limits of those principles, however, are being tested. In the United States, efforts to expand party autonomy into the realm of consumer contracts and other contexts that lack basic trappings of consent are recognized, though widely criticized.[70] Most other countries would not recognize extending the concept of "consent" this far. Whether that amounts to a violation of international law, however, will be seen perhaps only if extraterritorial adjudicative jurisdiction is stretched that far.

Finally, another open frontier of adjudicative jurisdiction may relate to notice and service. The London Commercial Court, which is the prototype for many of these new international commercial courts,[71] largely bases adjudicative jurisdiction on service of process, with various regulations on how to serve parties within and outside the territory, be they individuals or other legal persons.[72] If adjudicative jurisdiction in international commercial courts follows this model

---

[66] See Latham & Watkins, *supra* note 48, at 2–3.

[67] Stephan Wilske, *International Commercial Courts and Arbitration—Alternatives, Substitutes or Trojan Horse?*, 11 CONTEMP. ASIA ARB. J. 153, 163 (2018); Requejo, *supra* note 63, at 9.

[68] See Erie, *supra* note 49 (discussing this as-yet-unused feature).

[69] Robin J. Effron, *Ousted: The New Dynamics of Privatized Procedure and Judicial Discretion*, 98 B.U. L. REV. 127, 128 (2018).

[70] See, e.g., Pamela K. Bookman, *The Arbitration-Litigation Paradox*, 72 VAND. L. REV. 1119 (2019) (describing these developments and criticism); David L. Noll, *Regulating Arbitration*, 105 CALIF. L. REV. 985, 1002–106 (2017).

[71] See Bookman, *supra* note 39, at 32.

[72] See generally *The Competence of the English Courts under the Traditional Rules*, in CHESHIRE, NORTH & FAWCETT: PRIVATE INTERNATIONAL LAW (Paul Torremans et al. eds., 15th ed. 2017).

and attempts to stretch it, that may put strains on international concepts of notice and service.[73]

## III. Finding Evidence of International Law

The debate sparked by the Restatement about the international law status of adjudicative jurisdiction is in part a debate about sources of international law. The reporters and their interlocutors agree that states rarely, if ever, object to exercises of adjudicative jurisdiction *on the basis of international law*. Far more likely, states may object to such jurisdiction as violating international comity. But at the same time, states almost always assert jurisdiction based on some kind of connection between the case and the forum. The controversy is in part a debate about starting points: Are we looking for evidence of states derogating from norms, which is difficult to find, or for evidence of states' objecting to others' derogating from norms, which is also difficult to find? Nevertheless, if the question is what might convince reporters to reconsider the Fourth Restatement's approach, we should look to what sources might move those reporters. This section will probe what the innovations discussed thus far might provide as evidence of state practice or *opinio juris* regarding the international law status of adjudicative jurisdiction.

## A. State Practice

The institutional design of new collective action mechanisms and new courts presents an interesting case study in the perceived limits on adjudicative jurisdiction. On one hand, notwithstanding several of these courts' openness to parties choosing them for contract disputes that have nothing to do with the locality, each of them has some kind of nexus requirement for asserting jurisdiction. But they also seem open to exercising jurisdiction even when there are scant connections between the defendant and the forum. Joinder jurisdiction, for example, based on other parties' consent to jurisdiction, may be allowable if the *case* requires it, even if that jurisdiction would seem unfair to the defendant. Notably, this perspective contrasts with recent developments in U.S. personal

---

[73] Cf., e.g., Rockefeller Tech. Investments (Asia) VII v. Changzhou Sinotype Tech. Co., 24 Cal. App. 5th 115 (Ct. App. 2018) (considering validity of international service by Federal Express where Chinese parties agreed in an international contract to accept service by FedEx in contravention of the Hague Service convention); John F. Coyle, Robin J. Effron, & Maggie Gardner, *Contracting Around the Hague Service Convention*, 53 U.C. DAVIS L. REV. ONLINE 53 (2019) (arguing that it is not possible to derogate from the Hague Service Convention by contract).

jurisdiction law, which requires connections between the defendant and the forum state.[74]

These courts are also likely to test the limits of consent-based jurisdiction. Consent could be found in contracts that were less than freely negotiated.[75] Likewise, the availability of opt-out class action settlements and judgments, for example through the Dutch WCAM process, may raise questions about the meaning of consent.

In short, new international commercial courts and courts responding to global forum shopping are primed to experiment with new extensions of exorbitant jurisdiction. As they do so, it will be important to watch how states respond to their nationals being subject to adjudicative jurisdiction on those terms. The same is true for more "old-fashioned" exorbitant exercises of jurisdiction, for example, based on the domicile of the complaining party (as is available before the DIFC Courts or possibly in the new French international commercial chambers), or jurisdiction based on consent where parties contest whether they truly consented to a forum selection clause.

When U.S. courts exercised exorbitant jurisdiction, foreign countries contested judicial imperialism in different ways. Some filed amicus briefs with the rendering court.[76] Some worked through diplomatic sources. Judicial independence made some diplomatic efforts less successful or less worth the candle. Indeed, the U.S. Supreme Court does not always seek or follow State Department advice in issues involving transnational litigation.

Different avenues for diplomatic protest may apply if the aspiring judicial imperialist is an authoritarian government. In the absence of judicial independence—for example, in China, where judicial independence is considered "a false Western ideal"[77]—there may be more fertile ground for diplomatic maneuvering.

Another sparring ground for these debates could be through courts themselves. For example, foreign courts will be called upon to recognize and enforce or block enforcement of judgments rendered on the basis of these expansions of exorbitant jurisdiction. In this context, one nation's judges' treatment of other nations' court decisions may shape the landscape of legal norms.[78] Decisions not to recognize foreign judgments rendered on the basis of exorbitant jurisdiction— whether for purposes of enforcement or for purposes of res judicata—may provide further evidence of state practice of rejecting such bases of jurisdiction.

[74] See, e.g., Walden v. Fiore, 571 U.S. 277 (2014).
[75] See, e.g., Carnival Cruise Lines, Inc. v. Shute, 499 U.S. 585 (1991).
[76] See Eichensehr, *supra* note 14, at 298.
[77] *A Belt-and-Road Court, supra* note 58.
[78] See generally Paul B. Stephan, *Courts on Courts: Contracting for Engagement and Indifference in International Judicial Encounters*, 100 VA. L. REV. 17 (2014).

## B. *Opinio Juris*

State objections will not be sufficient if they do not tie themselves to an objection on the basis of international law. Here, the Fourth Restatement could itself influence the arguments that states make about the content of international law. It is most likely to affect U.S. actors, who may be less likely to oppose foreign courts' exertion of jurisdiction over U.S. parties on the basis of international law. The Restatement, however, may have less influence on foreign states and their tendency to assert objections on the basis of international law. Conversely, it is conceivable that courts that otherwise were constraining themselves based on generally accepted limits of adjudicative jurisdiction will feel emboldened by the announcement that international law does not restrain them.

In the context of both institutional design and global forum shopping, the international law question will depend on how states define the debate. Over time, the question may be not only whether these courts may assert broader jurisdiction but also how other states react, for example, if states object to particular cases or if foreign courts refuse to enforce them. On the other hand, many of these new courts are signing memoranda of guidance with each other, committing to recognize each other's judgments and authority.[79] If these courts see each other as comrades, that may make it more likely that they will reinforce each other's exercises of jurisdiction, either out of an appreciation for reciprocity or based on reasoning that another's expansion of power could lead to one's own.

To move the needle on the question of international law's constraints on adjudicative jurisdiction, the courts' reactions must be put in international law terms. If the rendering courts then react to objections by cabining their jurisdictional reach, they could assert that those adjustments are meant to address international law restraints. As it now stands, courts in most nations will not recognize foreign judgments rendered without jurisdiction, as judged according to the receiving nation's standards of jurisdiction. Thus courts would have to rely on the rendering court's exercise of jurisdiction in violation of international law rather than simply in violation of the receiving court's domestic law understandings of the proper scope of jurisdiction.

These transnational litigation developments are also likely to involve powerful parties. Should those parties be subject to exorbitant adjudicative jurisdiction, they may be able to complain effectively to their political representatives. This could be a recipe for diplomatic protest against adjudicative jurisdiction. Such protest, once again, would need to be couched in international law terms to have an effect for purposes of this discussion.

---

[79] See Erie, *supra* note 49.

What might compel courts or diplomatic protest to reject exorbitant jurisdiction *on the basis of international law*? Some have argued that weaker states
are more likely to invoke international law in arguments against stronger states.
Alternatively, states trying to establish their own courts' legitimacy could argue
that staying within international law boundaries of adjudicative jurisdiction
furthers their claims to legitimacy.

In other contexts, Rebecca Ingber has explored reasons why states invoke international law that could likewise apply to states objecting to exorbitant jurisdiction. First, she suggests that states may invoke international law justifications
when they are trying to argue around what might otherwise be domestic law
hurdles.[80] In this context, parties or states may invoke international law to circumvent domestic law principles that would otherwise point in favor of enforcing or not enforcing foreign judgments. Second, Ingber explains that parties
invoke international law when they want to provide courts with a justification
for their decisions based in law.[81] This force may be particularly compelling in
high-stakes disputes, where parties may search ever further for legal principles
supporting their position. The Fortis WCAM settlement was worth $1.5 billion.
The CICC's jurisdiction covers only disputes worth *over* $40 million. It is pos-
sible that exorbitant jurisdiction in cases with so much at stake may be more
likely to offend first principles and the sense of what international law permits.

As a third possibility, the changing landscape of judgment enforcement could
alter parties' default assumptions. Customary international law does not require
courts to enforce other courts' judgments. But two new conventions—the new
Hague Convention on the Recognition and Enforcement of Foreign Judgments
in Civil or Commercial Matters and the Convention on Choice of Court
Agreements—do.[82] The Judgments Convention contains a long list of bases for
recognition and enforcement that track accepted bases for adjudicative jurisdiction, including general jurisdiction (e.g., if the defendant is habitually resident in
the rendering court's state)[83] and specific jurisdiction (e.g., if a tortious act giving
rise of the suit occurred in the rendering court's state).[84] If prevailing parties seek
recognition or enforcement of a judgment arising out of a contractual dispute
designating a particular forum, for example, but that extends jurisdiction over
nonconsenting third parties, that could trigger judicial discussions about the
scope of recognized jurisdiction and the customary international law that might

---

[80] Rebecca Ingber, *International Law Constraints as Executive Power*, 57 HARV. INT'L L.J. 49, 71 (2016).

[81] *Id.* at 66–67.

[82] Hague Conference on Private International Law, Convention of 2 July 2019 on the Recognition and Enforcement of Foreign Judgments in Civil or Commercial Matters (July 2, 2019), https://www.hcch.net/en/instruments/conventions/full-text/?cid=137.

[83] *Id.* at art. 5(1)(a).

[84] *Id.* at art. 5(1)(j).

fill in gaps not addressed by the Conventions.[85] The Conventions could also inform how parties and states more generally conceive of the appropriate international law boundaries for adjudicative jurisdiction. Moreover, the interaction between customary international law and these new Conventions could obscure the boundaries between the two. Ingber refers to parties' and states' use of "international law arguments as smokescreen," whether intentionally or not.[86] The interaction between Judgments Conventions and domestic and international law of adjudicative jurisdiction may provide fertile ground for such obfuscation.

It is also possible that these events never come to pass. That is, if adjudicative jurisdiction is not pushed that far or not objected to on the basis of international law—then the reporters of the Restatement (Fifth) will find themselves in much the same position as we are in today.

## IV. Questions Raised

This chapter has sought to evaluate current trends in international adjudication outside the United States to identify where the boundaries of adjudicative jurisdiction are most likely to be tested in the near future and to contemplate what developments could affect the reporters' understanding of international law restraints on adjudicative jurisdiction enough to call for a revision of the Fourth Restatement's position when future reporters consider the Fifth Restatement.

The dynamic future of adjudicative jurisdiction may leave out U.S. courts, although it may strongly impact U.S. parties. If other countries become "judicial imperialists," adjudicative jurisdiction—whether a matter of public international law or not—may become of greater concern for U.S. foreign relations.

The Third Restatement has been criticized for describing the domain of customary international law primarily by citing state practice by U.S. courts, omitting discussion of *opinio juris*.[87] The Fourth Restatement sought to correct that vision by searching for evidence of international law restraints on adjudicative jurisdiction outside the United States in the form of state practice and *opinio juris*. Finding none, the Restatement declared that international law imposed no such constraints. By the time the reporters of the Fifth Restatement reconsider this question, U.S. judicial practice may have little role in pushing the outer bounds of adjudicative jurisdiction. On the contrary, it is possible that U.S. political actors may oppose foreign courts' abuses of adjudicative jurisdiction. If other

---

[85] See generally Harlan Grant Cohen, *International Law's* Erie *Moment*, 34 MICH. J. INT'L L. 249 (2013) (discussing gap filling in international law).

[86] Ingber, *supra* note 80, at 100.

[87] See William S. Dodge, *International Comity in the Fourth Restatement*, in this volume.

states push the boundaries of adjudicative jurisdiction beyond the norms that require some connection between the forum and the dispute, there may emerge an important role for international law. If states, including the United States, continue not to invoke international law in these debates, the absence of international law limits may be felt with marked regret.

# 16

# *Forum Non Conveniens* in the Fourth Restatement

*Donald Earl Childress III*

The Fourth Restatement states succinctly the *forum non conveniens* doctrine: A U.S. federal court "may dismiss a case if: (a) there is an available and adequate alternative forum; and (b) despite the deference owed to the plaintiff's choice of forum, the balance of public and private interests favors dismissal."[1] The Fourth Restatement next details in the comments various intricacies of the doctrine and proposes rules derived from U.S. federal court decisions with the hope (one suspects) of constraining judicial discretion in applying the main rule. These rules, which do not appear in prior restatements, provide that the moving party has the burden of persuasion when invoking the doctrine;[2] federal courts apply federal common law in analyzing the doctrine while state courts apply state law, "even when the claim arises under a federal statute";[3] an "alternative forum is generally considered available if all parties are amenable to process" and jurisdiction, and it is generally "considered adequate if the parties will not be deprived or all remedies or treated unfairly";[4] a plaintiff's choice of forum is entitled to less deference when the plaintiff is not at home;[5] and federal courts should weigh "both private and public interest factors to determine if the presumption in favor of the plaintiff's choice of forum has been overcome."[6] As these rules illustrate, the Fourth Restatement treats the *forum non conveniens* doctrine as a doctrine of law—as opposed to one of judicial discretion. In so doing, the Fourth Restatement formulates clear rules for U.S. federal courts to apply in resolving a *forum non conveniens* motion.

This chapter evaluates the approach taken by the Fourth Restatement to the *forum non conveniens* doctrine in light of the doctrine's history and present usage. This chapter is divided into three sections. Section I considers Supreme

---

[1] FOURTH RESTATEMENT § 424 (2018).
[2] *Id.* cmt. *a.*
[3] *Id.* cmt. *b.*
[4] *Id.* cmt. *c.*
[5] *Id.* cmt. *d.*
[6] *Id.* cmt. *e.*

Donald Earl Childress III, Forum Non Conveniens *in the Fourth Restatement* In: *The Restatement and Beyond.* Edited by: Paul B. Stephan and Sarah H. Cleveland, Oxford University Press (2020). © Oxford University Press. DOI: 10.1093/oso/9780197533154.003.0017

Court decisions developing the doctrine to set the stage for assessing the Fourth Restatement's approach. Section II explores the doctrine as it has developed through various restatement projects, including the Fourth Restatement. Section III examines the role of party interests in the *forum non conveniens* analysis and explores tensions in the doctrine that should be accounted for by U.S. federal courts and in future restatement projects.

## I.  Background

According to the Supreme Court, the "doctrine of *forum non conveniens* has a long history."[7] Yet the doctrine as we know it in U.S. federal case law—not as a doctrine of comity or abstention, but as a multifactored test to be employed by U.S. courts—is of relatively recent vintage. The modern *forum non conveniens* doctrine arguably traces its roots in the United States to a law review article published by a New York law firm associate in 1929.[8] According to one commentator, it was not until 1948 that the doctrine was "accepted for general application in the federal courts, and it received little or no attention in the state courts until after the federal adoption."[9] The Supreme Court's decision in 1947 in *Gulf Oil Corp. v. Gilbert*[10] established the doctrine in U.S. federal courts.

In *Gulf Oil*, a Virginia plaintiff sued a Pennsylvania defendant doing business in Virginia for negligence that occurred in Virginia. Although the plaintiff could have sued in Virginia because Virginia was the place of the harm, he instead chose to sue in New York, where the defendant was registered to do business and had an agent appointed for service of process. Because all the conduct giving rise to the suit occurred in Virginia and the witnesses and evidence were in Virginia, the federal district court dismissed the case on *forum non conveniens* grounds. The U.S. Court of Appeals for the Second Circuit took a more restrictive view of the doctrine and reversed.

---

[7]   Piper Aircraft Co. v. Reyno, 454 U.S. 235, 248 n.13 (1981).

[8]   Paxton Blair, *The Doctrine of Forum Non Conveniens in Anglo-American Law*, 29 COLUM. L. REV. 1 (1929).

[9]   Allan R. Stein, *Forum Non Conveniens and the Redundancy of Court-Access Doctrine*, 133 U. PA. L. REV. 781, 796 (1985).

[10]   330 U.S. 501 (1947). A companion case with different facts, *Koster v. American Lumbermens Mutual Casualty Co.*, 330 U.S. 518 (1947), was decided the same day on the same legal principles. While not mentioning the doctrine by name, one precursor of the doctrine appears in the Supreme Court's decision in *Canada Malting Co. v. Patterson Steamships Ltd.*, 285 U.S. 413 (1932), where Justice Brandeis, writing for the Court, stated: "Courts of equity and of law also occasionally decline, in the interests of justice, to exercise jurisdiction, where the suit is between aliens or nonresidents, or where for kindred reasons the litigation can more appropriately be conducted in a foreign tribunal." *Id.* at 423. The doctrine arose mostly in the admiralty context, although some state court case law supported a broader doctrine outside of the admiralty context, as does the Supreme Court's opinion in *Slater v. Mexican National Railroad Co.*, 194 U.S. 120, 124–25 (1904).

On certiorari, the Supreme Court reversed the Second Circuit and clarified the doctrine. According to the Supreme Court, the *forum non conveniens* doctrine empowers a federal district court to dismiss a case in favor of another court (here, another U.S. court), even where there is jurisdiction and venue, when private and public interest factors weigh in favor of the suit being brought in an available and adequate alternative forum.[11] A federal district court's discretion to dismiss a case in favor of another adequate, alternative forum, the Court concluded, was subject to a series of private and public factors, and, as such, was not to be an exercise in unbounded judicial discretion. The Court detailed the factors to be balanced and considered as follows:

> [The private factors include] the relative ease of access to sources of proof; availability of compulsory process for attendance of unwilling, and the cost of obtaining attendance of willing, witnesses; possibility of view of premises, if view would be appropriate to the action; and all other practical problems that make trial of a case easy, expeditious, and inexpensive. There may also be questions as to the enforceability of a judgment if one is obtained. The court will weigh relative advantages and obstacles to fair trial. It is often said that the plaintiff may not, by choice of an inconvenient forum, "vex," "harass," or "oppress" the defendant by inflicting upon him expense or trouble not necessary to his own right to pursue his remedy.[12]

The Court also addressed the pertinent public interest factors:

> Administrative difficulties follow for courts when litigation is piled up in congested centers instead of being handled at its origin. Jury duty is a burden that ought not to be imposed upon the people of a community which has no relation to the litigation. . . . There is a local interest in having localized controversies decided at home. There is an appropriateness, too, in having the trial of a diversity case in a forum that is at home with the state law that must govern the case, rather than having a court in some other forum untangle problems in conflict of laws, and in law foreign to itself.[13]

According to the Court, a federal district court's discretion to dismiss a case on *forum non conveniens* grounds was to be used judiciously: "unless the balance is strongly in favor of the defendant, the plaintiff's choice of forum should rarely be disturbed."[14] Such limited circumstances would appear to be those cases where

---

[11] *Id.* at 507.
[12] *Id.* at 508.
[13] *Id.* at 508–509.
[14] *Id.* at 508.

the plaintiff's choice of an inconvenient forum causes injustice to the defendant, by choosing a forum with little or no nexus to the case at bar which compromises the defendant's ability to mount an appropriate defense.[15]

The Supreme Court developed further the *forum non conveniens* doctrine in 1981 in *Piper Aircraft Company v. Reyno*,[16] which applied the *Gulf Oil* test in the transnational context. In *Piper*, Scottish plaintiffs brought a wrongful death action in California state court against two American defendants who had manufactured the engine and propellers of a plane that crashed in Scotland. The defendants removed the case to a California federal district court, and then transferred the case to a Pennsylvania federal district court, where they then moved for dismissal on *forum non conveniens* grounds. Applying the *Gulf Oil* test, the federal district court granted dismissal in favor of a Scottish forum, but the U.S. Court of Appeals for the Third Circuit reversed, holding that dismissal was inappropriate because of Scottish law that was less favorable to the plaintiff's case.[17]

The Supreme Court reversed the Third Circuit and clarified the doctrine in two important respects. First, in evaluating the above *Gulf Oil* factors, the Court explained that when a plaintiff chooses her home forum, "it is reasonable to assume that this choice is convenient."[18] Yet, "[w]hen the plaintiff is foreign, ... this assumption is much less reasonable."[19] In short, "a foreign plaintiff's choice [of forum] deserves less deference" than a domestic plaintiff's choice.[20]

Second, the Court explained that even if an unfavorable change in law results from sending a case to a foreign jurisdiction, such a change does not by itself bar dismissal on *forum non conveniens* grounds.[21] So, for instance, even in a case where a foreign forum would not provide to the plaintiff similar relief as compared with a domestic forum, a federal court may still dismiss the case when the balance of private and public interests favors dismissal.[22] In the Court's most recent consideration of the doctrine in 2007 in *Sinochem International Co. Ltd. v. Malaysia International Shipping Corp.*, the Court clarified that a federal court may dismiss a case under the *forum non conveniens* doctrine even before determining subject matter and personal jurisdiction "when considerations of convenience, fairness, and judicial economy so warrant."[23]

---

[15]  See generally Koster v. (Am.) Lumbermens Mu. Cas. Co., 330 U.S. 518 (1947).
[16]  454 U.S. 235 (1981).
[17]  *Id.* at 241–46.
[18]  *Id.* at 256.
[19]  *Id.*
[20]  *Id.*
[21]  *Id.* at 261.
[22]  *Id.*
[23]  Sinochem Int'l Co. Ltd. v. Malaysia Int'l Shipping Corp., 549 U.S. 422, 432 (2007).

It is important to note that the private-public interest factors enunciated by the Supreme Court are only guideposts, and the Court to date has declined to catalog all of the circumstances where dismissal would be proper.[24] While it is hard to identify precisely a hierarchy of factors compelling dismissal, one of the leading rationales for doing so is whether a case requires complicated applications of foreign law.[25] Indeed, many lower federal courts have given this factor substantial and decisive weight in the *forum non conveniens* analysis.[26] While this factor is not conclusive,[27] the Court has emphasized that the doctrine

> is designed in part to help courts avoid conducting complex exercises in comparative law.... [T]he public interest factors point towards dismissal where the court would be required to "untangle problems in conflict of laws, and in law foreign to itself."[28]

The upshot of this Supreme Court case law is that a U.S. federal court is vested with wide discretion to dismiss a case with foreign elements, especially where a foreign plaintiff and foreign law is involved. In the federal system, such decisions are reviewed by appellate courts based on an abuse of discretion standard,[29] which confirms the significant discretion vested in federal district courts to resolve these motions.

## II. The Restatement Position

While the *forum non conveniens* doctrine is mentioned in various restatement projects,[30] its first substantial treatment was in the 1971 Second Restatement of Conflict of Laws. The Second Restatement states the doctrine crisply: "A state will not exercise jurisdiction if it is a seriously inconvenient forum for the trial of the action provided that a more appropriate forum is available to the plaintiff."[31] As to the factors to be considered by a U.S. court, the Second Restatement explains that:

---

[24] Gulf Oil Corp. v. Gilbert, 330 U.S. 501, 508 (1947).
[25] See *id.* at 509.
[26] See, e.g., Scottish Air Int'l, Inc. v. British Caledonian Grp., PLC, 81 F.3d 1224, 1234–35 (2d Cir. 1996); Ilusorio v. Ilusorio-Bildner, 103 F. Supp. 2d 672, 679 (S.D.N.Y. 2000).
[27] See Piper Aircraft Co. v. Reyno, 454 U.S. 235, 259–60 (1981).
[28] *Id.* at 251.
[29] *Piper*, 454 U.S. at 257.
[30] See, e.g., RESTATEMENT (FIRST) OF CONFLICT OF LAWS (Am. Law Inst. 1934); RESTATEMENT (FIRST) OF JUDGMENTS (Am. Law Inst. 1942); RESTATEMENT (SECOND) OF JUDGMENTS (Am. Law Inst. 1982).
[31] RESTATEMENT (SECOND) OF CONFLICT OF LAWS § 84 (Am. Law Inst. 1971).

[T]he two most important factors . . . are (1) that since it is for the plaintiff to choose his place of suit, his choice of forum should not be disturbed except for weighty reasons, and (2) that the action will not be dismissed unless a suitable alternative forum is available to the plaintiff.[32]

In addition to these factors, the Second Restatement notes that the remaining factors "may best be grouped under the two principal interests involved: those of the parties and those of the public."[33] It then cites and quotes *Gulf Oil* and basically leaves the rule at that. Besides providing very little guidance as to what a "seriously inconvenient" forum might be, the Second Restatement suffers from a distinctly domestic focus to the issue, as evidenced by the phrasing of the rule— namely, the use of the word "state" which, based on the comments, clearly means only U.S. states—and Comment i's sole concern with the doctrine's constitutional aspects in the interstate context.[34]

What is most interesting when comparing the 1971 restatement project to the Fourth Restatement is that the Second Restatement of Conflict of Laws engages forthrightly with the rationale for the doctrine in the very first comment following the black-letter law. According to the Second Restatement, because the Fifth and Fourteenth Amendments to the U.S. Constitution establish only the "outermost limits" of a U.S. state's jurisdiction, "the owner of a transitory cause of action will often have a wide choice of forums in which to sue. Some of these forums will have little relation to either the parties or the cause of action, and suit may increase greatly the burden to the defendant of making a defense."[35] On account of this concern, what animates the doctrine, according to the Second Restatement, is the desire to prevent a plaintiff from bringing "suit in such a forum in the belief that he may there secure a larger or an easier recovery or in the hope that" the burden on the defendant "will induce the defendant to enter a compromise, to contest the case less strenuously, or to permit judgment to be entered against him by default."[36] As explained in the Second Restatement, the *forum non conveniens* doctrine is designed to combat a plaintiff's forum shopping in domestic cases. It is important to note that the Second Restatement does not speak to the rationales for the doctrine in transnational cases, which is understandable given the limits of that project and the limited invocations of the doctrine in transnational cases as of the date of that restatement project.

Notably, the Fourth Restatement does not comment on the doctrine's rationales. This is an intriguing omission. One wonders why the reporters did not

---

[32] *Id.* cmt. *c.*
[33] *Id.*
[34] *Id.* cmt. *i.*
[35] *Id.* cmt. *a.*
[36] *Id.*

take account of the doctrine's rationales in transnational cases as the reporters did in the Second Restatement in domestic cases. This may tell us something about the Fourth Restatement's view of the doctrine. In placing comments on the rationales for the doctrine before the factors to be considered, and in providing such a short statement of the rule, the Second Restatement treats the doctrine as grounded in judicial discretion. Indeed, as that project explains, in a comment listed as "Discretion of the trial judge," whether a suit should be dismissed on *forum non conveniens* grounds "depends largely upon the facts of the particular case and is in the sound discretion of the trial judge."[37] One wonders why that project did not interrogate the trial judge's discretion more fully. It could be that the state of case law did not permit such an investigation. Alternatively, it could be that the domestic focus of that restatement project viewed other doctrines, such as personal jurisdiction in domestic cases, as a meaningful constraint on the doctrine.

In contrast, the Fourth Restatement also has a comment on the "discretion of the trial court."[38] But, unlike the Second Restatement, this comment does not merely confirm the trial court's discretion, but points to the ways in which a trial court may abuse its discretion, which include "failing to hold the moving party to its burden of persuasion, by dismissing without an adequate alternative forum" and "by failing to apply the appropriate level of deference to the plaintiff's choice of forum."[39] The Fourth Restatement thus trends toward what has been described as "rulification," which is the inherent pressure to identify rules as part of the common-law decision-making process.[40]

One question, however, is whether the rules identified by the Fourth Restatement are in keeping with the *Gulf Oil* Court's insistence that the private-public interest factors are only guideposts.[41] Certainly lower courts and litigants repeat this list as it comes from the Supreme Court, but putting the pieces together in the *forum non conveniens* puzzle may prove difficult. As explained by one court, "because there *is* a list, and a list sponsored by the Supreme Court, albeit in a case more than half a century old, parties find it difficult to resist trying to make their case correspond to the items in the list, however violent a dislocation of reality results."[42] Even if the Fourth Restatement is correct in its statement of the doctrine, future restatement projects should examine the doctrine's factors more fully in light of this critique.

---

[37] *Id.* cmt. *b.*
[38] FOURTH RESTATEMENT § 424 cmt. *h.*
[39] *Id.*
[40] See, e.g., Michael Coenen, *Rules Against Rulification*, 124 YALE L.J. 644, 654–55 (2014).
[41] Gulf Oil Corp. v. Gilbert, 330 U.S. 501, 508 (1947).
[42] Abad v. Bayer Corp., 563 F.3d 663 668 (7th Cir. 2009).

From this brief comparison of the exposition of the *forum non conveniens* doctrine by two restatement projects, we see the treatment of the doctrine shift from being one of a federal trial court's discretion to one of bounded discretion constrained by rules. We also see removal of the question of rationales for the doctrine from the analysis. This has the potential to provide clearer guidance for litigants and courts. It also presents the potential for greater scrutiny and checks on the doctrine as it is applied by U.S. federal courts in a given case. However, it also has the potential to obscure rationales for the doctrine, which is the subject of the next section.

## III. Party Interests

As noted, the Fourth Restatement states the *forum non conveniens* doctrine to capture three sets of interests: the interests of the plaintiff, the defendant, and the forum. A plaintiff presumably always chooses a forum that is convenient. But plaintiff convenience is mostly driven not by concerns of judicial efficiency or general litigation convenience but by litigation outcomes. A reasonable plaintiff should choose a forum where the likelihood of success on the merits is the greatest no matter the connection with the forum. Put another way, a reasonable plaintiff will select a forum where the applicable law, judicial procedures, and court or jury pool provide the greatest chance of a favorable outcome on the merits.

A defendant will have similar considerations in choosing a forum. In the federal system, doctrines such as removal and venue permit a defendant to challenge a plaintiff's forum choice in order to provide another adequate forum where the case can be heard. The defendant's considerations, like those of the plaintiff, are not made in a litigation vacuum. As with a plaintiff, a reasonable defendant should be assumed to identify a forum where her chance of success given substantive law, judicial procedures, and a favorable court or jury pool are paramount. Importantly, because the plaintiff is deemed to be the master of her case, significant deference is due to the plaintiff's forum choice. To be sure, loose doctrines of personal jurisdiction permitting significant discretion in a plaintiff's choice may work an injustice in an individual case. As such, the *forum non conveniens* doctrine permits the defendant to level the playing field and prevent egregious forum shopping, however that may be defined, where the forum has only an attenuated relationship with the case.

As explained by the Supreme Court, a forum court will have its own interest in the case. As the Court noted in *Gulf Oil*, the burdens on the forum include jury duty and the intricacies of applying foreign law as well as the "local interest in having localized controversies decided at home."[43] Yet it is unclear how this

---

[43] *Gulf Oil*, 330 U.S. at 508–509.

battle between a plaintiff and defendant for a favorable forum should be evaluated in the context of a forum's interests in hearing case.

How should a court evaluate these interests? The Fourth Restatement does not consider this question. Case law may be trending toward more precise rules, especially when evaluating motions to dismiss filed by home state defendants. Indeed, the question whether a forum defendant bears a heightened burden to establish that a suit brought by a foreign plaintiff should be subject to dismissal under the *forum non conveniens* doctrine is presently subject to a circuit split. This split is not considered by the Fourth Restatement, but it should be considered by federal courts and in future restatement projects.

A recent D.C. Circuit case identifies the issue, which is understandably not considered by the Fourth Restatement because the decision came after its publication. In *Shi v. New Mighty U.S. Trust*, the widow of a Taiwanese plastics billionaire sued three D.C.-based trusts created before her husband's death, alleging that the transfer of a large portion of the husband's assets to the trusts was unlawful under Taiwanese and District of Columbia law. The defendants moved to dismiss the case based on *forum non conveniens* on the grounds that complex and novel issues of Taiwanese family and inheritance law as well as the locations of witnesses and evidence in Taiwan counseled in favor of dismissal, which would be in keeping with the approach outlined by the Fourth Restatement.

The district court granted the defendants' motion and conditioned dismissal on the defendants' consent to personal jurisdiction and waiver of certain defenses in a Taiwanese forum. Applying the private-public interest factors, the district court concluded that the central claims in the case implicate Taiwanese concerns, especially Taiwanese law, and that the forum had only a weak interest in the case given the defendants' local incorporation. The district court also concluded that the locations of the witnesses and evidence also weighed in favor of dismissal.[44]

The D.C. Circuit, in reviewing the district court's dismissal for a clear abuse of discretion, examined the appropriate weight to be given to a foreign plaintiff's choice of a U.S. forum.[45] The D.C. Circuit began by noting, as does the Fourth Restatement, that while a U.S. plaintiff's choice of forum is entitled to substantial deference, a foreign plaintiff's choice of forum is entitled to less deference. But the deference due is a matter of degree, and deference "may be appropriate and certain considerations may make litigation in a U.S. court the most convenient choice even for foreign plaintiffs."[46] Returning somewhat to the rationales

[44] Chin-Ten Hus v. New Mighty U.S. Trust, 288 F. Supp. 3d 272 (D.D.C. 2018).
[45] Shi v. New Mighty U.S Trust, 918 F.3d 944 (D.C. Cir. 2019).
[46] *Id.* at 949 (citations omitted); see FOURTH RESTATEMENT § 424 cmt. d.

explained by the 1971 Second Restatement of Conflict of Laws, the D.C. Circuit explained that greater deference should be given to a plaintiff's choice of forum

> to the extent it was motivated by legitimate reasons, including the plaintiff's convenience and the ability . . . to obtain jurisdiction over the defendant, and diminishing deference to a plaintiff's forum choice to the extent that it was motivated by tactical advantage.[47]

Turning to the defendant's forum contacts, the D.C. Circuit noted that when evaluating the degree of deference owed to the plaintiff's choice of forum, where, as in the case at bar, a defendant is sued in their home jurisdiction, this "weighs heavily against dismissal."[48] In assessing the private-interest factors, the court concluded that the district court clearly failed to hold the defendants "to their 'heavy burden' to show that a foreign forum is significantly more convenient than a U.S. forum . . . that is their home jurisdiction."[49] In assessing the public-interest factors, the court observed that the defendants "can hardly complain now that they are burdened by being sued in their home jurisdiction," and any "economic burden to the forum is justified" given that the defendants are at home in the forum.[50]

In addition to the D.C. Circuit, the Eighth and Fourth Circuits have held that a defendant forum resident bears a heightened burden to establish dismissal under the *forum non conveniens* doctrine.[51] In contrast, the Seventh, Sixth, and Third Circuits have refused to impose a heightened requirement in similar circumstances.[52] The Fourth Restatement is silent on this question, even though some of the cases predate that project's publication.

As this circuit split shows, the Fourth Restatement leaves additional questions to be considered. In particular, how should federal courts evaluate *forum non conveniens* motions made by home forum defendants. The resolution of this split should tell one something about what the doctrine is designed to do, which takes

---

[47]  *Id.* at 950 (internal quotation marks and citations omitted).
[48]  *Id.*
[49]  *Id.* at 952.
[50]  *Id.* at 953 (quotation marks and citation omitted).
[51]  Reid-Walen v. Hansen, 933 F.2d 1390, 1395 (8th Cir. 1991) (holding that "where the forum resident seeks dismissal, this fact should weigh strongly against dismissal"); Galustian v. Peter, 591 F.3d 724, 732 (4th Cir. 2010) (holding that a foreign plaintiff is entitled to greater deference with respect to its forum choice "when the defendant is a resident and citizen of the forum he seeks to have declared inconvenient").
[52]  Abad v. Bayer Corp., 563 F.3d 663, 667 (7th Cir. 2009 (holding that "there is not reason to place a thumb on the scale . . . [w]hen the plaintiff wants to sue on the defendant's home turf, and the defendant wants to be sued on the plaintiff's home turf"); Barak v. Zeff, 289 F. App'x 907, 913 (6th Cir. 2008) (same); Windt v. Quest Commc'ns Int'l, Inc., 529 F.3d 183, 191 (3d Cir. 2008) (same).

us back to the relationship between rationales and factors that was discussed earlier.

If "the central focus on the *forum non conveniens* inquiry is convenience,"[53] one would be hard pressed to elevate the fact that a defendant brings a motion in their home jurisdiction to such significant influence. One wonders also whether the D.C. Circuit and other courts are animated more by creating rule-like factors that would be given central emphasis, as opposed to treating the doctrine as one of flexibility and discretion. It is unfortunate that the Fourth Restatement does not account for this case law. Perhaps future restatement projects will not only deal with the deference due to a foreign plaintiff's forum choice but also a forum defendant's desire to short-circuit that choice when they are at home in a given forum.

Future restatement projects may not be able to improve upon the factors outlined by the Supreme Court and developed by lower federal courts given the present state of case law. Nevertheless, some consideration is necessary of the forum defendant's interests in restating the doctrine.

## IV. Conclusion

The Fourth Restatement should be celebrated for undertaking a fulsome examination, especially compared to earlier projects, of the *forum non conveniens* doctrine that tries to discern rules for what is too often treated as pure judicial discretion. With that said, the Fourth Restatement presents an incomplete picture of the doctrine and fails to more precisely delineate the factors and rationales that should guide a U.S. federal court in employing the doctrine, especially in the case of a defendant domiciled in the forum where suit is brought.

As planned, the new Conflict of Laws Restatement will also restate the *forum non conveniens* doctrine.[54] The reporters plan to examine not only federal court decision making but also state court decision making in this area. In so doing, the restatement project should continue to focus not only on the rules that guide judicial decision-making but also on the rationales for the doctrine. It should also explore more completely the ways in which the doctrine is articulated and applied by U.S. federal courts in transnational cases. A more complete consideration of defendant interests will open up additional opportunities to evaluate the interests and rationales at stake when a U.S. federal or state court applies the

[53] *Piper*, 454 U.S. at 249.
[54] The Third Restatement proposes to comprise fifteen chapters, including Chapter 3 on judicial jurisdiction that will address *forum non conveniens*. RESTATEMENT (THIRD) OF CONFLICT OF LAWS xxiii–xxviii (Am. Law Inst. Preliminary Draft No. 5, Oct. 23, 2019). None of the five preliminary drafts produced to date, however, has taken up this task.

doctrine. Such a consideration will do much to counter or confirm recent academic commentary regarding the doctrine's usefulness in transnational cases. In so doing, doctrines of judicial discretion, like *forum non conveniens*, may be further restated as rules of law, or such doctrines may be returned to the rationales that animated prior restatement projects.

# 17

# Territoriality and Its Troubles

*George Rutherglen*

National boundaries have an appealing simplicity. For example, the 49th parallel divides western North America into the United States to the south and Canada to the north. Actions, events, and the allegiance of persons located entirely on one side of the parallel, no matter how close they are to the opposite side, fall within the power of either the United States or Canada, but not both. Like all territorial boundaries, if only more dramatically, this one establishes a simple rule for choice of law. It is a simple rule, however, only for simple cases. Complicate the geographical distribution of relevant events and the nationality of persons just a little, so that they are distributed across the border, and the simplicity of the solution offered by this rule disappears into the intricacies of conflict of laws, whether of the traditional rule-oriented variety or the later realist case-by-case approaches.

The same thing happens to the presumption against the extraterritorial application of statutes.[1] Taken literally, it is a simple rule suited for simple cases. The presumption works in complicated cases, when it works at all, only against the background of presumed rules that identify some geographically attributable feature of the case that can be used to select one sovereign's law over another's. Consider, for instance, *lex loci delicti*, which usually selects the law of the place of injury or damage for tort cases, ignoring the law of the place where the defendant might have acted.[2] The presumption against extraterritoriality, if it followed this background rule, would limit the coverage of federal statutes to cases where the place of injury was within the United States. Such "jurisdiction selecting" rules have been sharply criticized by generations of conflicts scholars.[3] The presumption against extraterritoriality sets its face against these criticisms. Why?

---

[1] Not to mention any presumption against application of statutes to extraterrestrials. The imagination of science fiction writers has not, to this author's knowledge, reached into the mysteries of choice of law. See Babak Shakouri Hassanabadi, *Legal Implications of an Encounter with Extraterrestrial Intelligence*, SPACE REV. (June 15, 2015), available at http://www.thespacereview.com/article/2770/1.

[2] RESTATEMENT (FIRST) OF THE LAW OF CONFLICT OF LAWS § 377 (Am. Law Inst. 1934).

[3] David F. Cavers, *Critique of the Choice-of-Law Problem*, 47 HARV. L. REV. 173 (1933).

George Rutherglen, *Territoriality and Its Troubles* In: *The Restatement and Beyond*. Edited by: Paul B. Stephan and Sarah H. Cleveland, Oxford University Press (2020). © Oxford University Press.
DOI: 10.1093/oso/9780197533154.003.0018

This chapter tries to answer this question in five sections.[4] It begins with a description of what the presumption against extraterritoriality means and how it operates. It then turns to the justification for territorial allocation of government power generally. It next examines the question whether any presumption about the territorial scope of statutes must await a new consensus on the appropriate rules of choice of law. The next section argues that the presumption against extraterritoriality requires a flexible interpretation that makes it more of a principle than a rule. From that premise, the final section examines the choice between an ad hoc and a principled application of the presumption, both of which are exemplified in recent decisions.

## I. The Misleading Meaning of Extraterritoriality

The presumption against extraterritoriality itself presumes a set of complicated rules about which features of a transnational case count: which features make a case territorial and within the scope of a federal statute because these features can be located within the United States or, if they cannot, make the case extraterritorial and outside the statute's scope.[5] The dependence of the presumption upon a network of other rules both complicates its operation and makes it a less than certain guide to statutory interpretation. The decision which regenerated reliance upon the presumption, *EEOC v. Arabian American Oil Co. (ARAMCO),*[6] illustrates this dependence perfectly.

The claim in *ARAMCO* arose from the employment of an American citizen of Lebanese descent by American corporations operating in Saudi Arabia. The U.S. Equal Employment Opportunity Commission (EEOC) alleged that he had been harassed and discharged because of his race, national origin, and religion. ARAMCO defended on the ground that the alleged conduct, all in Saudi Arabia, fell outside the coverage of Title VII of the Civil Rights Act of 1964. The lower courts dismissed the EEOC's complaint on this ground, and the U.S. Supreme Court affirmed. The opinion of the Court invoked the "longstanding principle of American law 'that legislation of Congress, unless a contrary intent appears, is meant to apply only within the territorial jurisdiction of the United States.'"[7] Despite the seemingly unqualified language of Title VII, covering "any individual" and any employer with fifteen or more employees "engaged in an

---

[4] For a defense of the presumption against extraterritoriality along similar lines, see William S. Dodge, *The New Presumption Against Extraterritoriality,* 133 HARV. L. REV. (forthcoming 2020).

[5] Caleb Nelson, *State and Federal Models of the Interaction between Statutes and Unwritten Law,* 80 U. CHI. L. REV. 657, 674 (2013).

[6] 499 U.S. 244 (1991).

[7] *Id.* at 248 (quoting Foley Bros., Inc. v. Filardo, 336 U.S. 281, 285 (1949)).

industry affecting commerce,"[8] the Court found no contrary intent expressed in the statute. It reached this conclusion, despite the fact that the employee was an American citizen and the defendants were American corporations, because all the relevant acts occurred in Saudi Arabia. In the technical terms of conflict of laws, the Court ignored passive personality—protecting American citizens abroad—and active personality—regulating the actions of American corporations abroad—because all of the employment and employment decisions occurred abroad. The Court selected the location of the actions, rather than the nationality of the parties, as the decisive issue for coverage.

Within a year, however, the precise holding in *ARAMCO* was superseded by Congress, in the Civil Rights Act of 1991. Congress limited the presumption only to situations in which compliance with Title VII in a foreign country would cause the employer "to violate the law of the foreign country in which such workplace is located."[9] This provision addressed the fact situation in *ARAMCO* but extended coverage of Title VII unless Saudi law required—not just permitted—the employer to engage in discrimination. This restricted exception to coverage was augmented by a further provision extending coverage of Title VII to foreign corporations operating in foreign countries but controlled by American employers, with a detailed explication of this last requirement.[10] Both provisions, in turn, operate in conjunction with the original exception in Title VII for "employment of aliens outside any State."[11] All these provisions together illustrate how intricate the legislative solution to the problem posed by *ARAMCO* turned out to be. It was not nearly as simple as just selecting the location where the alleged discriminatory acts occurred and determining the scope of Title VII accordingly.

The same theme of complexity dominated the scholarly reaction to *ARAMCO* and then to subsequent decisions extending the presumption against extraterritoriality to other federal statutes and other fact situations.[12] This was, of course, a staple in the Legal Realist critique of the determinate rules compiled in First Restatement of Conflict of Laws.[13] Before judges and legislators settle upon seemingly simple choice-of-law rules, they have to determine whether the rules further the same goals as the laws that might, or might not, be chosen. What holds true of *ARAMCO* also applies to many of the other cases in which the presumption of extraterritoriality has been invoked.

---

[8] §§ 701(b), (g), 703(a), 42 U.S.C. §§ 2000e(b), (g), 2000–2(a).

[9] § 702(b), 42 U.S.C. § 2000e-1(b).

[10] § 702(b), (c), 42 U.S.C. § 2000e-1(b), (c).

[11] § 702(a), 42 U.S.C. § 2000e-1(a).

[12] Larry Kramer, *Vestiges of Beale: Extra-territorial Application of American Law*, 1991 Sup. Ct. Rev. 179 ("the Court thoughtlessly attempted to revive the original principle [of extra-territoriality]").

[13] E.g., Brainerd Currie, *Married Women's Contracts: A Study in Conflict-of-Laws Method*, 25 U. Chi. L. Rev. 227 (1958).

For instance, *Argentine Republic v. Amerada Hess Shipping Co.*[14] held that the bombing of a neutral oil tanker on the high seas did not fall within the exception to foreign sovereign immunity for losses "occurring in the United States" from acts attributable to a foreign state.[15] The Court applied "[t]he canon of construction which teaches that legislation of Congress, unless a contrary intent appears, is meant to apply only within the territorial jurisdiction of the United States."[16] While the wording of this particular exception in the Foreign Sovereign Immunities Act (FSIA) invites application of the presumption, by the phrase "occurring within the United States," other exceptions in the FSIA contain a complex mixture of actions of various kinds and events with different degrees of connection with the United States. The commercial activity exception extends to "an act outside the territory of the United States in connection with a commercial activity of the foreign state elsewhere and that act causes a direct effect in the United States."[17] Just as with Title VII, legislative elaboration of the standards for applying U.S. law reaches into matters of ever greater detail.

The abiding defect in the presumption against extraterritoriality lies in the mismatch between its justification and its implementation. It rests on the indisputable truth that modern nation states have divided up the habitable surface of the earth (and adjacent waterways) by territorial boundaries which define the principal sphere of state sovereignty.[18] Yet the presumption tries to reduce this abstract principle to a clear-cut rule to resolve hard cases that, in one way or another, straddle the borders between sovereign states. The presumption neglects the advice offered by Justice Oliver Wendell Holmes that "[g]eneral propositions do not decide concrete cases."[19] Neither, upon examination, does the presumption against extraterritoriality. As Holmes goes on to say, "The decision will depend on a judgment or intuition more subtle than any articulate major premise."[20]

Perhaps it is only a fitting irony that not long after Holmes offered this advice, he seems not to have followed it in one of the decisions cited as the foundation of the presumption against extraterritoriality, *American Banana Co. v. United Fruit Co.*[21] Yet the rationale for that opinion might equally be grounded in the act of state doctrine, since the acts complained of were undertaken by the government

---

[14]   488 U.S. 428 (1989).

[15]   28 U.S.C. § 1605(a)(5).

[16]   488 U.S. at 440 (quoting Foley Bros. v. Filardo, 336 U.S. 281, 285 (1949)).

[17]   28 U.S.C. § 1605(a)(2).

[18]   For an apt summary of the arguments for territoriality, and pointed criticism of those who would abandon a territorial approach to sovereignty, see Douglas Laycock, *Equal Citizens of Equal and Territorial States: The Constitutional Foundations of Choice of Law*, 92 COLUM. L. REV. 249, 315–20 (1992).

[19]   Lochner v. New York, 198 U.S. 45, 76 (1905) (Holmes, J., dissenting).

[20]   *Id.*

[21]   213 U.S. 347 (1909).

of Costa Rica within its territory.[22] It is these facts that constitute the minor premise, "more subtle than any articulate major premise," that make the result in that case appear inevitable. We should be wary of similar influences that affect the application of the presumption to apparently easy cases. We should ask first why those cases appear to be easy.

## II. Sovereignty, Territoriality, and Political Authority

Cases appear to be easy when they respond to the principle of exclusive territorial sovereignty: as Justice Story put it, the principle "that every nation possesses an exclusive sovereignty and jurisdiction within its own territory."[23] The territorial division of power among modern nation states, often attributed to the Peace of Westphalia that ended the Thirty Years' War, establishes only the "*de facto* authority*" of state sovereigns over those subject to its control. It does not establish actual political authority based on the consent or acceptance by the governed. Those subject to the power of the state might find themselves subject to it only by birth, accident, or conquest. They might reluctantly acquiesce in the power of the state by not objecting to it, but without recognizing its legitimacy. They might prefer to be governed by another state or by none at all, and while receiving benefits from the existing state, not accept them as a form of consent because of the burdens that the state also imposes by way of restricting their freedom. Sovereignty as a form of de facto authority falls well short of genuine authority supporting an obligation to obey the laws and dictates of the state.

Nor does de facto authority, by itself, imply that it constitutes the exclusive authority over the individual. Only by manipulating the contested concept of sovereignty so that it entails exclusivity by definition does the power of a single state over defined territory come to be unique. The history of the concept of sovereignty reveals that it has been deployed in different controversies for different purposes with different meanings. Federal systems of government, or more generally, those in which "We the People" reserve the right to change the constitution, divide sovereignty in ways that compromise any unqualified principle of exclusivity. Separate states in a federal union can exercise concurrent power with the national government, and the power of any governmental unit remains subject to the ultimate power of the people to replace it. It turns out that the exclusivity of sovereignty depends on the framework of government and the purposes for which government acts.

---

[22] *Id.* at 354–55.
[23] JOSEPH STORY, COMMENTARIES ON THE CONFLICT OF LAWS § 18.1 (1834).

These considerations of authority and sovereignty add another layer of complexity to the presumption against extraterritoriality, one that goes to its justification as much as to its implementation. A plausible justification based on authority goes to the role of the presumption in identifying the limits of state power. If successful, the presumption gives notice to individuals when they are and when they are not subject to government power. This is at least a necessary condition of genuine authority, since notice enables individuals to decide whether to accept or reject government power. A traditional way of doing so, although hardly the only way, is to choose to remain in or to leave the territory controlled by the government. If the presumption gave individuals a clear choice to opt out by staying out or getting out, it would reinforce this traditional means of escaping government power.

This justification addresses only a necessary condition for genuine political authority, not a sufficient condition. Individuals might not have a genuine choice whether to emigrate, or they might simply prefer less costly means of expressing their rejection of government authority. But even putting these limitations of the argument to one side, others arise from the complex operation of the presumption against extraterritoriality. It does not, first of all, purport to be anything other than a presumption—one that can be overridden by the legislature without the consent of any individual who seeks to opt out. Moreover, just as individuals might not have a real choice over whether to emigrate, they might not have real understanding of how the presumption works in practice. In the terms of the Fourth Restatement, the presumption operates in combination with other principles, which are both numerous and indeterminate. Some expand the scope of prescriptive jurisdiction,[24] while others identify limits upon it.[25] Perhaps the limiting provisions dominate the expansive ones, but only an individual or an institution with expert counsel could discern the outer reaches of government power under this restatement (or any of its predecessors).

The noise accompanying the signal of obedience only grows louder when it might come to an individual from several different sovereigns. Sovereignty, without more, does not imply exclusivity. Even sovereigns who each adopted the presumption against extraterritoriality would find their laws in conflict if one followed the presumption in a particular fact situation and the other did not. The facts relevant to any case raising a serious choice-of-law issue cannot be confined to the law of a single state. Choice of law becomes controversial when the geographic attributes of a case cross sovereign boundaries. Hence any signal communicated to a party potentially subject to the law of two or more states must be the joint product of the law of all the states involved. They must agree not only

---

[24] FOURTH RESTATEMENT § 402 (2018).
[25] Id. §§ 403, 404.

on the principles to be applied, including the presumption against extraterritoriality, but also on its application to the case at hand.

Comity between nations does little to amplify or clarify the notice given to parties in such cases. Comity might, after the case has arisen, permit the states themselves to reconcile their differences, by allowing the state with the weaker connection to or interest in the case to defer to the state with the stronger connection or interest. The party subject to the law of competing states, however, has little say in how such deference operates or what result it achieves. The party's concern is not *ex post*—after a case is resolved by applying one state's law or the other—but *ex ante*—in determining whether to be bound by the law of either state. The presumption against extraterritoriality, coupled with the exercise of comity, might send a strong signal to states to cooperate with one another, while at the same time, sending only a very weak signal, if any at all, to those subject to state power.

Inquiries along these lines strongly support the conclusion that the presumption against extraterritoriality, despite its apparent simplicity, really is addressed to sophisticated institutions and individuals who can appreciate its complexity. States and their instrumentalities, officials, and representatives constitute one targeted group. Other large institutions like corporations constitute another. Untutored laypeople, unassisted by counsel, fall well outside the intended audience. Another group of intended recipients of the message sent by the presumption obviously is lawyers, whose role in implementing the presumption is discussed in the next section of this chapter.

## III. Extraterritoriality and Implied Rights of Action

The rise of the presumption against extraterritoriality coincided with the decline of implied private rights of action, in decisions either refusing to imply a new private right of action or restricting the scope of one already recognized. Both lines of decisions began to be consistently applied in the 1990s with *ARAMCO* in 1991 denying extraterritorial scope to Title VII and *Central Bank of Denver N.A. v. First Interstate Bank of Denver, N.A.*[26] in 1994 rejecting an implied right of action for aiding and abetting violations of the securities laws, which had previously been one of the hotbeds of implied claims for damages. The predecessors of *Central Bank* stretched back to Justice Powell's dissent in *Cannon v. University of Chicago*[27] in 1979, in which he would have refused to imply a private right of action under Title IX of the Education Amendments Act of 1972.[28] Justice Powell's

---

[26]  511 U.S. 164 (1994).
[27]  441 U.S. 677, 730–49 (1979) (Powell, J., dissenting).
[28]  20 U.S.C. § 1620 *et seq.*

reasoning has, since the 1990s, become the dominant line of analysis on implied rights of action.[29]

Both lines of decisions plausibly are addressed to the lower federal courts, sending them a warning to wait for Congress to act explicitly before imposing liability for violations of federal statutes, in the absence either of relevant conduct in this country on the one hand or in the absence of a provision for private enforcement on the other.[30] Both presumptions are most plausibly addressed to attorneys, particularly plaintiffs' attorneys, who are told that they are wasting their time and money (not to mention their clients') in pursuing claims that Congress has not expressly authorized. Defense attorneys receive the same signal about the vitality of such claims and can advise their clients accordingly.

On this view, the message conveyed by the presumption against extraterritoriality is twofold: first, that what used to support coverage and liability under federal statutes no longer does so, at least to the extent of expanding coverage beyond clearly settled law; and second, that the presumption primarily is directed against exposure to liability and the expense of litigation, rather than toward approval of the defendants' underlying conduct. To take *ARAMCO* as an example, the Supreme Court deployed the presumption not to approve of discrimination overseas but to disapprove of the risks of litigation in the United States. To be sure, the effects of the presumption on conduct outside litigation cannot be disentangled from its effects on litigation itself, but the latter can be ascertained much more easily than the former. The message, such as it is, comes down to "this far and no further" under federal statutes without explicit provisions for coverage overseas.

Taking the message in this narrow sense compensates for its uncertain signal to those who might be regulated by U.S. law. The lawyers who litigate cases with extraterritorial components can appreciate how the presumption operates in practice, or can educate themselves in the complex way in which it does so. If they get the message, then individuals and institutions arguably subject to U.S. law have some protection against bearing the costs and risks of litigation under it. This channel of communication has its own impediments to understanding, but at least the steps in its operation are discernible, and they are backed up by the inertia that any plaintiff must overcome in getting litigation started at all. If plaintiffs are discouraged from suing, defendants have nothing to fear from the risk of overreaching U.S. law.

---

[29] PETER W. LOW, JOHN C. JEFFRIES JR., & CURTIS A. BRADLEY, FEDERAL COURTS AND THE LAW OF FEDERAL-STATE RELATIONS 149–53 (8th ed. 2014).

[30] Paul B. Stephan, Bond v. United States *and Information-Forcing Defaults: The Work That Presumptions Do*, 90 NOTRE DAME L. REV. 1465, 1474–76 (2015).

Moreover, with such limited ambition, the presumption need not attempt the Herculean task of forging a consensus on choice of law. Cleaning out what most scholars regard as a particularly dirty stable can await more systematic interventions. The presumption does not need to make the hopeless choice between arbitrary rigidity in the First Restatement of Conflict of Laws[31] and the indefinite indeterminacy of the Second Restatement with its overriding appeal to an open-ended list of relevant factors.[32] The one goes too far in direction of rules, no matter how arbitrary they may be, and the other goes too far in the direction of case-by-case adjudication, no matter how erratic and unpredictable it may be. These are two extremes in search of an acceptable middle ground. The presumption against extraterritoriality does not supply the solution to this dilemma. It is just a provisional solution and, at best, a first approximation, rather than a powerful principle with far-reaching implications. It is a way station on the path toward consistent and widely accepted principles of choice of law.

## IV. The Presumption as Principle

If the presumption against the extraterritoriality presupposes a network of rules, like the First Restatement, that identifies the decisive geographic features of a transnational case, then it can hardly operate as a clear-cut rule itself in the absence of such supporting rules. The scholarly rejection of the First Restatement makes these "jurisdiction selecting" rules hard to defend, and the terms of the Second Restatement make any surviving rules subordinate to an indeterminate multifactor analysis. The absence of consensus on choice of law has effectively cut loose the presumption from the legal foundations that would make it operate smoothly and efficiently to determine the scope of federal statutes. It cannot therefore be treated as a rule and must be treated as a principle, with varying weight in different cases applying different statutes. The decisions endorsing the presumption do not contemplate this possibility, and apparently would find it unwelcome, but it seems inevitable given the vacuum of choice of law in which the presumption must operate.

Treated as a principle, the presumption nevertheless retains some value, or so I would suggest. Beginning with the premise, recognized even by Brainerd Currie, that legislatures frame statutes usually with domestic cases in mind,[33] the presumption calls attention to the fundamental territorial orientation with

---

[31] RESTATEMENT (FIRST) OF THE LAW OF CONFLICT OF LAWS § 384 (Am. Law Inst. 1934) (choice of the *lex loci delicti* for torts).

[32] RESTATEMENT (SECOND) OF THE LAW OF CONFLICT OF LAWS § 6 (Am. Law Inst. 1971) (listing a variety of choice-of-law principles).

[33] Currie, *supra* note 13, at 230–31.

which Congress usually acts. That does not, as argued earlier in this chapter, solve the hard cases which are, by definition, not entirely domestic. Yet it does supply one reason for extending enforcement to transnational transactions with elements beyond the borders of this country: to defeat avoidance and evasion by trying to achieve effects within the United States, prohibited in purely domestic cases, by engaging in conduct outside the United States.

On one reading of *United States v. Aluminum Co. of America*,[34] that is precisely what concerned Judge Hand in extending liability under the antitrust laws to anticompetitive activity overseas designed to target the aluminum market in this country.[35] One could characterize the decision as endorsing "extraterritorial" application of federal law based on an "effects test." Certainly, the decision has come to stand for that proposition, but a fresh reading of the opinion supports a different interpretation: that intent to target a domestic market was necessary to a finding of liability and that to this extent the application of the statute was not extraterritorial at all. As Professor Nelson has observed, even the most stringent decisions invoking the presumption against extraterritoriality do not purport to cast doubt on *Alcoa* itself.[36] Moreover, Congress has, to a significant degree, endorsed this qualified reading of *Alcoa* in the Foreign Trade Antitrust Improvements Act (FTAIA),[37] which applies the antitrust laws to foreign commerce, but only to the extent that it has direct effects on participants in domestic commerce.[38] The FTAIA preserves *Alcoa*, but also the focus of the antitrust laws on domestic markets.

A similar analysis at a similar level of generality could be offered of *Morrison v. National Australia Bank, Ltd.*,[39] which denied a private right of action for securities fraud in transactions on a foreign exchange between foreign parties involving securities not registered for trading on American exchanges. Transactions more directly connected to the domestic securities market could still give rise to private claims. No doubt *Morrison* could be read more broadly in favor of the presumption against extraterritoriality, just as *Alcoa* has been read broadly against the presumption, but the lower federal courts, so far, have not read *Morrison* that way.[40] They have imposed remedies for securities violations overseas when those violations would undermine domestic securities markets.

---

[34] 148 F.2d 416 (2d Cir. 1945).
[35] *Id.* at 444 (finding that "the intent to affect imports [of aluminum into this country] was proved").
[36] Nelson, *supra* note 5, at 718–19.
[37] 15 U.S.C. § 6a.
[38] F. Hoffman-LaRoche, Ltd. v. Empagran, S.A. 542 U.S. 155, 159 (2004).
[39] 561 U.S. 247, 250 (2010).
[40] E.g., Stoyas v. Toshiba Corp. 896 F.3d 933, 940–42 (9th Cir. 2018) (allowing securities fraud claim with respect to foreign transaction involving American Depository Receipts registered with the Securities and Exchange Commission).

At the same time, they have given notice to would-be violators how to avoid liability: do not trade in securities traded on domestic exchanges.

In striking contrast to these cases, those involving human rights violations overseas seem to pose little threat of evasion of purely domestic prohibitions. The refusal, in *Kiobel v. Royal Dutch Petroleum Co.*,[41] to recognize a claim under the Alien Tort Statute (ATS)[42] for human rights violations within another country, has to do with ending human rights violations overseas, not in this country. Hence the rationale for applying the ATS cannot rest on evasion of domestic prohibitions. The same can be said of the tort case involving the detention and alleged torture of an American citizen in Saudi Arabia. In *Saudi Arabia v. Nelson*,[43] the Supreme Court refused to apply an exception to the FSIA for "commercial activity carried on in the United States by the foreign state."[44] There was no question of preventing or compensating for similar torts in this country. The remedy, by way of a tort claim against the foreign sovereign, did not fit any wrong that could be localized in the United States.

Of course, in both *Kiobel* and *Nelson*, Congress could have legislated to further ends far beyond the borders of this country. The Commerce Clause does not contain any geographical limits on the power of Congress, nor do several other similar clauses in the Constitution.[45] Arguably, as the dissents in both cases contended, Congress did act in the ATS and in the FSIA to further ends in other countries. The presumption against extraterritoriality leaves this question open, and depending upon how strictly it is interpreted, it requires more or less compelling evidence of congressional intent to go beyond a primarily domestic focus. That question cannot be answered simply by returning to the breadth of congressional power, which has not been much constrained in this respect, as in many others, since the New Deal. The presumption, whatever else might be said about it, at least has the virtue of drawing attention to the right question.

What the presumption cannot do is rely upon an infrastructure of choice-of-law rules that no longer exists, and with its disappearance, the prospect of treating the presumption as a determinate rule also disappears. Instead, the presumption requires an ad hoc attempt to identify which features of a transnational case really count in deciding whether it falls within the scope of a particular federal statute.[46] This approach might be framed in traditional choice-of-law terms, but it has no durable basis in any such body of law. What it does have is the potential to direct inquiry into a more fruitful direction: to endorse application of a

---

[41] 569 U.S. 108 (2013).
[42] 28 U.S.C. § 1350.
[43] 507 U.S. 349 (1993).
[44] 28 U.S.C. § 1605(a)(2).
[45] Nelson, *supra* note 5, at 693.
[46] *Id.* at 722–23.

federal statute when necessary to serve domestic ends, in which case its application is best regarded as not extraterritorial at all; or to inquire whether Congress, more or less explicitly, enacted the statute to pursue ends in other countries, in which case the presumption is overcome.

## V.  Context and Consistency

Predictably enough, the presumption against extraterritoriality works for the benefit of defendants. It supplies an added argument why a claim under American law cannot apply to cases with extraterritorial elements. It leaves the plaintiff in the position of arguing that the presumption does not apply in the first place, or that it has been overcome by factors more or less unique to the claim or facts before the court. The dynamics and incentives of litigation ensure that the presumption will gain a permanent place in transnational disputes involving federal claims. It therefore can easily become a source for ad hoc restrictions on the scope of federal law and the availability of federal remedies. Some recent decisions of the Supreme Court support this conclusion. It is not a welcome one.

Returning the presumption to its proper role in regulating the exercise of federal power in transnational cases requires a step back from the immediate incentives of the parties: of the defendants to obtain dismissal of a federal claim and of the plaintiffs to obtain the unique advantages of suing under federal law. Neither perspective does justice to the necessary balance between legislative power and judicial interpretation, nor between federal law and the law of other countries. In striking that balance, courts necessarily must make a contextual judgment. Not all statutes are equally amenable to coverage of conduct and events in foreign countries. At one extreme, the Federal Tort Claims Act explicitly excludes "[a]ny claim arising in a foreign country,"[47] while at the other extreme the Foreign Corrupt Practices Act would lose most of its point and effectiveness if its prohibitions against bribing foreign officials did not reach into foreign countries.[48] This might be only to say that the presumption against extraterritoriality is no more than a presumption, which carries more or less weight depending upon the statute to which it is applied.

The implications of this point go further, however. Precedent interpreting the presumption tends to be specific to particular statutes. Decisions under the Securities Exchange Act, like *Morrison*, have limited force when applied to other statutes. Identifying the particular transactions subject to this statute has few immediate implications for identifying the transactions subject to the

---

[47]   28 U.S.C. § 2680(k).
[48]   15 U.S.C. § 78dd-1(a).

antitrust laws. The Supreme Court itself recognized the felt necessity of this approach in the recent decision in *RJR Nabisco, Inc. v. European Community*,[49] concerned with a claim under the Racketeer Influenced and Corrupt Organizations Act (RICO).[50] That statute created a civil action for treble damages from a long list of crimes that constitute a "pattern of racketeering activity." The Supreme Court held that RICO applied extraterritorially only if the statutes that defined those crimes, termed "predicate offenses," also applied extraterritorially.[51] The cross-reference to predicate crimes in RICO itself did not override the scope of the statutes defining those crimes. As the Court remarked, "Context is dispositive here."[52]

The opinion in *RJR Nabisco* then went on to hold that even though the predicate offenses were extraterritorial, the plaintiff's treble damage action required proof of "a *domestic* injury to its business or property."[53] This conclusion depended upon the precise terms of the provision in RICO for a private right of action, and in particular, the absence of any indication that the plaintiff's "injury to its business or property" could be suffered overseas.[54] The analysis specific to a particular statute entered at three different points into the Court's reasoning: in the cross-reference in RICO to predicate crimes; in the statutes defining the predicate crimes; and in the provision in RICO creating a private action for treble damages.

As *RJR Nabisco* makes clear, the presumption against extraterritoriality can be overcome. It is not "strict in theory but fatal in fact" to application of a federal statute beyond the borders of this country.[55] This is the good news, at least for plaintiffs bringing claims under federal law. The bad news is that presumption does not yield reliably predictable results. It might be consistently invoked by defendants, but not consistently deployed by the courts. In the end, it might do little to rationalize choice-of-law decisions.

A look at the statutes which, by their terms, address issues of extraterritoriality should dispel the need for a single-minded quest for predictability. Who would have predicted the precise scope of the amendments to Title VII superseding the decision in *ARAMCO* or the contours of the exceptions to sovereign immunity in the Foreign Sovereign Immunities Act?[56] Ex ante, before Congress

[49] 136 S. Ct. 2090 (2016).

[50] 18 U.S.C. §§ 1961–1968.

[51] 136 S. Ct. at 2102.

[52] *Id.*

[53] *Id.* at 2106 (emphasis in original).

[54] 18 U.S.C. § 1964(c); 136 S. Ct. at 2108–11.

[55] The quoted phrase originated as a description of heightened judicial review, for instance, for racial classifications by government. Gerald Gunther, *The Supreme Court, 1971 Term—Foreword: In Search of Evolving Doctrine on a Changing Court: A Model for a Newer Equal Protection*, 86 HARV. L. REV. 1, 8 (1972).

[56] See *supra* section I.

passed these laws, their content could only have been a matter of guesswork. *Ex post*, they provided detailed notice to defendants who might become subject to the accompanying statutes. That kind of predictability allows prospective defendants, with sufficient legal advice, to adapt their behavior to avoid the application or to comply with the obligations of federal law. It does not advise them how other statutes might affect their operations.

So, too, judicial decisions that determine extraterritorial coverage offer only locally predictable results confined to particular statutes after they have been interpreted. The presumption against extraterritoriality might promise more, by way of uniformity across different substantive claims, but it cannot deliver upon it. Neither, of course, can choice-of-law principles in their current state of disarray. At most, both deliver rationales that can justify judicial decisions that reach plausible results with a degree of prospective uniformity as applied to particular statutes.

Plausibility, in turn, depends largely upon three principles that emerge from the opinions of the Supreme Court. First, the incentives of plaintiffs to sue under federal law align very imperfectly with the interests of the federal government in determining the scope of its laws. All the plaintiffs want to preserve or to extend the scope of federal law. Second, the conflict of federal law with foreign law goes beyond the out-of-court conduct prohibited or permitted by each source of law, which might be largely subject to agreement in form. In practice, however, federal law might provide remedies where foreign law seldom if ever does. And third, just as plaintiffs have reasons to push the envelope of federal law, defendants have reason to squeeze it to gain advantage, as in the example of foreign firms that want to exploit the domestic U.S. market, while remaining immune from liability under U.S. law. Each of these principles bears upon the others, but each exerts its force in a different direction, making predictability illusive and judicial reconciliation of their opposing tendencies necessary. The presumption against extraterritoriality provides one means of bringing them into balance.

Lord Denning of the English Court of Appeal captured the governing motive underlying the first principle: "As a moth is drawn to the light, so is a litigant drawn to the United States."[57] Of course, not all litigants are drawn to the United States. Defendants who have no claim themselves would prefer to stay away and not be subject to liability. The migration of claims to the United States follows directly from the more generous remedies available to private parties under U.S. law. Those claimants have every reason to expand the available remedies still further by relying on the precedents establishing private rights of action,

---

[57]  Smith Kline & French Laboratories Ltd. v. Bloch, 1 W.L.R. 730 (C.A. 1983).

particularly under federal law. Accordingly, the confluence of private rights of action and extraterritoriality, noted earlier, should come as no surprise.

The fit between the two lines of cases, however, often remains uneven. The recent decision in *Jesner v. Arab Bank, PLC*[58] is a case in point. The Supreme Court interpreted the ATS to exclude foreign corporations from liability under the statute. This exclusion does not closely fit principles of extraterritoriality, since it excludes liability of foreign corporations on claims arising domestically but leaves liability open for domestic corporations on claims arising overseas.[59] The point of the decision must be sought elsewhere, in suspicion of aid-and-abetting liability for institutions not themselves directly involved in violations of the law of nations. As noted earlier, the Supreme Court restricted this form of liability under the federal securities laws partly in response to the restless search of plaintiffs for additional claims against additional defendants.[60] Presumably, they were looking for defendants they could sue and who could pay any resulting judgment. A plaintiff's lawyer who did any less would not be acting in the best interests of the client. Expansion of federal claims against additional defendants accentuates the departure of U.S. law from the more restrained remedies available in other legal systems.

That leads to consideration of the second principle: of avoiding genuine conflict between federal law and the law of other nations. At the abstract level of prohibiting securities fraud or protecting human rights, most nations reach agreement on the basic requirements of a market economy and civilized society. Their disagreements become more acute as the question of what to do about illegal behavior becomes more concrete. The gap between rights and remedies stretches particularly wide when it comes to international law and human rights violations. A plethora of prohibitions in the laws of almost all nations does not regularly result in effective enforcement.[61] Perhaps compromise over remedies, even if it does not amount to actual hypocrisy, is more salient in these fields than elsewhere, but it is pervasive throughout the law. "Remedial equilibration," as Daryl Levinson has drily described it,[62] often leaves violations of the law and denial of individual rights subject to no remedy at all.

---

[58] 138 S. Ct. 1386 (2018).

[59] Symeon C. Symeonides, *Choice of Law in the American Courts in 2018: Thirty-Second Annual Survey*, 67 Am. J. Comp. L. 1 (2019).

[60] See *supra* note 39 and accompanying text.

[61] O'Nora O'Neill, Justice Across Boundaries: Whose Obligations? 140 (2016) (state obligations under covenants on rights "have been repeatedly emphasised, sometimes extended and frequently ignored").

[62] Daryl J. Levinson, *Rights Essentialism and Remedial Equilibration*, 99 Colum. L. Rev. 345 (2000).

Any single legal system that attempts to restore equilibrium between rights and remedies faces a likely influx of claims from elsewhere. Addressing one imbalance leads to another. To forestall multiple discrepancies of this kind, the Supreme Court handed down decisions like *RJR Nabisco*, which admit the existence of substantive violations, in that case of RICO and the predicate statutes, but limits the remedy. The same holds for *Kiobel*, in which the Supreme Court conceded the existence of human rights violations for the sake of argument, but denied any remedy under the ATS because these violations occurred within the boundaries of another country.[63] These decisions take the gap between rights and remedies seriously, but do not propose to narrow it, beyond devising a modus vivendi that makes it tolerable in a world of divided sovereignty and imperfect remedies.

As it typically operates, the presumption against extraterritoriality seeks to narrow the gap in the opposite direction: by limiting the scope of prohibitions and correlative rights under federal law. That strategy detracts from a universal view of rights, which takes the moral force of a claim to be correlated with its scope. Universal jurisdiction over piracy, for instance, has been justified on the ground that pirates "have declared war against all mankind."[64] Yet even in that instance, the absence of national sovereignty over the "high seas" creates a vacuum that must be filled by some form of law.[65] Universal coverage of legal norms has its origins in natural law, which elides any question of enforcement by operating outside the scope of any legal system. It purports, instead, only to offer abstract norms to be implemented by the laws actually in force in any existing legal system. Only in exceptional cases, like piracy, does the principle of "one law, eternal and immutable" map directly onto enforceable legal norms.[66] The division of labor among actual legal systems and sovereigns counsels against conflicting remedies in the run of ordinary cases.

The incentives of defendants to evade and defeat this division of labor bring the third principle into play: preventing defendants from gaining the benefit of the forum while evading its prohibitions, rights, and remedies. Attempts by defendants to evade the law represent the mirror image of attempts by plaintiffs

---

[63] 569 U.S. at 115 ("The question is not whether petitioners have stated a proper claim under the ATS, but whether a claim may reach conduct occurring in the territory of a foreign sovereign.").

[64] *Kiobel*, 569 U.S. at 132–34 (Breyer, J., concurring in the judgment) (internal quotation marks, brackets, and citation omitted).

[65] *Id.* at 121 (opinion of the Court).

[66] The quoted phrase comes from the discussion of natural law by MARCUS TULLIUS CICERO, ON THE REPUBLIC 98 (David Fott transl. 2014):

> There will not be one law in Rome, another at Athens, one now, another later, but one law both everlasting and unchangeable will encompass all nations and for all time.

Justice Story famously invoked this phrase to support internationally uniform maritime law. DeLovio v. Boit, 7 Fed. Cas. 418, 443 (1815).

to expand its scope. The third principle serves as the necessary qualification and complement to the first. It applies most directly in cases, like those under the antitrust law, in which the defendant allegedly exploited the domestic market by actions undertaken overseas. The somewhat inaccurately labeled "effects test" in antitrust attempted to reach such evasion, and as noted earlier, was subsequently endorsed by Congress in the FTAIA, although with some baffling complications, in the Foreign Trade Antitrust Improvements Act. In *F. Hoffman-La Roche, Ltd. v. Empagran, S.A.*,[67] the Supreme Court sensibly interpreted the act to exclude claims based on an anticompetitive foreign effect independent of any domestic effect.

As *Hoffman-LaRoche* indicates, the presumption against extraterritoriality becomes harder to rebut as the harm to U.S. interests becomes weaker. It poses particular obstacles to claims like those under the ATS, in which the harm often occurs overseas and in which, by the terms of the statute itself, the plaintiff is an alien. Neither traditional conceptions of territorial sovereignty nor "passive personality" jurisdiction based on protection of U.S. nationals[68] support application of the ATS. It is therefore no surprise that the Supreme Court has offered a narrow interpretation of the ATS for harms that occur outside the United States. The existence of domestic harm works as a two-edged sword, rebutting the presumption where it is present and making it all the more difficult to rebut when it is absent. Critics of the presumption might decry this result as territoriality with a vengeance, and they might likewise denounce any attempt to limit the scope of U.S. interests, as the principle of passive personality jurisdiction does. The clarity of these limitations, however, gives fair warning to potential defendants when their conduct might trigger a claim under federal law and fair notice to Congress when it might need to act to override the presumption itself.

## VI. Conclusion

Analyzed as a stage in the development of legal doctrine, the presumption against extraterritoriality seems more acceptable, or at least explicable, as a path out of the maze of the contemporary conundrums of the complexity of choice of law. Whether it leads legislators and treaty negotiators to a better consensus on choice of law remains as imponderable as the question, suggested earlier in this chapter, about the correct balance between private and public enforcement of statutory rights. No one answer seems plausible for all times and all rights, yet moving the issue to the right sphere of deliberation—in the legislature and

---

[67]   542 U.S. 155, 159 (2004).
[68]   FOURTH RESTATEMENT § 402(1)(c).

among nations—is certainly a worthwhile goal. Grudging respect for the presumption against extraterritoriality recognizes that it is severable from the seemingly intractable general questions of choice of law and that it might, in the end, contribute to making them more amenable to solutions that command a wide consensus.

# PART V
# THE RESTATEMENT
# AND IMMUNITY

# 18

# The Fourth Restatement, International Law, and the "Terrorism" Exception to the Foreign Sovereign Immunities Act

*Beth Stephens*

The Fourth Restatement sets out to "restate" the law of the United States and "relevant portions of international law,"[1] not to critique U.S. law or settle debates about the content of international law. But that task is complicated when the law of the United States triggers questions about unresolved international law issues.

The "terrorism" exception to the Foreign Sovereign Immunities Act (FSIA)[2] illustrates this complexity. Congress, the executive branch, and the judiciary have employed the exception as a politically motivated weapon to target disfavored states, while excluding U.S. allies, politically powerful states, and the United States itself from the reach of the statute. The text of the Fourth Restatement merely restates the U.S. law governing the "terrorism" exception, without identifying international law concerns or analyzing the issues they raise.[3] This chapter, by contrast, offers a critique of the "terrorism" exception, focusing on the statute as written, as amended to reach particular targets, and as applied in practice.

A well-crafted statutory exception to sovereign immunity for state human rights violations would be a welcome addition to human rights accountability. The "terrorism" exception falls far short of that goal.

---

[1] Fourth Restatement intro. at 2.

[2] Foreign Sovereign Immunities Act of 1976, Pub. L. No. 94-583, 90 Stat. 2891, codified at 28 U.S.C.A. §§ 1330, 1332(a)(4), 1391(f), 1441(d), 1602–611. The "terrorism" exception is at 28 U.S.C. § 1605A. In 2016, Congress enacted an additional "terrorism" exception, the Justice Against Sponsors of Terrorism Act (JASTA), 28 U.S.C. § 1605B. This chapter does not address JASTA, although the basic provision is described *infra* note 38.

[3] See Kristina Daugirdas, *The Restatements and the Rule of Law*, in this volume (critiquing the Fourth Restatement's failure to address the international law issues triggered by the "terrorism" exception and JASTA).

Beth Stephens, *The Fourth Restatement, International Law, and the "Terrorism" Exception to the Foreign Sovereign Immunities Act* In: *The Restatement and Beyond*. Edited by: Paul B. Stephan and Sarah H. Cleveland, Oxford University Press (2020). © Oxford University Press. DOI: 10.1093/oso/9780197533154.003.0019

# I. The "Terrorism" Exception and Human Rights Accountability

The FSIA generally grants foreign states immunity from suit in U.S. courts.[4] One exception to that immunity permits claims against a handful of foreign states labeled "sponsors of terrorism."[5] Litigation under the "terrorism" exception has produced tens of billions of dollars in default judgments that often reflect unreliable allegations and include enormous awards of punitive damages based on specious expert calculations. Liability frequently rests on claims that the foreign state provided support to a nonstate actor, whether or not that support directly contributed to the abuses. When litigants run into difficulty in obtaining or collecting judgments, Congress has repeatedly amended the statute, including enacting targeted amendments aimed at facilitating particular claims.

No international body has assessed whether the "terrorism" exception complies with international law. By comparison, when the Italian domestic judiciary issued a judgment against Germany awarding compensation for World War II war crimes, Germany challenged the judgment in the International Court of Justice (ICJ), which held that Italy had violated the customary international law governing foreign sovereign immunity.[6] The United States, however, has refused to allow the ICJ to consider whether the "terrorism" exception violates sovereign immunity.[7] In the absence of any international check, U.S. litigants are free to obtain U.S. judgments and enforce them by seizing assets found in the United States or elsewhere, although other states may refuse to enforce the judgments.

The "terrorism" exception occupies an uneasy place in the movement for human rights accountability, triggering opposing views from those who otherwise agree that sovereign immunity does not protect states that violate human rights. While some advocates view the provision as a useful step toward accountability for human rights abuses, I view it as a perversion of accountability, both as written and as applied. Although the exception provides remedies to a cohort of people who have been grievously harmed, it is fundamentally politicized and hypocritical. The one-sided, outsized judgments and frequent amendments to

---

[4]  28 U.S.C. § 1604 ("[A] a foreign state shall be immune from the jurisdiction of the courts of the United States and of the States except as provided in sections 1605 to 1607 of this chapter.").

[5]  28 U.S.C. § 1605A.

[6]  Jurisdictional Immunities of the State (Ger. v. It.: Greece intervening), Judgment, 2012 I.C.J. Rep. 99 (Feb. 3, 2012).

[7]  Iran sought ICJ review under the terms of the 1955 Treaty of Amity between the United States and Iran, but the ICJ accepted the U.S. government argument that the treaty did not require the parties to respect international norms of sovereign immunity and the court, therefore, will not reach that issue. Certain Iranian Assets (Iran v. U.S.), Preliminary Objections (Feb. 13, 2019), https://www.icj-cij.org/files/case-related/164/164-20190213-JUD-01-00-EN.pdf. The United States later announced that it was withdrawing from the treaty, id. ¶ 30, part of a pattern of U.S. withdrawals from international agreements that grant international tribunals jurisdiction to resolve disputes.

target particular claims make a mockery of the basic notions of due process and fair play that are essential to the enforcement of human rights norms.[8]

Equally important, the United States uses the label "terrorism" to justify denying immunity to a handful of disfavored states, while demanding immunity for itself and granting immunity to allies and strategically important states accused of comparable acts. Legislators and courts alike jump on the bandwagon, using the exception to demonstrate that they are tough on terrorism. The relentless focus on claims of terrorism attributed to a few foreign states has real consequences in today's world, drawing attention away from domestic hate crimes, violence by the U.S. government and other states, and egregious human rights violations around the world.[9] And to the extent that the statute focuses primarily on states that are predominantly Muslim, it contributes to Islamophobia and the selective demonization of "Islamic terrorism."

A word about terminology: I refrain from calling the immunity exception the "state sponsors of terrorism" or "terrorist state" exception because the U.S. government has developed and amended the list of "state sponsors of terrorism" through an opaque political process that renders it suspect. I am also uncomfortable caricaturing any state as a "terrorist state," thereby ignoring the state's complexity and history. Given the need for a manageable label, I default to *"terrorism" exception*, putting "terrorism" in quotation marks when I refer to the statute to reflect the international debate about the definition of the term.[10] Even that is misleading, however, given that—as explained in the following section—there is no statutory requirement that the violation that triggers the exception actually constitute "terrorism."

## II. An Overview of the "Terrorism" Exception

The FSIA, enacted in 1976, codifies the presumption that foreign states are immune from the jurisdiction of U.S. courts and lists a handful of exceptions to that immunity, most importantly for certain commercial activity and torts committed within the United States.[11] The "terrorism" exception, added in 1996,

---

[8] See Chimène I. Keitner, *Personal Jurisdiction and Fifth Amendment Due Process Revisited*, in this volume (discussion of possible due process limits on claims involving allegations of terrorist acts in foreign states).

[9] For additional discussion of the politicized use of "terrorism" accusations by the United States, see Beth Stephens, *Accountability Without Hypocrisy: Consistent Standards, Honest History*, 36 NEW ENG. L. REV. 919, 919–22 (2002).

[10] THE ROUTLEDGE HANDBOOK OF TERRORISM RESEARCH 99–200 (Alex P. Schmid ed., 2011), compiled 260 definitions of "terrorism."

[11] 28 U.S.C. § 1605(a). The statute adopted the "restrictive" approach to sovereign immunity, whereby states are generally immune for "claims arising out of governmental activities (de jure imperii)" but not for acts "of a kind carried on by private persons," including commercial activity. FOURTH RESTATEMENT § 451 cmt. *a*.

denies immunity to foreign states designated as "state sponsors of terrorism" by the U.S. executive branch, in cases on behalf of U.S. nationals in which:

> money damages are sought against a foreign state for personal injury or death that was caused by an act of torture, extrajudicial killing, aircraft sabotage, hostage taking, or the provision of material support or resources for such an act if such act or provision of material support or resources is engaged in by an official, employee, or agent of such foreign state while acting within the scope of his or her office, employment, or agency.[12]

The statute defines a "state sponsor of terrorism" as "a country, the government of which . . . has repeatedly provided support for acts of international terrorism" and has been designated as a "sponsor of terrorism" by the secretary of state pursuant to one or more statutorily authorized lists.[13] Iran, North Korea, Sudan, and Syria are currently on the list.[14] Three states have been removed since the statute was enacted in 1996—Iraq (2004), Libya (2006), Cuba (2015). North Korea was removed in 2008 and then added back in 2017. No new states have been added since 1996.[15]

Note that the exception does not explicitly target acts of "terrorism." That is, by its terms, it removes immunity for four violations (torture, extrajudicial execution, aircraft sabotage, and hostage taking) when an official (or employee or agent) of a state on the U.S. list of "state sponsors of terrorism" has committed one of those acts or provided material support or resources for the act. Not all such acts constitute "terrorism."[16]

The "terrorism" exception also alters the FSIA's approach to execution of judgments against foreign state property. As enacted in 1976 and still applicable to other claims against foreign states, only commercial property connected in some way with the claim can, in general, be attached to satisfy a judgment against a foreign state,[17] and funds "blocked" or "frozen" by the U.S. government

---

[12] 28 U.S.C. § 1605A(a)(1). In addition to U.S. nationals, claims can be brought on behalf of members of the U.S. armed forces and employees or contractors of the U.S. government. 28 U.S.C. § 1605A(a)(2)(A)(ii).

[13] 28 U.S.C. §§ 1605A(h)(6), 1605A(a)(2)(A)(i)(I). "State sponsors of terrorism" are designated by Section 6(j) of the Export Administration Act of 1979, Section 620A of the Foreign Assistance Act of 1961, or Section 40 of the Arms Export Control Act. 28 U.S.C. § 1605A(h)(6).

[14] U.S. Dep't of State, State Sponsors of Terrorism, available at https://www.state.gov/j/ct/list/c14151.htm.

[15] Congressional Research Service, State Sponsors of International Terrorism 1, 8–9 (Nov. 30, 2018), available at https://fas.org/sgp/crs/terror/R43835.pdf.

[16] See, e.g., Martinez v. Republic of Cuba, No. 99-18208 (Fla. 11th Cir. Ct. Mar. 9, 2001), discussed text at *infra* notes 61–64. For a more recent example, see Colvin v. Syrian Arab Republic, 363 F. Supp. 3d 141 (D.D.C. 2019) (awarding damages for Syria's targeted killing of journalist during armed conflict).

[17] 28 U.S.C. § 1610.

are immune from execution. Congress, however, has steadily expanded the categories of state property available for the execution of "terrorism" exception judgments.

## III. The Fourth Restatement's Analysis of International Law and the "Terrorism" Exception

Sections 460 and 464 of the Fourth Restatement and the accompanying comments and reporters' notes together provide a mostly nuts-and-bolts account of the "terrorism" exception. In keeping with the task of "restating" the law, there is no discussion of possible conflicts with contested norms of international law. Reporters' Note 11 to Section 460 contains the only mention of international law as it relates to the exception, and includes two points.

First, the note suggests that the exception violates no norms of international law because it addresses widely condemned acts of concern to the international community:

> Given its focus on injuries to U.S. nationals resulting from acts that have been condemned as illegal by the international community, and the frequently repeated exhortation that states should provide relief and means of compensating victims of terrorism, it is not clear that § 1605A contravenes any presumptive jurisdictional constraint under international law.[18]

This language seemingly accepts that customary international law imposes some constraints on what immunity exceptions states can recognize: It suggests that this particular exception may not violate any "presumptive" rules of international law[19] because of a history of state condemnations and exhortations to compensate victims. But, significantly, this sentence suggests that customary international law permits states to deny immunity to illegal acts that harm a state's citizens if the international community has condemned those acts and called for providing relief to victims. The same logic presumably would apply to other human rights violations, including, for example, genocide, torture, war crimes, and crimes against humanity. The analysis thus has far-reaching consequences: The reporters appear to support the view that international law

---

[18] FOURTH RESTATEMENT § 460 reporters' note 11.
[19] The use of the word "presumptive" is confusing. I assume here that it means a background rule that can be overridden by a state's domestic law, but I'm not clear whether it is distinct from a rule of customary international law, which can (arguably) be rejected, but only if a state is a "persistent objector," opting out at the time the rule develops into binding law.

permits a state to deny foreign state immunity when widely condemned illegal acts harm the forum state's citizens.

Second, however, and without further analysis, the note quotes language from the ICJ that may be intended to limit that conclusion:

> In Jurisdictional Immunities of the State (Ger. v. It.: Greece intervening), Judgment, 2012 I.C.J. Rep. 99 (Feb. 3), the International Court of Justice observed (in the context of claims arising from alleged violations of the laws of war) that "States are generally entitled to immunity in respect of *acta jure imperii*" without regard to the illegality of those acts. *Id.* at ¶ 61.[20]

Do the reporters read the ICJ language as limited to violations of the laws of war?[21] If so, the quotation seems irrelevant to an analysis of the "terrorism" exception. If not, it at least raises questions about an exception to immunity that applies to *acta jure imperii*, or public acts.[22] There is nothing in the "terrorism" exception that limits its scope to nonpublic acts. Some "terrorism" exception cases do address acts that would be classified as illegal public acts—a Cuban Air Force attack on a civilian aircraft, for example,[23] or a Syrian military attack on a journalist during an ongoing armed conflict.[24]

Some scholars—myself included—argue that sovereign immunity does not bar states from asserting jurisdiction over claims against other states or their officials for egregious human rights violations.[25] William Dodge, one of the reporters for the jurisdiction section of the Fourth Restatement, argues that international law leaves states great discretion in deciding whether to grant foreign sovereign immunity and concludes that the discretion includes denying immunity for acts of terrorism.[26] Others disagree, including Curtis Bradley, a reporter for the treaty section, who has written that international law "guarantee[s] immunity, even for alleged egregious crimes."[27] As a result, Bradley concludes that the "terrorism" exception is "almost certainly contrary to international law."[28]

---

[20] FOURTH RESTATEMENT § 460 reporters' note 11.

[21] See Chimène I. Keitner, Germany v. Italy *and the Limits of Horizontal Enforcement*, 11 J. INT'L CRIM. JUSTICE 167, 171 (2013) (noting that "[t]he ICJ was persuaded by Germany's emphasis on the special circumstances of armed conflict....").

[22] For criticism of the view that international crimes constitute *acta jure imperii* entitled to immunity, see *id.*, at 172.

[23] See Alejandre v. Republic of Cuba, 996 F. Supp. 1239 (S.D. Fla. 1997).

[24] See Colvin v. Syrian Arab Republic, 363 F. Supp. 3d 141 (D.D.C. 2019).

[25] Beth Stephens, *Abusing the Authority of the State: Denying Foreign Official Immunity for Egregious Human Rights Abuses*, 44 VAND. J. TRANSNAT'L L. 1163 (2011).

[26] William S. Dodge, *Does JASTA Violate International Law?*, JUST SECURITY (Sept. 30, 2016), available at https://www.justsecurity.org/33325/jasta-violate-international-law-2/.

[27] Curtis Bradley & Jack Goldsmith, Op-Ed, *Don't Let Americans Sue Saudi Arabia*, N.Y. TIMES, at A27 (Apr. 22, 2016), available at https://www.nytimes.com/2016/04/22/opinion/dont-let-americans-sue-saudi-arabia.html.

[28] *Id.*

The reporters' note ignores this debate, with the ambiguous assertion that the exception violates no "presumptive" rule of international law.

Further, given its focus on restating the law as it currently exists, the Fourth Restatement's analysis of the "terrorism" exception does not address either the statute's repeated amendments tailored to prejudice the small set of potential defendants or the questionable judgments issued pursuant to the exception. My analysis of the provision begins with this history and practice.

## IV. The Troubling History of the "Terrorism" Exception

To understand the evolution of the "terrorism" exception, it is useful to begin with the events that led to its passage in 1996. In the late 1980s and early 1990s, the FSIA stymied several lawsuits against foreign states seeking damages for human rights violations. In 1989, the Supreme Court held both that the FSIA provided the only means by which to sue a foreign state in U.S. courts and that it did not authorize an immunity exception for claims of fundamental violations of human rights.[29] Later cases alleging human rights violations sought unsuccessfully to avoid the FSIA bar, including lawsuits on behalf of a man tortured by security officials in Saudi Arabia; the families of 270 people killed in the 1988 bombing of Pan Am 103 over Lockerbie, Scotland; and a survivor of genocide in Nazi Germany.[30]

In 1993, members of Congress proposed an amendment to the FSIA that would have denied sovereign immunity to all foreign states for the torture or extrajudicial killing of a U.S. citizen.[31] The Department of State strenuously opposed the proposal, and the bill died.[32] In 1996, however, in the wake of the Oklahoma City bombing (committed by a far-right, non-Muslim U.S. citizen), Congress fast-tracked wide-ranging tough-on-crime and tough-on-immigrants legislation, and folded the earlier proposal to create an exception to sovereign immunity into the Anti-Terrorism and Effective Death Penalty Act of 1996.[33] The Pan Am 103 families joined the Oklahoma City families in supporting the legislation. At the last minute, however, Congress narrowed the sovereign immunity provision to apply only to states on one of the U.S. government's lists of "state sponsors of terrorism."[34] The result was the basic provision that survives today.

---

[29] Argentine Republic v. Amerada Hess, 488 U.S. 428 (1989) (finding that FSIA barred suit in case involving the bombing of a civilian oil tanker).

[30] Saudi Arabia v. Nelson, 507 U.S. 349 (1993); Smith v. Socialist People's Libyan Arab Jamahiriya, 101 F.3d 239 (2d Cir. 1996); Princz v. Fed. Republic of Germany, 26 F.3d 1166 (D.C. Cir. 1994).

[31] See ALLAN GERSON & JERRY ADLER, THE PRICE OF TERROR 212 (2001). A revised version introduced in 1994 added claims for aircraft sabotage, hostage taking, and genocide. Id. at 213–14.

[32] Id. at 212, 214–15.

[33] Pub. L. No. 104-132, 110 Stat. 1214.

[34] GERSON & ADLER, supra note 31, at 224–25, 227–38.

The subsequent history of the provision has followed a clear pattern: As litigants faced obstacles in obtaining or enforcing judgments, Congress responded with a dizzying series of amendments to facilitate judgments and the collection of damages, often tailoring the amendments to benefit specific claimants. In response to concerns raised by a U.S. citizen whose noncitizen wife was killed on Pan Am 103, for example, a "technical amendment" clarified that the exception encompassed suits by U.S. citizen plaintiffs, not just suits on behalf of U.S. citizen victims.[35] The belated recognition that the immunity exception granted U.S. courts subject matter jurisdiction but did not create a cause of action led to a 1997 amendment that created a cause of action against the employees and agents of foreign states. It also specified that damages against those individuals could include pain and suffering, emotional distress, and punitive damages.[36] With the courts split on whether the provision created a cause of action against the foreign state as well, a 2008 amendment specifically created such a cause of action.[37] In a stunning display of legislative disregard for international law, Congress made multiple attempts to enact legislation to enable the Iran hostages to sue Iran, but failed each time: Courts held that none of the provisions stated clearly that Congress intended to abrogate the Algiers Accords—the executive agreements that had led to the release of the hostages and barred any civil actions on their behalf.[38]

Congress also took steps to facilitate the collection of damage awards. As originally enacted, the exception authorized collection of judgments from assets in the United States that were used for commercial purposes and from assets

---

[35] *Id.* at 249–51.

[36] Pub. L. No. 104-208, § 589, 110 Stat. 3009, 172, codified at 28 U.S.C. § 1605 note.

[37] Pub. L. No. 110-181, § 1083, 122 Stat. 3, 338–44, codified at 28 U.S.C. § 1605A.

[38] See Stephen J. Schnably, *The Transformation of Human Rights Litigation: The Alien Tort Statute, the Anti-Terrorism Act, and JASTA*, 24 U. Miami Int'l & Comp. L. Rev. 285, 312, 348–50, 360–62 (2017); W. Michael Reisman & Monica Hakimi, *Illusion and Reality in the Compensation of Victims of International Terrorism*, 54 Ala. L. Rev. 561, 575–77 (2003).

In 2016, over President Barack Obama's veto, Congress enacted the Justice Against Sponsors of Terrorism Act (JASTA), designed to revive lawsuits against Saudi Arabia for the September 11 attacks that had been dismissed because Saudi Arabia is not on the "sponsors of terrorism" list. Pub. L. No. 114-222, 130 Stat. 852, codified at 28 U.S.C. § 1605B; see *In re* Terrorist Attacks on September 11, 2001, 298 F. Supp. 3d 631, 639 (S.D.N.Y. 2018). JASTA added a new provision to the FSIA, Section 1605B, that denies immunity for injuries or deaths occurring within the United States and caused by (a) an act of international terrorism and (b) a state's tortious act (no matter where that tortious act occurs). With its focus on harms caused within the United States, JASTA invokes the common exception to sovereign immunity for territorial torts. Note that JASTA, unlike the "terrorism" exception, applies to all foreign states, not a short list of states selected by the U.S. executive branch.

JASTA has triggered formal protests, including from the European Union, which stated that the statute "would be in conflict with fundamental principles of international law and in particular the principle of State sovereign immunity." European Union Delegation to the United States of America (Sept. 19, 2016); see also Carmen-Cristina Cirlig & Patryk Pawlak, European Parliamentary Research Service, Justice against sponsors of terrorism: JASTA and its international impact 8–9 (Oct. 2016) (listing complaints from Saudi Arabia, the Gulf Cooperation Council, Morocco, Russia, France, the Netherlands, and the United Kingdom).

"blocked" pursuant to one of several U.S. statutes. The statute authorized the president to waive access to blocked assets, which President Bill Clinton promptly did.[39] Contentious debates over the waiver led to a compromise that authorized payment of compensatory damage awards from U.S. government funds, but only for claimants who had final judgments against Cuba or Iran as of July 2000 and for the plaintiffs in five specific lawsuits identified in the statute—each of whom had been represented in the negotiations leading to the amendment.[40] As characterized in a note by a somewhat outraged law student, "Congress chose simply to pay off the plaintiffs party to the negotiation" with a statute that enabled Congress to "claim a victory for victims' rights over terrorist countries."[41]

In 2002, Congress went further, creating a fund drawn from blocked assets to satisfy "terrorism" exception judgments.[42] When the complexities of the various blocking statutes rendered that provision inadequate, a 2008 amendment authorized execution of judgments against a broader range of blocked assets belonging to a state's agency or instrumentality.[43] Over the years, executive branch officials have strenuously opposed the use of frozen assets in this way, pointing out the value of such funds in resolving disputes with foreign states.[44] Some four years later, in response to lobbying by the families of the U.S. service members killed in the 1983 suicide bombing of the Marine barracks in Lebanon, Congress passed yet another narrow statute, this one stating that plaintiffs in that case could seize a particular account belonging to the Iranian Central Bank.[45] In an attempt at a more global solution, Congress in 2015 established a compensation fund,

---

[39] 28 U.S.C. § 1610(f). See DAVID P. STEWART, FEDERAL JUDICIAL CENTER, THE FOREIGN SOVEREIGN IMMUNITIES ACT: A GUIDE FOR JUDGES 130–31 (2d ed. 2018), available at https://www.fjc.gov/content/337316/foreign-sovereign-immunities-act-guide-judges-2ed.

[40] Pub. L. No. 106-386, § 2002, 114 Stat. 1464 (2000). The statute authorized the president to reimburse the U.S. government by liquidating blocked funds of Cuba and Iran. For a detailed analysis of the statute, see Sean K. Mangan, *Compensation for "Certain" Victims of Terrorism Under Section 2002 of the Victims of Trafficking and Violence Protection Act of 2000: Individual Payments at an Institutional Cost*, 42 VA. J. INT'L L. 1037 (2002).

[41] Mangan, *supra* note 40, at 1055–56.

[42] Terrorism Risk Insurance Act of 2002, Pub. L. No. 107-297, 116 Stat. 2322, codified at 28 U.S.C. § 1610 note. For a discussion of the complicated interactions among these provisions and the statutes defining and regulating blocked assets, see STEWART, *supra* note 39, at 131–34.

[43] 28 U.S.C. § 1610(g). See STEWART, *supra* note 39, at 134–36.

[44] See, e.g., Victims' Access to Terrorist Assets: Hearing on Amendments to the Foreign Sovereign Immunities Act Before the Senate Comm. on the Judiciary, 106th Cong. (1999) (prepared statement of Stuart E. Eizenstat, Deputy Secretary, Department of the Treasury), cited in Allison Taylor, *Another Front in the War on Terrorism? Problems with Recent Changes to the Foreign Sovereign Immunities Act*, 45 ARIZ. L. REV. 533, 547 n.141 (2003). For a discussion of diplomatic resolutions involving blocked assets, see *id.* at 545–46.

[45] Iran Threat Reduction and Syria Human Rights Act of 2012, Pub. L. No. 112-158, § 502, 126 Stat. 1214, codified at 22 U.S.C. § 8772. For a detailed description of the statute and the legislative negotiations, see Pamela K. Bookman & David L. Noll, Ad Hoc *Procedure*, 92 N.Y.U. L. REV. 767, 816–23 (2017). The statute—which explicitly applied only to the plaintiffs in that one case—was held constitutional by the Supreme Court in 2013. Bank Markazi v. Peterson, 136 S. Ct. 1310 (2016). Bookman and Noll, at 823, characterize the statute as "the raw exercise of state power."

financed with fines assessed against violators of various sanction regimes, to compensate plaintiffs who obtain judgments under the "terrorism" exception and (finally) the Iran hostages.[46]

These repeated amendments reflect a Congress bound and determined to facilitate litigation under the "terrorism" exception. Not surprisingly, foreign states accused of supporting "terrorism" have proven to be easy targets for members of Congress seeking to show that they are both tough on terrorism and supportive of victims and survivors. As one commentator explained:

> [W]hen terrorism litigation follows a path through Congress, it is unlikely that Congress will effectively hear from both sides, since—as Saudi Arabia and Iran both discovered—foreign states accused of supporting terrorism meet with little sympathy, at least in public. . . . The danger . . . is that because any bill emanating from Congress will be "fighting terrorism," the usual scrutiny one might hope to see of such a fraught process . . . may be diminished.[47]

As a result, "Congress's main approach to responsibility for terrorism turns out to be to use it an instrument for pressuring states in disfavor with the U.S. foreign policy."[48]

## V. Litigation under the "Terrorism" Exception

Many of the judgments under the "terrorism" exception reflect one or more of a series of flaws. Some are based on faulty facts, ascribing liability based on unproven claims and unreliable expert testimony. Others demonstrate blatant disregard for the statutory requirements. And the level of damages in most cases is head-spinning, even as compared to the high damages often awarded in U.S. litigation. These errors are possible in part because the foreign state defendants generally reject the jurisdiction of the U.S. courts and refuse to defend the lawsuits or appeal problematic judgments—and because the courts are eager to show that they are tough on terrorism.

Cases holding both Iraq and Iran liable for the attacks on September 11, 2001, demonstrate the problem of faulty fact-finding.[49] In the 2003 Iraq decision,

---

[46] Justice for United States Victims of State Sponsored Terrorism Act, 34 U.S.C. § 20144. In late 2019, the fund was processing applications for a third round of payments due to be paid by January 1, 2020. See U.S. Victims of State Sponsored Terrorism Fund Website, available at https://www.usvsst.com.

[47] Schnably, *supra* note 38, at 400–402.

[48] *Id.* at 407.

[49] See E. Perot Bissell V & Joseph R. Schottenfeld, *Exceptional Judgments: Revising the Terrorism Exception to the Foreign Sovereign Immunities Act*, 127 YALE L.J. 1890, 1890–91 (2018) (Iran); Sean D. Murphy, *Terrorist State Litigation in 2002–2003*, 97 AM. J. INT'L L. 966, 972 (2003) (Iraq).

relying on two experts who listed circumstantial and speculative connections to Iraq, a district court judge awarded over $67 million to the families of two people killed in the attacks.[50] Just four months later, President George W. Bush famously acknowledged that there was no evidence linking Iraq to the September 11 attacks.[51] Years later, a federal court held Iran liable for the September 11 attacks, based largely on evidence that Iran had enabled the hijackers to travel through Iran.[52] The 9/11 Commission convened by the government to examine the attacks, however, concluded that there was "no evidence" that Iran was aware of the planned attacks and pointedly did not conclude that Iran had assisted al-Qaeda.[53] Today, the evidence relied on by the court continues to be hotly contested—and highly politicized.[54] There is little reason to believe that the one-sided presentation of evidence to the district court resulted in a reliable factual conclusion.

Equally suspect, courts have granted judgments against Sudan for two earlier al-Qaeda attacks—the 1998 bombing of the U.S. embassies in Kenya and Tanzania, and the 2000 attack on the USS *Cole*—relying on evidence suggesting that Osama bin Laden had been based in Sudan during the early 1990s and had received support at that time from the Sudanese government.[55] But the 9/11 Commission noted that, in response to pressure from the U.S. government, bin Laden and his supporters had been expelled from Sudan in 1996, two years before the embassy bombings and four years before the attack on the USS *Cole*.[56] Despite noting that the plaintiffs' allegations were "somewhat imprecise" both as to the timing of Sudan's support for al-Qaeda and the "causal connection"

---

[50]  Smith v. Islamic Emirate of Afghanistan, 262 F. Supp. 2d 217, 228–32, 240–41 (S.D.N.Y. 2003).

[51]  See White House Press Release on Remarks by President After Meeting with Members of the Congressional Conference Committee on Energy Legislation (Sept. 17, 2003), cited in Murphy, *supra* note 49, at 972 n.41.

[52]  Havlish v. bin Laden, 30-MDL-1570, 2012 U.S. Dist. LEXIS 143525, *78–82 (S.D.N.Y Oct. 3, 2012); Havlish v. bin Laden (*In re* Terrorist Attacks on September 11, 2001), 2011 U.S. Dist. LEXIS 155899, at 125–34 (S.D.N.Y. Dec. 22, 2011); Bissell & Schottenfeld, *supra* note 49, at 1891, 1891 nn.9–10. Commentators have questioned the reliability of the expert testimony that forms the foundation for the court's decision. *Id.* at 1908.

[53]  *Id.* at 1891, 1891 n.9 (citing NAT'L COMM'N ON TERRORIST ATTACKS UPON THE U.S., THE 9/11 COMMISSION REPORT 241 (2011)). For more on politicized efforts to link Iran to the 9/11 attacks, debunking the significance of the travel facilitation, see Kristen Breitweiser, *Iran and 9/11: Down the Rabbit Hole of Blame,* HUFFPOST (Oct. 25, 2017), available at https://www.huffpost.com/entry/iran-and-911-down-the-rabbit-hole-of-blame_b_59ef7e1be4b04809c0501194.

[54]  Alex Ward, *How the Trump Administration Is Using 9/11 to Build a Case for War with Iran,* Vox (June 14, 2019), available at https://www.vox.com/2019/6/14/18678809/usa-iran-war-aumf-911-trump-pompeo.

[55]  See Michael T. Kotlarczyk, *"The Provision of Material Support and Resources" and Lawsuits Against State Sponsors of Terrorism,* 96 GEO. L.J. 2029, 2040–41 (2008) (discussing Owens v. Republic of Sudan, 412 F. Supp. 2d 99 (D.D.C. 2006) (embassy bombings), and Rux v. Republic of Sudan, 461 F.3d 461 (4th Cir. 2006) (USS *Cole*).

[56]  9/11 COMMISSION REPORT, *supra* note 53, at 62–63.

between that support and the bombings, the courts found the claims sufficient to uphold jurisdiction under the "terrorism" exception.[57]

Default judgments based on attenuated connections are possible in part because the courts require only a weak link between a foreign state's conduct and the tortious conduct. The statute imposes liability for injuries "caused by . . . the provision of material support or resources" for one of the listed acts.[58] The legislative history of the statute suggests that Congress intended the statute to sweep broadly, with members of Congress emphasizing their intent to hold states liable for supporting groups that are later accused of terrorist acts, whether or not the state had the ability to control the actions of those groups or knew of, condoned, or contributed directly to the commission of the acts.[59] Since the cases are decided on default judgments, the courts require only that the complaint demonstrate a "reasonable connection" between the foreign state's acts and the acts underlying the claim.[60] As a result, multibillion dollar judgments based on untested and faulty factual findings are the basis for enforcement proceedings in the United States and around the world.

In addition to factual errors, courts—in their eagerness to take stand against terrorism—often ignore the basic requirements of the statute. A series of cases against Cuba illustrates this problem.[61] In *Martinez v. Republic of Cuba*, the court awarded a Cuban American woman damages for torture after she learned that her husband was actually a Cuban spy.[62] The Florida State court held that she had been tortured without considering the statutory definition of torture,[63] which explicitly requires that the victim be under the "physical control" of the perpetrator, sets a high standard for physical torture, and limits claims based on mental suffering to that resulting from one of three specific acts.[64] Although the

---

[57]  Owens v. Republic of Sudan, 531 F.3d 884, 895 (D.C. Cir. 2008), quoting *Rux*, 461 F.3d at 474.

[58]  28 U.S.C. § 1605A(a)(1).

[59]  Kotlarczyk, *supra* note 55, at 2035–42.

[60]  *Owens*, 531 F.3d at 895 (quoting *Rux*, 461 F.3d at 474).

[61]  The 2002 amendments that made blocked assets available to satisfy "terrorism" exception judgments led to "a flurry of cases" against Cuba, all filed in a Florida State court in Miami, in "the heart of the Cuban exile community hostile to" the Cuban government. Andrew Lyubarsky, *Clearing the Road to Havana: Settling Legally Questionable Terrorism Judgments to Ensure Normalization of Relations Between the United States and Cuba*, 91 N.Y.U. L. REV. 458, 468 (2016).

[62]  Martinez v. Republic of Cuba, No. 99-18208 (Fla. 11th Cir. Ct. Mar. 9, 2001). See discussion of *Martinez* case in Diane L. Dick, *The Case of the Little Yellow Cuban Biplane: Can Interest Analysis Reconcile Conflicting Provisions in Federal Statutes and International Treaties?* 57 FLA. L. REV. 91, 93–95 (2005).

[63]  See 28 U.S.C. § 1605A(h)(7), incorporating the definition of torture set forth in the Torture Victim Protection Act (TVPA), § 3(b), codified at 28 U.S.C. § 1350 note.

[64]  The statute limits actionable mental pain or suffering to that resulting from threats of severe physical pain or suffering, administration of mind-altering substances, or the threat of imminent death. TVPA, § 3(b)(2). See Martinez v. Republic of Cuba, 221 F. Supp. 3d 276, 282–84 (N.D.N.Y. 2016) (refusing to enforce Florida judgment, noting Florida court did not consider statutory definition of torture and rejecting argument that conduct met that definition).

plaintiff's mental anguish was clear, it is just as clear that it did not meet the statutory definition of torture.

Several judgments issued against Cuba for killings and torture in the early years after the 1959 Cuban revolution, or at the time of the 1961 U.S.-sponsored Bay of Pigs invasion of Cuba, also involve egregious failures to apply the language of the statute.[65] The "terrorism" exception explicitly requires either that "the foreign state was designated as a state sponsor of terrorism at the time the act . . . occurred" or that the state was designated "as a result of" the act.[66] Neither option applies to these cases: Cuba was designated in 1982 (long after the acts at issue in these cases occurred), based on administration claims that Cuba was assisting revolutionary movements elsewhere in Latin America (not because of the earlier acts at issue in these cases).[67] The "terrorism" exception clearly did not apply to these cases.

This pattern of shaky factual and legal foundation lends credence to the conclusion that "terrorism" exception judgments often have "transparently political motivations."[68] Despite these flaws, however, multiple courts around the country have enforced the judgments. A federal court judge in the Northern District of New York broke with this pattern, refusing to recognize the *Martinez* judgment for lack of subject matter jurisdiction.[69] In another case, however, a judge from the same district court held that a similarly flawed Florida court's finding of subject matter jurisdiction was entitled to *res judicata*, and noted that *seven* other district courts had already enforced the judgment.[70] The district court later reversed its decision in light of an intervening Second Circuit case[71]—but other enforcement decisions remain in place.

Finally, and further compounding the problem, some U.S. judges have approached the assessment of damages in "terrorism" exception cases with the zeal of avenging angels. Most—but not all—of the claims involve nefarious conduct that inflicted egregious harms. But does that justify billion dollar judgments? A Florida State court awarded $4 billion to two brothers who alleged

Although not relevant to the "terrorism" exception, the Florida court's separate conclusion that the conduct triggered the noncommercial tort exception to sovereign immunity, 28 U.S.C. § 1605(a)(5), was equally unfounded. See *id.* at 284–88 (explaining that, under Florida law, sexual relations based on fraud do not constitute battery and rejecting other possible tort theories).

[65] See Lyubarsky, *supra* note 61, at 468–73.

[66] 28 U.S.C. § 1605A(a)(2)(A)(i)(I).

[67] Lyubarsky, *supra* note 61, at 466 (citing repeated executive branch testimony before Congress), 477–78 (noting that executive branch affirmed in 2013 court filing that Cuba was placed on list because of its support for armed groups abroad).

[68] See Bissell & Schottenfeld, *supra* note 49, at 1906–07.

[69] *Martinez*, 221 F. Supp. 3d at 288–89.

[70] Volloldo v. Castro Ruz, No. 1:14-mc-0025 (LEK/CFH) (N.D.N.Y. Jan. 7, 2016), at 8–12 (explaining decision to grant "full faith and credit" to Florida court decision on subject matter), 7 n.3 (listing cases).

[71] Volloldo v. Castro Ruz, 2017 WL 4838780, 1:14-MC-25 (LEK/CFH) (N.D.N.Y. Oct. 24, 2017),

that their father had been harassed and tortured in Cuba in 1959, leading him to commit suicide.[72] As of 2016, eighty-nine default judgments had been entered against Iran under the statute, totaling $56 billion, with twenty-nine additional cases pending.[73]

Meanwhile, a small industry of lawyers is engaged in hunting for the assets of states with outstanding judgments, particularly Iran and Cuba. In response to lobbying by plaintiffs and their advocates, amendments have systematically expanded the types of assets available to enforce judgment.[74] Current enforcement efforts include Iranian assets held outside the United States.[75]

As early as 2003, in congressional testimony critical of "piecemeal" legislation enacted to address "the suffering of victims of international terrorism," the Department of State noted the problematic practice under the "terrorism" exception.[76] As the State Department Legal Adviser testified, "The current litigation-based system of compensation is inequitable, unpredictable, occasionally costly to the U.S. taxpayer and damaging to the foreign policy and national security goals of this country."[77] Sixteen years later, these problems have only become more extreme.

## VI. The "Terrorism Exception" and International Law

The "terrorism" exception is bad policy for multiple reasons. It undermines human rights by contributing to a global fixation on a politicized definition of "terrorism" to the exclusion of other human rights violations. As part of the "war on terrorism," it contributes to the demonization of Muslims around the world. The fixation on a short list of states promotes the view that other states are not responsible for equally reprehensible human rights violations. In particular, the use of the exception by the United States to punish disfavored political targets

---

[72] See Lyubarsky, *supra* note 61, at 473.

[73] Application Instituting Proceedings (Iran v. United States), app. 2, tbls. 1, 2 (June 14, 2016).

[74] After a judge's order blocked collection of an Iranian account in New York, for example, "plaintiffs decided, in the words of their attorney Steve Perles, that seeking legislation was the 'prudent thing to do.'" Bookman & Noll, *supra* note 45, at 818. Those efforts led to a "bespoke" statute that authorized plaintiffs to seize an account belonging to the Iranian Central Bank. *Id.* at 822.

[75] See Peterson v. Islamic Republic of Iran, 876 F.3d 63, 87–95 (2d Cir 2017) (holding that FSIA by its terms only provides immunity from execution to property within United States, so U.S. court can order multinational institution to transfer Iranian assets held by its Luxembourg affiliate to United States) vacated and remanded in light of new legislation, 140 S. Ct. 813 (2020); see also cases in foreign jurisdictions discussed *infra* notes 102–104 and accompanying text.

[76] Testimony of U.S. Department of State Legal Adviser William H. Taft IV on S. 1275, Benefits for Victims of International Terrorism Act, Before the Senate Committee on Foreign Relations, at 7–12 (July 17, 2003), quoted in Murphy, *supra* note 49, at 973.

[77] *Id.*

reinforces a world order in which the United States abuses the law to pursue political goals.

But in addition to the policy issues, international law constrains a state's power to act in this manner, not because states are entitled to immunity for human rights violations, including terrorism,[78] but rather because of the relentless way in which the U.S. government has used the statute as a political weapon against a small handful of states, without concern for fair play and consistency.[79] While some of these governments may have supported terrorism, the U.S. government decision to deny them immunity is not based on any rational assessment of their conduct compared to that of other states. Under the principle of reciprocity, the same standards should be applied to the United States, its allies, and other powerful states. Reciprocity—the concept that states should treat others as they themselves demand to be treated—is a basic building block of international law.[80] In particular, reciprocity demands that "a State basing a claim on a particular norm of international law must accept that rule as also binding on itself."[81] The United States, however, adamantly opposes any effort to hold itself or its officials accountable in its own courts or the courts of other countries. The United States has punished a small set of disfavored states without accepting for itself the standards it imposes on others.

Fear of reciprocity has been a major driver of the executive branch's opposition to the "terrorism" exception, raised repeatedly in futile attempts to dissuade Congress from enacting and expanding the provision.[82] Advocates of the exception maintain that the United States has nothing to fear because it does not engage in the conduct addressed by the statute, including torture and summary execution. As one proponent wrote in 2004, "The United States does not and will not engage in this kind of terrorism around the world. Moreover, were American officials to do so, there is likely already both criminal and civil liability under our own national law."[83] Victims of the counterrevolutionaries (Contras) who

---

[78] But see Daugirdas, *supra* note 3, at 539–40 (noting that governments have objected to the exception as a violation of sovereign immunity and that "some scholars . . . and many within the U.S. executive branch share this view.")

[79] See Schnably, *supra* note 38, at 355–56, noting that the "sponsors of terrorism" list "is notoriously politicized, its composition heavily influenced by strategic questions of U.S. foreign policy," and has "turned liability for torture or extrajudicial killing into a weapon against disfavored states, with the shield retained for others in U.S. favor."

[80] Bruno Simma, *Reciprocity*, in MAX PLANCK ENCYCLOPEDIA OF PUBLIC INTERNATIONAL LAW ¶ 19 (Apr. 2008) ("International law rests upon the logic of reciprocity in its entirety.").

[81] *Id.* ¶ 2.

[82] States targeted by the "terrorism" exception have enacted legislation authorizing reciprocal litigation against the United States. For an overview, see Troy C. Homesley III, *"Towards a Strategy of Peace": Protecting the Iran Nuclear Accord Despite $46 Billion in State-Sponsored Terror Judgments*, 95 N.C. L. REV. 795, 813–15 (2017); Law Library of Cong., Laws Lifting Sovereign Immunity in Selected Countries 1–16 (2016), https://www.loc.gov/law/help/sovereign-immunity/lifting-sovereign-immunity.pdf.

[83] John Norton Moore, *Introduction*, in CIVIL LITIGATION AGAINST TERRORISM 1, 14–15 (2004).

sowed terror among civilians in Nicaragua in the 1980s or survivors of torture by U.S. officials in the aftermath of September 11, to cite just two examples, would, of course, take issue with that claim.[84]

Indeed, my long-standing frustration with this statute stems in part from the years I lived in Nicaragua, at a time when the United States openly provided "material support and resources"—weapons, training, financing—to the Nicaraguan Contras. To further illustrate the reciprocity problem, imagine that, during the 1980s, Nicaragua had enacted a statute equivalent to the U.S. "terrorism" exception and had labeled the United States a "sponsor of terrorism" based on its well-documented support of the Contras and their equally well-documented acts of terrorism. Imagine that Nicaraguan victims of the Contras then sued the United States in a Nicaraguan court and that, after an unsuccessful challenge to the court's assertion of jurisdiction, the United States withdrew from the lawsuit, leading to a default judgment against it for billions of dollars, seizure of U.S. assets in Nicaragua, and efforts to seize U.S. assets in other countries.

But this is not a purely fictional example: Nicaragua did bring a claim for damages against the United States, not in its own courts but in the neutral forum of the International Court of Justice.[85] After losing a challenge to jurisdiction, the United States withdrew from the proceedings, and the ICJ eventually issued a multibillion dollar judgment against it. The United States disdainfully refused to honor the judgment. After a change of government in Nicaragua, the United States pressured the new government until it abandoned the claim.[86]

Reciprocity is also relevant to the causation standard applied to "terrorism" exception cases. The exception holds states liable for damages caused by "the provision of material support or resources" for one of the listed violations.[87] "[M]aterial support or resources," defined by reference to the Anti-Terrorism Act, offers a long list of possible assistance, including property, services, financing, lodging, training, equipment, weapons, personnel, and transportation.[88] U.S. courts have interpreted this broad provision even more broadly, denying immunity to states that provide funding or other support to a group that is later held responsible for one of the "terrorism" exception's enumerated acts.[89]

---

[84] For an overview of the doctrines used by the U.S. government to block lawsuits seeking accountability for human rights violations, see Beth Stephens, *The Curious History of the Alien Tort Statute*, 89 NOTRE DAME L. REV. 1467, 1530–35 (2014). For more on the human rights abuses committed by the Contras, see Stephens, *supra* note 9, at 919–22.

[85] Military and Paramilitary Activities in and Against Nicaragua (Nicar. v. U.S.), Merits, 1986 I.C.J. Rep. 14 (June 27).

[86] See Mark A. Uhlig, *U.S. Urges Nicaragua to Forgive Legal Claim*, N.Y. TIMES (Sept. 30 1990), available at https://nyti.ms/29uS5J0; Council on Hemispheric Relations, Nicaragua Seeks Retribution (July 21, 2011), available at http://www.coha.org/nicaragua-seeks-retribution/(describing 2011 Nicaraguan interest in reviving and enforcing judgment).

[87] 28 U.S.C. § 1605A(a)(1).

[88] 18 U.S.C. § 2339A(b).

[89] See *supra* notes 55–57 and accompanying text (discussion of claims against Sudan).

The material support need not have "directly contributed" to the acts giving rise to the claim.[90] As one court explained the standard, the "terrorism" exception requires evidence that a defendant state "generally provided material support or resources" to the nonstate actor that "contributed to its ability to carry out the terrorist act."[91]

By contrast, international law holds states accountable for the conduct of non-state actors only under narrow circumstances, requiring that the nonstate actors act under the instructions or the direction or control of the state.[92] Ironically, the United States was the beneficiary of this rule when the ICJ found that the United States could only be held liable for its own acts against Nicaragua—such as mining a Nicaraguan harbor—not for violations committed by the Contras, even though the United States had admittedly supplied them with essential funding and other support.[93] The ICJ concluded that a state must have "effective control" over nonstate actors in order to be held accountable for their actions.[94] Although some argue for a looser international law standard ("overall control" rather than "effective control"),[95] neither formulation bears any resemblance to the loose domestic law standard applied in the "terrorism" exception cases.[96] Notably, "[t]he United States did not criticize the International Court of Justice's holding of law on this point, and it is unlikely that the United States would do so today."[97]

Finally, much "terrorism" exception litigation now focuses on the collection of damages and breaches standard rules governing damages and execution of judgments against foreign states. As originally enacted in 1976, the FSIA barred punitive damage awards against foreign states, because, as the legislative report accompanying the statute explained, "[u]nder current international practice, punitive damages are usually not assessed against foreign states."[98] That restriction remains in place for all other claims against foreign states. In 2008, President George W. Bush vetoed an attempt to permit punitive damages in "terrorism" exception cases, stating that permitting punitive damages would be "[c]ontrary

[90] Flatow v. Islamic Republic of Iran, 999 F. Supp. 1, 18 (D.D.C. 1998). See STEWART, *supra* note 39, at 117.
[91] Fraenkel v. Islamic Republic of Iran, 248 F. Supp. 3d 21, 36 (D.D.C. 2017).
[92] Articles on State Responsibility, art. 8.
[93] ICJ, Nicaragua v. United States, *supra* note 85, ¶¶ 115–116.
[94] *Id.* ¶ 115; see also Application of the Convention on the Prevention and Punishment of the Crime of Genocide (Bosn. & Herz. v. Serb. & Montenegro), Judgment, 2007 I.C.J. Rep. 43, ¶¶ 399–400 (Feb. 26).
[95] See Judgment, Tadic (ICTY-94-1-A), Appeals Chamber (Tadic AC), 15 July 1999, at ¶ 137.
[96] Reisman & Hakimi, *supra* note 38, at 580 ("With respect to the decisions against Iran arising out of Iran's support for terrorist organizations, the standard of derivative liability statutorily imposed by Congress and then strictly applied by the courts is not consistent with contemporary international law.").
[97] *Id.*
[98] H.R. Rep. 94-1487, 94th Cong., 2d Sess. 1976 at *22, 1976 WL 14078 (Leg. Hist.).

to international legal norms."[99] Congress, however, included the amendment in a bill enacted later that same year.[100] Since then, restrictions on the categories of foreign state property subject to attachment and execution have followed similar patterns, with Congress expanding the categories of property available for execution and enacting legislation to assist particular litigants.[101]

Armed with these fraught multibillion dollar default judgments, litigants have attempted to seize Iran's assets both within and outside the United States. Since enforcement procedures generally do not consider the fact-findings or damage assessments of the underlying judgment, many of the flaws of the "terrorism" exception judgments are overlooked. Nevertheless, although a Canadian court has enforced a U.S. judgment based on the Canadian law that parallels the U.S. "terrorism" exception,[102] other foreign judicial systems have been skeptical about the U.S. judgments. In March 2019, a court in Luxembourg held that the exception violated international law and refused to enforce the judgment against Iran for the September 11, 2001, attacks.[103] A court in Italy also refused to enforce a "terrorism" exception judgment.[104]

# VII.  Conclusion

An exception to sovereign immunity that offered redress for state-sponsored violence would constitute a valuable advance in human rights accountability. The "terrorism" exception is not such a tool. As enacted, amended, and applied, the exception functions as a tool of U.S. domestic politics and foreign policy, targeting states based on political calculations and ignoring violence committed by U.S. allies, strategically important states, and the United States itself. With its

---

[99] Memorandum to the House of Representatives Returning Without Approval the "National Defense Authorization Act for Fiscal Year 2008," 2 Pub. Papers 1592 (Dec. 28, 2007), cited in Ashley Deeks, *Statutory International Law*, 57 VA. J. INT'L L. 263, 280 n.72 (2018).

[100] President Bush signed the later version, despite the punitive damages provision, after Congress added a section allowing him to waive application of the statute to Iraq. Ronald J. Bettauer, *The Law and Politics of Foreign Sovereign Immunity*, 102 AM. SOC'Y INT'L L. PROC. 101, 103–04 (2008).

[101] See, e.g., the statute that enabled seizure of funds belonging to Iran's Central Bank in order to satisfy one particular claim, discussed in Bookman & Noll, *supra* note 45, at 816–22.

[102] Tracy v. Iran (Information and Security), 2017 ONCA 549 (June 30, 2017) (Ontario Court of Appeals upheld decision permitting enforcement of U.S. judgment against Iran in "terrorism" exception case).

In yet another twist, the Second Circuit has held that a U.S. court can order a banking clearinghouse to transfer funds held in Luxembourg to the United States, where the funds would be subject to the jurisdiction of the U.S. courts, a decision that may be reviewed by the U.S. Supreme Court. Peterson v. Islamic Republic of Iran, 876 F.3d 63, 87–95 (2d Cir. 2017) (petition for certiorari pending, request for the views of the Solicitor General pending, 139 Sup. Ct. 306 (2018)).

[103] *In re* Republic of Iran, Judgement civil 2019TALCH01/00116, No. 177266 (Mar. 27, 2019).

[104] Thomas Weatherall, *Flatow v. Iran*, 110 AM. J. INT'L L. 540 (2016) (summarizing decision of the Italian Court of Cassation).

focus on states that are predominantly Muslim, the exception also contributes to Islamophobia and the vilification of Muslims.

The Fourth Restatement accurately "restates" the provisions of the "terrorism" exception. In their notes, however, the reporters choose not to grapple with international law issues triggered by the troubling history and practice under the exception, or with a broader debate over the scope of sovereign immunity. To the contrary, the notes suggest that the exception complies with international law.

The decision to ignore these issues does a disservice to the government officials, judges, scholars, and practitioners who rely on the notes to guide their understanding of U.S. foreign relations law. Equally important, the treatment of the "terrorism" exception by the Fourth Restatement leaves unchallenged a seriously flawed provision of U.S. law that deserves rigorous analysis and rebuke.

# 19

# The Jurisdictional Immunities of International Organizations

## Recent Developments and the Challenges of the Future

*David P. Stewart & Ingrid Wuerth*

International organizations (IOs) experienced explosive growth in the years after the United Nations was established. They expanded not only in number but also in the scope of their activities, becoming important global economic and social actors and changing the nature of international system. They also became important employers in many countries. As international (supranational) entities, IOs are generally entitled to some measure of immunity from the jurisdiction of domestic courts—similar in some ways to (and yet very different in other ways from) the immunity given to foreign states at the domestic level. Immunity allows IOs to fulfill their missions without interference from the domestic courts of the countries in which they locate and operate. This area of the law initially posed relatively few issues.

As IOs grew, the domestic and international legal regulation of their activities also expanded. A variety of social harms were increasingly addressed by positive law and resolved through private litigation, both in the United States and around the world. Laws prohibiting employment discrimination, most of which were enacted after many IOs were founded, serve as an important example, as does the growing jurisprudence of the European Court of Human Rights. As a consequence of these developments, immunity for international organizations today may shield them from more conduct that would otherwise be actionable in court than it did when most treaties and statutes conferring IO immunity were adopted. In addition, the immunity of foreign states has generally become subject to more exceptions during this period, another factor that makes absolute immunity for IOs appear anomalous to some observers, despite the differences between IOs and foreign states. Although IOs generally remain entitled to a high level of immunity in the United States as they do around the world, cases in the United States and elsewhere have begun to indicate ways in which that immunity will be limited going forward.

David P. Stewart & Ingrid Wuerth, *The Jurisdictional Immunities of International Organizations* In: *The Restatement and Beyond.* Edited by: Paul B. Stephan and Sarah H. Cleveland, Oxford University Press (2020). © Oxford University Press. DOI: 10.1093/oso/9780197533154.003.0020.

This chapter describes developments in the law of IO immunity, focusing on the United States. It argues that in some places courts appear poised to limit IO immunity too much, while other cases confer broader immunity than desirable. IOs themselves should do a better job of compensating for harms that they cause, to avoid political pressure that may lead to the further erosion of immunity. Finally, we suggest that the Fourth Restatement take up the topic of IO immunity.

# I. Growth in Numbers, Functions, and Challenges

International organizations are a relatively recent arrival on the international stage. While one can point to a few earlier institutions,[1] the first such organization in the contemporary sense was the League of Nations, established in 1920 in the wake of World War I as part of the effort to prevent such catastrophic conflicts in the future.[2] Today, just a century later, over 250 international organizations exist, touching almost every aspect of international life worldwide. Although their influence is not always visible to or appreciated by people in their daily lives, the reach of international organizations is pervasive.

Best known, of course, is the United Nations, founded in 1945 in the wake of World War II, and its primary mission (the maintenance of international peace and security) is not dissimilar to that of the League of Nations. The Cold War circumscribed its role, but after the demise of the Soviet Union, the Security Council become more active, in part through wide-ranging peacekeeping missions and in part by imposing a wide range of sanctions on individuals and organizations.

Today, the U.N. organization—including not only its principal organs but its various specialized agencies and other affiliated entities—has a pervasive (if often poorly appreciated) role in virtually every aspect international life, including trade and development, financial regulation, telecommunications, scientific research, intellectual property, food, health, migration and refugees, environment and human settlements, air and water quality, telecommunications and civil aviation, and even deep space research. It has become an essential part of the international community.

---

[1] Examples include the International Telegraphic Union (1865) and the Universal Postal Union (1874). Their forebears included the Rhine Commission and European Commission for the Danube, established in 1815 and 1856, respectively. See Robert Kolb, *History of International Organizations or Institutions*, in MAX PLANCK ENCYCLOPEDIA OF PUB. INT'L L. §§ 15–16 (Rüdiger Wolfrum ed.), https://opil.ouplaw.com/view/10.1093/law:epil/9780199231690/law-9780199231690-e501?rskey=V cWg0I&result=1&prd=MPIL (last updated 2011).

[2] See League of Nations Covenant arts. 8 & 10; see also Jose E. Alvarez, *International Organizations: Then and Now*, in A CENTURY OF INTERNATIONAL LAW 141 (2006).

Dozens of globally focused organizations exist today outside the U.N. system and others have proliferated at the regional level, including the European Union, the Organization of American States, the Organization of African Unity, the Organization of Islamic Cooperation, the Commonwealth of Nations, and the Organization of Eastern Caribbean States, to name only a few. When one includes specialized entities, as well as organizations that have nongovernmental entities (in addition to states) as members, the numbers swell into the many hundreds.

In the decades following the end of World II and especially since the end of the Cold War, international organizations have become key actors in the international legal order. They enjoy a unique legal status, in that generally speaking they have international legal personality but lack the sovereignty of states. They are creatures of state action yet do not belong to or represent any particular country, instead acting on behalf of their member states and (to varying degrees) the international community as a whole.

Collectively, jurists increasingly understand the varied structures and practices of international organizations as having created a new (if not entirely coherent) field of law and practice, sometimes described as "international institutional law" or the "law of international organizations."[3] International organizations are typically creatures of multilateral conventions or other international agreements. They are established to carry out specific (and often specialized) tasks considered by states as critically important to the evolving international community. Unlike a simple alliance between states, an international organization has an international institutional structure; as compared to a confederation of states, the focus of an international organization is the international community rather than the specific interests of their constituting members.[4] While international organizations lack the sovereignty of nation-states, some have been recognized as having "international legal personality" in their own right.[5]

The several hundred international organizations in existence today reflect significant variations in structure, purpose, authority, and scope of activity.[6] Some

[3] See, e.g., IMMUNITY OF INTERNATIONAL ORGANIZATIONS (Niels Blokker & Nico Schrijver, eds. 2015); SNEŽANA TRIFUNOVSKA, THE LAW OF INTERNATIONAL ORGANIZATIONS: DOCUMENTS AND CASES (2015) (providing a compilation of key documents and cases regarding the Law of International Organizations as a branch of Public International Law).

[4] See Robert Kolb, *History of International Organizations or Institutions*, in MAX PLANCK ENCYCLOPEDIA OF PUB. INT'L L. § 2 (Rüdiger Wolfrum ed., last updated 2011), https://opil.ouplaw.com/view/10.1093/law:epil/9780199231690/law-9780199231690-e501?rskey=VcWg0I&result=1&prd=MPIL.

[5] See Reparation for Injuries Suffered in the Service of the United Nations, Advisory Opinion, 1949 I.C.J. Rep. 174, 205 (Apr. 11); see generally T. Gazzini, *Personality of International Organizations*, in RESEARCH HANDBOOK ON THE LAW OF INTERNATIONAL ORGANIZATIONS (Jan Klabbers & Åsa Wallendahl eds., 2011).

[6] See JAN KLABBERS, ADVANCED INTRODUCTION TO THE LAW OF INTERNATIONAL ORGANIZATIONS 2–7 (2015); HENRY G. SCHERMERS & NIELS BLOKKER, INTERNATIONAL INSTITUTIONAL LAW (6th ed. 2018).

have global functions, while others are regionally focused. Some have broad mandates, others are specialized. Collectively, they engage in an ever-widening range of important international areas and activities, contributing to such vital areas as peacekeeping, global health and environmental protection, international trade and finance, and regulation of the internet, to name only a few. In one way or another, IOs affect the lives of every person on the planet. As institutions, they also engage in more quotidian matters such as hiring and firing employees, purchasing supplies and materials, and leasing vehicles and buildings. IOs increasingly engage in various types of lawmaking (consider sanctions and international rulemaking), and many are associated with an international tribunal such as the International Court of Justice or the Court of Justice of the European Union.[7]

All have a physical presence somewhere (at least in the form of headquarters or main offices), and most operate in multiple domestic jurisdictions, meaning that they interact with the domestic laws (and potentially the courts) of multiple countries. The United States and Switzerland host many international organizations, but other countries also serve as hosts, in particular France, Austria, Italy, Netherlands, Belgium, Canada, and the United Kingdom, as well as the Peoples' Republic of China, Singapore, Kenya, Nepal, Philippines, Indonesia, Chile, Costa Rica, Spain, Jamaica, Japan, and Thailand.

Historically, international organizations may at times have claimed the immunity of their member states as a derivative matter, but as IOs developed greater independence and international legal personality, they also became directly entitled to immunity.[8] Today, an overlapping regime of multilateral treaties, customary international law, and statutes (such as "headquarters agreements") typically address the immunity of international organizations from the jurisdiction of domestic courts for most matters.[9] Some observers question whether the current immunities to which international organizations are entitled has kept pace with the evolution of the nature and scope of their activities and responsibilities over the past six decades, and whether a fresh look is required—especially in light of changes in immunity rules applicable to foreign states and their agencies and instrumentalities.[10]

---

[7] See JOSE E. ALVAREZ, INTERNATIONAL ORGANIZATIONS AS LAW-MAKERS 459 (2005).

[8] See THIRD RESTATEMENT, pt. IV, intro. note (Am. Law Inst. 1987); see also *id.* at § 467 reporters' note 4 (noting that the European Economic Community was afforded the tax status of its constituent member states).

[9] See generally August Reinisch, *Privileges and Immunities*, in THE OXFORD HANDBOOK OF INTERNATIONAL ORGANIZATIONS 1048 (Jacob Katz Cogan, Ian Hurd, & Ian Johnstone eds., 2016).

[10] See EDWARD CHUKWUEMEKE OKEKE, JURISDICTIONAL IMMUNITIES OF STATES AND INTERNATIONAL ORGANIZATIONS xi–xiii (2018); William M. Berenson, *Squaring the Concept of Immunity with the Fundamental Right to a Fair Trial: The Case of the OAS*, 3 WORLD BANK LEGAL REV. 133, 134–35 (Hassane Cissé, Daniel Bradlow, & Benedict Kingsbury eds., 2012); Eric De Brabandere, *Immunity of International Organizations in Post-Conflict International Administrations*, 7 INT'L ORG.

In performing their various functions, international organizations can do great good, but on occasion they may also cause or otherwise be responsible for significant harm. When that happens, victims may have only limited ability to obtain redress within the organizations themselves. At the same time, the IO's immunity may leave those victims with little or no opportunity to seek compensation through suit in a domestic court, especially in the country in which that IO is located (headquartered). When such a gap in remedies occurs, that situation necessarily raises important legal and policy issues pitting principles of accountability and access to justice against the independence and optimal functioning of the organization themselves.

Since IOs are detached in theory from supervision by any one state, to what extent should they be subject to domestic litigation in respect of various aspects of their operations?

## II. Domestic U.S. Legal Framework

Many international organizations (in particular the United Nations and its specialized agencies) benefit from specific treaty provisions, and even separate treaties, with respect to their immunities.[11] Absent such provisions, however, these issues are governed primarily by domestic law.

In the United States, the statutory framework rests on the seventy-four-year-old International Organization Immunities Act (IOIA).[12] That statute, adopted in 1945 in anticipation that the U.N. Headquarters would be situated in New York, provides that:

> [i]nternational organizations, their property and their assets, wherever located, and by whomsoever held, shall enjoy the same immunity from suit and every form of judicial process as is enjoyed by foreign governments, except to the extent that such organizations may expressly waive their immunity for the purpose of any proceedings or by the terms of any contract.[13]

L. Rev. 79, 89–91 (2010); Anthony Miller, *The Privileges and Immunities of the United Nations*, 6 Int'l Org. L. Rev. 7, 41 (2009); August Reinisch, *The Immunity of International Organizations and the Jurisdiction of Their Administrative Tribunals*, 7 Chinese J. Int'l L. 285, 285–86 (2008) [hereinafter *IO Immunity and Administrative Tribunals*].

[11] E.g., U.N. Charter art. 105; Convention on the Privileges and Immunities of the Specialized Agencies of the United Nations, Nov. 21, 1947, 33 U.N.T.S. 521 (United States not a party). See generally Third Restatement § 467 & reporters' note 2.
[12] The International Organizations Immunities Act (IOIA), 59 Stat. 669 (1945), codified as amended 22 U.S.C. §§ 288–288l. In specific cases, of course, other statutory provisions will be relevant, see, e.g., the Headquarters Agreement with the United Nations, June 26, 1947, 61 Stat. 756, 22 U.S.C. § 287 note, T.I.A.S. No. 1676, 11 U.N.T.S. 11.
[13] 22 U.S.C. § 288a(b).

Some subsections of the statute extend the benefits of the IOIA specifically to named organizations, while others permit the president to make the necessary designations (which has typically been done by executive order). The statute also permits the president to withhold or withdraw immunities from any such organization.[14]

Today, of course, the immunity of "foreign governments," to which the IOIA refers, is governed in the United States by the Foreign Sovereign Immunities Act (FSIA), adopted in 1976.[15] But in 1945, when the IOIA was passed, no such statute existed, and states enjoyed virtually absolute immunity from suit in U.S. courts as a matter of customary international law. Moreover, recognition of such immunity was considered to be (at least in significant part) a function of the executive, in that courts were informed by "suggestions of immunity" transmitted by the Department of State.[16]

For the first forty years of the IOIA's life, this area of the law remained relatively confined, with only a few judicial decisions of significance. For example, when the Third Restatement was published in 1986, it was possible to summarize developments in four comparatively short sections: Section 467 Privileges and Immunities of International Organizations; Section 468 Immunity of Premises, Archives, Documents, and Communications of International Organizations; Section 469 Immunity of Officials of International Organizations; and Section 470 Immunity of Member Representatives to International Organizations.[17]

Despite the equivalence drawn by the IOIA itself between IO immunity and the immunities accorded to foreign states, the Third Restatement described the privileges and immunities of international organizations as conceptually distinct from those of states, focusing heavily on the United Nations. It recognized that IO immunity is based not on sovereignty—which IOs lack—but instead on the functional needs of the organization, including the immunity of officials necessary to carry out those functions, and immunity from any exercise of jurisdiction that would interfere with the IO's use of its premises, archives, documents, and

---

[14] See 22 U.S.C. § 288.

[15] Foreign Sovereign Immunities Act of 1976, Pub. L. No. 94-583, 90 Stat. 2891, codified at 28 U.S.C.A. §§ 1330, 1332(a)(4), 1391(f), 1441(d), 1602–611.

[16] See generally Ingrid Wuerth, *Foreign Official Immunity Determinations in U.S. Courts: The Case Against the State Department*, 51 Va. J. Int'l L. 915, 925–26 (2011).

[17] Third Restatement §§ 468–69. The Second Restatement of Foreign Relations Law discussed these issues in Sections 83–93, noting that because "[m]ost questions with respect to immunities relating to international organizations are governed by international agreements (including the constitutions of such organizations) or national legislation" it would deal "primarily with general principles and with only some of the more important specific problems that have arisen or that seem to present special difficulty." Restatement (Second) of Foreign Relations Law ch. 4, Topic 4, intro. note *a* (Am. Law Inst. 1965). "Since international agreements and national legislation regarding immunities have accompanied the development of international organizations, there has been little occasion for the development of rules of international law." Reporters' note (b).

communications.[18] IO immunity thus lacks the principle of bilateral reciprocity that is sometimes said to undergird the doctrine of state immunity, and appropriately so, since the organization represents (at least in theory) the international community as a whole, and officials working for or accredits to the organization will have various nationalities, including that of the state from which immunity is sought.[19]

The approach adopted by the IOIA was perhaps adequate in the early years of its existence, given the relatively small number of international organizations. Since then, however, many significant developments have occurred—not merely the growth in the number and diversity of international organizations but also the extent of their interactions with domestic legal systems. In consequence, a significant (and growing) body of domestic decisions has emerged around the world related to the privileges and immunities of international organizations.[20] In the United States alone, the courts have rendered some 110 judicial decisions interpreting and applying the IOIA since 1986, and altogether nearly 300 mention the privileges and immunities of the United Nations, the Organization of American States, the World Bank, and other international organizations.

Two kinds of cases have proven the most difficult and controversial in the United States. One category poses direct challenges to decisions and activities that are core to the mission of the IO itself, such as suits based upon the lending practices of an international financial organization or upon the way the relief is distributed by an aid organization. Another broad set of cases arise not from challenges to an IO's core functions, but instead from its labor and employment practices. Suits in this category involve topics like wages and tax withholding, unemployment, retirement, or other benefits, and discrimination based on age, gender, race, or other protected classes.

In these two categories of cases, the general trends described here converge to produce contested results. Growth in the scope of activity by IOs means that they are more pervasive economic and social actors, so that their missions have greater impact and their mistakes are more costly, giving rise to more lawsuits challenging their core function. Growth in the number and size of IOs means

---

[18]  See THIRD RESTATEMENT, intro. note, §§ 467–69.

[19]  See *id.*

[20]  E.g., Georges v. United Nations, 834 F.3d 88 (2d Cir. 2016); Laventure v. United Nations, 279 F. Supp. 3d 394 (E.D.N.Y. 2017); Amaratunga v. Northwest Atlantic Fisheries Organization, [2013] 3 S.C.R. 866 (Can.); HR 16 June 2014, ECLI:NL:RBDHA:2014:8562 m.nt. (Mothers of Srebrenica Association/State of the Netherlands) (Neth.), (trans.), https://uitspraken.rechtspraak.nl/inziend ocument?id=ECLI:NL:RBDHA:2014:8748; Case T-315/01, Yassin Abdullah Kadi v. Council of the Eur. Union and Comm'n of the Eur. Cmtys., 2005 ECJ II-3659; Z.M. v. Permanent Delegation of the League of Arab States to the United Nations (Switzerland 1993); Arab Monetary Fund v. Hashim and Others, House of Lords (1991) [reprinted in 6 ARAB L.Q. 90, https://brill.com/view/journals/alq/6/1/article-p90_7.xml]; Waite and Kennedy v. Germany, 1999-I Eur. Ct. H.R., http://hudoc.echr.coe.int/eng?i=001-58912.

that they collectively employ larger numbers of people, giving rise to more employment-related cases. Moreover, a growing number of social harms are resolved through private litigation, both in the United States and around the world. Laws prohibiting employment discrimination serve as an important example, as does the growth of the case law of the European Court of Human Rights and the importance of access to courts under the European Convention on Human Rights.[21] Providing near absolute immunity for international organizations now shields them from legal challenges to much conduct that might otherwise be actionable in court.

Finally, foreign states, as discussed here, have less immunity from suit than they did when the IOIA was enacted, another factor that makes absolute immunity for IOs appear anomalous. As a consequence of these developments, a substantial amount of scholarly and academic attention has been given in recent years to the "privileges and immunities" of international organizations from the supervision of domestic courts.[22]

## III.  Cases Challenging Conduct Core to an IO's Mission

The increasing scope and significance of IO activities, along with the growing use of law and litigation to resolve social and international legal issues and the reduction of immunity available to nation-states, has led to challenges to the conduct of international organizations in domestic courts, even in cases that where that conduct goes to the core of an IO's mission. Two important U.S. cases illustrate these trends.

### A.  IO and Foreign State Immunity: *Jam v. International Finance Corporation*

The International Finance Corporation (IFC) was established in 1956 as the private-sector arm of the World Bank Group. Its aim is to promote economic development by mobilizing financial resources for private enterprise, promoting accessible and competitive markets, supporting businesses and other

---

[21]  See generally EUROPEAN UNION AGENCY FOR FUNDAMENTAL RIGHTS & COUNCIL OF EUROPE, HANDBOOK ON EUROPEAN LAW RELATING TO ACCESS TO JUSTICE (2016), https://www.echr.coe.int/Documents/Handbook_access_justice_ENG.pdf.

[22]  See, e.g., Anthony Cooper, Jam v. International Finance Corporation: *Access to Remedy, But Only When We Say So*, 26 TUL. J. INT'L & COMP. L. 417, 428–31 (2018); Carson Young, *The Limits of International Organization Immunity: An Argument for a Restrictive Theory of Immunity under the IOIA*, 95 TEX. L. REV. 889, 894–901 (2017); R.J. Oparil, *Immunity of International Organizations in United States Courts: Absolute or Restrictive*, 23 VAND. J. TRANSNAT'L L. 689, 696–704 (1991).

private-sector entities, and creating jobs and delivering necessary services to those who are poverty stricken or otherwise vulnerable.

The IFC describes itself as "a sister organization of the World Bank and member of the World Bank Group ... [and] the largest global development institution focused exclusively on the private sector in developing countries."[23] Under its Articles of Agreement, the IFC is charged with furthering economic development "by encouraging the growth of productive private enterprise in member countries, particularly in the less developed areas, thus supplementing the activities of" the World Bank.[24] According to the IFC's website, "[o]ur financial products enable companies to manage risk and expand their access to foreign and domestic capital markets. IFC operates on a commercial basis. We invest exclusively in for-profit projects in developing countries, and we charge market rates for our products and services."[25] An executive order in 1957 designated the IFC as an international organization under the IOIA.[26]

The case brought by Jam against the IFC gave the U.S. Supreme Court a chance to consider whether, in light of the subsequent adoption of limitations on the immunity of foreign states (first, in the so-called "Tate Letter" in 1952 and then in the FSIA itself), the language of the IOIA should be read to afford international organizations more extensive immunities than are today afforded foreign states.[27] It arose out of a loan by the IFC to an Indian power company for the purpose of developing a new power plant. Under the terms of the loan, the power plant was supposed to comply with an environmental and social plan. The agreement allowed the IFC to revoke financial support for the project for lack of compliance with the plan. The IFC allegedly provided inadequate supervision of the dam's construction, which apparently caused severe environmental harm to the air and water, resulting in damages to local farmers and fishermen.[28]

Those farmers and fishermen brought suit against the IFC in federal court in Washington, D.C. They argued that the IOIA must be read in light of the FSIA, so that the IFC should be entitled only to the immunity due to foreign states under the FSIA. This meant that exceptions to immunity might apply, including the one for commercial activity. The plaintiffs based their argument on language

[23] See International Finance Corporation, https://www.ifc.org/wps/wcm/connect/corp_ext_content/ifc_external_corporate_site/home(last visited Aug. 25, 2019) ("Since 1956, IFC has leveraged $2.6 billion in capital to deliver more than $285 billion in financing for businesses in developing countries.").

[24] Articles of Agreement of the International Finance Corporation art. I, Dec. 5, 1955, 7 U.S.T. 2193, T.I.A.S. No. 3620.

[25] International Finance Corporation, https://www.ifc.org/wps/wcm/connect/corp_ext_content/ifc_external_corporate_site/solutions/products+and+services/investment-proserv(last visited Aug. 25, 2019).

[26] See Exec. Order No. 10,680, 21 Fed. Reg. 7,647 (Oct. 2, 1956).

[27] See Jam v. Int'l Fin. Corp., 139 S. Ct. 759, 765 (2019).

[28] See Jam v. Int'l Fin. Corp., 860 F.3d 703, 708 (D.C. Cir. 2017), rev'd, 139 S. Ct. 759 (2019).

in the IOIA providing that international organizations "shall enjoy the same immunity from suit and every form of judicial process as is enjoyed by foreign governments."[29]

The District Court dismissed their complaint holding that, under prevailing precedent, the IOIA conferred "absolute immunity upon international organizations like IFC" and that the IFC had not waived its immunity as permitted under the statute.[30] The D.C. Circuit Court of Appeals affirmed that decision, agreeing (somewhat reluctantly) that the IFC was entitled to absolute immunity, consistent with its prior decisions.[31]

### 1. The Majority Decision

The U.S. Supreme Court granted certiorari and reversed. Resolving a long-standing split in the circuits,[32] the Court concluded that the statutory language of the IOIA is more naturally read to refer to a standard that changes over time, reasoning bolstered by other statutes with similar language that have been interpreted that way.

The IFC had argued, in language echoing that of the Third Restatement, that the IOIA should not be tied to changing norms of foreign state immunity, because the purpose of international organization immunity differs from the purpose of foreign sovereign immunity. The latter is based on reciprocity and sovereign respect, while the former is designed to allow international organizations to function without undue interference from the courts of any one member country. The IFC contended that the IOIA does not (was not intended to) tether the immunity of international organizations to the shrinking scope of foreign state immunity.

The Court found these arguments unconvincing in light of the language of statute itself.[33] It was also unconvinced by policy arguments against affording international organizations only restrictive immunity. For example, exposing international organizations to more lawsuits makes it more expensive for them to operate, an argument with particular force in the case of investment banks because their activities may well qualify as "commercial" so that an exception to immunity applies. Domestic lawsuits also allow courts to second-guess the work

---

[29]  28 U.S.C. § 288a(b).

[30]  Jam v. Int'l Fin. Corp., 172 F. Supp. 3d 104, 109, 112 (D.D.C. 2016). Under the IOIA, a designated IO may waive its immunity "for the purpose of any proceedings or by the terms of any contract." 22 U.S.C. § 288a(b).

[31]  See Jam v. Int'l Fin. Corp., 860 F.3d 703, 704–13 (2017) (relying heavily on Atkinson v. Inter-American Development Bank, 156 F.3d 1335, 1340 (D.C. Cir. 1998)).

[32]  The D.C. Circuit had long held that international organizations were entitled to absolute immunity. The Third Circuit had held to the contrary for reasons that ultimately led the Supreme Court to reject the D.C. Circuit's reasoning. See OSS Nokalva, Inc. v. European Space Agency, 617 F.3d 756, 760–66 (3d Cir. 2010).

[33]  Jam v. Int'l Fin. Corp., 139 S. Ct. 759, 768–69 (2019).

that international organizations perform. The Court rejected these arguments in part because the IOIA sets only default rules, meaning that the treaties that create international organizations can specify a higher level of immunity.[34]

## 2. Justice Breyer's Dissent

The Supreme Court's analysis rested on the so-called "reference canon" of statutory interpretation, according to which a statute that refers to a general subject "adopts the law on that subject as it exists whenever a question under the statute arises. . . [but] a statute that refers to another statute by specific title or section number in effect cuts and pastes the referenced statute as it existed when the referring statute was enacted, without any subsequent amendments."[35]

The Supreme Court interpreted the IOIA's reference to the immunity enjoyed by foreign governments as a general rather than specific reference. The reference, the majority concluded, is to an external body of potentially evolving law—the law of foreign sovereign immunity—not to a specific provision of another statute. The IOIA should therefore be understood to link the law of international organization immunity to the law of foreign sovereign immunity, so that the one develops in tandem with the other.[36]

In lone dissent, Justice Breyer emphasized "the differences between international organizations and nation states, along with the Act's purposes and the risk of untoward consequences," noting that maintaining the broader interpretation would be more consonant with the likely intent of Congress "to facilitate international organizations' ability to pursue their missions in the United States."[37]

One can question whether the majority's analysis imputes an intention to the legislature for which (at best) scant basis exists in the record. As Jam's attorneys noted, the legislative history of the IOIA itself gives no indication of any intent to afford IO's any degree of immunity other than the absolute immunity enjoyed at the time of its adoption by foreign states, and perhaps more importantly, no support can be found in the legislative history of the FSIA to indicate that the executive branch had such congruence in mind in proposing the statute, or that Congress did so in adopting it.

In the face of that silence, and given the possible ramifications of such a change in the substantive law, some may incline to the view that deferring the issue to the legislature would have been an outcome more appropriate to the

---

[34] *Id.* at 771–72; see also Charles H. Brower II, *United States*, in THE PRIVILEGES AND IMMUNITIES OF INTERNATIONAL ORGANIZATIONS IN DOMESTIC COURTS 303, 304–306 (August Reinisch ed., 2013) (describing the various forms of international agreements that confer immunity on international organizations).

[35] 139 S. Ct. at 769.

[36] *Id.* at 763.

[37] *Id.* at 777–81.

judicial function. Structural differences between the two statutes make it difficult to read the two statutes together: For instance, the IOIA vests primary discretion in the president, while the FSIA places the decision largely in the hands of the judiciary (indeed, one of its primary goals was removing immunity decisions from the hands of the executive). In any event, it is clear that the *Jam* decision will inevitably generate considerable litigation requiring the lower courts to apply the general direction of the Supreme Court to particular cases.

### 3. Commercial Activities and Other Exceptions

Perhaps the most important difficulty one can anticipate is in defining exactly what scope the term "commercial activities" has in relation to the activities of international organizations. As Justice Breyer noted, a consequence of the *Jam* decision will likely be civil lawsuits against many of the international organizations to which the United States belongs "based on their (U.S.-law-defined) commercial activity. . . ."[38] Notwithstanding that (unlike foreign states and state-owned enterprises) IO's do not engage in "commercial activities" for their own profit, the lower courts will presumably be bound to follow the Supreme Court's interpretation of the FSIA's "commercial activities" exception—meaning either a regular course of commercial conduct or a particular commercial transaction or act. The commercial character of an activity shall be determined by reference to the nature of the course of conduct or particular transaction or act, rather than by reference to its purpose.[39]

As the Court itself pointed out, it is not clear whether loans by entities such as the IFC, made for public purposes, will or should qualify as "commercial" under the FSIA. More broadly, the Supreme Court has sometimes defined "commercial" in terms of conduct that is not "sovereign," a definition that provides little assistance in the context of international organizations because they inherently lack sovereignty.[40]

In the case of the IFC, the issue is even more fraught. As the IFC's website indicates, it "operates on a commercial basis" and it "invest(s) exclusively in for-profit projects in developing countries." Its purpose, however, is a public one, to stimulate economic growth and development, not to generate profits for

---

[38] 139 S. Ct. at 778.

[39] 22 U.S.C. § 1603(d). Following *Jam*, a lower court held that the World Bank lacks immunity from a suit related to employer-provided health insurance because providing such insurance to an employee is a commercial activity. Francisco S. v. Aetna Life Ins. Co., 2020 WL 1676353 (D. Utah 2020).

[40] See Saudi Arabia v. Nelson, 507 U.S. 349, 359–60 (1993); Republic of Argentina v. Weltover, 504 U.S. 607, 614 (1992).

shareholders. It is an international organization, established by states for sovereign purposes related to economic development.

Even if the conduct involved is properly deemed "commercial," the suit must also have an adequate nexus to the United States under the FSIA, a further restriction on cases against foreign states under the commercial activity exception. Since the IFC invests exclusively in projects in developing countries, the question will be whether the fact that decisions are made at its headquarters in Washington, D.C., will be sufficient to vest jurisdiction in U.S. courts. How this and other limitations are interpreted in cases involving international organizations will determine exactly how far the *Jam* case opened the courthouse door. Indeed in the *Jam* case itself, the District Court held on remand that the commercial activities exception did not apply precisely because plaintiffs failed to establish that the "gravamen" or "core" of their complaint (which it described as "the IFC's failure to ensure the Tata Mundra Power Plant was designed, constructred, and operated with due care so as not to harm plaintiffs' property, health, and way of life) was "based upon" conduct carried on in the United States as required for application of the FSIA's commercial activities exception.[41]

The *Jam* decision left unclear whether international organizations are now subject just to the FSIA's "commercial activities" exception or whether some or all of the statute's other exceptions to immunity apply—in particular, the noncommercial tort and arbitration exceptions. Some of the FSIA's other provisions, such as the expropriation and "state-sponsored terrorism" exceptions, seem impossible to apply to international organizations, meaning that the "same immunity" language of the IOIA cannot resolve all cases.[42]

## 4. International Law

The extent to which U.S. courts will consider customary international law and its focus on the functional needs of the organization is also unclear, both in cases purportedly involving commercial activity and those involving other exceptions.[43] Other domestic legal systems and the treaties governing immunity do not equate foreign states and IOs; instead, they generally provide that IOs are immune from suit for conduct necessary to perform their functions.[44]

---

[41] Jam v. International Finance Corporation, 2020 WL 759199 (D.D.C. 2020). See 28 U.S.C. §§ 1603, 1605(a)(2).

[42] See Ingrid Wuerth, *How the Supreme Court Should Decide Jam v. International Finance Corp.*, LAWFARE BLOG (Oct. 24, 2018), https://www.lawfareblog.com/how-supreme-court-should-decide-jam-v-international-finance-corp.

[43] See Julian Arato, *Equivalence and Translation: Further Thoughts on IO Immunities in Jam v. IFC*, EJIL: TALK! (Mar. 11, 2019), https://www.ejiltalk.org/equivalence-and-translation-further-thoughts-on-io-immunities-in-jam-v-ifc/.

[44] See HAZEL FOX & PHILIPPA WEBB, THE LAW OF STATE IMMUNITY 574–75 (3d ed. 2014).

Although the two approaches are different, there may be some overlap. In particular, whether the conduct is "commercial" might in some cases be relevant to (or overlap with) whether the conduct is necessary for the IO to perform its functions. Other exceptions to foreign state immunity might also overlap with the necessary functions test.

The *Jam* case accordingly represents a big departure from the near-absolute immunity that IOs previously enjoyed, but it is unclear whether it will result in significant departures from functional test more commonly used in international law. Recall, as well, that treaty commitments may give IOs more immunity from U.S. courts than does the IOIA. Whether the decision will result in violations of customary international law or whether it shapes that law moving forward remains to be seen.

The stakes are high, and the *Jam* case itself may subject the organization to litigation that goes to the heart of its purpose, contrary to a functional necessity approach. As Justice Breyer pointed out in his dissenting opinion, many international organizations engaged in the financial sector, including the World Bank, the Inter-American Development Bank, and the Multilateral Investment Guarantee Agency, may find themselves subject to litigation in the United States for conduct at the core of their missions: the promotion of international development through investment.[45]

### 5. Scope of Application

*Jam* itself involved immunity from jurisdiction to adjudicate. The reasoning should also apply to immunity from execution or attachment jurisdiction, however. The IOIA provides that international organizations, including "their property and their assets, wherever located, and by whomsoever held, shall enjoy the same immunity from suit and every form of judicial process as is enjoyed by foreign governments."[46] The "same immunity" language protects property and applies to "every form of judicial process," meaning that efforts to attach the assets of, or execute judgments against, international organizations will now be governed by the FSIA's requirements. Immunity from execution or attachment jurisdiction is broader than immunity from adjudication under the FSIA, so treating IOs like states may have less of an impact in enforcement cases than it will in cases involving jurisdiction to adjudicate.[47]

---

[45] See Jam v. Int'l Fin. Corp., 139 S. Ct. 759, 778–79 (2019) (Breyer, J. dissenting).

[46] 22 U.S.C. § 288a(b).

[47] See, e.g., Peterson v. Islamic Rep. of Iran, 563 F. Supp. 2d 268, 276 (2008) (dismissing enforcement action against international organization because they were entitled to absolute immunity, but also dismissing the action against foreign states (and their agencies or instrumentalities) because the requirements of the FSIA were not satisfied).

## B. Alternative Resolution of Claims:
## The Haiti Litigation (*Georges*)

After the devastating 2010 earthquake in Haiti, the U.N. Security Council voted to expand its peacekeeping mission there. The U.N. Stabilization Mission in Haiti (MINUSTAH) had been established in 2004, when President Bertrand Aristide was exiled. The 2010 expansion was intended to support recovery and reconstruction after the earthquake.

Instead, U.N. peacekeepers apparently caused a major cholera outbreak that resulted in the death of more than nine thousand people. Evidently, personnel from Nepal were stationed at a facility that allegedly discharged raw sewage into a river that serves as an important source of drinking water. Victims and their families brought class action lawsuits in federal court in New York against the United Nations and certain high-level officials, alleging that they had failed to provide adequate health screening for members of the mission and to ensure sanitary conditions for its mission in Haiti.[48] In particular, the plaintiffs alleged that the United Nations deployed personnel from Nepal to Haiti without testing or screening for cholera, although they knew that the disease was widespread in Nepal.

The district court dismissed the suits because all of the defendants were immune, an outcome upheld on appeal.[49] In distinction to the *Jam* litigation, the United Nations' claim of immunity rested not on the IOIA but rather on two treaties: (1) the Charter of the United Nations (U.N. Charter), which states that the United Nations "shall enjoy in the territory of each of its Members such privileges and immunities as are necessary for the fulfillment of its purposes,"[50] and (2) the Convention on the Privileges and Immunities of the United Nations (CPIUN), which was adopted less than a year after the U.N. Charter and provides that the United Nations shall enjoy immunity from "every form of legal process."[51]

The plaintiffs argued that immunity for all defendants was inapplicable because the United Nations had violated CPIUN Article 29, which requires the United Nations to "make provisions for appropriate modes of settlement of . . . disputes arising out of contracts or other disputes of a private law character to which the [United Nations] is a party." The United Nations had not created

---

[48]  See Georges v. United Nations, 84 F. Supp. 3d 246, 247–48 (S.D.N.Y. 2015).

[49]  See Georges v. United Nations, 834 F.3d 88, 94 (2d Cir. 2016); Laventure v. United Nations, 279 F. Supp. 3d 394 (E.D.N.Y. 2017), *aff'd*, 746 F. App'x 80 (2d Cir. 2018).

[50]  U.N. Charter art. 105, ¶ 1.

[51]  Convention on the Privileges and Immunities of the United Nations, Feb. 13, 1946, T.I.A.S. No. 6900, 21 U.S.T. 1418 (1970). It also provided absolute immunity for the senior U.N. officials named because they were entitled to the same immunity as diplomats.

a claims commission or other dispute resolution process for those injured or killed by the cholera outbreak, a failure that plaintiffs claimed violated not only the CPIUN but also an obligation under the Agreement Between the United Nations and the Government of Haiti Concerning the Status of the United Nations Operation in Haiti (SOFA) to provide a settlement process for third-party private-law claims.[52]

The Second Circuit reasoned that, absent an express waiver, the United Nations is absolutely immune from suit under the CPIUN. Compliance by the United Nations with Article 29's requirements was not, the court held, a condition precedent for absolute immunity. Although the defendants did not enter an appearance in the case, the executive branch of the U.S. government argued that absolute immunity applied under the CPIUN whether or not the United Nations had violated Article 29, and the court gave the government's view "great weight."[53]

The *Georges* decision is consistent with a Dutch case interpreting the same language of the CPIUN. In that matter, *Mothers of Srebrenica et al. v. State of The Netherlands and the United Nations*, plaintiffs alleged that the United Nations was liable for a 1995 attack on a U.N. safe haven established in the Bosnian enclave of Srebrenica. Bosnian-Serb forces under the command of General Mladic allegedly killed between eight thousand and ten thousand people who had taken refuge in the safe haven. The Court rejected an analogy between states and international organizations, reasoned that neither the European Convention on Human Rights nor the International Covenant on Civil and Political Rights required a denial of immunity, and held that the United Nations was immune whether or not alternative means of securing redress were available.[54]

International practice may nevertheless be moving toward a system in which immunity before domestic courts depends upon the availability of alternative dispute resolution mechanisms.[55] The trend is most pronounced in Europe, in part because the European Convention on Human Rights safeguards the right of access to justice.[56] The European Court of Human Rights has reasoned that although the immunity is an essential means of ensuring that international organizations can function properly, a "material factor" in determining whether it is

---

[52] See Georges v. United Nations, 84 F. Supp. 3d 246, 247–48 (S.D.N.Y. 2015), *aff'd*, 834 F.3d 88 (2d Cir. 2016).

[53] See Georges v. United Nations, 834 F.3d at 93.

[54] See HR 13 April 2012, ECLI:CE:ECHR:2013:0611DEC006554212 m.nt. (Mothers of Srebrenica Association/State of the Netherlands) (Neth.), https://hudoc.echr.coe.int/eng#{%22itemid%22: [%22001-122255%22]}.

[55] See Reinisch, *IO Immunity and Administrative Tribunals, supra* note 10.

[56] Convention for the Protection of Human Rights and Fundamental Freedoms, arts. 6 ("right to a fair trial") & 13 (access to "an effective remedy"), Nov. 4, 1950, E.T.S. No.005; see also Charter of Fundamental Rights of the European Union, art. 47 ("right to an effective remedy and to a fair trial"), Dec. 18, 2000, [2000] O.J. 20.

permissible to deny an applicant access to court (through immunity), is whether a "reasonable alternative means" is available to protect the applicants' interests.[57] A variety of administrative tribunals have recognized the related principle that IO employees should have access to dispute settlement for the resolution of employment-related issues.[58] None of these cases involves the language of the CPIUN at issue in *Georges* and *Mothers of Srebernica*, but they do suggest a trend toward accountability, especially in the context of employment-related disputes, which are discussed in the next section.

The foregoing examples illustrate developments in the law of IO immunity, as the well as the importance of immunity in shielding IOs from potentially costly lawsuits. The examples also highlight the social costs of conferring immunity and preventing an adjudication on the merits of cases involving allegations of egregious misconduct by IOs and their employees and officers.[59] In particular, the outcome of the Haitian litigation has met with substantial criticism as a policy matter and seems unfair to the many people who experienced extreme suffering. The United Nations eventually suggested that it may make some form of reparations available.[60] To date, however, it does not appear to have adopted such alternative arrangements.

The outcome of the *Jam* case should, perhaps, put international organizations on notice that they cannot rely solely upon absolute immunity going forward. They should put in place meaningful and effective means of resolving meritorious claims when their conduct causes unnecessary suffering and harm, both as a matter of basic decency and to prevent regulation and reductions in immunity by national courts.[61]

---

[57] Waite and Kennedy v. Germany, 1999-I Eur. Ct. H.R. ¶ 68, http://hudoc.echr.coe.int/eng?i=001-58912. In some tension with the *Waite and Kennedy* case, the European Court of Human Rights has refused to consider the availability of other means of dispute settlement in cases involving the immunity of foreign states. See Mizushima Tomomori, *Denying Foreign State Immunity on the Grounds of the Unavailability of Alternative Means*, 71 MOD. L. REV. 734, 739–43 (2008); see also Philippa Webb, *The Immunity of States, Diplomats and International Organizations in Employment Disputes: The New Human Rights Dilemma?*, 27 EUR. J. INT'L L. 745, 747 (2016); see generally August Reinisch & Ralph Janik, *The Personality, Privileges, and Immunities of International Organizations before National Courts—Room for Dialogue*, in THE PRIVILEGES AND IMMUNITIES OF INTERNATIONAL ORGANIZATIONS IN DOMESTIC COURTS 332–37 (August Reinisch ed., 2013) (describing the impact of *Waite and Kennedy*).

[58] See Reinisch, *IO Immunity and Administrative Tribunals, supra* note 10, at 293.

[59] See Kristen E. Boon, *The United Nations as Good Samaritan: Immunity and Responsibility*, 16 CHICAGO J. INT'L L. 341, 358–62 (2016); Bruce Rashkow, *Above the Law: Innovating the Legal Response to Build a More Accountable UN: Where Is the UN Now?*, 23 ILSA J. INT'L & COMP. L. 345, 346–50 (2017).

[60] For a discussion of the United Nations' response to complaints of sexual misconduct by peacekeeping troops, see Kristina Daugirdas, *Reputation as a Disciplinarian of International Organizations*, 113 AM. J. INT'L L. 221 (2019).

[61] See *id.* at 254 (noting that "[o]ver the years, NGOs, UN officials, and academic commentators have decried the 'culture of silence' that pervades the United Nations when it comes to sexual violence and other kinds of abuse and exploitation perpetrated by UN-affiliated individuals" and arguing that the United Nations should improve the way it responded to allegations of misconduct); Paul R

## IV. Employment-Related Litigation against International Organizations

International organizations usually do provide an internal procedure for aggrieved employees, one that does not subject them to the interference and oversight of domestic courts. As mentioned earlier, in some cases in Europe the availability of such a procedure has been relevant to determining whether the IO is entitled to immunity.[62] In the United States, courts have conferred very broad immunity on IOs and their officials in the employment context—perhaps more than is warranted—even for conduct apparently covered by a waiver or that appears to fall outside of official functions.

### A.  Waivers of Immunity

In waiver cases, the D.C. Circuit has been protective of international organizations, as it was in the *Jam* case before the Supreme Court's reversal. In *Mendaro v. World Bank*, for example, a staff member alleged discrimination and sexual harassment.[63] The World Bank's Articles of Agreement provided that "[a]ctions may be brought against the Bank" in "a court of competent jurisdiction," with few limitations.[64] Plaintiffs argued that this open-ended waiver allowed their case to go forward. The D.C. Circuit held to the contrary. It emphasized the importance of immunity from suits by employees, warned against the dangers of inadvertent waivers, and reasoned that a general waiver is inapplicable unless the international organization would get a "corresponding benefit." The possibility of legal recourse would encourage investors and other commercial actors to do business with the bank, and waiver accordingly applied in such cases.

Employment claims, by contrast, would provide no benefit and would "lay the Bank open to disruptive interference with its employment practices."[65] One might argue that a workplace free of discrimination would provide a benefit to

---

Stephan, *What Should We Ask Reputation to Do?*, 113 AJIL UNBOUND 223, 225 (2019) (noting the need for alternative accountability mechanisms in light of the immunity to which IOs are entitled).

[62]  See Webb, *supra* note 57 at 755–57.

[63]  Mendaro v. World Bank, 717 F.2d 610, 615 (D.C. Cir. 1983); see also Smith v. World Bank Grp., 99 F. Supp. 3d 166, 167 (D.D.C. 2015), *aff'd*, 694 F. App'x 1 (D.C. Cir. 2017).

[64]  Articles of Agreement of the International Bank for Reconstruction and Development art. VII, § 3, Dec. 27, 1945, 60 Stat. 1440, 1447, 2 U.N.T.S. 134, 180 ("Actions may be brought against the Bank only in a court of competent jurisdiction in the territories of a member in which the Bank has an office, has appointed an agent for the purpose of accepting service or notice of process, or has issued or guaranteed securities."); see also Agreement Establishing the Inter-American Development Bank art. XI, § 3, Apr. 8, 1959, 10 U.S.T. 3029, 3095, 389 U.N.T.S. 69, 128 (same language).

[65]  *Mendaro*, 717 F.2d at 618.

the IO by improving the workplace environment for all employees. The "corresponding benefit" doctrine has, however, been applied to prevent employment discrimination cases from going forward,[66] while allowing commercial cases to precede, even those in which the defendant itself argued that it received no benefit from the type of litigation in question.[67]

The D.C. Circuit applied the "corresponding benefit" reasoning to the waiver issue in the *Jam* case. It acknowledged that the IFC charter "read literally, would seem to include a categorical waiver."[68] It also noted that it is "a bit strange" that the *courts* determine when a claim "benefits" the international organization when "one would think that the organization would be a better judge as to what claims benefit it than the judiciary."[69] The plaintiffs in *Jam* argued that waiver should apply to their claims because "holding the IFC to the very environmental and social conditions it put in the contract, conditions which the IFC itself formulated, would benefit the IFC's goals" by ensuring that it is properly managed and by helping to generate community support. The D.C. Circuit rejected this argument, in part because the lawsuit arose out of the IFC's "core operations," would "threaten the policy discretion of the organization," and would mean that "every loan the IFC makes to fund projects in developing countries could be the subject of a suit in Washington."[70] Judge Pillard agreed that the case was controlled by precedent, but wrote separately to argue that the court should revisit "the amorphous waiver-curbing doctrine that has developed under *Mendaro*."[71]

The Supreme Court did not address the waiver issue in *Jam*, but its decision will make the "corresponding benefit" doctrine less important in one sense. The commercial cases against the World Bank (and other organizations with the same waiver language in their charters) in which courts found a "corresponding benefit," and therefore found immunity had been waived, might now go forward under the commercial activity exception, making waiver irrelevant. However, the "corresponding benefit" doctrine will continue to limit noncommercial cases brought against international financial organizations that have broad waiver language in their charters. It may be best for courts to abandon the judge-made

---

[66] See, e.g., Atkinson v. Inter-Am. Dev. Bank, 156 F.3d 1335 (D.C. Cir. 1998); Morgan v. Int'l Bank for Reconstruction & Dev., 752 F. Supp. 2d 492, 493–94 (D.D.C. 1990).

[67] See Osseiran v. Int'l Fin. Corp., 552 F.3d 836, 839 (D.C. Cir. 2009) (permitting a suit by a potential investor); see also Vila v. Inter-American Investment, Corp., 570 F.3d 274, 276, 279–82 (D.C. Cir. 2009) (permitting suit by a consultant).

[68] Jam v. Int'l Fin. Corp., 860 F.3d 703, 706 (D.C. Cir. 2017).

[69] *Id.* at 707.

[70] *Id.* at 708.

[71] *Id.* at 708 (opinion of Judge Pillard); see also Vila v. Inter-Am. Inv. Corp., 583 F.3d 869 (D.C. Cir. 2009) (noting that "Judge Williams has filed a statement inviting a challenge to the interpretation of a waiver of immunity provision in the articles of agreement adopted by an international organization."); Young, *supra* note 22, at 908 (arguing that the "corresponding benefit" test should be abandoned).

"corresponding benefit" doctrine and instead rely on the text of the waivers themselves.

## B.  Immunity of Individual Officials

Individual officials of international organizations are generally entitled, at a minimum, to immunity for actions they take as part of their official functions. The CPIUN provides, for example, that the "Secretary-General and all Assistant Secretaries-General shall be accorded" the immunity given "to diplomatic envoys, in accordance with international law."[72] The Second Circuit has held that the CPIUN is self-executing, meaning that it can be applied directly in court even absent implementing legislation.[73]

The CPIUN reference to diplomatic immunity leads to the Vienna Convention on Diplomatic Relations (VCDR), which governs the issue of immunity for diplomats. Pursuant to the VCDR, currently accredited diplomats have absolute immunity from civil and criminal process, while former diplomats have immunity "with respect to acts performed by such a person in the exercise of his functions."[74] Lower level U.N. officials are also entitled to immunity for their official acts.[75] Under the IOIA, immunity extends to acts performed in an official capacity.[76]

Courts have generally interpreted "official capacity" to include almost all conduct related to the employment relationship, although the limits of that reasoning are not clear. The Second Circuit held that allegations of employment discrimination, retaliation, intentional infliction of emotion distress, and of violations of the Racketeer Influenced and Corrupt Organizations Act all related to the "management of the office" and thus fell within the defendants' official functions.[77] The D.C. Circuit reached the same conclusion in a case in which an investment officer at the International Finance Corporation sued her supervisor for assault, battery, and intentional infliction of emotional distress, based on allegations that he had sexually harassed her, grabbed her by the wrist, twisted her arm painfully, and kicked her.[78] The IFC filed an amicus brief stating that the supervisor's

---

[72] Convention on the Privileges and Immunities of the United Nations, art. V, § 19, Feb. 13, 1946, 1 U.N.T.S. 15 [hereinafter U.N. Convention on Privileges and Immunities].

[73] See Brzak v. United Nations, 597 F.3d 107, 112 (2d Cir. 2010).

[74] Vienna Convention on Diplomatic Relations, art. 39, ¶ 2, Apr. 18, 1961, 500 U.N.T.S. 95, T.I.A.S. 7502, 23 U.S.T. 3227 (1972).

[75] See U.N. Convention on Privileges and Immunities, supra note 72, at art. V, § 18.

[76] See 22 U.S.C. § 288d(b).

[77] See Brzak v. United Nations, 597 F.3d 107, 113 (2d Cir. 2010).

[78] See Rendall-Speranza v. Nassim, 107 F.3d 913, 915 (D.C. Cir. 1997).

conduct was appropriate because he was preventing the plaintiff from stealing IFC files. Note, however, that the Second Circuit has declined to hold that an allegation of battery in the workplace constituted official conduct.[79] The battery count was dismissed for other reasons, leaving open the possibility that physical assault in the workplace may fall outside of official functions.

Courts have interpreted waivers of immunity for officials more broadly than they have interpreted waivers for international organizations themselves. In *United States v. Bahel*,[80] a Chief of the Commodity Procurement Section within the United Nations' Procurement Division was convicted of fraud, bribery, and corruption for his role in helping applicants receive contracts in return for kickbacks for himself. The Secretary-General of the United Nations wrote that he had "waived, under Article V, Section 20 of the [U.N.] Convention, the immunity from legal process of Mr. Bahel" for "crimes allegedly committed during his employment as a procurement officer at the [United Nations] from in or about May 2003 through in or about May 2005."[81] Bahel was convicted for conduct that took place prior to May 2003. He argued that the waiver did not apply.

Despite the specificity of the dates in the waiver, the Second Circuit reasoned that there had been an express waiver of Bahel's immunity. The United Nations' participation in the investigation and prosecution of Bahel, as well as reference in the waiver letter to the criminal proceedings in question, led the Court to conclude that dates were meant only to identify the proceedings, not to limit the scope of the waiver. The reasoning is in some tension with the narrow interpretation of waivers in cases like *Mendaro*. As the court also reasoned in *Bahel*, however, no express waiver was necessary for a U.N. official (as opposed to the United Nations itself),[82] and there were strong reasons to conclude that waiver could be implied under the circumstances.

---

[79] See Brzak v. United Nations, 597 F.3d 107, 113–14 (2d Cir. 2010). The District Court had held that the alleged battery was part of the defendant's official functions. Brzak v. United Nations, 551 F. Supp. 2d 313, 319–20 (S.D.N.Y. 2008), *aff'd*, 597 F.3d 107 (2d Cir. 2010) (reasoning that "[t]he allegations of sexual harassment and 'indecent battery'" are "allegations of abuse of authority in the workplace" and thus qualify as official activity). The District Court's opinion also noted that "courts have consistently held that employment-related issues lie at the core of an international organization's immunity." *Brzak*, 551 F. Supp. 2d at 319.

[80] 662 F.3d 610, 624 (2d Cir. 2011).

[81] *Id.* at 621.

[82] *Id.* at 624. Article II, Section 2 of CPIUN provides that "[t]he United Nations . . . shall enjoy immunity from every form of legal process except insofar as in any particular case it has expressly waived its immunity." Article V, which governs official immunity, provides that the Secretary-General may waive such immunity, but lacks the language requiring an express waiver.

## V. Need for a Re-evaluation

Moving forward, courts should interpret the *Jam* decision with care, as it is neither possible nor desirable to subject IOs to suit on precisely the same terms as foreign states. On the other hand, courts should reconsider the judicially created "corresponding benefit" doctrine, which confers more immunity than is required or desirable in certain circumstances. International organizations should provide more effective self-regulation (and opportunity for recourse) when their conduct causes substantial harm, as unfortunately the United Nations did in Haiti.

Finally, developments over the past few decades mean that the Third Restatement can no longer serve as an authoritative resource. For example, whatever the ultimate effect of the *Jam* opinion, it means that the immunity of foreign states and of international organization are put on comparable footing in certain respects, contrary to some language in the Third Restatement.

More broadly, there is a need for an authoritative survey of domestic practice in other host country legal systems. Can one conclude that the entitlement of IOs to immunity is now a matter of customary international law, not dependent on specific agreements? This is the question expressly avoided by the Second Restatement and addressed to a limited extent in the Third,[83] but it needs to be re-evaluated in light of growing practice.[84]

If answered in the affirmative, then a second question arises: What is the content of the relevant customary international legal obligations? A comparative inquiry is appropriate, since customary international law is relevant to the interpretation of statutes and treaties to which the United States is a party and which govern international immunity in U.S. law. Such an endeavor would properly focus on the interface between the activities of the IOs and the domestic laws of the host country in which they are hosted or operate (mainly privileges and immunities), rather than on "internal" questions concerning the organization, structure, functions, procedures, and dissolution of IOs. Nor would it engage the broader substantive (policy) questions about the optimal level of IO accountability, although those questions serve as important background that highlights the significance of the project. As the field of IO immunity continues to change and develop, a new Restatement would serve as invaluable guide to judges, practitioners, and scholars.

---

[83] Of the four sections of the Third Restatement that address IO immunity, only one addressed customary international law in the black letter.

[84] See THIRD RESTATEMENT § 467 ("Under international law, an international organization generally enjoys such privileges and immunities from the jurisdiction of a member state as are necessary for the fulfillment of the purposes of the organization, including immunity from legal process, and from financial controls, taxes, and duties.").

# 20

# Foreign-Official Immunity under the Common Law

*John B. Bellinger III & Stephen K. Wirth*

The Fourth Restatement does not yet include a section on the immunity of foreign officials in U.S. Courts. The American Law Institute may consider including this passionately debated topic in a future volume. In the meantime, we provide here background on the state of the case law and executive-branch practice, identify several challenging open questions, and outline some principles that we think will be useful to the eventual drafters of the Fourth Restatement's section on the topic.

U.S. courts have long recognized three types of foreign immunity: the immunity enjoyed by foreign states; the immunity enjoyed by foreign diplomats, consular officers, and members of special diplomatic missions; and the immunity enjoyed by other foreign officials. Foreign-official immunity is further divided into status-based immunity (immunity *ratione personae*), which affords absolute immunity to sitting heads of state, heads of government, and foreign ministers (and potentially other senior officials), and conduct-based immunity (immunity *ratione materiae*), which affords immunity to sitting and former foreign officials for official conduct undertaken on behalf of the foreign sovereign. Each of these immunities has deep roots in customary international law and the common law. And for nearly two centuries, U.S. courts applied common-law principles of immunity, as articulated by the executive branch in court filings known as "suggestions of immunity," to assess whether a foreign state or foreign official was immune from suit in the United States.[1]

---

[1] Diplomatic and consular immunities, by contrast, have long been governed by statute. In 1708, the British Parliament codified diplomatic immunity and banned the arrest of foreign envoys. See Diplomatic Privileges Act 1708, 7 Anne c 12. And the first Congress passed similar legislation in 1790 that provided absolute immunity for diplomats and their families and servants, as well as for lower ranking diplomatic-mission personnel. See Crimes Act of 1790, ch. 9, §§ 25–27, 1 Stat. 117–18. The 1790 law remained in force until 1978, when Congress enacted the Diplomatic Relations Act, Pub. L. No. 95-393, 92 Stat. 808, to implement the United States' treaty obligations. See Vienna Convention on Diplomatic Relations, Apr. 18, 1961, 23 U.S.T. 3227, T.I.A.S. No. 7502; Vienna Convention on Consular Relations, Apr. 24, 1961, 21 U.S.T. 77, T.I.A.S. No. 6820. The executive branch separately recognizes a related immunity for members of qualifying "special missions" to the United States,

John B. Bellinger III & Stephen K. Wirth, *Foreign-Official Immunity under the Common Law* In: *The Restatement and Beyond*. Edited by: Paul B. Stephan and Sarah H. Cleveland, Oxford University Press (2020). © Oxford University Press.
DOI: 10.1093/oso/9780197533154.003.0021

That regime was upturned in 1976, when Congress enacted the Foreign Sovereign Immunities Act (FSIA).[2] The FSIA set out a statutory scheme governing the immunity of foreign states, including their political subdivisions, their agencies, and their instrumentalities.[3] And following the FSIA's enactment, most courts applied the act to suits against foreign officials (other than heads of state) for actions taken in their official capacities.[4] As a result, for years, the common law of foreign-sovereign and foreign-official immunity was almost entirely supplanted by statutory interpretation of the FSIA, and the executive branch was largely ousted from its traditional role in the immunity analysis.

But in 2010, in the watershed immunity decision *Samantar v. Yousuf*,[5] the Supreme Court revived the common law of foreign-official immunity along with the executive branch's role in articulating the common law. The Court held that "[a]lthough Congress clearly intended to supersede the common-law regime for claims against foreign states" with the enactment of the FSIA, nothing in the act's text or legislative history "indicate[s] that Congress similarly wanted to codify the law of foreign official immunity."[6] The Court further noted that it had "been given no reason to believe that Congress saw as a problem, or wanted to eliminate, the State Department's role in determinations regarding individual official immunity."[7] The Court thus held that suits against foreign officials are "properly governed by the common law," not by the FSIA, and outlined the historical two-step framework for analyzing immunity under the common law.[8] Under that framework, if the executive branch issued a "suggestion of immunity" the district court would "surrender its jurisdiction."[9] But where the executive branch had not taken a position, the district court "had authority to decide for itself whether all the requisites for such immunity existed."[10]

Using *Samantar*'s two-step framework as a guide, we examine the historical development and modern implementation of the common law of foreign-official immunity. We begin by tracing the doctrine's historical roots, as expressed in statements by the executive branch and the case law. We next discuss some of

which draws upon principles of diplomatic and consular immunity. See Suggestion of Immunity at 4–11, Li Weixum v. Bo Xilai, 568 F. Supp. 2d 35 (D.D.C. 2008).

Closely related, but governed by different principles, is the immunity of international organizations and their officials. See David P. Stewart & Ingrid Wuerth, *The Jurisdictional Immunities of International Organizations: Recent Developments and the Challenges of the Future*, in this volume.

[2]  Pub. L. No. 94-583, 90 Stat. 2891.
[3]  See 28 U.S.C. § 1603(a).
[4]  See *infra* notes 66–67 and accompanying text.
[5]  See 560 U.S. 305 (2010).
[6]  *Id.* at 325.
[7]  *Id.* at 323.
[8]  *Id.* at 325.
[9]  *Id.* at 311.
[10]  *Id.* (citation omitted).

the challenging questions that have arisen in the decade after *Samantar* and pro-pose some answers. We then describe, from a more practical perspective, current executive-branch practice for issuing statements of interest. And we conclude with a brief statement of principles that we believe should guide a future section on foreign-official immunity in the Fourth Restatement.

## I. Historical Development of the Doctrine

Foreign-official immunity has deep roots in the common law. In 1797, Attorney General Charles Lee opined that it was "well settled in the United States as in Great Britain, that a person acting under a commission from the sovereign of a foreign nation is not amenable for what he does in pursuance of his commis-sion, to any judiciary tribunal in the United States."[11] Fifteen years later, in *The Schooner Exchange v. M'Faddon*, the Supreme Court first articulated the immu-nity enjoyed by foreign *states* by analogizing to two long-standing principles of immunity afforded foreign *persons*: first, "the exemption of the person of the sovereign from arrest or detention within a foreign territory" (what is today known as status-based immunity); and, second, "the immunity which all civ-ilized nations allow to foreign ministers" (what is today known as diplomatic immunity).[12]

It was not until 1876, in *Underhill v. Hernandez*,[13] that the Supreme Court first endorsed the principle of conduct-based foreign-official immunity. In *Underhill*, the Court affirmed the dismissal of a suit brought by a U.S. citizen against a Venezuelan military commander for unlawful assault and detention in Venezuela. *Underhill* is most widely known for first articulating the act-of-state doctrine, under which "the courts of one country will not sit in judgment on the acts of the government of another done within its own territory."[14] But in so holding the Court also acknowledged "[t]he immunity of individuals from suits brought in foreign tribunals for acts done within their own states, in the exercise of governmental authority . . . as civil officers."[15] That reasoning was the basis of the Second Circuit's decision below, which had held that "because the acts of the official representatives of the state are those of the state itself, when exercised within the scope of their delegated powers, courts and publicists have recognized the immunity of public agents from suits brought in foreign tribunals for acts done within their own states in the exercise of the sovereignty thereof."[16]

[11] *Case of Sinclair*, 1 Op. ATT'Y GEN. 81, 81 (1797).
[12] See The Schooner Exchange v. M'Faddon, 11 U.S. (7 Cranch) 116, 137–39 (1812).
[13] 168 U.S. 250 (1897).
[14] *Id.* at 252.
[15] *Id.*
[16] 65 F. 577, 579 (2d Cir. 1895).

Notwithstanding these scattered early endorsements of foreign-official immunity, court decisions and executive-branch statements addressing the immunity of individual foreign officials during this period were "few and far between."[17] The scant sources available show that the law was unsettled, even in the executive branch. For example, early Attorney General opinions took contradictory positions on whether foreign-official immunity served as a jurisdictional defense or an affirmative defense on the merits.[18] And it appears that, at least in the early days of the Republic, the executive branch considered intervention in a civil suit against a foreign official to be outside the scope of its constitutional and statutory authority.[19] During this period, both the courts and the executive branch were instead primarily focused on foreign sovereign immunity, especially with regard to warships and other vessels owned or operated by foreign states. Although these cases raise different issues than cases against foreign officials, they are nonetheless useful for understanding how the judiciary's and executive branch's respective roles evolved with respect to determinations of immunity.

In the late nineteenth and early twentieth centuries, courts afforded foreign sovereigns essentially absolute immunity, even for purely commercial conduct. During this period, the executive branch's role in court proceedings was largely as a factual adviser to the courts. Courts deferred to the executive branch's statements of fact—for example, whether the foreign sovereign was recognized by the United States or whether the foreign sovereign had claimed a ship as its property—but largely engaged in independent immunity determinations. For example, in *The Pesaro*, a case involving claims against a commercial steamship owned by the Italian government, the State Department submitted a suggestion of nonimmunity to the district court: "It is the view of the Department that government-owned merchant vessels . . . employed in commerce should not be regarded as entitled to the immunities accorded public vessels of war."[20] The

---

[17] *Samantar*, 560 U.S. at 323; but see Chimène I. Keitner, *The Forgotten History of Foreign Official Immunity*, 87 N.Y.U. L. REV. 704 (2012) (recounting six cases from the 1790s).

[18] Compare *Case of Sinclair*, 1 OP. ATT'Y GEN. at 81 ("If the cause of action is fully and truly stated in the memorial, Henry Sinclair, *upon a plea to the jurisdiction of the court*, ought to prevail before the court; for it is as well settled in the United States as in Great Britain, that a person acting under a commission from the sovereign of a foreign nation is *not amenable* for what he does in pursuance of his commission, to any judiciary tribunal in the United States." (emphasis added)), with Actions Against Foreigners (*Case of Collot*), 1 OP. ATT'Y GEN. 45, 46 (1797) ("With respect to his suability, he is on a footing with any other foreigner (not a public minister) who comes within the jurisdiction of our courts. If the circumstances stated form of themselves a sufficient ground of defence, they must, nevertheless, be regularly *pleaded*; and the court will not hear them upon motion, for the purpose of quashing the writ or setting aside the arrest."), and Actions Against Foreigners (*Case of Cochram*), 1 OP. ATT'Y GEN. 49, 50 (1794) (similar).

[19] See *Case of Sinclair*, 1 OP. ATT'Y GEN. at 81 ("[A]ccording to the constitution and laws of the United States, the Executive cannot interpose with the judiciary proceedings between an individual and Henry Sinclair, whose controversy is entitled to a trial according to law. . . .").

[20] 277 F. 473, 480 n.3 (S.D.N.Y. 1921).

court granted that the State Department's view "is not without significance," but added that it "did not mean to say that immunity should be refused in a clear case simply because the executive branch has failed to act."[21] Only after engaging in a thorough independent analysis of international law did the court agree with the State Department that the ship was not immune.[22] The Supreme Court, moreover, later rejected the State Department's views in *Berizzi Bros. Co. v. The Pesaro*, instead holding that merchant vessels owned by a foreign sovereign enjoy the same immunity as foreign warships.[23]

Executive-branch suggestions of immunity began to take on a more central role with the Supreme Court's 1921 decision in Ex parte *Muir*.[24] Prior to that decision, foreign governments had employed a variety of techniques to establish immunity in cases involving foreign ships, such as special appearance of counsel as amicus curiae or suggestions of immunity submitted directly to the court by foreign officials.[25] In Ex parte *Muir*, however, the Court declared that in order to establish immunity a foreign government had only two options: it could "appear in the suit, to propound its claim to the vessel and to raise the jurisdictional question"; or, "if there was objection to appearing as a suitor in a foreign court," it could secure "an appropriate suggestion to the court" from the executive branch.[26] Despite the case's relatively narrow holding that suggestions of immunity can serve as an alternative method of establishing immunity, Ex parte *Muir* set the stage for a trio of cases—*The Navemar*,[27] Ex parte *Peru*,[28] and *Republic of Mexico v. Hoffman*[29]—that transformed the State Department's role in immunity determinations.

*The Navemar*, decided in 1938, was an admiralty suit to recover a ship expropriated by the Spanish Republican government. After the State Department declined to file a suggestion of immunity, the Spanish ambassador entered the suit to assert immunity on behalf of the Spanish government, as authorized in Ex parte *Muir*. The Second Circuit, reversing the district court, held that the ship was immune based entirely on the Spanish ambassador's assertion of immunity.[30] The Supreme Court reversed. Although nominally endorsing Ex parte *Muir*, the Court dramatically reframed the case's two-pronged framework. The

[21] *Id.* at 481. The court apparently construed the State Department's express suggestion of nonimmunity as a failure to act.
[22] *Id.* at 481–85.
[23] 271 U.S. 562, 574 (1926).
[24] 254 U.S. 522 (1921).
[25] G. Edward White, *The Transformation of the Constitutional Regime of Foreign Relations*, 85 VA. L. REV. 1, 135 (1999).
[26] 254 U.S. at 532.
[27] Compania Espanola de Navegacion Maritima, S.A. v. The Navemar, 303 U.S. 68 (1938).
[28] Ex parte Peru, 318 U.S. 578 (1943).
[29] 324 U.S. 30 (1945).
[30] The Navemar, 90 F.2d 673, 676–77 (2d Cir. 1937).

Court held that an assertion of immunity by a foreign sovereign was merely evidence of immunity, which courts could take into account in making an independent determination.[31] But the Court contrasted that scenario with a suggestion of immunity from the executive branch, which it held was binding and conclusive: "If the claim [of immunity] is recognized and allowed by the executive branch of the government, it is then the duty of the courts to release the vessel upon appropriate suggestion by the Attorney General of the United States, or other officer acting under his direction."[32] Because the executive branch had not suggested immunity, the Court concluded that "the alleged public status of the vessel and the right of the Spanish Government to demand possession of the vessel as owner if it so elected, were appropriate subjects for judicial inquiry upon proof of the matters alleged."[33]

The Court's decision in *The Navemar* did not acknowledge (much less provide a rationale for) the shift in approach from Ex parte *Muir*. But in Ex parte *Peru* and *Hoffman*, the Court explained that its absolute deference to the executive branch was based on the foreign-relations interests implicated by immunity determinations. In Ex parte *Peru*,[34] a district court took possession of a steamship allegedly owned by the Peruvian government. Peru requested the State Department's intervention, and the executive branch subsequently requested " 'that the claim of immunity made on behalf of the said Peruvian Steamship Ucayali and recognized and allowed by the State Department be given full force and effect by this court'; and 'that the said vessel proceeded against herein be declared immune from the jurisdiction and process of this court.' "[35] The district court nonetheless denied Peru's motion to release the vessel and dismiss the case, holding that Peru had waived its immunity by applying for extensions of time within which to answer and by taking the deposition of the ship's master.[36] The Supreme Court granted mandamus, holding conclusively that courts are bound by suggestions of immunity:

> The [executive branch's] certification and the request that the vessel be declared immune must be accepted by the courts as a conclusive determination by the political arm of the Government that the continued retention of the vessel interferes with the proper conduct of our foreign relations. Upon the submission of this certification to the district court, it became the court's duty, in

---

[31]   *The Navemar*, 303 U.S. at 75–76.
[32]   *Id.* at 74.
[33]   *Id.* at 75.
[34]   318 U.S. 578 (1943).
[35]   *Id.* at 581.
[36]   *Id.* at 581–82.

conformity to established principles, to release the vessel and to proceed no further in the cause.[37]

The Court explained that "[t]his practice is founded upon the policy, recognized both by the Department of State and the courts, that our national interest will be better served in such cases if the wrongs to suitors, involving our relations with a friendly foreign power, are righted through diplomatic negotiations rather than by the compulsions of judicial proceedings."[38]

In *Hoffman*, decided two years after Ex parte *Peru*, the Supreme Court went even further, elevating the executive branch as the sole source of the common law of immunity. The issue in *Hoffman* was whether a foreign state that owned but was not in possession of a merchant ship could assert sovereign immunity in an admiralty action against the ship. The dispute arose out of a collision between an American fishing vessel and a freighter owned by the Mexican government but leased to a Mexican corporation. In two suggestions filed in the district court, the executive branch "accepted as true" that the Mexican government owned the vessel and "would meet any liability decreed against the vessel as a binding international undertaking," but did not take a definitive position on immunity.[39] The district court denied immunity on the ground that mere ownership without possession was insufficient to establish immunity.[40] And the Supreme Court affirmed. Faced with silence from the executive branch on the immunity question, the Court looked "to the principles accepted by the [executive branch]" in prior cases, observing that the executive branch had never asserted immunity based on ownership without possession.[41] The Court also appeared to read between the lines of the executive branch's two suggestions, both of which, through their conspicuous silence on the immunity issue, strongly suggested that the executive branch in fact considered the ship not immune.[42]

The new regime of absolute judicial deference to executive-branch statements of immunity coincided with a shift in international law and U.S. policy away from the absolute approach to immunity embraced by both branches of government in the nineteenth century and toward a "restrictive" approach. One of the first statements of this new doctrine came in *The Pesaro*, in which the executive branch asserted that a commercial vessel was not subject to immunity.[43] More broadly, under the restrictive approach, foreign sovereigns are entitled to

---

[37] *Id.* at 589.
[38] *Id.*
[39] *Hoffman*, 324 U.S. at 32 (1945).
[40] *Id.* at 32–33.
[41] *Id.* at 35.
[42] *Id.* at 32–33.
[43] 277 F. at 481.

sovereign immunity only when they act in their sovereign capacities, but when foreign sovereigns act like private entities, such as by operating a commercial enterprise, they are subject to suit like private entities.

From the early to mid-twentieth century, the restrictive approach was incorporated ad hoc into U.S. law by way of individual suggestions, such as in *The Pesaro* and *Hoffman*, and through bilateral agreements with other states.[44] But in 1952, in a letter from the State Department's Acting Legal Adviser, Jack Tate, to the Acting Attorney General, the State Department formally announced that it had fully embraced the restrictive approach. The letter—titled, "Changed Policy Concerning the Granting of Sovereign Immunity to Foreign Governments," but now known simply as the "Tate Letter"—explained that "the widespread and increasing practice on the part of governments of engaging in commercial activities makes necessary a practice which will enable persons doing business with them to have their rights determined in the courts."[45] Accordingly, the letter announced the State Department's adoption of the restrictive approach, under which "the immunity of the sovereign is recognized with regard to sovereign or public acts (*jure imperii*) of a state, but not with respect to private acts (*jure gestionis*)."[46] Notably, and notwithstanding the Supreme Court's unequivocal statements in Ex parte *Peru* and *Hoffman*, the letter assumed that courts would give deference to the State Department's new policy but would not be bound by it: "It is realized that a shift in policy by the executive cannot control the courts but it is felt that the courts are less likely to allow a plea of sovereign immunity where the executive has declined to do so."[47]

From 1952 until the enactment of FISA in 1976, immunity determinations were made according to the *Navemar/Peru/Hoffman* framework, under which foreign sovereigns could formally request immunity from the State Department or could request immunity directly from the district court.[48] That framework applied in all cases implicating foreign sovereign immunity—including cases against foreign heads of state and other officials—notwithstanding that the foundational cases all involved foreign vessels.[49] Nevertheless, during this period, there were very few recorded cases brought against individual foreign officials. From May 1952 to January 1976, the State Department recorded only six cases

---

[44] See William W. Bishop Jr., *The Problem of Jurisdictional Immunities of Foreign States*, 47 AM. J. INT'L L. 93, 96 (1953).

[45] Letter from Jack B. Tate, Acting Legal Adviser, U.S. Dep't of State, to Philip B. Perlman, Acting Att'y Gen. (May 19, 1952), *reprinted in* 26 DEPT. ST. BULL. 984, 985 (1952) [hereinafter Tate Letter].

[46] *Id.* at 984.

[47] *Id.* at 985.

[48] *Sovereign Immunity Decisions of the Department of State, May 1952 to January 1977*, 1977 DIG. U.S. PRAC. IN INT'L L. 1017, 1018–19 (1977) [hereinafter 1977 DIGEST].

[49] The executive branch apparently lost whatever constitutional objections it once had about "interpos[ing]" in civil suits against foreign officials. *Case of Sinclair*, 1 OP. ATT'Y GEN. at 81; see *supra* note 19 and accompanying text.

involving foreign officials.[50] In one case, the Department granted immunity to foreign officials where there was "no allegation that the officials . . . acted other than in their official capacities and on behalf of [their foreign sovereign]."[51] And, in a related case, the Department granted immunity, despite an allegation that the officials had "acted in excess of their authority," because it was "not alleged that these officials acted other than in their official capacities and on behalf of [their foreign sovereign]."[52] By contrast, the Department denied immunity in a case where the allegations concerned "activities . . . of a private nature under the standards set forth in the Tate Letter."[53] That said, the executive branch did not always apply its own standards consistently, but, where the executive branch did suggest immunity, courts gave conclusive effect to the executive branch's suggestion, even when it was ostensibly contrary to the principles laid out in the Tate Letter. For example, in *Isbrandtsen Tankers v. President of India*, the Second Circuit granted immunity at the executive branch's suggestion, despite strong indications that "the actions of the Indian government were . . . purely commercial decisions."[54]

In 1965, the Second Restatement of the Foreign Relations Law of the United States included several sections on foreign sovereign immunity. Under the Second Restatement, the heads of state, heads of government, and foreign ministers all enjoy absolute immunity from suit,[55] whereas other foreign officials enjoy immunity "with respect to acts performed in [their] official capacity if the effect of exercising jurisdiction would be to enforce a rule of law against the state."[56] While the first half of this statement ("with respect to acts performed in [their] official capacity") is familiar, the second half ("if the effect of exercising jurisdiction would be to enforce a rule of law against the state") is not. Despite purporting to summarize the common law, the Second Restatement does not explain where this latter qualification comes from, nor does it explain what it means. And, although the comments to this section include two illustrations, neither illustration much illuminates the contours of the rule. The first states that a foreign official is immune from a suit seeking to compel payment of state funds in the official's possession.[57] But immunity in such a case should be entirely uncontroversial because the foreign sovereign is the real party in interest. The second illustration describes an automobile accident negligently caused by a foreign

---

[50] See 1977 DIGEST, *supra* note 48, at 1020.

[51] *Id.* at 1076 (ellipsis in original).

[52] *Id.*

[53] *Id.* at 1063.

[54] 446 F.2d 1198, 1200–101 (2d Cir. 1971).

[55] RESTATEMENT (SECOND) OF FOREIGN RELATIONS LAW OF THE UNITED STATES § 66(a)–(e) (Am. Law Inst. 1965) [hereinafter SECOND RESTATEMENT].

[56] *Id.* § 66(f).

[57] *Id.* § 66 cmt. *b*, illus. 2.

official during an official mission in the nation in which the suit is brought.[58] According to the Second Restatement, that official is not immune because a negligence action would not have the effect of enforcing a rule of law against the foreign state.[59] Even assuming that this illustration is correct (and it may not be[60]), it says nothing about tortious conduct committed by foreign officials in their own country, which is a qualification found in earlier descriptions of foreign-official immunity.[61] The meaning of the Second Restatement and whether it remains relevant today are issues discussed in greater detail later.[62]

In 1976, Congress enacted the FSIA, which marked a sea change in the law of foreign sovereign immunity. The FSIA was enacted in large part to address criticisms of ad hoc immunity determinations made by the executive branch and the courts, which many lawmakers and commentators saw as producing inconsistent decisions that were subject to undue political influence.[63] The FSIA removed immunity determinations from the province of the executive branch and codified the restrictive approach to immunity, with express exceptions for waiver, commercial activity, takings of property in violation of international law, noncommercial torts committed within the United States, enforcement of arbitral awards, certain suits in admiralty, and (as added in a later amendment) certain suits against state sponsors of terrorism.[64]

The FSIA, on its face, applies only to "foreign state[s]" and their "agenc[ies]" and "instrumentalit[ies]"—not to their officials.[65] But, beginning with the Ninth Circuit's decision in *Chuidian v. Philippine National Bank*[66]—and over

[58]   *Id.* § 66 cmt. *b*, illus. 3.

[59]   *Id.*

[60]   Take, for example, a government-sanctioned military mission in a foreign country that results in the negligent wrongful death of a civilian. Or consider a case in which the foreign government has agreed to indemnify its officers for negligent conduct committed in the scope of their duties.

[61]   See *Underhill*, 168 U.S. at 252; *Underhill*, 65 F. at 579; see also Hatch v. Baez, 14 N.Y. Sup. Ct. 596, 599 (Gen. Term 1876) (holding that the former president of the Dominican Republic was not "amenable to the jurisdiction of the courts of this State" for "the acts of another government done within its own territory.").

[62]   For its part, the Third Restatement included almost no reference to foreign-official immunity, aside from a cursory mention of head-of-state immunity and an incorrect description of the immunity enjoyed by former heads of state. See THIRD RESTATEMENT § 464 reporters' note 14.

[63]   See, e.g., Hearings on H.R. 11315 Before the Subcomm. on Admin. Law and Governmental Relations of the H. Comm. on the Judiciary, 94th Cong. 58 (1976) (testimony of Peter Trooboff); Mark B. Feldman, *The United States Foreign Sovereign Immunities Act of 1976 in Perspective: A Founder's View*, 35 INT'L & COMP. L.Q. 302, 303–304 (1986); Andreas F. Lowenfeld, *Litigating a Sovereign Immunity Claim—The Haiti Case*, 49 N.Y.U. L. REV. 377, 390 (1974).

[64]   28 U.S.C. §§ 1605, 1065A.

[65]   28 U.S.C. §§ 1603–104. The State Department's a review of pre-FSIA immunity decisions in the 1977 *Digest of U.S. Practice in International Law* specifically noted that the FSIA "does not deal with the immunity of individual officials." 1977 DIGEST, *supra* note 48, at 1020.

[66]   912 F.2d 1095, 1099–103 (9th Cir. 1990). The *Chuidian* court reasoned that it would be "illogical" to think that Congress intended the FSIA to implicitly eliminate common-law foreign-official immunity. *Id.* at 1102. To avoid that outcome the court held that foreign officials could reasonably be considered "agencies or instrumentalities" of the foreign state under the FSIA. See *id.* But the court started with a faulty premise, namely, that if the FSIA did not apply to foreign officials, they would not

the objections of the executive branch—most courts extended the FSIA to suits against foreign officials (other than heads of state) for actions taken in their official capacities.[67] As a result, for years, the common law of state and foreign-official immunity was almost entirely supplanted by statutory interpretation of the FSIA, and the executive branch was largely ousted from its traditional role in the immunity analysis.[68]

In 2006, the State Department decided to reassert its authority to determine conduct-based immunity under the common law, appearing in a suit against Avi Dichter, the former Israeli intelligence chief.[69] The complaint alleged that Dichter had authorized, planned, and directed a bombing that killed fourteen civilians in the Gaza Strip.[70] Upon the district court's invitation for the views of the State Department, the executive branch filed a fifty-page statement of interest in the district court, arguing that Dichter enjoyed immunity under customary international law, as recognized by the State Department.[71] In addition to arguing that neither the text of the FSIA nor its legislative history supported its application to foreign officials, the executive branch also argued that allowing foreign officials to be sued for their official conduct would depart from customary international law, aggravate relations with foreign states, and expose our own officials to similar suits abroad.[72]

The district court did not accept the executive branch's position, instead applying the FSIA to find Dichter immune.[73] On appeal, the executive branch reiterated its position to the Second Circuit, while also explaining that the

enjoy any immunity whatsoever. See *id.* The court should have considered whether foreign officials continued to enjoy common-law immunity even after the FSIA's enactment.

[67] See, e.g., *In re* Terrorist Attacks on September 11, 2001, 538 F.3d 71, 81 (2d Cir. 2009); Guevara v. Republic of Peru, 468 F.3d 1289, 1305 (11th Cir. 2006); Keller v. Cent. Bank of Nigeria, 277 F.3d 811, 815–16 (6th Cir. 2002); Byrd v. Corporación Forestal y Industrial de Olancho, SA, 182 F.3d 388–89 (5th Cir. 1999); El-Fadl v. Cent. Bank of Jordan, 75 F.3d 668, 671 (D.C. Cir. 1996); Leutwyler v. Office of Her Majesty Queen Rania al-Abdullah, 184 F. Supp. 2d 277, 289 (S.D.N.Y. 2001); Jungquist v. Al Nahyan, 940 F. Supp. 312, 317 (D.D.C. 1996).

[68] See John B. Bellinger III, *The Dog that Caught the Car: Observations on the Past, Present, and Future Approaches of the Office of the Legal Adviser to Official Acts Immunities*, 44 VAND. J. TRANSNAT'L L. 819, 822–23 (2010). To the extent that the executive branch filed statements of interest or amicus briefs in foreign-official-immunity cases during this period, its arguments were consistent with its position on the limited scope of the FSIA, even if it did not attempt to relitigate the issue. *Id.* at 822–23 & n.14. That is in contrast to cases involving foreign heads of state, in which the State Department continued to argue that the FSIA did not supplant the executive branch's sole authority to determine immunity, notwithstanding *Chuidian*. See, e.g., Doe v. Roman Catholic Diocese of Galveston-Hous., 408 F. Supp. 2d 272, 279 (S.D. Tex. 2005).

[69] Matar v. Dichter, 500 F. Supp. 2d 284 (S.D.N.Y. 2007), *aff'd*, 563 F.3d 9 (2d Cir. 2009).

[70] *Id.* at 286.

[71] Order, Matar v. Dichter, No. 05 Civ. 10270 (S.D.N.Y. July 20, 2006); Statement of Interest at 19–22, Matar v. Dichter, 500 F. Supp. 2d 284 (S.D.N.Y. 2007) (No. 05 Civ. 10270) [hereinafter Dichter SOI].

[72] Dichter SOI, *supra* note 71, at 10–13, 19–23.

[73] *Dichter*, 500 F. Supp. 2d at 291.

"principles" set out in its brief "are susceptible to general application by the judiciary without the need for recurring intervention by the Executive, particularly in the form of suggestions of immunity filed on a case-by-case basis."[74] The Second Circuit affirmed, in a nuanced opinion that came much closer to adopting the views of the executive branch.[75] The court accepted that the common law provides immunity for the official acts of former officials, although the court stopped short of holding that the FSIA was inapplicable.[76] Because the executive branch filed a statement of interest recognizing that Dichter was entitled to immunity, the Second Circuit deferred to the executive branch and held that Dichter was "immune from suit under common-law principles that predate, and survive, the enactment of [the FSIA]."[77]

*Dichter* contributed to a circuit split on the application of the FSIA to foreign officials, which the Supreme Court resolved in 2010 in *Samantar v. Yousuf*.[78] The case was brought by citizens of Somalia against a former high-ranking Somali official, Mohamed Ali Samantar, alleging acts of torture, extrajudicial killing, and wrongful detention by Somali forces under Samantar's control. In its opinion, the Court first described the *Navemar/Peru/Hoffman* two-step framework for analyzing immunity under the common law. At step one, if the executive branch issued a "suggestion of immunity," the district court would "surrender its jurisdiction."[79] Where the executive branch had not taken a position, at the second step, the district court would "decide for itself whether all the requisites for such immunity existed."[80] Turning to the FSIA, the Court rejected Samantar's argument that he was immune under the statute, holding that "[a]lthough Congress clearly intended to supersede the common-law regime for claims against foreign states" with the enactment of the FSIA, nothing in the act's text or legislative history "indicate[s] that Congress similarly wanted to codify the law of foreign official immunity."[81] The Court further noted that it had "been given no reason to believe that Congress saw as a problem, or wanted to eliminate, the State Department's role in determinations regarding individual official immunity."[82]

---

[74] U.S. Amicus Brief at 21 n.*, Matar v. Dichter, 563 F.3d 9 (2d Cir. 2009) (No. 07-2579-cv) [hereinafter U.S. Dichter Brief].

[75] Matar v. Dichter, 563 F.3d 9 (2d Cir. 2009).

[76] *Id.* at 14. Although it expressed strong skepticism that the FSIA applied to foreign government officials, the court did not definitively resolve the question, as it found that Dichter would be entitled to common-law immunity in any event. See *id.*

[77] *Id.*

[78] 560 U.S. 305 (2010). The *Chuidian* doctrine remained the uniform view among the circuit courts until 2005, when the Seventh Circuit became the first to hold that the FSIA was inapplicable to foreign officials in *Enahoro v. Abubakar*, 408 F.3d 877, 881–82 (7th Cir. 2005).

[79] *Id.* at 311.

[80] *Id.* (quoting Ex parte *Peru*, 318 U.S. at 587).

[81] *Samantar*, 560 U.S. at 325.

[82] *Id.* at 323.

The Court thus held that suits against foreign officials are "properly governed by the common law," not by the FSIA.[83] And the Court remanded for the lower courts to determine immunity under the common law in the first instance.[84]

In the decade following the Court's decision in *Samantar*, the executive branch and the lower courts have continued to grapple with the content and scope of foreign-official immunity under the common law. By our count, since *Samantar*, the executive branch has suggested immunity in twenty-two cases and nonimmunity in only two (including *Samantar* on remand).[85] Of the suggestions of immunity, the overwhelming majority (seventeen) were filed in suits brought against a sitting head of state, head of government, or foreign minister,[86] whereas only five were filed in suits against other officials or former officials.[87] In every

---

[83]  *Id.* at 325.

[84]  *Id.* at 325–26.

[85]  On remand in *Samantar* and in another case involving a different former Somali official, the executive branch suggested nonimmunity because there was, at the time, no recognized government of Somalia. See Statement of Interest 7–9, Ahmed v. Magan, No. 10 Civ. 342 (S.D. Ohio Mar. 15, 2011); Statement of Interest 7–9, Yousuf v. Samantar, No. 04 Civ. 1360 (E.D. Va. Feb. 14, 2011) [hereinafter Samantar SOI]. The executive branch reasoned that, because foreign-official immunity is for the benefit of the state, if there is no state, there can be no immunity. *Id.*

[86]  See Suggestion of Immunity, Miango v. Democratic Republic of the Congo, No. 15 Civ. 1265 (D.D.C. Dec. 3, 2018) (president of the Democratic Republic of the Congo); Statement of Interest, Savang v. Lao People's Democratic Republic, No. 16 Civ. 2037 (E.D. Cal. May 1, 2018) (president and prime minister of Laos); Suggestion of Immunity, Burma Task Force v. Sein, No. 15 Civ. 7772 (S.D.N.Y. Feb. 12, 2016) (president and foreign minister of Burma); Suggestion of Immunity, Hmong I v. Lao People's Democratic Republic, No. 15 Civ. 2349 (E.D. Cal. Feb. 12, 2016) (president and prime minister of Laos); Suggestion of Immunity, He Nam You v. Japan, No. C 15-3257 (N.D. Cal. Feb. 11, 2016) (emperor and prime minister of Japan); Suggestion of Immunity, Yongtian v. Xi Jinping, No. 15 Civ. 6968 (S.D.N.Y. Oct. 6, 2015) (president of China); Suggestion of Immunity, American Justice Center v. Modi, No. 14. Civ. 7780 (S.D.N.Y. Oct. 19, 2014) (prime minister of India); Suggestion of Immunity, Rendon v. Funes, No. 2014-2756-CA-01 (11th Fla. Jud. D. May 23, 2014) (president of El Salvador); Suggestion of Immunity, Sikhs for Justice v. Singh, 64 F. Supp. 3d 190 (D.D.C. 2014) (No. 13 Civ. 1460) [hereinafter Singh SOI] (former prime minister of India); Suggestion of Immunity, Jibreel v. Hock Seng Chin, No. C 13-3470 (N.D. Cal. Apr. 14, 2014) (prime minister of Singapore); Suggestion of Immunity, Fotso v. Republic of Cameroon, No. 12 Civ. 1415 (D. Ore. Dec. 21, 2012) (president of Cameroon); Suggestion of Immunity, Devi v. Rajapaksa, No. 11 Civ. 6634 (S.D.N.Y. Apr. 26, 2012) (president of Sri Lanka); Suggestion of Immunity, Tawfik v. al-Sabah, No. 11 Civ. 6455 (S.D.N.Y. Apr. 5, 2012) (emir of Kuwait); Suggestion of Immunity, Manoharan v. Rajapaksa, 845 F. Supp. 2d 260 (D.D.C. 2012) (No. 11 Civ. 235) (president of Sri Lanka); Government Response, United States v. al-Nashiri, No. AE 037C (Mil. Comm'ns Trial Judiciary, Guantanamo Bay Feb. 6, 2012) (third-party deposition of president of Yemen); Suggestion of Immunity, Habyarimana v. Kagame, 821 F. Supp. 2d 1244 (W.D. Okla. 2011) (No. 10 Civ. 437) (president of Rwanda); Suggestion of Immunity, Hassen v. Nahyan, No. 09 Civ. 1106 (C.D. Cal. July 26, 2010) (president of UAE).

[87]  See Suggestion of Immunity, Doğan v. Barak, No. 15 Civ. 8130 (C.D. Cal. June 10, 2016) [hereinafter Barak SOI] (former Israeli defense minister); Suggestion of Immunity, Ben-Haim v. Edri, No. L-003502-15 (N.J. Super. Ct. Dec. 3, 2015) [hereinafter Edri SOI] (Israeli rabbinical judges); Statement of Interest, Rosenberg v. Lashkar-e-Taiba, 980 F. Supp. 2d 336 (E.D.N.Y. 2013) (No. 10 Civ. 5381) [Lashkar-e-Taiba SOI] (former directors of Pakistani intelligence service); Suggestion of Immunity, Doe v. Zedillo Ponce de León, No. 11 Civ. 1433 (D. Conn. Sept. 7, 2012) [hereinafter Zedillo SOI] (former president of Mexico); Suggestion of Immunity, Giraldo v. Drummond Co., 808 F. Supp. 2d 247 (D.D.C. 2011) (No. 10 Misc. 764) [hereinafter Giraldo SOI] (third-party subpoena of former president of Colombia).

case where the executive branch suggested immunity, except for one, the court dismissed the suit.[88] And where the executive branch suggested nonimmunity, the court exercised jurisdiction—though, as we discuss later, not always for the same reasons suggested by the executive branch.[89]

These *Samantar* step-one cases were not the only cases filed against foreign officials during this period, however—just the ones in which the executive branch expressed its views. In many other cases, the executive branch did not weigh in,[90] which left the district court, at *Samantar* step two, to determine for itself whether the foreign official was entitled to immunity. In several cases, courts found common-law status-based or conduct-based immunity on the pleadings without input from the executive branch.[91] Courts have also granted motions to

[88] For the one exception, see Sikhs for Justice v. Singh, 64 F. Supp. 3d 190 (D.D.C. 2014). We discuss this case later. See *infra* notes 124–130 and accompanying text. The cases that resulted in dismissal include Ben-Haim v. Edri, 183 A.3d 252, 259 (N.J. App. Div. 2018); Order, Miango v. Democratic Republic of Congo, No. 15 Civ. 1265 (D.D.C. Jan. 19, 2019); Order, Savang v. Lao People's Democratic Republic, No. 16 Civ. 2037 (E.D. Cal. July 23, 2018); Doğan v. Barak, No. 15 Civ. 8130, 2016 WL 6024416, at *7 (C.D. Cal. Oct. 13, 2016); Order, Yongtian v. Xi Jinping, No. 15 Civ. 6968 (S.D.N.Y. June 30, 2016); Order, He Nam You v. Japan, No. C 15-3257 (N.D. Cal. June 21, 2016); Hmong I v. Lao People's Democratic Republic, No. 15 Civ. 2349, 2016 WL 2901562, at *8–10 (E.D. Cal. May 17, 2016), *R&R adopted*, 2016 WL 3254066 (E.D. Cal. June 13, 2016); Burma Task Force v. Sein, No. 15 Civ. 7772, 2016 WL 1261139, at *3 (S.D.N.Y. Mar. 30, 2016); "American Justice Ctr." (AJC), Inc. v. Modi, No. 14 Civ. 7780, slip op. at 3 (S.D.N.Y. Jan. 14, 2015); Order, Rendon v. Funes, No. 2014-2756-CA-01 (11th Fla. Jud. D. May 27, 2014); Jibreel v. Hock Seng Chin, No. 13 Civ. 3470, 2014 WL 12600278, at *5 (N.D. Cal. Apr. 17, 2014), *R&R adopted*, 2014 WL 12617420 (N.D. Cal. May 5, 2014); Doe v. Zedillo Ponce de León, 555 F. App'x 84, 85 (2d Cir. 2014); Rosenberg v. Lashkar-e-Taiba, 980 F. Supp. 2d 336, 343 (E.D.N.Y. 2013), *aff'd sub nom.* Rosenberg v. Pasha, 577 F. App'x 22, 23 (2d Cir. 2014); Fotso v. Republic of Cameroon, No. 12 Civ. 1415, 2013 WL 664158, at *1–2 (D. Or. Jan. 25, 2013), *R&R adopted*, 2013 WL 665618 (D. Or. Feb. 22, 2013); Manoharan v. Rajapaksa, 845 F. Supp. 2d 260, 263–64 (D.D.C. 2012), *aff'd*, 711 F.3d 178 (D.C. Cir. 2013); Devi v. Rajapaksa, No. 11 Civ. 6634, 2012 WL 3866495, at *2–4 (S.D.N.Y. Sept. 4, 2012), *aff'd*, No. 12-4081, 2013 WL 3855583 (2d Cir. 2013); Tawfik v. al-Sabah, No. 11 Civ. 6455, 2012 WL 3542209, at *3 (S.D.N.Y. Aug. 16, 2012); Opinion, United States v. al-Nashiri, No. AE 037F (Mil. Comm'ns Trial Judiciary, Guantanamo Bay Feb. 17, 2012); Habyarimana v. Kagame, 821 F. Supp. 2d 1244, 1263–64 (W.D. Okla. 2011), *aff'd*, 696 F.3d 1029 (10th Cir. 2012); Giraldo v. Drummond Co., 808 F. Supp. 2d 247, 250–51 (D.D.C. 2011), *aff'd*, 493 F. App'x 106 (D.C. Cir. 2012); Hassen v. Nahyan, No. 09 Civ. 1106, 2010 WL 9538408, at *5–6 (C.D. Cal. Sept. 17, 2010).

[89] See Ahmed v. Magan, No. 10 Civ. 342, 2011 WL 13160129, at *2 (S.D. Ohio Nov. 7, 2011); Yousuf v. Samantar, No. 04 Civ. 1360, 2011 WL 7445583, at *1 (E.D. Va. Feb. 15, 2011), *aff'd*, 699 F.3d 763 (4th Cir. 2012).

[90] As discuss later, the executive branch may decline to weigh in for a variety of practical, legal, and political reasons. See *infra* notes 205–218 and accompanying text.

[91] See, e.g., In Chambers Order, Wickrematunge v. Rajapaksa, No. 19 Civ. 2577 (C.D. Cal. Oct. 17, 2019) (finding conduct-based immunity where plaintiff alleged that Sri Lankan defense secretary acted in official capacity); Eliahu v. Jewish Agency for Israel, 919 F.3d 709, 712–13 (2d Cir. 2019) (finding conduct-based immunity where plaintiffs alleged that Israeli cabinet member, judge, and civil servants acted in official capacities); Doe 1 v. Buratai, 318 F. Supp. 3d 218, 238 (D.D.C. 2018) (finding conduct-based immunity where Nigeria ratified its official's conduct), *aff'd on other grounds*, No. 18-7170, 2019 WL 668339 (D.C. Cir. Feb. 15, 2019); Farhang v. Indian Inst. of Tech., 655 F. App'x 569, 571 (9th Cir. 2016) (finding conduct-based immunity where plaintiffs alleged that Indian official acted in official capacity); *In re* Terrorist Attacks on Sept. 11, 2001, 122 F. Supp. 3d 181, 189 (S.D.N.Y. 2015) (finding conduct-based immunity for Saudi official where only nonconclusory allegations were official acts); Weiming Chen v. Ying-jeou Ma, No. 12 Civ. 5232, 2013 WL 4437607, at *3 (S.D.N.Y. Aug. 19, 2013) (finding head-of-state immunity for sitting president of the Republic

quash third-party subpoenas served on former officials.[92] And courts have found immunity under the FSIA where the officials were sued in an official capacity such that the foreign state was the real party in interest.[93]

Other courts have denied immunity to foreign officials in the absence of a suggestion of immunity. In *Lewis v. Mutond*, a decision we discuss at length later, the D.C. Circuit denied immunity to two high-ranking Congolese officials because plaintiffs sued them in their personal capacities and because, the court held, the Torture Victim Protection Act of 1991 (TVPA) abrogated common-law immunity for claims arising under the statute.[94] In another case, a district court denied immunity because the plaintiffs alleged that the defendants had not acted in their official capacities.[95] And courts have denied immunity to consular officers involved in automobile accidents, in situations similar to the illustration in the Second Restatement, discussed earlier.[96]

These *Samantar* step-two cases—because of the lack of executive-branch guidance—have proven fertile ground for new and complex immunity questions, which we discuss in the following section.

## II. Open Questions (and Some Proposed Answers)

*Samantar* conclusively established that foreign-official immunity is governed by the common law, not the FSIA. But it did not say much else. It did not, for example, define the source or contours of common-law immunity; it did not identify any common-law or statutory exceptions to immunity; and it did not endorse the Second Restatement's formulation of the doctrine. In the decade since *Samantar*, the executive branch and the lower courts have grappled with these issues and more, developing an expanding body of case law and executive-branch

---

of China (Taiwan)); Smith v. Ghana Commercial Bank, Ltd., No. 10 Civ. 4655, 2012 WL 2930462, at *7–10 (D. Minn. June 18, 2012), *R&R adopted*, 2012 WL 2923543 (July 18, 2012), *aff'd*, No. 12-2795 (8th Cir. Dec. 7, 2012) (finding head-of-state immunity for president of Ghana and conduct-based immunity for attorney general).

[92] See, e.g., Moriah v. Bank of China Ltd., 107 F. Supp. 3d 272, 277–80 (S.D.N.Y. 2015) (former Israeli official); Wultz v. Bank of China Ltd., 32 F. Supp. 3d 486, 492–98 (S.D.N.Y. 2014) (same).

[93] See, e.g., Smith Rocke Ltd. v. Republica Bolivariana de Venezuela, No. 12 Civ. 7316, 2014 WL 288705, at *11 (S.D.N.Y. Jan. 27, 2014); Mohammadi v. Islamic Republic of Iran, 947 F. Supp. 2d 48, 72 (D.D.C. 2013), *aff'd*, 782 F.3d 9 (D.C. Cir. 2015); Odhiambo v. Republic of Kenya, 930 F. Supp. 2d 17, 35 (D.D.C. 2013), *aff'd*, 764 F.3d 31 (D.C. Cir. 2014).

[94] 918 F.3d 142, 144 (D.C. Cir. 2019) (interpreting Torture Victim Protection Act, Pub. L. No. 102-256, 106 Stat. 73, codified at 28 U.S.C. § 1350 note).

[95] See *Hassen*, 2010 WL 9538408, at *6.

[96] See C.G. *ex rel.* Garcia v. Gutierrez, No. 16 Civ. 158, 2017 WL 1435720, at *3 (E.D.N.C. Apr. 21, 2017); Rishikof v. Mortada, 70 F. Supp. 3d 8, 11–17 (D.D.C. 2014); cf. *supra* notes 58–61 and accompanying text.

statements. In this section we describe some of the most important recurring questions that have arisen, identify where the law is still developing (and where we think consensus has been reached), and offer our views on some of the thornier doctrinal problems.

## A. What Is the Source of the Common Law of Foreign-Official Immunity?

Perhaps the first question in every immunity determination is: What law applies? The Supreme Court in *Samantar* directed courts to apply "the common law of official immunity," but it did not identify what that common law is or where courts should locate it.[97] This has resulted in some confusion in the lower courts, with one federal circuit judge musing that "[i]t may well be that there is not now and never was any common law of immunity for foreign officials sued in the United States."[98] The executive branch's answer is: "Principles adopted by the executive branch, informed by customary international law, govern the immunity of foreign officials acting in their official capacity."[99] Likewise, the Department has stated that its suggestions of immunity, statements of interest, and amicus briefs set out "principles [that] are susceptible to general application by the judiciary."[100] In other words, the common law of official immunity is founded in customary international law, but courts must follow the executive branch's interpretation of it.

We think that this approach—whereby courts apply the immunity principles articulated by the executive branch—is appropriate (though we recognize that it is not without detractors).[101] As a policy matter, it prevents courts from contradicting or "embarrassing" the executive branch's position in sensitive diplomatic negotiations, especially considering the executive branch's acute interest in ensuring that foreign courts afford reciprocal immunities to our own officials.[102] As a legal matter, we think that the executive branch's authority is a necessary component of the president's constitutional responsibility for

---

[97] *Samantar*, 560 U.S. at 320.

[98] Lewis v. Mutond, 918 F.3d 142, 149 (D.C. Cir. 2019) (Randolph, J., concurring in the judgment).

[99] U.S. Amicus Brief at 7, Samantar v. Yousuf, 560 U.S. 305 (2010) (No. 08-1555).

[100] U.S. Dichter Brief, *supra* note 74, at 21 n.*.

[101] For the detractors' views, see Christine E. Ganley, *Reevaluating the Common Law of Foreign Official Immunity: Ascertaining the Proper Role of the Executive*, 21 Geo. Mason L. Rev. 1317, 1336–46 (2014); Peter B. Rutledge, *Samantar and Executive Power*, 44 Vand. J. Transnat'l L. 885, 909 (2011); Ingrid Wuerth, *Foreign Official Immunity Determinations in U.S. Courts: The Case Against the State Department*, 51 Va. J. Int'l L. 915, 975 (2011).

[102] See *Hoffman*, 324 U.S. at 35; Ex parte *Peru*, 318 U.S. at 589. See U.S. Dichter Brief, *supra* note 74, at 25.

conducting the foreign relations of the United States.[103] It is also fully consistent with the Supreme Court's statement in *Hoffman* that "it is ... not for the courts to deny an immunity which our government has seen fit to allow, or to allow an immunity on new grounds which the government has not seen fit to recognize."[104] But in order for courts to buy in to this approach—which entails the judiciary ceding, to some extent, its role in the articulation of the common law—the State Department will have to clearly state its principles for determining immunity, and the courts will have to know where to find them.[105] To that end, we offer two recommendations.

First, we recommend that the State Department publish a new "Tate Letter" defining the principles that will guide the executive branch's immunity determinations going forward.[106] This document would provide courts, foreign governments, and litigants with a useful general statement of the law of foreign-official immunity applicable in cases where the executive branch has declined to submit its views.[107] Second, we recommend that the Department collect and publish the suggestions of immunity and other statements of interest that the executive branch files in cases implicating foreign-official immunity, much like it did between 1952 and 1976.[108] A compendium or database containing these filings would provide the courts (and litigants) with a valuable resource; it would promote transparency into the Department's approach to determining immunity (even in the absence of an overriding statement of policy); and it would encourage consistency and predictability in immunity determinations, both within the Department and in the courts. By making this body of law more easily accessible, such a database would also serve the Department's institutional interests in having courts apply the executive branch's articulation of the common law of

[103] See Lewis S. Yelin, *Head of State Immunity as Sole Executive Lawmaking*, 44 VAND. J. TRANSNAT'L L. 911, 951–75 (2011).

[104] *Hoffman*, 324 U.S. at 35.

[105] Notwithstanding the executive branch's insistence that courts rely on its statements in prior cases, courts have overwhelmingly relied on the cases themselves, not the executive branch's submissions. We think this fact is likely due to force of habit (both on the part of litigants and the courts, who are both more accustomed to citing cases) and to the difficulty of identifying prior executive-branch filings.

[106] See Harold Hongju Koh, *Foreign Official Immunity After Samantar: A United States Government Perspective*, 44 VAND. J. TRANSNAT'L L. 1141, 1147 (2011) (noting that "it may be some time before the Executive Branch develops a full-fledged U.S. Government statement of official immunity principles ... parallel to those principles found in the 1952 Tate Letter").

[107] We do not think such a statement would have to be comprehensive, so long as it also directs courts and litigants to review the executive branch's corpus of suggestions of immunity. Moreover, the Department can expressly reserve the right to deviate from or revise these principles on as necessary, in the national interest or to conform U.S. practice to customary international law.

[108] See 1977 DIGEST, *supra* note 48. The Office of the Legal Adviser does publish many of its suggestions of immunity, but they are scattered throughout the annual editions of the *Digest of United States Practice in International Law* and thus difficult to locate. Our recommendation is that these suggestions of immunity (and other filings not always published by the Department) should be collected in one easily accessible and searchable compendium or database.

foreign-official immunity without having to file a statement of interest in every case involving a foreign official.[109] We think that the Fourth Restatement could serve a helpful function in this regard by directing courts to the statements of the executive branch and explaining that those filings are authoritative and conclusive statements of the common law of foreign-official immunity in U.S. courts.

## B. Are Suggestions of Immunity Binding, or Is There Room for Courts to Conduct Independent Analysis?

A second important preliminary question is whether the executive branch's suggestions of immunity (or nonimmunity) are conclusive and binding on the courts. The Supreme Court, in our view, has already provided a definitive answer to this question. In *The Navemar*, the Court stated that "[i]f the claim [of immunity] is recognized and allowed by the executive branch of the government, it is then the duty of the courts" to accept it.[110] Likewise, in Ex parte *Peru*, the Court stated that the executive branch's "certification . . . must be accepted by the courts as a conclusive determination by the political arm of the Government," and "[u]pon the submission of this certification to the district court, it became the court's duty . . . to proceed no further in the cause."[111] And in *Hoffman*, the Court held that "it is an accepted rule of substantive law governing the exercise of the jurisdiction of the courts that they accept and follow the executive determination" of immunity.[112] *The Navemar*, Ex parte *Peru*, and *Hoffman* all involved foreign vessels, but the Court in *Samantar* relied on those precedents when explaining that the two-step framework established in those cases also applies to foreign officials.[113]

Likewise, it is the long-held view of the executive branch that a suggestion of immunity or nonimmunity is conclusive and binding on the courts— notwithstanding the hesitation expressed in the Tate Letter.[114] This position has been expressed in numerous suggestions of immunity, statements of interest, and amicus briefs filed by the executive branch.[115] For example, the executive

---

[109] See U.S. Dichter Brief, *supra* note 74, at 21 n.*.

[110] 303 U.S. at 74.

[111] 318 U.S. at 589.

[112] 324 U.S. at 36.

[113] 560 U.S. at 312 (citing Heaney v. Government of Spain, 445 F.2d 501, 504–505 (2d Cir. 1971); Waltier v. Thomson, 189 F. Supp. 319 (S.D.N.Y. 1960)). We recognize that, as a technical matter, *Berizzi Bros. Co. v. The Pesaro*, 271 U.S. 562 (1926), in which the Supreme Court rejected the executive branch's suggestion of nonimmunity, has not been overruled. But we doubt that the case survives *The Navemar*, Ex parte *Peru*, *Hoffman*, and *Samantar*; cf. *Hoffman*, 324 U.S. at 39–42 (Frankfurter, J., concurring).

[114] See *supra* text accompanying note 47.

[115] See, e.g., U.S. Amicus Brief at 12–14, Doğan v. Barak, 932 F.3d 888 (9th Cir. 2019) (No. 16-56704) [hereinafter U.S. Barak Brief]; U.S. Amicus Brief at 12–19, Samantar v. Yousuf, No. 12-1078

branch recently stated in an amicus brief to the Ninth Circuit that "the State Department's determinations are controlling under the common law of foreign-official immunity."[116] And the lower courts have overwhelmingly accepted the executive branch's position, according absolute deference to executive-branch suggestions of immunity—both for sitting heads of state (status-based immunity), and for other foreign officials (conduct-based immunity).[117]

Only the Fourth Circuit has ruled that the courts are not bound by executive-branch immunity determinations. On remand in *Samantar*, the Fourth Circuit held that it would give absolute deference only in cases against a sitting head of state, but not for former heads of state or other foreign officials, such as Samantar.[118] Instead, the court held that suggestions of conduct-based immunity (specifically, in that case, *non*immunity) carry only "substantial weight."[119] The

(U.S. Dec. 2013) [hereinafter U.S. Samantar Brief (No. 12-1078)]; Barak SOI, *supra* note 87, at 2–7; U.S. Amicus Brief at 5–10, Doe v. Zedillo Ponce de León, No. 13-3122 (2d Cir. Jan. 22, 2014); Lashkar-e-Taiba SOI, *supra* note 87, at 7–9; U.S. Amicus Brief at 5–8, Manoharan v. Rajapaksa, 711 F.3d 178 (D.C. Cir. 2013) (No. 12-5087) [hereinafter U.S. Rajapaksa Brief]; Zedillo SOI, *supra* note 87, at 4–6; U.S. Amicus Brief at 9–13, Giraldo v. Drummond Co., No. 11-7118 (D.C. Cir. Aug. 3, 2012) [hereinafter U.S. Giraldo Brief]; U.S. Dichter Brief, *supra* note 74, at 5–8; U.S. Amicus Brief at 13–22, Wei Ye v. Jiang Zemin, 383 F.3d 620 (7th Cir. 2004) (No. 03-3989) [hereinafter U.S. Jiang Brief].

[116] U.S. Barak Brief, *supra* note 115, at 12 (capitalization altered); see also U.S. Samantar Brief (No. 12-1078), *supra* note 115, at 12.

[117] Status-based immunity: see, e.g., Manoharan v. Rajapaksa, 711 F.3d 178, 179 (D.C. Cir. 2013), *aff'g*, 845 F. Supp. 2d 260, 261 (D.D.C. 2012) ("The Court finds that the United States' Suggestion of Immunity is binding on the Court and dispositive of the Court's jurisdiction."); Habyarimana v. Kagame, 696 F.3d 1029 (10th Cir. 2012) ("For more than 160 years American courts have consistently applied the doctrine of sovereign immunity when requested to do so by the executive branch . . . with no further review of the executive's determination."); Isbrandtsen Tankers, Inc. v. President of India, 446 F.2d 1198, 1201 (2d Cir. 1971) ("[O]nce the State Department has ruled in a matter of this nature, the judiciary will not interfere."); see also Devi v. Rajapaksa, No. 11 Civ. 6634, 2012 WL 3866495, at *2 (S.D.N.Y. Sept. 4, 2012); Saltany v. Reagan, 702 F. Supp. 319, 320 (D.D.C. 1988); cf. Li Weixum v. Bo Xilai, 568 F. Supp. 2d 35, 38 (D.D.C. 2008) (special-mission immunity).
Conduct-based immunity: see, e.g., Doe v. Zedillo Ponce de León, 555 F. App'x 84, 85 (2d Cir. 2014) ("'[U]nder our traditional rule of deference to such Executive determinations,' the United States' submission is dispositive." (quoting *Dichter*, 563 F.3d at 13)); Rosenberg v. Pasha, 577 F. App'x 22, 23 (2d Cir. 2014) ("[T]he District Court correctly determined that, in light of the Statement of Interest filed by the State Department recommending immunity for Pasha and Taj, the action must be dismissed."); *Dichter*, 563 F.3d at 15 ("Here, the Executive Branch has urged the courts to decline jurisdiction over appellants' suit, and under our traditional rule of deference to such Executive determinations, we do so."); Wei Ye v. Jiang Zemin, 383 F.3d 620, 621 (7th Cir. 2004) ("[T]he Executive Branch's suggestion of immunity is conclusive and not subject to judicial inquiry."); Doğan v. Barak, No. 15 Civ. 8130, 2016 WL 6024416, at *7 (C.D. Cal. Oct. 13, 2016) ("To avoid 'embarrass[ing] the [Executive Branch] by assuming an antagonistic jurisdiction,' and to afford the political branches the much-needed discretion to resolve the issue through diplomacy, the Court should follow the Executive's suggestion." (citation omitted)); Ben-Haim v. Edri, 183 A.3d 252, 259 (N.J. App. Div. 2018) ("[W]e . . . hold that a[] [suggestion of immunity] is controlling on a court when the immunity determination is based on a finding by the State Department that foreign officials were acting within the scope of their authority for a foreign sovereign nation."); see also *Magan*, 2011 WL 13160129, at *2 (deferring to suggestion of nonimmunity).

[118] Yousuf v. Samantar (*Samantar II*), 699 F.3d 763, 773 (4th Cir. 2012).
[119] *Id.*

court drew this distinction on constitutional grounds, reasoning that the executive branch was due absolute deference for suggestions of immunity involving sitting heads of state based on the president's constitutional authority to "'receive Ambassadors and other public Ministers' to the Executive Branch, which includes, by implication, the power to accredit diplomats and recognize foreign heads of state."[120] The court then proceeded to conduct its own analysis to determine that Samantar was not immune under a broad exception for allegations of jus cogens violations, which we discuss in the following section.[121]

While agreeing with the Fourth Circuit's ultimate holding (that Samantar was not immune), the executive branch has expressed strong disagreement with the court's decision not to defer to its determination. In a suggestion of immunity filed in a subsequent case, the executive branch referred to the Fourth Circuit's position as "legal error" and explained:

> [T]he Executive Branch's authority to make foreign official immunity determinations, and the requirement of judicial deference to such determinations, flow from the Executive's constitutional responsibility for conducting the Nation's foreign relations, and not just from the more specific constitutional power to recognize diplomats and foreign heads of state on which the Fourth Circuit relied.[122]

Likewise, in its brief urging the Supreme Court to vacate the Fourth Circuit's decision, the executive branch invoked the "separation of powers" to argue that the Fourth Circuit's decision not to defer to the executive branch had usurped the president's constitutional role as "'the guiding organ in the conduct of our foreign affairs.'"[123]

Notwithstanding the Fourth Circuit's decision on remand in *Samantar*, we are aware of only one modern case in which a U.S. court has exercised jurisdiction over a foreign official in the face of a suggestion of immunity from the executive branch. In *Sikhs for Justice v. Singh*, the plaintiff alleged that then-sitting Indian prime minister Manmohan Singh was personally culpable for crimes committed by the Indian government against Indian Sikhs while Singh served as prime minister and finance minister before that.[124] The executive branch filed a suggestion of immunity on behalf of Singh, but shortly thereafter, he was voted out of office, raising the question whether the executive branch's suggestion of

---

[120] *Id.* at 772 (quoting U.S. CONST. art. II, § 3).

[121] *Id.* at 776–77.

[122] Barak SOI, *supra* note 87, at 6 (citing Ex parte *Peru*, 318 U.S. at 589).

[123] U.S. Samantar Brief (No. 12-1078), *supra* note 115, at 18 (quoting Ludecke v. Watkins, 335 U.S. 160, 173 (1948)).

[124] 64 F. Supp. 3d 190, 192 (D.D.C. 2014).

status-based immunity still controlled.[125] The executive branch then filed a reply brief reaffirming that Singh was "immune from this suit" because the executive branch "ha[d] not withdrawn [its previous] assertion of immunity," which "remain[ed] binding."[126] Oddly, the executive branch did not assert that Singh was entitled to conduct-based immunity for his official conduct as prime minister and finance minister, instead noting, somewhat cryptically, that the case did not present the question whether Singh "would enjoy immunity in a new suit, filed after he left office."[127] The district court was not convinced, calling the executive branch's position "overly formal," in part because, as the government seemed to suggest, "Plaintiff could simply refile his suit."[128] Embarking on an independent analysis, the court concluded that Singh was entitled to "residual" immunity for acts done in his capacity as prime minister.[129] But the court held that there were "no grounds for a suggestion of immunity as to acts Singh took as Finance Minister," and allowed the case to go forward.[130] The court notably did not consider whether conduct-based immunity would apply to Singh's official acts undertaken as finance minister.

We think the district court's decision is plainly wrong for two reasons. First, it failed to defer to the executive branch's unequivocal statement that Singh was immune from that suit. Second, it failed to consider that conduct-based immunity would apply to Singh's official acts as finance minister. The case was eventually dismissed and never appealed after plaintiffs failed to effect service, but the court's opinion remains a (nonprecedential) outlier—albeit one of limited applicability considering the unusual circumstances of Singh losing head-of-state status after the executive branch had suggested immunity.

## C. What Is the Scope of Conduct-Based Immunity, and Does the Second Restatement's Formulation of Foreign-Official Immunity Remain Relevant?

*Samantar* did not define the scope of common-law immunity or how courts should apply it, nor did it endorse (or disavow) the Second Restatement's formulation.[131] Instead, it left the executive branch and the lower courts to fill the gap.

---

[125] See Singh SOI, *supra* note 87, at 1–3.

[126] Reply in Support of Suggestion of Immunity at 2, Sikhs for Justice v. Singh, 64 F. Supp. 3d 190 (D.D.C. 2014) (No. 13 Civ. 1460).

[127] *Id.* at 3 n.1.

[128] 64 F. Supp. 3d at 195.

[129] *Id.* at 193–94.

[130] *Id.* at 194.

[131] *Samantar*, 560 U.S. at 311.

Following *Hoffman's* directive, we begin with the executive branch's position. The executive branch has explained that foreign-official immunity "is not a personal right" but is "for the benefit of the official's state," and can thus be asserted or waived by the foreign state.[132] As for status-based immunity, the executive branch's view is straightforward. Sitting heads of state, heads of government, and foreign ministers are absolutely immune from any U.S. suit while in office.[133] As far as we are aware, no court has ever adopted a contrary position.[134] Conduct-based immunity, on the other hand, is more complicated. The formulation consistently articulated by the executive branch is: "As a general matter, under principles of customary international law accepted by the Executive Branch, a foreign official enjoys immunity from suit based upon acts taken in an official capacity."[135] But that raises two questions: What acts are official acts? And when does this "general" rule not apply?

The executive branch has explained some of the considerations that guide its determination whether an official had acted in an official capacity:

> In making the immunity determination, the Department of State considers, *inter alia*, a foreign government's request (if there is such a request) that the Department of State suggest the official's immunity. Notwithstanding such a request, the Department of State could determine that a foreign official is not immune. That would occur, for example, should the Department of State conclude that the conduct alleged was not taken in an official capacity, as might be the case in a suit challenging an official's purely private acts, such as personal financial dealings. In making that determination, it is for the Executive Branch, not the courts, to determine whether the conduct alleged was taken in a foreign official's official capacity.[136]

Where the executive branch has not spoken, however, courts must apply these principles for themselves. One open question is whether courts can (or should) look to foreign domestic law to determine whether an official acted within the scope of his or her authority. Most courts avoid the issue by relying on allegations in the complaint or on the foreign sovereign's ratification of its official's conduct to determine that the alleged conduct was undertaken on behalf of the sovereign.[137]

---

[132] Samantar SOI, *supra* note 85, at 9; see *Wultz*, 32 F. Supp. 3d at 493–95 (holding that Israel had standing to challenge subpoena of former official).

[133] See *supra* note 86.

[134] See *supra* note 88.

[135] Barak SOI, *supra* note 87, at 7.

[136] *Id.* at 7–8 (citing *Hoffman*, 324 U.S. at 35).

[137] See, e.g., Lewis v. Mutond, 258 F. Supp. 3d 168, 174 (D.D.C. 2017) ("[T]his Court finds the DRC Ambassador's ratification of the defendants' actions sufficient to establish that they were acting in their official capacities in the present case."), *vacated and remanded on other grounds*, 918 F.3d 142 (D.C. Cir. 2019).

But, in at least one case, the executive branch directed the court to make a finding about the scope of an official's authority under foreign domestic law.[138] Relatedly, some plaintiffs have attempted to avoid immunity by alleging that the official, although acting in an official capacity, violated the domestic laws or constitution of the foreign sovereign. But, to our knowledge, every court to consider this so-called ultra vires exception to conduct-based immunity has rejected it,[139] and the executive branch has disavowed it.[140]

Another open question is whether the Second Restatement's description of foreign-official immunity should play any role in courts' decisions.[141] As far as we are aware, the executive branch has never endorsed this formulation, although it has cited to it in passing.[142] *Hoffman*, therefore, would foreclose any application of the Second Restatement to limit immunity in a way that has not been accepted by the executive branch.[143]

Nonetheless, many courts have cited the Second Restatement approvingly, although only a few courts have substantively addressed in what circumstances "exercising jurisdiction" over a foreign official would have the effect of "enforce[ing] a rule of law against the state."[144] A 2018 district court decision, *Doe 1 v. Buratai*, contains perhaps the most thorough discussion.[145] In that case, the court held that a personal-capacity suit against Nigerian officials for alleged TVPA violations "would have the effect of enforcing a rule of law against Nigeria" because "[t]he Nigerian government claimed the defendants' actions

---

[138] See, e.g., Statement of Interest at 1, Abi Jaoudi & Azar Trading Co. v. Cigna Worldwide Ins. Co., No. 91 Civ. 6785 (E.D. Pa. Dec. 5, 2011) ("[T]he United States suggests that Respondents . . . are immune from suit *to the extent the Court finds* that, *under Liberian law*, they acted in their official capacities when they took the acts that are the basis for Defendant's contempt motion against them." (emphasis added)). This approach brings with it a host of potential pitfalls: It risks interfering with the U.S. government's diplomatic relations and intruding on the sovereignty of foreign states—especially where a plaintiff invites a U.S. court to interpret foreign law contrary to the foreign state's own interpretation. Cf. *Underhill*, 168 U.S. at 252.

[139] See, e.g., *Lewis*, 258 F. Supp. 3d at 174; *Giraldo*, 808 F. Supp. 2d at 250; see also *Belhas*, 515 F.3d at 129 (Williams, J., concurring) (rejecting argument "that [plaintiffs'] characterization of [the foreign official's] conduct as violating . . . Israeli law establishes an irrebuttable presumption that he acted without official authority").

[140] U.S. Giraldo Brief, *supra* note 115, at 14.

[141] SECOND RESTATEMENT, *supra* note 55, § 66(f) (foreign officials enjoy immunity "with respect to acts performed in [their] official capacity if the effect of exercising jurisdiction would be to enforce a rule of law against the state").

[142] E.g., Dichter SOI, *supra* note 71, at 8–9.

[143] *Hoffman*, 324 U.S. at 35.

[144] See, e.g., *Barak*, 932 F.3d at 893–94; *Dichter*, 563 F.3d at 14; *Heaney*, 445 F.2d at 504; Ivey for Carolina Golf Dev. Co. v. Lynch, No. 17-cv-439, 2018 WL 3764264, at *3 (M.D.N.C. Aug. 8, 2018); Mireskandari v. Mayne, No. 12-cv-3861, 2016 WL 1165896, at *16 (C.D. Cal. Mar. 23, 2016); *In re* Terrorist Attacks on Sept. 11, 2001, 122 F. Supp. 3d 181, 187 (S.D.N.Y. 2015); Smith v. Ghana Commercial Bank, Ltd., No. 10-cv-4655, 2012 WL 2930462, at *9–10 (D. Minn. June 18, 2012), *R&R adopted*, 2012 WL 2923543 (July 18, 2012), *aff'd*, No. 12-2795 (8th Cir. Dec. 7, 2012).

[145] 318 F. Supp. 3d 218 (D.D.C. 2018), *aff'd*, No. 18-7170, 2019 WL 668339 (D.C. Cir. 2019); see also *Barak*, 932 F.3d at 893–94.

as the country's own" by ratifying their conduct in a diplomatic note to the State Department.[146] The court concluded that, because Nigeria had ratified its officials' conduct, "a decision . . . on the legality of the defendants' actions would amount to a decision on the legality of Nigeria's actions."[147] The court rejected plaintiffs' argument that they had sued the Nigerian officials in their personal capacities only, reasoning that holding them personally liable for state conduct "would affect how Nigeria's government, military, and police function, regardless whether the damages come from the defendants' own wallets or Nigeria's coffers."[148]

The only outlier on this issue is *Lewis v. Mutond,* an oddly fractured 2019 decision from the D.C. Circuit that produced two holdings split among three opinions.[149] In *Lewis,* an American citizen was arrested and detained in the Democratic Republic of the Congo (DRC) on grounds that he was illegally working as a foreign mercenary. Upon his release, he sued two high-ranking DRC officials raising claims under the TVPA. The central allegations of the complaint concern prosecutorial and police powers, including deciding "whether to detain, charge, try, or release [plaintiff]," "giving orders to and supervising" government personnel, and "order[ing] the general prosecutor of the DRC to open a judicial case."[150] And the DRC expressly ratified its officials' conduct in two diplomatic notes to the State Department.[151] Applying the Second Restatement's formulation of foreign-official immunity, the district court held that the DRC officials were immune.[152] With regard to whether exercising jurisdiction over the officials would "enforce a rule of law" against the DRC, the district court noted that exercising jurisdiction would require the court to conclude, contrary to the DRC's own determination, that the foreign officials had violated the DRC's laws and constitution.[153] The D.C. Circuit vacated and remanded, holding that, under the Second Restatement, conduct-based immunity does not apply where a plaintiff seeks money damages from foreign officials only in their personal, rather than official, capacities.[154] The court concluded that because the DRC would not have to pay a judgment against its officials, exercising jurisdiction would not "enforce a rule of law" against the DRC.[155] A petition

---

[146] *Id.* at 233.

[147] *Id.*

[148] *Id.*

[149] 918 F.3d 142 (D.C. Cir. 2019). We should note that we represent the defendant DRC officials in the Supreme Court petition for certiorari with respect to this decision.

[150] Complaint at ¶¶ 4, 5, 33, Lewis v. Mutond, 258 F. Supp. 3d 168 (D.D.C. 2017) (No. 16 Civ. 1547).

[151] *Lewis,* 258 F. Supp. 3d at 173.

[152] *Id.* at 172–75.

[153] *Id.* at 174.

[154] *Lewis,* 918 F.3d at 147.

[155] *Id.*

for a writ of certiorari in this case is currently pending before the Supreme Court.[156]

Our view, consistent with *Hoffman*, is that courts cannot apply the Second Restatement to deny immunity in ways not accepted by the executive branch. The executive branch has suggested immunity in numerous personal-capacity suits and has never intimated that a plaintiff's choice to sue a foreign official in his or her personal capacity (for official conduct) is relevant to the immunity analysis, much less dispositive.[157] But even applying the Second Restatement's standard on its face—unconstrained by the executive branch's views—we agree with the district court in *Buratai* that even a personal-capacity suit against a foreign official would have the effect of enforcing a rule of law against a foreign state where the official has engaged in quintessentially sovereign conduct on behalf of, and ratified by, the state.[158] This scenario is different from lawsuits where the foreign sovereign is the real party in interest, or a necessary party to the suit.[159] Even if a lawsuit does not seek a judgment against the state, where a foreign state has claimed its officials' actions as its own, a decision on the legality of the officials' actions amounts to a decision on the legality of the state's actions.[160] And holding individual officials personally liable for conduct in furtherance of sovereign functions can adversely affect the "government's ability to perform its traditional functions" by chilling officials' conduct.[161]

## D. Is There an Exception to Foreign-Official Immunity for Jus Cogens Violations?

Another recurring question is whether there is an exception to foreign-official immunity for alleged violations of jus cogens—that is, "a norm accepted and recognized by the international community of States as a whole as a norm from which no derogation is permitted."[162] The theory is that, because foreign-official

[156] Petition for a Writ of Certiorari, Mutond v. Lewis, No. 19-185 (U.S. filed Aug. 9, 2019).

[157] See, e.g., Barak SOI, *supra* note 87, at 7–10; Edri SOI, *supra* note 87, at 6–8; Lashkar-e-Taiba SOI, *supra* note 87, at 9–11; Dichter SOI, *supra* note 71, at 4; U.S. Jiang Brief, *supra* note 115, at 23–34.

[158] See *Buratai*, 318 F. Supp. 3d at 233.

[159] As to whether the foreign sovereign is the real party in interest, see *Samantar*, 560 U.S. at 324–25. If an official is sued in an official *capacity*, not merely for official *acts*, then the FSIA may apply. See *supra* note 93 and accompanying text. As to whether the foreign sovereign is a necessary party to the suit, see Republic of Philippines v. Pimentel, 553 U.S. 851, 863–72 (2008). If a foreign sovereign is a necessary party to a lawsuit but cannot be joined for any reason (including immunity under the FSIA), then the suit may have to be dismissed. See *id.*

[160] See *Buratai*, 318 F. Supp. 3d at 233.

[161] Wyatt v. Cole, 504 U.S. 158, 167 (1992); see Ziglar v. Abbasi, 137 S. Ct. 1843, 1866 (2017).

[162] *Samantar II*, 699 F.3d at 775 (quotation marks omitted); see also THIRD RESTATEMENT § 702 & reporters' note 11 (describing as jus cogens violations: genocide; slavery or slave trade; murder or causing the disappearance of individuals; torture or other cruel, inhuman, or degrading treatment or punishment; prolonged arbitrary detention; and systematic racial discrimination).

immunity flows from the foreign sovereign and no nation endorses torture or extrajudicial killing, foreign officials cannot assert immunity for those acts.

The executive branch, however, has determined that there is no consensus in customary international law recognizing an exception for alleged violations of jus cogens.[163] And nearly all courts to have addressed the issue have rejected any such exception.[164] In *Matar v. Dichter* and *Doğan v. Barak*, the executive branch had submitted a suggestion of immunity, and the courts declined to craft an exception to immunity that would override the executive branch's determination.[165] The district court in *Buratai* did not have the benefit of a suggestion of immunity in that case, but the court relied on the fact that "the executive branch has not recognized a blanket *jus cogens* exception" in other cases.[166] The court also recognized numerous prudential reasons, including that such an exception "would likely place an enormous strain not only upon our courts but, more to the immediate point, upon our country's diplomatic relations with any number of foreign nations."[167]

Only one court, the Fourth Circuit, has recognized a jus cogens exception to immunity.[168] On remand in *Samantar*, executive branch suggested nonimmunity on behalf of Samantar for two reasons: First, Somalia did not have a recognized government "to assert or waive [Samantar's] immunity"; and, second, Samantar was a legal permanent resident of the United States, "who enjoy[ed] the protections of U.S. law" and therefore "should be subject to the jurisdiction of our courts, particularly when sued by U.S. residents."[169] The Fourth Circuit agreed with the executive branch that Samantar was not immune, but it disagreed as to why. Rather than simply defer to the suggestion of nonimmunity, the court crafted a jus cogens exception to foreign-official immunity for alleged acts of torture and extrajudicial killing.[170] The court based this exception on what it identified as "an increasing trend in international law to abrogate foreign official immunity for individuals who commit acts, otherwise attributable to the State, that violate *jus cogens* norms."[171]

---

[163] See, e.g., U.S. Barak Brief, *supra* note 115, at 21–26; U.S. Samantar Brief (No. 12-1078), *supra* note 115, at 19–22; U.S. Dichter Brief, *supra* note 74, at 19–25.

[164] See, e.g., *Barak*, 932 F.3d at 897; *Dichter*, 563 F.3d at 14–15; *Pasha*, 577 F. App'x at 23–24; *Buratai*, 318 F. Supp. 3d at 233–36; *In re* Terrorist Attacks on Sept. 11, 2001, 122 F. Supp. 3d at 189; see also *Belhas*, 515 F.3d at 1287–88 (rejecting jus cogens exception under the FSIA).

[165] *Dichter*, 563 F.3d at 14–15; *Doğan v. Barak*, 932 F.3d 888, 897 (9th Cir. 2019).

[166] *Buratai*, 318 F. Supp. 3d at 235.

[167] *Id.* at 234 (quoting *Giraldo*, 808 F. Supp. 2d at 250).

[168] *Samantar II*, 699 F.3d at 776–77; see also Warfaa v. Ali, 33 F. Supp. 3d 653 (E.D. Va. 2014), *aff'd*, 811 F.3d 653 (4th Cir. 2016) (applying *Samantar II*).

[169] 699 F.3d at 767.

[170] *Id.* at 776–77.

[171] *Id.* at 776.

We think that the Fourth Circuit's decision is wrong for three independent—and independently important—reasons. First, the executive branch has not recognized a jus cogens exception to immunity and, in fact, has expressly stated that no such exception exists.[172] Under *Hoffman*, that is the end of the analysis.[173] In numerous cases, both before and after the Supreme Court's decision in *Samantar*, the executive branch has suggested immunity for former foreign officials who were alleged to have committed jus cogens violations.[174] And the courts deferred to the executive branch's suggestions of immunity in each of these cases.[175] Second, the court is wrong about the state of international customary law. The court purported to base its holding on an emerging consensus, while admitting that "the *jus cogens* exception appears to be less settled in the civil context."[176] That is an understatement, to say the least. In fact, the court identified no case recognizing a jus cogens exception in the civil context. And the only foreign court decision the panel cited finding a jus cogens exception was an Italian decision finding liability against Germany for war crimes during World War II.[177] Germany subsequently sued Italy in the International Court of Justice (ICJ) over the Italian decision, and in 2012 the ICJ ruled in favor of Germany, concluding that Italy had violated Germany's sovereign immunity and that there is no jus cogens exception to sovereign immunity.[178] In so holding, the ICJ documented that courts in the United Kingdom, Canada, Poland, Slovenia, New Zealand, and Greece, as well as the European Court of Human Rights, had all rejected a jus cogens exception to state immunity.[179] Third, policy considerations counsel against such an exception. It is easy to allege jus cogens violations and thus to evade immunity (at least at the pleading stage), thus subjecting foreign officials to the "attendant burdens of litigation" that immunity is meant to protect against.[180] And, as the executive branch has explained, if U.S. courts permit lawsuits against former officials for alleged jus cogens violations, there is a substantial risk that foreign courts will permit similar suits against our own former officials.[181]

---

[172] *Id.* at 767; see also, e.g., U.S. Barak Brief, *supra* note 115, at 21–26; U.S. Dichter Brief, *supra* note 74, at 19–25.

[173] 324 U.S. at 35.

[174] See, e.g., U.S. Dichter Brief, *supra* note 74, at 19–25; U.S. Jiang Brief, *supra* note 115, at 23–34; Lashkar-e-Taiba SOI, *supra* note 87, at 7–11; Zedillo SOI, *supra* note 87, at 6; see also Giraldo SOI, *supra* note 87, at 5–6 (third-party testimony was sought from former Colombian president in a suit in which he was alleged to have committed jus cogens violations).

[175] See *Dichter*, 563 F.3d at 14–15; *Wei Ye*, 383 F.3d at 626–27; Rosenberg v. Lashkar-e-Taiba, No. 10 Civ. 5381, 2013 WL 5502851, at *5–7 (E.D.N.Y. Sept. 30, 2013); Transcript of Ruling at 3:8–6:4, Doe v. Zedillo, No. 11 Civ. 1433 (D. Conn. July 18, 2013); see also *Giraldo*, 808 F. Supp. 2d at 250–51.

[176] *Samantar II*, 699 F.3d at 776.

[177] *Id.* (citing Ferrini v. Germany, Appeal Decision, Cass. No. 5044/04, I.L.D.C. 19 (It. Cass. 2004)).

[178] Jurisdictional Immunities of the State (Ger. v. Italy: Greece intervening), Judgment, 2012 I.C.J. 99 (Feb. 3).

[179] See *id.* at ¶ 96 (collecting cases).

[180] *Giraldo*, 808 F. Supp. 2d at 250–251 (citation omitted).

[181] See U.S. Dichter Brief, *supra* note 74, at 25.

We recognize that foreign states may at some point recognize a jus cogens exception to foreign-official immunity. And we are sympathetic to those who want to see the worst human rights abusers held responsible for their crimes. But until such an exception is recognized by the executive branch, under *Hoffman*, courts cannot craft such an exception on their own. In the meantime, however, suits alleging jus cogens violations may still proceed in certain circumstances. For example, a foreign sovereign may waive its official's immunity or disavow its official's conduct, thus stripping the official of immunity.[182] Or the executive branch may issue a suggestion of nonimmunity, as it did in *Samantar*.[183]

## E.  Does the Torture Victim Protection Act Abrogate Foreign-Official Immunity?

On March 16, 1992, President George H.W. Bush signed into law the TVPA, which created a civil cause of action for damages against individuals who, "under actual or apparent authority, or color of law, of any foreign nation," commit acts of "torture" or "extrajudicial killing."[184] The TVPA notably does not speak to immunity, but there is evidence in the legislative history that Congress understood that at least head-of-state and diplomatic immunity would not be affected by the TVPA's enactment.[185] And although conduct-based immunity is not directly addressed in the legislative history, there is some indication that Congress understood that a foreign official could claim immunity if the foreign sovereign ratified the official's conduct.[186] Putting aside the (somewhat equivocal) legislative history, however, it is clear that liability under the TVPA overlaps conspicuously with the central element of conduct-based immunity—official conduct—such that, in many cases, pleading a claim under the TVPA necessarily implicates conduct-based immunity. This overlap raises the question of whether the TVPA impliedly abrogated the common law of conduct-based immunity, such that former heads of state and other lower-level foreign officials can never claim immunity for acts of torture or extrajudicial killing.

The executive branch's consistent view on this question has been that the TVPA does not abrogate the common law of conduct-based foreign-official immunity—a position which, perhaps not surprisingly, maintains its authority

---

[182] See, e.g., Hilao v. Estate of Marcos, 25 F.3d 1467, 1472 (9th Cir. 1994); *In re* Doe, 860 F.2d 40, 45–46 (2d Cir. 1988); see also Samantar SOI, *supra* note 85, at 9.

[183] *Samantar II*, 699 F.3d at 767; see also *Magan*, 2011 WL 13160129, at *1.

[184] TVPA § 2(a).

[185] S. REP. NO. 102-249, at 7-8 (1991); H.R. REP. NO. 102-367, at 5 (1991).

[186] S. REP. NO. 102-249, at 8.

to make immunity determinations in this arena.[187] The executive branch's argument is that the TVPA does not expressly abrogate immunity, so it should be read consistently with background common-law principles of immunity.[188] But, unlike the question of whether there is an exception for jus cogens violations— where (under *Hoffman*) the executive branch's statement of customary international law is the last word on the matter in U.S. courts—the executive branch's view on this question of statutory interpretation is entitled to no more deference than its view on any other statute. Courts have to interpret the TVPA for themselves.

Although the issue is still percolating—and the Supreme Court has not yet weighed in—a consensus is emerging in the lower courts that the TVPA does not abrogate the common law, and that foreign officials can assert immunity in suits alleging TVPA violations. In *Matar v. Dichter*, the Second Circuit rejected plaintiffs' argument that "any immunity [the defendant] might enjoy is overridden by his alleged violations of the TVPA."[189] And district courts in that circuit have repeatedly applied that case to reject claims that the TVPA abrogates both status-based and conduct-based immunity.[190] Likewise, in *Doğan v. Barak*, the Ninth Circuit "h[e]ld that the TVPA does not abrogate foreign official immunity."[191] The district court in *Buratai* came to the same conclusion.[192] And the D.C. Circuit, in *Manoharan v. Rajapaksa*, held that the TVPA does not abrogate status-based immunity.[193]

Only one court has held that the TVPA impliedly abrogated common-law *conduct-based* immunity. In *Lewis v. Mutond*, the same decision that held that plaintiffs can plead around immunity by suing foreign officials in their personal capacities, two judges held in the alternative that common-law conduct-based immunity "must give way" to claims under the TVPA because the statute "imposes liability for actions that would render the foreign official eligible for immunity."[194] As noted earlier, a petition for a writ of certiorari is currently pending in that case.[195]

---

[187] See, e.g., U.S. Barak Brief, *supra* note 115, at 15–21; Barak SOI, *supra* note 87, at 10–12; U.S. Rajapaksa Brief, *supra* note 115, at 8–12; U.S. Dichter Brief, *supra* note 74, at 25–28; Dichter SOI, *supra* note 71, at 33–35.

[188] See, e.g., U.S. Barak Brief, *supra* note 115, at 15–21.

[189] 563 F.3d at 15.

[190] E.g., Burma Task Force v. Sein, No. 15 Civ. 7772, 2016 WL 1261139, at *3 (S.D.N.Y. Mar. 30, 2016); "American Justice Ctr." (AJC), Inc. v. Modi, No. 14 Civ. 7780, slip op. at 3 (S.D.N.Y. Jan. 14, 2015); Devi v. Rajapaksa, No. 11 Civ. 6634, 2012 WL 3866495, *3-4 (S.D.N.Y. Sept. 4, 2012), *aff'd*, No. 12-4081, 2013 WL 3855583 (2d Cir. 2013); Tawfik v. al-Sabah, No. 11 Civ. 6455, 2012 WL 3542209, at *3-4 (S.D.N.Y. Aug. 16, 2012).

[191] 932 F.3d at 896.

[192] *Buratai*, 318 F. Supp. 3d at 236–38.

[193] 711 F.3d 178, 180 (D.C. Cir. 2013).

[194] 918 F.3d at 150 (Randolph, J., concurring in the judgment); *id.* at 148 (Srinivasan, J., concurring).

[195] See *supra* note 156.

We believe that the *Lewis* decision is wrong and that the executive branch, the Second Circuit, and the Ninth Circuit are correct. Our reasoning largely tracks the Ninth Circuit's thorough and well-reasoned decision in *Doğan v. Barak.*[196] The plaintiffs in that case sued former Israeli Defense Minister Ehud Barak for his role in "plann[ing]," "direct[ing]," and "authoriz[ing]" an Israeli military action that resulted in their son's death.[197] In considering the plaintiffs' abrogation arguments, the court began with the presumption that "common-law principles of . . . immunity were incorporated into our judicial system and that they should not be abrogated absent clear legislative intent to do so."[198] Reasoning by analogy from 42 U.S.C. Section 1983—which creates a right of action against "[e]very person who, under color of [law]," deprives another of his or her legal rights—the court noted that "[e]ven with this all-encompassing language ('[e]very person'), the Supreme Court has held that, in passing Section 1983, Congress did not 'abolish wholesale all common-law immunities.'"[199] The court also took into account the "Pandora's box of liability" that a contrary holding would open:

> Under the Doğans' reading, the TVPA would allow foreign officials to be haled into U.S. courts by "any person" with a family member who had been killed abroad in the course of a military operation conducted by a foreign power. The Judiciary, as a result, would be faced with resolving any number of sensitive foreign policy questions which might arise in the context of such lawsuits. It simply cannot be that Congress intended the TVPA to open the door to that sort of litigation.[200]

We grant that reading the TVPA in harmony with common-law immunity will result in some foreign officials being immune to TVPA claims. But such a reading provides ample room for the TVPA's application. The statute would still apply where a foreign official abuses his or her apparent authority for personal gain.[201] And it will still apply with respect to acts performed "under color of law" but that are not properly attributable to a foreign state, or where there is no recognized government.[202] A foreign sovereign, moreover, may waive its official's

---

[196] 932 F.3d 888 (9th Cir. 2019) (Bea, J.).

[197] *Id.* at 890–91.

[198] *Id.* at 896 (quoting Filarsky v. Delia, 566 U.S. 377, 389 (2012)); see also United States v. Texas, 507 U.S. 529, 534 (1993); Pulliam v. Allen, 466 U.S. 522, 529 (1984); Norfolk Redevelopment & Hous. Auth. v. Chesapeake & Potomac Tel. Co. of Va., 464 U.S. 30, 35 (1983); Fairfax's Devisee v. Hunter's Lessee, 11 U.S. (7 Cranch) 603, 623 (1812).

[199] *Barak,* 932 F.3d at 895 (quoting Pierson v. Ray, 386 U.S. 547, 554 (1967)).

[200] *Id.*

[201] See, e.g., Kadic v. Karadžić, 70 F.3d 232, 250 (2d Cir. 1995).

[202] See, e.g., *Samantar II,* 699 F.3d at 777.

immunity or disavow the conduct.[203] Or the executive branch may issue a suggestion of nonimmunity.[204]

## III. Modern Executive-Branch Practice

Thus far, we have discussed the development of the doctrine of foreign-official immunity and explored some difficult and unresolved questions that have arisen after *Samantar*. But in this section we would like to briefly explain how suggestions of immunity work in practice, both from the perspective of the executive branch and from the perspective of a foreign sovereign requesting a suggestion of immunity. We hope that this section will shed some daylight on an otherwise nontransparent process, with a focus on the sometimes competing institutional interests at stake.

The Supreme Court's decision in *Samantar* vindicated the long-held view of the executive branch that the FSIA does not apply to foreign officials, and it reaffirmed the executive branch's central role in immunity determinations under the *Navemar/Peru/Hoffman* framework. But the experience of the past decade has shown that the State Department's victory was not without some costs. The decision has placed a significant burden on the Office of the Legal Adviser, which is now regularly asked to submit its views on the potential immunity of every foreign government official sued in the United States.[205] The State Department, likewise, is now regularly solicited both by foreign governments who want to protect their officials and by plaintiffs and human rights advocates who would like to recognize exceptions to official immunities. The State Department has not issued a new "Tate Letter" outlining the principles that will govern individual immunity decisions in the post-*Samantar* era—though, as discussed in the following, we think it should. In the meantime, we have made the following observations based on our experience within the Department and representing foreign officials.

The process for obtaining a suggestion of immunity tends to follow a common script. Generally, if one of its officials has been sued in U.S. court, a foreign sovereign initiates a request for a suggestion of immunity by submitting to the State Department a diplomatic note, which states the grounds for immunity and requests that the United States submit a suggestion of immunity on the official's behalf.[206] Within the State Department, requests for immunity are managed by

---

[203] See, e.g., Hilao v. Estate of Marcos, 25 F.3d 1467, 1472 (9th Cir. 1994); *In re* Doe, 860 F.2d 40, 45–46 (2d Cir. 1988).

[204] See, e.g., *Magan*, 2011 WL 13160129, at *1.

[205] See Bellinger, *supra* note 68, at 827–33.

[206] As a matter of best practice, the foreign sovereign should specifically state (if true) that its official acted entirely in an official capacity at all times during the events alleged in the lawsuit and that

the Office of the Legal Adviser, with input from the relevant policy bureaus. If there are factual or legal questions that bear on the question of immunity, the State Department may ask for more information or pose specific interrogatories. These can include questions about the allegations in the lawsuit, about the official's identity and position, or about the scope of the official's legal authority. The Department may also request documents or other evidence. The Office of the Legal Adviser typically invites counsel for the defendants and plaintiffs to meet to make their arguments for immunity or nonimmunity. The Legal Adviser will then make a determination regarding whether the foreign official is entitled to immunity. If the Legal Adviser makes a determination of immunity that determination is submitted to the secretary of state (or the secretary's delegee) for approval. If approved, the Legal Adviser drafts a letter to the Assistant Attorney General for the Civil Division of the Department of Justice, setting forth the basis for the State Department's immunity determination and formally requesting that the Department of Justice file a suggestion of immunity. The lawyers in the Federal Programs Branch of the Civil Division then draft and file a suggestion of immunity, usually attaching the letter from the Legal Adviser. At the appellate stage (or on writ of certiorari), the Office of the Legal Adviser is generally closely involved with appellate attorneys in the Civil Division or the Office of the Solicitor General in drafting the brief of the United States, and the Legal Adviser is often a signatory.

Just because a foreign government asks for a suggestion of immunity, however, does not guarantee that it will get one. The executive branch's general practice has been to assert status-based immunity on behalf of sitting heads of state and foreign ministers immediately upon receipt of a diplomatic note requesting immunity on behalf of such an official.[207] But that is not the usual practice for cases implicating conduct-based immunity. The executive branch generally will not file a suggestion of immunity or other statement of interest on behalf of lower-level foreign government officials (or former heads of state) in district

exercising jurisdiction would have the effect of enforcing a rule of law against the sovereign. The sovereign may also wish to formally ratify its official's conduct and adopt that conduct as its own.

[207] See, e.g., *supra* note 86. During the Obama administration, however, the Legal Adviser's office would sometimes delay issuing a determination of immunity until the foreign head of state or minister had been served. See John B. Bellinger III, *TVPA Lawsuit Against Sri Lanka President Dismissed, after Administration Submits Delayed Suggestion of Immunity*, LAWFARE (Mar. 1, 2012), https://www.lawfareblog.com/tvpa-lawsuit-against-sri-lanka-president-dismissed-after-administration-submits-delayed-suggestion; see also Koh, *supra* note 106, at 1158–59; cf. Lashkar-e-Taiba SOI, *supra* note 87, at 8 n.3 ("[C]ourts need not address the immunity question until they have first reached determinations on threshold issues, including whether a foreign official defendant has been properly served and whether the court has personal jurisdiction.").

court—even when requested by a foreign government—unless the United States' views are solicited by the court.[208]

The Department's divergent approach to status-based and conduct-based suggestions of immunity reflects institutional concerns of limited resources and political capital. As a practical matter, the Office of the Legal Adviser, which is a relatively small group of attorneys and staff, has only limited resources to review and respond to lawsuits against foreign officials. Status-based suggestions of immunity are relatively straightforward, as they only require the department to ascertain that the defendant is a sitting head of state or foreign minister of a recognized government to suggest immunity. Absolute immunity, moreover, is a bright-line rule, which makes it less likely that political considerations will bleed into status-based immunity determinations (especially considering the Department's very strong institutional interests in maintaining reciprocal immunities in foreign courts for the U.S. president and secretary of state). Cases implicating conduct-based immunity, by contrast, raise more-nuanced questions (e.g., whether the alleged conduct was undertaken on behalf of the state or within the scope of the official's authority) and can be much more legally and factually intensive.[209] Conduct-based immunity, moreover, can raise politically sensitive questions, for example in cases where the defendant is alleged to have *personally* committed torture or extrajudicial killing.[210]

Silence from the State Department, however, should not be taken as a signal that the Department has determined that an official is not entitled to immunity. The Department's view is that, in many cases, courts can apply common-law principles of conduct-based immunity for themselves, looking to suggestions of immunity filed in other cases, which the Department has stated set forth "principles . . . susceptible to general application by the judiciary without the need for recurring intervention by the Executive, particularly in the form of suggestions of immunity filed on a case-by-case basis."[211] That approach is consistent with *Hoffman*'s admonition that courts should not expand or contract immunity in ways that have not been endorsed by the executive branch.[212] In other cases, a suit against a foreign official may have to be dismissed for some other reason,

---

[208] This is the general practice, but it is not a fixed policy. Indeed, the executive branch has occasionally filed suggestions of immunity for lower-level foreign officials in trial-court proceedings, even in highly political cases. See *supra* note 87 and accompanying text.

[209] See, e.g., Statement of Interest at 7–10, Miango v. Democratic Republic of the Congo, No. 15-cv-1265 (May 1, 2019) (suggesting that the court "undertake limited factual finding" to determine whether foreign officials acted in their official capacities).

[210] See, e.g., Filártiga v. Peña-Irala, 630 F.2d 876, 878 (2d Cir. 1980) (alleging that police inspector general tortured and murdered plaintiffs' brother). Cases against foreign heads of state, by contrast, are often pleaded at a higher level of generality (often under a command theory of responsibility). See, e.g., *Manoharan*, 845 F. Supp. 2d at 261–62.

[211] U.S. Dichter Brief, *supra* note 74, at 21 n.*; see also Koh, *supra* note 106, at 159–61.

[212] 324 U.S. at 35–36.

such as lack of personal jurisdiction, failure to state a claim, failure to join the foreign state as a necessary party, or where the foreign state is the real party in interest.[213] In each of these instances, the court would not have to reach the immunity issue, which, from the Department's perspective, conserves resources.[214]

From the perspective of foreign sovereigns, of course, the Department's silence can create substantial burdens that are contrary to the purpose of immunity, which is to protect foreign sovereigns and their officials not merely from adverse judgments but from all the "attendant burdens of litigation."[215] But even if the State Department does not respond positively to a foreign government's request for a suggestion of immunity, the fact that the foreign government made the request is, in itself, potentially helpful in litigation as powerful (if not dispositive) evidence that the foreign sovereign has ratified its official's conduct and considers the official to have acted on its behalf.[216]

As noted, in most cases, the executive-branch process is initiated by the foreign government through diplomatic channels, but in others, a court will directly solicit the views of the State Department—despite *Samantar*'s instruction that courts should determine immunity for themselves when the executive branch has not weighed in.[217] In most cases, the Legal Adviser will respond substantively to such a request, but it is not uncommon for the Legal Adviser to decline the court's invitation, sometimes without explanation, sometimes providing reasons why an immunity determination could not be made.[218]

## IV.  Toward a Restatement of the Common Law of Foreign-Official Immunity

To conclude, we propose a series of principles, largely summarizing what we have written in the foregoing pages, which we believe should inform a future section on foreign-official immunity in the Fourth Restatement. We have not drafted these principles with the precision and nuance that we are sure the drafters of

---

[213]  See *Samantar*, 560 U.S. at 324–25.

[214]  As early as the 1960s, it was Department practice "generally [to] refuse[] to decide immunity claims while jurisdictional defenses remained to be decided by the court." 1977 DIGEST, *supra* note 48, at 1019 (citing cases); see also *supra* note 207.

[215]  *Giraldo*, 808 F. Supp. 2d at 250–251 (citation omitted).

[216]  See, e.g., *Buratai*, 318 F. Supp. 3d at 233; *Lewis*, 258 F. Supp. 3d at 174.

[217]  E.g., Letter from Hon. Amy Berman Jackson to Jennifer Gillian Newstead, Legal Adviser, U.S. Dep't of State, Miango v. Democratic Republic of Congo, No. 15-1265 (D.D.C. Oct. 25, 2019).

[218]  See, e.g., *Dichter*, 563 F.3d at 11 (describing substantive response); Statement of Interest, Doe v. Ali, No. 05 Civ. 701 (Sept. 19, 2013) (declining invitation); Statement of Interest, Doe v. Ali, No. 05 Civ. 701 (Apr. 24, 2014) (explaining that the government had been unable to discuss the immunity issue with the foreign government and therefore could not come to a conclusion about whether the foreign official was entitled to immunity).

that section will bring to their work, nor are these principles proposed as black-letter statements of the law. Instead, we hope that these final thoughts will inspire further discussion of this complex and evolving area of law.

Above all, we think that two fundamental principles should be central to the Fourth Restatement's section on foreign-official immunity. First, the executive branch's suggestions of immunity are conclusive and binding on the courts. And, second, where the executive branch has not submitted a suggestion of immunity, the district courts are bound to follow the principles of common-law immunity adopted by the executive branch in prior suggestions of immunity and other court filings. Accordingly, the "common law of official immunity" identified in *Samantar* is found, first and foremost, in the executive branch's suggestions of immunity, statements of interest, and amicus briefs, and, second, in the case law, to the extent that courts do not expand or contract immunity in ways that have not been accepted by the executive branch. It necessarily follows that only the executive branch can identity new exceptions to immunity based on its interpretation of customary international law.

As for the substantive law of foreign official immunity, the following statements have been accepted by the executive branch and, we believe, represent a general (if not entirely settled) consensus. First, sitting heads of state, heads of government, and foreign ministers enjoy absolute immunity from suit while in office. Second, other foreign officials and former officials enjoy immunity from suit based upon acts taken in an official capacity.[219] A foreign official's immunity is not a personal right but is for the benefit of the official's state, and can thus be asserted or waived by the foreign state. And, although the executive branch may recognize new exceptions to foreign-official immunity based on its interpretation of customary international law, it does not now recognize any exception for violations of jus cogens or for ultra vires acts. Finally, notwithstanding the Fourth Circuit's decision on remand in *Samantar* and the D.C. Circuit's recent decision in *Lewis v. Mutond*, we believe that the consensus view of the courts (and certainly of the executive branch) is that there is no jus cogens exception to foreign-official immunity and that the TVPA does not abrogate the common law, and we anticipate that the Supreme Court will ultimately affirm these positions.

---

[219] We note that the executive branch has not endorsed the Second Restatement's qualification that conduct-based immunity applies only where exercising jurisdiction over a foreign official would have the effect of enforcing a rule of law against the state. See *supra* notes 141–161 and accompanying text. We therefore think that this language, which seems to have no foundation in the case law (aside from the cases that have subsequently applied the Second Restatement), should not appear in the Fourth Restatement.

# PART VI

# THE RESTATEMENT'S FUTURES

# 21

# Constitutional Authority for the
# Transboundary Deployment
# of Armed Force

*Bakhtiyar Tuzmukhamedov*

The initial volume of the Fourth Restatement does not ponder general matters of separation of powers and specifically in the realm of foreign affairs and national security. Apparently, this discussion is left to subsequent installments.[1] The Third Restatement briefly addressed the separation of powers in foreign relations, in particular referring to the "continuing controversy as to whether the President can deploy the forces of the United States on his own authority for foreign policy purposes *short of war*, and, if so, whether that authority is subject to Congressional control [ . . . ] Nor is it agreed to what extent Congress can control decisions of the President as Commander in Chief in the conduct of wars authorized by Congress."[2] The United States is not unique in that respect, and similar controversies, whether in law or in practice, may and do occur in other jurisdictions.

While the Restatement is, by definition, focused on the U.S. foreign relations law, as are most chapters in this collection, this author was asked to offer a comparative perspective, primarily, as his citizenship and most affiliations would suggest, drawing from experiences of the Russian Federation and, to the extent applicable, its predecessor, the Soviet Union and its heirs. This contribution will discuss the formal constitutional framework of authorization of foreign deployments of uniformed personnel, both formed units and individual service members. As appropriate, overview of that experience will be supplemented with examples from other jurisdictions.[3]

---

[1] As the Director of the American Law Institute indicated in the Foreword, "my hope is that, in the not-too-distant future, we will undertake a new project designed to complete the Restatement Fourth." FOURTH RESTATEMENT intro. at xvii.

[2] THIRD RESTATEMENT § 1(3) at 9–10 (emphasis added).

[3] The author wishes to acknowledge collegial tips and leads, which shall be referenced further on, that he received from Mr. Nobuo Hayashi, of Faculty, the United Nations Interregional Crime and Justice Research Institute; Dr. Vladimir Vardanyan, Chair, Standing Committee on State and Legal Affairs of the National Assembly of Armenia; and Prof. Wenqi Zhu, Professor of International Law, Renmin University of China.

Bakhtiyar Tuzmukhamedov, *Constitutional Authority for the Transboundary Deployment of Armed Force* In: *The Restatement and Beyond.* Edited by: Paul B. Stephan and Sarah H. Cleveland, Oxford University Press (2020).
© Oxford University Press. DOI: 10.1093/oso/9780197533154.003.0022

# I. War vs. "Short of War"

Apparently, reference to "war" in the Third Restatement implies armed hostilities accompanied by a declaration of war envisaged by Section 8 (Subsection 11) of Article I of the Constitution of the United States.[4] Considering that the three most recent declarations of war (of eleven in total[5]) on three junior members of the Axis by the act of Congress date back to 1942,[6] it would appear that most armed conflicts involving the United States formally did not amount to war, their magnitude, intensity, duration, and human losses notwithstanding. Neither did the Algerian War of Independence,[7] in which France fought from 1954 to 1962, nor an almost decade-long, from December 1979 until February 1989, involvement of the Soviet Union in civil war in Afghanistan.[8]

A situation "short of war" implies engagement of armed forces and attainment of level of violence, exceeding, "because of its scale and effects," the level of "a mere frontier incident."[9] Such "hostile resort to armed force involving two or more States" amounts to an armed conflict, that is, an international armed conflict.[10] As to a non-international armed conflict, international authority defines it

---

[4] "The Congress shall have Power . . . to declare War . . ."

[5] Official Declarations of War by Congress, available at https://www.senate.gov/pagelayout/history/h_multi_sections_and_teasers/WarDeclarationsbyCongress.htm.

[6] Declarations of War with Bulgaria, Hungary, and Rumania, June 4 1942, available at https://www.senate.gov/artandhistory/history/resources/pdf/HJRES319_WWII_Bulgaria.pdf; https://www.senate.gov/artandhistory/history/resources/pdf/HJRES320_WWII_Hungary.pdf; https://www.senate.gov/artandhistory/history/resources/pdf/HJRES321_WWII_Rumania.pdf.

[7] "The brutal Algerian War of Independence saw atrocities committed on both sides with Algerian historians putting the death toll at 1.5 million Algerian victims while French historians say around 400,000 people from both sides were killed." France Remembers the Algerian War, 50 Years On, available at https://www.france24.com/en/20120316-commemorations-mark-end-algerian-war-independence-france-evian-accords.

[8] The Russian Federal News Agency TASS puts casualties among Soviet uniformed personnel at 15,051. See Istoriya uchastiya SSSR v afganskom konflikte (History of the participation of the USSR in the Afghan conflict), available at https://tass.ru/info/6116588. Human losses among fighters and Afghan civilians cannot be reliably verified. According to *Encyclopaedia Britannica*, "Afghanistan has never conducted a full census, and it is thus difficult to gauge the number of casualties suffered in the country since the outbreak of fighting. The best estimates available indicate that some 1.5 million Afghanis were killed before 1992—although the number killed during combat and the number killed as an indirect result of the conflict remain unclear." Afghan War, available at https://www.britannica.com/event/Afghan-War. While the Soviet forces completed withdrawal from Afghanistan in February 1989, President Najibullah, initially supported by the Soviet Union, stayed in power until his overthrow and execution by the Taliban in April 1992.

[9] Military and Paramilitary Activities in and Against Nicaragua (Nicar. v. U.S.), Merits, 1986 I.C.J. Rep. 14, 98, ¶ 195 (June 27).

[10] INT'L COMM. OF THE RED CROSS, COMMENTARY ON THE FIRST GENEVA CONVENTION: CONVENTION (I) FOR THE AMELIORATION OF THE CONDITION OF THE WOUNDED AND SICK IN ARMED FORCES IN THE FIELD ¶ 219 (2d ed. 2016). An earlier source stated that "any difference arising between two States and leading to the intervention of armed forces is an armed conflict within the meaning of Article 2, even if one of the Parties denies the existence of a state of war. It makes no difference how long the conflict lasts, or how much slaughter takes place." Int'l Comm. of the Red Cross, Commentary, IV Geneva Convention Relative to the Protection of Civilian Persons in Time of War 20 (Jean S. Pictet ed., 1958).

as "protracted armed conflict between governmental authorities and organized armed groups or between such groups," with a caveat that such armed conflict takes place "in the territory of a State."[11]

While the terms "war" and "armed conflict" might seem synonymous, they are distinct in a legal sense. Common Article 2 of the Geneva Conventions states that they "shall apply to all cases of declared war or of any other armed conflict which may arise between two or more of the High Contracting Parties."[12] An earlier authority considered formal declaration of war a *conditio sine qua non* for "opening of hostilities."[13]

War is a form of relationship between states, a supreme type of an armed conflict, a violent confrontation engaging sovereigns or their coalitions. War should be declared—even though such a declaration may not be immediately followed by resort to armed violence between a state that declares war and those against which the declaration is made—"even if the state of war is not recognized by one of them."[14] If laws of a state do not provide for a declaration of war, then a state of war and martial law may be proclaimed, providing for extraordinary means of exercising the government's powers, including derogation from fundamental human rights and freedoms. In international affairs of opposing states, war is accompanied by suspension of diplomatic and consular relations, which may even be broken off entirely, or termination or restriction of implementation of international treaties, and may lead to other consequences for those states and their citizens and legal entities.

Armed conflict is a form of relationship between a broader range of subjects than in a formal war.[15] Parties to an international armed conflict could be sovereign states or, in the case of a non-international armed conflict, government forces and "dissident armed forces or other organized armed groups"[16] or, as stated earlier, such groups fighting each other. A non-international armed

[11] Rome Statute of the International Criminal Court, art. 8(2)(f), 2187 U.N.T.S. 98.

[12] Geneva Convention (I) for the amelioration of the condition of the wounded and sick in armed forces in the field, art. 2 (1), 75 U.N.T.S. 32.

[13] According to 1907 Convention on the Opening of Hostilities, "the Contracting Powers recognize that hostilities between themselves must not commence without previous and explicit warning, in the form either of a reasoned declaration of war or of an ultimatum with conditional declaration of war." The Hague Convention (III) Relative to the Opening of Hostilities of 1907, The Hague, Oct. 17, 1907, art. 1.

[14] Geneva Convention (I), art. 2(1).

[15] "The determination of the existence of an armed conflict within the meaning of Article 2(1) [of Geneva Convention (I)] must be based solely on the prevailing facts demonstrating the *de facto* existence of hostilities between the belligerents, even without a declaration of war." INTERNATIONAL COMMITTEE OF THE RED CROSS, COMMENTARY ON THE FIRST GENEVA CONVENTION: CONVENTION (I) FOR THE AMELIORATION OF THE CONDITION OF THE WOUNDED AND SICK IN ARMED FORCES IN THE FIELD § 211 (2016).

[16] Protocol Additional to the Geneva Conventions of 12 August 1949 and relating to the protection of victims of non-international armed conflicts (Protocol II), art. 1, 1125 U.N.T.S. 611.

conflict can spill over international boundaries or, while being confined to a territory of a single state, may become internationalized through involvement of foreign actors, both state, whether or not invited by the territorial sovereign, and nonstate.[17] Whether and when a non-international armed conflict may morph into an international armed conflict should be determined by review of factual circumstances.

Likewise, the determination of a type of conflict in which a state or a coalition of states engage a transnational nonstate entity pursuing terrorist goals should be based on facts. A view expressed by plurality of the Supreme Court of the United States in *Hamdan v. Rumsfeld* is not without merit:

> The term "conflict not of an international character" is used here in contradistinction to a conflict between nations. . . . [It] is distinguishable from the [international armed] conflict . . . chiefly because it does not involve a clash between nations.[18]

A situation where a coalition force under the U.N. mandate or that of a duly authorized "Chapter VIII" regional arrangement is introduced into the territory of a state to disengage warring parties and to freeze an armed conflict until political settlement could be reached constitutes yet another type of external interference in a non-international armed conflict.[19] However, in such a situation an international contingent does not become a party to an armed conflict and enjoys privileges and protection afforded by international law to persons and entities not participating in hostilities. The situation changes if the international coalition force receives a robust mandate, as did the U.N. Multidimensional Integrated Stabilization Mission in Mali (MINUSMA), which was authorized by the U.N. Security Council "to use all necessary means,"[20] and in particular, "in support of the transitional authorities of Mali, to stabilize the key population centres, especially in the north of Mali and, in this context, to deter threats and take active steps to prevent the return of armed elements to those areas."[21] In such circumstances, the international mission, siding with or using armed force in support of the official government in its confrontation with organized armed opposition, becomes a party to an armed conflict.

---

[17] See KUBO MACAK, INTERNATIONALIZED ARMED CONFLICTS IN INTERNATIONAL LAW (2018).

[18] Hamdan v. Rumsfeld, 548 U.S. 557, 630 (2006).

[19] Nothing in the present Charter precludes the existence of regional arrangements or agencies for dealing with such matters relating to the maintenance of international peace and security as are appropriate for regional action provided that such arrangements or agencies and their activities are consistent with the Purposes and Principles of the United Nations. U.N. Charter, art. 52(1).

[20] S/RES/2100, para. 17 (2013).

[21] *Id.*, para. 16(a)(i).

## II.  Declaration of War vs. Proclamation of State of War
## in Modern Constitutions

Among the four permanent members of the U.N. Security Council that have
written constitutions, aside from the United States, it is the Constitution of the
French Republic which explicitly provides for the declaration of war: "A declaration of war shall be authorized by Parliament."[22] What used to be a single
phrase in Article 35 has been amended by the Constitutional Law in 2008 to
include provisions which would be activated to authorize foreign deployments
of French forces.[23] In the absence of a written Constitution, it may be less clear
whether the declaration of war still exists as a constitutional option in the
United Kingdom. On the one hand, "under the Royal prerogative powers, the
Government can declare war,"[24] such declaration being made "in the Monarch's
name but by the Prime Minister, acting under the prerogative."[25] Yet on the other
hand, "the United Kingdom has made no declaration of war since that against
Siam (modern Thailand) in 1942, and it is unlikely that there will ever be another."[26] Presumably, under the current interpretation of the Constitution there
is no place for the declaration of war.

Under the Constitution of the People's Republic of China, the power to declare a state of war is shared by the National People's Congress, its Standing
Committee (if the Congress is not in session), and the president.[27] The National
People's Congress, which is the highest representative and legislative authority,
under Article 62(14) enjoys the power "to decide on questions of war and peace."
When the Congress is not in session, the Standing Committee, acting in accordance with Article 67(18), will decide "on the proclamation of a state of war in the
event of an armed attack on the country or in fulfilment of international treaty
obligations concerning common defense against aggression." Acting in pursuance of the decision of either the Congress or the Committee, the president will
proclaim a state of war (Article 80). However, the Constitution does not prescribe
procedures for authorization of foreign deployments of units of the People's

---

[22] The English version of the Constitution is available on the website of the Constitutional Council
at https://www.conseil-constitutionnel.fr/sites/default/files/as/root/bank_mm/anglais/constiution_
anglais_oct2009.pdf.

[23] Loi constitutionnelle no 2008-724 du 23 juillet 2008 de modernisation des institutions de la V$^e$
République (1), JOURNAL OFFICIEL DE LA RÉPUBLIQUE FRANÇAISE, 24 juillet 2008, Texte 2 sur 149,
available at https://www.legifrance.gouv.fr/jo_pdf.do?numJO=0&dateJO=20080724&numTexte=2
&pageDebut=11890&pageFin=11895.

[24] Waging war: Parliament's role and responsibility, House of Lords Select Committee on the
Constitution 15th Report of Session 5 (2005–06).

[25] Id. at 7.

[26] Id.

[27] An English version of the Constitution is available on the website of the National People's
Congress at http://www.npc.gov.cn.

Liberation Army as part of international missions and to other situations "short of war." It may be assumed that decisions to that effect are made by the Central Military Commission, which is established under Section 4 of the Constitution and, according to Article 93, "directs the armed forces of the country." However, as some observers opine, "the precise decision-making process remains unclear."[28] In reality, since the Central Military Commission is chaired by the president, who is also the secretary-general of the omnipotent Central Committee of the Communist Party of China, it is safe to assume that the decision-making process is concentrated within the Communist Party institutions and the Central Committee's own Military Council.[29]

Similar to the Constitution of China, the Constitution of the Russian Federation makes no reference to a declaration of war.[30] Rather, it authorizes the president to introduce martial law "in the event of aggression against the Russian Federation or of a direct threat of aggression" (Article 87(2)) by a decree that shall be approved by the Council of the Federation (Article 102(1)(b)), a chamber of the bicameral parliament, the Federal Assembly. In an apparent reference to foreign deployments, including situations "short of war," the same chamber decides "on the possibility of using the Armed Forces of the Russian Federation outside the territory of the Russian Federation" (Article 102(1)(d)).

Several other constitutions of the post–World War II era provide for a formal declaration of war, one example being the 1978 Constitution of Spain. Section 163(3) makes it "incumbent upon the King, following authorization by the Cortes Generales, to declare war and to make peace."[31] Or consider the Constitution of Armenia, which empowers with the authority of "declaring war" either the National Assembly, acting on proposal made by the government (Article 118(1)), or the government (the executive branch), if the National Assembly cannot convene (Article 118(2)).[32] Yet others turn to the concept of "declaration of state of war," as does the Constitution of Turkey in Article 92: "The power to authorize the declaration of a state of war . . . is vested in the Grand National Assembly of

---

[28] Yasuhiro Matsuda, China's UN Peacekeeping Operations Policy: Analysis of the Factors behind the Policy Shift toward Active Engagement, International Circumstances in the Asia-Pacific Series (China), Japan Digital Library (Mar. 2016), at 58, http://www2.jiia.or.jp/en/digital_library/china.php.

[29] The author appreciates clarifications he received from Professor Wenqi Zhu.

[30] The English version of the Constitution is available on the website of the Constitutional Court of the Russian Federation at http://www.ksrf.ru/en/INFO/LEGALBASES/CONSTITUTIONRF/Pages/default.aspx.

[31] The English version of the Constitution is available on the website of Congress of Deputies, a chamber of the bicameral parliament, at http://www.congreso.es/portal/page/portal/Congreso/Congreso/Hist_Normas/Norm/const_espa_texto_ingles_0.pdf.

[32] An English version of the Constitution is available on the website of the National Assembly of the Republic of Armenia at http://www.parliament.am/legislation.php?sel=show&ID=5805&lang=eng.

Turkey."[33] Such declarations may be triggered by an armed attack or, as some constitutions state, "an armed aggression," even though this author strongly doubts the propriety of such use of the term "aggression."[34]

And, of course, there is the textbook example of Article 9 of the Constitution of Japan, which states:

> the Japanese people forever renounce war as a sovereign right of the nation and the threat or use of force as means of settling international disputes . . . The right of belligerency of the state will not be recognized.[35]

However, notwithstanding that and the next paragraph of Article 9, which pledges that "land, sea, and air forces, as well as other war potential, will never be maintained,"[36] Japan boasts an impressive military organization under the guise of "Self-Defense Forces" (SDF) with considerable assets and power projection capability.[37] The legal grounds for overseas deployments of the SDF may be found in the Self-Defense Forces Act of 1954, which, as amended, authorizes SDF missions to engage in activities that contribute to the maintenance of international peace and security through U.N.-led international peace efforts and other international cooperation.[38] Interaction with the U.N. missions is further elaborated in the Act on Cooperation with United Nations Peacekeeping Operations and Other Operations of 1992,[39] while broader international military activities are regulated be a recent Act Concerning Cooperation and Support Activities to Armed Forces of Foreign Countries, in Situations where the International Community Is Collectively Addressing for International Peace and Security of 2016.[40]

[33] An English version of the Constitution is available on the website of the Grand National Assembly of Turkey at https://global.tbmm.gov.tr/docs/constitution_en.pdf.

[34] See Bakhtiyar Tuzmukhamedov, *Russian Forces in the Former USSR and Beyond*, in THE HANDBOOK OF THE LAW OF VISITING FORCES 692–94 (2d ed. Dieter Fleck ed., 2018) (discussing said improper usage of the term "aggression").

[35] An English version of the Constitution is available on the website of the Prime Minister and Cabinet at https://japan.kantei.go.jp/constitution_and_government_of_japan/constitution_e.html.

[36] For a discussion of interpretations of Article 9, including proposals for its amendment, see Japan: Interpretations of Article 9 of the Constitution, The Law Library of Congress, Global Legal Research Center, September 2015.

[37] For further discussion, see a Foreign Policy comment on the deployment of Ground SDF officers to Multinational Force & Observers (MFO) in Sharm el-Sheikh, available at https://foreignpolicy.com/2019/05/03/with-little-fanfare-japan-just-changed-the-way-it-uses-its-military/#.

[38] The authoritative Japanese Law Translation service maintained by the Ministry of Justice of Japan (http://www.japaneselawtranslation.go.jp/) does not offer the English translation of the SDF Act. The author is indebted to Mr. Nobuo Hayashi for guidance with respect to this and other pieces of Japanese legislation.

[39] An English version of the act is available from the Japanese Law Translation Service at http://www.japaneselawtranslation.go.jp/law/detail/?ft=1&re=2&dn=1&x=30&y=14&co=01&ia=03&ky=united+nations&page=16.

[40] The act, also referred to as International Peace Support Act, envisages three types of activities other than those covered by the U.N. Peacekeeping Operations and Other Operations Act. These

## III. Evolution of Constitutional Authority to Dispose of the Military Arm of Government from the USSR to the Nascent Russian Federation

Russia deploys forces abroad, as do other major powers, albeit in less numbers and to fewer locations then do several other states.[41] As multiple other states, Russia has developed a system of participation of several branches of government in decisions on transboundary deployments. And, as in several other states, the judicial branch has made its own contribution to development of the system by way of constitutional review and interpretation.

This author discussed elsewhere the evolution of constitutional national security powers from the early Soviet constitutions to the latest and profoundly amended version of the Constitution of the USSR and on to the Constitution of the Russian Federation of 1978, which in 1993 was superseded by the current Constitution.[42] The power of the government to dispose of its military forces, as defined by the early Soviet Constitutions of 1918, 1924, and 1936, as well as the original version of the Constitution of the USSR of 1977, did not include specific authority to use the armed forces beyond national borders. A latest version of the Constitution of 1936 before it was superseded by the Constitution of 1977, as well as the latter, authorized the Presidium of the Supreme Soviet—a standing body of the legislature acting when the Supreme Soviet was not in session—to declare a state of war "in case of a military attack against the USSR or the need to fulfill international treaty obligations on mutual defense against aggression" (respectively, Article 49(m) and Article 121(17)).[43] The powers of the executive

---

three types of activities, to be taken where a situation threatening international peace and security requires concerted action by the international community in conformity with the purposes of the U.N. Charter and where Japan, as a member of the international community, needs to contribute proactively to such action, are as follows: first, provision of material and facility to the armed forces of other states; second, search and rescue of foreign combat personnel in distress; and third, visitation and inspection of marine vessels pursuant to a separate piece of legislation. The International Peace Support Act specifically designates the SDF as the entity whose material and function are to be provided for the first type, and the SDF as the entity that is to conduct search-and-rescue operations for the second type (source: author's written briefing with Mr. Nobuo Hayashi, on file with the author). See also Defense of Japan 2019, Pt. II, Ch. 5, Development of Legislation for Peace and Security and the SDF Activities since Legislation's Enforcement, https://www.mod.go.jp/e/publ/w_paper/pdf/2019/DOJ2019_Full.pdf.

[41] It does not take to be a major power to deploy considerable military assets to foreign lands. Consider Ethiopia, which ranks first among states contributing troops to U.N. peace operations, with 6,797 military personnel deployed to U.N. missions, https://peacekeeping.un.org/en/troop-and-police-contributors, which amounts to 4.9 percent of its armed forces, estimated at 138,000 (https://data.worldbank.org/indicator/MS.MIL.TOTL.P1).

[42] Tuzmukhamedov, *supra* note 34, at 686–89.

[43] *Konstitutziya Obshchenarodnogo Gosudarstva* [The Constitution of the All-Peoples State, hereinafter KOG]. Hereinafter, Cyrillic-lettered paragraphs of legislative acts will be replaced by corresponding Latin letters in alphabetical order. For example, a paragraph identified as "b" in the original

branch, that is, the Council of Ministers, under both Constitutions were formally limited to supervision of the development of the armed forces and the setting of annual draft quotas (respectively, Article 68(e) and Article 131(5)).

In reality, the decision-making took place in neither the executive nor the legislative branch, but in the highest echelons of the Communist Party of the Soviet Union (CPSU), its Central Committee, and the ruling body thereof, the Politburo. Any significant military and foreign-policy action required a decision of the Politburo. The only applicable constitutional provision giving grounds for that real "supremacy" appeared in Article 6 of the Constitution of 1977, which named the CPSU "the guiding and leading force of Soviet society, the nucleus of its political system, its government and public organizations." Early deployments to international missions, including the first ever dispatch of a group of Soviet officers to the U.N. Truce Supervision Organization (UNTSO) in 1973, suggest that decisions had been taken at the level of affected departments of the government (Ministry of Foreign Affairs and Ministry of Defense, including the General Staff of the Armed Forces) and the leadership superstructure of the Central Committee of the Communist Party—the Politburo, of which the heads of both ministries were members.[44]

The legislative transformation and preparation for the fundamental constitutional reform, launched in the 1980s and largely associated with the name of Mikhail Gorbachev, affected that area as well. The reinstatement of the national representative body, the Congress of People's Deputies, and the introduction of the office of the President of the USSR resulted in redistribution of authority among branches of the government, primarily the president and the Supreme Soviet, as well as in curtailing of authority of the Communist Party. Much of this was achieved by a single amendment to the Constitution, adopted by Law No. 1360-I of March 14, 1990.[45] Article 113(14), a new and noteworthy provision introduced by that amendment, authorized the Supreme Soviet "to decide on the use of contingents of the armed forces of the USSR to fulfill international treaty obligations on the maintenance of peace and security." On its face, it provided, first, that the Communist Party apparatus (Politburo, the Central Committee,

---

text will become paragraph "c," or as in this case, paragraph "H" in the Russian text will be identified as "m."

[44] The United Nations Truce Supervision Organization, the first ever U.N. peacekeeping operation, was established in 1948 to monitor cessation of hostile activities in the Middle East. See U.N. Security Council Resolution S/48 (1948). On Soviet decision-making processes regarding such missions, see Bakhtiyar Tuzmukhamedov, *Russian Federation: The Pendulum of Powers and Accountability*, in DEMOCRATIC ACCOUNTABILITY AND THE USE OF FORCE IN INTERNATIONAL LAW 258–60 (Charlotte Ku & Harold K. Jacobson eds., 2003).

[45] *Vedomosti S"yezda Narodnikh Deputatov i Verkhovnogo Soveta SSSR* [The Bulletin of the Congress of People's Deputies and the Supreme Soviet of the USSR], 1990, No. 12, Item 189.

and its Secretariat) was to be excluded from the decision-making process regarding foreign deployments of Soviet military personnel. Second, although the president was made the Supreme Commander-in-Chief of the Armed Forces of the USSR, the Supreme Soviet, that is the parliament, was made the ultimate authority with regard to a deployment of forces, other than war fought by the nation to repel an armed attack. In the latter case, the power to use military force was vested in the president.

The new distribution of authority was largely influenced by the unpopular involvement in Afghanistan, which incurred heavy human and economic losses, and by revelations of how secret decisions to intervene had been taken. The new provision, however, never had a chance to be activated. There were no new deployments in the brief period during which it was part of the law. The reforms initiated in the mid-1980s became history with the demise of the Soviet Union in December 1991. Subsequent convoluted legislative reform was exacerbated by the constitutional crisis which pitched the president and parliament against each other. This confrontation between branches of power was reflected in the final version of the Russian Constitution, originally adopted in 1978 as a Constitution of the Russian Soviet Socialist Federal Republic, as were constitutions of fourteen other entities comprising the USSR. This instrument was a modified and adapted version of the 1977 Constitution of the Union.

The 1978 Constitution of the Russian Federation did not contain any provision similar to Article 113(14) of the Soviet Constitution. Until September 1992 there was no legislation to cover the gap. Before adoption of a regulatory act, Russia had to meet the challenge of authorizing the deployment of its forces abroad under international auspices. On March 6, 1992, the Supreme Soviet of the Russian Federation decided on the placing of a formed combat unit under the authority of the U.N. Protection Force (UNPROFOR) in the former Yugoslavia. In the absence of any established and formalized procedure, the president and the Supreme Soviet had to engage in legislative improvisation. The president requested that the Supreme Soviet consent to deployment of one infantry battalion. By Resolution No. 2462-I of March 6, 1992,[46] the parliament decided to "give consent to detail the requested military contingent." It referred to the request of the president, Russian obligations under the U.N. Charter, the resolution of the U.N. Security Council, an appeal from the U.N. Secretary-General, and its own desire "to contribute by practical steps to the early restoration of peace and stability in Yugoslavia." By the same resolution, the Supreme Soviet tasked the Council of Ministers with dealing with all issues related to the deployment of

---

[46] *Vedomosti S"yezda Narodnikh Deputatov i Verkhovnogo Soveta Rossiyskoy Federatsii* [The Bulletin of the Congress of People's Deputies and the Supreme Soviet of the Russian Federation], 1992, No. 12, Item 619.

the unit. Four months later, responding to a request by the president to reinforce the unit, which in turn had been prompted by an appeal by the U.N. Secretary-General and a U.N. Security Council resolution, the Supreme Soviet acted again. It consented to an additional deployment of four hundred service personnel "to participate in the UN operation to provide the necessary conditions for unhampered delivery of humanitarian aid to Bosnia and Herzegovina."[47]

Concurrently the parliament was deliberating the draft Law on Defense, which was finally enacted on September 24, 1992, as Law No. 3531-I. It had a provision that resembled Article 113(14) of the Soviet Constitution, but the broader Russian version authorized the Supreme Soviet "to decide on the use of the Armed Forces of the Russian Federation beyond the boundaries of the Russian Federation according to its international obligations."[48] Article 113(14), in contrast, had restricted the USSR's Supreme Soviet to authorizing instances when military units were to be used "to fulfill international treaty obligations regarding the maintenance of peace and security."

The brief period of immediate post-Soviet legislative reforms came to a violent end as tensions growing between the president and parliament reached a violent climax. The president suspended the representative bodies by his Decree No. 1400 of September 21, 1993, and used the military and security forces and their firepower to enforce that suspension.[49] However, even during those several months, the competing branches of government had been able to develop and test certain decision-making methods that would be embodied in legislative acts soon to be adopted.

## IV. Current Regulation in the Space of the Former USSR

The concentration of considerable authority within a single personified body of power, be that the czar, the General Secretary of the Central Committee of the Communist Party, or the president, has never been unusual for, respectively, the Russian Empire, the USSR, or the post-Soviet entities. The constitutions of most former Soviet republics provide for a strong presidency. And, as in Russia, several of them ensure that presidents enjoy the broadest prerogatives in general, and in national security matters in particular.

---

[47] Resolution No. 3336-I of July 17, 1992, *Vedomosti S"yezda Narodnikh Deputatov i Verkhovnogo Soveta Rossiyskoy Federatsii*, 1992, No. 12, Item 1839.

[48] *Vedomosti S"yezda Narodnikh Deputatov i Verkhovnogo Soveta Rossiyskoy Federatsii*, 1992, No. 42, Item 2331.

[49] *Sobraniye Aktov Preszidenta i Pravitelstva Rossiyskoy Federatsii* [Collection of the Acts of the President and the Government of the Russian Federation], 1993, No. 39, Item 3597.

In Azerbaijan, the Constitution makes the president the Supreme Commander-in-Chief of the Armed Forces (Article 9(III)).[50] Unlike his Russian counterpart, the president of Azerbaijan submits to the *Milli Majlis* (Parliament) the state's military doctrine (Article 109(11)), which the latter then approves (Article 95(7)). But appointments of senior military officers rest within the Office of the President (Article 109(12)), as they do in Russia. Unlike in Russia, the Constitution of Azerbaijan recognizes the power to declare war, which is proclaimed by the president with the consent of the *Milli Majlis* (Articles 95(17) and 109(30)).

In Belarus, the Constitution vests in the president the power, in his capacity as Commander-in-Chief of the Armed Forces, to unilaterally appoint and relieve senior military commanders (Article 84(28)).[51] Similar to the Russian Constitution, the Constitution of Belarus authorizes the president to introduce martial law "in the event of a military threat or attack," which act should then be approved by the Council of the Republic (Article 84(29)).[52] However, it is the House of Representatives that passes a law on declaration of war (Article 97(2)), subject to approval by the Council of the Republic.

A notable feature of several post-Soviet constitutions are provisions for deployments of armed forces outside of national territory. Most of those cite international obligations as primary grounds for sending service personnel to foreign missions, whether under international auspices or in accordance with mutual defense and security arrangements.

In Kazakhstan, the joint session of Parliament makes a decision "to use the Armed Forces of the Republic pursuant to the proposal of the President of the Republic to fulfil international obligations for the maintenance of peace and security" (Article 53(5) of the Constitution),[53] that authority being further specified in the Law on Defense and the Armed Forces of the Republic of Kazakhstan (Article 32 "International Cooperation of the Republic of Kazakhstan in Defense Matters").[54]

The Constitution of Kyrgyzstan does not indicate the branch of government which initiates consideration of foreign military deployment, it merely states that the *Jogorku Kenesh*—the Parliament, shall "decide on the possibility of using

---

[50] An English version of the Constitution is available on the website of the President of the Republic of Azerbaijan at https://en.president.az/azerbaijan/constitution.

[51] An English version is available on the official National Legal Internet Portal of the Republic of Belarus at http://law.by/document/?guid=3871&p0=V19402875e.

[52] The Council of the Republic and the House of Representatives make up the National Assembly, the Parliament of Belarus.

[53] An English version is available on the website of the President of the Republic of Kazakhstan at http://www.akorda.kz/en/official_documents/constitution.

[54] Kazakh and Russian versions are available on the website of the Ministry of Defense of the Republic of Kazakhstan at https://www.mod.gov.kz/rus/dokumenty/zakony/ob_oborone_vooruzhennyh_silax/?cid=0&rid=1938.

the Armed Forces of the Kyrgyz Republic beyond its borders if need arises to fulfill international treaty obligations on the maintenance of peace and security" (Article 74(5.3)).[55] The gap is filled by the Law on Defense and Armed Forces of the Republic of Kyrgyzstan, which, in Article 11(19) authorizes the president in his capacity as commander-in-chief to introduce the respective motion in Parliament.[56]

The Constitution of Georgia—or maybe only the English translation that is available from Parliament—uses rather stringent language when it states that "the use of the armed forces for the honoring international obligations shall be impermissible without the consent of the Parliament of Georgia" (Article 100(1)).[57]

The Constitution of Ukraine does not provide for any specific authority of the president, other than making him the Commander-in-Chief of the Armed Forces (Article 106(17)),[58] whereas it is the Verkhovna Rada (the Parliament) that approves "decisions on providing military assistance to other states, on sending units of the Armed Forces of Ukraine to a foreign state" (Article 85(23)). Whether those are "decisions" of and by parliament, or made by another entity and then submitted for approval, is not clear from the text. The Constitution only states that "the procedure for deploying units of the Armed Forces of Ukraine to other states" shall be "established exclusively by the law of Ukraine" (Article 92(2.2)), that law having been adopted by the Verkhovna Rada. However, the tools and resources available to this author could only unearth the Law on the Participation of Ukraine in International Operations for the Maintenance of Peace and Security,[59] which details the interaction between branches of government in developing the aforementioned "decision" on foreign military deployments. The legal grounds for each deployment shall be a law passed by the Verkhovna Rada (Article 4), which codifies a decision of the president, based on advice given by the Ministry of Foreign Affairs in coordination with the Ministry of Defense and approved by the National Security and Defense Council (Article 3)—a

---

[55] Kyrgyz and Russian versions are available on the website of Jogorku Kenesh at http://www.kenesh.kg/ru/article/show/31/konstitutsiya-kirgizskoy-respubliki.

[56] Kyrgyz and Russian versions are available on the website of the Ministry of Justice of the Republic of Kyrgyzstan at http://cbd.minjust.gov.kg/act/view/ru-ru/202668.

[57] An English version is available on the website of the Parliament of Georgia at http://www.parliament.ge/files/68_1944_951190_CONSTIT_27_12.06.pdf.

[58] An English version is available on the website of the Constitutional Court of Ukraine at http://www.ccu.gov.ua/en/kategoriya/legal-documents.

[59] The official text of the Law on Participation of Ukraine in International Operations for the Maintenance of Peace and Security, as amended, is available on the website of the Verkhovna Rada only in Ukrainian at https://zakon.rada.gov.ua/laws/show/613-xiv. A Russian version can be retrieved, from a service with credentials that could not be verified by this author, at https://kodeksy.com.ua/ka/ob_uchastii_ukrainy_v_mezhdunarodnyh_operatsiyah_po_podderzhaniyu_mira_i_bezopasnosti/download.htm.

consultative body similar to, and presumably modeled on, the National Security Council that advises the president of the United States.

The Constitution of Armenia, following profound amendments adopted in the wake of the Constitutional Referendum of December 6, 2015, which transformed the system of government from presidential to parliamentary, does not contain any provisions setting a general outline for decisions on foreign deployments of Armenian service personnel.[60] It may be assumed that this power is implicitly embedded in the subordination of the armed forces to the government (the executive branch), which has the authority to "pass resolutions" on their use (Article 155(1)).[61] And indeed, the Law on Defense, enacted in 2017 in compliance with the amended Constitution, states that the government shall "adopt in accordance with international treaties of the Republic of Armenia a resolution on the participation of units of the armed forces in peacekeeping or military activities beyond boundaries of the Republic" (Article 7(1.1)).[62] It may appear though, that the term "international treaty" in the context of foreign deployments is interpreted quite broadly. While both the previous and current versions of the Constitution provide for ratification of "treaties of military character" (Article 81(2.a) and Article 116(1.2), respectively), it was, for example, the interagency Memorandum of Understanding between the Ministry of Defense of the Republic of Armenia and the United States Army Europe Regarding Deployment of the Rotational Unit of the Peacekeeping Brigade of the Armed Forces of the Republic of Armenia to Kosovo, signed on June 21 and 22, 2011, that served as grounds for sending Armenian military abroad.[63]

According to the Constitution of Estonia, which is a republic with a longer parliamentary tradition than Armenia, "on the proposal of the President, the *Riigikogu* [Parliament] . . . decides on the use of the Defense Forces to fulfil international obligations of the Estonian government" (Section 128).[64] Further details regarding procedures may be found in the National Defense Act of 2015, which includes Chapter 4 "International military co-operation."[65] The law establishes

---

[60] An English version is available on the website of the National Assembly of the Republic of Armenia at http://www.parliament.am/parliament.php?id=constitution&lang=eng#6.

[61] *Postanovleniye* [Resolution], which appears in the Russian version of the text (http://www.parliament.am/parliament.php?id=constitution&lang=rus#6), would be more precise than the term "decision" in this source's English version.

[62] The Russian version is available on the website of the National Assembly of the Republic of Armenia at http://www.parliament.am/legislation.php?sel=show&ID=5936&lang=rus.

[63] On file with this author, courtesy of Dr. Vladimir Vardanyan. For further reading about Armenia's participation in international missions, see Samvel Sargsyan, Small Nations in Multinational Operations and Armenian Perspectives, Master's Thesis, U.S. Army Command and General Staff College (2014).

[64] An English version is available on the website of *Riigi Teataja*, the Official Gazette published by the government, at https://www.riigiteataja.ee/en/eli/530102013003/consolide.

[65] Text available at https://www.riigiteataja.ee/en/eli/517112015001/consolide.

separate procedures for deployments to collective defense operations (Section 33) and "other international military operations" (Section 34), with the *Riigikogu* remaining the principal actor.

## V. Current Regulation in Russia

Even a cursory look at the distribution of authority in deciding on transboundary deployments of armed forces under the Constitution of 1993 and relevant laws reveals an apparent imbalance between branches of government.[66] The Constitution vests the bulk of those powers in the president, who is the head of state and the Supreme Commander-in-Chief of the Armed Forces (Article 87(1)). The authority of the Office is broad, and the Constitution, along with specific powers, stipulates in rather general terms that the president "shall adopt measures to protect the sovereignty of the Russian Federation, its independence and State integrity" (Article 80(2)).

As the Supreme Commander-in-Chief, the president, "in the event of aggression against the Russian Federation or of a direct threat of aggression" is authorized to "introduce martial law on the territory of the Russian Federation or on certain parts thereof." While a presidential decree may authorize the initial introduction of martial law, the president must notify both chambers of the Federal Assembly without delay and seek approval of that decree by the Council of the Federation. The decree will apply temporarily until the chamber votes to approve it. According to the Federal Constitutional Law on Martial Law, it will become ineffective should the majority of the total membership of the Council not vote to approve it (Article 4(6)).[67] That would seem to be one of few checks that the legislature has over the authority of the president in military matters.

Presidential authority is further solidified by the subordination to the president of several ministries and agencies of the government (the executive branch), including the ministries of defense, of internal affairs (internal security), and of civil defense and emergency management, the Federal Security Service (counterintelligence), the Foreign Intelligence Service, and several other agencies and

---

[66] An English version of the Constitution of the Russian Federation of 1993, as amended, is available on the website of the Constitutional Court of the Russian Federation at http://www.ksrf.ru/en/INFO/LEGALBASES/CONSTITUTIONRF/Pages/default.aspx.

[67] For the original text, see *Sobraniye Zakonodatelstva Rossiyskoy Federatzii* [Collection of Laws of the Russian Federation] [hereafter SZ RF], No. 5, Item 375 (2002). The current consolidated text inclusive of all amendments to this and other acts cited hereafter, is available from CONSULTANT PLUS, a Russian electronic legal reference tool. Federal constitutional laws stand above ordinary federal laws and are adopted in pursuit of a specific regulatory objective set by the Constitution, for example, the provision of Article 87(3) of the Constitution, which states that "the regime of martial law shall be defined by federal constitutional law."

departments, including the recently established Federal Service of the National Guard, incorporating former Internal Forces of the Ministry of Internal Affairs.[68] The government merely "coordinates activities" of those ministries and services.

Furthermore, the president approves the military doctrine of the Russian Federation; without seeking the consent of either chamber of the Federal Assembly, he appoints the senior military officers who make up the supreme command of the armed forces and can relieve them of their posts. The president also appoints and chairs the Security Council of the Russian Federation, which advises him on national security matters.

The corresponding powers of the legislative branch in Russia are rather modest. They are distributed between the two chambers of the Federal Assembly: the State Duma, formed by a mix of majority and proportional voting, and the Council of the Federation, comprising equal representation from constituent entities of the Federation. They share the budgetary power, and both participate in the ratification of international treaties. Federal laws on budget and on ratification of international treaties, passed by the Duma, must then be considered on their merits by the Council of the Federation, which otherwise has the authority only to implicitly approve several other categories of laws. Another notable provision makes it the Council's legislative obligation to hold debates on laws "on matters of war and peace."[69] Little may be inferred from the Constitution or laws as to what specifically that provision implies, or as to whether it is the president, or the Federal Assembly, or either of its chambers that may raise "matters of war and peace."

The Federal Law on Defense provides for the declaration of a state of war by adoption of a federal law "in case of an armed attack against the Russian Federation by another State or group of States, or in case of need to execute international treaties of the Russian Federation" (Article 18(1)).[70] Both scenarios, the latter in particular, may require deployment of forces across national boundaries, in addition to any already existing treaty-based presence of forces on foreign soil. The "declaration of war" is a concept that has been alien to the Russian or Soviet constitutional system since the Constitution of 1936; moreover, under the Federal Constitutional Law on Martial Law, a declaration of war on Russia by a foreign entity amounts to an "imminent threat of aggression" (Article 3(3)).[71] And, according to the Constitution, the imminent threat of aggression is sufficient for the declaration of martial law, nationally or in several regions, by authority of the president with immediate notification of both chambers of the

---

[68] Federal Constitutional Law on the Government of the Russian Federation, art. 32, SZ RF, No. 51, Item 5712 (1997).

[69] RF Constitution 1993, art. 106(f).

[70] SZ RF, No. 23, Item 2750 (1996).

[71] SZ RF, No. 5, Item 375 (2002).

Federal Assembly (Article 87(2)), and subsequent approval of the president's decree by the Council of the Federation (Article 102(1)(b)). In light of the debates in Russia in the early 2000s regarding preemptive use of armed force, it might be argued that "imminent threat of aggression" could meet the *Caroline* test and justify resort to transboundary use of armed force.[72] It might further be argued that a reference to Russia as a state that has committed an "act of armed aggression" in Ukrainian legislation, in the absence of determination of existence of the act of aggression by the U.N. Security Council, acting under Chapter VII of the UN Charter, amounts to such an "imminent threat."[73]

The only specific constitutional power of parliament to dispose of military force is the authority of the Council of the Federation to decide "on the possibility of using the armed forces of the Russian Federation outside the territory of the Russian Federation" (Article 102(1)(c)), which has been used on multiple occasions. The decision on such a deployment is the responsibility both of the president in his dual constitutional capacity as the Supreme Commander-in-Chief and the most senior authority in the realm of foreign affairs, and of the Council of the Federation, the consent of which is required for such deployments and which reviews on the merits federal laws on ratification of international treaties that provide for collective security, collective self-defense, and mutual military assistance.

The Constitution provides for approval by the Council of the Federation of a presidential decree introducing a state of war. The Federal Constitutional Law on Martial Law, which is the principal subconstitutional authority in matters of national defense, specifies that the approval shall be given within forty-eight hours, or as soon as practicable (Article 4(5)). But the Law also envisages a hypothetical situation when the decree fails to get that approval. In that event, however unlikely, the decree becomes null and void on the next day after action by the chamber (Article 4(6)). The Constitution and laws remain silent as to what would happen to the troops that may have already deployed beyond national boundaries and are engaging an adversary. In theory, a legal requirement may upset military exigency, even though such scenario is hard to imagine, that is, either the approval would be given in a timely manner, or troops would have

---

[72] See, e.g., Bakhtiyar Tuzmukhamedov, *Preemption by Armed Force of Trans-boundary Terrorist Threats: The Russian Perspective*, 83 INT'L L. STUD. 83 (2007).

[73] See Resolution of the Verkhovna Rada of Ukraine on the Appeal to the United Nations Organization, the European Parliament, the Parliamentary Assembly of the Council of Europe, The Parliamentary Assembly of the OSCE, the Parliamentary Assembly of GUAM, national parliaments of the states of the world, regarding recognition of Russian Federation as aggressor state, 27 January 2015, at https://zakon.rada.gov.ua/laws/show/ru/129-19?lang=ru; Law of Ukraine on Particularities of State Policy to Ensure State Sovereignty of Ukraine over Temporarily Occupied Territories in Donetsk and Luhansk Oblast's, in force as of 24 February 2018, available at https://zakon.rada.gov.ua/laws/show/ru/2268-19?lang=ru.

to stay in battle without comprehensive constitutional support, relying only on presumption of legality and lawfulness of orders coming from their Supreme Commander-in-Chief.

As to other Russian legislation regulating the transboundary use of armed force in situations other than a large-scale attack that may qualify as an act of aggression, regard should be had to the Federal Laws on Defense, on Countering Terrorism,[74] on the Federal Security Service,[75] on the Procedure for the Provision by the Russian Federation of Military and Civilian Personnel for Participation in Activities for the Maintenance and Restoration of International Peace and Security,[76] and, presumably, to the recent Federal Law on the Forces of the National Guard of the Russian Federation.[77] According to the Federal Law on Defense, the primary role in national defense is performed by the armed forces of the Russian Federation as administered by the Ministry of Defense (Article 13(2)). Other uniformed services that may perform national defense-related tasks are the National Guard, civil defense, the Foreign Intelligence Service, the Federal Security Service, and other agencies (Article 1(6)). A literal reading of regulating acts may lead to a conclusion that only the armed forces, under the Federal Law on Defense, and special purpose units of the Federal Security Service, under the Federal Law on the Federal Security Service,[78] may be assigned tasks involving the transboundary use of armed force. However, laws regulating other services do not explicitly preclude their use of armed force outside of national territory. For example, while the Federal Security Service is the lead counterterrorism agency and may be tasked with transboundary deployment, the National Guard shall participate in "combatting terrorism" (Article 2(1.3)) and is given a supporting role in enforcing martial law and "legal regime of counterterrorist operation" (Article 2(1.4)). Foreign Intelligence Service personnel are unlikely not to bear and be ready to use arms while performing the statutory task of "ensuring security of staff of institutions of the Russian Federation located outside the territory of the Russian Federation, and of their family members, in the receiving state" (Article 6(7)).[79]

On balance, the current Russian legislation provides for six "short of war" scenarios for deployment of armed forces and other uniformed services beyond the national boundary: (a) participation in international peace operations under the U.N. or regional mandates; (b) counterterrorist engagements outside the Russian territory; (c) repulsion of an armed attack against Russian military units

---

[74]  SZ RF, No. 11, Item 1146 (2006).
[75]  SZ RF, No. 15, Item 1269 (1995).
[76]  SZ RF, No. 26, Item 2401 (1995).
[77]  SZ RF, No. 27 (Part I), Item 4159 (2016).
[78]  SZ RF No. 15, Item 1269 (1995).
[79]  Federal Law on Foreign Intelligence, SZ RF, No. 3, Item 143 (1996).

and associated bodies stationed abroad; (d) repulsion or prevention of an armed attack against another state at that state's request; (e) protection of Russian citizens beyond national boundaries from an armed attack; (f) repression of piracy and ensuring safety of maritime navigation.

## VI.  A Note on Practice

As indicated earlier, the Constitution delegates to the Council of the Federation the power of "deciding on the possibility of using the armed forces of the Russian Federation outside the territory of the Russian Federation" (Article 102(1)(d)). That provision is further elaborated in several federal laws, as well as in the Rules of the Council.[80] The initiative rests with the president, who submits a proposal to the Council, on which it votes. An approval does not necessarily entail the actual "use of the Armed Forces," as the Council decides on the possibility of such use, leaving the final decision to the Supreme Commander-in-Chief.

The practice of applying the respective constitutional provisions is most developed—and, with few exceptions, transparent—in the instances when Russia deploys military personnel on peacekeeping operations under international auspices and pursuant to the respective Federal Law. Grounds for such deployments include U.N. Security Council resolutions and duly authorized requests from regional arrangements—the OSCE, EU and others.

Although the Rules of the Council provide for *in camera* debates on international deployments (Article 162(4)), most often the Chamber deliberates in open sessions. The resolution giving consent to a deployment, along with an international decision, will serve as the grounds for a subsequent presidential decree. It should be noted, though, that the president seeks approval of the Council only when Russia contributes units. Individual service members and police officers are assigned to international missions by an executive order of the president. It should also be noted that, while the Federal Law on the Procedure for the Provision by the Russian Federation of Military and Civilian Personnel for Participation in Activities for the Maintenance and Restoration of International Peace and Security obliges the executive branch to submit annual reports to both chambers of the Federal Assembly on participation in peacekeeping or peace restoration activities (Article 16), this author is not aware of any such reports, unless they were classified.

Less developed—and not as transparent—is the practice of implementation of provisions of the Federal Laws on Defense and on Countering Terrorism, related

---

[80]  SZ RF, No. 6, Item 279 (2002).

to transboundary use of armed force. As compared to deployments on multi-lateral peacekeeping operations, there are fewer instances when the president requested an approval from the Council of the Federation of the prospective use of armed force—broadly speaking, that is, not only the Armed Forces—beyond the territory of the Russian Federation invoking those laws.

On June 3, 2006, four staff members of the Russian Embassy in Baghdad were kidnapped from their vehicle, while the fifth was shot dead as he fought back the assailants. All four were brutally murdered before the end of that month. Responding to the request of the president and citing, among other sources, Article 51 of the U.N. Charter, as well as the Constitution and both laws, the Council of the Federation authorized the president to

> use elements of the Armed Forces of the Russian Federation and special pur-pose units beyond the territory of the Russian Federation to interdict interna-tional terrorist activities directed against the Russian Federation or the citizens of the Russian Federation, or stateless persons permanently residing on the ter-ritory of the Russian Federation.[81]

Although the Resolution was passed by the Council on July 7, 2006, it was re-ported that on or before June 28 the president already had given orders to "find and eliminate" those responsible for the murder of the Russian embassy per-sonnel.[82] The Resolution and respective presidential decree and orders were not time-limited and may still be in the process of execution, unbeknown to researchers, observers, and the general public.

The other instance was the general and, likewise, not time-limited authori-zation given by the Council of the Federation to the president to use the armed forces in contingencies that require prompt action. Presumably, this was a reac-tion to the failure of constitutional and legislative mechanisms to function prop-erly and efficiently when hostilities erupted in the South Ossetia on the night of August 7 to 8, 2008.[83] It took more than two weeks after fighting broke out for the president to submit a request to augment the strength of Russian units that were components of collective forces in South Ossetia and Abkhazia, both being

---

[81] Resolution of the Council of the Federation No. 219-SF, 7 July 2006, SZ RF No. 29, Item 3144 (2006).

[82] *Rossiyskaya Gazeta* (Russian Gazette), June 29, 2006 (No. 4104).

[83] The armed conflict between Russia and Georgia started during the night of August 7 to 8, 2008, with a sustained artillery attack by Georgian forces on the South Ossetian town of Tskhinvali and other locations, including positions of the Russian component of tripartite (Russian, Georgian, and South Ossetian) Joint Peacekeeping Forces. The EU-mandated Independent International Fact-Finding Mission on the Conflict in Georgia (IIFFMCG) acknowledged those attacks and concluded that "the use of force by Georgia against Russian peacekeeping forces in Tskhinvali in the night of 7/8 August 2008 was contrary to international law." I IIFFMCG REPORT 23 (2009).

parts of Georgia at that time, and for the Council of the Federation to grant approval, on August 25,[84] following deliberations *in camera*. Hostilities ended on or around August 12, which means that fighting had taken place in a constitutional void and without due authorization.

Apparently to offset similar legal and practical embarrassments in the future, the president sought authority from the Council to decide on contingency deployments of forces beyond national territory, "proceeding from the need to protect interests of the Russian Federation and her citizens, maintenance of international peace and security, with due account of the generally recognized principles and norms of international law and international treaties of the Russian Federation."[85] The Resolution granting the requested authority was passed by the Council on December 16, 2009, and was not time-limited.[86]

It might seem that this Resolution vested sufficient authority in the Supreme Commander-in-Chief for contingency deployment of military forces if, in the wake of forced removal of the Ukrainian President Yanukovich from office amid violence in the capital city Kiev and elsewhere throughout the country, he were to consider using armed force to protect Russian citizens, including service personnel deployed in Crimea and ethnic Russians whom he perceived as being threatened by events. Notwithstanding that possibility, the president sought specific authority from the Council of the Federation "to use the Armed Forces of the Russian Federation in the territory of the Ukraine till public and political situation in that country is normalized."[87] Despite broad language ("the territory of the Ukraine") at the time it seemed that both actors, the president and the Council, had a common understanding that such prospective use of military force would be limited to the territory of the then Autonomous Republic of Crimea. Backed by that Resolution, which was adopted on March 1, 2014, the president could order that Russian forces deployed in Crimea under bilateral agreements with the Ukraine be augmented to 25,000 personnel, as authorized by the then effective Agreement Between the Russian Federation and Ukraine on Parameters of Division of the Black Sea Fleet (Article 2, Annex 2).[88]

However, when on June 25, 2014, the Council of the Federation voted to approve the request of the president to repeal the Resolution of March 1, both the wording of the request and statements made during the meeting referred to that action as directed at "normalization of conditions and settlement of the situation

---

[84] Resolution of the Council of the Federation No. 297-SF, SZ RF, No. 35, Item 3995 (2008).

[85] Records of the 260th Session of the Council of the Federation, available at http://council.gov.ru/activity/meetings/?date=16.12.2009.

[86] Resolution of the Council of the Federation No. 456-SF of 16 December 2009, SZ RF, No. 51, Item 6168 (2009).

[87] Records of the 347th (Extraordinary) Session of the Council of the Federation, available at http://council.gov.ru/media/files/41d4c8b9772e9df14056.pdf.

[88] SZ RF, No. 31, Item 3990 (1999).

in Eastern regions of the Ukraine in light of the commencement of tri-partite negotiations."[89] This could be an indication that, after all, the original authorization implied the possibility of using the armed forces not only in the Crimea.

A more recent instance of granting the president's request to use military force occurred on September 30, 2015, when the Council of the Federation meeting *in camera* gave tersely worded consent to "the use of the Armed Forces of the Russian Federation beyond the boundaries of the Russian Federation in accordance with the generally recognized norms and principles of international law."[90] No reference was made to a governing statute, aside from an overall authority granted by the Constitution, nor did the Resolution provide any details about nature of the mission and its duration, personnel, and materiel to be involved. Later on the same day, the Ministry of Defense reported that Russian warplanes flew first combat missions over Syria and destroyed several Islamic State targets.[91] It was only one year later, on September 28, 2016, that the Council acknowledged the obvious when it released a special statement to appraise the implementation of its own Resolution of the prior year. In particular, the Council commended the Russian service personnel participating in the combat operation in Syria "for honest and brave fulfilment of military duty."[92]

As to the judiciary, one should consider a single relevant decision of the Constitutional Court rendered in response to a petition filed on June 15, 1995, by the Council of the Federation.[93] As the interpretation of the Constitution is the prerogative of the Constitutional Court, the Council approached the Court with a request to elaborate on the meaning of Article 102(1)(d), which authorizes the Council to decide on the possibility of transboundary deployments of the armed forces. However, the petition itself revealed, firstly, a narrow understanding by the petitioner of options of lawful uses of the armed forces and, secondly, the apparent inclination of the Council to impose limitations on its own participation in the procedure.

The legal grounds for the employment of the armed forces listed in the petition were limited to those found in treaties. Moreover, the Council found its participation inexpedient whenever there was a ratified treaty, considering its prior approval expressed during the ratification as a carte blanche both in duration and substance. The petition did not raise such specific possibilities of the deployment of the armed forces as peacekeeping operations and enforcement measures

---

[89]    Records of the 357th Session of the Council of the Federation, available at http://council.gov.ru/media/files/41d4edaba79402ac3d4e.pdf.

[90]    Resolution of the Council of the Federation No. 355-SF of Sept. 20, 2015, SZ RF, No. 40, Item 5469 (2015).

[91]    Missiya v Sirii [The Mission in Syria], available at http://syria.mil.ru/news/more.htm?id=12059172@egNews.

[92]    SZ RF, No. 40, Item 5721 (2016).

[93]    Copy of petition on file with the author.

under Chapter VII of the U.N. Charter, and similar regional arrangements provided for in Chapter VIII and in respective regional treaties. It also ignored cases of extra-treaty collective and individual self-defense under Article 51 of the Charter. Neither did it mention situations to which the precedent of the "Uniting for Peace" Resolution of the U.N. General Assembly could apply.[94]

Surprisingly, the petitioner seemed to be unaware of the fact that while the Council was drafting its petition to the Constitutional Court, the State Duma was about to vote on two laws of immediate relevance to the petition. One was the Federal Law on International Treaties of the Russian Federation;[95] the other, the Federal Law on the Procedure for the Provision by the Russian Federation of Military and Civilian Personnel for the Participation in the Activities for the Maintenance and Restoration of International Peace and Security of 1995.[96] Both laws offered clear answers to several questions raised in the petition.

The Constitutional Court found itself confined to the rather narrow limits of the petition and its imperfect contents and, citing lack of clarity in the request for constitutional interpretation, refused to consider the petition on its merits.[97] It could be convincingly argued that a body of constitutional review ought not reject petitions to interpret the Constitution. Such rejection would be especially inappropriate if, as was the case, the Court were asked to expound the meaning of an important prerogative of the government, on which the Constitution and laws were quite terse.

One should bear in mind, though, that the petition was filed with the Court only three months after it resumed its activities, having been suspended in October 1993 when the government crisis reached its violent peak. The Council of the Federation barely concealed its willingness to put most of the burden of the decision to use the armed forces on the president and the government through its petition. The Constitutional Court, had it decided to consider the case on its merits, could hardly have avoided taking one side in the dispute, thus identifying itself with either the president or the legislature. By doing so, it would have got involved in a new confrontation between the president and lawmakers. By rejecting the petition, the Court might have been driven by an instinct of self-preservation, thus developing a Russian version of the American "political question" judicial doctrine. Ironically, Valeriy Zorkin, the president of the Constitutional Court, in a recent article published by the official gazette of the Russian government expressed disappointment with the "absence in the

---

[94] UNGA Res. 377 V (3 November 1950).

[95] SZ RF, No. 29, art. 2757 (1995).

[96] SZ RF, No. 26, art. 2401 (1995).

[97] Text of ruling available on the official website of the Constitutional Court of the Russian Federation at http://doc.ksrf.ru/decision/KSRFDecision31585.pdf.

Constitution of a proper system of checks and balances, and a tilt towards the executive branch of the Government."[98]

## VII. Conclusion

This chapter's glancing look at various jurisdictions reveals diverging trends in the allocation of authority to dispose of the armed capacities of governments. The picture is inconclusive, at best.

In the post-Soviet space, it is apparent that respective authority is more often concentrated in the executive branch, be it an individualized presidency or, like in Armenia, the prime minister and the Cabinet. There does not appear to be any ongoing constitutional development similar to the one in Germany, ever since the seminal judgment of the Federal Constitutional Court in 1994, which stated that any foreign deployment of the *Bundeswehr* for combat or peacekeeping purposes, regardless of whether German military personnel may engage in hostilities, would require the consent of the *Bundestag*, and in principle that consent should be sought and obtained prior to deployment.[99] And yet subsequently the Court ruled that

> in cases of imminent danger, the Federal Government may, by way of exception and for the time being, decide upon deployments alone . . . However, in such a case the Federal Government must immediately involve the Bundestag in the thus decided deployment and withdraw the armed forces upon the request of the Bundestag.[100]

Or, conversely, consider France's Law on Modernization of Institutions of the Fifth Republic of July 23, 2008, which allows the executive to decide on foreign deployment and to actually "have the armed forces intervene abroad" and only then to inform the Parliament "at the latest three days after the beginning of said intervention."[101] Or look at the short-lived May 1, 2018, amendments to Israel's Basic Law (The Government), tilting the balance within the executive branch and concentrating critical authority to use armed force at the Ministerial Committee on National Security, or even in the hands of the prime minister and minister of defense, albeit in "extreme circumstances."[102] Less than three months later, on

---

[98] Valeriy Zorkin, *Letter and Spirit of the Constitution*, ROSSIYSKAYA GAZETA (Sept. 9, 2018).

[99] *International Military Operations (German Participation) Case*, 106 INT'L L. REP. 320 (1997).

[100] BVerfG, Judgment of the Second Senate of 23 September 2015–2 BvE 6/11, para. 83, redacted English version available on the official website of the Federal Constitutional Court at http://www.bverfg.de/e/es20150923_2bve000611en.html.

[101] Loi constitutionnelle no 2008-724, *supra* note 23.

[102] Available at https://main.knesset.gov.il/EN/News/PressReleases/Pages/Pr13851_pg.aspx.

July 18, the Knesset voted to remove the provisions authorizing the prime minister and another member of the Cabinet to deploy *Tzahal* (Israeli Self-Defense Forces) into combat.[103]

The Third Restatement quoted Justice Jackson's concurring opinion in *Youngstown Sheet & Tube Co. v. Sawyer*, where he defined the "twilight zone" of concurrent authority of the executive and legislative branches of the government in foreign affairs.[104] That brings to mind another quote from Justice Jackson, this one from his dissenting opinion in *Korematsu v. United States*, and even more relevant to matters raised in this chapter:

> If the people ever let command of the war power fall into irresponsible and unscrupulous hands, the courts wield no power equal to its restraint. The chief restraint upon those who command the physical forces of the country, in the future as in the past, must be their responsibility to the political judgments of their contemporaries and to the moral judgments of history.[105]

---

[103] Available at https://main.knesset.gov.il/EN/News/PressReleases/Pages/Pr13974_pg.aspx; see also Avindam Sharon, Recent Developments in Israeli Law, July 25, 2018, VERSA, available at http://versa.cardozo.yu.edu/viewpoints/recent-developments-israeli-law-2.

[104] THIRD RESTATEMENT §1 reporters' note 3.

[105] 323 U.S. 214, 248 (1944).

# 22

# Sleeping Dogs

## The Fourth Restatement and International Humanitarian Law

### Ashley Deeks

Six years ago, I wrote about a phenomenon I termed "domestic humanitarian law."[1] Even though by 2013 the international community had established no new *international* rules to regulate how states fight transnational armed conflicts against nonstate actors, I argued that important new rules nevertheless had emerged from *domestic* judicial decisions in several states in the post–September 11 era. Courts were producing decisions about how to characterize a state's extraterritorial armed conflicts against nonstate actors; who a state lawfully may detain or target during those conflicts; the detention review processes a state must conduct; and what restrictions should attach to detainee transfers, among other topics.[2] I termed this case law "domestic humanitarian law" (DHL). The DHL emerging from different jurisdictions offered a way to develop international humanitarian law, akin to the U.S. constitutional idea that U.S. States serve as experimental "laboratories" in which different approaches to problems are tested.[3] U.S. courts were a major player in this undertaking. The decisions they produced, and the congressional and executive reactions to those decisions, fall squarely within what we think of as U.S. foreign relations law.

Notwithstanding the stated interest by the Fourth Restatement of Foreign Relations Law's reporters in updating the Third Restatement to better reflect major geopolitical changes since 1987,[4] however, and notwithstanding the fact that DHL is a new, plentiful, and important reflection of those changes, there seems to be an unspoken consensus that DHL would be a poor subject for the

---

[1] Ashley Deeks, *Domestic Humanitarian Law: Developing the Law of War in Domestic Courts*, in Applying International Humanitarian Law in Judicial and Quasi-Judicial Bodies (Derek Jinks, Jackson Maogoto & Solon Solomon eds., 2014).

[2] *Id.* at 134.

[3] *Id.* at 158.

[4] Paul B. Stephan & Sarah H. Cleveland, Proposal for a Fourth Restatement of the Foreign Relations Law of the United States 1 (copy on file with author).

Ashley Deeks, *Sleeping Dogs* In: *The Restatement and Beyond*. Edited by: Paul B. Stephan and Sarah H. Cleveland, Oxford University Press (2020). © Oxford University Press. DOI: 10.1093/oso/9780197533154.003.0023

Fourth Restatement to take up. This chapter considers why this is the case and what it says about U.S. "war on terror" jurisprudence.

This chapter begins by describing basic developments in U.S. "DHL" since the September 11 attacks and shows why this jurisprudence theoretically would fit squarely into a Fourth Restatement. It then explores why there is no enthusiasm for including the topic in a future Restatement, even from groups whom we might expect to support such an idea. It focuses on academics who support broad executive power, academics who emphasize the importance of U.S. compliance with international law, and officials in the executive branch, including members of the State Department's Office of the Legal Adviser ("L"). Substantively, it surveys why each group may have unique reasons to resist the inclusion of DHL in a Restatement, and why all three groups may share general, strategic reasons to resist. It concludes that this pessimism reflects dissatisfaction from virtually all quarters about the state of U.S. law in this area, even from those actors who ostensibly "won" their cases.

## I.  U.S. *Jus in Bello* Cases as Paradigmatic Foreign Relations Law

U.S. DHL appears to be a paradigmatic example of U.S. foreign relations law.[5] The Fourth Restatement of Foreign Relations Law encompasses both "domestic law bearing on foreign relations and relevant portions of international law."[6] It also implicitly adopts the Third Restatement's statement about what is covered: "international law as it applies to the United States" and "domestic law that has substantial significance for the United States or has other substantial international consequences."[7] Curt Bradley, a leading foreign relations scholar and one of the Fourth Restatement reporters, similarly defines foreign relations law to "encompass the domestic law of each nation that governs how that nation interacts with the rest of the world."[8]

DHL reflects court decisions that purport to identify U.S. legal obligations in armed conflicts with nonstate actors such as al-Qaeda. Some of these obligations flow from international law, although the precise nature of the court decisions

---

[5]  See CURTIS BRADLEY, ASHLEY DEEKS & JACK GOLDSMITH, FOREIGN RELATIONS LAW (7th ed. 2020) (treating the use of force and the war on terror as important foreign relations issues).

[6]  FOURTH RESTATEMENT intro.

[7]  THIRD RESTATEMENT § 101.

[8]  Curtis A. Bradley, *What Is Foreign Relations Law?*, in COMPARATIVE FOREIGN RELATIONS LAW 3 (Curtis A. Bradley ed., 2018); see also Sarah H. Cleveland, *The Legacy of Louis Henkin: Human Rights in the "Age of Terror", an Interview*, 38 COLUM. HUM. RTS. L. REV. 499, 499–500 (2007) (praising Louis Henkin's work on foreign relations law, which included discussions of the application of law during war).

that comprise DHL admittedly is not entirely clear. As I asked in my earlier DHL essay:

> Are the decisions best thought of as purely domestic law? Treaty interpretation? A "common law of war"? Hybrid domestic/international law? It is difficult to reach definitive conclusions on this point; indeed, specific domestic judicial decisions will have different characters, depending on the extent to which the court is (i) interpreting international law directly; (ii) interpreting domestic law through the lens of international law; or (iii) crafting new law in a field of interest to international law, reasoning by analogy from related bodies of international law.[9]

Regardless of which of these descriptions most accurately captures what DHL is, DHL squarely fits within the Restatement's scope. Indeed, it may be precisely the type of body of law for which a Restatement can be useful.

Further, Sarah Cleveland and Paul Stephan, who initiated the process that led to the current Fourth Restatement and who ultimately became reporters, asserted that one rationale for undertaking a Fourth Restatement was that the September 11 attacks wrought immense changes in the international sphere. As Cleveland and Stephan argued, the end of the Cold War and the growth of the internet have forced us to confront issues today that "either did not exist or were understood very differently at the time of the Third Restatement's drafting," including "terrorism, global warming, failed states, [and] pandemics. . . ."[10] Moreover, they argued that the focus of international law has shifted from "managing potential conflicts between states" to "organizing collective international responses to common problems."[11] Cleveland and Stephan concluded, "If all goes well, we eventually will cover every relevant topic that a comprehensive restatement might encompass."[12] DHL—which wades into difficult questions about the rules regulating how states fight terrorist groups—is an obvious manifestation of the changes in the problems that states face and in the way they manage those problems, and clearly constitutes a "relevant topic" for the Fourth Restatement.

Third, there has been a significant amount of case law emanating from the "war on terror." In the years since the Third Restatement, dozens of federal cases have fed into today's body of DHL, including four important Supreme Court cases. The Court's cases address the extraterritorial application of the U.S. Constitution;[13] the application of habeas corpus to wartime detainees;[14] the

[9] Deeks, *supra* note 1, at 152.
[10] Stephan & Cleveland, *supra* note 4, at 1.
[11] *Id.*
[12] Stephan & Cleveland, *supra* note 4, at 2.
[13] Boumediene v. Bush, 553 U.S. 723 (2008).
[14] Hamdi v. Rumsfeld, 542 U.S. 507 (2004); Rasul v. Bush, 542 U.S. 266 (2004).

transfers of American citizen detainees to third states;[15] and rules regulating military commissions, in a case that also considered how legally to characterize the conflict.[16] There are also scores of lower court cases spelling out wartime habeas corpus requirements, including the appropriate standards of evidence and proof to support continued detention. Beyond case law, there is extensive executive and legislative practice related to DHL. The length of the conflicts in Afghanistan and Iraq and the conflict with al-Qaeda have forced the executive to make a host of statements about legal topics, such as when two groups are co-belligerents and how to identify the end of a conflict.[17] Further, these conflicts have stimulated Congress to enact several statutes related to the scope of detention, war crimes, and detainee treatment.

Finally, war is a repeating problem, and the challenges posed by violent and capable terrorist groups are unlikely to disappear in the short term. In those conflicts, the United States is likely to detain individuals, and private sector and nongovernmental lawyers are likely to litigate cases about those detentions.

What would a Fourth Restatement section on the *jus in bello* consider? It presumably could include rules on the rights of habeas corpus for wartime detainees and the specific processes due; the geographic reach of habeas corpus; a list of war crimes; minimum standards of treatment; the permissibility of detainee transfers to third states; a recognition of the political nature of a decision about when conflict ends; and perhaps rules about which types of actors are detainable.

Notwithstanding the fact that DHL falls squarely within foreign relations law, that the Fourth Restatement was inspired in part by changes wrought by September 11, that there is extensive new case law, and that armed conflicts against terrorist groups seem unlikely to wane in the near term, the prospects for a section in the Fourth Restatement on DHL are very dim.

## II. A Consensus to Let Sleeping Dogs Lie?

At least in a vacuum, we might expect the Fourth Restatement's reporters to seriously consider whether to include some rules related to the U.S. use of force against nonstate actors. This section explores why there has been almost no interest in pursuing this path. It concludes that there is significant dissatisfaction with the substantive state of the law, and therefore little interest in achieving the kind of legal stability that Restatements can provide.[18] In fact, all of the groups

---

[15] Munaf v. Geren, 553 U.S. 674 (2008).

[16] Hamdan v. Rumsfeld, 548 U.S. 557 (2006).

[17] Jeh Charles Johnson, General Counsel, U.S. Dep't of Defense, "The Conflict Against Al Qaeda and its Affiliates: How Will It End?," Address at the Oxford Union, Oxford Univ., Nov. 30, 2012.

[18] See Jide Nzelibe, *Can the Fourth Restatement of Foreign Relations Law Foster Legal Stability?*, in this volume (discussing when and how Restatements can provide legal stability).

considered in this section may affirmatively favor legal instability in this area of the law, in the hope that the law will shift in the future.

At least three groups have an interest in whether the Fourth Restatement takes up DHL: (1) proponents of robust executive powers, (2) internationalists in the U.S. legal academy, and (3) executive branch lawyers, including those in the Departments of State, Defense, and Justice. Of course, others may care about the question (including foreign actors), and there may be overlap among the views of these three groups. This portrait necessarily simplifies what are surely more nuanced views of the members of these groups. Each of these groups, however, is likely to hold considered views on the substance of DHL as it currently stands. Some of the reasons they seem to oppose DHL's inclusion are unique to each group, while others are likely shared by all three groups.

## A. The Postures of Specific Groups

First, consider those who believe that the president must have significant flexibility in fighting armed conflicts, and that the role for courts during wartime should necessarily be limited. This group objected to a number of Supreme Court decisions on DHL. Its members criticized decisions such as *Hamdi*, which insisted that the government must provide American citizen detainees with some modicum of process to challenge their detention.[19] They objected to *Boumediene* on the ground that foreign detainees outside the United States should not receive the protection of the U.S. Constitution.[20] And they viewed *Hamdan* as showing a problematic lack of deference to executive interpretations of international law and statutes.[21] In their view, these cases weakened executive power and made it more difficult for future presidents to fight conflicts. Indeed, at least some in this group would prefer that courts not be involved in adjudicating wartime issues.[22]

---

[19] See, e.g., Michael Stokes Paulsen, *The Constitutional Power to Interpret International Law*, 118 YALE L.J. 1762 (2009); BENJAMIN A. KLEINERMAN, THE DISCRETIONARY PRESIDENT: THE PROMISE AND PERIL OF EXECUTIVE POWER 11 (2009).

[20] See, e.g., Richard Klingler, *The Court, the Culture Wars, and Real Wars*, ABA NAT'L SEC'Y L. REP. (June 2008). For a related critique that Boumediene reflects "judicial cosmopolitanism," see Eric A. Posner, Boumediene *and the Uncertain March of Judicial Cosmopolitanism*, 2008 CATO S. CT. REV. 23.

[21] See, e.g., Julian Ku & John Yoo, Hamdan v. Rumsfeld: *The Functional Case for Foreign Affairs Deference to the Executive*, 23 CONST. COMMENT. 102, 103 (2006).

[22] See, e.g., Andrew Kent, *Judicial Review for Enemy Fighters: The Court's Fateful Turn in* Ex Parte Quirin, *the Nazi Saboteur Case*, 66 VAND. L. REV. 153, 159–60 (2013) (identifying "unjustifiably high costs" when courts are involved in habeas litigation related to unlawful enemy combatants). In enacting the Military Commissions Act of 2006, which stripped U.S. federal and State courts of jurisdiction to consider habeas petitions by individuals to hear applications for habeas corpus by aliens properly determined to be enemy combatants, Congress aggressively attempted to narrow the scope of judicial review for detainee-related litigation. See Military Commissions Act of 2006, sec. 7, P.L. 109-366, Oct. 17, 2006.

Another group with a significant interest in the Restatement process has a different perspective on these cases (and related statutes): scholars who advocate robust adherence to the United States' international law commitments. Those scholars have critiqued the way in which the courts have interpreted international law in decisions such as *Hamdi*, arguing that "the court did not engage in a rigorous examination of the treaties and customary international law applicable to the armed conflict in Afghanistan" and that the Court "embarked on a questionable path toward creating its own, new constitutional common law of war, ungrounded either in international humanitarian law" or U.S. statutes.[23] In *Hamdan*, the Court arguably misinterpreted Articles 1 and 3 of the Geneva Conventions.[24] (On the other hand, members of this group generally support *Hamdan*'s holding, which applied Common Article 3 to the U.S. conflict with al-Qaeda and rejected certain aspects of the military commissions as then constituted.) Others have criticized the *Al Bahlul* opinion, which wrestled with the extent to which the United States could properly try wartime detainees for the crimes of conspiracy and material support for terrorism.[25] Further, scholars have expressed dismay about the D.C. Circuit's jurisprudence setting forth the procedural standards for detainee habeas cases.[26]

These critiques tend to argue that the courts have misinterpreted international law in a way that leaves the United States in violation of that law or, at the very least, in the position of holding controversial and minority opinions about how international law applies to the conflicts with al-Qaeda, the Taliban, ISIS, and other similar nonstate armed groups. This group is surely not satisfied with the outcomes of many of the cases and would prefer a jurisprudence that adheres more closely to what they see as international standards. In their view, crafting

---

[23]  See Jenny S. Martinez, *Recent Decision,* Hamdi v. Rumsfeld, *124 S. Ct. 2633*, 98 AM. J. INT'L L. 782, 785, 787 (2004).

[24]  Hamdan v. Rumsfeld, 548 U.S. 557 (2006).

[25]  Steve Vladeck, *Al Bahlul and the Long Shadow of Illegitimacy*, LAWFARE, Oct. 22, 2016; Brief of International and Constitutional Law Experts as Amici Curiae in Support of Petitioner, Al Bahlul v. United States, No. 16-1307, May 31, 2017; Jonathan Hafetz, *The D.C. Circuit's En Banc Ruling in Al Bahlul: Innovation, Tradition, and America's Domestic Common Law of War*, OPINIO JURIS, July 22, 2014.

[26]  Stephen I. Vladeck, *The D.C. Circuit After* Boumediene, 41 SETON HALL L. REV. 1451, 1488 (2011) ("[O]n the 'merits' of the detainee cases, the analysis and the holdings reflect a profound tension with both *Boumediene* and *Hamdi*, and a fundamental unwillingness by the D.C. Circuit—especially Judges Brown, Kavanaugh, Randolph, and Silberman—to take seriously the implications of the Supreme Court's analysis in either case."); Jonathan Hafetz, *Calling the Government to Account: Habeas Corpus in the Aftermath of* Boumediene, 57 WAYNE L. REV. 99, 129 (2011) ("The D.C. Circuit has deviated from [*Boumediene*'s] requirement by effectively depriving the courts of authority to order a prisoner's release from Guantánamo."). For a general discussion of the rules that emerged from the D.C. Circuit on detention procedures, see Benjamin Wittes et al., *The Emerging Law of Detention 2.0: The Guantanamo Habeas Cases as Lawmaking* 13 (2011), available at http://www.brookings.edu/~/media/ research/files/reports/2011/5/guantanamo%20wittes/05_guantanamo_wittes.pdf.

a DHL section of the Restatement at this point in time would memorialize case law that might reflect a time of judicial overreaction.[27] The courts decided key detainee cases when the terrorist threat remained tangible, but generally have declined to revisit these cases in the past five years, when the perceptions of the threat to the homeland have decreased.[28]

This group might also disfavor the development of Restatement provisions on these issues because there are alternative international alternatives that address at least some of the subjects of U.S. DHL case law. For example, the International Committee of the Red Cross has produced its Customary International Humanitarian Law Study, a report on the concept of "direct participation in hostilities," and newly revised Commentaries on the Geneva Conventions.[29] Unsurprisingly, these documents take a more rights-protective approach to international humanitarian law than U.S. case law has taken.

A third group that pays close attention both to the creation of Restatements and to the laws of armed conflict are executive branch lawyers. This group includes lawyers from L, as well as from the Defense and Justice Departments. Members of the State and Justice Departments, as well as other agencies, have historically provided comments during the Restatement drafting process,[30] and presumably

---

[27] See JACK GOLDSMITH, POWER AND CONSTRAINT: THE ACCOUNTABLE PRESIDENCY AFTER 9/11, at 248–50 (2012) (discussing cycles of over- and under-reaction to terrorist threats); Neal Katyal, *Stochastic Constraint*, 126 HARV. L. REV. 990, 1008–109 (2013) (describing *Boumediene* as "constitutionalizing military detention").

[28] Justice Breyer recently filed a statement regarding denial of certiorari in Al-Alwi v. Trump, 139 S. Ct. 1893 (2019), in which he suggested that it was time to revisit the Court's approach to the nineteen-year-old U.S. conflict with al-Qaeda and the underlying detention authorities based thereon. He was the only Justice who showed any appetite to revisit this question, however, which indicates that the Court is unlikely to address the continued validity of the Court's approach in *Hamdi* any time soon.

[29] JEAN-MARIE HENCKAERTS & LOUISE DOSWALD-BECK, CUSTOMARY INTERNATIONAL HUMANITARIAN LAW (2004); Nils Meltzer, Interpretive Guidance on the Notion of Direct Participation in Hostilities (2009), available at https://www.icrc.org/en/doc/assets/files/other/icrc-002-0990.pdf. In 2015, the Defense Department issued a Law of War Manual, which also addresses some of these issues. However, that Manual does not purport to represent the views of the U.S. government as a whole, and some in L and the Department of Justice may disagree with certain of its contents. See generally Georg Nolte, *The Effectiveness of International Law*, 108 AM. SOC'Y INT'L L. PROC. 27 (2014) (noting that, unlike the drafters of the original Restatement, the Third Restatement's drafters faced larger number of alternatives to the Restatement, such as the Customary International Humanitarian Law study).

[30] See *Statement of President Roswell B. Perkins*, 62 A.L.I. PROC. 374–77 (1985) (stating that those preparing the Third Restatement postponed the adoption of the final revisions to give the Departments of State and Justice the chance to review them); *The Restatement of Foreign Relations Law of the United States, Revised: How Were the Controversies Resolved?*, 81 AM. SOC'Y INT'L L. PROC. 180 (1987) [hereinafter Restatement Controversies] (discussing the substantial role that the State Department played in the ALI's work product); *Remarks of Prof. Louis Henkin*, 63 A.L.I. PROC. 105 (1986) (stating that the drafters altered the way in which the Third Restatement identified the standard it followed for crafting black-letter rules because the administration was "very allergic" to the International Court of Justice); John Houck, *Restatement of the Foreign Relations Law of the United States (Revised): Issues and Resolutions*, 20(4) INT'L LAW. 1361, 1364–65 (Fall 1986) (discussing inputs on the Third Restatement from the State, Justice, and Treasury Departments, the Securities and Exchange Commission, and the Federal Reserve),

those comments reflect the shared views of other executive agencies. In the post–
September 11 era, the Justice Department played a much more significant role
than it had previously in establishing U.S. views on the laws of armed conflict because a host of detainee cases ended up in federal court. The Justice Department
thus developed expertise in the laws of armed conflict, supplementing its existing expertise on the separation of powers issues that were relevant to the wartime detainee cases. And of course the Defense Department, as the U.S. agency
that fights wars, has long-standing expertise in the laws of armed conflict. Thus,
State, Justice, and Defense all would have views not only about whether generally to include DHL in a Fourth Restatement but also about what the contents
of that DHL should be. Complicating matters, these three agencies might differ
among themselves about what the contents of any Restatement provisions on
DHL should be.

First, consider career members of the Legal Adviser's Office. This group, like
the U.S. international law scholars just discussed, is committed to helping the
United States comply with its international law obligations, even though it might
interpret those obligations somewhat differently. Lawyers in L might share the
view of the internationalist scholars that much of the DHL case law and some
of the "war on terror" statutes stand in tension with international law. As actors
on the front lines of U.S. legal diplomacy, these lawyers are undoubtedly sensitive to the critiques of allies, which have become more muted in recent years
but which were highly salient during the George W. Bush administration. If the
American Law Institute (ALI) were to produce a document that highlighted the
differences between the U.S. positions on international humanitarian law (IHL)
and the views of many European states and the ICRC, it might reopen difficult
discussions that have moved into the background in the past decade. This alone
is a reason that L as an institution might want to avoid having these rules memorialized in a Restatement. Further, there could be a divide between career L
attorneys and L's political leadership about the extent to which it would be to the
government's benefit to memorialize certain aspects of DHL in a Restatement.
Finally, L might worry that it stands in a relative position of weakness in the
Donald Trump administration and might be concerned that its voice would lose
out during interagency debates.

In contrast, the Justice Department might share the view of the "broad executive power" group that some of the court decisions that comprise DHL are
insufficiently sensitive to the needs of a wartime president. It was the George
W. Bush Justice Department that took aggressive positions about the impro-
priety of having courts review wartime detainee claims, and, having won some of
those cases, DOJ presumably would favor memorializing rules drawn from cases
that reflected broad deference by Congress and the courts toward the president's

detention power. This approach may find less favor in the State Department, though.

The Defense Department might wish to pursue a third approach: de-emphasizing the aspects of DHL that support the "broad executive power" claims but emphasizing the ways in which DHL and IHL differ. That is, the Defense Department (DOD) might have less of a concern than the State Department about the fact that the U.S. approach to the laws of armed conflict differs in important ways from the "international" approach to the laws of armed conflict.[31] The Defense Department might find it helpful for the Restatement to clearly set out the Defense Department's DHL approach, whether or not there is daylight between that approach and those of foreign governments. In short, there may be significant interagency disagreement about what a DHL Restatement section should look like; the agencies likely would prefer to avoid those difficult conversations by skirting the topic entirely.

In addition to possible concerns about the inability of the U.S. government to formulate a shared position about discrete draft DHL rules, the government has generally been cautious about having the ALI establish black-letter rules in a Restatement because there is a chance that those rules will not precisely track the government's positions. During the writing of the Third Restatement, U.S. officials and the reporters fought about how to proceed. Specifically, "[g]overnment officials sought to avoid being burdened by black-letter conclusions in legal areas that they viewed as still in a state of flux."[32] That same concern likely would apply here, especially if the U.S. international law academy were able to exert a robust influence on the rules' content. In any case, the U.S. government historically has evidenced significant interest in Restatements and would pay close and critical attention to any effort to handle DHL in new Restatement provisions.

[31] As noted earlier, the State and Justice Departments declined to formally attach their imprimatur to the Defense Department's Law of War Manual. This suggests some level of disagreement among those agencies about the substance of U.S. DHL. See David Glazier, Zora Colakovic, Alexandra Gonzalez & Zacharias Tripodes, *Failing Our Troops: A Critical Assessment of the Department of Defense Law of War Manual*, 42 YALE J. INT'L L. 215, 227 (2017) ("The lack of formal Justice and State Department concurrence are thus major red flags, highlighting the Manual's unsuitability for U.S. military use until this shortcoming is rectified.").

[32] See Restatement Controversies, *supra* note 30, at 182; see also Houck, *supra* note 30, at 1362 (describing L's and other government agencies' concerns about the draft and noting that "the decision on the part of the reporters at various junctures not to adopt the U.S. view is, of course, a major source of the controversies that have surrounded the new Restatement").

## B. Collective Concerns

Although each group just discussed has its own reasons to resist a Restatement section on DHL, these groups likely also share some reasons for finding its inclusion unattractive.[33]

First, all of these groups surely recognize how difficult it would be to reach consensus about what issues within DHL to address and what the content of those rules should be.[34] Even actors within a single group might disagree about the rules' content, as the earlier discussion about the State, Defense, and Justice Departments illustrates. One key area of dispute would be a conceptual fight about the extent to which the Restatement is an exercise in reasoning inductively and stating what the law is, or an exercise in pushing the law in a particular direction. The groups discussed earlier will favor one or the other, at least for particular subtopics. (One group might even seek a *lex lata* approach on one rule and a *lex ferenda* approach on another, given that the case law does not pull uniformly in a rights-protective, international law–favoring direction or an executive power direction.)

Second, it will be difficult to achieve consensus because it is not obvious how to characterize the legal nature of DHL, as discussed previously. Some of the holdings in the DHL cases appear to be U.S. interpretations of international law; others appear to constitute constitutional holdings informed by international law; and yet others appear to be domestic *jus in bello* rules crafted from whole cloth. The Fourth Restatement sometimes distinguishes the "international principle and the U.S. rule in successive Sections or subsections."[35] This suggests that the drafters will face self-imposed pressure to identify the nature of DHL and, in cases where a DHL rule seems to differ from international law, what the content of the international rule is. Even that latter determination is challenging: It is genuinely difficult to identify which paradigm of armed conflict to use, and if non-international conflict is the correct paradigm, that body of law does not contain details about detention and review procedures. To the extent that international law is clear in some areas, Restatement discussions likely would highlight the deltas between international law and U.S. domestic law, differences that leave L lawyers and international academics dissatisfied.

---

[33] The reporters themselves (whose views or group associations this chapter does not purport to predict) will in any case likely want to avoid "backwards propagation" of suspicions about a section on the laws of armed conflict to spread to other chapters of the Restatement.

[34] Nolte, *supra* note 29 (arguing that the zeitgeist changed between the lead-up to the Third Restatement and the Fourth because in the United States "international law is now much contested, not just certain of its rules, but also with respect to its basic functions").

[35] FOURTH RESTATEMENT intro. at 2.

Third, these groups might agree that it simply may not be necessary to produce "black-letter" rules on these issues. This might be because they believe that
the case law is clear enough on its own; most of these cases were decided in the
D.C. Circuit and D.C. District Courts, so there is little need to harmonize case
law across circuits. Just as likely, the groups might doubt that there will be a future spate of detainee cases that will force courts and lawyers to re-confront these
issues. Further, as Nzelibe has argued, it may be less important to establish black-
letter rules in public law than it is private law.[36] Although the United States continues to fight conflicts with nonstate armed groups, including al-Qaeda and its
associated forces, the U.S. military has shied away from detaining individuals
from these groups, in part because it is now so legally complicated to do so.

In sum, there may be collective resistance to seeking stability in this area of
foreign relations law.[37] The three groups may recognize that it might be worse
to try to reach consensus and fail than to simply avoid the topic in the first
place.[38] Even if some of the groups are satisfied with the outcomes in specific
areas of DHL, none of them likely favors the DHL case law across all possible
topics. In Nzelibe's construct, each group will lose something in a Restatement
codification, and therefore will fear legal entrenchment.[39] Nzelibe argues that
a Restatement's goal of fostering legal stability can be realized only under very
specific conditions: when the political stakes in a legal controversy are low, or
when they implicate technical issues that do not obviously favor one side over
the other.[40] DHL fails this test: Though less salient now than it was a decade ago,
it continues to embody high political stakes, and the issues are neither technical
nor neutral. In short, all of the actors discussed here likely consider that they have
something to lose in seeking to memorialize DHL in the Fourth Restatement,
and they presumably view the challenges of the negotiations around DHL's content and nature as so formidable that any gains they may achieve are not worth
the candle.

## III. Conclusion

Contemplating the sheer possibility of including DHL rules at a future stage of
the Fourth Restatement provides a stimulus to step back and consider in toto

[36] Jide Nzelibe, *Remarks*, 104 Am. Soc'y Int'l L. Proc. 313 (2010). Of course, the "war on terror"
cases involved many private lawyers, even if the issues were public law issues.

[37] Nolte, *supra* note 29, at 29–30 ("Those who advocate progressive development, but see little likelihood of this, may want to aim at reducing the scope of the project in order to leave room for further
debate in the U.S. context.").

[38] Nzelibe, *supra* note 18 (noting consensus norm).

[39] *Id.*

[40] *Id.*

fifteen years of *jus in bello* jurisprudence in U.S. courts. This investigation leads to the conclusion that almost no one is satisfied in full with where the law came out, and that there is, accordingly, little appetite to cement a host of DHL-related topics in black-letter rules. Taking a more positive view, we might conclude that U.S. DHL in the post–September 11 era has a Goldilocks quality: The cases reflect some amount of push-pull between the courts and the executive about the breadth of executive power in wartime, and push-pull between the executive and those advocating interpretations of international law that are more favorable to individuals than states in wartime. It is overly facile to suggest that, if no one group is satisfied, the courts might have gotten it right, but the outcomes of these cases, taken collectively, do highlight the potential for international law to serve as a check on executive power and courts' periodic willingness to use it that way.

In the absence of a single group driving to include this body of foreign relations law in the Restatement, DHL will remain where it is: scattered among a host of cases, unsynthesized, and possibly left as a legal artifact of a unique moment in time. That seems like the best possible outcome: All three groups surely would agree that it would be desirable not to have to revisit these difficult legal questions again any time soon.

# 23

# Consider the Source

## Evidence and Authority in the Fourth Restatement

*Edward T. Swaine*

Discussions of the Fourth Restatement appropriately focus on its substance. Attention is directed, for example, to instances in which those provisions deviate from the Third Restatement. Like every offspring of a prior Restatement, there is always the potential for unflattering comparisons to its parent, or even worse, suggestions that it was too early to bring a new generation into the world.

Methodological questions receive less attention, understandably enough. The American Law Institute (ALI) process tends to smooth methodological variation, even across fields. Variation within a given subject, like foreign relations law, seems still less likely, suggesting that a new Restatement—even the first of the Fourth—is unlikely to pursue any revolutionary course. It is especially difficult, given the yet-partial progress of the Fourth Restatement project, to say anything decisive about which direction its approach might ultimately take.

And yet. The Fourth Restatement is a distinctive project: Other recent ALI projects touch on international law, U.S. constitutional law, and federal statutes, but none blends these diverse bodies of law so comprehensively. Continuity between the Third Restatement and Fourth Restatement—surely more evident than any discrepancies—may indeed diminish the odds of any sea changes, but may also show deeper and more sustained tendencies. Most important, discussion of the Fourth Restatement's methodology may be valuable precisely *because* it is a work in progress: sufficiently determinate as to the work already completed, but sufficiently unresolved as a whole that criticism, including self-criticism, is constructive.

With that in mind, what is the Fourth Restatement exhibiting about how foreign relations law is established and evidenced? As would be expected, it appears to have a conventional sense of how that law is to be reckoned; that is surely easier to accept than had it pursued something untested and unrecognizable to those in the field. At the same time, its methods not only to follow a path on which the law is developing but also reinforce it, and it is worth exploring where choices are being made and might be made differently. After briefly recounting how the analogous issue of international law sources and evidence was managed

Edward T. Swaine, *Consider the Source* In: *The Restatement and Beyond*. Edited by: Paul B. Stephan and Sarah H. Cleveland, Oxford University Press (2020). © Oxford University Press. DOI: 10.1093/oso/9780197533154.003.0024

in the Third Restatement—to the dissatisfaction of at least some audiences—this chapter takes up whether similar developments are afoot in connection with the Fourth Restatement's methodology for reckoning U.S. foreign relations law.

## I. International Law in the Third Restatement

Not long after publication of the Third Restatement, Stephen McCaffrey wrote about those volumes' treatment of international law's sources and evidence.[1] As he explained, addressing such fundamental questions was not radical stuff: detailing what counted as international law,[2] and how it might be established,[3] were conventional inquiries in public international law, and setting them out in the Third Restatement might assist American lawyers less familiar with such matters.[4] Peering under the hood, he noted approvingly that the reporters had taken a broader view of sources than had the first Restatement,[5] though he thought that certain voices—those of international organizations and their resolutions—had been exaggerated.[6] McCaffrey largely avoided appraising the substance of the resulting rules perceived by the reporters.[7] Other contemporaries went straight to the substance: The Third Restatement's account of reasonableness in prescriptive jurisdiction, for example, was extensively criticized. Indeed, the Fourth Restatement wrestled with that exact issue, on essentially the same criteria, and took a different course.[8]

Behind reactions to the Third Restatement's approach to international law was a question of perspective: "international law" to whom, exactly? The reporters took pains to avoid parochial understandings, seeking to describe the rules

---

[1]  Stephen C. McCaffrey, *The Restatement's Treatment of Sources and Evidence of International Law*, 25 INT'L L. 311 (1991).

[2]  THIRD RESTATEMENT § 101 ("International law, as used in this Restatement, consists of rules and principles of general application dealing with the conduct of states and of international organizations and with their relations inter se, as well as with some of their relations with persons, whether natural or juridical.").

[3]  *Id.* § 103(1) (indicating that appropriate evidence depended on the particular source), (2) (indicating "substantial weight" was to be accorded to "(a) judgments and opinions of international judicial and arbitral tribunals; (b) judgments and opinions of national judicial tribunals; (c) the writings of scholars; (d) pronouncements by states that undertake to state a rule of international law, when such pronouncements are not seriously challenged by other states").

[4]  McCaffrey, *supra* note 1, at 312; see also THIRD RESTATEMENT intro. at 4 ("Further experience has suggested . . . the desirability of guidance in matters not likely to be familiar to the average lawyer, for example, the sources of international law. . . .").

[5]  McCaffrey, *supra* note 1, at 314.

[6]  In his view, this had been dialed back from the initial drafts, but not far enough, and the result was not especially coherent. *Id.* at 323–24, 326–30.

[7]  He did suggest that some were not so clear-cut as had been presented. *Id.* at 315–16.

[8]  See FOURTH RESTATEMENT § 407 reporters' note 3.

applicable to states in general, not just those applicable to the United States.[9] Their overall ambition, as ultimately stated, was to restate "the opinion of The American Law Institute as to the rules that an impartial tribunal would apply if charged with deciding a controversy in accordance with international law"—not just the views that might be held by U.S. courts.[10]

This attempted objectivity proved controversial. Some argued that the Third Restatement erred fundamentally because it did not focus on the "U.S. view of international law." The rationales varied. To a degree, it was just a matter of internal consistency; it was named, after all, the "Restatement of Foreign Relations Law of the United States." The truth-in-labeling argument actually ran a bit deeper than that. Because the Restatement would invariably be perceived as indicating a U.S. perspective, one argument ran, it might be better to embrace that role. At the same time, government representatives also indicated concerns about purporting to represent the U.S. view of international law—which, in the international legal system, is not just politically salient, but actually contributes to rules formed by state practice and *opinio juris*.[11] Perhaps the U.S. government could have publicly disassociated itself from the project (conceivably, liberating an even *more* international perspective), but the government might have accepted the association as inevitable, and in any case sought to align the Third Restatement more closely with its views.

As matters developed, this might have been the worst of all worlds. The U.S. government played a conspicuous role, but remained dissatisfied with some of the results. International critics, dissatisfied with those and other conclusions, could discount the Third Restatement's analysis as peculiarly American and less true to international law than had been purported. And the reporters emerged with a composite voice—addressing public international law neither as disinterested, neutral observers, nor from any systematic and coherent alternative perspective—that might have left the Third Restatement's audience in doubt as to whether its provisions were gospel, required comparison with other global perspectives, or required comparison instead with positions espoused by the U.S. government.

The Fourth Restatement has to this point unfolded more peacefully, not having yet to establish any comprehensive method for reckoning international law. Of necessity, it already assesses whether certain propositions are established

[9] THIRD RESTATEMENT intro. note, at 5 ("Unless otherwise indicated, normative statements in this Restatement set forth rules or principles of international law that apply to states generally, including the United States.").

[10] THIRD RESTATEMENT intro. at 3; see McCaffrey, *supra* note 1, at 313.

[11] For snapshots of these controversies, see *The Restatement of Foreign Relations Law of the United States, Revised: How Were the Controversies Resolved?*, 81 AM. SOC'Y INT'L L. 180–82 (1987) (remarks by Professor Maier); *id.* at 183–86 (remarks by Detlev Vagts); *id.* at 189–94 (remarks by Monroe Leigh).

by international law; of necessity, this requires some basic assumptions about how that law is established. This is evident, for example, in the Jurisdiction topic's discussion of categories of jurisdiction, which explains the relevance and derivation of customary international law while carefully distinguishing domestic law on the subject.[12] Other parts even convey basic methodological propositions.[13]

One might argue that this made it incumbent upon the reporters to set out their method, like the Third Restatement. All things considered, the failure to do so is defensible. It would have been premature to propose anything, given that important sources, like customary international law, had not been authorized for general inquiry—at least absent certainty that such work would never be taken up (so that any externalities would be minimal), or a deep-seated conviction that the Third Restatement approach had to be repudiated before progress could be made. Caution might have been particularly appropriate given concerns, evident in both the Third Restatement and Fourth Restatement, that incorrect U.S. understandings of international norms by the United States should be avoided where possible,[14] and awareness that there were other efforts afoot to restate principles of customary international law.[15]

## II. Foreign Relations Law in the Fourth Restatement

The question of what counts as foreign relations law seems more inescapable. The Third Restatement attempted to define U.S. foreign relations law, at least "as dealt with in [that] Restatement." This consisted both of:

(a) international law as it applies to the United States; and
(b) domestic law that has substantial significance for the foreign relations of the United States or has other substantial international consequences.[16]

---

[12] See, e.g., FOURTH RESTATEMENT § 401 cmt. *a-d* & reporters' note 1; see also *id.* § 402 reporters' note 2 (prescriptive jurisdiction).

[13] See, e.g., *id.* § 401 reporters' note 1 (describing forms of state practice); *id.* § 451 cmt. *c* ("Judicial decisions and domestic legislation, if enacted or decided out of a sense of international legal obligation, constitute state practice and evidence of opinio juris, the two elements of customary international law").

[14] See, e.g., *id.* § 406.

[15] Most prominently, at the International Law Commission. See Int'l Law Comm'n, Draft Conclusions on Identification of Customary International law, with Commentaries (2018); see also Int'l Law Association, Committee on Formation of Customary (General) International Law, Statement of Principles Applicable to the Formation of General Customary International Law, Final Report of the Committee (2000).

[16] THIRD RESTATEMENT § 1.

Although this question seems central to the Fourth Restatement's enterprise, that centrality may have heightened concerns about prejudging the compatibility of a working definition with subjects not yet authorized by the American Law Institute. In any event, the Fourth Restatement has not yet published any comparable statement, so presumably what the Third Restatement provided—however limited to "this Restatement" it purported to be—still goes, at least for the time being.

Ultimately, some of the quandaries the Third Restatement suggested regarding the range of foreign relations law, like the nature of domestic law with "substantial significance" for U.S. foreign relations or having "other substantial international consequences," are likely to be revisited. Drafts of a successor Section 1 for the Fourth Restatement vary the wording at least a bit.[17] In practice, the authoritative answer as to what counts as an *output* of U.S. foreign relations law will consist of the topics authorized by the ALI and addressed in the Fourth Restatement, and what the reporters say about the field's theoretical scope seems considerably less interesting.

In contrast, the issue of what counts as foreign relations law *within* the range of potential topics—its sources and evidence, as it were—is more present and deserving of interrogation. The best description in the present Fourth Restatement lies in its Introduction, which states:

> The foreign relations law of the United States is drawn from different sources, including the Constitution, congressional legislation, judicial decisions, actions of the executive, customary international law, international agreements, and State law. This Restatement attempts to distinguish clearly among these different sources and to explain their interrelationships with respect to the particular topics covered here.[18]

This is quite similar to the view taken in the Third Restatement; each is vulnerable, accordingly, to similar objections. The Fourth Restatement, however, is positioned to gain insight from the Third Restatement—including, by analogy, from the latter's approach to international law—and perhaps even to course-correct.

---

[17] See Reporters' Memorandum, Section 1: Definition of the Foreign Relations Law of the United States (on file with author).
[18] FOURTH RESTATEMENT intro. at 1.

## III. The Positive (and Negative) Law of U.S. Foreign Relations

The Introduction's statement concerning the "foreign relations law of the United States" is cautious and, cautiously construed, suited to the field as it is generally perceived. If one thinks of U.S. foreign relations law as a cityscape, the skyscrapers are easily viewed, even if their outlines may be more or less hazy on a given day or from a particular vantage point. These skyscrapers are certainly visible in the Fourth Restatement's Introduction. The more interesting and difficult questions concern the other components of the skyline.

## A. The Positive Law of U.S. Foreign Relations

The core of the Fourth Restatement's approach to sources of U.S. foreign relations law is its focus on *law*: that is, authority that would be regarded as binding in any dispute regarding a foreign-relations topic. This is most evident, but with most limited import, in regard to "State law." On its face, this encompasses every means by which States might generate law bearing on U.S. foreign relations law. The Fourth Restatement does not state what those means are, but it does clearly address only "law" as such.[19]

Finer distinctions are made concerning federal law, which is delineated by type. As the Fourth Restatement indicates at numerous junctures, the Constitution establishes the controlling law in any domestic legal dispute, notwithstanding contrary indication from another source of law.[20] Naturally, deriving constitutional law is more complex than reading the text itself, which is just one of the warrants for including "judicial decisions." In international law, judicial decisions are merely "evidence" of some other "source,"[21] even if in practice they seem more significant than that suggests. The Restatement exhibits no such ambivalence about domestic decisions. Lawyers trained in the common-law tradition are more inclined to treat judicial precedent on matters of constitutional, statutory, and treaty law (among others) as having much the same force as the underlying source. This conviction was on display during the Third Restatement's drafting; while the participants differed as to whether international

---

[19] The most substantial example might be State law concerning the recognition of foreign judgments. See FOURTH RESTATEMENT ch. 8 intro. note; *id.* § 481 cmt. *a.*

[20] See, e.g., *id.* § 307 cmt. *a* (relationship between treaties and constitutional prohibitions, such as those relating to individual rights).

[21] See Statute of the International Court of Justice art. 38, ¶ 1(d), June 25, 1945, 59 Stat. 1055, 1060, 33 U.N.T.S. 993 (describing "judicial decisions and the teachings of the most highly qualified publicists of the various nations, as subsidiary means for the determination of rules of law").

tribunals should be expressly included as hypothetical arbiters, there was no question as to whether domestic courts helped set the standard.[22] Citations to judicial decisions are ubiquitous in the Fourth Restatement.

The types become more interesting as they engage the work of the political branches. "Congressional legislation," as the Introduction puts it, is surely part of the mix. This probably means statutes and joint resolutions: This is how the term seems to be used in the draft Section 1, and Section 1 of the Third Restatement explicitly addressed U.S. statutes.[23] The chapter on jurisdiction to prescribe, for example, emphasizes statutory prescription (although the commentary makes clear that either the executive branch or the judiciary could also be responsible for such exercises).[24] To an even greater degree, the sovereign immunity provisions make clear that the main task is making sense of the Foreign Sovereign Immunities Act (FSIA), subject of course to its judicial interpretation.[25] The direct relationship between the statute and the Fourth Restatement's black-letter provisions leave little doubt as to the positive-law basis.

"International agreements" are also a part and also require only slight amplification. Part III, which addresses the status of Senate-approved Article II treaties in U.S. law, surely takes those agreements to be part of U.S. foreign relations law, and numerous sections concerning jurisdiction and immunity bear that out by citing treaties as authoritative. There is, as yet, little formal discussion of other, non–Article II international agreements. Still, it would be fair to assume that these, too, directly and authoritatively govern foreign-relations matters for the United States. The scope, in any event, is almost certainly international agreements *of the United States*, the only ones binding on the United States under international law.[26] Other international agreements, to which the United States is not a party, might bear on U.S. foreign relations law, but that is principally or exclusively because they contribute through other source-of-law mechanisms.

"Customary international law" and "actions of the executive" are a little hazier. As previously indicated, the Fourth Restatement to this point has neither reiterated nor replaced the Third Restatement's attempts to define customary international law, instead proceeding at least provisionally on a similar footing.[27] And while the Fourth Restatement does not address long-controverted questions regarding the relationship between customary international law and

---

[22] See *supra* text accompanying note 10; see also *The Restatement of Foreign Relations Law of the United States, Revised: How Were the Controversies Resolved?, supra* note 11, at 190–91 (remarks by Monroe Leigh) (discussing switch from standard of an "international tribunal" to that of an "impartial tribunal").

[23] See THIRD RESTATEMENT § 1 cmt. *b*.

[24] See FOURTH RESTATEMENT § 402 cmt. *a*.

[25] See *id.* pt. IV, ch. 5 intro. note; *id.* § 451 cmt. *c* & reporters' note 2.

[26] See *id.* § 301.

[27] See, e.g., *id.* § 401 reporters' note 1 (describing customary international law),

other American law, it appears to accept that customary international law is a part of U.S. foreign relations law. For example, many sections of the Treaties topic resemble provisions of the Vienna Convention on the Law of Treaties (VCLT).[28] Superficially, deriving black-letter sections from a treaty may seem like deriving black-letter sections from the FSIA. But the United States is not a party to the VCLT. The principal warrant for relying on the VCLT, rather, is that the relevant norms are binding on the United States as a matter of customary international law.[29]

What counts as "actions of the executive" is not defined. It plainly includes matters like agency rules, which may prescribe law,[30] and executive orders that are intended to have the force of law.[31] In foreign relations, this means including, for example, programmatic exercises of prescriptive jurisdiction.[32] Whether it encompasses actions with less well-recognized status is less obvious. For example, actions involving the application of prescriptive jurisdiction—such as "the search of a plane, the arrest of a person, imprisonment after criminal conviction, and seizure of a plane"—are worth capturing, and accurately described as "performance" and part of "United States Practice," but it is less clear that they are "actions of the executive" that embody U.S. foreign relations law.[33]

The uncertainty can be illustrated by how executive practice intersects with other types of law. Return for a moment to the topic of customary international law and VCLT principles. The Fourth Restatement indicates their relevance by citing corresponding U.S. conduct,[34] as well as statements by the U.S. government that recognize particular sets of norms as binding or appropriate for the United States.[35] Materials like this function, together with the perception that

---

[28] See, e.g., *id.* § 306 cmt. *a* (citing Vienna Convention on the Law of Treaties, May 23, 1969, arts. 31–32, 1155 U.N.T.S. 331).

[29] FOURTH RESTATEMENT pt. III, intro. note; *id.* § 301 reporters' note 1.

[30] 5 U.S.C. § 551(4).

[31] Contrast (at least potentially) one "devoted solely to the internal management of the executive branch." Meyer v. Bush, 981 F.2d 1288, 1296 n.8 (D.C. Cir. 1993).

[32] The vast majority of the examples of prescriptive jurisdiction involve statutes, but in some cases the ability of the executive branch to implement those statutes is highlighted, and in others the capacity to temper them—in all instances, by actions that unambiguously have the force of law. See, e.g., FOURTH RESTATEMENT § 402 reporters' note 7 (noting authority of the Secretary of Treasury to adopt regulations exempting certain business organizations from nationality jurisdiction); *id.* § 402 reporters' note 7 (noting capacity of "regulations of the President" to exempt other organizations owned or controlled by U.S. persons); § 402 reporters' note 9 (noting Treasury Department regulations restricting re-exports based on the protective principle); see also *id.* § 402 reporters' note 3 (explaining, with citations to the Code of Federal Regulations, that "[a]dministrative agencies exercise prescriptive comity when they issue regulations defining the geographic scope of statutory requirements . . . or recognizing exceptions for compliance with foreign law").

[33] The first two quotes are from *id.* § 431 cmt. *a*, the last from the title to § 431.

[34] See, e.g., *id.* § 302 reporters' note 6 (describing U.S. executive branch indications of support for manifest violation standard); *id.* § 304 reporters' note 8 (same, for interim obligation).

[35] See, e.g., *id.* § 304 reporters' note 8 (describing U.S. view that interim obligation was established as a customary obligation).

the norms are obligatory under customary international law, in something like a belt-and-suspenders fashion. Because acceptance of nonconventional norms by a subject state is not, strictly speaking, required—at least under modern conceptions of customary international law—statements by the U.S. government are not controlling in establishing custom; they may contribute to it, if they are coincident with the views of other states, but that is all.[36] It seems unlikely that U.S. domestic law confers on such practice the status of law simply by virtue of its possible contribution to international law. At the same time, treaty-related practice by the executive does meaningfully suggest U.S. subscription to a customary norm that the VCLT exemplifies, such as how provisional application is governed or how treaties are interpreted,[37] at the very least indicating acceptance of this proposition by a key actor in U.S. foreign relations law—and a key participant in its elaboration.

The easiest diagnosis, of which we should not lose sight, is that the Fourth Restatement both describes U.S. foreign relations law and describes other features that, while not necessarily "law," contribute to our understanding of how that law works in practice. The question of which is which is not, however, wholly inconsequential, and it is worth exploring whether anything more systematic is going on.

## B. The Soft Law of U.S. Foreign Relations

"Soft law" actions or instruments generally earn that description because they are not legally binding—usually because they do not comply with legal formalities.[38] Soft law plays a part in U.S. foreign relations, and previous scholarship has explained why at least some such law—such as agreements between U.S. agencies and their foreign counterparts—should be acknowledged as part of U.S. foreign relations law.[39] Whether one type of soft law or another is worth restating may pose interesting questions for the Fourth Restatement. But what role does soft law play in relation to the other, already acknowledged forms of foreign relations

---

[36] See, e.g., the reporters' notes relating U.S. practice to foreign practices concerning prescriptive jurisdiction over terrorism and immunity for state sponsorship of terrorism. *Id.* § 412 reporters' note 2, & § 460 reporters' note 11.

[37] See *id.* §§ 304, 306.

[38] For a broad definition, see Jacob E. Gersen & Eric A. Posner, *Soft Law: Lessons from Congressional Practice*, 61 STAN. L. REV. 573, 579 (2008) (defining soft law "as a rule issued by a lawmaking authority that does not comply with constitutional and other formalities or understandings that are necessary for the rule to be legally binding").

[39] See Jean Galbraith & David Zaring, *Soft Law as Foreign Relations Law*, 99 CORNELL L. REV. 735 (2014); Jean Galbraith, *From Treaties to International Commitments: The Changing Landscape of Foreign Relations Law*, 84 U. CHI. L. REV. 1675 (2017); Jean Galbraith, *The Fourth Restatement's Treatment of International Law and Administrative Law*, in this volume.

law indicated in the Fourth Restatement? That is, putting aside whether future work should include sections addressing particular types of soft law, does the project already account for it somehow?

The answer depends on the type of "U.S. foreign relations law" in question—but clearly, and unsurprisingly, "actions of the executive" (in a broad sense) have been the most frequent vehicle. It is widely agreed, for example, that the Constitution's meaning may be established not just by its original meaning, or by judicial interpretation, but also by the practice of the political branches—at least on matters relating to the assignment of powers to those branches.[40] The independent significance of this practice may be dampened once the Supreme Court has construed the Constitution; paying attention to such practice is also more derivative, and less autonomous, if it simply aims at predicting what the courts would do.[41] Regardless, political branch practice, typically at the initiative of the executive branch, plays a major role in foreign-relations matters. Highlighted by Justice Frankfurter, among others, in *Youngstown Sheet & Tube v. Sawyer*,[42] such practice has proved relevant in vindicating the president's authority to settle claims touching on private rights,[43] the president's foreign relations authority to preempt State law,[44] and the president's recognition power relative to congressional encroachments.[45]

These particular examples have not yet been addressed in the Fourth Restatement, which has to date taken up only a few discrete subjects. Even so, the tendency to defer to political branch practices are already on display, as are some of the quandaries this poses. The areas in questions are not only those involving constitutional law. The possible contributions of practice to particular customary international law rules has already been mentioned.[46] Deference to the executive branch also plays a conspicuous role in the interpretation of treaties, even though it plays no comparable role in the Vienna Convention on the Law of Treaties.[47] There is no general pronouncement regarding deference in statutory interpretation, but it is emphasized substantially, and possibly controversially, in relation to prescriptive jurisdiction and the presumption against extraterritoriality.[48]

---

[40]  NLRB v. Noel Canning, 573 U.S. 513, 524 (2014).

[41]  That vantage, certainly, is fundamental to the Restatement's own gaze. See *supra* text accompanying notes 10, 22.

[42]  Youngstown Sheet & Tube Co. v. Sawyer (Steel Seizure), 343 U.S. 579, 610–11 (1952) (Frankfurter, J., concurring); see also *id.* at 635–38 (Jackson, J., concurring).

[43]  Dames & Moore v. Regan, 453 U.S. 654, 677–88 (1981).

[44]  Am. Ins. Ass'n v. Garamendi, 539 U.S. 396, 414 (2003).

[45]  Zivotofsky ex rel. Zivotofsky v. Kerry, 135 S. Ct. 2076, 2086 (2015)

[46]  See *supra* text accompanying notes 34–37.

[47]  FOURTH RESTATEMENT § 306(6) (providing that "[c]ourts in the United States have final authority to interpret a treaty for purposes of applying it as law in the United States. In doing so, they ordinarily give great weight to an interpretation by the executive branch"); *id.* cmt. *a*, *g*, & reporters' notes 10 & 11.

[48]  *Id.* § 404 cmt. *e* & reporters' note 12.

What is the status of these materials? Put aside, for these purposes, any that clearly serve as a "source" of U.S. foreign relations law, as international lawyers would use that term. In some other instances, they seem evidentiary. In yet other instances, they seem a bit more like background: not intended, exactly, as displays of U.S. foreign relations law themselves, nor to evidence some otherwise-grounded proposition, but rather to illustrate, explain, or provide context. Finally, some seem more like inputs. Foreign laws, for example, are relevant to U.S. foreign relations law under the Act of State Doctrine and foreign-state compulsion defenses,[49] and foreign judgments may be due recognition and enforcement;[50] these are certainly "law," and pertinent to U.S. foreign relations law rules, but few would describe them as being part of it.

Quite often it is unclear which category (or categories) is intended. Not infrequently, the Fourth Restatement cites authority without clearly tying it to another, paradigmatic source of U.S. foreign relations law, leaving it unclear whether they are to stand as authority in their own right or might establish persuasive evidence of some other authority. Citations to the Digest of United States Practice, common in the Treaties topic, are sometimes left to speak for themselves,[51] as are citations to Office of Legal Counsel and Attorney General opinions.[52] In other cases, illustrations are provided without unpacking their significance.[53] This is difficult to avoid and, in the main, uncontroversial. Even if they are viewed as more than merely descriptive, the indicated practices typically reflect the considered view of the U.S. government as a whole, at least sometimes with the participation and approval of U.S. courts.

In some instances, however, greater clarity may be material. For example, in discussing the authority to suspend, terminate, or withdraw from treaties, the Fourth Restatement takes the view that—at least so long as such action is justified on the basis of the treaty's terms, or otherwise consistent with international law—the president can act on the United States' behalf on the international plane, apparently determining all relevant domestic legal effects simultaneously.[54] The comments and reporters' notes make clear that this view is based on historical practice, which can establish or evidence a constitutional or statutory

---

[49] *Id.* §§ 441–42.

[50] *Id.* §§ 481–90.

[51] See, e.g., *id.* § 302 reporters' note 6 (noting expressions of U.S. concern regarding domestic-law excuses for treaty violations, principally to illustrate rationale for narrow international rule); see also §§ 303, 304, 305, 306, 313.

[52] See, e.g., *id.* § 302 reporters' note 6; see also §§ 309, 313.

[53] For example, § 402 elaborates "United States Practice with Respect to Jurisdiction to Prescribe," which shows how the United States has opted to employ bases of jurisdiction permitted it under customary international law. Similarly, § 305 reporters' note 5 elaborates ways in which the United States has used treaty conditions.

[54] *Id.* § 313.

gloss.[55] Even so, the proposition is tempered as one reckoned "[a]ccording to established practice."[56] This arguably implies that it is contingent or defeasible somehow: open to the courts to re-evaluate on their own, given the lack of precedent in the area, and perhaps open as well for reconsideration by the political branches or other actors.

This illustrates more general, structural distinctions. Political practice by the executive or legislature—perhaps examples of "actions of the executive" or "congressional legislation" as those terms are used in the Fourth Restatement, or perhaps not—might contribute to U.S. foreign relations law with quite different results. If a practice amounts to or contributes to law, as that concept is generally used, it will help establish something that binds other actors and may prevail over other, hierarchically inferior sources of law. Alternatively, the practice may simply bind the branch in question, without necessarily requiring that other actors yield, or it may bind the political branches without binding the courts.[57] Whether described as soft law, or some form of nonjudicial precedent, the implications for other actors, and other forms of foreign relations law, may be quite different.[58]

The discussion to this point has foreshadowed another, long-standing, question: Does diversifying the range of materials that count toward U.S. foreign relations law unduly compound the advantages of the executive branch? Most agree that Congress is at a serious disadvantage in establishing foreign relations law and international law.[59] If and to the extent that the Fourth Restatement suggests a distinction between "actions of the executive" and "congressional legislation," marking a higher standard for Congress, that may simply reflect the realities of the field. Similar distinctions, and similar distributions of power, are reflected in international practice.[60] Domestically, it is also well understood that apart from

---

[55] They also make clear that such practice does not resolve other questions, such as whether this authority extends to instances not consistent with international law or inconsistent with congressional limitations. *Id.* § 313 cmt. *c* & reporters' notes 5–6.

[56] *Id.* § 313(1).

[57] See, e.g., MICHAEL J. GERHARDT, THE POWER OF PRECEDENT ch. 4 (2011).

[58] Foreign relations law, established by one means or another, might even establish substantive micro-principles of this form: for example, the idea that if a president ratifies a treaty after the Senate's advice and consent, he or she will be deemed to have accepted any accompanying conditions. RESTATEMENT § 305(2).

[59] See, e.g., HAROLD HONGJU KOH, THE NATIONAL SECURITY CONSTITUTION (1990); Curtis A. Bradley & Jack L. Goldsmith, *Presidential Control Over International Law*, 131 HARV. L. REV. 1201 (2018); Jean Galbraith, *From Treaties to International Commitments: The Changing Landscape of Foreign Relations Law*, 84 U. CHI. L. REV. 1675 (2017); Galbraith, *The Fourth Restatement's Treatment of International Law and Administrative Law*, supra note 39; Oona A. Hathaway, *Presidential Power over International Law: Restoring the Balance*, 119 YALE L.J. 140 (2009); Harold Hongju Koh, *Could the President Unilaterally Terminate All International Agreements? Questioning Section 313*, in this volume.

[60] For example, the International Law Commission's recent description of state practice contributing to customary international law mentioned—in addition to diplomacy, which is overwhelmingly executive—both "executive conduct, including operational conduct 'on the ground'" and

a few special procedures, like treaty-making and impeachment, Congress acts only through bicameralism and presentment.[61]

Even so, one might distinguish between the means by which Congress can legislate and the broader class of activities by which it can contribute to U.S. foreign relations law. For the latter, more might be made of softer legislative input, such as vetoed bills and joint resolutions, concurrent resolutions, and simple one-house resolutions. As others have explained, Congress frequently employs simple and concurrent resolutions to express its views regarding foreign affairs;[62] while nonbinding, such outputs can offer more acute insight into congressional preferences because (unlike the "hard" law of statutes) they need not seek to accommodate the views of the president.[63] That virtue might be diminished for vetoed bills and joint resolutions, which usually seek presidential approval. Yet these may have failed precisely because they were uncompromising—or failed despite offering a compromise that fairly reflected the long-term views of both branches, if not the immediate political reality.

The Fourth Restatement, consistent with the field as a whole, devotes relatively little space to legislative "soft law";[64] greater (if still marginal) attention is paid to the presidential messages accompanying vetoes and to executive-branch legal opinions concerning proposed legislation.[65] It arguably signals a more accommodating view via the deference given to treaty conditions like declarations of non-self-execution, which accords weight to an unorthodox means of legislating through the treaty-making process.[66] And the reporters' notes fairly reflect the divided views regarding the propriety of Byrd-Biden conditions, which sought to compel acquiescence by the executive branch in Senate views regarding treaty interpretation.[67] At the same time, discussion of possible legislative limitations on unilateral treaty termination by the president seemed to consider formal

"legislative and administrative acts." The distinction between executive "conduct" and legislative (as well as administrative) "acts" arguably suggests the kind of formalism associated with legislative action in the United States. Int'l Law Comm'n, Draft Conclusions, 6(2) (2018). But cf. id. at 13 (Commentary) (explaining that "'executive conduct'... refers comprehensively to any form of executive act, including executive orders, decrees and other measures; official statements on the international plane or before a legislature; and claims before national or international courts and tribunals," while "'legislative and administrative acts' similarly embraces the various forms of regulatory disposition effected by a public authority").

[61] See, e.g., Clinton v. City of New York, 524 U.S. 417 (1998) (line item veto); INS v. Chadha, 462 U.S. 919 (1983) (legislative veto).
[62] Gersen & Posner, supra note 38, at 580–82.
[63] Id. at 577–79, 586–99.
[64] One exception is in discussing attempted regulation of treaty negotiations, when nonbinding resolutions gain mention. See FOURTH RESTATEMENT § 303 reporters' notes 2–3.
[65] For examples, see, respectively, id. § 313 reporters' notes 2 & 3.
[66] See generally id. § 305; for non-self-execution declarations, see also id. § 305 reporters' note 6; id. § 310 cmt. e & reporters' note 9.
[67] Id. § 305 reporters' note 5.

measures like treaty conditions and statutes—each requiring consent by a prior president—as a prerequisite.[68]

More might be counted. Under Justice Jackson's famed approach, the scope of presidential authority may be mitigated even by legislative measures that are less than authoritative.[69] How this applies to nonconstitutional issues, or to matters involving sustained practice by one branch or another, is less clear. But it appears to open up space for citations to a diverse range of legislative measures—certainly bills and resolutions, and perhaps even committee product—to counteract other less-than-definitive elements of U.S. foreign relations law.

## C. The Negative, Soft Law of U.S. Foreign Relations

Assume, with the Fourth Restatement to this point, that a diverse range of materials—including, at least, executive-branch statements and practice of foreign relations law, perhaps accompanied by comparable legislative emissions—are noteworthy, even if their precise legal import is not always clear or elaborated. What significance should be attributed to the *absence* of such statements? Their absence from the pages of the Fourth Restatement will often signify only the reporters' conviction that more definitive evidence was available and sufficient. But when any material concerning a given proposition is difficult to identify, what significance might be attributed to that?

This raises difficult questions. Reasonable people will differ—assuming they are willing to entertain the issue in the abstract at all—regarding the quantum of evidence that is required before reporters may consider a given proposition to be established, including as to when it is tenable to reason from more basic or related propositions to address a different one. All the same, the permissible range of answers are consequential, and have pronounced distributional effects. Applying a low threshold for establishing government authority, or applying a high threshold for restrictions on it, will produce a familiar *Lotus*-like enhancement of U.S. power. The Fourth Restatement does not endorse the *Lotus* itself,[70] but its reasoning concerning jurisdiction over certain acts of terrorism, and immunity relating to those acts, bears a certain resemblance in the ease with which it extrapolates permissibility from a pair of states.[71]

---

[68] *Id.* § 313 reporters' note 6.

[69] Youngstown Sheet & Tube Co. v. Sawyer, 343 U.S. 579, 637 (1952) (Jackson, J., concurring) ("When the President takes measures incompatible with the expressed *or implied* will of Congress, his power is at its lowest ebb, for then he can rely only upon his own constitutional powers minus any constitutional powers of Congress over the matter.") (emphasis added).

[70] See FOURTH RESTATEMENT § 407 reporters' note 1.

[71] See *id.* § 412 cmt. *b* & reporters' note 2; *id.* § 413; *id.* § 460 & reporters' note 11.

There are other distributional effects on the domestic level. It is common, during the process of drafting a Restatement, to receive astute advice to the effect that a particular proposition ought to be omitted (or confined to the reporters' notes) in light of the limited case law or practice. It is not uncommon for that advice to be tendered by executive-branch personnel, key participants in that process. Their advice on that score is wholly legitimate, but—given that many foreign relations issues do not come before the courts or before legislatures—it tends to relegate matters on which the executive branch has not taken a definitive view. Such tendency is particularly marked, again not unreasonably, as to diplomatic issues on which the president enjoys considerable deference; the absence of a considered formulation by the United States, it may be urged, is good reason to avoid other pronouncements that might thereby be speculative or premature. The practical effect, however, is to creep toward an agenda-clearing authority for the executive branch, even in excess of what appropriate caution recommends.

A related, slightly more tractable question concerns a different kind of negative: What significance should be attributed to the failure of some identifiable practice to take another, more conclusive form? Again, the relative disadvantage of the legislature is widely noted and acute. Congressional acquiescence in an executive-branch practice—often, measured in terms of its failure to take definitive action prohibiting that practice—may be cited as lending significance to executive-branch assertions, even though there is every reason to attribute it to the transaction costs in the legislative process . . . including, but not limited to, the prospect of opposition from those within the president's party and that of a presidential veto.[72]

For whatever reason, less attention is typically paid to comparable executive-branch failures or half-measures. Foreign relations scholars are well familiar with debates about signing statements, which are not much cited in the Fourth Restatement.[73] Apart from whether they have significance in their own right, it may be asked whether it matters that the president did not, or could not, veto the legislation, or whether it should matter that Congress (in all probability) did not share the president's view. Similarly, executive branch positions that are not reflected in final agency or legislative actions might be questioned. In the Treaties topic, the Circular 175 procedure provided valuable context,[74] but there was no discernible downgrade in the significance of procedural tendencies and

---

[72] For further discussion, see, e.g., NLRB v. Noel Canning, 573 U.S. 513, 593 (2014) (Scalia, J., concurring); Curtis A. Bradley & Trevor W. Morrison, *Historical Gloss and the Separation of Powers*, 126 Harv. L. Rev. 411, 439–47 (2012); cf. Edward T. Swaine, *The Political Economy of Youngstown*, 83 S. Cal. L. Rev. 263 (2010); Shalev Roisman, *Constitutional Acquiescence*, 84 Geo. Wash. L. Rev. 668 (2016).

[73] See Fourth Restatement § 303 reporters' note 3.

[74] See 11 F.A.M. § 721 et seq.

pronouncements that were *not* incorporated. Support by the executive branch for a treaty and its substance, even if it does not result in any ratification, is essentially risk-free. As to the VCLT, for example, it is forthrightly acknowledged that the United States is not conventionally bound, but falling short is not presented as a substantial negative, nor is that the case with the Law of the Sea Convention.[75] Yet one might wonder, for example, whether any domestic implications of rules concerning interim obligations might factor in the long-standing failure to secure advice and consent, or consider (as with the Kyoto Protocol) concerted, if nonbinding, Senate opposition in the form of a simple resolution.[76]

In these respects, the Fourth Restatement largely reflects the way the legal world is tilted. If the legislative branch conducted more hearings and turned out more resolutions and reports on international affairs, or facilitated more commentaries like the Congressional Research Service's Treaties and Other International Agreements (or even updated that document),[77] doubtless the Fourth Restatement would take note, and if courts and other actors took such materials more readily into account, reporters would follow suit. But it also has its own agency. In each restatement, the American Law Institute has its own *dédoublement fonctionnel*: It digests available sources and evidence, while at the same time aspiring to count as evidence, or maybe even a source, in its own right.

Relative to courts, this role-splitting tends generally to produce a kind of harmony, as a restatement and the subjects of inquiry gravitate toward one another. Relative to courts, the Fourth Restatement will ideally behave similarly, but the interaction with the executive branch and with legislatures is likely to be a mixture of harmonization and mutual obliviousness. This can be improved. The executive branch, particularly the State Department, has played an invaluable, collegial, and constructive role,[78] but it naturally follows its own muse with respect to foreign-relations law. There is much less interaction with legislative and committee staff, who can and should be consulted more extensively in further work. The experience with the Third Restatement, at least, suggests that a deep

---

[75] See, e.g., FOURTH RESTATEMENT §§ 408 reporters' note 3 (referencing Law of the Sea Convention with respect to prescriptive jurisdiction); 432 reporters' note 4 (same, with respect to enforcement jurisdiction).

[76] Byrd-Hagel Resolution, S. Res. 98, 105th Cong. (1997).

[77] CONG. RESEARCH SERV., TREATIES AND OTHER INTERNATIONAL AGREEMENTS: THE ROLE OF THE UNITED STATES SENATE (Comm. Print 2001).

[78] The Third Restatement relationship occasionally showed strains. See *Perspectives on the Fourth Restatement Project*, 109 AM. SOC'Y INT'L L. PROC. 209, 215 (2015) (remarks by John Bellinger) (reporting that "the experience of the Third Restatement had been a bitter experience where the views of the Legal Adviser's Office were ignored in many ways," and that "[t]he acrimony between the U.S. government and the ALI got to be so great at the time of the Third Restatement, that the Secretary of State and the Attorney General wrote to the ALI asking the ALI to put off the project, which was a remarkable thing"); e.g., Davis R. Robinson, *Conflicts of Jurisdiction and the Draft Restatement*, 15 LAW & POL'Y INT'L BUS. 1147, 1152–53, 1155 (1983) (explaining U.S. view that draft Third Restatement "does not accurately reflect the state of international law").

commitment to the process—there, defining the approach to international law—can also contribute deeply to defining the scope of the field.

## IV.  Conclusion

When the American Law Institute first undertook the Restatements, its founders are said to have considered such undertakings as reaffirming not only the science of law but also the role of courts—at the expense not only of arid and overly abstract treatises but also inferior and inexpert legislators.[79]

Were that actually the contemporary standard, the Fourth Restatement would probably be regarded as a failure. True, it is not evidently beholden to treatises, nor does it bend toward legislative supremacy; these fairly reflect the field it surveys. But courts are not the clear beneficiaries. What the ALI's founders appear not to have anticipated was the remarkable influence that the executive branch would hold over modern law. The Fourth Restatement has at this point stopped short of the most fundamental questions, very much at issue in this day and age, concerning the unilateral capacity of the president to establish foreign relations law.[80] It is worth reflecting whether future invocations of executive branch statements and activities—which may assign them an important evidentiary role, without entirely foreclosing the possibility that they are to be regarded as authoritative in their own right—require clearer ground rules, and worth contemplating what else might be weighed in the balance.

---

[79] See G. Edward White, *The American Law Institute and the Triumph of Modernist Jurisprudence*, 15 LAW & HIST. REV. 1, 11–13 (1997).

[80] See *supra* text accompanying note 59. Such claims are presently noted only in passing, in comments and notes. See, e.g., FOURTH RESTATEMENT § 313 cmt. *c* (indicating that "it has long been accepted that the President and his or her agents represent the United States in international diplomacy and discourse") (citing, inter alia, United States v. Curtiss-Wright Exp. Corp., 299 U.S. 304, 320 (1936)). But see *id.* cmt. *c* (noting that the "'sole organ' characterization may not take full account of Congress's substantial powers relating to foreign relations"); *id.* § 403 reporters' note 6 (noting parallel but distinct role of "one voice" doctrine, involving Congress, in Dormant Commerce Clause jurisprudence).

# 24

# The Restatements and the Rule of Law

*Kristina Daugirdas*

In drafting and publishing Restatements of the Law of Foreign Relations, both the American Law Institute and the reporters have understood the projects as contributing to the rule of law at the international level, at the domestic level, or both. Herbert Wechsler described 1965—the year that the first such Restatement was published—as a time "when the maintenance and development of law in the governance of international relationships increasingly engages the attention and the hopes of all mankind."[1] This publication was formally captioned the Second Restatement, as others have explained.[2] Some twenty years later, when a comprehensive revision—the Third Restatement—was published, the introduction returned to and elaborated on this theme. The Restatement should be understood as a "reaffirmation" of the role of law along two dimensions: "Relations between nations are not anarchic; they are governed by law"; so too are "Presidents, members of Congress, and public officials when they conduct the foreign relations of the United States."[3] Finally, the recently published Fourth Restatement reiterated the point that "this project is a reaffirmation of the rule of law."[4]

It is easy to cheer promotion of the rule of law. Indeed, reaffirmations of the rule of law seem especially welcome, even urgent, at this historical moment, when the president of the United States has repeatedly manifested disdain for legal rules and legal institutions, national and international alike. But, as is often the case when it comes to slogans that garner widespread endorsement, things are more complicated than they initially appear. This chapter surfaces some of

---

[1] RESTATEMENT (SECOND) OF THE FOREIGN RELATIONS LAW OF THE UNITED STATES intro. at vii (Am. Law Inst. 1965).
[2] Sarah H. Cleveland & Paul B. Stephan, *Introduction: The Roles of the Restatements in U.S. Foreign Relations Law*, in this volume.
[3] THIRD RESTATEMENT intro. at 5.
[4] FOURTH RESTATEMENT intro. at 2. The Introduction continues: "Responsible officials—domestic, foreign, and international alike—face legal constraints on their choices in the conduct of foreign relations. Particular rules may demand revision in the face of changes in international relations and the world economy, but the fundamental importance of the rule of law remains beyond question. This Restatement, as much as the work of our distinguished predecessors, seeks to direct attention to law as a means of expressing, supporting, and reinforcing the decisions that make up international relations." *Id.*

Kristina Daugirdas, *The Restatements and the Rule of Law* In: *The Restatement and Beyond.* Edited by: Paul B. Stephan and Sarah H. Cleveland, Oxford University Press (2020). © Oxford University Press. DOI: 10.1093/oso/9780197533154.003.0025

the tensions that are built into the project of reaffirming or promoting the rule of law.

To start, there are at least three distinct ways that Restatements of foreign relations law might promote the rule of law. First, they might do so by clarifying the content of the law. With respect to international law, which is largely unfamiliar to a significant fraction of the Restatement's audience, clarifying content involves both explaining the sources of international law and identifying specific rules. As Thomas Franck has observed, rules that are clear are generally perceived to be more legitimate, in part because, when rules are clear, they are easier to follow—and violations are easier to identify.[5]

Second, the Restatements might contribute to the development of new legal rules—specifically to the evolution and consolidation of customary international law.[6] Of course, as a formal matter, the American Law Institute lacks the authority to promulgate new rules of international law. But the Restatement nevertheless has significant capacity to influence their development. When U.S. courts rely on the Restatement for an articulation of a rule of customary international law and apply it, the resulting opinions supply data points that are relevant to assessing the existence and content of such rules. As the audience for the Restatement extends beyond the borders of the United States, the Restatement can also influence the practice and *opinio juris* of other states as well.

Clarification of the law always involves some degree of development of the law. As a result, contributing to the development of new rules of international law is, at least to some degree, inevitable. Of course, the greater the degree of development, the more controversial the exercise. Efforts to nudge the development of the law can backfire, leaving the authors vulnerable to charges that they are engaged in advocacy and that they are undermining the credibility of the Restatement as a restatement—and of customary international law as a source of law.[7]

---

[5] THOMAS FRANCK, THE POWER OF LEGITIMACY AMONG NATIONS 55–83 (1990); cf. Frederick Schauer, *Official Obedience and the Politics of Defining Law*, 86 S. CAL. L. REV. 1165, 1190, 1992 (2013) (arguing that clear rules are especially important when courts or other formal institutions for adjudicating disputes are unavailable).

[6] Karl M. Meessen, *Conflicts of Jurisdiction and the New Restatement*, 50 L. & CONTEMP. PROBS. 47, 53 (1987) ("[T]oday's *lex ferenda* might be tomorrow's *lex lata* if only due to the impact of the *Restatement* itself.").

[7] See, e.g., David B. Massey, *How the ALI Influences CIL*, 22 YALE J. INT'L L. 419 (1997) ("The usefulness of the entire Restatement diminishes when the accuracy of one of its key sections is called into question. Judges and practitioners who rely on the Restatement because of its user-friendliness will do so only as long as they perceive that it is authoritative."); W.T. Burke, *Customary Law of the Sea: Advocacy or Disinterested Scholarship?*, 14 YALE J. INT'L L. 508, 527 (1989) ("Expanding the rule of law in international affairs is unquestionably worthy and important, but it is not a service to that goal for allegedly objective observers to endorse official views about customary law irrespective of the amount or probity of the evidence supporting those views.").

Finally, the Restatements might promote the rule of law by promoting compliance with the law. In a variety of ways, U.S. courts have the potential to play an important role in promoting compliance with international law, by the United States and by other actors if they are subject to suit in U.S. courts.[8] Separately, the Restatements of Foreign Relations Law might provoke or support action by foreign governments or other actors abroad that promotes compliance with international law.[9]

The Third and Fourth Restatements have taken quite different approaches to promoting the rule of law. To some extent these different approaches are a consequence of changes in the legal landscape over the past three decades. They also reflect different choices that the reporters and the American Law Institute have made about how to carry out the project of restating foreign relations law.

Part I identifies some developments in U.S. case law since the publication of the Third Restatement that have rendered the promotion of the rule of law a more complicated task. While the United States remains a "semi-monist" system,[10] during that interlude, the United States moved closer to the dualist end of the spectrum. These steps were not inevitable—in fact, some of them were quite controversial. Regardless, these developments have begun to drive a wedge between promoting the rule of domestic law and promoting compliance with international law.

Part II turns to the diverging approaches of the Third and Fourth Restatements with respect to articulating rules of customary international law. The Third Restatement is notably quick—according to some critics, too quick—to articulate rules of customary international law. In doing so, the reporters of the Third Restatement were quite willing to disagree with the views of the U.S. government. By contrast, the Fourth Restatement is more reticent on both fronts. The approach taken by the Fourth Restatement avoids some of the downsides of that taken by its predecessor, but also forfeits some of the advantages.

Part III argues that future installments of the Fourth Restatement ought to promote the rule of international law by updating and expanding the sections of the Third Restatement that address the architecture of international law on two key issues: international responsibility and the evolution of customary international law over time. The Fourth Restatement need not directly exhort litigants and judges to comply with international law. But by providing this basic

---

[8] This capacity is by no means limited to U.S. courts; it is shared by all national courts. See ANDRÉ NOLLKAEMPER, NATIONAL COURTS AND THE INTERNATIONAL RULE OF LAW (2011).

[9] See, e.g., Karl M. Meessen, *Foreword to Special Review Essays: The Restatement (Third) of Foreign Relations of the United States*, 14 YALE J. INT'L L. 433, 435 (1989) ("[I]n disputes with the U.S. government, foreign governments can be expected to rely on the Restatement whenever it supports their case.").

[10] Cleveland & Stephan, *supra* note 2.

information about the international legal system, the Restatement would wave a caution flag and encourage courts to take the procedural steps that would avoid unwitting (and potentially deleterious) engagement with international law.

## I. Promoting International vs. Domestic Rule of Law

When it comes to implementing the United States' treaty obligations, the reporters for the Fourth Restatement confronted a legal landscape that looked quite different from that faced by the reporters for the Third Restatement. This section describes two Supreme Court decisions that have created tension between the promotion of international and domestic rule of law. They don't make it impossible to do both simultaneously, but—especially in combination—they do make it make it harder, and therefore less likely.

First, there was the Supreme Court's 2008 decision in *Medellín v. Texas*.[11] The case concerned a decision by the International Court of Justice (ICJ) about the required remedy for the United States' breach of the Vienna Convention on Consular Relations (VCCR). Pursuant to Article 36 of the VCCR, the United States has an obligation to inform foreign nationals arrested in the United States that they have a right of access to their consular officials.[12] Implementation of this obligation was spotty at best, and no one so informed José Ernesto Medellín when he was arrested for murder in Texas. Medellín was subsequently convicted and sentenced to death. On behalf of Medellín and a number of other individuals, Mexico pursued action against the United States before the ICJ, which ruled that, as a consequence of this breach, the United States was obliged to permit "review and reconsideration" of these individuals' cases to ascertain whether the breach of Article 36 "caused actual prejudice to the defendant in the process of administration of criminal justice."[13]

There was no doubt that the United States had an international obligation to comply with this decision.[14] The problem was that Texas law precluded such review and reconsideration. If the ICJ's decision were self-executing, Texas law would have to give way.

The black-letter provisions of the Third Restatement suggest that, as a default matter, international agreements are self-executing. Section 111 provides that such agreements are non-self-executing only if "the agreement manifests an

[11]  552 U.S. 491 (2008).
[12]  Vienna Convention on Consular Relations, art. 36(1)(b), Apr. 24, 1963, 21 U.S.T. 77, 596 U.N.T.S. 261.
[13]  Case Concerning Avena and Other Mexican Nationals (Mex. v. U.S.), Merits, 2004 I.C.J. Rep. 1 (Mar. 31), para. 121.
[14]  *Medellín*, 552 U.S. at 504.

intention that it shall *not* become effective as domestic law without the enactment of the implementing legislation," "if the Senate in giving consent to a treaty, or Congress by resolution, requires implementing legislation," or "if implementing legislation is constitutionally required."[15] A reporters' note explains that "compliance is facilitated and expedited" where treaties are self-executing.[16] Thus, "if the Executive Branch has not requested implementing legislation and Congress has not enacted such legislation, there is a strong presumption that the treaty has been considered self-executing by the political branches, and should be considered self-executing by the courts."[17]

The approach taken by the Supreme Court in *Medellín* diverged from that prescribed by the Third Restatement. Instead of looking for evidence that ICJ judgments were not meant to be self-executing, the Supreme Court engaged in a search for affirmative indications that ICJ judgments were intended to be self-executing, and did not find them.[18] Moreover, the Court appeared untroubled by the risk of noncompliance with international law. Instead, the Court was anxious to preserve the option of violating international law: The Court did not want to "undermin[e] the ability of the political branches to determine whether and how to comply with an ICJ judgment."[19]

Ultimately, the Court concluded that the ICJ's decision was not self-executing. In doing so, the Court raised the costs of compliance with treaty obligations. The federal government could try to cajole states into compliance, but in the wake of *Medellín*, those efforts repeatedly failed to deliver results.[20] In theory, Congress could still enact federal legislation to require review and reconsideration. In practice, Congress did not.[21] This omission is no great surprise: inaction in Congress is overdetermined. Had the Supreme Court's opinion gone the other way, noncompliance with an ICJ decision would remain possible. But the default would be set to compliance, and a president who wanted to disregard an ICJ opinion would have to secure legislation requiring or permitting this course of action.

While *Medellín* insisted that implementing legislation was the solution for implementing non-self-executing treaties, a decision that followed several years later, *Bond v. United States*, made this solution harder to obtain. In particular,

---

[15] THIRD RESTATEMENT § 111(4) (emphasis added).

[16] *Id.* reporters' note 5.

[17] *Id.*

[18] *Medellín*, 552 U.S. at 517 ("Given that ICJ judgments may interfere with state procedural rules, one would expect the ratifying parties to the relevant treaties to have clearly stated their intent to give hose judgments domestic effect, if they had so intended. Here there is no [such] statement. . . .").

[19] *Id.* at 510–11.

[20] Kristina Daugirdas & Julian Davis Mortenson, *Another Mexican National Executed in Texas in Defiance of Avena Decision*, 108 AM. J. INT'L L. 322 (2014).

[21] *Id.*

*Bond* made it harder to enact implementing legislation that would comprehensively implement certain treaty obligations—specifically those that address
matters that have been traditionally regulated by state governments. In this way,
*Bond* further increased the obstacles to complying with treaty obligations.

*Bond* concerns a challenge to the constitutionality of the Chemical Weapons
Convention Implementation Act. As the statute's title suggests, it was enacted
to implement the United States' obligations as a party to the Chemical Weapons
Convention. That treaty prohibits States Parties from using chemical weapons
"under any circumstances,"[22] and separately imposes an obligation on states parties
to enact legislation that would prohibit individuals from "undertaking any activity
prohibited to a State Party under this Convention."[23] Accordingly, Section 229 of the
implementing legislation includes a provision that forbids, among other things, the
possession or use by any person of "any chemical weapon."[24] Both the treaty and the
legislation define "chemical weapons" as toxic chemicals and their precursors, except where the chemicals are intended for industrial, agricultural, and certain other
narrowly defined uses.[25] And both the treaty and the legislation define "toxic chemical" as "any chemical which through its chemical action on life processes can cause
death, temporary incapacitation or permanent harm to humans or animals."[26]

Federal prosecutors had charged Carol Anne Bond with two counts of
possessing and using a chemical weapon pursuant to this statute.[27] Bond, a mi-
crobiologist, had sought to poison her former friend, Myrlinda Hanes, upon
learning that Hanes was pregnant—and that Bond's husband was the father.[28]
Apparently hoping that Haynes would "develop an uncomfortable rash," Bond
spread the chemicals on Haynes's car door, mailbox, and doorknob.[29] Haynes
was largely able to avoid the chemicals, and suffered only a "minor chemical burn
on her thumb."[30]

This unlikely set of facts laid the groundwork for the Supreme Court to reconsider the scope of Congress's authority to implement treaties under the necessary
and proper clause. Bond argued that Section 229 exceeded Congress's enumerated authorities under the Constitution. The U.S. government had disavowed
the interstate commerce clause as a source of authority.[31] As a result, Bond's

---

[22] Convention on the Prohibition of the Development, Production, Stockpiling and Use of
Chemical Weapons and on Their Destruction, art. I, ¶ 1(b), S. Treaty Doc. No. 103-21, 1974 U.N.T.S.
317 [hereinafter CWC].

[23] *Id.* art. VII, ¶ 1(a).

[24] 18 U.S.C. § 229(a)(1).

[25] CWC art. II(1)(a); art. II(9)(a); 18 U.S.C. § 229F(1)(A); 229F(7).

[26] CWC art. II(2); 18 U.S.C. 229F(8)(A).

[27] Bond v. United States, 572 U.S. 844, 852 (2014).

[28] *Id.*

[29] *Id.*

[30] *Id.*

[31] *Bond*, 572 U.S. at 854–55.

challenge set the stage for the Supreme Court to revisit *Missouri v. Holland*, the 1920 case in which the Supreme Court held that "[i]f the treaty is valid there can be no dispute about the validity" of the implementing legislation "as a necessary and proper means to execute the powers of the Government."[32]

Two Justices were ready and willing to overturn *Missouri v. Holland*.[33] The majority, however, was not. Instead, the majority interpreted the statute as not reaching Bond's conduct. Reading the Implementation Act to reach a "purely local crime[]" like Bond's would intrude on the police power of the States, according to the majority. The Court declined to do so in the absence of a clear statement from Congress that the legislation was meant to reach such conduct. In this way, the majority avoided reaching the constitutional challenge.

The majority opinion suggested that—unlike in *Medellín*—the United States' international obligations were not in play. Chief Justice Roberts wrote: "[T]here are no apparent interests of the United States Congress or the community of nations in seeing Bond end up in federal prison, rather than dealt with (like virtually all other criminals in Pennsylvania) by the State."[34] In making this observation, Roberts relied on the Solicitor General's statement during oral argument that it was unlikely that the failure to prosecute Ms. Bond would "give rise to an international incident."[35] Perhaps this characterization was a strategic choice on the part of the executive branch to downplay the risk of a breach (more on this later).[36] But "not giv[ing] rise to an international incident" is not the same thing as saying the United States' compliance with the Chemical Weapons Convention was not at risk. And, indeed, an amicus brief filed by several former diplomats who negotiated the Chemical Weapons Convention argued forcefully that the treaty's prohibitions did reach Bond's conduct.[37] Moreover, they explained, the United States could not fulfill its obligations under the Chemical Weapons Convention by relying on State criminal laws:

> The CWC requires states parties to enact criminal prohibitions that apply not only to use of chemical weapons but also development, manufacture, possession, and transfer—acts that State law generally leaves unregulated. Even if all 50 States could be persuaded to enact compliant implementing legislation,

---

[32] Missouri v. Holland, 252 U.S. 416, 432 (1920).
[33] See *Bond*, 572 U.S. at 873–82 (Scalia, J., dissenting). Justice Thomas joined this dissent.
[34] *Bond*, 572 U.S. at 865.
[35] *Id.*
[36] See *infra* text accompanying note 109.
[37] Brief of Amici Curiae Chemical Weapons Convention Negotiators and Experts in Support of Respondent, Bond v. United States, 2013 WL 4518601 (2013), at *16 ("In this case, the plain text, structure and context of the CWC make clear, and the *travaux* confirm, that the CWC's prohibitions reach Bond's conduct.").

the laws must apply not only within the country but to U.S. nationals located abroad.[38]

Importantly, the effects of the Supreme Court's decision in *Bond* were not confined to implementing the Chemical Weapons Convention. The United States is party to a number of other treaties that require the United States to enact particular domestic penal regimes, including treaties related to biological and nuclear weapons and to hostage-taking.[39] A number of other treaties likewise require action on "local" matters in order to comply, including the Hague Convention on Civil Aspects of Child Abduction and the Convention on Road Traffic.[40] After *Bond*, the legislation that implements these treaties is vulnerable to challenge.

The Fourth Restatement takes a cautious approach to characterizing both *Medellín* and *Bond*, and is careful not to overstate their holdings. In fact, the Fourth Restatement may understate the extent to which *Medellín* reflected a change from past practice. The black-letter text on evaluating whether a treaty provision is self-executing retains the Third Restatement's references to the Senate's views and to constitutionally required implementing legislation; it also provides that "Courts will evaluate whether the text and context of the provision, along with other treaty materials, are consistent with an understanding by the U.S. treatymakers that the provision would be directly enforceable in courts in the United States."[41] In a comment that follows, the Fourth Restatement elaborates that while "[m]odern practice has made inquiry into self-execution more routine," the case law "has not established a general presumption for or against self-execution, in the sense of a clear statement or default rule that dictates a result in the absence of contrary evidence."[42] It is true that *Medellín* didn't expressly establish a presumption against self-execution, but— as a reporters' note acknowledges[43]—some lower courts have characterized it as doing so. Such a characterization is, at a minimum, entirely plausible in light of the Court's demanding search for affirmative indications of self-execution. The establishment of a de facto presumption against self-execution is all the more plausible in light of Justice Breyer's observation that such affirmative evidence is unlikely to be found, at least in the context of multilateral treaties, in light of the range of national practices with respect to incorporating treaty provisions into domestic law.[44]

---

[38] *Id.* at *4.

[39] *Id.* at *34; Brief of Former State Department Legal Advisers as Amici Curiae in Support of Respondent, Bond v. United States, 2013 WL 4518602 (2013), at *23–*24.

[40] Brief of Former State Department Legal Advisers as Amici Curiae in Support of Respondent, Bond v. United States, 2013 WL 4518602 (2013).

[41] FOURTH RESTATEMENT § 310.

[42] *Id.* § 310 cmt. *d.*

[43] *Id.* § 310 reporters' note 3.

[44] *Medellín*, 552 U.S. at 552.

Likewise, the Fourth Restatement avoids anticipating how the Supreme Court might build on these cases in the future. Thus, for example, the Fourth Restatement follows the lead of the majority in *Bond* and does not address the vulnerability of *Missouri v. Holland* to future challenges.[45] Instead, the Fourth Restatement reiterates *Missouri's* holding in black letter.[46]

All that said, it may well be the case that the Supreme Court will drive a bigger wedge between national and international law in years to come. Since *Medellín* and *Bond* were decided, the Court's composition has changed. On the D.C. Circuit, now-Justice Kavanaugh went out of his way to reject international law as relevant to either statutory or constitutional interpretation. In *Al-Bihani v. Obama*, he wrote a concurrence that rejected the *Charming Betsy* canon of interpretation[47] with respect to non-self-executing treaties and customary international law.[48] In *Bahlul v. United States*, he wrote another concurrence that dismissed as "extraordinary"—in other words, implausible, if not ridiculous—an argument that Congress has the constitutional authority to establish military commissions only for offenses recognized by the international law of war.[49] Justice Gorsuch's views regarding international law remain unknown. As a Tenth Circuit judge, he wrote almost nothing about international law or foreign affairs.[50]

## II. Clarifying the Content of Customary International Law

When it comes to customary international law, the Restatements agree on the appropriate methodology for ascertaining such rules, at least as a formal matter. In this sense, the legal landscape has not shifted over the past thirty years. The Third Restatement supplies a definition of customary international law that closely tracks—and arguably even improves on—that found in Article 38 of the Statute of the International Court of Justice. Section 102 explains that "[c]ustomary

---

[45] FOURTH RESTATEMENT § 312 cmt. *e* & reporters' note 5.

[46] *Id.* § 312(2) ("Congress has constitutional authority to enact legislation that is necessary and proper to implement treaties, even if such legislation would otherwise fall outside of Congress's legislative authority.").

[47] Section 406 of the Fourth Restatement articulates the *Charming Betsy* canon of construction in the context of jurisdiction to prescribe: "Where fairly possible, courts in the United States construe federal statutes to avoid conflict with international law governing jurisdiction to prescribe." For further discussion of the Restatement's treatment of the canon, see Anthony J. Bellia Jr. & Bradford R. Clark, *Restating* The Charming Betsy *as a Canon of Avoidance*, in this volume.

[48] 619 F.3d 1, 9–11 (D.C. Cir. 2010) (Kavanaugh, J., concurring).

[49] 840 F.3d 757, 759–63 (D.C. Cir. 2016) (Kavanaugh, J., concurring).

[50] Congressional Research Service, Judge Neil M. Gorsuch: His Jurisprudence and Potential Impact on the Supreme Court 85 & n.685 (2017), available at https://fas.org/sgp/crs/misc/R44778.pdf.

international law results from a general and consistent practice of states followed by them from a sense of legal obligation."[51] The next section elaborates on evidence of international law. For customary international law, the "'best evidence' is proof of state practice, ordinarily by reference to official documents and other indications of government action" while for international agreements, the key evidence is the "text of the agreement, but appropriate supplementary means to its interpretation are not excluded."[52] Thus, the Third Restatement's black-letter description of the secondary rules regarding customary international law hews to a traditional, positivist approach.[53]

The Fourth Restatement does not (yet) include a comparable introduction to the international legal system. Nevertheless, scattered in comments and reporters' notes is an affirmation of the same methodology for identifying rules of customary international law. Thus, for example, a comment following Section 401, which introduces categories of jurisdiction, explains that customary international law "results from a general and consistent practice of states followed out of a sense of international legal right or obligation."[54] A later comment explains that the Foreign Sovereign Immunities Act (FSIA) "and cases applying it may also contribute to the content, interpretation, and development of international law. Judicial decisions and domestic legislation, if enacted or decided out of a sense of international legal obligation, constitute state practice and evidence of *opinio juris*, the two elements of customary international law."[55]

Notwithstanding their parallel descriptions of the elements of customary international law, the Restatements take quite different approaches to identifying such rules. The Third Restatement does not shy away from articulating rules of customary international law on a wide range of topics. Its reporters seemed to embrace the status of that Restatement as a subsidiary means for identifying rules of customary international law.[56] In identifying such rules, the reporters for the Third Restatement disagreed, sometimes quite vehemently, with the positions taken by the U.S. government with respect to such rules.[57] Indeed, a number of

---

[51] THIRD RESTATEMENT § 102(2).

[52] *Id.* § 103.

[53] Anthea Roberts, *Traditional and Modern Approaches to Customary International Law: A Reconciliation*, 95 AM. J. INT'L L. 757 (2001).

[54] FOURTH RESTATEMENT § 401 cmt. *a.*

[55] *Id.*; see also *id.* § 402 cmt. *c* (explaining why actions and decisions based on international comity are not evidence of what customary international law requires).

[56] THIRD RESTATEMENT § 103 reporters' note 1.

[57] See *id.* Foreword at ix ("In a number of particulars the formulations in this Restatement are at variance with positions that have been taken by the United States Government."); *The Restatement of Foreign Relations Law of the United States, Revised: How Were the Controversies Resolved?*, 81 PROC. AM. SOC'Y INT'L L. 180, 184 (1987) (remarks of Detlev Vagts) ("While in our last round we adjusted quite a few things to meet government objections, particularly of The Legal Adviser of the State Department, we didn't change our view of the law. There are some things in there that The Legal Adviser does not like.").

participants described the process of drafting the Third Restatement as rife with tension between the reporters, the American Law Institute, and the U.S. executive branch.[58]

Reviews of the Third Restatement's analysis of customary international law were mixed.[59] Among the criticisms that emerged, one common theme was that the reporters were too quick to claim the status of customary international for the rules that they articulated: They did so with what was, at best, a cursory review of evidence of practice and *opinio juris*.[60]

A comment following Section 103's discussion of evidence of customary international law suggests the reporters deliberately established a lower evidentiary threshold for certain rules: "A determination as to whether a customary rule has developed is likely to be influenced by assessment as to whether the rule will contribute to international order."[61] As drafted, this sentence could be taken as descriptive—as meaning something like: Notwithstanding the black-letter rules, one can observe that tribunals and others take this consideration into account. The sentence could also be read as taking a normative position endorsing the appropriateness of this consideration. Employing a laxer approach to evaluating evidence for desirable rules (in the eyes of the reporters and the American Law Institute) is one way that the Third Restatement might seek to promote the rule of international law.

Indeed, by influencing judges and other actors at home and abroad, the Third Restatement's contestable assertions that certain rules had already attained the status of customary international law could become self-fulfilling prophecies. Precisely because collecting and analyzing evidence of customary international

---

[58] See *The Restatement of Foreign Relations Law of the United States, Revised: How Were the Controversies Resolved?*, 81 PROC. AM. SOC'Y INT'L L. 180, 181 (1987) (remarks of Harold Maier) (noting the "unusually vituperative controversy that accompanied the development, promulgation, and eventual adoption" of the Third Restatement).

[59] Massey, *supra* note 7, at 423–24 (collecting and summarizing reviews).

[60] See, e.g., Burke, *supra* note 7, at 509 (arguing that the Restatement "mistreats" customary international law by "declaring that some principles have that quality when there is no evidence that customary international law has anything effective to say on the matter; second, by declaring unqualified customary law principles when the evidence of state practice is unclear at best; and finally, by identifying principles as customary law which are supported only by distorted and misleading characterizations of sources."); David Caron, *The Law of the Environment: A Symbolic Step of Modest Value*, 14 YALE J. INT'L L. 528, 534 (1989) ("The legal propositions in these sections [on transfrontier pollution] are sometimes conservative, sometimes progressive, and almost always stated with too much conviction. The recurring certainty with which propositions are stated in Part VI gives an impression of overall stability to this area of law that is unwarranted, if not inappropriate."); *The Restatement of Foreign Relations Law of the United State, Revised: How Were the Controversies Resolved?*, 81 AM. SOC'Y INT'L L. PROC. 180, 192 (1987) (remarks of Monroe Leigh) ("This brings me to my first general criticism of the new Restatement—that the Reporters have been a bit too prone, perhaps we can say too willful, to finding new customary international law.").

[61] THIRD RESTATEMENT § 103, cmt. *a*.

law is difficult and resource-intensive, judges and other actors rely on sources like the Restatement without undertaking an independent analysis.[62]

At the same time, allowing such normative considerations to infuse analyses of customary international law is risky. It could invite unflattering assessments of the reporters' motivations.[63] More consequentially, such a normatively infused approach could disserve the goal of promoting the rule of law by fueling skepticism about customary international law as a source of law.[64] On what basis should, or could, the world possibly be bound by the subjective assessment of the American Law Institute about which rules conduce to the global good?

By contrast to the Third Restatement, the Fourth approaches customary international law with greater humility, reflecting the view that a rigorous analysis of practice and *opinio juris* is genuinely difficult. In the area of immunity, one reporter explained that uncovering the practice of foreign states was challenging: "Many states have not codified their rules of state immunity, and in many of these states, the courts have not been require to address the full range of issues that are addressed by the FSIA."[65] Identifying *opinio juris* was likewise difficult: "Even when there is a controlling statutory provision or judicial decision, it can be challenging to determine whether the particular rule is followed out of a sense of international legal obligation or whether the foreign country has extended or curtailed immunity beyond what may legitimately be viewed as the requirements of customary international law."[66]

At the same time, unlike the Third Restatement, the Fourth reflects a more collaborative approach with the U.S. government. In fact, one reporter described the reporters as "trying assiduously to avoid finding ourselves in a box where we are declaring, based on our understanding of international law, that U.S. practice might be inconsistent with international law."[67] An example cited in this volume by the chief reporters is the Fourth Restatement's handling of "tag" jurisdiction.[68] Faced with a conflict between U.S. practice and the customary international law

---

[62] Cf. David D. Caron, *The ILC Articles on State Responsibility: The Paradoxical Relationship between Form and Authority*, 96 AM. J. INT'L L. 857, 866–68 (2002) (expressing the concern that arbitrators would "defer too easily and uncritically" to apparently neutral external sources describing rules of customary international law like the draft articles on state responsibility).

[63] Monroe Leigh, *supra* note 60, at 192 (suggesting that international lawyers in general are susceptible to "the addiction of declaring that a favorite proposition of law has now become customary international law and is therefore binding on everybody. Especially if the favorite proposition is close to the goal line of acceptance, international lawyers, in their writings, in their decisions, and even in restatements such as this, find it difficult to resist the temptation to nudge that favorite proposition across the goal line and into the end zone of customary international law.").

[64] Burke, *supra* note 7, at 527.

[65] *Perspectives on the Restatement (Fourth) Project*, 109 AM. SOC'Y INT'L L. PROC. 209, 212 (2015) (remarks by William S. Dodge).

[66] *Id.*

[67] *Id.* (remarks by Paul B. Stephan).

[68] Cleveland & Stephan, *supra* note 2.

rule articulated by the Third Restatement, the Fourth Restatement refrains from addressing the latter.[69]

## A. Prescriptive Jurisdiction

The Third and Fourth Restatements' respective handling of prescriptive jurisdiction illustrates their diverging approaches to customary international law—as well as the risks and advantages of those diverging approaches.

The Third Restatement garnered significant attention—at the time of publication and subsequently—for declaring that customary international law imposes a requirement of reasonableness on exercises of prescriptive jurisdiction. In particular, after setting out the accepted bases of prescriptive jurisdiction,[70] Section 403 explains that an exercise of jurisdiction is "nonetheless unlawful if it is unreasonable."[71] To structure the analysis of this question, the Third Restatement sets out a list of eight factors to consider when evaluating reasonableness.[72] Among these factors were "the extent to which another states may have an interest in regulating the activity" and the "likelihood of conflict with regulation by another state."[73]

Louis Henkin, the Chief Reporter for the Third Restatement, explained that, in drafting this section, the reporters

> tried to combine what American courts have done in developing this balancing and these standards, and foreign objections to what they call extravagant and exorbitant exercises of jurisdiction—combining those two approaches into a principle of international law which we think our courts would accept, and has a good chance of being accepted by the people abroad as a restatement of what they are doing.[74]

The executive branch objected to Henkin's approach as a matter of both law and policy. In the view of the State Department Legal Adviser, Section 403 neither accurately reflected international law nor did it "constitute a desirable change in the law."[75]

---

[69] *Id.*
[70] THIRD RESTATEMENT § 402.
[71] *Id.* § 403 & cmt. *a*.
[72] *Id.* § 403(2).
[73] *Id.*
[74] *Thursday Morning Session, May 21, 1981*, 58 AM. L. INST. PROC. 255, 262 (1981).
[75] Davis R. Robinson, *Conflicts of Jurisdiction and the Draft Restatement*, 15 LAW & POL'Y INT'L BUS. 1149, 1152 (1983) (describing the opinion of the Office of the Legal Adviser).

Of course, even if the Third Restatement was wrong about the status of the reasonableness requirement at the moment that it was published, it could become right over time. Within the United States, the reasonableness rule did get some traction. Justice Scalia, writing a dissent on behalf of four Justices in *Hartford Fire Insurance v. California*, relied on Section 403's characterization of customary international law to interpret the extraterritorial reach of the Sherman Act.[76] In 2004, the Supreme Court decided another antitrust case in line with the reasonableness requirement. The Court wrote that it "ordinarily construes ambiguous statutes to avoid unreasonable interference with the sovereign authority of other nations," and observed that this "rule of construction reflects principles of customary international law—law that (we must assume) Congress ordinarily seeks to follow."[77] A handful of lower courts likewise relied on Section 403.[78]

In at least one instance, the State Department itself adopted the Third Restatement's characterization of the reasonableness requirement as part of customary international law. Communicating with Congress, the Legal Adviser's Office objected to certain proposed sanctions on the grounds that "international law . . . requires a state to apply is laws to extraterritorial conduct only when doing so would be reasonable in view of certain customary factors."[79]

Ultimately, however, neither the U.S. executive branch nor foreign governments endorsed the reasonableness requirement, and most scholars of international law remained unpersuaded that the reasonableness requirement was part of customary international law.[80]

Reflecting these developments, the Fourth Restatement departs from the Third in delineating permissible exercises of prescriptive jurisdiction:

> Customary international law permits exercises of prescriptive jurisdiction if there is a genuine connection between the subject of the regulation and the state seeking to regulate. The genuine connection usually rests on a specific connection between the state and the subject being regulated, such as territory, effects, active personality, passive personality, or protection. In the case of universal jurisdiction, the genuine connection rests on the universal concern of states in suppressing certain offenses.[81]

---

[76] Hartford Fire Ins. Co. v. California, 509 U.S. 764, 818–19 (1993).

[77] F. Hoffmann-La Roche v. Empagran, 542 U.S. 155, 164 (2004).

[78] Massey, *supra* note 7, at 437–39.

[79] *Id.* at 439.

[80] See, e.g., Phillip R. Trimble, *The Supreme Court and International Law: The Demise of Restatement Section 403*, 89 AM. J. INT'L L. 53, 55 (1995); CEDRIC RYNGAERT, JURISDICTION IN INTERNATIONAL LAW 178–79 (2008). But see Hannah Buxbaum & Ralf Michaels, *Reasonableness as a Limitation on the Extraterritorial Application of U.S. Law: From 403 to 405 (via 404)*, in this volume.

[81] FOURTH RESTATEMENT § 407.

Reasonableness isn't entirely irrelevant to this inquiry, the Fourth Restatement explains: "Reasonableness, in the sense of showing a genuine connection, is an important touchstone for determining whether an exercise of jurisdiction is permissible under international law."[82] But, the Fourth Restatement continues,

> state practice does not support a requirement of case-by-case balancing to establish reasonableness as a matter of international law. . . . Nor does international law require a state with a legitimate basis for asserting prescriptive jurisdiction to refrain from exercising such jurisdiction because another state has a stronger interest in exercising jurisdiction.[83]

One might view the demise of the reasonableness requirement as confirmation of the problematic nature of the Third Restatement's approach to customary international law. In my view, however, this assessment misses the value added by the Third Restatement, which was wrong in a constructive way. Even if the reasonableness rule articulated by the Third Restatement was not supported by widespread practice and evidence of *opinio juris*, the reasonableness rule did reflect a good-faith effort to assimilate the practice of U.S. courts and the protests of foreign governments. The rule that the Third Restatement articulated supplied a focal point to which courts, scholars, and governments could react. Article 38(1)(d) of the ICJ Statute affirms that "the teachings of the most highly qualified publicists of the various nations" constitute a "subsidiary means for the determination of rules of law." Such "teachings" are worth consulting not because they are infallible, but because they can reflect good-faith efforts to collect and analyze the data points that supply evidence of customary international law.

## B. The Terrorism Exceptions to the FSIA

The terrorism exceptions to the FSIA resulted from a series of amendments to that statute permitting lawsuits and facilitating enforcement of judgments against states that the U.S. executive branch had designated sponsors of terrorism. The consistency with international law of the terrorism exceptions is questionable: The exceptions have elicited protests from foreign governments. For example, in 2016, the Coordinating Bureau of the Non-Aligned Movement issued a communiqué protesting the United States' unilateral waiver of sovereign immunity:

[82] *Id.* § 407 reporters' note 3.
[83] *Id.*

This practice runs counter to the most fundamental principles of international law, in particular the principle of sovereign immunity as one of the cornerstones of the international legal order and a rule of customary international law. . . .[84]

Some scholars have likewise concluded that some or all of the exceptions violate customary international law[85]—and many within the U.S. executive branch share this assessment.[86]

Because the terrorism amendments are a relatively new feature of the legal landscape, the reporters for Third Restatement did not have to wrestle with them.[87] The Fourth Restatement generally downplays the controversy associated with these amendments, either declining to address their consistency with international law or omitting references to protests by other governments and negative assessments by scholars.[88] At a minimum, the Restatement ought to have acknowledged more directly the contested status of the terrorism amendments.[89]

---

[84] Communiqué of the Coordinating Bureau of the Non-Aligned Movement in rejection of unilateral actions by the United States in contravention of international law, in particular the principle of State immunity, reproduced in U.N. Doc. A/70/861-S/2016/420 (May 6, 2016). For other examples, e.g., Kristina Daugirdas & Julian Davis Mortenson, *Congress Overrides Obama's Veto to Pass Justice Against Sponsors of Terrorism Act*, 111 AM. J. INT'L L. 156 (2017) (cataloging responses of foreign governments to JASTA's enactment); Beth Stephens, *The Fourth Restatement, International Law, and the "Terrorism" Exception to the Foreign Sovereign Immunities Act*, in this volume.

[85] ROSANNE VAN ALEBEEK, THE IMMUNITY OF STATES AND THEIR OFFICIALS IN INTERNATIONAL CRIMINAL LAW AND INTERNATIONAL HUMAN RIGHTS LAW 355 (2008) ("This study asserts that the terrorist exception to the FSIA causes the United States to violate its obligations under international law. . . . The entertainment of claims against 'rogue' states for payment of damages suffered as a result of human rights violations and terrorist acts is illegal under international law."); Paul B. Stephan, *Sovereign Immunity and the International Court of Justice: The State System Triumphant*, in FOREIGN AFFAIRS LITIGATION IN UNITED STATES COURTS 67, 78–82 (John Norton Moore ed., 2013) (explaining reasons to doubt the consistency with international law of the terrorism exception as codified in 2008).

[86] Ashley Deeks, *Statutory International Law*, 57 VA. J. INT'L L. 263, 280 (2018) ("Many, including the executive branch, believe that the [terrorism] exception violates the rule of international law that immunizes states from being sued in each other's courts for their sovereign acts.").

[87] For the drafters of the Third Restatement, foreign sovereign immunity was quite straightforward. As Louis Henkin put it during the deliberations of the American Law Institute, "[i]t is my impression that there are no serious substantive issues about sovereign immunity. There is a statute." 58 ALI PROC. 255, 256 (1981).

[88] Austen Parrish makes this same critique with respect to the Fourth Restatement's treatment of adjudicatory jurisdiction. Austen Parrish, *Adjudicatory Jurisdiction and Public International Law: The Fourth Restatement's New Approach*, in this volume.

[89] Unlike the final published version of the Fourth Restatement, the reporters' first draft of the chapter on the immunity of states from jurisdiction did acknowledge the contested status of 28 U.S.C. § 1605A. See Restatement of the Law Fourth, The Foreign Relations Law of the United States: Sovereign Immunity § 460 reporters' note 1 (Preliminary Draft No. 1, Sept. 13, 2013) (including the following text: "Some suggest that by denying immunity to state sponsors of terrorism, the United States may have gone beyond what the international law of sovereign immunity permits."). This acknowledgment disappeared in the first Council Draft, which was circulated one year later. See Restatement of the Law Fourth, The Foreign Relations Law of the United States: Sovereign Immunity 37–39 § 460 reporters' notes 1–10 (Council Draft No. 1, Sept. 29, 2014).

More broadly, the Fourth Restatement missed an opportunity to contribute to the rule of law by addressing more comprehensively the terrorism exceptions' consistency with international law. Such a contribution could provide useful guidance to judges, who must interpret the terrorism amendments, and to members of Congress, who face persistent efforts to enact additional amendments. Such guidance would be especially useful because—perhaps surprisingly—the U.S. executive branch has remained steadfastly silent about this issue, at least in public.

By way of background, the initial version of the terrorism exception was enacted as part of the Anti-Terrorism and Effective Death Penalty Act (AEDPA) in 1996.[90] It permitted lawsuits against states that had been designated sponsors of terrorism:

> in which money damages are sought against a foreign state for personal injury or death that was caused by an act of torture, extrajudicial killing, aircraft sabotage, hostage taking, or the provision of material support or resources . . . for such an act if such act or provision of material support is engaged in by an official, employee, or agent of such foreign state while acting within the scope of his or her office, employment, or agency. . . .

Since 1996, Congress has repeatedly legislated to expand on that initial terrorism exception. Some of these provisions made it easier for plaintiffs to win such suits on the merits or expanded the damages they could seek; other provisions were designed to facilitate enforcement of judgments.[91] Many of these enactments were narrowly targeted to aid particular plaintiffs. To cite just one example, in 1997, the requirement that both the claimant *and* the victim be U.S. nationals was modified so that only one *or* the other had to be a U.S. national.[92] The House Report indicates this change was made to allow lawsuits brought by families of individuals who were killed when Pan Am 103 exploded over Lockerbie, Scotland.[93] Some of the victims were aliens whose close family members were U.S. nationals, so they couldn't satisfy the nationality requirement in the terrorism exception as originally enacted.

Remarkably, in many cases these amendments were adopted over the strenuous objections of the executive branch. In 1994, when Congress was considering

---

[90] Pub. L. No. 104-132 (1996). The terrorism exception was initially codified as 28 U.S.C. § 1605(a) (7).

[91] See, e.g., Sean Murphy, *Satisfaction of U.S. Judgments Against State Sponsors of Terrorism*, 94 Am. J. Int'l L. 117 (2000); Sean Murphy, *2002 Victims of Terrorism Law*, 97 Am. J. Int'l L. 187 (2003); Stephens, *supra* note 84.

[92] An Act to make a technical correction to title 28, United States Code, relating to jurisdiction for lawsuits against terrorist states, Pub. L. No. 105-11, 111 Stat. 22 (1997).

[93] H.R. Rep. No. 105-48; Stephens, *supra* note 84.

creating a terrorism exception to the FSIA, officials from the State and Justice Departments made a range of arguments against such an amendment.[94] They pointed out that Congress's expansion of courts' jurisdiction reflected a departure from the practice of other states regarding foreign sovereign immunity,[95] and warned that this divergence from state practice could erode the credibility of the FSIA as a whole and undermine foreign states' willingness to defend other lawsuits that the FSIA permits.[96] Furthermore, the State Department maintained that the terrorism exception could interfere with the United States' calibration of sanctions against state sponsors of terrorism and its ability to develop joint positions with other nations regarding acts of terrorism.[97] Finally, the State Department observed there was a risk that other states would expand the jurisdiction of their own courts to reach acts of alleged wrongdoing by foreign states—and would do so in a way that would potentially harm the United States.[98] These objections did not sway many members of Congress. In the end, AEDPA included many provisions that President Bill Clinton had specifically requested Congress to enact.[99] And so, notwithstanding the administration's objections to the terrorism exception, Clinton not only signed AEDPA but hailed its enactment as "an important step forward in the Federal Government's continuing efforts to combat terrorism."[100]

On two subsequent occasions, legislation expanding the terrorism exception generated presidential vetoes. In 2007, Congress included language in that year's National Defense Authorization Act to expand the original terrorism exception along multiple dimensions, including by expressly creating a cause of action and allowing the recovery of punitive damages. President George W. Bush vetoed that legislation and secured an exception for Iraq in a subsequent version of the bill, which he signed in 2008.[101] The other expansions of the terrorism exception the 2007 legislation had contained were enacted and codified in 28 U.S.C. Section 1605A. In 2016, Congress overrode President Barack Obama's veto to enact the Justice Against Sponsors of Terrorism Act (JASTA).[102] JASTA allows

[94] The Foreign Sovereign Immunities Act: Hearing on S. 825 Before the Subcomm. on Courts and Administrative Practice of the Judiciary Comm., 103d Cong. (1994).

[95] Id. at 13–14 (prepared statement of Jamison S. Borek) ("We are not aware of any instance in which a state permits jurisdiction over such tortious conduct of a foreign state without territorial limitations.").

[96] Id. at 14.

[97] Id.

[98] Id. at 15.

[99] Pub. L. No. 104-32 (1996).

[100] Statement of President William J. Clinton on Signing S. 1965, 32 Weekly Comp. Pres. Doc. 719 (Apr. 29, 1996).

[101] National Defense Authorization Act for Fiscal Year 2008, Pub. L. 110-81, Jan. 28, 2008, 122 Stat. 338.

[102] Kristina Daugirdas & Julian Davis Mortenson, Congress Overrides Obama's Veto to Pass Justice Against Sponsors of Terrorism Act, 111 AM. J. INT'L L. 156 (2017).

Americans to sue foreign states for playing a role in terrorist attacks on U.S. soil. While the statute is written in general terms, it was drafted specifically to allow families of the victims of the 9/11 attacks to sue Saudi Arabia for its suspected role in those attacks. In his veto message, President Obama expressed concern that JASTA would "reduce the effectiveness of our response to indications that a foreign government has taken steps outside our borders to provide support for terrorism, by taking such matters out of the hands of national security and for-eign policy professionals and placing them in the hands of private litigants and courts"; would "upset longstanding international principles regarding sovereign immunity"; and "threatens to create complications in our relationship with even our closest partners."[103] Notably, these objections were not framed in terms of in-ternational legal obligations governing foreign sovereign immunity.[104]

To analyze the consistency of the terrorism exceptions with international law, it is necessary to draw some distinctions among them. The basic objection is that any kind of "terrorism exception" is inconsistent with the restrictive theory of sovereign immunity, pursuant to which foreign sovereigns maintain immunity from adjudicative jurisdiction for their sovereign acts (but not their commercial acts).[105] The ICJ recently affirmed that this immunity subsists even for serious human rights violations.[106] Exceptions like JASTA that address events on the ter-ritory of the United States may be easier to justify: numerous states and the U.N. Convention on Jurisdictional Immunities of States and Their Properties recog-nize exceptions to sovereign immunity with respect to some territorial torts.[107] By contrast, terrorism exceptions that permit enforcement against foreign states are generally harder to justify because customary international law requires more robust protections with respect to exercises of enforcement jurisdiction.[108]

A key motivation for the U.S. executive branch's silence is to avoid supplying ammunition to challenge or critique the United States to foreign states ad-versely affected by the provisions in the event they are enacted into law.[109] An unequivocal public statement that proposed legislation expanding the terrorism

---

[103] *Id.* at 159.

[104] When asked directly whether JASTA violates international law, the White House press secre-tary sidestepped the question. *Id.* at 161.

[105] The analysis for different terrorism exceptions will vary in the particulars. For example, foreign sovereign immunity from enforcement is generally considered broader than foreign sovereign im-munity from adjudication. In addition, there is support in state practice for an exception to foreign sovereign immunity for territorial torts.

[106] Jurisdictional Immunities of the State (Ger. v. It.), Judgment, 2012 I.C.J. Rep. 99, ¶ 88 (Feb. 3).

[107] *Id.* ¶¶ 64–79; United Nations Convention on Jurisdictional Immunities of States and Their Properties art. 12, Dec. 2, 2004, 44 I.L.M. 803 (not yet in force).

[108] Jurisdictional Immunities of the State, *supra* note 106, ¶ 113.

[109] HAZEL FOX & PHILIPPA WEBB, THE LAW OF STATE IMMUNITY 285 (3d rev. ed. 2015) (noting the "consequences of disregarding the rules of state immunity" include "potential liabilities of the US before international tribunals").

exceptions violates international law could become a liability once that legislation is actually enacted. Other states could cite it as a definitive concession that the United States has violated its international obligations.

This concern is not merely hypothetical. In 2016, the U.S. Supreme Court rejected Iran's challenges to a legislative provision that was designed to help certain plaintiffs who had obtained default judgments against Iran to enforce them against assets held in New York on behalf of the Central Bank of Iran.[110] Iran subsequently initiated proceedings against the United States before the International Court of Justice based on the dispute resolution provision of the 1955 Treaty of Amity, Economic Relations, and Consular Rights between Iran and the United States. Iran argued that this bilateral treaty incorporates customary international law rules regarding foreign sovereign immunity, and therefore confers jurisdiction to decide whether the United States had violated those customary international law obligations. Ultimately, the ICJ concluded that the treaty did not supply such jurisdiction.[111]

The Fourth Restatement's discussion of foreign sovereign immunity offers little indication that the terrorism exceptions are widely—albeit not universally—viewed as contrary to international law. The Fourth Restatement begins with a statement that addresses both international law and U.S. law regarding adjudicative jurisdiction: Under both sources of law, "a state is immune from the jurisdiction of the courts of another state, subject to certain exceptions."[112] This formulation leaves open the question of whether those exceptions align. Section 460 describes Section 1605A. A reporters' note observes that the United States was the first country to enact a terrorism exception, that Canada followed some years later, and that the U.N. Convention on Jurisdictional Immunity of States and Their Property "neither endorses nor precludes the removal of immunity for acts of state-sponsored terrorism."[113] Strikingly, the Fourth Restatement omits any mention of scholarship or protests by foreign governments charging that these exceptions violate international law. Instead, the Fourth Restatement adduces reasons to doubt a violation: "Given its focus on injuries to U.S. nationals resulting from acts that have been condemned as illegal by the international community, and the frequently repeated exhortation that states should provide relief and means of compensating victims of terrorism, it is not clear that Section 1605A contravenes any presumptive jurisdictional constraint under

[110] Bank Markazi v. Peterson, 136 S. Ct. 1310 (2016); see also Kristina Daugirdas & Julian Davis Mortenson, *U.S. Supreme Court Upholds Law Facilitating Compensation for Victims of Iranian Terrorism*, 110 AM. J. INT'L L. 555 (2016); Pamela K. Bookman & David Noll, Ad Hoc *Procedure*, 92 N.Y.U. L. REV. 767, 816–23 (2017) (describing the background of the contested provision).

[111] Certain Iranian Assets (Islamic Republic of Iran v. U.S.), Preliminary Objections, Feb. 13, 2019, ¶ 80.

[112] FOURTH RESTATEMENT § 451.

[113] *Id.* § 460 reporters' note 11.

international law."[114] The Fourth Restatement describes JASTA in a reporters' note, but says nothing at all about how it aligns with international law.[115] When it comes to enforcement jurisdiction, the Fourth Restatement acknowledges that customary international law imposes some limits but does not describe them, and does not address whether the terrorism exceptions regarding enforcement align with customary international law.[116]

The Fourth Restatement could have made a valuable contribution by saying more about whether and how the various terrorism exceptions align with customary international law. Judges sometimes turn to customary international law to interpret the FSIA,[117] but they need help ascertaining the content of those rules. Legislators too are often swayed by arguments that proposed legislation would contravene international law[118]—but they can only be swayed by such arguments if they know what international law requires.

Separately, keeping in mind the educational role of the Restatements of Foreign Relations Law and the importance of "showing" as well as "telling" how to work with customary international law, the Fourth Restatement could have illustrated how to assess evidence for (or against) a given rule of customary international law. There is little doubt that American litigators and judges would benefit from such demonstrations. Ryan Scoville has demonstrated in an empirical study of U.S. judicial opinions that American judges rarely undertake rigorous and comprehensive analyses before pronouncing rules of customary international law.[119] Moreover, it is quite likely that Congress will continue to legislate additional terrorism exceptions, and that foreign governments will continue to protest those expansions. American judges and legislators would benefit from an illustration of how to interpret those protests and what significance to assign to them.

Finally, to the extent that the Fourth's Restatement assessment of Section 1605A rests in part on the absence of clear statements by foreign governments that they believe customary international law requires foreign sovereign

---

[114] Id.

[115] Id. reporters' note 9.

[116] Id. § 464 & reporters' notes 10 & 16.

[117] Id. § 451 reporters' note 2 (citing examples of courts' use of international law to help interpret the FSIA).

[118] See generally Deeks, supra note 86; Kevin Cope, Congress's International Legal Discourse, 113 MICH. L. REV. 115 (2015).

[119] Ryan M. Scoville, Finding Customary International Law, 101 IOWA L. REV. 1893 (2016). As it turns out, American judges are hardly alone along this dimension: international courts and tribunals rarely undertake such analyses either. Stephen J. Choi & Mitu Gulati, Customary International Law: How Do Courts Do It?, in CUSTOM'S FUTURE 117 (Curtis A. Bradley ed., 2016); Stefan Talmon, Determining Customary Int'l Law: The ICJ's Methodology Between Induction, Deduction, and Assertion, 26 EUR. J. INT'L L. 417 (2015) (finding that, "in a majority of cases, the ICJ has not examined the practice and opinio juris of states but, instead, has simply asserted the rules that it applies.").

immunity for terrorist acts, a statement to that effect may have spurred precisely such statements. In turn, such statements would contribute to the clarification of customary international law on this topic.

## III. Architecture of the International Legal System

While the Third Restatement aimed for comprehensive coverage of foreign relations law, the Fourth Restatement has, so far, tackled only a limited set of topics. Two topics ought to be a priority for future installments of the Fourth: International responsibility and the evolution of customary international law over time. Addressing these topics would educate American lawyers and judges about the basic architecture of the international legal system. Even today, many, and perhaps most, practitioners have had very limited exposure to international law. No State bar exam tests international law, and international law is not part of the Federal Judicial Center's curriculum for new federal judges.[120]

Because it addresses only selected topics, the Fourth Restatement periodically touches on international responsibility but does not address it systematically. For example, the reporters' note following Section 401, which sets out the three categories of jurisdiction, explains that "if a state exercises jurisdiction beyond the limits of international law, the state in question will violate international law, and such a violation will entail international responsibility."[121] This note cites the International Law Commission's Draft Articles on State Responsibility, but does not go on to elaborate what international responsibility entails. As another example, a comment in a subsequent section explains: "If Congress were to violate international law governing jurisdiction to prescribe, the United States would not be relieved of its obligations under international law or of the consequences of a violation of those obligations."[122]

Systematically addressing the law of international responsibility is important—and even urgent—in light of the developments described in Part I. In recent years the United States' legal system has become more dualist, and there are some indications that in future years it may move further in this direction. The more insulated U.S. law becomes from international law, the greater the risk of international responsibility. Judges and lawyers ought to understand these risks so that they can make deliberate decision about how to handle them. Judges have various tools at their disposal that they can deploy to better understand the

---

[120] John Coyle, *The Case for Writing International Law into the US Code*, 56 B.C. L. REV. 433, 468 (2015).

[121] FOURTH RESTATEMENT § 401 reporters' note 1.

[122] *Id.* § 406 cmt. *b.*

international legal consequences of their decisions. They might seek the views of the executive branch. Alternatively, or in addition, judges might take additional steps to discern the content of rules of international law to more precisely ascertain the risk of breach, or what is needed to avoid one.[123]

Moreover, the law of international responsibility is "ripe" for inclusion in future installments of the Fourth Restatement because its contents are largely settled since the International Law Commission completed its work on state responsibility in 2001. The draft articles the Commission produced are increasingly accepted and cited as reflecting customary international law.[124] At the time that the Third Restatement was being developed and published, the Commission had not yet figured out how it would handle a number of controversial issues.[125]

The Third Restatement addresses responsibility mainly in Part IX, which is captioned Remedies in International Law. This part briefly addresses "defenses," or what the Commission referred to as "circumstances precluding wrongfulness";[126] obligations to cease wrongful conduct and make reparation;[127] and the possibility that a state that is a victim of a breach may take countermeasures.[128]

One issue that merits attention in a future installment of the Fourth Restatement is attribution. Section 207 of the Third Restatement addresses attribution of conduct to States, providing: "A state is responsible for any violation of its obligations under international law resulting from action or inaction by . . . any organ, agency, official, employee or other agent of a government or of any political subdivision, acting within the scope of authority or under color of such authority."[129] This remains an accurate statement of the law of international responsibility, but judges who are unfamiliar with international law could easily miss two points that merit emphasis, especially in the wake of the *Medellín* and *Bond* decisions. First, the acts and omissions of the individual U.S. States are attributable to the United States as a matter of international law. A reporters' note states: "The United States has consistently accepted international responsibility for actions or omissions of its constituent States and has insisted upon similar

---

[123] See, e.g., Scoville, *supra* note 119, at 1947 (noting that courts can deploy Federal Rule of Civil Procedure 44.1 to gather additional evidence of practice and *opinio juris*).

[124] See, e.g., Report of the Secretary-General, Responsibility of States for Internationally Wrongful Acts: Compilation of Decisions of International Courts, Tribunals, and Other Bodies, U.N. Doc. A/71/80 (2016).

[125] See generally Alain Pellet, *The ILC's Articles on State Responsibility for Internationally Wrongful Acts and Related Texts*, in THE LAW OF INTERNATIONAL RESPONSIBILITY 75, 84 (James Crawford, Alain Pellet, & Simon Olleson eds., 2010) (noting that, even by 1996, nearly a decade after the Third Restatement was published, the Commission had not yet resolved a number of controversial issues, including the notion of State international crime, countermeasures, and settlement of disputes).

[126] THIRD RESTATEMENT § 901 cmt. *a* & reporters' note 1.

[127] *Id.* § 901.

[128] *Id.* § 905.

[129] *Id.* § 207.

responsibility on the part of the national governments of other federal states." The problem is the implication that this is a discretionary, and perhaps idiosyncratic, position on the part of the United States. A second point that warrants emphasis is that decisions of individual U.S. courts are likewise attributable to the United States.

Separately, future installments of the Fourth Restatement ought to explain in general terms how rules of customary international law may change over time. On this topic, the Third Restatement offers no information at all. The Fourth Restatement, once again, includes some scattered notes about the evolution of customary international law. Thus, a reporters' note observes: "National legislation, executive action, and the decisions of national courts on jurisdiction represent forms of state practice and may contribute to the *development* and interpretation of customary international law on jurisdiction if done out of a sense of legal right or obligation."[130] Systematic discussion of how customary international law evolves over time would, among other things, help judges and legislators understand how to cope with new developments relating to the terrorism exceptions of the FSIA. Supplementing the Fourth Restatement in this way would have another positive effect: It would extend its shelf life, preserving the Fourth Restatement's utility over the decades to come as both international law and U.S. law will continue to shift.

## IV. Conclusion

Promoting the rule of law is not exactly a straightforward task. All three of the Restatements of Foreign Relations Law have advanced this goal in various ways. There remains room for future installments of the Fourth Restatement to further advance this goal.

---

[130] FOURTH RESTATEMENT § 401 reporters' note 1.

# 25

# Can the Fourth Restatement of Foreign Relations Law Foster Legal Stability?

*Jide Nzelibe*

Can the Fourth Restatement of Foreign Relations serve as a useful road map for promoting legal stability? At some level, the desire for stability in the law of foreign relations may be as unassailable as are the numerous anxieties to which the very notion of stability gives rise. On the one hand, legal stability may make it easier for litigants and diplomats to predict what rules govern their behavior and plan accordingly; on the other hand, stability may seem like legal entrenchment, and groups may be loath to entrench in the law a position that gives their opponents an advantage. Indeed, the more social groups are polarized, the greater the fear of legal entrenchment is likely to be, especially with respect to those issues that touch on the social and moral identity of such groups. Given these realities, I wish to explore whether the kind of legal stability one may expect the Restatement to foster is even feasible, and if it is, whether it is desirable.[1]

This chapter makes two key points. First, it argues that in the current political climate, the objective of fostering legal stability in foreign relations law may no longer be as feasible as it once was. For much of the postwar era until

---

[1] One important caveat: The claim here is not that legal stability is the only discernible justification or explanation for the drafting of Restatements. Commentators on the Restatements often point to a variety of other objectives, including reforming the law in a more progressive direction or advancing the narrow policy goals of interest groups; at some level, these other objectives may be in tension with achieving legal stability. See Alan Schwartz & Robert E. Scott, *The Political Economy of Private Legislatures*, 143 U. PA. L. REV. 595 (1995) (describing the role of interest groups in shaping the Restatements); V. William Scarpato, *"Is" v. "Ought." or How I Learned to Stop Worrying and Love the Restatement*, 85 TEMP. L. REV. 413, 420–21 (2013) (describing those who believed the Restatement could be used as a tool for moving the law in a progressive direction). But there is also a long-standing tradition that links the Restatement drafting efforts with the need to bring predictability, coherence, and uniformity to disparate areas of common and statutory law. See Kristen D. Adams, *The Folly of Uniformity? Lessons from the Restatement Movement*, 33 HOFSTRA L. REV. 423, 443–45 (2004) (exploring the arguments that the restatements lend predictability and stability to case law); Randy E. Barnett, *The Death of Reliance*, 46 J. LEGAL EDUC. 518, 527 (1996) (arguing that the Restatement (Second) of Contracts provides the law with a "safe-haven framework"). And in her contribution to this volume, Ashley Deeks points out that one of the reasons various constituencies are hesitant to include domestic humanitarian law as a subject of the Restatement is because of an aversion to legal stability in that area of the law. See Ashley Deeks, *Sleeping Dogs: The Fourth Restatement and International Humanitarian Law*, in this volume.

Jide Nzelibe, *Can the Fourth Restatement of Foreign Relations Law Foster Legal Stability?* In: *The Restatement and Beyond.* Edited by: Paul B. Stephan and Sarah H. Cleveland, Oxford University Press (2020). © Oxford University Press. DOI: 10.1093/oso/9780197533154.003.0026

the administration of President George W. Bush, various commentators have suggested that even though there were occasional partisan skirmishes, a relatively bipartisan consensus on liberal internationalism prevailed.[2] Under those conditions, the drafters of both the Third Restatement in 1987 and the Second Restatement in 1965 might have hoped that the product of their efforts would help stabilize the rule of law in foreign policy.[3] However, today, the conditions that produced that moderate bipartisan consensus no longer hold, and thus the quest to foster stability in foreign relations law is likely to face even more of an uphill battle.[4] Throughout this chapter, I will illustrate these claims by looking at the ebb and flow in efforts to use the Restatement to nail down a rule regarding the self-execution of treaties.

Second, and more speculatively, it suggests that while the Restatement may occasionally foster stability in foreign relations law, there is also the possibility that it may do so in undesirable circumstances. This point assumes that whereas too little legal stability can sometimes be disruptive, too much of it could be inhibiting. In circumstances where there is too little political conflict, and thus less of an incentive for parties to challenge or re-examine outdated and redundant legal understandings, there is a risk that judges and practitioners may overrely on the Restatement. Thus, it is plausible that under certain circumstances, the Restatement may actually contribute to the unwelcome ossification of foreign relations law.

Before proceeding, a brief historical digression is in order. The proponents of the Third Restatement in 1987 were not necessarily oblivious of the political forces that might trigger legal instability in foreign relations. But they believed

---

[2] Charles A. Kupchan & Peter L. Trubowitz, *Dead Center: The Demise of Liberal Internationalism in the United States*, 32 INT'L SECURITY 7, 8 (2007) (observing that the administration of President George W. Bush marked a crucial break with the postwar bipartisan consensus on liberal internationalism that would not likely be reversed); Tim Dunne & Matt McDonald, *The Politics of Liberal Internationalism*, 50 INT'L POL. 1, 12 (2013) (discussing literature that connects the end of the consensus on international liberalism to the George W. Bush administration). To be clear, there are other commentators who have argued that the collapse in the bipartisan consensus on liberal internationalism might have occurred earlier. See Thomas L. Hughes, *The Twilight of Internationalism*, FOR. POL. 25–48 (Winter 1985–1986). For purposes of this project, however, the exact period in which the postwar consensus broke down is not too important. What matters more was that the decline in such consensus was perceived as continuous and uninterrupted through crucial parts of the post–Cold War period. Thus, legal regimes that once seemed firmly rooted in liberal internationalism gradually became even more vulnerable to intense dissensus.

[3] Of course, by the time of the drafting of the Third Restatement in 1987, there were already signs of significant disagreement over certain aspects of the project. See *infra* note 8.

[4] See Kupchan & Trubowitz, *supra* note 2, at 7–9 (describing when the consensus broke down); Jide Nzelibe, *Our Partisan Foreign Affairs Constitution*, 97 MINN. L. REV. 838, 841–42 (2013) (same); Ganesh Sitaraman & Ingrid Wuerth, *The Normalization of Foreign Relations Law*, 128 HARV. L. REV. 1897 (2015) (arguing that the constitutional treatment of foreign policy was becoming more like domestic policy); but cf. David H. Moore, *Beyond One Voice*, 98 MINN. L. REV. 953 (2014) (suggesting that the historical importance of the sole organ vision of presidential power might have been exaggerated).

such forces could be domesticated by judicialization and by the intervention of specialized and neutral experts. Understandably, much of the drafting of the Third Restatement focused on seemingly arcane and procedurally complex issues, such as jurisdiction, immunity, treaty interpretation, and various abstention doctrines.[5] Nevertheless, there was one problem. Efforts to draw sharp distinctions between technical legal procedures and substantive policy outcomes would prove to be somewhat illusory; on the contrary, since the choice of a set of technical procedures could sometimes shape substantive policies in ways that favored certain groups at the expense of others, these procedures themselves often became the source of conflict.

To be clear, the claim here is not that mutually beneficial and stable constraints in foreign relations are never feasible, or that tinkering with the Restatement cannot help progress toward this end. But one needs to be circumspect about the conditions under which legal stability can arise. Where the veil of ignorance is thick, and thus where groups cannot predict with certainty whether certain legal procedures will have distributional effects, opportunities to foster stable legal arrangements may exist. But a realist account of the evolution of foreign relations law suggests that such circumstances are likely to be quite rare.

## I. Some Preliminary Issues

At first blush, the question as to whether some version of the Restatement of Foreign Relations Law is worth preserving seems misplaced. Rarely is the complete revision or abandonment of any particular Restatement ever on the table; indeed, once the original decision to draft a Restatement provision is made, it seems to take on a life of its own, and there is not much precedent for reversing course. At bottom, whether for normative or expediency considerations, Restatements of Law tend to be particularly sticky.

Thus, the more relevant question might be this: Given that we already have a Third Restatement of Foreign Relations, which for better or for worse is being relied upon by various courts and foreign authorities, should we continue to stick to that old text, even when it might seem to be superseded by recent developments?[6] Alternatively, should we make our best effort to update the

---

[5] THIRD RESTATEMENT §§ 901–907; RESTATEMENT (SECOND) OF THE FOREIGN RELATIONS LAW OF THE UNITED STATES (Am. Law Inst. 1965).

[6] Paul Stephan delves into some of the weaknesses associated with the Third Restatement, including that version's preference for the nationalization of foreign relations law. See Paul B. Stephan, *The Waning of the Federal Common Law of Foreign Relations*, in this volume; see also Paul B. Stephan, *Courts, the Constitution, and Customary International Law: The Intellectual Origins of the Restatement (Third) of the Foreign Relations Law of the United States*, 44 VA. J. INT'L L. 33 (2003); but cf. Leila N. Sadat, *The Proposed Restatement (Fourth) of the Foreign Relations Law of the United States: Treaties— Some Serious Procedural and Substantive Concerns*, 2015 B.Y.U. L. REV. 1673 (questioning whether it

Restatement from a partial perspective, even if any such effort is likely to be fraught with its own limitations, including the concern as to whether the drafters will be merely restating the law or modifying it?

Of course, even if one concedes that some partial revision of the Restatement is desirable, one may still wish to avoid making some of the same kinds of errors made by previous efforts. For instance, in an era of polarization, where views of the appropriate legal boundaries may swing back and forth faster than normal, may we find ourselves in a situation where the recent revisions to the Restatement might once again be rendered obsolete in the very short term?

Perhaps two key arguments can be made in favor of why the current approach to revision should assuage the skeptics. First, there is the claim that the scope of the current revision effort is fairly modest and circumscribed and that the more contentious issues, such as the status of customary international law in the U.S. legal system,[7] have been studiously avoided or kicked down the road. Instead, the drafters have prudently focused on more technical and less politically loaded concerns, such as jurisdiction, sovereign immunity, and treaty interpretation. Second, and more broadly, there is also the claim that any updates to the Restatement only become finalized after wide consultation with experts in the field, including practitioners, legal academics, State Department lawyers, judges, and other key stakeholders. Thus, one key feature of the Restatement revision effort is the norm of consensus: the drafters presumably try as much as possible to solicit input from a wide range of actors and then try to reach agreement before presenting a final draft for approval by the American Law Institute.

Against this view, one can raise two objections. First, the legal issues that are contentious today may not be the same ones that will bedevil future political actors; conversely, issues that seem technical and boring today may very well become the axis of future polarizing conflicts. Indeed, one of the principal challenges of previous Restatement efforts has been that no sooner than certain doctrinal fires were quenched have those battles been rendered obsolete by new ones. A case in point was the controversy surrounding the customary international law rules for expropriation during the drafting of the Third Restatement

---

is worthwhile to engage in a revision of the Restatement if it is simply going to be a fragmented and piecemeal project).

[7] The academic debate over the status of customary international law in the United States is quite extensive. See Curtis A. Bradley & Jack L. Goldsmith, *Customary International Law as Federal Common Law: A Critique of the Modern Position*, 110 HARV. L. REV. 815 (1997) (staking out the revisionist position on customary international law); William S. Dodge, *Customary International Law and the Question of Legitimacy*, 120 HARV. L. REV. F. 19 (2007) (same); Harold H. Koh, *Is International Law Really State Law?*, 111 HARV. L. REV. 1824 (1998); Gerald L. Neuman, *Sense and Nonsense About Customary International Law: A Response to Professors Bradley and Goldsmith*, 66 FORDHAM L. REV. 371 (1997) (defending the modern position).

in 1986.[8] Initially, the drafters considered backing away from the language in the 1965 Restatement that required just compensation for an expropriation be "prompt, adequate, and effective."[9] But that suggestion provoked a strong reaction by certain prominent critics who eventually prevailed over the reporters to withdraw the proposed revision.[10] In any event, the geopolitical controversies over expropriation in the 1970s and early 80s that likely prompted that debate in 1986 eventually subsided, and the fault line of political conflict has since moved onto other issues, mostly of a noneconomic variety, such as the scope of the Alien Tort Statute and the domestic reach of customary international law in the United States.[11]

Second, and more importantly, sometimes consensus may not necessarily reflect deep agreement over the direction and trajectory of recent court decisions. Instead, it may camouflage the reality that the protagonists in these debates have reached a political stalemate. However, any such stalemate may be fragile. If, for instance, the willingness to adapt to certain doctrinal developments in foreign relations law reflects the current balance of power within the U.S. Supreme Court, then those developments may only be as stable as long as that balance exists. Of course, given how long various justices tend to serve on the Court, the change in that configuration could actually take a long time. As it stands, however, the justices on the Court cannot even lay claim to exclusive or even primary authority in shaping the contours of foreign relations law; indeed, the political branches, especially the president, happen to play an outsized role in this domain. And this has significant consequences for the stability of various doctrines in foreign relations law, as the various political actors may have both

---

[8] With respect to the debates over expropriation during the drafting of the Third Restatement, one commentator observed: "While this was going on, a group headed by Peter D. Trooboff and Brice M. Clagett of the District of Columbia Bar mounted a well-organized attack on the treatment of expropriation in sections 712 and 713 of the draft Restatement. They proposed at the 1982 ALI annual meeting that these sections be disapproved and that the reporters be instructed to go back to what the previous Restatement had said on the subject of expropriation. This proposal was defeated but it began a process (explained in greater detail below) by which the reporters finally arrived at a version more nearly reflecting the Trooboff-Clagett view." John B. Houck, *Restatement of the Foreign Relations Law of the United States (Revised): Issues and Resolutions*, 20 INT'L LAW. 1361, 1363 (1986).

[9] See *id.*

[10] See *id.*

[11] For the debates about customary international law, see the articles referenced in note 7, *supra*. For some of these debates about the Alien Tort Statute, see Daniel Abebe, *Not Just Doctrine: The True Motivation for Federal Incorporation and International Human Rights Litigation*, 29 MICH. J. INT'L L. 1 (2007) (using international relations realism to argue for greater judicial deference to executive branch views in ATS cases); Sarah H. Cleveland, *The Alien Tort Statute, Civil Society, and Corporate Responsibility*, 56 RUTGERS L. REV. 971 (2004) (arguing that ATS litigation does not harm U.S. foreign relations, nor America's standing as an international leader in the promotion and protection of human rights); Julian Ku & John Yoo, *Beyond Formalism in Foreign Affairs: A Functional Approach to the Alien Tort Statute*, 2004 SUP. CT. REV. 153 (2004); Beth Stephens, *The Curious History of the Alien Tort Statute*, 89 NOTRE DAME L. REV. 1467 (2014); Ernest A. Young, *Universal Jurisdiction, the Alien Tort Statute, and Transnational Public-Law Litigation after Kiobel*, 64 DUKE L.J. 1023 (2015).

the incentives and opportunities to disrupt conventional legal understandings, albeit in somewhat predictable ways.

## II.  Is Legal Stability Even Feasible?

In theory, we may expect that political actors lack the incentives to manipulate the boundaries of foreign relations law, since they tend to implicate procedural rather than substantive values or policies. There are plausibly two reasons why this may be the case.

First, if we assume that the relevant actors operate behind a Rawlsian veil of ignorance, they may be unable to predict which institutional arrangements will favor them in the future, and so they may all agree to coordinate around procedural safeguards that protect them from their most feared outcomes. Thus, all else equal, we may expect guarantees that either enhance or weaken treaty supremacy will be unlikely to hurt or benefit any one side in any systematic way, especially if the various groups anticipate that they will spend equal amounts of time in and out of office. Second, the presence of an external threat may amplify the value of vesting more authority in a strong executive who has the flexibility to counter such threats. Thus, at the height of the Cold War, when the Soviet threat loomed large, actors across the political spectrum might have had an incentive to resist the fragmentation of foreign affairs authority, and so there might have been little wiggle room to exploit the law of foreign affairs for political purposes.

In the modern era, however, two obstacles may prevent any kind of legal understanding favored by the Restatement from being "locked in." First, after multiple electoral cycles, political actors are likely to update their beliefs about their chances of pursuing their policy objectives under alternative institutional arrangements. In addition, to the extent that particular constraints in foreign affairs once believed to produce symmetric policy outcomes no longer do so, those constraints are likely to be re-evaluated.[12] Second, the kind of legal consensus that commanded allegiance across the partisan divide during the Cold War era had a temporary shelf life; in other words, the further removed one was from the external crisis that inspired the need to overcome differences, the more likely the consensus would break down.

One illustration: take, for instance, the ebb and flow in both the Restatement and federal case law as to whether there should be a strong presumption in favor

---

[12] See, e.g., DAVID L. SLOSS, THE DEATH OF TREATY SUPREMACY: AN INVISIBLE CONSTITUTIONAL CHANGE 219–25, 248–56 (2016) (discussing how partisan and ideological disagreements in the 1940s and early 1950s weakened the doctrine of treaty supremacy).

of treaty self-execution.[13] In the Third Restatement, the drafters favored a strong presumption toward self-execution. In the most recent revision, the drafters backtracked and staked out a more neutral position, neither favoring a presumption in favor or against the self-execution of treaties.[14] This change reflected the reality that the case law had evolved in a more uncertain direction since the mid-1980s, especially in the wake of the Supreme Court's decision in *Medellín v. Texas*.[15]

What may these shifts and inconsistencies in judicial positions have to do with the larger political context? If one believes that political groups across the political spectrum are likely to place the same or similar values on treaties that are self-executing, then the debates about this issue may seem largely academic and esoteric. In the contemporary era, however, the presumption in favor of the self-execution of treaties is likely to produce a predictable bundle of policy outcomes; under fairly reasonable assumptions, the distribution of such benefits is likely to favor left-leaning groups at the expense of conservative-leaning groups.[16] Indeed, in large measure, these debates have tracked the polarizing divisions over human rights treaties in the United States; at bottom, if one strongly dislikes the policy implications of enforcing human rights treaties, then one is likely to favor a strong presumption against the self-execution of treaties, and vice versa.[17]

The challenge is that since the choice of any judicial presumption regarding the self-execution of treaties may implicate the redistribution of social and moral values, it will tend to foster a zero-sum mindset among warring groups.[18] Of

---

[13] There is a rich and long-standing scholarly debate on the desirability of a strong presumption toward the self-execution of treaties. See Martin S. Flaherty, *Response, History Right?: Historical Scholarship, Original Understanding, and Treaties as "Supreme Law of the Land,"* 99 COLUM. L. REV. 2095, 2128–29 (1999) (contending that the opinion during Convention and ratification debates support the notion that "treaties would be presumptively self-executing"); Carlos M. Vázquez, *Laughing at Treaties*, 99 COLUM. L. REV. 2154, 2169–70 (1999) (defending a reading of Supremacy Clause that favors the self-execution of treaties). But see John C. Yoo, *Globalism and the Constitution: Treaties, Non-Self-Execution, and the Original Understanding*, 99 COLUM. L. REV. 1955, 1961, 2024–74 (1999) (contending that evidence supports the view that Founders intended treaties to be non-self-executing).

[14] Compare THIRD RESTATEMENT § 111 reporters' note 5, with FOURTH RESTATEMENT § 310 reporters' notes 3, 14. For a critical analysis of the positions taken by both the Third and Fourth Restatements on the issue of self-execution, see Carlos M. Vázquez, *Four Problems with the Draft Restatement's Treatment of Treaty Self-Execution*, 2015 B.Y.U. L. REV. 1747 (2015).

[15] 552 U.S. 491, 504–10 (2008) (denying relief on the ground that the treaty being invoked was non-self-executing). Certain justices have also voiced objections to the expansive scope of treaty powers endorsed by the Third Restatement. See Bond v. United States, 572 U.S. 844, 877–78 (2014) (Scalia, J., concurring) (disagreeing with the broad treaty powers under the Third Restatement); see also *id.* at 883 (Thomas, J., concurring) (criticizing the Third Restatement for not recognizing the federal limits placed on the Treaty Power).

[16] See Nzelibe, *supra* note 4, at 842–43.

[17] See *id.* at 843 ("In the United States, however, such debates about human rights agreements often expose a particularly deep fault-line that has divided core constituencies aligned with the Republican and Democratic Parties since the end of World War II.").

[18] To be sure, the preceding argument brackets all the legal nuances that might underpin the doctrine of self-execution, including the fact that the doctrine may go beyond the simple

course, it is plausible that one day the tide may shift, and social conservatives may plausibly profit from a regime that favors the self-execution of treaties. In the meantime, however, it is unlikely that they will be willing to trade off certain present costs for uncertain future benefits. Thus, regardless of how one tries to couch the legal issues at stake, as long as there are serious disagreements about the current policies and values that may be produced by certain judicial presumptions, then there are likely to be serious disagreements about those presumptions.

Nevertheless, in realizing that certain judicial presumptions regarding the domestic effects of treaties can have distributive effects, one should resist the impulse to go overboard in the other direction. There may still be significant constraints on the politicization of judicial presumptions in foreign relations. Judges may strongly balk at the notion that they are simply playing the role of "politicians in robes," especially in foreign affairs. Moreover, since these doctrinal debates are likely to come up in a variety of concrete disputes, judges are likely to face strong institutional incentives to be consistent in their interpretive approaches. Finally, it is plausible to think they may privilege their interpretive commitments over their policy preferences, especially when the two come into conflict.

Nonetheless, the actual choice of any single interpretive approach may still have significant policy implications that favor certain groups' treaty preferences over others. As Adrian Vermeule has keenly observed:

> Interpretation is not a pure exercise in coordination across judges and courts; interpretive method also largely determines whose values or preferences the legal system promotes, and to what degree. . . . It is a mixed game of coordination and distribution, in which judges desire to coordinate, but some judges [will] prefer that all coordinate on one particular rule, while other judges would prefer that all coordinate on a different rule.[19]

Furthermore, elected officials are hardly passive players in this game. To the contrary, both the president and Congress have an extensive inventory of tools to shape public opinion of what they think the appropriate legal standards in

---

direct enforcement of treaties or that it may implicate other separation of power concerns. See Jean Galbraith, *The Fourth Restatement's Treatment of International Law and Administrative Law*, in this volume; Jean Galbraith, *What Should Restatement (Fourth) Say About Treaty Interpretation?*, 2015 B.Y.U. L. REV. 1499, 1515–17 (2015); David L. Sloss, *Taming Madison's Monster: How to Fix Self-Execution Doctrine*, 2015 B.Y.U. L. REV. 1691 (2015); Edward T. Swaine, *Taking Care of Treaties*, 108 COLUM. L. REV. 331 (2008); Vázquez, *supra* note 14, at 1747–50; Samuel Estreicher, *Taking Treaty-Implementing Statutes Seriously*, in this volume.

[19] Adrian Vermeule, *The Judiciary Is a They, Not an It: Interpretive Theory and the Fallacy of Division*, 14 J. CONTEMP. LEGAL ISSUES 549, 571–72 (2005).

foreign relations ought to be, praising some and denigrating others. And since the development of foreign relations law has as one of its dominant characteristics the infrequent involvement of the judiciary, the political branches (especially the president) have significant leeway in shaping norms and practices of legally permissible actions.[20] At bottom, instead of viewing the structure of foreign relations law as an inflexible and binding constraint, these politicians may instead treat it as one of many malleable considerations in their quest to entrench their favored political programs.

Finally, one of the common tropes of foreign relations law is that the political branches are primarily preoccupied with protecting their institutional interests; in other words, we often expect presidents to be avaricious empire builders, while members of Congress are presumably constrained by collective action problems. But there is an alternative interpretation: instead of advancing institutional objectives, the political branches may also rank their institutional preferences in purely partisan terms and focus on how much each preference advances the objectives of their core constituencies. For instance, such asymmetric constraints might take place if conservative-leaning presidents favor more extensive and cumbersome procedures for both the passage and implementation of self-executing treaties, even when a conservative president occupies the White House. As long as left-leaning groups stand to benefit more from self-executing treaties, then this strategy may seem to make sense. In this picture, the right-leaning president may appear to be constraining herself when she agrees to abide by such cumbersome procedures, but in reality she may be constraining the discretion of future presidents who may have more progressive policy leanings.

## III. Is Legal Stability Necessarily Desirable?

At first glance, a dispassionate and technical approach to foreign relations law may seem to have an unambiguous upside; after all, without clumsy and parochial interventions from political actors, the path of foreign relations law can rest on a more predictable footing shaped by objective experts. Thus, in order to avoid undue politicization, one of the plausible aims of the Restatement may be

---

[20] Of course, some have argued that the Restatement should soften the language on the weight of deference that courts should accord to the executive branch's interpretation of treaties. See Galbraith, *supra* note 18, at 1522–23. For a broader discussion of the role of judicial deference to the executive branch in treaty and customary international law, see Robert M. Chesney, *Disaggregating Deference: The Judicial Power and Executive Treaty Interpretations,* 92 Iowa L. Rev. 1723, 1749 (2007); Harlan G. Cohen, *The Death of Deference and the Domestication of Treaty Law,* 2015 B.Y.U. L. Rev. 1467, 1471–83 (2015) (discussing the deference trends of the Supreme Court).

to encourage the orderly and stable evolution of the law, based upon expert judgment about our legal past as well as informed conjectures about the future.

But here is the rub. Too much stability in foreign relations law may be as suffocating as too little is disruptive. Where to strike the right balance cannot simply be determined by reference to refined legal texts or doctrinal niceties embodied in the Restatement; indeed, it might be as much (if not more) of an artifact of political judgment. But even if it were possible to isolate the more politically contentious issues in foreign relations law and focus only on the more technical and mundane aspects, entrenching legal stability through the Restatement could still be problematic for two reasons.

First, there is the question of the epistemic plausibility of discovering consensus about the existing state of public law. In a society where there are likely to be hundreds of deeply vested stakeholders across different levels of government with conflicting interests, knowledge of what the stakeholders' preferences may be in stabilizing the law is likely to be very hard to uncover. Moreover, while some modicum of legal stability can be achieved by judicial reliance on the Restatement, it may still be important to ask why this is so.

Of course, it is possible that legal stability will be the result of widespread public satisfaction with the Restatement drafters' efforts to capture the current state of the law. But stability may also be the result of relative apathy, and apathy can be caused by a variety of factors. One likely cause may be that groups have not been spurred into action because they happen to perceive the current stakes of the legal rules as too trivial. But if that is the case, the legal stability that one observes can be somewhat illusory. Eventually, seemingly trivial issues may become salient for certain groups. At some stage, if the pent-up anxieties of these disaffected groups are not addressed, the system is liable to break down at the margins.

In the absence of immediate distributional effects, social groups may be willing to accept a rule proposed by the drafters of the Restatement—perhaps any rule—on a temporary basis. However, if the rule evolves down the line to favor certain groups over others, then the "outs" may seek to revisit their initial choice, while the "ins" may seek to retain it. From the perspective of the "outs," changes to the rule may no longer seem forbidding if they do not involve wholesale and sweeping transformations of constitutional structure or customary international law, but only marginal tinkering in a more favorable direction. In this picture, any attempt to justify the freezing of the law through the Restatement may then look like a disguised effort to suppress conflict, or to favor the "ins" at the expense of the "outs," and thus it may exacerbate rather than mitigate political conflict. More importantly, there is no reason to assume that a legal rule that owes its long survival to apathy will necessarily be an efficient rule; indeed, if the

THE FOURTH RESTATEMENT OF FOREIGN RELATIONS LAW    561

collective action costs of changing rules are sufficiently high, a particularly bad rule can last a long time.

Second, the perceived net benefits of legal stability may not be uniform across stakeholders. There may be reason to believe that it will tend to privilege the career and professional interests of bureaucrats and judges. But interest groups of a certain stripe may have different preferences. As repeat players in the domain of public law, such groups are aware that foreign relations law sometimes implicates significant aspects of their core social and moral identities. In addition, since the demand for social identity tends to be high relative to its supply, the initial losers may become vested in upsetting the legal status quo. Put differently, these groups may be more willing to trade off the benefits of legal stability in order to have a decent chance of continuing to fight hard for their ideal rule, even if a moderate degree of legal uncertainty ensues in the interim.

Of course, a tacit compromise to settle on a specific rule may occasionally result from a stalemate in which neither party is able to impose its will, but such a stalemate rarely rests on solid ground.[21] As one commentator put it, "political life in democracy—or indeed in any voting body—consists of a continual efforts to dislodge the temporary authorities who have authoritatively but temporarily allocated despised values."[22] Once the circumstances become propitious again, the groups will reignite conflict and try to improve their chances of realizing those rules of the game that will allow them to impose their own values or policy objectives on the rest of society.

By contrast, unlike politicians and interest groups, career insiders often fear unpredictability in the larger political and legal environment as a threat to their core institutional and professional interests. These career insiders may tend to view efforts to undermine settled legal understandings as imperiling what they perceive as the rational management of foreign policy. In the view of these insiders, the rancor and divisive tenor of outside ideological groups will be associated with gridlock and the inability to achieve basic policy goals, while the quiet and deliberate approach they favor will be linked with cohesive policy behavior.

There is, however, an alternative and less cynical account of legal change. The resistance to change may simply reflect a kind of institutional stasis, and the disruptive elements may reflect an effort to undo an enduring logjam in the system.

---

[21] Indeed, one might consider the Fourth Restatement's approach on the self-execution of treaties as reflecting some sort of tacit compromise. By staking out a position that neither endorses not rejects the presumption toward self-execution of treaties, the Restatement adopts a position that is vague enough that it is not likely to alienate any of the key constituencies. However, it is not likely to quench their efforts to push the courts toward one side or the other on this issue.

[22] WILLIAM H. RIKER, LIBERALISM AGAINST POPULISM: A CONFRONTATION BETWEEN THE THEORY OF DEMOCRACY AND THE THEORY OF SOCIAL CHOICE 208 (1982).

In this respect, Terry Moe summarizes one common view of the bureaucratic mindset:

> If [careerists] cannot control the environment, they can try to shut themselves off from it in various ways. They can promote further professionalization and more extensive reliance on the civil service. They can formalize and judicialize their decision procedures. They can base decisions on technical expertise, operational experience, and precedent, thus making them "objective" and agency-centered . . . These insulating strategies are designed, moreover, not simply to shield the agency from its political environment, but also to shield it from the very appointees who are formally in charge.[23]

The bottom line is that we may not be able to resolve the wisdom of preserving legal stability in foreign relations law in the abstract. We may need to know more about its actual implications for various constituencies. In performing this analysis, we should not assume that if legal stability happens to make the professional lives of judges or diplomats easier, it also serves the public interest. To be sure, if all or most of the indispensable interest groups rank durability in foreign relations law higher than any other legal objective, then all is well.

But the nirvana fallacy counsels against assuming the best intentions of one set of institutional actors while assuming the worst in others. Just as bureaucrats might sometimes be motivated to shun blame-generating situations, so too must we suppose that judges might sometimes prefer to avoid making hard and unpleasant choices. Given these incentives, and the reinforcing tendencies of judicial citations, overreliance by judges on precedent or the Restatement might create a distorted picture of whether the relevant rules continue to serve current needs or have become outdated.

At some level, judges may find the technicalities and nuances of foreign relations law too removed from their usual, daily professional routines, and thus they might be tempted to use the Restatement as a legal crutch. Moreover, a stable legal crutch may be more valuable than an unstable one; however, a constituency who believes its ox is being gored by the "stable" rule might feel otherwise. Of course, there is no reason to conclude that any particular group's preference for a different interpretation or rule will be good for the rest of society, but there is no reason to assume that it will be bad either. To the dissenting groups, the claim that the disputed Restatement provision happens to embody the wisdom of the ages, or the judgment of a wide swath of experts, might not be particularly reassuring. As one commentator has keenly observed, "[t]he *Burkean paradox* is

---

[23] Terry M. Moe, *The Politics of Bureaucratic Structure*, in CAN THE GOVERNMENT GOVERN? 267, 284 (John E. Chubb & Paul E. Peterson eds., 1989).

that an epistemic strategy of relying on precedent or tradition for its embodied collective wisdom works only if, or to the extent that, past decision makers were not themselves Burkeans and thereby contributed independent information to the stream of decisions."[24]

## IV.  Conclusion

The narrow claim made here is that the Restatement's ambition to cultivate legal stability in foreign relations law may only be realized under very specific conditions. In those circumstances where the political stakes in a legal controversy are low, or where they implicate technical issues that do not obviously favor certain groups over others, then it may make sense for various stakeholders to coordinate around a common rule, rather than fight to change it. In a polarized environment, however, the boundary between what is merely technical and procedural in foreign relations law and what embodies substantive values favoring particular groups will often be difficult to define. Moreover, once this boundary starts to blur, social groups may become vested in either tearing down or modifying the legal edifice so carefully erected by the technical experts who drafted the Restatement. Thus, given these considerations, the law of foreign relations may become increasingly prone to the similar kinds of contingencies one sees in other areas of constitutional law, where conflicts over substantive policies soon collapse into conflicts over constitutional structure.

[24] Adrian Vermeule, *Collective Wisdom and Institutional Design*, in COLLECTIVE WISDOM: PRINCIPLES AND MECHANISMS 338, 353 (Hélène Landemore & Jon Elster eds., 2012).

# Index